A Practitioner's Guide to Wills

FIFTH EDITION

A Practitioner's Guide to Wills

FIFTH EDITION

Lesley King, Keith Biggs and
Peter Gausden

CONSULTING EDITOR
Meryl Thomas

WS
&H

Wildy, Simmonds & Hill Publishing

Contains public sector information licensed under the Open Government Licence v3.0

ISBN: 9780854902965

British Library Cataloguing in Publication Data

A catalogue record for this book is available from the British Library

Third edition 2010
Fourth edition 2017

This edition published in 2023 by

Wildy, Simmonds & Hill Publishing
Wildy & Sons Ltd
Lincoln's Inn Archway
Carey Street
London WC2A 2JD
www.wildy.com

Typeset by Heather Jones, North Petherton, Somerset.
Printed in Great Britain by CPI Group (UK) Ltd, Croydon CR0 4YY.

Preface

The fifth edition of *A Practitioner's Guide to Wills*, as with its predecessors, is intended to provide a wide-ranging guide to the drafting of wills. In addition to the selection of precedents and specimen wills which are included, the text also examines the major areas of law which are likely to be relevant to the practitioner – capacity, formal requirements, executors and trustees, administrative provisions and construction, for example. The closing chapters provide a review of the inheritance tax and capital gains tax regimes, along with some introductory advice on settlements and tax planning.

The effect of the residence nil rate band that became available after publication of the previous edition is considered. Emphasis is given to the conditions that must be met, and the pitfalls to avoid if a claim is to be successful, particularly if drafting will trusts. The residence nil rate band now has a major role as a tax planning strategy alongside the traditional use of discretionary trusts and flexible life interests, which are also looked at, along with the availability of the reduced rate for charitable giving that meets the statutory criteria.

This edition takes account of recent important legislative changes that will be relevant to those drafting wills, including the changes to the execution requirements enacted during the COVID-19 pandemic allowing remote witnessing. It also looks at the requirement to register details of beneficial owners of trusts on HMRC's trust register. The work also covers many important case-law developments since the previous edition, particularly the way in which courts now deal with family provision claims after the Supreme Court decision in *Ilott v The Blue Cross and Others* [2017] UKSC 17.

Lesley King
Keith Biggs
Peter Gausden
2 August 2022

Contents

Appendices

Table of Precedents

Table of Cases

Table of Statutes

Table of Statutory Instruments

Table of Non-UK Materials

References are to page numbers

Table of Codes of Guidance, Manuals, etc

References are to page numbers

Chapter 1

Introduction

Before drafting a client's will, the will drafter must enquire into all the testator's circumstances, including their family, assets and liabilities. The will drafter must ensure the client is aware of the value of the assets currently held and any that they are likely to acquire. The will drafter must also be sure that the client is not under any disability (such as mental illness or minority) which would prevent the making of a valid will. The will drafter must ascertain what the testator wants to do and consider whether or not that is possible, and the likely consequences.

The will drafter must enquire about the client's marital status – whether they are married or a partner in a civil partnership, or whether they intend in the foreseeable future to marry or enter a civil partnership; and about the composition of their family. Any intended provisions must be looked at in the light of the Inheritance (Provision for Family and Dependants) Act 1975. The testator must be advised of the effects of the Act and the applications that could be made under it if adequate provision is not made for those eligible to make applications under the Act. In *Ilott v Mitson and Others* [2015] EWCA Civ 797, an application under the 1975 Act, the deceased's daughter was awarded a substantial sum (£50,000) from her mother's estate despite an express provision in her will that her daughter be excluded from any benefit. This decision was appealed and after protracted litigation reached the Supreme Court (*Ilott v The Blue Cross and Others* [2017] UKSC 17) where the original award was restored. There is a clear need for the will drafter to consider possible claims under the Act.

The will drafter must ensure that any intended gift to relatives not being made by name but using their family relationship – for example 'issue' (see *Reading v Reading* [2015] EWHC 946 (Ch)) and 'nephews and nieces' (see *Wales and Another v Dixon and Others* [2020] EWHC 1979 (Ch)) – will accurately identify those whom the testator wishes to benefit.

If the testator intends to be married or enter into a civil partnership in the near future then special provision may be needed in the will to prevent revocation of the whole or part of the will on the occurrence of that event. The will should include a statement that the testator is expecting to marry (or form a civil partnership with) a named person and that the will is to survive the marriage or formation of a civil partnership (see also *Court and Others v Despallieres* [2009] EWHC 3340 (Ch)).

Apart from the testator's duties to provide for family and dependants, the will drafter must also ascertain whether the client has any contractual obligations or other duties requiring certain dispositions to be made in the will.

The will drafter must be fully aware of the size and nature of the estate. It is also necessary to find out whether the client has any power of appointment or disposition to be exercised by the will. Further, the will drafter should find out whether any recent lifetime gifts have been made, as these may affect the inheritance tax position.

The will drafter should find out the size and nature of the testator's debts and liabilities so that these can be taken into account.

If the testator has a business, or is a partner in a firm or a director of a company, special provision may have to be made in the will. The partnership deed or the articles and memorandum of association of the company must be inspected before the will is drafted, to check that the provisions of the will are not inconsistent with the provisions of those documents.

If the testator owns property outside England and Wales, enquiry should be made to ascertain how that property is held and whether it can be disposed of by the proposed will under the law applicable to the place where the property concerned is situated. It may be that the testator has already made a will in the country or territory concerned disposing of the property there, so the effect of that will must be considered. Any revocation clause must make provision for the survival of the will already made disposing of the foreign asset. Alternatively, the testator may need advice about making a will in the country or territory where their property is held in order to comply with the applicable law. In the case of property held in one of the EU states which has accepted EU Regulation 650/2012 ('the Succession Regulation') (see Precedent 2C and Chapter 11), it is necessary to consider whether a statement should be included choosing the law of the testator's nationality to govern succession to property.

The will drafter should make a full record of the client's instructions and ensure the will complies with the instructions. Once drafted, the provisions should be fully explained to the testator before the will is executed, to ensure that the testator understands and approves the contents of the will. In *Franks v Sinclair and Others* [2006] EWHC 3365 (Ch), the court found that the will drafted by the deceased's son (a solicitor) raised 'a significant degree of suspicion'. The will differed from an earlier will by including the will drafter son but excluding the other son and the deceased's grandson who were the former beneficiaries. There was criticism of the will-making process as the main residuary clause, which was drafted in a convoluted and complex way, was simply read verbatim to the testatrix without explanation in everyday language. The judge held that the lay person would consider the language used as 'gobbledygook' and accordingly the will failed through the testatrix's lack of knowledge and approval. The lesson to be learned was that will drafters should seek to avoid the preparation of wills for members of their family when the will drafter is to be a major beneficiary.

Although Administration of Justice Act 1982, section 20 allows for the rectification of a will where a mistake has arisen by reason of a clerical error or a misunderstanding of instructions, the section does not enable every mistake to be corrected. If an error occurs, it is likely to be the will drafter (or their firm) who pays the costs of any application to rectify, and the will drafter or firm may be sued for negligence. See also *Kell v Jones and Others* [2012] EWHC B30 (Ch), [2013] All ER (D) 153 (Jan), in which it was confirmed that the only grounds for rectification were those specified in section 20(1)(a).

The will drafter's duty does not end when the will is drafted; it is also necessary to ensure that it is properly and validly executed. In the case of *Esterhuizen v Allied Dunbar Assurance plc* [1998] 2 FLR 668, the disappointed beneficiaries sued the will drafters (who were not solicitors) for failure to ensure proper execution (there was only one witness).

In *Humblestone v Martin Tolhurst Partnership (A Firm)* [2004] EWHC 151 (Ch), the testator executed his will at home and returned it to the drafting solicitors for safe custody. On receipt, the will was checked and pronounced in order. However, after the testator's death it was discovered he had not signed his will. The disappointed beneficiary sued for negligence. The court held the solicitors who were instructed, knowing the will was to be executed outside their supervision, had a duty to ensure proper execution by checking the will and ensuring it was ostensibly valid and were therefore negligent.

The will drafter not only has a contractual duty to the client, but also owes a duty of care to potential beneficiaries (see *Ross v Caunters* [1980] Ch 297 and *White v Jones* [1995] 2 AC 207). In *Ross v Caunters*, Megarry VC held that a solicitor was negligent where he:

(i)   failed to warn a testator that the spouse of a beneficiary should not witness a will;

(ii) failed to check whether the will was properly attested when it was returned to the solicitor;

(iii) failed to observe that the attesting witness was the spouse of a beneficiary; and

(iv) failed to draw this to the testator's attention.

In *White v Jones*, the House of Lords found that a solicitor who had accepted instructions to prepare a will was liable to the disappointed beneficiary where, as a result of an unacceptable delay, the testator died before the will was prepared.

The will drafter must ensure that other matters necessary to give effect to the testator's wishes contained in the will, for example, severing a joint tenancy, are done before execution. The will drafter should draw their client's attention to the effects of dealing with property (such as the doctrines of ademption and lapse). Property passing outside the will (such as joint property, the proceeds of insurance policies and payments from pension funds or assets held abroad) should also be discussed. Tax aspects should be looked at and discussed in relation to the particular circumstances of the client and their family.

In *Hawes v Burgess and Another* [2013] EWCA Civ 74, the court held that it is good practice to send a draft will to the testator for him to consider before the execution of it. At the meeting when execution took place, the solicitor read over the content of the will, but this was done in the presence of another. The fact that the deceased had not had an opportunity to check and approve the contents of the draft will before she went to the solicitor's office to execute it, in addition to the deteriorating state of her mental and physical health, were sufficient to support the conclusion that the will was invalid on the basis of want of knowledge and approval.

The will drafter must act promptly in preparing the will. The greater the age of the testator and the degree of any infirmity dictate the speed with which the will drafter must act. Delay in preparation of a draft should be avoided (see *White v Jones* [1995] 2 AC 207). The decision in *White v Jones* was followed in *Feltham v Bouskill* [2013] EWHC 1952 (Ch), [2013] All ER (D) 172 (Jul). In the latter case, the will drafter was found negligent, and considerable damages awarded, because the will drafter had failed to prepare and have executed with appropriate alacrity the will of a 90-year-old lady already suffering from mild dementia and living in a care home.

The form of the will adopted is largely a matter of choice for the will drafter, although the formalities under Wills Act 1837, section 9 must always be complied with. There are certain conventions that are usually followed, such as the absence of punctuation from the text. Words of command such as 'I GIVE' or 'I APPOINT' are usually in capital letters. The usual structure of a will is as follows:

- opening words;
- revocation clause;
- appointment of executors, trustees, etc;
- specific gifts (if any);
- general legacies (if any);
- a gift of residue;
- extension of executors' and trustees' powers (if appropriate);
- attestation clause.

Most wills can be prepared from a selection of standard clauses modified to suit the needs of the individual client. In *Austin v Woodward* [2011] EWHC 2458 (Ch), the solicitors, who had drafted the earlier will of the testatrix in 1993, had revised their precedents before drafting the later 2003 will. The new will inadvertently included provision for the testatrix's house to pass into residue, whereas it was the testatrix's clear intention that the provision in her earlier will for the property to pass to her daughter as an absolute gift was to be retained. The court allowed rectification of the will, finding that the new precedents had been applied without proper consideration of their impact on the dispositions as a whole.

This book provides a comprehensive selection of precedents from which to work.

Chapter 2

The Nature of a Will

2.1 DEFINITION

A will is an expression by a person of wishes intended to take effect only at their death. It is ambulatory in nature, which means that it has no effect until the testator dies. It does not therefore limit the testator's rights of ownership or their right to make lifetime dispositions of the property referred to in the will. Until the testator's death, the will is no more than a declaration of intention, and may be revoked or varied at any time until death.

Although a document which is intended to operate as a will need not describe itself as such in order to be valid, any professionally drafted document should expressly state that it is a will and whose will it is. If the document is intended to be supplementary to a will, it should state, usually at the beginning, that it is a codicil to a will of the testator. However clearly a paper may appear to be testamentary on the face of it, it will not be admitted to probate if there is evidence to show that it was not made with testamentary intention.

The usual forms of commencement are as follows.

2A FORMS OF COMMENCEMENT OF WILL

THIS IS THE LAST WILL of me [testator] of [address].
or
I [testator] of [address] HEREBY REVOKE all former wills and testamentary documents made by me and declare this to be my last will.

As regards revocation, see also **7.1.3** and the effect of such a clause on foreign property.

2B   FORM OF COMMENCEMENT OF CODICIL

> I [testator] of [address] DECLARE this to be the [first] codicil to my will
> dated the ... day of ...

The commencement clause should include the testator's full name and address
(including postcode) so that the testator is identified clearly.

**2C   DECLARATION OF CHOICE OF LAW UNDER
EU REGULATION 650/2012**

> I DECLARE that I am a United Kingdom national who is most closely
> connected with the jurisdiction of [England and Wales] [Scotland]
> [Northern Ireland] and I choose the law of [England and Wales]
> [Scotland] [Northern Ireland] to govern succession to my assets, rights
> and obligations as a whole, including any not disposed of by this will.

This declaration is relevant if a testator owns property in an EU state. It is now
possible to provide for property disposal under the law of England and Wales
(allowing testamentary freedom) rather than, as previously, having to submit to
the civil law applicable at the property's location (which might have been subject
to forced heirship rules). As to the effect of EU Regulation 650/2012 ('the
Succession Regulation') (applicable to deaths after 17 August 2015) on the
disposition by will of non-UK property located in an EU state, see further in
Chapter 11.

A declaration such as that in Precedent 2C may not strictly be necessary because
as long as the testator is 'habitually resident' in England and Wales, the
Succession Regulation provides that the domestic court will have jurisdiction to
determine the succession to property located in an EU state. However, including
such a declaration avoids doubt as to which law is to apply. Notwithstanding the
change made by the Succession Regulation, it may still be better to put in place
separate wills made in each jurisdiction where assets are owned. This is because
it is likely to be easier to administer assets in a foreign jurisdiction if there is a
will both in the language of that jurisdiction and made in a way which is compliant
with the law of that jurisdiction. Of course, each will should contain the same
declaration.

2.2   A WILL DISTINGUISHED FROM OTHER CONCEPTS

A will is to be distinguished from other legal devices which may be used
effectively to dispose of property.

2.2.1   Lifetime settlement

A testator may leave realty to a beneficiary by means of a will, but a similar succession result may be achieved by a lifetime transfer of the property to trustees to hold for the settlor for life, with the remainder to the beneficiary. If the beneficiary survives the settlor, the effect of the settlement will be similar, in many respects, to a gift contained in a will. However, on the creation of the settlement, the beneficiary receives an interest in remainder, with the result that if the beneficiary predeceases the settlor, then provided the settlor has not revoked the settlement, the beneficiary's interest forms part of their (the beneficiary's) estate. The family home is often the most valuable asset, so care, consideration and advice must be given if the testator is to make a lifetime gift of it but continue to live in it. In the light of the pre-owned asset charge, the reservation of benefit rules and the effect of the gift for inheritance tax, income tax and capital gains tax, careful planning is called for. Such arrangements are rarely advisable from a tax perspective.

2.2.2   Nomination

A statutory nomination is a direction to a person (A) who holds a fund for another person (B) to pay the fund in the event of B's death to a person nominated by B to take the fund. Nominations operate by statute, by means of an occupational pension scheme, or by way of an insurance scheme.

Nominations pursuant to statute cover property in, for example, a provident society, up to the current limit of £5,000. To be valid, the nomination must be:

(i)   made in writing; and
(ii)   made by a person who is aged 16 or over; and
(iii)   attested by one disinterested witness.

In the case of nominations under a pension scheme, the rules of the scheme may provide that if an employee dies during the course of their employment without having retired, the amount of their contributions paid to the fund may be paid to any person nominated in writing by the employee. In the absence of any such nomination, the fund is paid directly to the personal representatives of the deceased employee and forms part of their estate. Some schemes require the funds to be paid to the nominee. However, many schemes are discretionary in form, in which case the nomination is merely an indication of how the employee would like the trustees to exercise their discretion. Sums payable under discretionary schemes are not part of the deceased's inheritance tax estate.

A nomination does not in any way operate as part of the will (see *Baird v Baird* [1990] 2 AC 548 (PC)) and is therefore not subject to the rules for the creation of a valid will (see Chapter 4). If a nomination is invalid, but is executed in accordance with Wills Act 1837, section 9, it may operate as a will (see *Re Baxter's Goods* [1903] P 12).

Many of the schemes which facilitated nominations, such as National Savings, have now ceased. The Administration of Estates (Small Payments) Act 1965 (as amended) allows many of the benefits that were nominated to pass without obtaining a grant. Enquiry should be made about any asset which could still pass by nomination.

2.2.3   Donatio mortis causa

A gift *donatio mortis causa* has been described as a gift of an 'amphibious nature' (see Buckley J in *Re Beaumont, Beaumont v Ewbank* [1902] 1 Ch 889, 892) because it is neither entirely *inter vivos* nor entirely testamentary. It is a gift made *inter vivos* which is conditional upon, and which takes effect upon, death. It is in no way governed by the provisions relating to properly executed wills, nor is it governed by the rules relating to the effective disposition of *inter vivos* gifts, but it is subject, in general, to the rules relating to satisfaction and ademption (see Chapter 20).

Inheritance tax is payable on any property which is the subject matter of a *donatio mortis causa*, since it forms part of the donor's estate on death.

According to Lord Russell CJ in *Cain v Moon* [1896] 2 QB 283, three requirements must be fulfilled for there to be a valid *donatio mortis causa*:

(i)   the gift must be made by the donor in contemplation, although not necessarily in expectation, of death;
(ii)   the gift must be conditional on death, so that if the donor recovers from the contemplated cause of death, the gift is revoked;
(iii) before the donor dies, they must part with dominion over the subject matter of the gift, i.e. the subject matter must be delivered to the donee.

The donor must have the mental capacity to make the gift, which capacity may not be of such a high degree as that to make a will, depending on the substance of the gift (see *Re Beaney* [1978] 1 WLR 770). If there is an allegation of lack of capacity to make a gift, the evidential burden of proof passes to the donee(s). The donee(s) must satisfy the court that the donor had capacity when making the gift (see *Williams v Williams and Another* [2003] EWHC 742 (Ch)).

In addition, the subject matter of the gift must be such that it is capable of passing as a *donatio mortis causa*. Most personalty is so capable. Since the Court of Appeal's decision in *Sen v Headley* [1991] Ch 425, it seems that realty is also capable of being the subject matter of a valid *donatio mortis causa* if there is constructive delivery of the deeds. There are conflicting opinions as to whether stocks and shares can be the valid subject of a *donatio mortis causa*. The case of *Re Weston* [1902] 1 Ch 680 seems to suggest that they cannot, but *Staniland v Willott* (1852) 3 Mac & G 664 indicates otherwise.

In *Vallee v Birchwood* [2013] EWHC 1449 (Ch), [2014] Ch 271, the court considered, *inter alia*, point (i) of the conditions for a gift prescribed by Lord Russell CJ in *Cain v Moon* [1896] 2 QB 283, and concluded that the gift was valid as it had been made in contemplation of death because the donor thought he might die within 5 months, which he did. The Court of Appeal has since considered the question in *King v Chiltern Dog Rescue* [2015] EWCA Civ 581, [2015] WTLR 1225 and held that *Vallee v Birchwood* had been wrongly decided, and therefore allowed the appeal. The facts in *King v Chiltern Dog Rescue* were that at the time of the purported gift, made by the donor some 4 to 6 months before her death, the donor was not contemplating her death in the sense required by the authorities, i.e. a reason to anticipate death in the near future from a known cause. At the time of making the purported gift, the donor had given the intended recipient the deeds to her property and an epitome of title, and said 'this will be yours when I go'. The court concluded that for a *donatio mortis causa* to be effective, it must be made in the contemplation of death in the near future and not merely a possibility of death at some future date weeks or even months ahead.

Jackson LJ at [53] expressed 'some mystification as to why the common law has adopted the doctrine of DMC at all', and continued, 'In my view therefore it is important to keep DMC within its proper bounds'.

Lastly, a valid *donatio mortis causa* cannot be revoked by a will (see *Jones v Selby* (1710) Prec Ch 300).

2.3   CONTRACTS TO MAKE A WILL

A promisor can execute a contract to make a will. The contract may contain clauses relating to the contents of the will to ensure, for example, that particular property is given by the will to the promisee. A contract merely to make a will is discharged by the execution of the will. If this is not done the promisee is, in theory, entitled to be placed in the same position as if the will had been made, but the problem is that the promisee has no knowledge of what property, if any, they would have received under the will had it been made. In any event, such a contract does not imply that the testator would not revoke a will made pursuant to the contract.

If the contract contains terms that specified property is to pass to the promisee, and the promisor alienates that property during their lifetime to a third party, then the promisee may sue the promisor (or their estate) for damages, or obtain a declaration of their right to the property, or obtain an injunction to prevent the alienation.

Contracts not to revoke a will can be executed and are valid. The court will not intervene to prevent the revocation of the will itself, but it will enforce the terms of the contract and grant an injunction and/or damages where the promisor seeks to alienate property in contravention of the agreement (see *Synge v Synge* [1894] 1 QB 466 and *Hammersley v De Biel* (1845) 12 Cl & Fin 45). Such a contract is not breached where revocation occurs by operation of law; it is breached only by the act(s) of the promisor. If the promisor remains bound by the contract to ensure that the property concerned passes to the promisee on death, the promisor may be obliged to execute a further will to give effect to the agreement.

For there to be a valid contract to make a will, or a valid contract not to revoke a will, there must be present the same basic elements as feature in any other contract:

(i)   an intention on the part of the promisor to enter into a contractual relationship;
(ii) offer and acceptance;
(iii) certainty of subject matter;
(iv) consideration or execution in the form of a covenant.

Where the contract is to make a will disposing of land then, if executed after 27 September 1989, it falls within the provisions of Law of Property (Miscellaneous Provisions) Act 1989, section 2 and must be made in writing.

2.4   JOINT AND MUTUAL WILLS

Two or more persons may execute the same document as the will of both or all of them in order, in a single transaction, to dispose of property belonging to each of them, jointly or separately. Such a document constitutes a joint will and is treated as the separate will of both or all of the testators. On the death of each testator, the will is admitted to probate provided that it remains unrevoked. Each testator is free to revoke or vary the will at any time, whether or not the other person is still alive; any declaration in a joint will to the effect that it is to be irrevocable does not prevent the testator from subsequently revoking it (see *Re Duddell* [1932] 1 Ch 585).

The mere fact that two wills are executed in a similar manner is not, however, sufficient to establish a joint will. A joint will is generally used in two situations only. The first is to exercise a joint power of appointment, and the second is where there is an intention to make mutual wills.

A mutual will (see Appendix A1B for a precedent) is made where two or more persons execute wills, usually in similar terms, conferring reciprocal benefits on one another, following an agreement between them to make such wills and not to revoke them without the consent of the other. Such wills can be contained in a single document, but it is more usual and advisable to use separate documents. To be 'mutual', wills must be made pursuant to an agreement to make mutual wills and not to revoke them once made (see *Goodchild v Goodchild* [1997] 1 WLR 1216). This agreement may be incorporated into the will by recital or otherwise, or it may be proved by extrinsic evidence, as was the case in *Fry v Densham-Smith* [2011] EWCA Civ 1410. It is clearly advisable that such an agreement be incorporated into the recitals. It can be oral or written, but in so far as it relates to land, it must be in writing (see *Humphreys v Green* (1882) 10 QBD 148). The court has been willing to infer an agreement from the conduct of the parties, the circumstances and the terms of the will (see *Dufour v Pereira* (1769) 1 Dick 419). The mere simultaneity and similarity of wills are not sufficient *per se* to establish the necessary agreement, but see *Olins v Walters* [2008] EWCA Civ 782, [2009] Ch 212. In the case of *Re Hagger* [1930] 2 Ch 190, there was a declaration by the parties that the will should not be altered or revoked except by their mutual agreement. It was implicit in this declaration that the parties agreed that the survivor should be bound by the arrangement. The requirement can also be satisfied by an agreement to leave property by a will. In *Re Green Deceased* [1951] Ch 148, a husband and wife made mutual wills which recited an agreement between them that, if the survivor had the use of the other's property for life without any liability to account, the survivor would provide by will for the carrying out of the wishes expressed in the other's will.

In *Charles and Others v Fraser* [2010] EWHC 2154 (Ch), there was sufficient evidence to allow wills to be found to be mutual despite not containing a statement that they were intended to be mutual. However, Mr Jonathan Gaunt QC (sitting as a Deputy Judge of the Chancery Division) said at [66]:

> I think it was the plain duty of any solicitor, then as now, faced with two sisters wishing to make reciprocal wills, to ascertain their intentions as to revocation, to advise as to the effect of making mutual wills and to ensure that any agreement the testatrices wished to make was clearly and accurately recorded.

If two wills, though similarly worded, are not intended to be mutual wills in the technical sense, then it is advisable to expressly state this at the end of the revocation clause.

2D   CLAUSE NEGATING MUTUAL WILLS

> Notwithstanding that my [spouse] [civil partner] [sibling] [etc] is making a will in similar terms to this will we have agreed that these our said wills are not mutual wills and that each of us shall be free to revoke [his] [her] will at any time whether before or after the death of the other and shall not be under any obligation or trust to dispose of any of [his] [her] property in accordance with the terms of the said wills.

Mutual wills are most commonly executed between spouses and normally take one of two forms. The first creates between the spouses reciprocal life interests, with a remainder over to their child(ren). The second form provides for absolute gifts between the spouses with alternative provisions, for example, a gift over to a child, in the event of the other person's predeceasing.

The following is an example of an agreement that mutual wills are to be irrevocable.

2E   MUTUAL WILLS – AGREEMENT NOT TO REVOKE

> WHEREAS my [spouse] [civil partner] [sibling] [etc] and I have agreed with one another to execute wills of the same date and in substantially similar terms and have further agreed that such respective wills shall not hereafter be revoked or altered either during our joint lives [or so long as we remain [married] [civil partners]] or by the survivor of us [if surviving as the [lawful spouse] [civil partner] of the other] I relying upon such agreement HEREBY GIVE ...

Once one of the parties dies with the mutual will unaltered, the arrangement becomes irrevocable, at least if the survivor accepts the benefits that are conferred on them by the other's will, and it seems doubtful that acceptance is formally necessary (see *Stone v Hoskins* [1905] P 194, 197 and *Olins v Walters* [2008] EWCA Civ 782, [2009] Ch 212). Until the first party dies, however, either may withdraw from the arrangement despite an agreement not to revoke.

In the case of *The Thomas Carvel and Agnes Carvel Foundation v Carvel and Another* [2007] EWHC 1314 (Ch), it was held that under the doctrine of mutual wills a trust arises on the death of the first of the two testators to die. The trust does not arise from the will of the survivor, but from the agreement between the two testators not to revoke their wills. Where two people had agreed to make mutual wills on the basis they would be irrevocable, equity will enforce that agreement after the death of the first testator by means of a constructive trust.

Wills Act 1837, sections 18A and 18B provide that a will is revoked by the marriage of, or formation of a civil partnership by, the testator. Such an event revokes a mutual will, but the trust binding the property takes effect on the second death.

The effect of the whole arrangement is that the survivor holds the property concerned on a constructive trust for the beneficiaries named in the wills. If the survivor alters their will, the personal representatives of the latter take the property subject to the earlier trusts. It is important to identify the property which falls within the boundaries of the trust. The will itself should define this and may bind part or the whole of each person's residuary estate. If the will is not clear on this point then there are four possibilities:

(i)   the trust attaches to the property which the survivor receives from the estate of the first to die; or

(ii) the trust attaches to all the property that the survivor owned at the time of the first death; or

(iii) the trust attaches to all the property which the survivor owned at their death; or

(iv) the trust attaches to all the property which the survivor owned at any time since the first death.

The trust must include the property in point (i) above, but the position is more difficult with regard to the survivor's property. In *Re Hagger* [1930] 2 Ch 190, it was said that all the property which the survivor had at the time of the first death would also be subject to the trust.

With regard to points (iii) and (iv) above, there appears to be a divergence of opinion. It was said in *Paul v Paul* (1882) 20 Ch D 742 that the agreement acts like a covenant to settle after-acquired property, and the property becomes subject to the trust when it becomes vested in the trustee. If this is correct, the effect of mutual wills is to reduce the position of the survivor to that of a mere life tenant in respect of all their property. In the case of *Re Cleaver* [1981] 1 WLR 939, however, Nourse J adopted the view that the survivor could enjoy the property as an absolute owner in his lifetime 'subject to a fiduciary duty which ... crystallised on his death and disabled him only from voluntary dispositions *inter vivos*'. It is submitted that the correct view is probably that the trust attaches itself to the property in points (i) and (ii) above. In view of the uncertainties concerning mutual wills, many people consider it preferable not to use them.

The case of *Healey v Brown and Another* [2002] EWHC 1405 (Ch), [2002] WTLR 849 is important since it is the first case to deal with the effect on mutual wills of the Law of Property (Miscellaneous Provisions) Act 1989, which requires a contract for the disposition of land to be in writing and signed by both parties. In the case, the agreement in the mutual wills related to a bequest of land, which is the same as a contract for the disposition of land. Law of Property (Miscellaneous Provisions) Act 1989, section 2 was not complied with because either:

(i)   the mutual wills could be regarded together as one agreement and there was no single document signed by both parties; or
(ii) the mutual wills could be regarded as two contracts, one made by the husband to leave the property to C if his wife died without revoking the will, and the other made by the wife in reverse terms. Section 2 is not satisfied in such a situation since the document must be signed by both parties, and the husband's will did not contain any terms as to consideration for his under-taking – namely that his wife should have maintained her will unrevoked to her death. Hence it did not incorporate all the terms.

In *Birmingham v Renfrew* (1937) 57 CLR 666, the Australian High Court held that the equivalent statute in Victoria was in principle engaged in a case where husband and wife made mutual wills. The statute was held inapplicable and the claim succeeded only on the basis that the will (and therefore the promise) referred simply to the entirety of the testator's estate on death, and therefore it could not be said, at the date of the agreement, that it concerned an interest in land, even if, at the time of death, the estate turned out to include such an interest.

In *Healey v Brown and Another* [2002] EWHC 1405 (Ch), [2002] WTLR 849, the agreement related to a specific gift of land and the statute was therefore relevant since the bequest of the survivor was explicitly of land. The disappointed beneficiary was prevented by reason of Law of Property (Miscellaneous Provisions) Act 1989, section 2 from establishing the contract at law which, according to *Goodchild v Goodchild* [1997] 1 WLR 1216, is necessary for the doctrine of mutual wills to operate.

In *Olins v Walters* [2007] EWHC 3060 (Ch), however, Norris J held that section 2 is only relevant where the agreement is expressed to relate to land. In *Olins*, the deceased's will simply asked her executors to convert her estate (which included land) and then disposed of the proceeds. In these circumstances the lack of a signed document was not fatal. The Court of Appeal upheld the judge's finding that the wills were mutual without expressing a view on this point ([2008] EWCA Civ 782, [2009] Ch 212).

In *Legg and Another v Burton and Others* [2017] EWHC 2088 (Ch), Paul Matthews J said at [23] that to make the success of a claim for mutual wills depend on whether a gift of land in a will is drafted as a gift of a particular interest in land or as a gift of residue happening to contain land seemed to him 'rather capricious, even unprincipled'. The form of the gift should not defeat its substance. He suggested the necessary equitable obligation to bind the conscience of the testator might arise from a proprietary estoppel rather than from a contract.

In view of the uncertainty where mutual wills relate to land, it is, therefore, important to have a document which complies with the requirements of Law of Property (Miscellaneous Provisions) Act 1989, section 2. These are that:

(i)   the agreement is in writing and incorporates all the terms which the parties have expressly agreed in one document;
(ii) the document incorporating the terms is signed by or on behalf of each party to the contract.

The easiest solution is to have a separate document signed by both parties which sets out:

- what each party agrees to do (leave their property in a particular way);
- the consideration (the reciprocal promise from the other party);
- the precondition for the agreement to become binding (that the first party to die should have maintained their will unrevoked up to death).

The cases of *Birch v Curtis* [2002] EWHC 1158 (Ch), [2002] 2 FLR 847 and *Legg and Another v Burton and Others* (above) are each salutary reminders of how much cost and ill-feeling can result when wills do not make clear whether or not they are intended to be mutual. It may be wise, in cases where argument may be expected after the first death, to include a statement in the wills that they are not intended to be mutual (see **2.3**).

2.5   PROPERTY WHICH CAN VALIDLY BE DISPOSED OF BY WILL

Testators can dispose of any property vested in them at the time of death provided the interest in the property does not cease on death. Where the testator has a mere possessory title to land, then any devise or bequest of such land is good to the extent of that title or interest, but is subject to any superior rights of other parties (see *Asher v Whitlock* (1865) LR 1 QB 1). A mere life interest (but not an interest *per autre vie*) or an unsevered joint tenancy cannot be disposed of by means of a will and the will itself cannot act to sever the joint tenancy, although an agreement by joint tenants to dispose of the property subject to the joint tenancy in their respective wills, followed by the execution of those wills, operates to sever the joint tenancy (see *Re Hey's Estate* [1914] P 192; and for more modern examples, see *Re Woolnough, Perkins v Borden* [2002] WTLR 595, *Carr v Isard* [2006] EWHC 2095 (Ch), [2007] WTLR 409 and *Chadda v RCC* [2014] UKFTT 1061 (TC)). Tenants in common can bequeath their shares in the equity of the property. Incorporeal hereditaments may be devised by a will except where they are inseparable from the tenement. If they are devised to the owner of the servient tenement then clearly they are extinguished.

Testators may dispose of moneys payable under an assurance policy affected on their own life in whatever manner they wish, unless the policy provides otherwise, for example, by nomination.

Testators are at liberty to dispose by will of shares in a company subject to the articles of association of the company concerned, which may restrict or preclude the disposal of shares, and give other shareholders a right to buy them from the personal representatives (see Companies Act 2006, Part 3, Chapter 3). All contingent and future interests in property can be disposed of by will, whether or not they are vested in the testator at the time of their death.

Where the testator has agreed to buy or sell an interest in property, that interest may still be devised by will but subject to the contract.

Whether a *chose in action* can be bequeathed in a will depends on the nature of the *chose*; it must be one that is capable of assignment. Where the *chose* amounts to a contract for personal services, or a mere right of litigation, or is one where assignment is prohibited by statute (e.g. certain types of salary or pension), it cannot be bequeathed in a will. Other types of *chose in action* can be bequeathed, but the gift of a debt does not entitle the legatee to sue in their own right. Such a right is vested in the personal representatives.

Along with the subject matter of any gift there impliedly passes as accessory to the main gift all the rights and benefits that are necessary for the reasonable enjoyment of the gift.

Chapter 3

Testamentary Capacity

3.1 CHANGES IN CAPACITY

A will made by a person of full capacity is not revoked merely by the fact that the person subsequently becomes incapable of making a will. Conversely, a will made by a person who is incapable of so doing does not become valid merely by the fact that the incapacity ceases, unless the will is re-executed by the testator when of full capacity.

3.2 MINORS

Wills executed before 1 January 1970 are governed by Wills Act 1837, section 7, which provides that no will made by a person under the age of 21 years is valid (except for privileged wills within the special provisions affecting soldiers in actual military service and mariners or seamen at sea; see Chapter 4). For a will executed on or after 1 January 1970, however, the testator need be aged only 18 years or over (see Family Law Reform Act 1969, section 3(1)).

3.3 PERSONS WHO LACK CAPACITY

The testator must have testamentary capacity and must know and approve of the contents of the will at the time they give instructions for the drafting and when it is drawn up. In general, testators must have testamentary capacity at the time the will is executed, but this is subject to the rule in *Parker v Felgate* (1883) 8 PD 171.

Mental Capacity Act 2005, section 1 introduced a statutory test for capacity to make a decision. There was some doubt as to whether or not the statutory test had replaced the common law test of testamentary capacity contained in *Banks v*

Goodfellow (1870) LR 5 QB 549. There were initially some conflicting decisions, but the prevailing view is now that the common law test remains (see *Scammell and Another v Farmer* [2008] EWHC 1100 (Ch), [2008] WTLR 1261, *Re Estate of Elizabeth Jane Walker (Deceased) (Probate); Walker and Another v Badmin* [2014] EWHC 71 (Ch), [2015] WTLR 493, *James v James and Others* [2018] EWHC 43 (Ch) and *Re Jean Mary Clitheroe (Deceased); Clitheroe v Bond* [2021] EWHC 1102 (Ch), [2021] COPLR 380).

The rule in *Parker v Felgate* (1883) 8 PD 171 provides that a will may be valid even though the testator had lost capacity at the time of execution. In *Clancy v Clancy* [2003] EWHC 1885 (Ch), [2003] WTLR 1097, the testator was terminally ill, had capacity at the time of giving instructions, but probably lacked capacity, through sedation, at the time of execution. The rule has more recently been considered in *Perrins v Holland and Others* [2010] EWCA Civ 840, [2011] Ch 270. In the *Perrins* case, the deceased, who suffered from multiple sclerosis which affected his speech and confined him to a wheelchair, had given instructions for a will in April 2000. He wished to leave his estate to his carer; he had separated from his wife, and their young son remained living with the wife, although there was evidence there was a loving relationship between father and son. As the will drafter (an experienced legal executive with more than 40 years' experience in will drafting) had received no response to the sending of the draft will some 18 months before, he submitted his bill but was then asked by the carer to send a further draft as the deceased wanted to execute the will. It was executed in September 2001 by which time the deceased's condition had worsened. In both *Clancy* and *Perrins*, it was held that the lack of testamentary capacity at the time of executing a will does not invalidate it, provided the three conditions are fulfilled:

(i)   the testator had capacity at the time of giving instructions for the will;
(ii) the will is prepared in accordance with those instructions; and
(iii) at the time of execution, the testator remembers giving instructions for a will and believes the will has been prepared in accordance with those instructions.

It is immaterial whether the testator remembers the precise instructions or could not understand the will if read over before execution.

Testators need not understand the precise legal machinery, as long as they understand the broad effects of the will. The classic statement of the test of a person's mental capacity can be found in the judgment of Cockburn CJ in the case of *Banks v Goodfellow* (1870) LR 5 QB 549, 565:

> It is essential ... that a testator shall understand the nature of the act and its effects; shall understand the extent of the property of which he is disposing; shall be able to

comprehend and appreciate the claims to which he ought to give effect; and, with a view to the latter object, that no disorder of the mind shall poison his affections, pervert his sense of right, or prevent the exercise of his natural faculties – that no insane delusion shall influence his will in disposing of his property and bring about a disposal of it which, if the mind had been sound, would not have been made.

The testator must have 'a memory to recall the several persons who may be fitting objects of the testator's bounty, and an understanding to comprehend their relationship to himself and their claims upon him', *per* Sir J Hannen in *Boughton v Knight* (1873) 3 P&D 64, 65 to 66. In *Re Loxton Deceased; Abbott v Richardson* [2006] EWHC 1291 (Ch), [2006] WTLR 1567, the court found the testatrix lacked capacity as she was unable to recall or focus on all the persons she might be expected to benefit and to arrive at a rational decision as to which of them should benefit and to what extent.

In *Re the Estate of the Right Honourable Sydney William Baron Templeman of White Lackington (Deceased); Goss-Custard and Another v Templeman and Others* [2020] EWHC 632 (Ch), the question of the testator's capacity was considered. The main dispute arose from the difference in the gift in previous testamentary documents of the testator's property in which he lived and which had been his wife's before they married. It was accepted that the testator suffered short-term memory loss from 2006 until his death in 2014. He had made his last will, the disputed will, in 2008. The gift of the property was different to that made in his previous will.

The will was professionally drawn by an experienced private client solicitor who had seen and discussed the will with the testator on at least three occasions. At the time of execution there was evidence to show the solicitor had asked the testator questions which he fully answered and the will was read over to him before execution.

The judge found that Lord Templeman had not forgotten the terms of his earlier will but had wanted to change them. However, he said that even if Lord Templeman had been unable to remember what was included in his previous wills, this did not amount to a lack of capacity. He was able to comprehend and appreciate the claims to which he ought to give effect. The judge said at [133]:

> Comprehension and appreciation of the calls on a testator's bounty does not require actual knowledge of other gifts that have been made to, or the financial circumstances of, a potential object. A testator does not have to have all the facts with which to make a correct or justifiable decision; he has to have the capacity to decide for himself between competing claims. That means that he must have the ability to inform himself about those claims, to the extent that he wishes to do so, but not that he must remember the relevant facts about each of the potential objects or have correctly understood their financial circumstances.

In *Simon v Byford and Others* [2013] EWHC 1490 (Ch), [2013] All ER (D) 321 (May) and upheld on appeal [2014] EWCA Civ 280, the court made it clear that capacity does not have to be perfect. In this case, it was common ground that the deceased was suffering from mild to moderate dementia of such a degree as to put her testamentary capacity at the date of her will in doubt. The claimant unsuccessfully challenged the validity of the will.

It was settled law that testamentary capacity required the testatrix to be able to remember the claims which potential beneficiaries had on the estate, so as to achieve a rational and just testament. The test of capacity was issue-specific and was to be considered in relation to the particular transaction and its nature and complexity. It was not necessary that the testatrix should be able to understand the legal terminology which gave effect to her wishes. Once a court was satisfied that the testatrix had the capacity to understand what she had been doing, it was readily accepted that she had understood. Nevertheless, in some cases it was necessary to prove knowledge and approval. That was so where the testatrix was mentally or physically frail, or where beneficiaries had been part of the process of drawing up the will. In such cases, the judge had to consider whether the suspicion had been dispelled.

The testatrix had been capable of understanding (and had understood) the nature of a will and the effect of the will, which had been a very simple one. It was sufficient that she had understood that her late son's share would go to his family trust without further details. She had been capable, if she had wanted to know who the beneficiaries would be, of asking, but had not done so. She had been capable of understanding (and had understood) that her property had included her house, the flat and some shares. She was capable of understanding (and had understood) that she had owned other money and investments, but on the balance of probabilities, she had not been capable, without being told, of remembering the details. Since the testatrix, for the most part, had been leaving everything to her children in equal shares, she had not needed precise knowledge as to the extent of her estate, and the knowledge she had had been ample. Further, she had been capable of accessing the information about her previous will, which she would have understood, but had chosen not to do so. She had actually understood that her previous will had benefited the claimant in some way, but at the relevant time, wished to treat her four children equally.

HHJ Paul Matthews took the same approach in *James v James and Others* [2018] EWHC 43 (Ch) at [116], where the deceased had been diagnosed with dementia some years before making the challenged will. However, the will was simple, as were the assets and the family relationships. HHJ Matthews said 'the testator suffered from memory loss and confusion from time to time, and even some irrational behaviour. But there is also considerable evidence of normal behaviour and rational thought'. He also considered it important that:

> compared to some cases, this testator had relatively few claims upon his inheritance to consider, namely those of his wife and his three adult and emancipated children, and a fairly straightforward (if nevertheless valuable) estate to dispose of, largely consisting of land close by to him which he had worked on during his life and knew well, and some cash or cash-equivalent investments. The simpler the estate and the fewer claimants, the less difficult it is to dispose of, and accordingly the less acute the faculties required to do so successfully.

In *Key and Others v Key and Others* [2010] EWHC 408 (Ch), a will was executed within a few days of the testator's wife's death. In his judgment, Briggs J (as he then was) said at [94] to [95]:

> It was also common ground before me that the *Banks v Goodfellow* test for testamentary capacity has not been displaced by the Mental Capacity Act 2005, at least for the purposes of the present case, in which the 2006 will was made before that Act came into force.
>
> Without in any way detracting from the continuing authority of *Banks v Goodfellow*, it must be recognised that psychiatric medicine has come a long way since 1870 in recognising an ever widening range of circumstances now regarded as sufficient at least to give rise to a risk of mental disorder, sufficient to deprive a patient of the power of rational decision making, quite distinctly from old age and infirmity. The mental shock of witnessing an injury to a loved one is an example recognised by the law, and the affective disorder which may be caused by bereavement is an example recognised by psychiatrists. The symptomatic effect of bereavement [is] capable of being almost identical to that associated with severe depression. Accordingly, although neither I nor counsel has found any reported case dealing with the effect of bereavement on testamentary capacity, the *Banks v Goodfellow* test must be applied so as to accommodate this, among other factors capable of impairing testamentary capacity, in a way in which, perhaps, the court would have found difficult to recognise in the 19th century.

Care should therefore be exercised in taking instructions for a will, and having it executed soon after the death of someone close to the deceased. In the present case, it was the testator's wife of 65 years. Note, however, that the decision in *Key* was in the context of the unusual behaviour of the testator and pressure from outside sources.

A will is not invalid merely because the testator is motivated by frivolous or bad motives and spite. Eccentricity or mere foolishness is again insufficient to show want of capacity to make a will, although what amounts to mere eccentricity in one person may amount to incapacity in another (see *Mudway v Croft* (1843) 3 Curt 671).

3.3.1   Delusions

A testator lacks testamentary capacity if, at the time of making the will, they suffer from delusions which in any way influence, or are capable of influencing, the provisions of their will. A delusion is a belief in the existence of something in which no rational person could believe. Sir J Hannen in *Boughton v Knight* (1873) 3 P&D 64, 68 said that the jury must ask themselves, 'Can I understand how any man in possession of his senses could have believed such and such a thing? ... if the answer you give is, I cannot understand it, then ... you should say the man is not sane'. A delusion is not necessarily incompatible with the ability to act rationally, and it is a question of fact whether the delusion actually affected the disposition.

Cockburn CJ, in *Banks v Goodfellow* (1870) LR 5 QB 549, 565, said:

> If the human instincts and affections, or the moral sense, become perverted by mental disease; if insane suspicion, or aversion, take the place of natural affection; if reason and judgement are lost, and the mind becomes a prey to insane delusions calculated to interfere with and disturb its functions, and to lead to a testamentary disposition, due only to their baneful influence – in such a case it is obvious that the condition of the testamentary power fails, and that a will made under such circumstances ought not to stand.

Thus for delusions to be a cause of incapacity, the intelligence must be so adversely affected that the testator does not appreciate the testamentary act in all its bearings. In *Re Ritchie* [2009] EWHC 709 (Ch), the deceased had made a will leaving her £2.5 million estate to charity, disinheriting her four children. The deceased was a difficult woman with some elements of obsessive compulsive disorder. The solicitor will drafter, when giving evidence at the trial, said that the deceased had told him her sons were stealing from her and taking advantage of her; that one of her sons was violent to her and had tried to throttle her; and her daughters never came to see her and gave her no help. These allegations were strenuously denied by the children. The judge accepted the allegations were delusions and, pronouncing against the will, accepted the deceased would not have disinherited her children if she had not suffered from these delusions.

In *Re Estate of Charles Skillett, Deceased (Probate); Skillett v Skillett* [2022] EWHC 233 (Ch), [2022] WTLR 679, the testator and his wife had executed 'mirror image' wills on 19 May 2011. The testator's will was challenged on the grounds of lack of mental capacity and want of knowledge and approval. The wills were professionally drawn and made in accordance with the instructions given.

The testator had been diagnosed with Parkinson's disease in 2007 and suffered from hallucinations. The medical evidence showed that it was likely that the testator had progressed from a mild degree of impairment to a moderate degree of impairment by 2011 when he made his will. Although hallucinations were a very marked feature of the testator's illness, there is nothing to suggest that they affected the testamentary disposition. They were unpleasant and intrusive, and at times they produced aggressive behaviour towards those close to him, but their content does not appear to have driven his decisions about the will. On the balance of probability, the testator's impairment of cognitive function was not sufficient to have undermined his testamentary capacity at the time of the 2011 will.

It was held that this was not a case where the evidence was so lacking that the court needed to decide it on the burden of proof. HHJ Mott QC (sitting as a Deputy High Court Judge) went on to say at [62]:

> The accepted diagnosis of [Parkinson's disease], together with the persistent hallucinations recorded in the medical records, as well as the descriptive evidence of family members, makes it necessary to scrutinise the evidence as a whole. I cannot simply presume capacity from the due execution of the will, even though it appears rational on its face.

The court was satisfied on all the evidence that the testator did have testamentary capacity at the time he executed his will on 19 May 2011.

In *Re Jean Mary Clitheroe (Deceased); Clitheroe v Bond* [2021] EWHC 1102 (Ch), [2021] COPLR 380, the court accepted that the testatrix had been suffering from delusions which had affected her testamentary capacity when she had made either of her two wills.

Falk J said that to be delusional the belief must be irrational and fixed in nature. The point in issue was what was necessary to prove that the belief is irrational and fixed in nature? Falk J made the following points:

- Where the belief is obviously extreme and irrational (e.g. belief by a testatrix that she was a member of the Holy Trinity), it is unlikely to be difficult to demonstrate that it amounts to a delusion.
- Where a belief does not fall into that category, one way of demonstrating that it amounts to a delusion is to show by evidence that the individual could not, in fact, be reasoned out of it. However, it is not necessary to show that such an attempt was actually made.
- Another way is to show that the belief was formed and maintained in the face of clear evidence to the contrary, of which the individual was plainly aware (such that there is no sensible basis on which to conclude that the

individual was simply mistaken or had forgotten the true position, as opposed to being delusional).
- A further alternative is to demonstrate that the individual had no basis on which they could rationally have formed and maintained the mistaken belief.

The key question in each case is whether the relevant irrational belief is fixed.

3.3.2　Drink and drugs

The use of alcohol or drugs by the testator is not, *per se*, proof of incapacity. Even though a person is an habitual drunkard, they are, when not drunk, capable of making a will (see *Billinghurst v Vickers* (1810) 161 ER 956). For drunkenness to vitiate a will, it must have the effect on the testator that they do not know the nature of the act they are performing (see *Chana v Chana* [2001] WTLR 205).

3.3.3　Evidence of lack of mental capacity

In questions relating to lack of capacity, the legal burden of proof always lies upon the person propounding the will to prove that the testator had testamentary capacity at the time the will was made. If a duly executed will is rational on the face of it, there is a presumption that the testator had testamentary capacity. This may be rebutted by evidence to the contrary.

In *Key and Others v Key and Others* [2010] EWHC 408 (Ch), Briggs J (as he then was) summarised at [97] the rules on burden of proof as follows:

> The burden of proof in relation to testamentary capacity is subject to the following rules:
>
> (i)　While the burden starts with the propounder of a will to establish capacity, where the will is duly executed and appears rational on its face, then the court will presume capacity.
> (ii)　In such a case the evidential burden then shifts to the objector to raise a real doubt about capacity.
> (iii)　If a real doubt is raised, the evidential burden shifts back to the propounder to establish capacity nonetheless.

If there is any doubt about an intending testator's mental capacity, then, to prevent a later challenge to the will, it is a wise precaution to have a medical practitioner present at the time of execution. The medical practitioner should either sign as a witness to the will or be referred to in the attestation clause.

The 'golden rule' expressed by Templeman J in *Kenward v Adams* (*The Times*, 29 November 1975) was that when a solicitor is drawing up a will for an aged or infirm testator, or one who has been seriously ill, the will should be witnessed and approved by a medical practitioner, who should record their examination of the testator and their findings.

It is often helpful to carry out a mini mental state examination, but care must be exercised in interpreting the results. In *Tchilingirian v Ouzounian* [2003] EWHC 1220 (Ch), [2003] WTLR 709, the testatrix had scored 15 out of 30 points and appeared lucid and articulate, but the court still found she lacked capacity to execute her will.

It is important to make a full attendance note, including matters relevant to the client's mental capacity in case there is a challenge. See for example *Coles v Reynolds and Another* [2020] EWHC 2151 (Ch), where HHJ Paul Matthews (sitting as a Judge of the High Court) gave weight to the checklists attached to the solicitor's attendance notes, which were full and contemporaneous. He said at [73] to [74]:

> I have already mentioned the checklists attached to the attendance note of the solicitor. They deal with a number of matters, including testamentary capacity. But the solicitor also notes that the deceased 'seemed relaxed', and 'answered all questions put to her'. Moreover, in a section headed 'Undue Influence,' the solicitor is asked the following questions:
>
>> 'Would you consider the client to be vulnerable to undue influence? Does anything in the discussion raise any suspicions of undue influence in your mind? Is there anything in the proposed gifts in the will or disclosed lifetime gifts that gives rise to a concern about undue influence?'
>
> The answers given by the solicitor are as follows:
>
>> 'Client of a certain age with certain requirements who is cared for by one daughter over another. Asked daughter to leave meeting which she was happy to do and client was happy to see [solicitor] alone also. Noted that [earlier solicitor] also asked daughter to leave during initial meeting.'
>
> From this, I infer that the only circumstance which the solicitor thought worth noting was the fact that the deceased's needs were being met by one daughter rather than another, but that there was nothing else. I add only that I am entirely satisfied on the

basis of this material that the deceased had capacity to make it, and that it was duly executed.

3.3.4   Wills made by the court

Mental Capacity Act 2005, section 16, which came into force on 7 October 2007 provides for the Court of Protection to make an order for a will to be made on behalf of an adult mental patient where the court believes that the patient is incapable of making a will for themselves. Section 5 provides that 'An act done, or decision made, under this Act for or on behalf of a person who lacks capacity must be done, or made, in his best interests'.

In determining for the purposes of the Mental Capacity Act 2005 what is in a person's best interests, the person making the determination must not make it merely on the basis of the person's age or appearance, or a condition of theirs, or an aspect of their behaviour, which might lead others to make unjustified assumptions about what might be in that person's best interests. The person making the determination must also consider all the relevant circumstances and, in particular, whether it is likely that the person will at some time have capacity in relation to the making of a will, and if it appears likely that they will, when that is likely to be.

The person making the determination must, so far as reasonably practicable, permit and encourage the person to participate, or to improve their ability to participate, as fully as possible in any act done for them and any decision affecting them. In *Re P* [2009] EWHC 163 (Ch), Lewison J expressed the view that the Mental Capacity Act 2005 marks a radical change in the treatment of persons lacking capacity, imposing an overarching requirement that any decision (making a will) must be made in the person's best interests. 'Best interests' requires the application of an objective test not a substituted judgment. This approach was also adopted in *ITW v Z and Others* [2009] EWHC 2525 (Fam). The issue of 'best interests' in statutory wills was further considered in *Re JC; D v JC (Statutory Will Application)* [2012] WTLR 1211. The judge said that assessing the best interests of P was only of limited use when making a statutory will as opposed to cases where lifetime gifts were being sought. In the instant case, the intestate beneficiaries on P's death would be his children whom it was sought to benefit under the proposed will (P had four children but one child had been adopted). Although P had had a generally poor relationship with his second and third children, he had been closer to two of them, but that was no reason to exclude the first, even though P wrongly doubted his paternity. So the three children entitled on intestacy would share his estate equally under the statutory will.

The former approach to a statutory will – making the will the person would have made if they had a lucid moment – is no longer appropriate. The current test is a 'best interests' test not a 'substituted judgement' test.

Such a will should be signed by the person authorised by the order, with the name of the patient and with their own name, in the presence of two or more witnesses present at the same time, and these witnesses should attest and subscribe in the usual way (see Mental Capacity Act 2005, Schedule 2). The will is then authenticated with the official seal of the Court of Protection.

Where an order has been made for a will to be executed on behalf of a patient, the will is valid even though it is not sealed by the Court of Protection before the patient's death (see *In Re Hughes*, *The Times*, 8 January 1999), the sealing required by Mental Health Act 1983, section 97(1) under Court of Protection Rules 2001 (SI 2001/824), rule 90 being an 'evidential act' and not a 'formal' requirement to validate the will. See also the Court of Protection Practice Directions to the Court of Protection Rules 2007 (SI 2007/1744).

The form of commencement for such a will can take the following form.

3A   FORM OF COMMENCEMENT OF WILL MADE UNDER THE MENTAL CAPACITY ACT 2005

I [testator] of [address (including postcode)] HEREBY REVOKE all former wills and testamentary dispositions made by me and declare this to be my last will which is executed for me by [name of authorised person] of [address] [he] [she] being the person authorised to execute it by an Order made on [date] by the Court of Protection pursuant to Mental Capacity Act 2005, section 16 and Schedule 2.

For an attestation clause for such a will, see Precedent 4I.

The power of the court can also be invoked to remedy an injustice caused by the effect of ademption on a specific legacy, or to avoid an undesired intestacy (see *Re Davey* [1981] 1 WLR 164).

3.4   INTENTION

The testator must have the intention, or the *animus testandi*, to make a will. The test is whether, by their act, the testator intends to make a disposition of their property which is to take effect on their death, whether or not the testator knows at that time that the disposition is in law a will.

Where the transaction was effected by a document which has been executed in a manner satisfying the requirements of Wills Act 1837, section 9 (see Chapter 4), but it is unclear whether it is to be a will, extrinsic evidence will be admitted by the court to decide the issue.

3.5   KNOWLEDGE AND APPROVAL

Before a will is admitted to probate, the court must be satisfied that the testator knew and approved of the contents at the time they signed it. Usually, proof of testamentary capacity and due execution suffice to establish knowledge and approval, but in certain cases the court may require further evidence. These cases include where the person who prepared the will is also to receive a benefit under it (see **3.7.4**, and *Franks v Sinclair and Others* [2006] EWHC 3365 (Ch), [2007] WTLR 439), and where the testator is deaf and dumb, illiterate or blind. A will executed in accordance with Wills Act 1837, section 9 (see Chapter 4) will be accepted to proof in common form without supporting evidence, unless the probate district judge or registrar has any cause for concern, such as where the testator's signature is frail.

Judges used to apply a two-stage approach to the issue of knowledge and approval (see, e.g. *Barry v Butlin* [1838] 2 Moo PCC 480 and *Tyrrell v Painton* [1894] 1 P 151):

(i)   Are the facts sufficient facts to rebut the presumption of knowledge and approval and 'excite the suspicion of the court'?
(ii)   Has the person seeking to prove the will managed to allay those suspicions?

However, in *Gill v Woodall and Others* [2010] EWCA Civ 1430, Neuberger LJ said at [22] that where a judge had heard evidence of fact and expert opinion over a period of many days, 'the value of such a two-stage approach to deciding the issue of the testatrix's knowledge and approval appears to me to be questionable'.

In his view, the approach which it would, at least generally, be better to adopt was that summarised by Sachs J in *Crerar v Crerar* (unreported) but followed by Latey J in *Re Morris, Deceased* [1971] P 62, 78E to G, namely that the court should:

> consider all the relevant evidence available and then, drawing such inferences as it can from the totality of that material, it has to come to a conclusion whether or not those propounding the will have discharged the burden of establishing that the testatrix knew and approved the contents of the document which is put forward as a valid testamentary disposition. The fact that the testatrix read the document, and the fact that she executed it, must be given the full weight apposite in the circumstances, but in law those facts are not conclusive, nor do they raise a presumption.

In *In the Estate of Sherrington; Sherrington and Others v Sherrington* [2005] EWCA Civ 326, [2005] 3 FCR 538, the court of first instance (having pronounced against the will for lack of due execution) held that it was for the person seeking to propound a will to establish that the testator had knowledge of, and approved, its contents (see **4.4**).

The rule in *Parker v Felgate* (1883) 8 PD 171 considered at **3.3** in relation to capacity applied equally to knowledge and approval. In *Perrins v Holland and Others* [2010] EWCA Civ 840, [2011] Ch 270 at [32], Sir Andrew Morritt C approved the trial judge's finding that 'in a case in which the principle in *Parker v Felgate* is applied it is not necessary to prove knowledge and approval of the will, provided that (a) the testator believes that it gives effect to his instructions and (b) it does in fact do so'.

Where the testator has read their will, or where it has been read over to them before execution, or where the contents of the will have been brought to the testator's attention in any other way, for example by sign language or through a translator, and the will has been executed, this gives rise to a rebuttable presumption that the testator knew and approved of the contents of the document. In *Hawes v Burgess and Another* [2013] EWCA Civ 74, the court held it was good practice to send a draft will to the testator for him to consider before execution of it. In the instant case, the will had been read over by the solicitor to the testatrix immediately before execution, but this had been done in the presence of another (her daughter), leaving cause for concern for lack of knowledge and understanding.

The question of the provision of evidence was considered in *Re Devillebichot (Deceased); Brennan v Prior and Others* [2013] EWHC 2867 (Ch), where the court held it was settled law that an assertion that the testator did not know and approve of the will required the court to be satisfied that the testator understood what he was doing and its effect. In the instant case, the will had not been drawn up by a solicitor, and had instead been encouraged and drawn up by members of the family who stood to benefit under it. However, looking at the evidence, the testator did know and approve the contents of the will. The law did not require a testator to be shown to have had knowledge and approval of every effect and consequence of their will. All that was required was satisfactory evidence that the testator knew and approved the contents of their will. In the instant case, the necessary requirements had been satisfied.

The question of knowledge and approval was considered in *Sharp v Hutchins; Re the Estate of Ronald Hubert Butcher Deceased* [2015] EWHC 1240 (Ch), [2015] WTLR 1269, in which the claimant was the executor and sole beneficiary under a will made by the deceased in 2013 (the 2013 will). He and the deceased had struck up a friendship after meeting about 6 years prior to the deceased's death, when the claimant, a builder, had been doing some work in the same area in which the deceased lived. The defendant was the executor and one of three beneficiaries under an earlier will made by the deceased in 2011 (the 2011 will). The defendant challenged the 2013 will for want of knowledge and approval. It was agreed that the deceased had had capacity at the time he had executed both the 2011 and 2013 wills. The court ruled there was sufficient evidence from which to reach the conclusion, applying the single-stage test in authority, that the claimant had discharged the burden of proving, on the balance of probabilities, that the deceased had understood what was in the 2013 will when he had signed it and what its effect would be. The court was satisfied that the 2013 will had been executed with the knowledge and approval of the deceased, and that he had intended it to give effect to his testamentary wishes.

The question of knowledge and approval was more recently considered in *Re Estate of Charles Skillett, Deceased (Probate); Skillett v Skillett* [2022] EWHC 233 (Ch), [2022] WTLR 679 (see **3.3.1**).

3.6 MISTAKE

There are three possible mistakes which may occur:

(i)   the wrong document may be executed;
(ii)   the testator may mistakenly believe certain circumstances or facts exist, and these affect their motives for the provisions of the will;
(iii) the testator may be mistaken as to the effect of a will, or of one or more of its provisions.

Where a document is executed by mistake, it is not admitted to probate. In *Re Meyer's Estate* [1908] P 353, it was held that, where two sisters executed codicils in similar terms and by mistake each executed the codicil intended for, and purporting to be that of, the other sister, probate would be refused. There was no intention to execute the document propounded, even though it contained some testamentary dispositions which were in fact intended by the testatrix, and which were common to the two documents executed. If the testator intended certain words to be used in the will, and they are, but the testator is mistaken as to their legal effect, the will is nevertheless admitted to probate. However, see now the decision of the Supreme Court in *Marley v Rawlings and Another* [2014] UKSC 2, [2015] AC 129 (where the husband and wife each executed the other's will), in which the court directed the wills be rectified under Administration of Justice Act 1982, section 20(1)(a), holding that the signatures on the wrong wills were a clerical error (see Chapter 24).

Courts have three limited powers to alter the words in a will:

(i) A court of probate may omit from the will any words which the testator did not know of and approve. However, the court will refuse to omit part of the will from probate if the effect of the remainder is altered (see *Re Horrocks* [1939] P 198). If a testator died before 1983, the court, when admitting the will to probate, had no power to add any words which the testator intended. It had power to omit words from the will if such words were considered offensive, libellous or blasphemous, and it was immaterial that the effect of this might indeed render a clause in the will ambiguous or even meaningless.

(ii) Where the testator died after 31 December 1982, Administration of Justice Act 1982, section 20 empowers the court to order that a will be rectified so as to carry out the intention of the testator. This can be done only if the court is satisfied that the will fails to carry out the testator's intentions because of a clerical error, or a failure to understand their instructions.

If a court rectifies a will under section 20 then it may add to the will words that were intended by the testator. If, however, the will does not carry out the testator's intentions for some other reason, section 20 does not apply (see also *Kell v Jones and Others* [2012] EWHC B30 (Ch), [2013] All ER (D) 153 (Jan)). Most applications to rectify are made before the grant, but an application for rectification must be made not later than 6 months from the date on which a grant of probate or letters of administration to the deceased's estate is first taken out, although the court does have a discretion to extend this time limit. An unopposed application to rectify may be made in the Family Division to a district judge of the Principal Registry or district probate registrar. An opposed application must be made to the Chancery Division.

(iii) A court of construction can construe the will as though certain words were inserted, omitted or changed, provided it is clear from the will that an error has been made in the wording and it is clear what the substance of the intended wording was (see Chapter 24 for a further discussion on this point).

3.7 FORCE, FEAR, FRAUD OR UNDUE INFLUENCE

If a will is made as a consequence of force, fear, fraud or undue influence, it is not regarded as the act of the testator and is not admitted to probate. The burden of proof is on the person alleging the irregularity, and there are no presumptions to assist.

3.7.1   Force and fear

If a testator made a will as a result of having been injured or threatened with injury then the will may be admitted to probate only if pronounced for in solemn form in a probate claim. A disappointed beneficiary in a later will was entitled to the benefit they would have received under an earlier will where the testator had been induced by threats of violence to omit the legacy from their later will (see *Betts v Doughty* (1879–80) LR 5 PD 26).

3.7.2   Fraud

Fraud is something which misleads the testator. Lord Langdale said, in *Giles v Giles* (1836) 1 Keen 685, 692, 'a legacy given to a person in a character which the legatee does not fill, and by the fraudulent assumption of which character the testator has been deceived, will not take effect'. Fraud includes making false representations about the character of others in order to induce the testator to make or revoke gifts, or to exclude persons from a proposed will.

3.7.3   Undue influence

Undue influence is something that overpowers the volition of the testator. It is permissible to persuade a testator, but not to coerce them. Undue influence is not presumed (see *Parfitt v Lawless* (1872) LR 2 P&D 462). It may be difficult in some situations to distinguish between persuasion and undue influence, but provided the testator retained real freedom of choice a court does not normally interfere. If, on the other hand, the testator surrendered to intolerable pressure the court will intervene. *Pesticcio v Huet; Niersmans v Pesticcio* [2004] EWCA Civ 372, [2004] WTLR 699 is a good example of undue influence in making a lifetime gift.

The court is more inclined to find undue influence where the testator is physically or mentally weak. The concept of undue influence in probate is confined to actual undue influence. Therefore, any challenge to a will based on undue influence must be alleged and proved (see *In the Estate of Sherrington; Sherrington and Others v Sherrington* [2005] EWCA Civ 326, [2005] 3 FCR 538). The mere proof of the relationship of parent and child, confessor and penitent, guardian and ward, husband and wife, doctor and patient, or tutor and pupil, does not of itself raise a presumption of undue influence sufficient to vitiate a will.

The burden of evidence of undue influence was considered in *Re Devillebichot (Deceased); Brennan v Prior and Others* [2013] EWHC 2867 (Ch), where the court held the execution of a will as a result of undue influence had to be proved, as a fact, by those who asserted that influence. They had to establish that there was coercion, pressure that had overpowered the freedom of action of the testator without having convinced his mind. If the evidence established only persuasion, then a case of undue influence would not be made out. In the instant case, there was plenty of evidence that two of the testator's siblings had had the opportunity to influence the testator in the making of the will, and indeed that they had done so. However, there was no evidence of coercion or pressure so as to have overpowered the testator's freedom of action. There had been persuasion, but no coercion. The point had arisen in *Cowderoy v Cranfield* [2011] EWHC 1616 (Ch), [2011] WTLR 1699 and *Wharton v Bancroft and Others* [2011] EWHC 3250 (Ch), [2012] WTLR 693, both of which were applied in *Re Devillebichot*. *Wharton v Bancroft and Others* was quoted in *Coles v Reynolds and Others* [2020] EWHC 2151 (Ch).

In *Sifri v Clough and Willis* [2007] EWHC 985 (Ch), [2007] WTLR 1453, the judge was critical of the solicitor will drafter who was sued for negligence in drafting the will. The solicitor had not ensured the instructions were from the testator. In his judgment, HHJ Roger Kaye QC (sitting as a Judge of the High Court) said at [17]:

> if a solicitor does fail to take instructions from the proposed testator, does take them from a third party and does not check to see he has understood his instructions properly and moreover, as alleged in this case, does not keep a proper note of his instructions, it is reasonably foreseeable that a challenge to whatever will is executed as a result will in turn ensue and the costs thereby incurred are also foreseeable.

In *Coles v Reynolds and Others* [2020] EWHC 2151 (Ch) (in which one of two daughters was excluded from the will), the solicitor drafting the will made a note that the testatrix was in her eighties, but she knew exactly what she was doing when she made her will, she explained why she was not leaving her daughter anything in her will and she was sound of mind when writing her will. The drafter also suggested that the testatrix might want to get a doctor's note showing that the testatrix knew what she was doing in case the excluded daughter did contest the will as it would provide more evidence to support knowledge and approval. Such evidence was obtained.

The court held that the allegation of undue influence in the making of the will was not made out. The deceased was independently advised by her solicitors, who were not acting for anyone else and who interviewed her on her own, and she satisfied them that she wished to make the will in the form that she executed. Given the breakdown in relations between the deceased and the claimant, the change in the deceased's testamentary wishes was quite understandable, and, on that basis, it was hard to see what more she could have done to put it into effect.

It was evident that the claimant did not like the change. But that did not mean that there must have been undue influence.

3.7.4 Will prepared by a beneficiary

Where a person who prepared a will for a testator is one of the beneficiaries of the will, a suspicion of undue influence arises and must be dispelled by the person propounding the will. The degree of suspicion varies according to the circumstances of the case. In the case of *Wyniczenko v Plucinska-Surowka* [2005] EWHC 2794 (Ch), [2006] WTLR 487, the testatrix had made a new will differing from her previous will by excluding charitable bequests and a gift to her niece (the claimant and only relative), and leaving all her estate to the defendant. The defendant had drafted the will for the testatrix. The court held that where a beneficiary is involved in the making of the will the court's suspicions are aroused. The defendant did not satisfy the court that the will reflected the testatrix's true wishes, and therefore failed (see also *Franks v Sinclair and Others* [2006] EWHC 3365 (Ch), [2007] WTLR 439; **3.5**).

Those regulated by the Solicitors Regulation Authority (SRA) are subject to special rules of conduct set out in the SRA Standards and Regulations 2019 replacing the SRA Code of Conduct 2011.

The SRA Standards and Regulations 2019, unlike the Code of Conduct, makes no specific references to legacies to those preparing wills. However, the obligatory Principles which underpin the Standards require those regulated to act with honesty and integrity (principles 4 and 5) and in the best interests of the client (principle 7).

The SRA issued the following Ethics Guidance for Private Client practitioners entitled *Drafting and Preparation of Wills* on 6 May 2014 (updated 25 November 2019, available at www.sra.org.uk/solicitors/guidance/drafting-preparation-wills/). The guidance is not mandatory and is issued to help those regulated by the SRA understand their obligations and how to comply with them. However, the SRA may have regard to it when exercising its regulatory functions:

Gifts to you or someone in your business
If you draft a will where the client wishes to make a gift of significant value to you or a member of your family, or an employee of your business or their family, you should satisfy yourself that the client has first taken independent legal advice with regard to making the gift.
This includes situations where the intended gift is of significant value in relation to the size of the client's overall estate, but also where the gift is of significant value in itself. Paragraph 6.1 of each of the Codes requires you not to act if there is an own interest conflict or a significant risk of an own interest conflict. In a situation like this, you will

usually need to cease acting if the client does not agree to taking independent legal advice.

There may be some exceptions where you can continue to draft the will even if the client has not received independent legal advice for example, if you draft wills for your parents and the surviving parent wishes to leave the residuary estate to you and your siblings in equal shares.

However, whether it is appropriate to do so will depend upon the specific circumstances of each situation, and in each case you should consider whether your ability to advise, and be seen to advise, impartially is undermined by any financial interest or personal relationship which you have.

A testator may wish to give property to their solicitor to be held on a secret trust for specified beneficiaries, the solicitor receiving no personal benefit. The solicitor is free to prepare such a will, but the Council of the Law Society, and now the SRA, advises that the instructions from the client be preserved and the terms of the trust be embodied in a written document signed or initialled by the testator.

A solicitor is also perfectly entitled, with their client's approval, to include a charging clause in a will, authorising the solicitor to charge for services performed in connection with the administration of the estate (or of any trust arising under the will). See Chapter 22 for specimen charging clauses.

Practitioners' attention is drawn to the following Law Society practice notes, which are available on the 'Advice and practice notes', 'Topics and Resources/ Private Client' section of the Law Society website:

- *Appointment of a Professional Executor*, 3 September 2020, www.lawsociety.org.uk/Topics/Private-client/Practice-notes/Appointment -of-a-professional-executor.
- *Preparing a Will when your Client is Leaving a Gift for You, Your Family or Colleagues*, 4 September 2020, www.lawsociety.org.uk/Topics/ Private-client/Practice-notes/Preparing-a-will-when-your-client-is-leaving-a-gift-for-you-your-family-or-colleagues.

Chapter 4

Formal Requirements for the Creation of a Will

4.1   GENERAL

Wills Act 1837, section 9, as substituted by Administration of Justice Act 1982, section 17, provides that a will or any form of testamentary disposition is valid if:

(a)   it is in writing, and signed by the testator, or by some other person in his presence and by his direction; and

(b)   it appears that the testator intended by his signature to give effect to the will; and

(c)   the signature is made or acknowledged by the testator in the presence of two or more witnesses present at the same time; and

(d)   each witness either—

    (i)   attests and signs the will; or

    (ii)   acknowledges his signature, in the presence of the testator (but not necessarily in the presence of any other witness),

but no form of attestation shall be necessary.

This amended section applies to cases where the testator died after 31 December 1982.

The Wills Act 1837 (Electronic Communications) (Amendment) (Coronavirus) Order 2020 (SI 2020/952) amended Wills Act 1837, section 9, as set out above, on a temporary basis to allow wills to be witnessed remotely for a limited period. The change ceases to apply for wills executed on or after 31 January 2024 (see Appendix 3):

(2)   For the purposes of paragraphs (c) and (d) of subsection (1), in relation to wills made on or after 31 January 2020 and on or before 31 January 2024, 'presence' includes presence by means of videoconference or other visual transmission.

To constitute a will, the document must contain the testator's wishes as to the disposition of their estate, or appoint an executor. A validly executed will containing no dispositions but appointing an executor must be proved, the executor distributing the estate as though the testator had died intestate (see *O'Dwyer v Gear* [1859] 1 Sw & Tr 465).

4.2   WRITING

No will is valid unless it is made in writing, although there is an exception in the case of members of forces on actual military service and seamen and mariners at sea (see **4.6**). The Interpretation Act 1978 extended the term 'writing' to include 'typing, printing, lithography, photography and other modes of representing or reproducing words in a visible form' and 'expressions referring to writing are construed accordingly'. A will written in shorthand or braille is therefore acceptable. When submitting such a will to proof, a verified transcription must be provided.

A will may be written in any language and on any material by any means. Where a will is written partly in pencil and partly in ink, there is a presumption that the pencil writing is deliberative and it is not admitted to probate unless the court decides it represents the testator's definite intention. If words have been written onto a will in pencil, and the court determines that they were included intentionally, those words are underlined on the original will by the court. The will so marked forms a perpetual copy and is then reproduced to create the probate and record copies.

4.3   SIGNATURE

4.3.1   Form of signature

In general, any mark, sign or signature made by the testator on their will is a valid signature, provided it was intended to be a signature. The testator should, though, sign with their usual signature so as to avoid any doubt about validity.

The following have all been held to be sufficient to amount to a valid signature provided that was the testator's intention:

- initials (see *Re Savory's Goods* (1851) 15 Jur 1042);
- a stamped signature (see *Re Jenkins* (1863) 3 Sw & Tr 93);
- a mark such as a cross;
- an inked thumb mark (see *Re Finn's Estate* (1935) 105 LJP 36);

- a mark of any shape (see *In the Estate of Holtam* (1913) 108 LT 732);
- an unfinished signature (see *In the Goods of Chalcraft* [1948] P 222);
- a signature in pencil (see *Bateman v Pennington* (1840) 3 Moo PC 223);
- the words 'your loving mother' (see *Re Cook's Estate; Murison v Cook* [1960] 1 WLR 353);
- a rubber stamp (see *Perrins v Holland and Others* [2010] EWCA Civ 840, [2011] Ch 270).

In *Payne and Another v Payne* [2018] EWCA Civ 985, [2018] 1 WLR 3761, the Court of Appeal held that the term 'sign' used in Wills Act 1837, section 9 (as amended with effect from 1 January 1983 by the Administration of Justice Act 1982) should be construed as meaning the same as the original requirement to 'subscribe'. A signature as an identifiable and personal mark as when signing a cheque or other formal document was not required. The court further held that a witness merely had to write their name with the intention that the act of writing it should operate as an attestation.

4.3.2   Signature on the testator's behalf

A person other than the testator may sign on the testator's behalf provided the signature is made in the presence of, and by the direction of, the testator. The person so signing may be one of the witnesses, but does not need to be. The person signing for the testator may either sign their own name or that of the testator. The best course is for them to sign their own name and write that the signature is on behalf of the testator, in their presence and by their direction. The testator must be present when the signature is made and must in some way indicate to the witnesses that the signature has been requested.

This has been clarified by the decision in *Barrett v Bem and Others* [2011] EWHC 1247 (Ch), [2011] 3 WLR 1193, where there was a dispute over the testator's signature. The trial judge had held, on the balance of probabilities, the testator had tried and had failed, on account of his physical condition, to sign the will himself, and then by his conduct had directed his sister to assist him by doing so on his behalf. There might well also have been an intermediate attempt to sign with the sister assisting the testator by steadying his hand. The will was initially declared valid, but that decision was reversed by the Court of Appeal [2012] EWCA Civ 52. The Court of Appeal held that the court should not find that a will had been signed by a third party at the direction of the testator unless there was 'a positive and discernible communication by the testator that he wished the will to be signed on his behalf by a third party'. In this case, there had been no such communication by the testator, so the signing of the will by the sister (as had been found by the court below) meant the will was not properly executed.

4.3.3   Signature by a blind or illiterate testator

Non-Contentious Probate Rules 1987 (SI 1987/2024), rule 13 provides:

> Before admitting to proof a will which appears to have been signed by a blind or illiterate testator or by another person by direction of the testator, or which for any other reason raises doubt as to the testator having had knowledge of the contents of the will at the time of its execution, the district judge or registrar shall satisfy himself that the testator had such knowledge.

Where the testator's signature is feeble, the district judge or registrar needs to be satisfied that the testator had testamentary capacity and had knowledge of, and approved the contents of, the will before execution.

4.3.4   Position of signature

The original Wills Act 1837, section 9 required that the signature be 'at the foot or end' of the will and this was strictly interpreted, invalidating a number of wills which did not comply with it. The Wills Act Amendment Act 1852 was then passed to extend the meaning of the term 'foot or end', and as a result the court could in certain circumstances admit part of a document to probate while excluding other parts which appeared physically after the signature.

The amended section 9 repealed the 1852 Act. Where the testator dies on or after 1 January 1983, section 9 no longer requires the signature to be at the foot or end of the will. It is sufficient that 'it appears that the testator intended by his signature to give effect to the will'. The new section 9 contemplates the signature validating all or none of the will. In *Weatherhill v Pearce* [1995] 1 WLR 592, it was accepted that a signature in the attestation clause was sufficient. In *Wood v Smith* [1993] Ch 90, the Court of Appeal held that where the testator wrote his name in the heading of the will, that was sufficient to constitute signature.

A signature on a separate page attached to the beginning or end of the will probably satisfies the requirement of section 9. This is likely to require evidence from a witness to support due execution even for proof in common form.

Where the testator has enclosed the will in an envelope and signed the envelope, it is thought that, provided the signature was intended to give effect to the will and there is evidence to support that, this is sufficient. But if the signature is merely to identify the contents of the envelope this is insufficient.

4.3.5 Acknowledgement of signature in the presence of at least two witnesses

The testator must sign the will or acknowledge their signature in the presence of two or more witnesses present at the same time, who must then sign or acknowledge their signatures in the testator's presence. The witnesses must both remain until the testator's signature is complete. If the testator has not signed in the simultaneous presence of both witnesses then the testator must acknowledge their signature in the joint presence of the witnesses.

The acknowledgement must be made by words or by conduct, but the witnesses must at the time of the acknowledgement see, or have the opportunity of seeing, the signature of the testator. If the signature is concealed there is, therefore, no valid acknowledgement. The witnesses need not know, however, that the document is a will, nor need they look at the signature itself. A will may be executed and republished by the acknowledgement of the signature. As to acknowledgement by a witness of an earlier signature, see below.

4.4 ATTESTATION

Section 9 requires that each witness must either attest and sign the will, or acknowledge their signature, in the presence of the testator. Before 1983, a witness who had signed before the testator was not able to acknowledge an earlier signature and the will would fail unless that witness signed again after the testator. Since 1 January 1983 the invalidity caused by the testator's signing in the presence of one witness who signs, the testator then acknowledging their signature in the presence of both witnesses and the second witness signing, can be remedied. To do so, the testator acknowledges their prior signature in the presence of both witnesses. Then the first witness acknowledges their prior signature, and the second witness then signs.

Both attesting witnesses must be present at the same time and both must attest and subscribe or acknowledge after the testator's signature has been made or acknowledged in their presence. Nevertheless, it is not essential that they sign in each other's presence. Their signatures may appear anywhere on the will and need not be next to or after the testator's signature. If, however, they appear above the testator's signature, there is a presumption that they signed in this order. Acknowledgement by a witness of a previously made signature requires the testator and witness to be in visible contact. Where a witness expressed doubt about the sufficiency of a previously made signature this was held to be sufficient acknowledgement (see *Couser v Couser* [1996] 1 WLR 1301).

In *Kayll and Others v Rawlinson* [2010] EWHC 1269 (Ch), [2010] WTLR 1443, the court found it was sufficient to constitute an acknowledgement that the will bearing the testator's signature was put before the witnesses, both of whom, or one of whom in the presence of the other, were asked by the testator in his presence to sign as a witness or witnesses. The witness had to be in the visual presence of the testator, but it was not necessary for him to have actually seen the witness sign, provided he could have done if he had chosen to look.

In *Channon and Another v Perkins and Others* [2005] EWCA Civ 1808, [2006] WTLR 425, the Court of Appeal, reversing the decision of the court below, held that the defective memory of a witness was insufficient to overturn a will *prima facie* properly executed. The witnesses recognised their signatures on the will but could not remember signing the will. As a period of 8 years had elapsed since the date of execution, the court found this enough time to explain the witnesses' loss of recollection of events.

In *In the Estate of Sherrington; Sherrington and Others v Sherrington* [2005] EWCA Civ 326, [2005] 3 FCR 538, the Court of Appeal, again reversing the decision of the court below, held that the strongest evidence is necessary to rebut the presumption of due execution where the will is signed and witnessed and contains an attestation clause, i.e. where the will is *prima facie* properly executed.

There is no special form of attestation clause, but the usual forms are as follows.

4A   ATTESTATION CLAUSE

> Dated this ... day of ... 20 ...
> Signed by the testator in our presence and then by us in the testator's presence.
> [Signature of testator]
> [Signatures, addresses and descriptions of two witnesses]

Although it is preferable to do so, there is no requirement in English law for a witness to give their address or description.

This form is recommended for use in all cases except where there are unusual circumstances. The fewest words lead to fewest errors.

## 4B	ATTESTATION CLAUSE TO A CODICIL

Dated this ... day of ... 20 ...
Signed by the testator as a [first, or as the case may be] codicil to their will dated the ... day of ... in our presence and then by us in the testator's presence.
[Signature of testator]
[Signatures, addresses and descriptions of two witnesses]

## 4C	ATTESTATION CLAUSE WHERE THE WILL HAS BEEN ALTERED

Signed by the testator in our presence and then by us in the testator's presence the alteration [or erasure or interlineation] [in line ...] on page ... thereof and [signed] [initialled] by the testator and us having been made previously to the execution hereof.
[Signature of testator]
[Signatures, addresses and descriptions of two witnesses]

## 4D	ATTESTATION CLAUSE WHERE THE TESTATOR SIGNS WITH THEIR MARK

Signed by the testator with their mark (they being otherwise unable to sign their name) (the will having been previously read over to them by [name] [me the undersigned [name]] when they seemed thoroughly to understand and approve the content of the same) in our presence and then signed by us in the testator's presence.
[Testator's mark]
[Signatures, addresses and descriptions of two witnesses]

## 4E	ATTESTATION CLAUSE WHERE ANOTHER SIGNS ON BEHALF OF A TESTATOR WHO CANNOT READ OR WRITE

Signed by [person signing] with the name of the testator (the will having been previously read over to [him] [her] by [name] [me the undersigned [name]] when [he] [she] seemed thoroughly to understand and approve the same) in [his] [her] presence and by [his] [her] direction and in our presence and then signed by us in [his] [her] presence.
[Signature of testator]
[Signatures, addresses and descriptions of two witnesses]

4F   ATTESTATION CLAUSE WHERE ANOTHER SIGNS ON BEHALF OF A TESTATOR WHO IS ABLE TO READ BUT UNABLE TO SIGN

The testator being [able to read the will but] temporarily unable to sign the will [because of a hand injury] the same was signed by [person signing] with the name of the testator in [his] [her] presence and by [his] [her] direction and in our presence and then signed by us in the testator's presence.
[Signature of testator]
[Signature, address and description of two witnesses]

4G   ATTESTATION CLAUSE WHERE THE TESTATOR IS BLIND

This will having first been read over to the testator (who is blind) [in our presence] by me the undersigned [name] in the presence also of me the undersigned [name] when [he] [she] appeared thoroughly to understand and approve the same was signed by [him] [her] in our presence and then by us in the testator's presence.
[Signature of testator]
[Signatures, addresses and descriptions of two witnesses]

4H   ATTESTATION CLAUSE WHERE THE TESTATOR HAS AN IMPERFECT KNOWLEDGE OF ENGLISH

This will having first been read over to the testator (who understands the French language but has an imperfect knowledge of and cannot read the English language) by me the undersigned [first witness] in English and having been truly interpreted to the said [testator] by me the undersigned [second witness] [who understands both the English and French languages] [both of whom the said [witnesses] understand both the English and French languages] which reading and interpretation were both done in our presence when the testator appeared thoroughly to understand and to approve the contents thereof was signed by the said [testator] in our presence and then by us in [his] [her] presence.
[Signature]
[Signatures, addresses and descriptions of two witnesses]

In *Kassim and Others v Saeed* [2019] EWHC 2763 (Ch), the High Court, in *obiter* comments, suggested it is best practice when advising a testator with an imperfect command of the English language, to ask them to paraphrase the contents of the will once the adviser had explained its terms. This should put beyond doubt any question of lack of knowledge and approval of the will. The testator was originally from Yemen and had lived in the United Kingdom for many years as a businessman, but, was illiterate in all languages and also had very little knowledge of spoken English. The case also includes a useful summary of the law concerning illiterate and non-English-speaking testators as a reminder of particular issues to be addressed when advising such testators.

4I   ATTESTATION CLAUSE OF A WILL MADE PURSUANT TO AN ORDER OF THE COURT OF PROTECTION

> Signed by the said [testator/person lacking capacity] by the said [authorised person] and by the said [authorised person] with their own name pursuant to the said order in our presence and attested by us in the presence of the said [authorised person]
> [Signature made by authorised person in testator's name]
> [Signature of authorised person in their own name]
> [Signatures, addresses and descriptions of two witnesses]
> Sealed with the official seal of the Court of Protection the ... day of ... 20 ...

After execution, the will must be authenticated with the official seal of the Court of Protection (see **3.3.4**).

4.5   CAPACITY OF WITNESSES

There are no particular rules about who may act as a witness. The only test seems to be whether the witnesses are capable of attesting at the time they sign. Thus a minor may witness a will provided they are not too young to understand the significance of their act, and providing they understand the nature of witnessing a signature (see *In the Estate of Sherrington; Sherrington and Others v Sherrington* [2005] EWCA Civ 326, [2005] 3 FCR 538; **4.4**). Someone who is visually impaired cannot act as a witness if unable to see the signature. A person who is drunk or lacks capacity to understand what is involved in witnessing a signature would also be incapable of attesting.

In choosing witnesses, have regard to the fact that a person chosen may be required to give evidence of due execution, and therefore persons who are old or who may be difficult to trace should be avoided. A beneficiary under the will or a beneficiary's spouse (or partner in a civil partnership) should not be chosen since, although their signatures are perfectly valid, they will lose their legacies (Wills Act 1837, section 15), except where the will would have been valid without that signature.

There are, however, several exceptions to the rule in section 15. This rule does not apply:

(i)   to an informal will made by a privileged testator (see **4.6**), since such a will does not require witnessing;

(ii)   where the beneficiary or their spouse (or civil partner) signed the will not as an attesting witness, but in some other capacity. There is, however, a rebuttable presumption that any person, except the testator, whose signature appears at the end of a will signed the will as an attesting witness;

(iii)   to a beneficiary who marries (or enters into a civil partnership with) an attesting witness after the will has been executed. Section 15 applies only to a beneficiary who is the spouse (or civil partner) of an attesting witness at the time the will was executed;

(iv)   to gifts to attesting witnesses as trustees, including trustees of a secret trust, since such gifts are not beneficial;

(v)   if the gift to the beneficiary is contained in a will or a codicil which was not attested by the beneficiary or their spouse (or civil partner), but some other document was so attested;

(vi)   if the gift to the beneficiary is contained in a document which was attested by the beneficiary or their spouse (or civil partner), but the document was confirmed by a will or codicil not so attested;

(vii)   in relation to deaths occurring after 1 February 2001, if a will makes provision for a trustee or personal representative (acting in a professional capacity) to receive payment from the estate (a 'charging clause'); such payment is not treated as a gift and hence is not subject to Wills Act 1837, section 15 (Trustee Act 2000, section 28).

In *Barrett v Bem and Others* [2012] EWCA Civ 52, the Court of Appeal drew a distinction between a person signing a will on behalf of the testator and the effect of Wills Act 1837, section 15. Whereas a witness will lose their benefit from the will, the person signing will not. However, the Court of Appeal did make the point that it is not desirable for a beneficiary to sign for the testator and that it would be likely to raise an issue as to knowledge and approval.

4.6   PRIVILEGED WILLS

The formal requirements for the execution of a valid will are waived for a testator who has privileged status. Such a will can be made in any form and may even be an oral statement provided it shows an intention to dispose of property in the event of the testator's death. The testator need not know that they are making a will. Such a will is valid even if made by a minor. Since no attestation by witnesses is required, a gift to a witness in a soldier's, sailor's or airman's will is effective. Since such a will requires no formalities for its execution, it requires none for its revocation (see *Re Gossage's Estate* [1921] P 194). A privileged will is revoked by a subsequent marriage (see *Re Wardrop's Estate* [1917] P 54) or formation of a civil partnership.

The privilege extends to soldiers in actual military service and to mariners or seamen at sea. The term 'soldier' includes members of the Royal Air Force and naval or marine personnel serving on land. The meaning of the term 'actual military service' is not certain, but includes activities closely connected with warfare, whether or not war has been declared and whether or not the testator has actually arrived at the scene of fighting. A soldier stationed in Northern Ireland as part of the armed forces deployed there at the request of the civil authorities to assist in the maintenance of law and order has been held to be in actual military service (see *Re Jones* [1981] Fam 7). The fact that there was not an actual state of war or that the enemy was not a uniformed force engaged in regular warfare was irrelevant. The privilege attaches to members of the military forces in Bosnia, Afghanistan and Iraq.

The term 'being at sea' again cannot be defined precisely, but this privilege is wider in its scope than 'actual military service'. In *Re Rapley* [1983] 1 WLR 1069, it was said that the privilege can be invoked if the following conditions are met:

(i)   that the testator was serving or employed in, or by, the Royal Navy or the Merchant Navy, on service of whatever nature, that could be regarded as sea-service;

(ii)   that the testator was 'on maritime service' in the sense that the testator was:

–   at the time of making the will, in a post as ship's officer; or
–   at the time of making the will, a member of a particular ship's company serving in that ship or on shore leave, or on long leave ashore; or
–   at the time of making the will, employed by the owners of a fleet of ships, and having been discharged from one ship, was under orders to join another ship in that fleet.

It is often forgotten that the privilege applies to a seaman or mariner being at sea at all times and not only when warlike circumstances exist. In a more recent case the court held that 'being at sea' includes the time when making preparation and travelling to take up a position on board a ship. In *Re Servoz-Gavin Deceased; Ayling v Summers and Others* [2009] EWHC 3168 (Ch), [2009] WTLR 1657, the deceased who was a merchant seaman (a radio officer) made an oral statement of his testamentary wishes ('What I told you before still applies. If anything happens to me, if I snuff it, I want everything to go to Auntie Anne') in February 1990 to his cousin while in England before setting out on his journey to his ship in Bombay. He had made a previous statement of his wishes in 1985. He died in April 2005. The court held the privilege existed at the time of making the statement and having pronounced for the will in solemn form directed the will should be admitted to proof.

The privilege does not apply to the will of a seaman made while on shore leave, at a time when they are not a member of the crew of a particular ship and when they have not received orders to join a ship.

4.7   INCORPORATION OF UNATTESTED DOCUMENTS

It is usually preferable to set out all the provisions of a will in one properly executed document; any alterations may be made by codicils to the original will or by the execution of a new will. An unattested document in the form of a list, schedule or memorandum can, however, be incorporated into a will and admitted to probate as part of the will provided the following conditions are satisfied:

(i)   the unattested document must be dispositive and in existence at the time the will is executed or at the time the will is republished by codicil. This is a question of fact;

(ii)   the unattested document must be referred to in the will as being in existence at the time of execution. A future intention to make the list, schedule or memorandum does not suffice. This means that a will which states 'I leave £1,000 to each of the persons named in my notebook called "My Notebook 2004" to be found in my desk drawer' satisfies this condition, whereas one that says 'I leave £1,000 to each of the persons named in my notebook which I shall write before my death' does not satisfy the condition. The notebook would not be admitted to probate even if it was written before the will was executed, as the will refers to its coming into existence at a later date. If a will is republished by a codicil (see Chapter 8), this may have the effect of incorporating an unattested document which was in existence at the time of execution of the codicil and is referred to as in existence in either the will or the codicil;

(iii)   the unattested document must be clearly identified in the will.

A reference in the will to another document, which is not dispositive, but sets out the reasons for the dispositions in the will or for the omission of any disposition, will not be admitted by incorporation. Non-Contentious Probate Rules 1987 (SI 1987/2024), rule 14(3) provides the district judge or registrar with discretion to decide whether any document should be incorporated.

4J GIFT BY REFERENCE TO A DOCUMENT ALREADY IN EXISTENCE

I GIVE my watches jewellery trinkets and other articles of personal use and ornament to [name] UPON TRUST to distribute the same to the persons if living and in the manner set out in a [list] [schedule] [memorandum] dated ... which I have already prepared and signed and which will be found with this my will at my death and in so far as there may be any such articles at the date of my death which are not subject to any directions contained in the said list I GIVE the same to [name] absolutely.

Chapter 5

Beneficiaries

See also Chapter 3, at **3.7.3** on undue influence, and, for the position of attesting witnesses, Chapter 4, at **4.4**.

5.1 GENERAL

Any legatee in a will must always be clearly described; otherwise the gift, unless charitable (see **5.7**), may be void.

5.2 GIFT TO A BENEFICIARY WHO PREDECEASES THE TESTATOR

Where the beneficiary under a will is either dead at the time the will is made, or dies after the will is executed but before the death of the testator, then the gift, in general, is invalid and lapses.

The doctrine of lapse cannot be excluded from a will (see *Re Ladd* [1932] 2 Ch 219), but a gift may be worded so that the subject matter passes to some other beneficiary if the original beneficiary predeceases the testator. The testator may provide that, in the event of the death of the beneficiary, the property is to pass to the beneficiary's personal representatives to be held as part of the beneficiary's estate; or the testator may include a gift over to the beneficiary's children or to any named person or body.

5A GIFT TO BENEFICIARY'S CHILDREN WITH GIFT OVER

I DECLARE that if [name] my [son] [daughter] shall die in my lifetime or if this gift shall fail for any other reason [leaving children living at my death or then *en ventre sa mère* but born alive afterwards] the share of residue hereby given to my said [son] [daughter] shall not lapse but shall pass to such of [his] [her] children who are alive at the date of my death and who attain the age of [eighteen] years or marry or enter into a civil partnership under that age and if more than one in equal shares.

The doctrine of lapse has no application where the testator makes a gift to two or more persons as joint tenants (unless all such persons predecease), but does apply where the beneficiaries take as tenants in common. If the beneficiary dies before the testator, there is no charge to inheritance tax on the property given as part of the beneficiary's estate as well as part of the testator's estate. This is because at the time of the beneficiary's earlier death, the beneficiary was not entitled to anything under the testator's will.

5B   GIFT OVER TO BENEFICIARY'S PERSONAL REPRESENTATIVES

I DECLARE that if [name] shall die during my lifetime or if this gift shall fail for any other reason the share of residue [legacy of ...] hereby given to [him] [her] shall not lapse but shall in that event pass to [his] [her] personal representatives as part of [his] [her] estate.

Note that the testator effectively has no control over the destination of the gift which will be determined by the terms of the deceased beneficiary's will (if any) or intestacy. Also, the property stands to be lost through payment of the deceased beneficiary's debts if their own estate is not sufficient.

A further option for a testator in anticipation of lapse is to include a provision that the lapsed interest will be used primarily for the payment of debts and legacies by way of exonerating other property which might otherwise have been liable. See Administration of Estates Act 1925, Schedule 1, Part II as to the order of application of assets where the estate is solvent.

5C   CLAUSE AS TO THE APPLICATION OF A LAPSED SHARE OF RESIDUE

I DIRECT that if any gift of any share of residue shall lapse [whether the Beneficiary predeceases me or for any other reason] then where such lapse in the absence of this provision would give rise to an intestacy or partial intestacy then such lapsed share shall be primarily applied in or towards the payment of my debts funeral and testamentary expenses and pecuniary legacies hereby or by any codicil hereto bequeathed first recourse to be had to the said lapsed share before any other property hereby or by any codicil hereto bequeathed or devised.

5.2.1 Class gifts and lapse

In the case of class gifts, the members of the class are not generally ascertained until after the testator's death. For this reason any person who would have formed part of the class but who dies before the testator is not included as a member of the class and thus the doctrine of lapse has no application. A gift may still be a class gift even if some particular member is named in the gift, for example a gift to 'my children including [or excluding] A' (see *Shaw v M'Mahon* (1843) 4 Dr & War 431).

Class gifts are to be distinguished from gifts to a distinct group of individuals. A gift to a number of defined individuals, such as named sisters as tenants in common in equal shares, would not be a class gift where the share of each is distinct and quantifiable, regardless of which of the individuals survive the testator. The doctrine of lapse would apply if one of the sisters predeceased the testator. A gift to such of 'my children as survive me in equal shares' would create a class gift and the doctrine of lapse would apply only if there were no children of the testator alive at their death.

5.2.2 Exceptions to the doctrine of lapse

There are two situations where the doctrine of lapse does not operate:

- gifts in discharge of a moral obligation;
- under Wills Act 1837, section 33.

The precise ambit of the common law exception in respect of gifts in discharge of a moral obligation is uncertain, but it applies, *inter alia*, to a gift in discharge of a debt which is statute barred, and to a direction that creditors of a deceased beneficiary be paid. It may be that the rule extends only to directions to pay debts and not to other forms of moral obligation.

Wills Act 1837, section 33 (as substituted by the Administration of Justice Act 1982) applies where a testator dies after 31 December 1982, and provides that where:

(a) a will contains a devise or bequest to a child or remoter descendant of the testator; and

(b) the intended beneficiary dies before the testator, leaving issue; and

(c) the issue of the intended beneficiary are living at the testator's death,

then, unless there is a contrary intention in the will, the devise or bequest shall take effect as a devise or bequest to the issue living at the testator's death.

Section 33(3) provides that:

> Issue take through all degrees according to their stock, in equal shares if more than one, any gift or share which their parent would have taken, and so that no issue shall take whose parent is living at the testator's death and so capable of taking.

Wills Act 1837, section 33 applies to contingent gifts. In *Ling v Ling* [2002] WTLR 553, [2001] All ER (D) 322 (Nov), Etherton J expressed the view at [33] that a substituted beneficiary under the section was subject to the same contingency (in that case, attaining the age of 21) as his parent (who predeceased the testator) would have been. In *Naylor and Another v Barlow and Others* [2019] EWHC 1565 (Ch), HHJ Hodge QC (sitting as a Judge of the High Court) accepted that a substituted beneficiary takes subject to any conditions imposed on the original gift saying at [16], 'In my judgment, the substituted beneficiaries step into the shoes of the original deceased beneficiary for all purposes'.

When drafting any contingent or conditional gift, it is helpful to make it clear by means of an express provision as to whether or not any substitutional gift is subject to the contingency.

Section 33(2) deals with class gifts. It provides that where:

(a) a will contains a devise or bequest to a class of person consisting of children or remoter descendants of the testator; and
(b) a member of the class dies before the testator, leaving issue; and
(c) the issue of that member are living at the testator's death,

then, unless there is a contrary intention in the will, the devise or bequest shall take effect as if the class included the issue of its deceased member living at the testator's death.

The issue take according to their stock, in equal shares if more than one, the share which their parents would have taken, and no issue whose parent is living at the time of testator's death may take (section 33(3)).

Section 33(4) provides that:

> For the purpose of this section the illegitimacy of any person is to be disregarded and a person conceived before the testator's death and born living thereafter is to be taken to be living at the testator's death.

Section 33 applies only where a gift is made to a child or remoter descendant of the testator. In all other cases a substitutional gift takes effect only if expressly provided for in a will. For avoidance of doubt and in order clearly to express the testator's intentions a substitutional gift should, as a matter of practice, always be made the subject of an express provision, notwithstanding the fact that section 33 will apply if the gift is to a child or remoter descendant of the testator. (See also Chapter 17 for substitutional gifts.)

5D   DECLARATION EXCLUDING WILLS ACT 1837, SECTION 33

> Wills Act 1837, section 33 (as amended) shall not apply to my will or any codicil thereto.

In *Rainbird v Smith* [2012] EWHC 4276 (Ch), the will contained the words 'to such of them my daughters ... as shall survive me', and the clause containing those words went on to provide 'and if more than one in equal shares'. It was held that had the intention been to leave the bequest merely to the daughters, the language would not have included the words 'such of them as shall survive me', it would have been upon trust for my daughters A, B and C. The use of the language 'and if more than one in equal shares' indicated the testatrix's intention that the amount each one of them might get would increase if any of the daughters pre-deceased her. It was clear from the will as properly construed that section 33 was not to apply in the event a daughter predeceased. However, in *Hives v Machin* [2017] EWHC 1414 (Ch), the court was presented with virtually identical wording and instead followed the earlier decision in *Ling v Ling* [2002] WTLR 553, [2001] All ER (D) 322 (Nov), saying that section 33 is the default position and if it is to be excluded, clear words must be included in the will (in the absence of admissible extrinsic evidence) to show the testator did not wish the issue of a deceased child to benefit.

5.2.3   Presumption where uncertainty as to which survived

Because of the effect of the doctrine of lapse it may be necessary to establish whether the testator or the beneficiary died first. Law of Property Act 1925, section 184 provides that:

> In all cases where, after the commencement of this Act, two or more persons have died in circumstances rendering it uncertain which of them survived the other or others, such deaths shall (subject to any order of the court), for all purposes affecting the title to property, be presumed to have occurred in order of seniority, and accordingly the younger shall be deemed to have survived the elder.

Consequently, the younger is deemed to inherit the elder's property, which then passes under the terms of the younger's will or intestacy.

This section applies whether the deaths occurred in a common disaster (*commorientes*) or separately.

The statutory presumption where the order of deaths is uncertain does not apply between spouses or civil partners if the elder dies intestate (Intestates' Estates Act 1952, section 1(4)). When the estate of the elder is being administered, the younger is presumed not to have survived the elder intestate. When the estate of the younger spouse or civil partner is being administered, section 184 applies in its usual way. It should be remembered that to acquire a benefit under intestacy, the spouse or civil partner has to survive the deceased by 28 days (Law Reform (Succession) Act 1995). To avoid property passing through two estates, it is wise to include a survivorship clause in the will (see Chapter 17).

5E   CONTINGENT GIFT OF PROPERTY WHICH CARRIES IMMEDIATE INCOME DURING SURVIVORSHIP PERIOD

I GIVE [property] to [donee] absolutely provided that [he] [she] survives me for [twenty-eight days] and if [he] [she] shall fail to survive me for the said [twenty-eight days] then [he] [she] shall be treated as if [he] [she] had predeceased me and income from the said [property] arising after my death and prior to the death of [donee] shall not belong to [him] [her] and in that event [I GIVE the said [property] including the intermediate income thereof to [alternative donee]] [the said [property] including the intermediate income thereof shall form part of my residuary estate].

5F   'OMNIBUS' SURVIVORSHIP PROVISION AGAINST COMMORIENTES EXTENDING TO ALL GIFTS IN THE WILL

No person shall take any benefit under the provisions of this my will UNLESS they shall survive me for [one* calendar month] and if any person shall fail to survive me for that period then each and every such person shall be treated for all purposes connected with the devolution of my estate [[including] [but not including] Wills Act 1837, section 33] as if [he] [she] had predeceased me and my estate and the intermediate income thereof shall devolve accordingly.

* The period in brackets must not exceed six months.

In the case of spouses or civil partners, it may be advisable to add words to provide that, should deaths occur in circumstances where it is uncertain which survived, the survivorship requirement does not apply. This is because an inheritance tax advantage can be obtained. There is also a possibility that legacies intended to be paid on the death of the surviving spouse or civil partner will have to be paid under each will, as was the case in *Jump and Another v Lister and Another* [2016] EWHC 2160 (Ch), [2017] WTLR 61. See **17.8**.

5.2.4   Effect of disclaimer

A beneficiary is not obliged to accept a gift in a will and may choose to disclaim their benefit. The Estates of Deceased Persons (Forfeiture Rule and Law of Succession) Act 2011 added section 33A to the Wills Act 1837 as follows:

33A Disclaimer or forfeiture of gift
(1)   This section applies where a will contains a devise or bequest to a person who—

    (a)   disclaims it, or
    (b)   has been precluded by the forfeiture rule from acquiring it.

(2)   The person is, unless a contrary intention appears by the will, to be treated for the purposes of this Act as having died immediately before the testator.
(3)   But in a case within subsection (1)(b), subsection (2) does not affect the power conferred by section 2 of the Forfeiture Act 1982 (power of court to modify the forfeiture rule).
(4)   In this section 'forfeiture rule' has the same meaning as in the Forfeiture Act 1982.

If the intended beneficiary disclaims their interest, the beneficiary is treated as having predeceased the deceased (see section 2 above) but see also **25.2**.

5.3   UNLAWFUL KILLING

It is a rule of public policy that a person must not be allowed to benefit from their crime. An intended beneficiary convicted of the murder or manslaughter of the testator generally cannot receive a benefit under the testator's will or the deceased person's intestacy. This is subject to any relief under the Forfeiture Act 1982 (see below). The rule extends to all unlawful killings, including, for example, causing death by dangerous driving. It has also been applied where death was caused by careless driving (see *Re Estate of Amos (Deceased); Amos v Mancini and Others* [2020] EWHC 1063 (Ch), although relief against forfeiture was granted). The definition of 'unlawful killing' in the 1982 Act includes aiding, abetting, counselling or procuring the death. Motive and moral guilt are irrelevant, except where unsoundness of mind or justifiable homicide is proved. Relief under the Act was refused in *Dalton v Latham and Others, sub nom Re Estate of Bernard Joseph Murphy* [2003] EWHC 796 (Ch), [2003] WTLR 687 to a person convicted of manslaughter on the grounds of diminished responsibility. The court of first instance stated that Parliament had not intended to abrogate the forfeiture rule in all cases involving diminished responsibility and it was not in the interests of justice to modify the forfeiture rule in the circumstances of this case. In *Chadwick v Collison and Others* [2014] EWHC 3055 (Ch), on the application of the forfeiture rule, the applicant sought relief based on the mental disorder from which he was suffering on the date of the killing of his partner and her child. It was held, dismissing the claim, that while the level of culpability was reduced or even perhaps significantly reduced by the impact of the mental disorder from which the claimant was suffering on the day of the killings, it had not been eliminated or reduced to the level where it could properly be said to be so low that to give effect to the forfeiture rule would be contrary to the public interest.

Similarly, the claim was dismissed in *Henderson v Wilcox and Others* [2015] EWHC 3469 (Ch), in which the claimant, who had been found guilty of the manslaughter of his mother, sought to inherit his mother's estate under her will, as justice did not require modification of the forfeiture rule. However, the court held that the forfeiture rule had no application to any interest presently or in future created under two trusts relating to his mother's home. The interests that the claimant had or might acquire under the trusts did not arise from, or result from, the death of his mother. Insofar as he was a discretionary beneficiary of her trust, he had acquired that status on the execution of the trust and his interest had been neither created not enlarged by her death.

Where an intended beneficiary is disqualified by the rule, the gift devolves as if that beneficiary had died immediately before the testator (see *In the Estate of Crippen* [1911] P 108, and see now Wills Act 1837, section 33A). If the beneficiary is a member of a class to receive a benefit under the will then they are excluded from the class as if they had predeceased the testator, and the remainder of those eligible will take. The effect of the forfeiture rule is to sever a joint tenancy so that the beneficial interest vests in the personal representatives of the deceased and the survivor as tenants in common.

Strangely, although since the decision in *Crippen* a person was precluded from benefiting from the illegal act, there was no bar to that person acting as executor or administrator of the deceased's estate. Unless the convicted person renounced, an application to pass over that person's title to the grant had to be made under Senior Courts Act 1981, section 116. This is no longer the case for deaths after 1 February 2012 when the Estates of Deceased Persons (Forfeiture Rule and Law of Succession) Act 2011 came into force. The 2011 Act added section 33A to the Wills Act 1837 and section 46A to the Administration of Estates Act 1925, whereby the convicted person is treated as having predeceased the deceased.

The decision of the Court of Appeal in *Re DWS (Deceased); In Re EHS (Deceased); TWGS (A Child) v JMG and Others* [2000] EWCA Civ 282, [2001] Ch 568 caused concern. In this case, a son, R, murdered his parents, both of whom died intestate. He was disqualified from taking their estates under the rule of public policy, but the issue arose as to where the father's estate should go. The court said R's son was ineligible to take the estate. The definition of 'statutory trusts' for issue in Administration of Estates Act 1925, section 47(1)(i) must be construed literally, so that the issue of a child of the intestate could inherit only if the intestate's child had *actually predeceased* the intestate. R was disqualified from taking the estate and hence R's child could not take it. The majority of the Court of Appeal said the estate devolved to the executors of the grandfather's sister, since the sister had died after the murder but before the case was decided. Sedley LJ, however, said that the property devolved to the Crown as *bona vacantia* (see now Wills Act 1837, section 33A).

The confusion above arose because of the interpretation of Administration of Estates Act 1925, section 47(2). This section provided that if the statutory trusts fail because none of the issue attains an absolutely vested interest, the estate must be distributed as if the deceased died without issue. The majority of the Court of Appeal said the subsection dealt with the failure to attain an interest for whatever reason (including reasons external to the scheme of the Act), whereas Sedley LJ said the subsection applied only where the child or other issue failed to obtain an absolutely vested interest for reasons foreseen in the Act, namely he did not attain the age of 18 or marry under that age.

However, the Estates of Deceased Persons (Forfeiture Rule and Law of Succession) Act 2011, in force from 1 February 2012, amended the Administration of Estates Act 1925 so that a person who forfeits or disclaims an interest on intestacy is to be treated as having died immediately before the intestate.

The forfeiture rule is not to be taken as precluding any person from making an application under the Inheritance (Provision for Family and Dependants) Act 1975. In *Land v Land's Estate* [2006] EWHC 2069 (Ch), [2006] WTLR 1447, the claim for relief under the 1982 Act failed as it had been brought out of time. However, the claimant succeeded in his claim under the 1975 Act on the grounds that to deny the claimant relief would be a breach of European Convention for the Protection of Human Rights and Fundamental Freedoms (European Convention on Human Rights), Articles 9 and 14 and that the legislation should now be construed in accordance with Human Rights Act 1998, section 3 in a manner which was compliant with the Convention.

The problem that arose in *Re DWS (Deceased); In Re EHS (Deceased); TWGS (A Child) v JMG and Others* [2000] EWCA Civ 282, [2001] Ch 568 did not arise in *Re Callaway; Callaway v Treasury Solicitor* [1956] Ch 559, where the deceased actually left a will. Here it was held that although the deceased had given all her estate to her daughter by her will, on the daughter's conviction for her murder, the estate passed under the intestacy rules to the surviving son and not as *bona vacantia* to the Crown. This would not now be so for deaths after 1 February 2012. The Estates of Deceased Persons (Forfeiture Rule and Law of Succession) Act 2011 provides that the convicted person is deemed to have predeceased the deceased so the deceased's estate will pass accordingly.

5.3.1   Relief from forfeiture

The Forfeiture Act 1982 allows the person who has killed the testator to apply to the court to modify the rule of public policy in so far as it affects them. An application must generally be made within 3 months of the conviction (Forfeiture Act 1982, section 2(3)). Where the conviction was for murder, however, the court has no power to modify the effect of the rule. In all other cases the court may, if it thinks fit to do so, allow the applicant and any person claiming through them to take:

- under the will;
- on intestacy;
- under a nomination;
- under a *donatio mortis causa*;
- the deceased's share of jointly owned property;
- other property held in trust.

The court may apply the forfeiture rule to some parts of the deceased's property and not others (see *Re Forfeiture Act 1982 (Manslaughter: Forfeiture of Widow's Pension)* [1999] Pens LR 1).

A recent example of relief against forfeiture is *Re Challen (Deceased); Challen v Challen and Another* [2020] EWHC 1330 (Ch), [2021] 2 All ER 738, where the widow was initially found guilty of murder and sentenced to life imprisonment but after a re-trail, a verdict of manslaughter was substituted and her sentence reduced to 9 years and 4 months.

HHJ Paul Matthews (sitting as a Judge of the High Court) described the circumstances of the case, which involved coercive control of the wife by her husband over 40 years, as 'tragic'. He said that when deciding whether or not to exercise the discretion contained in section 2(2) of the Act, the court was entitled to take into account a whole range of circumstances, quite apart from the conduct of the offender and the deceased, such as the relationship between them; the degree of moral culpability for what had happened; the nature and gravity of the offence; the intentions of the deceased; the size of the estate and the value of the property in dispute; the financial position of the offender; and the moral claims and wishes of those who would be entitled to take the property on the application of the forfeiture rule.

In *Re Estate of Amos (Deceased); Amos v Mancini and Others* [2020] EWHC 1063 (Ch), Mrs Amos (aged 74) was convicted of causing the death of her husband (aged 81) by careless driving. She had been driving all day and ran into a car at the back of a line of traffic which had come to a stop at a roundabout, causing a four-vehicle shunt. It was held that it would be unjust for the forfeiture rule to apply in this case so as to deprive Mrs Amos of her husband's share in their former matrimonial home or the gift in his will. The loss of either would be significantly out of proportion to her culpability in the offence in question.

5.3.2   Family provision and forfeiture

It is expressly provided that the forfeiture rule is not to be taken as precluding any person from making an application under the Inheritance (Provision for Family and Dependants) Act 1975. In the case of *Re Royse; Royse v Royse* [1985] Ch 22, however, a woman who was convicted of unlawfully killing her husband and who was disinherited by the forfeiture rule was not able to make an application under the 1975 Act, since the absence of reasonable financial provision could not be attributed to the deceased's will or intestacy, but to the rule of public policy. An application may be made only if the requirements of the 1975 Act are complied with (see Chapter 26).

5.4   GIFTS FOR THE UPKEEP AND MAINTENANCE OF GRAVES

Gifts for the upkeep and maintenance of graves take effect only as trusts of imperfect obligation and are void if worded so as to last for an indefinite period. They must be limited to the perpetuity period (see Chapter 23). This effectively means that they can continue for a period of 21 years only; the alternative 125-year period provided for by the Perpetuities and Accumulations Act 2009 has no application (see Perpetuities and Accumulations Act 2009, section 18). A bequest to trustees to provide for the upkeep of graves 'so far as they can legally do so and in any manner they may in their discretion arrange', is a valid form of wording (see *Re Hooper* [1932] 1 Ch 38). The testator should be advised that the trustees of a trust of imperfect obligation are not obliged to comply with the wishes of the testator, and that a resulting trust arises if the trustees do not carry out the terms of the trust.

5G   GIFT FOR THE UPKEEP OF A GRAVE

> I GIVE to my Trustees the sum of £ .... UPON TRUST to invest the same as they in their absolute discretion think fit and during the period of twenty-one years from my death (which period shall be the perpetuity period applicable to the disposition hereby effected) to apply the income thereof for the upkeep of the grave and gravestone of [name] at [place] to maintain the same in good order and repair and to keep any lettering on the said gravestone legible causing the same to be recut from time to time when necessary for that purpose.

A 'condition' requiring the maintenance of a grave or gravestone can be attached to a gift to charity A, with a gift over to charity B if charity A should fail to fulfil the condition (see *Christ's Hospital v Grainger* (1845) 1 Mac & G 460). However, the 'condition' must be discretionary in its nature if it is to be upheld. If the gift over is not to a charity, but to an individual, the gift is subject to the perpetuity rule. If the gift over falls outside the perpetuity period the original charitable legatee takes free from the condition (see *Re Cooper's Conveyance* [1956] 3 All ER 28). The original gift may impose only a moral obligation on the trustees.

Parish Councils and Burial Authorities (Miscellaneous Provisions) Act 1970, section 1 (as amended by Local Authorities Cemetery Order 1974 (SI 1974/628), article 9(5)), provides an alternative method of maintaining a grave, which avoids any perpetuity problems. A local authority or burial authority may agree with any person, in consideration of a sum of money payable to the authority, to maintain a grave or other memorial in a burial ground which is maintained by the authority. The maximum period of such an agreement is 100 years from the date of it. A testator can direct their executors to enter into such an agreement, although they would not be obliged to do so.

5H   DIRECTION TO EXECUTORS TO ENTER INTO AGREEMENT TO MAINTAIN GRAVE

> I DIRECT my Executors to enter into an agreement with the appropriate authority having responsibility for the place of my burial for the maintenance of my grave and I GIVE to my Trustees UPON TRUST such sum as is provided for in the said agreement for the maintenance of my grave.

5.5   GIFTS FOR ANIMALS

A gift for the maintenance of a particular animal or animals is a valid gift, but again creates a trust of imperfect obligation and so is restricted in duration to

21 years. Some gifts for animals are valid charitable gifts if they are shown to be for purposes beneficial to the community (see **5.7.1**).

51   GIFT FOR THE MAINTENANCE OF A PARTICULAR ANIMAL

> I GIVE to my Trustees the sum of £ .... UPON TRUST to invest the same as they in their absolute discretion think fit and to apply the income thereof for the upkeep and maintenance of my [dog] [other animal, describing it] for the duration of its life or for the period of twenty-one years from the date of my death whichever period shall be the shorter and after the death of my [dog] [other animal] or after the expiration of the period of twenty-one years whichever shall first happen the gift shall fall into and form part of my residuary estate.

5.6   GIFTS TO SOCIETIES AND CLUBS

A gift may be made to a society or club, but where the society or club is not charitable the gift must comply with the perpetuity rule. The rule can be avoided, however, if the members are left free to dispose of the gift as they think fit (see *Re Clarke* [1901] 2 Ch 110).

Special problems arise if the society or club is non-charitable and unincorporated. Such an institution is not a legal person, and, with the exception of trade unions (see Trade Union and Labour Relations (Consolidation) Act 1992, section 10), cannot hold property in its own right as a society. The validity of a gift to such an institution depends on the construction of the gift by the courts and there are four possible interpretations:

(i)   it may be construed as a gift to the individual members of the association, at the date the gift takes effect, as joint tenants. Such a construction gives every member the right to sever their share and take the value of it (see *Re Drummond* [1914] 2 Ch 90). As the members are joint tenants, the last surviving member is entitled to the property under the doctrine of survivorship (*Hanchett-Stamford v Attorney General and Another* [2008] EWHC 330 (Ch), [2009] Ch 173);

(ii) it may be construed as a gift not only to the present members, but also to future members, for ever or for an indefinite period of time. The problem with this construction is that, unless the period of time is limited to the perpetuity period, the gift would fail;

(iii) it may be construed as a gift for the trustees of the association, who hold the property on trust for the purposes of the association. If this construction is adopted, the gift will fail as an invalid purpose trust;

(iv) it may be construed as a gift for the existing members of the association beneficially, but on the basis that the gift is to be held as an accretion to the funds of the association and dealt with in accordance with the rules of the association which contractually bind the members of the association *inter se*. Such a gift is valid. The member, in such a case, cannot claim their share beneficially. On their death or resignation, their share will accrue to the other members of the association, including those who become members after the gift took effect (see *Re Recher's Will Trusts* [1972] Ch 526).

5J GIFT TO EXISTING MEMBERS OF A SOCIETY OR CLUB AS AN ACCRETION TO FUNDS

I GIVE to [name of society or club] the sum of £ .... as a gift to the members of the said [name of society or club] at the date of my death for the use and benefit of such members absolutely and this gift is made on the basis such sum is not available to each of them beneficially but is added to and forms part of the funds of [name of society or club] and is dealt with by the governing body of [name of society or club] according to either (as the case may be) the rules applying to the said [name of society or club] or to the contract which regulates its members *inter se* at the date of my death and I DIRECT that the receipt of the person who appears to my Trustees to be the treasurer or secretary or other proper officer of the [name of society or club] shall be a good discharge to my Trustees.

5.7 GIFTS TO CHARITIES

A charity may receive the benefit of a gift in a will by means of a charitable trust. No specific form of language is required, but the intention of the testator to give the property to charity must be clearly expressed and imperative in nature. Precatory words have even been held to be sufficient (see *AG v Davies* (1802) 9 Ves 535). It is also sufficient if the gift provides 'for such charities as my executors shall select' since it is necessary to show only certainty of intention to apply the property for charitable purposes. Charitable gifts receive concessionary treatment over other trusts in terms of enforcement, perpetuity, certainty and taxation, and are exempt from inheritance tax (Inheritance Tax Act 1984, section 23).

Charitable purposes are regarded as such if they fall within Charities Act 2011, section 3(1) or are for the public benefit. All purposes which were charitable under former legislation continue to be under the 2011 Act.

Formerly, for a gift to be charitable, three criteria had to be met:

(i)   the gift had to be of a charitable nature within the spirit of the preamble to the Statute of Elizabeth I as interpreted by the courts and extended by statute. Now the Charities Act 2011 is in force, sections 1 and 2 will apply;
(ii) the gift had to promote a public benefit of a nature recognised by the courts as a public benefit;
(iii) the purpose of the trust had to be wholly and exclusively charitable.

5.7.1   Charitable nature

The charitable purposes mentioned in the Statute of Elizabeth I became anachronistic and in *Income Tax Special Purpose Commissioners v Pemsel* [1891] AC 531, Lord MacNaghten categorised four groups of charitable trust, those:

- for the relief of poverty;
- for the advancement of education;
- for the advancement of religion;
- for other purposes beneficial to the community, not falling within the preceding heads.

The Charities Act 2011 states that a charitable purpose is one that comes within the following list:

(a)   the prevention or relief of poverty;
(b)   the advancement of education;
(c)   the advancement of religion;
(d)   the advancement of health or the saving of lives;
(e)   the advancement of citizenship or community development;
(f)   the advancement of the arts, culture, heritage or science;
(g)   the advancement of amateur sport;
(h)   the advancement of human rights, conflict resolution or reconciliation or the promotion of religious or racial harmony or equality and diversity;
(i)   the advancement of environmental protection or improvement;
(j)   the relief of those in need, by reason of youth, age, ill-health, disability, financial hardship or other disadvantage;
(k)   the advancement of animal welfare;
(l)   the promotion of the efficiency of the armed forces of the Crown or of the efficiency of the police, fire and rescue services or ambulance services;
(m) any other purposes—

(i)   that are not within paragraphs (a) to (l) but are recognised as charitable purposes by virtue of section 5 (recreational and similar trusts, etc) or under the old law,

(ii)   that may reasonably be regarded as analogous to, or within the spirit of, any purposes falling within any of paragraphs (a) to (l) or sub-paragraph (i), or this sub-paragraph,

(iii)   that may reasonably be regarded as analogous to, or within the spirit of, any purposes which have been recognised under the law relating to charities in England and Wales, as falling within sub-paragraph (ii) or this paragraph.

5K   GENERAL GIFT OF SPECIFIC SUM TO CHARITABLE INSTITUTION

I GIVE the sum of £ ... to [name of charity and its registered charity number] [and it is my wish without creating any binding obligation that this gift is used for [state specific benefit or purpose intended] and I DECLARE that the receipt of the person professing to be the treasurer or other proper officer for the time being thereof shall be a sufficient discharge to my Trustees.

If the charity is a national one with a local presence, a testator may wish to include a non-binding request that the gift is applied for purposes 'close to home'. Many large charities have a general policy regarding use of their funds and so testators often have to accept that a request that a gift is applied in a particular way cannot be made binding on the institution.

5L   LEGACY OF SPECIFIC SUMS TO SEVERAL CHARITABLE INSTITUTIONS

I GIVE to each of the following charitable institutions the amounts set forth below the receipt of the person professing to be the treasurer or other proper officer for the time being of each said institution being a sufficient discharge to my Trustees:
To [charity A] the sum of £ ...
To [charity B] the sum of £ ...

The Finance Act 2012 introduced a new inheritance tax relief to apply when a sufficiently large percentage of the estate is given to charity. See Chapter 27 for details of the relief. It is impossible to know when drafting a will what value it will have at death and therefore how much needs to be given to charity to obtain the rate reduction. Testators who wish to ensure that the relief is available must make use of a formula clause like the one set out below. Because of the uncertainty as to the size of the estate on death, it is helpful to set out whether or not a legacy is still to be paid if no inheritance tax is payable on the estate, and whether the testator wishes to set a maximum limit on the size of the gift.

5M   FORMULA CLAUSE IN FAVOUR OF CHARITY TO ENSURE REDUCED RATE OF INHERITANCE TAX APPLIES

1.1   I GIVE the Charitable Sum to [*name of charity*] [*or* to the several charities in the percentage shares set forth below:

To [charity A]   ...%
To [charity B]   ...%
To [charity C]   ...%
                                                                           100%]

such Charitable Sum being a sum as shall constitute a Donated Amount equal to 10 [or larger figure] % of the Baseline Amount in relation to the [General Component] [aggregate of the General, [Survivorship], [Settled Property] Components and [reservation of benefit property]] of my estate.

1.2   The Charitable Sum given by this clause shall in no event:

1.2.1   be less than £ ... whether or not the lower rate of inheritance tax shall be applicable; and

1.2.2   exceed £ ... ('the upper limit') even if in consequence of this restriction in the value of the Charitable Sum the lower rate of inheritance tax shall not apply. [If this proviso shall apply and in consequence the lower rate of inheritance tax shall not be payable, the amount of the Charitable Sum shall [be equal to the amount of the upper limit] [be reduced to £ ...] [lapse]].

1.3   My Executors shall have the power exercisable at their sole discretion to make, withhold or withdraw the elections under paragraphs 7 and 8 in Schedule 1A to the Inheritance Tax Act 1984.

1.4   For the purposes of this clause 'Baseline Amount', 'Donated Amount', 'General Component', 'lower rate of tax', 'qualifying component', 'Settled Property Component' and 'Survivorship Component' shall have the meanings they respectively bear in Schedule 1A to the Inheritance Tax Act 1984.

The above clause is based on wording used in HM Revenue & Customs, *Inheritance Tax Manual* at IHTM45008 (available at www.gov.uk/hmrc-internal-manuals/inheritance-tax-manual). It is readily apparent that if this clause is adopted, the amount of the legacy is unlikely to be known until the value of the estate is settled and so the amount of charity exemption will change as the value of the estate changes. Paragraph 1.1 ensures that the charitable legacy will meet the requirements for the reduced rate. The legacy is set by the reference to the components of the estate listed; but this only fixes the size of the legacy to be paid under the will and does not override the requirement for those liable for the tax of the different components to elect for the components to be merged before other components can benefit from the reduced rate. The proviso in 1.2.1 ensures that even if the estate is not liable to inheritance tax, the legacy is still payable to the charity, whilst the proviso in 1.2.2 ensures that the charitable legacy does not exceed a fixed amount, even though that could mean the estate does not qualify for the reduced rate.

For an alternative form to the above precedent, see **27.11** and Precedent 27A.

5N   GIFT OF LAND TO CHARITY

> I GIVE to [name of charity] absolutely my freehold property [description] and I DIRECT my Trustees to vest the same in or cause the same to be vested in the Trustees of [charity] to be held by them for the general purposes of the charity.

5O   GIFT TO CHARITY TO BE SELECTED BY THE TRUSTEES

> I GIVE the sum of £ ... to my Trustees UPON TRUST for such charitable object or objects or for such charitable purpose or purposes as my Trustees may in their absolute discretion select and I DECLARE that the receipt of the person professing to be the treasurer or other proper officer for the time being of any charity to which my Trustees may allocate any sums hereunder shall be a sufficient discharge to my Trustees.

Gifts for the relief of poverty

Poverty is a relative term and is not confined to the destitute in society (see *Re Coulthurst* [1951] Ch 661 (CA), and *IRC v Baddeley* [1955] AC 572 (HL)). The gift may be general or it may be confined to some particular section of the public defined by reference to a place, a religion or otherwise. The gift must be made by way of bounty, not bargain, but there is no objection to the beneficiaries being required to contribute to the cost of the benefit (see *Joseph Rowntree Memorial Trust Housing Association v AG* [1983] Ch 159). This heading of charity equates to Charities Act 2011, section 3(1). It should be noted that section 3(1) carries forward the provisions contained in Charities Act 2006, section 2(2)(a) and covers the *prevention* of poverty as well as the relief of poverty.

Gifts for the advancement of education

The Charities Act 2011 (following the Charities Act 2006) differentiates between the advancement of education (section 3(1)(b)), and the advancement of the arts, culture, heritage and science (section 3(1)(f)), and there may be a degree of overlap between these categories. Charitable gifts for the advancement of education extend to all kinds of educational services, and the courts have upheld as charitable, *inter alia*, gifts to libraries; gifts to facilitate a chess tournament for schoolboys; the provision of a field for a Sunday school; and a gift to the Boy Scouts Association (now re-named 'The Scout Association'). There is, however, a strict requirement that the gift must benefit a section of the public or be of a public nature (see **5.7.4** for changes to the public benefit requirement under the Charities Act 2006). (An educational establishment cannot be charitable if it is operated for the purpose of making a profit, and fee-paying schools operate on a non-profit-making basis in order to achieve charitable status. The Charities Act 2006 removed the presumption of public benefit in relation to private schools, and this must now be proved.) A trust to promote a particular sport does not, *per se*, qualify under this head, unless the gift is one to an educational institution for the purpose of improving or promoting its sporting facilities (see *Re Mariette* [1915] 2 Ch 284).

Any dispute over the identity of a particular charity falls to be determined by the Attorney General.

5P GIFT TO A SCHOOL FOR THE PROVISION OF PLAYING FIELDS

I GIVE to the Governors at the date of my death of ... School the sum of £ ... for the purchase by them of an area or areas of land to be used for the playing of games and for the sporting activities and other events of the school and its pupils and for similar purposes.

5Q GIFT TO A SCHOOL FOR THE ENDOWMENT OF A PRIZE FOR SPORT

I GIVE to the Governors at the date of my death of ... School the sum of £ ... to be invested by them as they see fit the income therefrom to be applied in the provision of a prize or trophy for the winners of [the one hundred metres relay] at the school's annual sports day.

Gifts for the advancement of religion

The law has taken a liberal view as to what amounts to a religion. It can include belief in one Supreme Being, many, or none. Charities Act 2011, section 3(2) carries forward the definitions contained in the previous legislation, providing that religion includes 'a religion which involves belief in more than one god', as well as one 'which does not involve belief in a god'. Religious gifts have included gifts for the provision and support of the clergy, building and maintenance of religious buildings, and the provision of graveyards and burial places. It has been held, however, that a gift for missionary work is not charitable on the ground that the description is so wide as to include non-charitable purposes (see *Scott v*

Brownrigg (1881) LR 9 Ir 246). In this case, however, as with many other phrases such as 'for God's work', 'for the service of God', 'for his work in the parish', the court often finds circumstances to indicate that the purposes are intended to be limited to charitable religious purposes (see *Re Moon's Will Trusts* [1948] 1 All ER 300).

Many testators who wish to leave a gift to the Church of England want to leave something for the work of their local parish church. The proper recipient in such a case is its Parochial Church Council (PCC). PCCs are the governing bodies of parish churches and are bodies corporate under the Parochial Church Councils (Powers) Measure 1956 (as amended). All Church of England churches have charitable status even if they do not have a registered charity number. Churches are excepted from registration with the Charity Commission, apart from those whose annual income exceeds £100,000.

If a testator wishes to leave a gift to the national Church, it needs to be remembered that the Church of England is itself not a legal entity and has a complex structure. However, there are options, with a number of different bodies an individual can leave a gift to, notably the Archbishops' Council, the Church and Community Fund or the Church of England Pensions Board.

5R   GIFT FOR RELIGIOUS PURPOSES IN A PARTICULAR PARISH

I GIVE the sum of £ ... to the Parochial Church Council of the parish of [name of parish] (registered charity number if applicable) in the Diocese of [name of Diocese] for its general religious purposes (including but not limited to the building or repair of buildings in the said parish used for religious purposes) as the Parochial Church Council shall in its absolute discretion think fit and I DIRECT that the Parochial Church Council shall be entitled to apply both the capital and income of the fund to any such purposes notwithstanding that the whole of the capital sum is thereby expended and I FURTHER DECLARE that the receipt of an officer of the Parochial Church Council shall be a sufficient discharge to my Trustees.

5S   GIFT TO A RELIGIOUS COMMUNITY

I GIVE the sum of £ ... to the Mother Superior at the date of my death of the Convent of ... at ... to be applied together with any income thereof for the general purposes of the convent and I DIRECT THAT the receipt of the Mother Superior or the person acting as such shall be a sufficient discharge to my Trustees in all respects.

5T GIFT TO PARISH PRIEST FOR THE OFFERING OF MASSES FOR THE DEAD

I GIVE the sum of £ ... to the priest in charge at the date of my death of ... Church at ... to be applied in the offering of masses in public for the repose of the soul[s] of ... and I DECLARE that the receipt of the priest in charge of the church at the time of the payment of the said sum shall be a sufficient discharge to my Trustees.

The validity of such gifts as charitable was re-affirmed in *Re Hetherington* [1990] Ch 1.

5U GIFT TO CHURCH OF ENGLAND PENSIONS BOARD

I GIVE the sum of £ ... to [the General Purposes Fund of the Church of England Pensions Board of 29 Great Smith Street, Westminster, London SW1P 3PS (registered charity no. 236627) as constituted by the Church of England Pensions Measures 1961–2003 or any statutory amendment or re-enactment of the same] and I DECLARE that the receipt by the secretary or other proper officer of the said Board shall be a full and sufficient discharge to my Trustees.

Other purposes beneficial to the community

GIFTS FOR THE ADVANCEMENT OF HEALTH OR THE SAVING OF LIVES

This category derives from the Preamble to the Charitable Uses Act 1601, which included charitable purposes for the relief of impotent people, which meant the sick or disabled. The advancement of health category in the Charities Act 2011 includes trusts to support hospitals and trusts to promote alternative or complementary medicine. The saving of lives includes gifts to the Air Ambulance Service and the Royal National Lifeboat Institution, although these may also fall within section 3(1)(l).

THE ADVANCEMENT OF ANIMAL WELFARE

Trusts for the welfare of animals have tended to be charitable, although trusts for the benefit of individual animals are not. Such trusts were said to 'stimulate humane and generous sentiments in man towards the lower animals, and ... promote feelings of humanity and morality generally, repress brutality, and thus elevate the human race', *Re Wedgwood* [1915] 1 Ch 113.

THE PROMOTION OF THE EFFICIENCY OF THE ARMED FORCES, POLICE AND RESCUE SERVICES

These were charitable under the previous law and continue to be so.

5V   GIFT FOR THE ADVANCEMENT OF HEALTH OR SAVING LIVES

(a)   I GIVE the sum of £ ... to ... [Hospital Foundation] [Healthcare Trust] for the benefit of [... Hospital] [the Trustees for the time being of ... Hospital] to be invested by the [Management Committee] [Board] [Trustees] of the said hospital in any investments authorised hereunder or by statute for the investment of trust funds with full power to transpose the same as the said [Committee] [Board] Trustees] think[s] fit into others of a like nature to be held UPON TRUST to apply the income therefrom for any one or more of the following purposes [list purposes desired]:

(i)   for the provision of facilities services or equipment or otherwise for the improvement of the general welfare of the staff of the said ... Hospital;

(ii)   for the assistance of the patients or former patients of the said ... Hospital in whatever manner including gifts of clothing or additional medical or surgical appliances to them on leaving the said ... Hospital;

(iii)   for the provision of accommodation for the use of relatives of critically ill patients;

(iv)   for the purpose of any research [or name a particular branch of research] carried on at the said ... Hospital.

[(b)   I DESIRE that the gift shall be known as the ... Fund.]

(c)   I DECLARE that a receipt signed by the [treasurer or other proper officer of the said [Board] [Trust]] [any two of the Trustees of the said hospital] shall be sufficient discharge to my Trustees in all respects.

In 2013, the National Health Service underwent a major transformation in terms of its organisation and structure. In most cases, financial matters are now dealt with by the appropriate foundation or healthcare NHS trust or special trustees for the hospital in question. There is usually an abundance of information available online to confirm the correct name of the recipient of donated funds and often precedents to assist the will drafter.

5.7.2   Political trusts

Trusts of a political nature are not charitable. Slade J said in the case of *McGovern v AG* [1982] Ch 321 that a trust is to be classified as 'political' where there is a direct or principal purpose:

(i)   to further the interests of a political party; or
(ii)   to procure changes in the laws of this or another country; or
(iii)   to procure a reversal of governmental policies in this country; or
(iv)   to procure a reversal of governmental policy or of particular decisions of governmental authorities in a foreign country.

Provided the main objects of the trust are charitable in nature, a secondary political purpose, incidental to the main objects, is irrelevant.

Despite the failure of political trusts as charities, gifts to political parties are nevertheless exempt from inheritance tax (Inheritance Tax Act 1984, section 24(1)), provided that the political party is a qualifying political party. To qualify, at the general election immediately preceding the transfer in question, either two members of the party must have been elected to the House of Commons, or one member elected and no fewer than 150,000 votes cast in favour of the party. Following the general election on 12 December 2019, the current political parties that qualify for this exemption are the Conservative Party, the Labour Party, the Liberal Democrats, the Social Democratic and Labour Party, the Scottish National Party, the Democratic Unionist Party, Plaid Cymru, Sinn Féin and the Green Party. For a list of parties which qualified for exemption following previous elections, see HM Revenue & Customs, *Inheritance Tax Manual* at IHTM11197 (available at www.hmrc.gov.uk/manuals/ihtmanual). Section 3(1)(h) allows purposes which advance human rights, conflict resolution and equality, which are political. This marks a radical change to the law, as does the Charity Commission's approach to political activity by charities. The guidance issued by the Charity Commission (*Speaking Out: Guidance on Campaigning and Political Activity by Charities*, March 2008, (CC9)) allows charities to carry out campaigning and political activities, if this would support their charitable purpose. However, changing the law cannot be a major, stated object of a charitable body, and political activities cannot be its only activities.

5.7.3   Social, recreational and sporting trusts

A gift to provide sporting facilities is not charitable, unless, as has been seen (see **5.7.1**), it is to provide facilities for pupils of schools, universities or institutes of higher education.

Charities Act 2011, section 5(1) provides that a gift to a recreational trust or registered sports ground qualifies under the Act if the beneficiary is charitable (and is to be treated as always having been charitable) to provide, or assist in the provision of, facilities for recreation, or other leisure-time occupation (if the facilities are provided in the interests of social welfare).

The requirement that the facilities are provided in the interests of social welfare cannot be satisfied if the basic conditions are not met. The basic conditions are that the facilities are provided with the object of improving the conditions of life for the persons for whom the facilities are primarily intended, and that those persons have need of the facilities because of their youth, age, infirmity or disability, poverty, or social and economic circumstances, or the facilities are to be available to members of the public at large or to male, or to female, members of the public at large.

Charities Act 2011, section 5(1) applies in particular to the provision of facilities at village halls, community centres and women's institutes, and the provision and maintenance of grounds and buildings to be used for purposes of recreation or leisure-time occupation, and extends to the provision of facilities for those purposes by the organising of any activity but this is subject to the requirement that the facilities are provided in the interests of social welfare. However, nothing in the section is to be treated as derogating from the public benefit requirement.

In *Gibbons and Another v Smith and Others* [2020] EWHC 1727 (Ch), the High Court said land held on trust for a sports and welfare club (an unincorporated association) was not held on charitable trusts, despite its governing document having been drafted with the intention of creating a charitable trust. Its objects were modelled on the Recreational Charities Act 1958 (since repealed and largely reproduced in Charities Act 2011, section 5(1)). However, it failed to fulfil the requirements of the 1958 Act. In particular, the facilities were not made available to members of the public at large as only members were entitled to access the club's benefits, and since membership was subject to approval of the club's committee, it was a private members' club. Also, the club's objects were too wide to be exclusively charitable.

5.7.4   Public benefit requirement

Charities Act 2011, section 4 continues the idea that in order for a trust to be charitable it must be for the public benefit, and it expressly provides that 'public benefit' refers to the concept as previously understood in charity law (section 4(3)). A gift can be charitable only if it is for public benefit, but this requirement differs from category to category. With regard to gifts for the relief of poverty, the test for public benefit is very wide, and some trusts or gifts have been upheld (under previous but similar legislation) as charitable even though limited in their application to some small group of individuals ascertained by reference to some personal nexus (e.g. of blood or contract).

In any gift for the advancement of education, the need for public benefit is not satisfied where the beneficiaries are to be ascertained merely by reference to a personal tie, as in the case of the relations of a particular person, or the employees of a particular firm. However, where there is a public element, the trust may be charitable even though such people benefit (see *Re Koettgen's Will Trusts* [1954] Ch 252). Here a trust was said to be charitable where it was to promote commercial education among members of the public who could not afford it, with a direction that a preference be given to the families of employees of a named company up to a maximum of 75% of the income.

Trusts for the advancement of religion must also be beneficial to the public (see *Gilmour v Coats* [1949] AC 426).

Charities Act 2006, section 3, changed the law on public benefit and this has been largely carried forward into Charities Act 2011, section 4. The presumption that organisations for the relief of poverty, the advancement of education or the advancement of religion are for the public benefit was abolished and this remains so. Thus the public benefit of all charitable purposes has to be demonstrated rather than assumed. Section 3(3) provided, as does section 4(3) of the 2011 Act, that any reference to the public benefit is a reference to the public benefit as that term is understood for the purposes of the law relating to charities in England and Wales.

Charities Act 2011, section 12 allows the Charity Commission to issue guidance as to the operation of the public benefit requirement, and to revise that guidance from time to time (see www.charitycommission.gov.uk).

5.7.5 Purposes wholly or exclusively charitable

For a charitable trust to be valid it is required to have as its object the furtherance of purposes which are wholly and exclusively charitable. This provision is now found in Charities Act 2011, section 1(1)(a). Phrases such as 'charitable or deserving', 'charitable or benevolent' and 'charitable or other objects' are to be avoided, since gifts expressed to be for such purposes could also be applied for purposes which are not charitable. If, however, a gift is drafted so that it is to have 'charitable and benevolent' or 'charitable and philanthropic' objects, then the terms do not necessarily invalidate the gift. The charitable purpose remains clear, although the type of charity may be restricted.

There are exceptions to the general rule:

(i)   where one gift is expressed to be for both charitable and non-charitable purposes and a power is given to the trustees to divide the gift between the purposes, as in *Re Douglas* (1887) 35 Ch D 472, 486, the court will hold that the gift is good: ' ... the mere addition to the general charitable purposes of certain definite objects does not make the gift bad because one of the objects is itself not a charity';

(ii)   where the primary purpose of the gift is charitable, but the gift is not exclusively charitable, the courts may overlook the non-charitable part, but the charitable purpose must have a greater weight than the non-charitable purposes (see *Re Coxen* [1948] Ch 747);

(iii)   under the Charitable Trusts (Validation) Act 1954 which perfects trusts made before December 1952. Where a trust is drafted in terms which could result in the property's being used exclusively either for charitable purposes, or for non-charitable purposes, retrospective validation may be possible provided that the invalid terms of the trust would have been considered valid had their object been exclusively charitable (section 2(1)).

5.7.6   Discrimination

Race Relations Act 1976, section 34 made express provision in relation to charities and charitable instruments. The Act dealt only with discrimination on the grounds of colour. Any provision in the charitable instrument which provides for conferring benefits on persons of a class defined by reference to colour has effect as if such reference to colour were disregarded and the benefits are conferred on the persons of the class which results. Where the original class is defined by reference to colour only, the gift takes effect in favour of persons generally.

The Race Relations Act 1976 and the Sex Discrimination Act 1975 are replaced by the provisions of the Equality Act 2010. This Act prohibits discrimination against persons who share 'protected characteristics', namely age, disability, gender reassignment, marriage and civil partnership, pregnancy and maternity, race, religion or belief, sex and sexual orientation (section 4). Section 193 contains special provisions in relation to charities, which basically mean that it is lawful to discriminate in favour of a group who fall within the category of protected characteristics, but not against them. In relation to provisions in charitable instruments which provide for benefits for a class who are defined by colour, the previous position remains, in that the gift will take effect without reference to colour (section 193(4), and see *Re Harding; Gibbs v Harding and Others* [2007] EWHC 3 (Ch), [2008] Ch 235).

5.7.7   The cy-près doctrine

The *cy-près* doctrine comes into operation where a testator, demonstrating a general charitable intention, creates a charitable trust, the objects of which are neither possible nor practicable. The trust may be saved by the doctrine and the court may, at its discretion, apply the intended subject matter of the trust to a purpose which resembles the original purpose as nearly as possible.

The question of the survival of a charitable gift where the intended recipient, a church, no longer existed was considered in *Re Schroder; Kings v Bultitude and Another* [2010] EWHC 1795 (Ch), [2010] All ER (D) 148 (Jul). The *cy-près* doctrine was applied.

Before the Charities Act 1960, the application of the *cy-près* doctrine was confined to cases where it was either impossible or impracticable to carry out the testator's intentions. As a result of the Act, it is no longer necessary to decide matters of impossibility or impracticability. A *cy-près* was previously permitted where the settlor had a clear charitable intention, and (Charities Act 1993, section 13(1)):

(a)   where the original purposes, in whole or in part,

(i)   have been as far as may be fulfilled; or
(ii)   cannot be carried out, or not according to the directions given and to the spirit of the gift; or

(b)   where the original purposes provide a use for part only of the property available by virtue of the gift; or
(c)   where the property available by virtue of the gift and other property applicable for similar purposes can be more effectively used in conjunction, and to that end can suitably, regard being had to the spirit of the gift, be made applicable to common purposes; or
(d)   where the original purposes were laid down by reference to an area which then was but has since ceased to be a unit for some other purpose, or by reference to a class of persons or to an area which has for any reason since ceased to be suitable, regard being had to the spirit of the gift, or to be practical in administering the gift; or
(e)   where the original purposes, in whole or in part, have, since they were laid down,

(i)   been adequately provided for by other means; or
(ii)   ceased, as being useless or harmful to the community or for other reasons, to be in law charitable;
(iii) ceased in any other way to provide a suitable and effective method of using the property available by virtue of the gift, regard being had to the spirit of the gift.

Charities Act 2011, Part 2 now prescribes the duties of the Charity Commission and the Official Custodian for Charities.

5.7.8   Charities wrongly named or having ceased to exist

Provided it can be shown from the wording of the disposition that a testator intended to benefit a charitable purpose, the gift need not fail even if the institution has never existed or cannot be identified. Where the beneficiary is an institution which has ceased to exist in the testator's lifetime, whether before or after the execution of the will, the gift lapses unless a general charitable intention is apparent. There is no lapse where there has simply been a change of name or an amalgamation with another institution. If the charity ceases to exist after the death of the testator but before payment, the gift still takes effect.

It is also advisable to provide for the possibility that an incorporated charity may be in the process of being wound up but not yet formally dissolved. In *Re ARMS (Multiple Sclerosis Research) Ltd* [1997] 1 WLR 877, it was held that legacies which vested in a charitable company after the winding-up order but before dissolution were available to the charity's creditors rather than being preserved for its charitable purposes.

Any dispute about, or difficulty in determining, the designation of a charitable gift falls to the Attorney General to decide.

5W   GENERAL PROVISION AGAINST LAPSE OF CHARITABLE GIFTS

Where any provision within this my will or any codicil hereto names any institution society or other body whether incorporated or not as an intended Beneficiary and that Beneficiary is stated to be a charity or the intended gift is stated to be for a charitable purpose and where the said intended Beneficiary is found never to have existed or to have ceased to exist [or in the case of a company to be subject to a winding up order or to have been dissolved] or to have changed its name or constitution either by amalgamation with another body or otherwise or to have transferred all its assets to another charitable body prior to my death then in such an event the benefit of such gifts for each such intended Beneficiary shall instead be given to such charitable body or bodies or applied to such charitable purpose or purposes as my Trustees shall in their absolute discretion think fit.

While a general provision such as this may be appropriate for a will with multiple charitable bequests covering a range of charitable objectives, if the testator has a specific objective in mind, the provision below added to the terms of a charitable bequest might better meet the testator's intentions.

5X   **SPECIFIC PROVISION AGAINST LAPSE OF A CHARITABLE GIFT**

... AND I DECLARE that if for any reason [name the charity beneficiary] has ceased to exist or cannot be identified then this gift shall not fail for such a reason but instead the gift shall take effect as a gift to my Trustees who shall pay it to such charity as they shall in their absolute discretion decide which they consider meets or most nearly fulfils the objectives of [name the charity beneficiary] being the objectives I intend to benefit [and I FURTHER DECLARE in exercising their discretion my Trustees may pay the gift to more than one charity meeting the above criteria in such shares as they may determine].

5.7.9   The rule against perpetuities

Charities form an exception to the general rule against perpetuities. A gift to one charity with a gift over to another charity upon a certain event is valid even if that event occurs at any time beyond the perpetuity period. The rule that a gift which purports to give income from property for an unlimited period is void has no application to a gift for a charitable purpose.

Chapter 6

Beneficiaries Identified by Description or Relationship

6.1 INTRODUCTION

Where a beneficiary in a will is referred to not by name but by description of relationship to the testator, such as 'my wife' or 'my gardener', then, unless a contrary intention is expressed in the will, it is the person who satisfies that description at the time the will is made who is entitled to the gift (see *Re Whorwood* (1887) 34 Ch D 446).

A person who is ascertained to be a beneficiary under a description continues to be entitled even if they cease to fit the description, unless a contrary intention is shown by the will or codicil.

6.2 RELATIONSHIP BY BLOOD AND AFFINITY

Where a relationship is specified in a will it is presumed that the only persons to take are the relations by blood, not those by marriage, unless a contrary intention is expressed or there are no blood relations in existence.

In *Re Daoust* [1944] 1 All ER 443, 444, Vaisey J stated that the strict and proper meaning of the word 'nephew' is 'son of a brother or sister'; and, similarly, 'niece' means, in the strict sense, 'daughter of a brother or sister'. But, he continued, the meaning could, having regard to the context and circumstance of the case, be extended in two directions:

(i)   the words may describe the child of a brother-in-law or of a sister-in-law; and
(ii)   'nephew' is often used to indicate a niece's husband and 'niece' is often used to describe the wife of a nephew.

Vaisey J said that, unless compelled by context or circumstances, the court will always construe a class gift to nephews and nieces as a gift confined to children of a brother or sister.

The question of who constitutes a nephew or niece was considered in *Wales and Another v Dixon and Others* [2020] EWHC 1979 (Ch). In his will, the testator gave his residuary estate to 'such all of my nephew's and niece's children'. At the date of his death, the testator had two blood nephews and two blood nieces. He also had three nephews by marriage and one niece by marriage. A further nephew by marriage had died in 1992 leaving a son.

Master Teverson found that in the light of the surrounding circumstances, it was clear that the testator intended to include the nephews and nieces of his dead wife as well as his own. The relevant circumstances included the fact that in a series of earlier wills made over many years, he had always included his wife's relatives. It was also relevant that instructions had been taken by telephone which increased the likelihood that the deceased's intention with regard to residue were not understood.

A description by relationship *prima facie* includes not only people of the whole blood, but also of the half-blood (see *Re Hammersley* (1886) 2 TLR 459) unless a contrary intention is evident. The words 'my own brothers and sisters' were said to exclude those of the half-blood (see *Re Dowson* (1909) 101 LTR 671).

Where a particular relationship is specified by the testator, relations of the exact degree only are presumed to benefit. Thus, if the testator refers to nieces, it is presumed they mean nieces and not great-nieces. Again, this presumption may be rebutted by the context or a contrary intention.

The term 'cousins' generally includes only first cousins; the term 'first cousins or cousins german' does not include the descendants of first cousins, i.e. first cousins once removed, and so on.

6.3   GENDER-SPECIFIC DRAFTING

The Gender Recognition Act 2004 affects gender-specific drafting. Section 9(1) of the Act provides that:

> Where a full gender recognition certificate is issued to a person, the person's gender becomes for all purposes the acquired gender (so that, if the acquired gender is the male gender, the person's sex becomes that of a man and, if it is the female gender, the person's sex becomes that of a woman).

Section 9(2) provides that:

> Subsection (1) does not affect things done, or events occurring, before the certificate is issued; but it does operate for the interpretation of … instruments and other documents made before the certificate is issued.

But wills are subject to section 15, which provides:

> The fact that a person's gender has become the acquired gender … does not affect the disposal or devolution of property under a will or other instrument made before 5 April 2004.

Thus, it might be wise to avoid gender-specific drafting whenever possible and refer to people by their names rather than as a class of a specific sex; or to provide that gifts depending on gender are to be construed as at the date the will is signed.

Section 18 provides for situations where the disposition of property under a will, whenever it is made, is affected by the provisions of the Act. In such a situation the court (if satisfied that it is just to do so) can vary the disposition.

6.4 ILLEGITIMACY AND ADOPTION

6.4.1 Illegitimate children

In the case of instruments made before 1 January 1970, a class includes only those who were born legitimate, unless there is a contrary intention. This is likely to be regarded as contravening the European Convention on Human Rights by analogy with *Hand and Another v George and Another* [2017] EWHC 533 (Ch) and *Re JC Druce Settlement* [2019] EWHC 3701 (Ch). See **6.4.2**.

In instruments made after that date, the presumption is reversed (Family Law Reform Acts 1969 and 1987). If the will was executed before 1970 it is not treated as made after that date even though a codicil made after that date republishes the will.

The 1987 Act provides that in the case of wills made after 4 April 1988, references to any relationship between two people are to be construed without regard to whether or not the parents of either of them, or the parents of any person through whom a relationship is traced, have or had been married.

It is possible to exclude the effect of the Acts by making contrary provision in the will. In the case of continuing trusts, if excluding the effect of the Acts, it may be appropriate to give the trustees power to add beneficiaries to deal with circumstances arising after the testator's death.

6A   DECLARATION AS TO MEANING OF CHILD

References to children, grandchildren and issue shall be construed so as to exclude:
(1)   illegitimate adopted and legitimated children, grandchildren and issue;
(2)   persons claiming descent through those so excluded.

6.4.2   Adopted children

A series of Acts deals with the entitlements of adopted children. The earliest was 1926 and the most recent 2002.

Before 1 January 1950, adoption gave the adopted child no right to share in the property of the adopting family (but did not deprive the child of its rights in relation to property of its original family).

Adoption of Children Act 1949, section 9 and Adoption Act 1976, section 39 reversed the position and provided that adopted children were to be treated as children of the adopters and of no other persons but only for the purposes of wills, intestacies and settlements made after the date of the adoption. The statutes were not in that sense retrospective.

Under the Adoption Act 1976, a will or codicil was to be treated as made on the date of death of the testator. Section 42(2)(a) provided that dispositions in wills were to be construed as if a child had been born on the date of the adoption, although this did not affect references to actual ages. Adoption and Children Act 2002, section 69(2), in force from 30 December 2005, repeats these provisions. Thus, for example, suppose a testator makes a gift to 'the children of A living at my death or born thereafter who reach the age of twenty-five'. The testator dies in 2005, and in 2006 A adopts a child aged 5. At the date of the testator's death the child was not a child of A, but the child is treated as 'born' in 2006 and so joins the class of beneficiaries. However, the child becomes entitled to their share of the capital on their 25th birthday, not 25 years after their adoption.

The European Court of Human Rights has consistently held that Article 14 in conjunction with Article 8 precludes legislation which confers more limited rights on adopted children to their adoptive parents' estate than are conferred on natural children. It has also consistently rejected arguments put forward by respondent governments that the discriminatory law should remain applicable to instruments that pre-date the change in social attitudes, which now requires equal treatment for adopted children. The European Court addressed the problem of retrospectivity of the Convention in this regard in *Marckx v Belgium* [1979] 2 EHRR 330. It held that arguments based on legal certainty or the need to protect the expectations of the deceased and their families must be subordinate to the imperative of equal treatment. Discrimination cannot be regarded as a proportionate response to such concerns.

In *Hand and Another v George and Another* [2017] EWHC 533 (Ch), [2017] Ch 449, Rose J had to consider the human rights issue. A testator had left the residue of his estate to his three children in equal shares for life with the remainder in each case to their 'child or children who attain the age of twenty one years'. When the will was made, Adoption of Children Act 1926, section 5(2) was in force, which provided that in any disposition 'children' was construed as not including adopted children. The testator died in 1948. The claimants were the adopted children of the testator's second son, who died in 2008. The defendants were the natural children of the testator's daughter.

The claimants argued that Human Rights Act 1998, section 3(1) required the court to construe Adoption Act 1976, Schedule 2, paragraph 6(1) (which provides that the reversal of the rule against including adopted children did not apply to existing instruments) to make it compliant with their Convention rights under Article 14, read with Article 8. In *Wilson v First County Trust Ltd* [2003] UKHL 40, the House of Lords had held that the 'reading down' of the legislation to make it compliant with the Convention must not be retrospective in the sense of interfering with vested rights or pending actions.

Rose J held that by retaining the discriminatory interpretative provision in Adoption of Children Act 1926, section 5(2), Adoption Act 1976, Schedule 2, paragraph 6(1) conferred more limited inheritance rights on adopted children than natural children. Such an interpretation infringed Article 14 in conjunction with Article 8. It was possible to read paragraph 6(1) pursuant to Human Rights Act 1998, section 3 to make it compliant with the claimants' Convention rights so that the reference to 'children' included biological and adopted children. This was not giving retrospective effect to the Human Rights Act 1998, which is generally impermissible, since the question only fell to be determined in 2008 when the claimants' father died. The defendants had 'vested interests', in the sense that this phrase is used in the law of inheritance. However, the House of Lords in *Wilson v First County Trust Ltd* [2003] UKHL 40 at [196] had not used the term in that way. In this context the word indicated that 'the particular beneficiary of the right must have done something to avail himself of it before the law is changed'.

Rose J therefore held (at [105]) that the restriction on adopted children being treated as 'children' under an instrument predating the relevant legislation should only apply to an existing instrument or enactment:

in so far as (i) it contains a disposition of property, and (ii) the beneficiary of the disposition has done something to avail himself or herself of the property right in question before the coming into force of the Human Rights Act 1998.

As beneficiaries of trusts and estates do not normally 'do' anything to obtain a property right, the restriction on adopted children inheriting under instruments pre-dating the adoption legislation is effectively removed.

This analysis has been followed in *Re JC Druce Settlement* [2019] EWHC 3701 (Ch), where a literal reading of 'beneficiaries' in clause 3I of a settlement made on 10 December 1959 would exclude certain potential members of the class because they or their parents were illegitimate or adopted.

The judge accepted that while the Human Rights Act 1998 cannot bring about a retroactive alteration of the identity of the beneficiaries at a past point in time, it can be applied when a power or duty falls to be exercised or performed post the implementation of the Human Rights Act 1998.

As with illegitimacy, it is possible to exclude the statutory provisions in the will. In the case of continuing trusts, it may be appropriate to give the trustees power to add or exclude beneficiaries to deal with circumstances arising after the testator's death.

6.4.3   Legitimated children

Under the Legitimacy Act 1976, a legitimated person (and any other person) is entitled to take any interest under the will of a testator who dies after 31 December 1975 as if the legitimated person had been born legitimate, subject to the expression of any contrary intention. Similar rules of construction apply to dispositions depending on the date of birth as apply on adoption. See section 5(4) and (5). Legitimacy Act 1976, section 2A provides that where, under the Human Fertilisation and Embryology Act 2008, a woman is a child's other parent as a result of written consent and subsequently forms a civil partnership with the child's mother, the child will be legitimated.

6.5   CHILDREN

Where a gift is to 'children' of the testator, the term is presumed to include immediate descendants, but not grandchildren or remoter issue. If the testator has adopted children, they are included in a gift to the testator's children generally, unless a contrary intention is expressed. A child adopted by a married couple is treated in law as a child of that marriage. If the adopters are not married, the child is treated in law as if born to the adopters. With effect from the making of an adoption order, a child in law ceases to be the child of its natural parents and becomes the child of the adopters (Adoption and Children Act 2002, section 67(1)). In *Hardy v Hardy and Another* [2013] EWHC 83 (Ch), [2013] All ER (D) 214 (Jan), the testator directed that his residuary estate be held in trust 'for such of my children as shall survive me and attain the age of 21 years and if more than one in equal shares absolutely'. The testator had three children who all attained the age of 21. However, one of his sons was adopted, and under section 67 was therefore to be treated as the child of the adopters and not as being the testator's child, unless there was a contrary indication in the will. The testator appointed his sons (which included his adopted son) and whom he described as 'my sons' as his executors and trustees. It was held on the true construction of the will the adopted son was considered to be one of the children of the testator and therefore entitled to his share of the residuary estate. The descriptions of the adopted son in the will and codicil as one of the testator's sons was a very clear indication that the intention was to regard that son as his child, and, therefore, as one of his 'children' within the meaning of the will, contrary to the effect of section 67.

The term 'children' may include grandchildren if the context shows the testator used the term in this broader sense.

A child *en ventre sa mère* is also included in the description of children born or living at a particular date if it is to the child's own benefit to be included.

6B   GENERAL CLAUSE FOR A CHILD EN VENTRE SA MÈRE

Any reference to a child or children in this will or any codicil hereto shall include any child *en ventre sa mère* at the date of my death or at such time as may be referred to therein provided that such person is born alive thereafter and I DECLARE that any such child shall be deemed to be living at that date.

No special clauses are required in respect of children born as a result of fertilisation techniques. On the Human Fertilisation and Embryology Acts 1990 and 2008, see **6.4.3** and **24.11**.

6.6   DESCENDANTS

The term 'descendants', when used in a will, generally includes anyone who is descended from a particular individual, however the descent is traced. It does not, however, include collateral relations, unless the will specifically defines the terms and indicates that it should do so.

Whenever drafting gifts to the testator's children (or remoter issue), it should be borne in mind that Wills Act 1837, section 33 (as amended) provides a statutory substitution clause in certain circumstances (see **5.2.2** and **14.1**).

The precedents which follow, for gifts to children and issue, include an optional age contingency. It is important to warn testators concerned about inheritance tax that the inclusion of an age contingency can result in anniversary and exit charges. To avoid such charges entirely, gifts to the testator's own children should be made contingent on an age no greater than 18, and gifts to others should be absolute, or of immediate post-death interests. Similarly, a contingent interest may result in the gift of a residence failing to attract the inheritance tax additional residence nil rate allowance. See Chapters 27 and 29.

If a contingency is included, provision should be made for failure of the contingency by way of a substitution or accruer clause. See Precedent 25C.

6C   GIFT IN TRUST FOR THE BENEFIT OF TESTATOR'S CHILDREN [OR THE CHILDREN OF ANOTHER] WITH SUBSTITUTED GIFT TO THE ISSUE OF DECEASED CHILDREN

IN TRUST for [all and every one of my children or child (if only one)] [the children or child (if only one) of ... deceased] [who attain the age of [eighteen] [twenty-one] years or marry [or form a civil partnership] under that age] and if more than one in equal shares as tenants in common PROVIDED THAT if any child of [mine] [the said ...] has died or shall die in my lifetime or otherwise fails to attain a vested interest leaving issue living at my death [who attain the age of [eighteen] [twenty-one] or marry [or form a civil partnership] under that age] such issue shall stand in the place of such deceased child and take *per stirpes* and equally between them if more than one the share which such deceased child would have taken if he or she had survived me and attained a vested interest but so that no issue shall take whose parent is alive at my death and so capable of taking.

6D   TRUST FOR CHILDREN IN UNEQUAL SHARES

IN TRUST as to three equal seventh parts for my son [name] absolutely as to two other equal seventh parts for my daughter [name] if and when she attains the age of [eighteen] [twenty-one] years and as to the remaining two equal seventh parts in trust in equal shares for my grandchildren ... and ... if and when they shall respectively attain the age of [eighteen] [twenty-one] years [or marry under that age].

6E   TRUST FOR CHILDREN OF QUANTIFIED AMOUNTS

IN TRUST as to £[50,000] or investments of that value at the date of [my death] [appropriation] for my son [name] if and when he attains the age of [eighteen] [twenty-one] years or [marries] [forms a civil partnership] under that age and as to £[75,000] or investments of that value at the date of [my death] [appropriation] for my daughter [name] if and when she attains the age of [eighteen] [twenty-one] years or [marries] [forms a civil partnership] under that age and as to the balance of the fund (if any) for my son [name] absolutely.

Provision should be made directing the trustees how investments are to be valued for this purpose.

6F   TRUST FOR TWO PERSONS AS TENANTS IN COMMON ON ATTAINING THE AGE OF TWENTY-ONE, WITH A GIFT OVER ON THE DEATH OF EITHER TO THE OTHER OF THEM

IN TRUST for [name] and [name] if and when they shall respectively attain the age of twenty-one years in equal shares as tenants in common but so that if either of them is already dead or shall die in my lifetime or before reaching the age of twenty-one years or if either fails to attain a vested interest for any other reason I GIVE the share [of residue] hereinbefore bequeathed to the one so dying to the other of them if and when [he] [she] shall attain the age of twenty-one years ALWAYS PROVIDED THAT if both [name] and [name] shall fail to take a vested interest hereunder for any reason I bequeath the said [property] (add gift over).

6G   TRUST FOR SPOUSE OR CIVIL PARTNER AND CHILDREN EQUALLY

IN TRUST for such of my [spouse] [civil partner] [name] and my children as survive me and if more than one in equal shares as tenants in common.

If this trust is in respect of the residuary estate, it gives rise to a partially exempt transfer for inheritance tax purposes. Although the will specifies 'equal shares', the amounts actually received by the beneficiaries may not be equal since the spouse's share is exempt from tax, while the shares taken by the children will be reduced by any tax which is payable from residue.

6.7   STEP-CHILDREN

In *Reading and Another v Reading and Others* [2015] EWHC 946 (Ch), Asplin J said at [41] that the ordinary and natural meaning of the word 'issue' does not include step-children. It connotes the actual children of the testator in the biological sense together with the descendants of those children. However, because of the circumstances of the case she felt able to construe the words 'issue of mine' and 'such of my issue' in a will to include children, step-children and their children.

In *Goodrich and Others v AB and Others* [2022] EWHC 81 (Ch), Chief Master Schuman had to rule on the interpretation of a number of terms used in the deed governing an Employee Benefit Trust. There was a question as to whether the term 'children' could be interpreted as including step-children. The Chief Master held that it could not. There was nothing in the context to suggest that they were intended to be included.

There was also a suggestion that drawing such a distinction might be discriminatory in contravention of the European Convention on Human Rights. Under Human Rights Act 1998, section 3, so far as possible, legislation must be read and given effect to in a way which is compatible with the rights guaranteed by the Convention. Under section 6, the court as a public authority is obliged to act in a way which is compatible with Convention rights. In this case the relevant articles were Article 8 (the right to respect for private and family life) and Article 14 (the right to non-discrimination on any ground such as sex, race, colour, language, religion, etc). The Chief Master completely rejected this argument (though he did accept it in relation to same sex spouses and civil partners: see below). He said at [102] that there is nothing discriminatory in drawing a distinction between a natural or adopted child, on the one hand, and a step-child, on the other hand; 'there is a difference between discriminatory law and the law drawing distinctions'.

6.8   ISSUE

The word 'issue', when used in its strict sense, means 'descendants in every degree'. The meaning may, however, be restricted by the wording of the will. For example, where the testator refers first to 'issue' but later speaks of the gift in question as a gift to children, or where the testator speaks of the 'issue of such issue', the meaning is restricted to 'children'. The same applies where property is directed to be settled on a person and their 'issue', so the word does not normally include step-children and their children (see *Reading and Another v Reading and Others* [2015] EWHC 946 (Ch)).

6.9   SURVIVORS

A gift may be made to such of a particular group of beneficiaries as survive the testator. Where the gift is immediate in nature, any beneficiary who outlives the testator becomes entitled to their share of the property on the testator's death.

Where the gift does not take immediate effect, the beneficiary's interest in the property does not vest immediately upon the death of the testator. For example, where a gift is expressed to be 'to A for life, with remainder to such of their children as survive them', only such of A's children as are living at the date of A's death will take, despite the fact that other children of A may have survived the testator.

See also **5.2.2** dealing with gifts saved under Wills Act 1837, section 33.

6.10   SPOUSES AND CIVIL PARTNERS

Where a testator expresses a gift to be 'to my wife' and he is married at the date the will is executed, there is a *prima facie* presumption that he is referring to his existing wife and not to any future wife. A reference to the 'wife' of any other person would be a reference to the wife at the time the will is created, unless a contrary intention is shown (e.g. 'the wife for the time being'), or that other person is unmarried at the date of the will, in which case the first person to answer the description would take.

The marriage or formation of a civil partnership of the testator following the execution of a will revokes the will unless the will is made in expectation of that marriage or civil partnership to a named person. A will containing a clause that any marriage or the formation of any civil partnership is not to revoke the will is ineffective; the survival of the will is dependent upon the formation of the relationship with a named person. In *Court and Others v Despallieres* [2009] EWHC 3340 (Ch), the testator had purportedly used the words 'that this, my last will and testament shall not be revoked by neither subsequent marriage, Civil Union Partnership nor adoption'. The court held that this wording was insufficient to comply with Wills Act 1837, section 18B(3), as inserted by the Civil Partnership Act 2004. To comply with the statutory requirement, a will which is intended to survive marriage or the formation of a civil partnership must be expressed to be made in contemplation of marriage or forming a civil partnership with a particular person.

A final decree dissolves a marriage and the parties cannot then be described as husband and wife. Likewise, the formation of a civil partnership may be dissolved or annulled by final decree so that the parties are no longer civil partners.

The generally accepted definition of the term 'widow' is the surviving legal wife until her death or remarriage. Where the testator is divorced, his ex-wife does not therefore become his widow, although a person not legally married has been held to be a widow (see *Re Wagstaff* [1908] 1 Ch 162, but compare *Re Lynch* [1943] 1 All ER 168). If a widow remarries, the widowhood ceases, provided the subsequent marriage is not annulled. A wife was held not to be entitled to an annuity payable 'so long as she shall continue my widow' where, after the date of the will, the testator's own marriage was declared null and void (see *Re Boddington* (1884) 25 Ch D 685).

Where a person is described as a 'wife', the gift does not fail merely because there was an invalid marriage, whether or not the parties knew of the invalidity. The gift remains valid provided the testator is not deceived for the purposes of the gift.

With effect from the coming into force of the Civil Partnership Act 2004 on 5 December 2005, the words, 'spouse', 'husband' or 'wife', when they appear in legislation, include a person who has formed a civil partnership. However, there is no provision stating that references in a will or other private instrument to 'spouse' or 'marriage' should be construed to include civil partners and civil partnerships. Therefore, a testator who wishes to include civil partners should make this clear in the will.

6H   DECLARATION AS TO MARRIAGE AND CIVIL PARTNERS

> 'Marriage' is to include civil partnership as defined in Civil Partnership Act 2004, section 1 (as amended) and 'husband', 'wife', 'widower', 'widow' and 'spouse' are to be construed accordingly.

Note the judgment in *Goodrich and Others v AB and Others* [2022] EWHC 81 (Ch) (see below), which considered that the failure of the UK government to legislate to remove differential treatment of spouses and civil partners was discriminatory and in contravention of the European Convention on Human Rights.

The Marriage (Same Sex Couples) Act 2013 provides that in the law of England and Wales marriage has the same effect in relation to same sex couples as it has in relation to opposite sex couples. It goes on at section 11(2) to state that the law of England and Wales, including legislation whenever passed or made, has effect in accordance with section 11(1).

However, Schedule 4, Part 1 expressly provides at paragraph 1, that section 11 'does not alter the effect of any private legal instrument made before that section comes into force'.

In wills drafted after the Act came into force (13 March 2014), therefore, a reference to 'spouse' will include same sex spouses unless a contrary intention is expressed. However, it is sensible to include a statement to this effect in the will for the avoidance of doubt.

If dealing with a will made before the Act came into force, it would appear that 'spouse' does not include a same sex spouse. However, in *Goodrich and Others v AB and Others* [2022] EWHC 81 (Ch) this was held to be in contravention of European Convention on Human Rights, Articles 8 and 14.

In *Goodrich*, Chief Master Schuman had to consider whether a reference to 'spouses' in a deed of settlement dated 11 April 1990 creating an Employee Benefit Trust should be construed to include civil partners and same sex spouses. He decided that for very specific reasons relating to the trust (in particular, to the fact that it was not feasible due to the huge number of beneficiaries to make an application to vary the terms under the Variation of Trusts Act 1958 as it would be with a private family trust), the trust instrument could be construed as including same sex spouses and civil partners.

That was sufficient to dispose of the issue. However, there was also an argument that UK legislation contravened European Convention on Human Rights, Articles 8 and 14.

The Chief Master held that it was discriminatory to treat civil partners differently from spouses.

He also held that Marriage (Same Sex Couples) Act 2013, Schedule 4 was discriminatory in providing at paragraph 1, that section 11 'does not alter the effect of any private legal instrument made before that section comes into force'.

In relation to same sex spouses, the Chief Master considered that it was possible to take the same approach that had been taken in *Hand and Another v George and Another* [2017] EWHC 533 (Ch) (see **6.4**) and read down the Schedule to make it compliant. He held at [93] that it should be read as follows:

(1) Section 11 does not alter the effect of any private legal instrument made before that section comes into force. ...

(2) In this paragraph 'private legal instrument' includes—
     ...

(b) an instrument (including a private Act) which settles property in so far as (i) it contains a disposition of property, and (ii) the beneficiary of the disposition has done something to avail himself or herself of the property right in question before the coming into force of the Human Rights Act 1998.

In relation to civil partners, he considered that it was not possible to read down the legislation in such a way as to make it Convention compliant. Civil partnerships are a new legal relationship created by parliament. Eliding spouses and civil partners would go beyond what the court should do. Therefore, unless and until there is legislation to extend the meaning of 'spouse', it remains necessary to include civil partners expressly.

6.11 NEXT OF KIN

The expression 'next of kin' is usually used to refer to the nearest relative of kin. The term 'statutory next of kin', however, refers to the persons who would be entitled to succeed to the estate on intestacy in the same manner and for such shares and amounts as they would have taken under the intestacy rules. Where there is more than one person in the same degree of kinship, each ranks equally and may take subject to any contrary intention expressed in the will.

6.12 HEIR

The word 'heir' has largely lost its significance since 1925. Before then, the heir succeeded by right to the real property of an ancestor on intestacy. Although descent to the heir on intestacy was abolished in 1925 (Administration of Estates Act 1925, section 45(1)(a)), the term 'heir' remained important in the creation of entailed interests. However, Trusts of Land and Appointment of Trustees Act 1996, section 2(6) and Schedule 1, paragraph 5 provide that no new entailed interests can be created after 1 January 1997. The word 'heir' may still be used to create an equitable interest for an heir taking by purchase (i.e. other than by descent). Hence, a gift of realty may be made as a remainder or immediately to the 'heir', the 'heirs' of X, or the 'heir of the body', and such a person would still be ascertained according to the old rules of descent under the Inheritance Act 1833.

Where the property comprises personalty alone, the term 'heirs' has been construed as meaning the next of kin, the widow or the executors and administrators. Its use in a certain context may result in its being given a different meaning, however. In the case of *Powell v Boggis* (1866) 35 Beav 535, the term was used several times in a will. It was construed to mean executors and administrators three times; next of kin twice; personal representatives and assigns once; and heir-at-law once. Law of Property Act 1925, section 132 now provides that the person taking as heir is to be ascertained according to the law in force immediately before the commencement of the Law of Property Act 1925.

6.13 HOLDERS OF AN OFFICE

Where donees are described by reference only to their office, they take the gift in a personal capacity unless the context and circumstances show that the holder for the time being was the intended donee. In the latter case, the gift is construed as a gift for the office or the association in which the office is held. In the absence of the words 'at the date of my death', the beneficiary is the holder of the office at the date of execution of the will.

6.14 PRECATORY WORDS

A testator may give a legacy to some person, often a trusted friend or relative, expressing a hope or wish that the legatee will apply the gift to a particular purpose, for example '£10,000 to my wife in the hope that she will provide for Aunt Matilda'. Such a gift takes effect as an absolute gift to the legatee; the legatee has only a moral obligation to fulfil the testator's wishes and cannot be impeached if she elects to take the gift herself for her own purposes. If anything more than a wish, hope or desire is expressed, there is a danger of creating a half secret trust (see below) and therefore it is necessary expressly to provide that no trust or legal obligation is intended.

6I   CLAUSE CREATING PRECATORY 'TRUST'

> I GIVE to [name] absolutely the sum of [£2,000] absolutely and I request without imposing any trust condition or legal obligation whatsoever on the said [name] that they give such sums to such persons as are described in any memorandum left by me with my solicitor at … PROVIDED ALWAYS that no such memorandum or expression of my wishes shall have any testamentary effect nor shall it create any trust right liability or obligation or be deemed to form any condition in relation to the gift herein.

The reference to 'any' memorandum ensures such a document is not capable of being incorporated into the will and so become a public document. See **4.7** and compare Precedent 4J where the reference makes clear the document is already in existence.

6.15 SECRET TRUSTS

A testator may wish to keep concealed the exact nature of a disposition they are making and not to set out the gift in a document such as a will, since such documents are open to public inspection once probate of them has been granted. Publicity may be avoided by creating a secret trust, the terms of which are not defined in the will. The testator must communicate the terms of the trust to the intended trustee, and there must be an intention to impose an obligation on the donee which the donee accepts. Where the trust is referred to but not defined in the will (a half secret trust), it is enforceable, but only if:

(i)   it is described in the will as having been defined and communicated to the trustees prior to, or contemporaneously with, the execution of the will; and

(ii) it is also proved that it was so defined and communicated to, and accepted by, some, even if not all, the trustees.

If the reference to the undefined trusts is not restricted to trusts defined and communicated prior to or contemporaneously with the execution of the will, the trusts are unenforceable. This is because a testator cannot confer on themselves the power of making future testamentary dispositions, by naming trustees and leaving the details of the trusts to be supplied afterwards.

Chapter 7

Revocation and Alteration

7.1   REVOCATION

A will is always revocable during the testator's lifetime, and a will or codicil can be revoked by:

(i)   the marriage of the testator or the formation of a civil partnership by them;
(ii)   destruction by the testator or by some other person at their direction and in their presence;
(iii)   the execution by the testator of another valid will or codicil; or
(iv)   a duly executed writing declaring an intention to revoke the will.

The legal burden of proving revocation falls on the person alleging that the will has been revoked. In *Re Sabatini* (1969) 114 Sol Jo 35, it was held that the *Banks v Goodfellow* (1870) LR 5 QB 549 test for mental capacity to make a will (see **3.3**) applies equally to a testator's capacity to revoke their will.

7.1.1   Marriage

Wills Act 1837, section 18, as substituted by the Administration of Justice Act 1982, provides that, for wills executed after 1 January 1983, the marriage of a testator automatically revokes any will made before the marriage (although a void marriage does not revoke a will). With effect from 5 December 2005, the Wills Act 1837 was amended by Civil Partnership Act 2004, Schedule 4 by the addition of sections 18B and 18C. Section 18B provides that a will is revoked upon the testator forming a civil partnership with another person. There are, however, three exceptions to this rule.

First exception

Sections 18(3) and 18B(3) now provide that, where it appears from a will that at the time it was made the testator was expecting to be married to or form a civil partnership with a particular person and that they intended that the will should not be revoked by the marriage or formation of the civil partnership, the will is not revoked by their marriage or formation of the partnership. It must 'appear from the will' that the testator is expecting to marry or form a civil partnership with a particular person at the time of execution, so that an express statement to that effect should be included. The will would still be revoked if the testator in fact marries or forms a civil partnership with another person. In the absence of such a statement it is thought that references to 'my fiancée', 'my intended civil partner', 'my future wife' or 'my future civil partner' would suffice, and such reference would include any fiancée or civil partner at the time the will was executed. It must also 'appear from the will' that the testator intended the will should not be revoked by the marriage or formation of the civil partnership. The Act is silent as to how such an intention should be manifested, but an express statement to that effect would suffice and should be included. (See now the decision in *Court and Others v Despallieres* [2009] EWHC 3340 (Ch), discussed at **6.10**.)

7A   CLAUSE DECLARING THE TESTATOR'S EXPECTATION TO MARRY OR FORM A CIVIL PARTNERSHIP – PREVENTION OF REVOCATION

I DECLARE that I make this will expecting to [be married to] [form a civil partnership with] [name of intended spouse or civil partner] and that I intend that this will shall not be revoked [by my marriage to] [the formation of a civil partnership with] the said [intended spouse or civil partner] [and I FURTHER DECLARE that this [will] [clauses 4 and 5] is [not] conditional on [my marriage to] [the formation of a civil partnership with] the said [intended spouse or civil partner] actually taking place].

Just because a will is expressed to be made in expectation of marriage or civil partnership to another, it is not implied that the will as a whole, or any gift in favour of the other party, is conditional on such event having taken place. So a future spouse or civil partner is still entitled to a gift in the will even if the marriage or civil partnership has not taken place by the testator's death. Whether or not the will as a whole, or a particular gift in it, is conditional, should be made clear.

Second exception

Sections 18(4) and 18B(4) provide that, where it appears from a will that at the time it was made the testator was expecting to be married to or to form a civil partnership with a particular person, and that they intended that a disposition in the will should not be revoked by the marriage to or formation of the civil partnership with that person:

- that disposition takes effect notwithstanding the marriage or formation of a civil partnership; and
- any other disposition in the will takes effect also,

unless it appears from the will that the testator intended the disposition to be revoked by the marriage or formation of a civil partnership.

The testator's intention should again be expressly stated in the will. Similarly, if some of the provisions are to be revoked by the marriage or formation of the civil partnership then that intention must be apparent from the will. Where a provision expressly saves a disposition from revocation by marriage or the formation of a civil partnership, the remaining dispositions are *prima facie* preserved by sections 18(4) and 18B(4). If this is not intended, a suitable provision should be added, either to the will or to each disposition.

Sections 18(3) and 18B(3) save the whole of a will made in contemplation of marriage or the formation of a civil partnership, but sections 18(4) and 18B(4) save only 'dispositions'. Thus in the latter case, any appointment clauses and similar administrative clauses (except powers of appointment) are revoked by the subsequent marriage or formation of a civil partnership, notwithstanding the provisions of the subsection (see *Court and Others v Despallieres* [2009] EWHC 3340 (Ch)).

7B CLAUSE PROVIDING FOR ALTERNATIVE DISPOSITIONS BY SCHEDULE ON MARRIAGE OR CIVIL PARTNERSHIP

I DECLARE that I make this will expecting to [be married to] [form a civil partnership with] [name of intended spouse or civil partner] and that I intend that until my said [marriage] [civil partnership] the provisions of Schedule 1 constitutes my will and upon my said [marriage] [civil partnership] Schedule 1 is revoked and Schedule 2 constitutes my will.

Third exception

Sections 18(2) and 18B(2) provide that the exercise of a power of appointment by will (see Chapter 18) remains effective notwithstanding a subsequent marriage or the formation of a civil partnership. This provision operates regardless of any intention of the testator to marry or form a civil partnership at the time the will is made. The sections have no application, however, where the subject matter of the appointment would pass to the testator's personal representatives in default of appointment.

Marriage (Same Sex Couples) Act 2013, section 9(1) provides that existing civil partners may convert their civil partnership into a marriage. There was some uncertainty as to whether such a marriage would revoke existing wills. A subsequent amendment was made to Wills Act 1837, section 18 to insert a new sub-section 5, to provide that the changing of a civil partnership into a same sex marriage does not revoke an existing will or codicil.

The Civil Partnership (Opposite-sex Couples) Regulations 2019 (SI 2019/1458) came into force on 2 December 2019 allowing opposite sex civil partnerships to take place. Part 8 of the Regulations limits the Marriage (Same Sex Couples) Act 2013 to maintain the current position on conversion rights, so that only same sex civil partners can convert their civil partnerships to marriage for the time being. Paragraph 91 of *Implementing Opposite-Sex Civil Partnerships: Next Steps* (the government guidance published with the Regulations in July 2019) states:

> This approach avoids making short-term changes ahead of the outcome of the public consultation on the future of conversion rights conducted earlier this year ... Further regulations on conversion rights may follow next year, depending on the outcome of the consultation.

7.1.2   Destruction

Under Wills Act 1837, section 20 a will may be revoked by an act of 'burning, tearing or otherwise destroying the same by the testator, or by some other person in his presence and by his direction, with the intention of revoking the same'. Two distinct elements are involved:

- an act of destruction; and
- an intention to revoke.

Neither alone is sufficient.

Destruction must be actual, not symbolic, and must be complete. Destruction of part of a will may be sufficient to revoke the whole will if the part destroyed is sufficiently vital (e.g. the signature of the testator and of the attesting witnesses). The danger is that the part actually destroyed may be relatively unimportant, and the act of destruction may be construed as revocation of only that part actually destroyed.

Writing on the will or crossing out words is not generally sufficient to revoke the will, but may have that effect if the signatures of both the attesting witnesses and the testator are rendered illegible or barely legible (see *Re Adams, Deceased* [1990] Ch 601).

Any act of revocation by the testator must be as complete as the testator themselves intended. If they are stopped for any reason before the will has been destroyed as intended, then the revocation is not effective (see *Doe d Perkes v Perkes* (1820) 3 B & Ald 489).

To establish the intention to revoke, the act of destruction must be carried out by the testator themselves or another person in their presence and by their direction. If the will is destroyed accidentally or without the testator's authority, or if the testator is not present at the time of destruction, then the will is not revoked and the destruction cannot be ratified at a later date. If the testator then wishes to revoke the will, they must do so by a written instrument. Destruction by a person lacking the appropriate mental capacity does not revoke the will. Further, if the testator destroys a will believing it to be invalid, there can be no intention to revoke a valid will and therefore no revocation.

Two rebuttable presumptions may apply in the following situations.

A will missing at death

In *Ferneley v Napier and Others* [2010] EWHC 3345 (Ch), [2011] WTLR 1303, the court held that it was established law that a will could be proved even if the piece of paper on which it had been written could not be produced. It could be proved if its terms and execution were properly demonstrated by acceptable evidence.

Where a will cannot be found after the testator's death but it is known to have been in the testator's possession immediately before their death, a presumption arises that the will has been destroyed by the testator with the intention of revoking it. The presumption is rebuttable by evidence of non-revocation, including evidence showing the testator's intention to adhere to the will, provided that evidence is clear. In *Rowe v Clarke* [2005] EWHC 3068 (Ch), [2006] WTLR 347, the court held that the presumption would always arise, but the strength of the presumption depended on the level or degree of security, or lack of it, with which the testator had custody of the will in his lifetime. Although the testator had not looked after the will carefully, there was nothing in his behaviour to show an intention to revoke his will by destruction. In *Re Zielinski, Korab-Karpinski v Lucas-Gardiner* [2007] WTLR 1655, there was evidence to show the will had been properly executed. There was no later will which could have revoked and no direct evidence of revocation by destruction. Nevertheless, the original will had been in the testatrix's possession immediately before her death and could not be found after her death. The presumption was rebutted by the circumstances of the making of the will and its return to the testatrix, the fact that the will had been made recently and there was no evidence to suggest the testatrix had changed her mind and the testatrix's inclination to instruct solicitors to carry out any act of legal significance.

More recently, in *Cooper and Another v Chapman and Others* [2022] EWHC 1000 (Ch), the claimant seeking probate was faced with the fact the only remaining trace of an alleged 2018 will, under which she benefited as the deceased's partner, was a draft in a file on the deceased's computer. Both parties to the dispute had instructed computer experts to examine this file, which they agreed had been created on 24 January 2018, amended on 20 March 2018, copied to another computer on 4 February 2019 and since then had remained unaltered. The claimant argued this file had been printed out and signed by the deceased on about 27 March 2018, and that he later acknowledged his signature on it in the presence of two relatives of the claimant acting as witnesses. The claimant therefore contended the 2018 will was valid as satisfying Wills Act 1837, section 9, despite no paper version being found at the deceased's home. The claimant was able to produce the witnesses, who confirmed her account. Taking all the evidence into consideration, the judge concluded on the balance of probabilities that it was a will and had been validly executed. The final question was whether the absence of the executed will in the deceased's house led to a presumption it was later revoked by the deceased having destroyed it. The judge decided that this was improbable, mainly because nothing apparently occurred after March 2018 to change the perspective the deceased had had at that point, so he probably continued to want to make significant testamentary provision for the claimant and did not intend to revoke the 2018 will.

A will found mutilated at death

A will found in the testator's possession at their death, which is torn or mutilated, is presumed to have been destroyed by the testator with the intention of revoking it in whole or in part. This presumption may again be rebutted by evidence to the contrary.

7.1.3   Execution of another valid will or codicil

Wills Act 1837, section 20 says that the whole or any part of a will may be revoked by another duly executed will or codicil. The clearest way in which a later will can revoke an earlier one is by the inclusion of an express revocation clause.

Where a testator already has a will dealing with property in another jurisdiction, and wants that will to continue, a limited revocation clause such as that at Precedent 7D should be used to avoid unwanted revocation.

7C   REVOCATION CLAUSE

I [testator] of [address] HEREBY REVOKE all former testamentary dispositions made by me.

7D   DECLARATION WHERE TESTATOR ALSO HAS A FOREIGN WILL

I [testator] of [address] HEREBY DECLARE that this will relates only to my property in the United Kingdom and does not affect any property outside the United Kingdom which is the subject of any separate will made according to the law of the country or territory where that property is situated.

A clause such as Precedent 7C should always be included in a new will and normally operates to revoke all previous testamentary instruments. Before including such a clause, however, the testator should be asked if they have made a will in any other country which would be revoked by such a clause. If so, a clause such as Precedent 7D should be included.

There are rare occasions when such a clause does not revoke all previous testamentary instruments, and an example of this is found in the case of *Re Wayland* [1951] 2 All ER 1041. Here a testator made two wills, the first dealing with his property in Belgium, made under Belgian law; the second, later, will was made in England and contained the revocation clause, but said 'this will is intended to deal only with my estate in England'. The court took the view that the revocation clause in the latter will had been restricted to testamentary dispositions relating to the testator's estate in England and admitted both the Belgian and the English wills to probate.

A revocation clause is excluded from a will if it was included without the testator's knowledge and approval, but not if the testator was mistaken only as to its effect.

A revocation clause in a conditional will has no effect if the condition remains unfulfilled, as the will itself is inoperative. Similarly, the revocation clause itself may be conditional and if the condition is not satisfied the clause has no effect.

A later will or codicil impliedly revokes a prior will or codicil if and in so far as the later will contains provisions which are inconsistent with those in the former. The provisions in the earlier will which are neither inconsistent with, nor replaced by, the later remain operative.

7.1.4　Intention to revoke declared in duly executed writing

Wills Act 1837, section 20 says that the whole or any part of a will may be revoked by 'some writing declaring an intention to revoke the same' and executed in the same manner as a will.

7.2　DIVORCE AND REVOCATION

Wills Act 1837, sections 18(1) and 18C(1) (as substituted by section 18(2) of the Administration of Justice Act 1982 and as further amended by the Law Reform (Succession) Act 1995 and the Civil Partnership Act 2004) provide that the dissolution or annulment of a marriage or civil partnership of the testator has two major effects on any will made before the dissolution or annulment:

(i)　provisions of the will appointing executors or trustees or containing a power of appointment, if they appoint or confer the power on the former spouse or civil partner, take effect as if the former spouse or civil partner had died on the date the marriage or partnership was dissolved or annulled; and

(ii)　any property or interest in property which is devised or bequeathed to the former spouse or civil partner passes as if the former spouse or civil partner had died on the date of dissolution or annulment of the marriage or civil partnership.

These provisions apply only where the testator was married and died after 1 January 1996, or for civil partnerships formed after 5 December 2005.

A decree of judicial separation, by contrast, has no effect in relation to dispositions made under the will (see Matrimonial Causes Act 1973, section 18).

The rights of a former spouse or civil partner under the Inheritance (Provision for Family and Dependants) Act 1975 are not affected by these provisions.

7.3　REVOCATION BY A PRIVILEGED TESTATOR

As has been said (see Chapter 4), a privileged testator can make a will free of any of the formal requirements of Wills Act 1837, section 9. They may also revoke the will in an informal manner, whether or not that will was made formally.

Where a privileged testator loses their privileged status, they must generally make any desired revocation formally. However, Family Law Reform Act 1969, section 3, allows a minor who has made a privileged will to revoke that will while still a minor, even though they no longer have privileged status. In this case the revocation must be either by destruction, or by the execution of a formal attested document of revocation.

7.4 CONDITIONAL REVOCATION

Where a testator destroys their will with the intention of revoking it, it must be determined whether the intended revocation was to be absolute or conditional. This is a question of fact, and extrinsic evidence as proof of that intention is admissible.

It may be the testator's intention to substitute one gift for another, perhaps by changing the amount of the original gift. If the testator revokes or alters their existing will with the intention of making a substituted provision, then it is presumed that the initial revocation is intended to be conditional upon the validity of the substituted provision.

This presumption is known as the doctrine of 'dependent relative revocation' and applies also where the testator revokes a will or a provision in a will giving property to one person, with the intention of replacing the first provision with another provision in favour of a second person. As long as it can be shown that the intention to revoke was conditional, then the original gift will stand if the substituted gift is invalid or ineffectual. Such a conditional intention may be inferred if it can be shown that the testator would rather have left the gift to the first person than have the gift fail entirely.

For example, where a testator destroyed a will in favour of his wife in the mistaken belief that she would be entitled to all his property on an intestacy, whereas she was in fact entitled to part only, it was held that the revocation of the will was conditional upon the testator's widow being entitled to the whole estate on intestacy. The will therefore remained valid (see *Re Southerden's Estate* [1925] P 177).

7.5 ALTERATION

The general rule is that any alteration to a will made after its execution should be executed by the testator and initialled by two witnesses, or the alteration should be made by a duly executed codicil to the will. Wills Act 1837, section 21 provides:

no obliteration, interlineation or other alteration made in any will after the execution thereof shall be valid or have any effect, except so far as the words or effect of the will before such alteration shall not be apparent, unless such alteration shall be executed in like manner as hereinbefore is required for the execution of the will ...

Wills should be returned to the will drafter after execution for the will drafter to ensure all the formal requirements have been complied with and any alteration is properly initialled. The will drafter has a duty of care to potential beneficiaries to ensure the due execution of the will (see *White v Jones* [1995] 2 AC 207, which was referred to and followed in *Feltham v Bouskill* [2013] EWHC 1952 (Ch), [2013] All ER (D) 172).

Where there is an alteration which is apparent on the face of the will, a rebuttable presumption arises that the alteration has been made after the execution of the will. For this reason, any apparent alteration should be referred to in the attestation clause as already made at the time of execution (see Precedent 4C) and any alteration should be executed in order to avoid uncertainty.

Alterations that are deliberative in nature and not intended to form part of the final will are excluded from probate. If a will is written partly in ink and partly in pencil, a rebuttable presumption arises that the parts in pencil are deliberative only. If the will is made on a typewritten form and partly completed in ink it is presumed to be in a final form if duly executed. Similarly, in a hand-written will a correction that elucidates an otherwise unintelligible clause or sentence and which is made in the same ink and handwriting as the rest of the will is sufficient to rebut the presumption of later alteration.

When a will is received after execution for safe custody and there could be doubt cast on due execution, it is suggested one of the following three procedures is adopted:

(i)   endorse a note on the reverse of the will explaining why the testator has signed in the manner/place they have, or why they have signed twice, or why the witnesses have signed where they have, or as to the form of their signatures or why the dating of the will has been changed or whatever is the defect;

(ii) complete a contemporaneous attendance note dealing with the problem; or

(iii) to be absolutely sure, have an affidavit of due execution, which also deals with the problem, sworn by a witness or other person present at execution.

Not surprisingly, special rules apply to the alteration of privileged wills. The presumption is that any informal alterations made to the will by the testator are made while the testator is still privileged, and the will and alterations are therefore valid.

If there is any doubt about an alteration which comes to the testator's attention, or that of their solicitor, it may be clarified by means of a codicil in the following form.

7E CODICIL CLARIFYING AN ALTERATION TO A WILL

> I [testator] of [address] DECLARE this to be a codicil to my will dated the ... day of ... WHEREAS in my said will at line ... on page ... and at line ... on page ... words ... and ... and the figure ... are crossed out and words ... and ... and the figure ... have been substituted by interlineations and such alterations were not executed on the said will by myself and the attesting witnesses nor referred to in the attestation clause.
>
> 1.   Now I HEREBY DECLARE that the said alterations were made prior to the execution of my said will and I DIRECT that my said will shall be read and construed subject to the said alterations and as if the said substituted words were the original words written in my said will.
> 2.   In all other respects I CONFIRM my said will.
> [Attestation clause.]

Where words have been crossed out or partly obliterated without the alteration being attested, then:

(i)   if the original wording is 'apparent' those words are admitted to probate. 'Apparent' means decipherable by ordinary means such as holding the document up to the light;

(ii) where the original wording is not apparent due to the attempted alteration, those words are excluded from probate provided the obliteration was made by the testator with an intention to revoke the words deleted.

If the testator had no such intention, or if the alteration was made by some other person, then extrinsic evidence (e.g. from solicitor's instructions or copies or infra-red photographs) is permitted to prove the original wording.

Where the testator made the obliteration with a conditional intention to revoke, the court will admit the original wording to probate under the principle of dependent relative revocation (see above), provided that wording can be proved by extrinsic evidence.

To avoid the possibility of unauthenticated alterations being made by the testator post execution of the will, it is suggested the original will be retained for safe custody by the solicitor will drafter.

Chapter 8

Codicils, Revival and Republication

8.1 CODICILS

A codicil is a testamentary instrument made supplemental to an existing will in order to add to, alter or revoke the original provisions, without revoking the whole. It is most useful to effect minor alterations to a complicated will. Major alterations may be better made by the execution of an entirely fresh will, revoking the existing one, as this is simpler to draft.

A codicil takes the same form as a will and is subject to the same legal formalities under Wills Act 1837, section 9. It must recite the will (crucially, the date of it) to which it is supplemental and must be executed and attested in the same manner as a will. It is not necessary for the witnesses of the codicil to be the same as those of the will.

The codicil should recite any changes in the testator's circumstances, including any change in the testator's name, a marriage, a civil partnership or divorce. The body of the codicil should recite the provisions of the original will that are to be amended or revoked, and should then set out in detail the exact alterations to be made and any new provisions to be added to the will.

The codicil should specifically state that the remainder of the will is confirmed in all other respects.

The Wills Act 1837 (Electronic Communications) (Amendment) (Coronavirus) Order 2020 (SI 2020/952) amends Wills Act 1837, section 9 to allow temporarily remote witnessing (see Appendix 3).

The provisions apply equally to the execution of a codicil.

8.2   REVIVAL

Where a will or codicil has been revoked but not destroyed it may be revived by the testator, either by re-execution of the original document or by the execution of a further codicil expressing an intention to revive the original will and any subsequent codicils to it (Wills Act 1837, section 22). It is important to remember to revive a will revoked by marriage or civil partnership if the provisions remain acceptable. This precedent can obviously be used with suitable amendments to revive a will revoked by the formation of a civil partnership.

8A   **CODICIL TO REVIVE WILL FOLLOWING THE TESTATOR'S SECOND MARRIAGE OR CIVIL PARTNERSHIP, SUBSTITUTING THE NAME OF THEIR SECOND SPOUSE OR CIVIL PARTNER FOR THAT OF THEIR FIRST, AND EXTENDING THE PROVISIONS IN FAVOUR OF THEIR EXISTING CHILDREN TO ANY CHILDREN OF THE SECOND MARRIAGE OR CIVIL PARTNERSHIP**

I [testator] of [address] DECLARE this to be a [first] codicil to my will dated the ... day of ...
WHEREAS
(1)   My [spouse] [civil partner] [name of late spouse or civil partner] referred to in my said will has since died and I have [married] [entered into a civil partnership with] [name of new spouse or civil partner].
(2)   By clause [8] of my said will I gave my residuary estate to my Trustees to hold the same in trust for my late [spouse] [civil partner] [name of late spouse or civil partner] for life with a gift over on [his] [her] death to my children and issue.
  1.   NOW I HEREBY DECLARE that the name of my [spouse] [civil partner] [name of spouse or civil partner] shall be substituted for the name of my late [spouse] [civil partner] [name of late spouse or civil partner] in clause [8] of my said will aforesaid and the same shall be read and construed accordingly [and I FURTHER DECLARE that any reference to 'child', 'children' or 'issue' in any provision of my said will shall include as well any child children or issue of mine by my second [marriage] [civil partnership]].
  2.   In all other respects I confirm and revive my said will and DECLARE that for all purposes my said will as hereby modified shall operate and take effect as if it had been made on the date of this codicil and after my [marriage] [civil partnership] with my [spouse] [civil partner] [name of late spouse or civil partner].
[Attestation clause.]

Once a will has been revived it takes effect as if executed on the date of its revival (Wills Act 1837, section 34).

Where one will has been revoked by a subsequent will it is not revived when the later will is revoked. To revive the first will a codicil should be used which shows an intention to revive the revoked will. As stated in *In the Goods of Steele* (1868) LR 1 P&D 575, 578, the intention must:

> appear on the face of the codicil, either by express words referring to a will as revoked and importing an intention to revive the same, or by a disposition of the testator's property inconsistent with any other intention, or by some other expression conveying to the mind of the Court, with reasonable certainty, the existence of the intention in question.

If the will revived by the codicil contains a revocation clause then any intervening will, i.e. a will made after the will now revived by the codicil, is revoked (see below). In *Hoare Trustees v Jacques and Others* [2008] EWHC 2022 (Ch), the testatrix had made a will and a first codicil then a second will. Later she made a second codicil to the earlier will reviving it and the first codicil. The solicitor will drafter of the second codicil was unaware of the second will. The court found that it was implicit if not expressed that the testatrix intended to revive her earlier will. The express reference in the second codicil to the first will, coupled with the terms of that codicil, varying clause 3.1 of the first will, constituted a clear expression of the testatrix's intention that the first will, and therefore necessarily the first codicil, were to be revived and the second will revoked.

In construing a codicil the usual rules on the admission of extrinsic evidence apply.

8.3   REPUBLICATION OR CONFIRMATION

Whereas revival operates to bring a revoked will or codicil back into effect, republication confirms an unrevoked will.

There are only two methods by which a will or codicil may be republished. First, the document may be formally re-executed. Second, a codicil referring to the previous will or codicil may be executed.

A codicil need not expressly confirm the contents of a previous will; the will is republished at the date of the codicil if it is referred to, as it is assumed the testator considered the will at that time. This is termed 'constructive republication'.

A republished will speaks from the date of republication, subject to any amendments and additions in any codicil. Where, however, the effect of the republication would be to defeat the intention of the testator in respect of a provision in the previous will or codicil, then the doctrine of republication does not apply to that gift.

Republication by codicil or re-execution may save a gift originally given to an attesting witness, their spouse or civil partner, provided the witnesses to the execution of the codicil are not the same as those of the original will. See Wills Act 1837, section 15, as amended by Civil Partnership Act 2004, Schedule 4.

Republication may save certain gifts in the original will from lapsing, as the construction may be altered. Where, for example, a gift in a will refers to 'the wife of my cousin Harvey' and Harvey's wife then dies, the gift to her lapses. If, however, the testator republished the will after the death of Harvey's wife and knowing of her death, then the gift will pass to the next wife of Harvey should he remarry; for a similar situation see *Re Hardyman* [1925] Ch 287. If, on the other hand, the gift had been to a named wife of Harvey and that wife had died, then the gift would lapse and could not be saved by the subsequent republication.

Chapter 9

Executors and Trustees

9.1 APPOINTMENT OF EXECUTORS

Executors are appointed, by testamentary document, to 'stand in the shoes' of the testator, administering the estate according to the law and the provisions of the will. An executor is not an agent of the deceased (see *Rickless v United Artists* [1988] QB 40 (CA)). Although a will does not have to appoint an executor, it is wise to do so; otherwise, there will be a period of time after the testator's death when there is no one in control of the testator's estate. This would continue until a grant of letters of administration (with will annexed) is issued.

An express provision should be included in the main body of the will appointing a named executor, or more than one if desired. If the executor is also named as a trustee they may appoint another trustee and delegate trust functions (see Trustee Act 2000, section 11).

Executors acquire their title and authority from the testator's will. The estate of the deceased testator vests in the executor from the date of the death. The executor's authority to administer the testator's estate derives from the grant of probate.

9A APPOINTMENT OF SOLE EXECUTOR

I APPOINT [name] of [address] to be the sole Executor of this my will (hereinafter called 'my Executor').

9B APPOINTMENT OF EXECUTORS

I APPOINT [name] of [address] and [name] of [address] to be the Executors of this my will (hereinafter called 'my Executors').

9C APPOINTMENT OF TWO PEOPLE AS EXECUTORS AND TRUSTEES

I APPOINT [name] of [address] and [name] of [address] (hereinafter referred to as 'my Trustees' which expression shall include the Trustees for the time being hereof) to be the Executors and Trustees of this my will.

No more than four executors may take out a grant of probate at one time in respect of the same part of an estate (Senior Courts Act 1981, section 114). Where more than four executors are appointed, then some may have power reserved to take a grant of (double) probate should a vacancy occur.

An executor must be clearly identified or the appointment will be void for uncertainty; see for example *In the Goods of Baylis* (1862) 2 Sw & Tr 613, where an appointment of 'any two of my sons' was void for uncertainty, and *Re Blackwell's Goods* [1877] 2 PD 72, where an appointment of 'one of my sisters' was similarly held to be void.

However, where the will shows a clear intention that a particular individual or particular person should act in the estate and perform the functions of an executor, then that person has implied authority to act as 'executor according to the tenor of the will'. An executor impliedly appointed in this way may act together with executors expressly appointed.

A conditional appointment, for example, on the named executor being resident in the United Kingdom is permissible, but it is normally preferable to make the appointment absolute. If the appointment of a sole executor is to be made, it is advisable to appoint a substitute in the event the condition is not satisfied. Executors can renounce or have power reserved if the circumstances at the date of death are such that one or more do not wish, or are unable, to take a grant.

9D APPOINTMENT OF THREE CHILDREN (ONE OF WHOM LIVES ABROAD AT DATE OF THE WILL) TO BE EXECUTORS AND TRUSTEES

I APPOINT my sons [name] and [name] and also if she is resident in the United Kingdom at the time of my death my daughter [name] to be the Executors and Trustees of this my will (hereinafter called 'my Trustees').

9.2 WHO CAN BE AN EXECUTOR?

Any person may be named as an executor in a will, but it is wise to choose someone who will be both willing and able to take up the office. Neither a minor

nor a person who lacks mental capacity will be granted probate; where such a person is appointed as sole executor, a grant of administration (with will annexed) may instead be given to another person for the use and benefit of the person under the disability.

Testators commonly appoint their spouses or civil partners as executors or trustees of their wills. If, following the making of the will, the marriage is dissolved or annulled, the effect on the appointment depends on the date of death. Where death occurred on or after 1 January 1983 but before 1 January 1996, the will takes effect as if any appointment of the former spouse as an executor and trustee were omitted. For deaths occurring on or after 1 January 1996, any provisions in the will appointing executors or trustees, or conferring a power of appointment upon the former spouse, take effect as if the former spouse had died on the date on which the marriage is dissolved or annulled (Wills Act 1837, section 18A(1)). A contrary intention may appear in the will, however. The same applies to a civil partnership which is dissolved on or after 5 December 2005 (see Wills Act 1837, section 18C).

When appointing a sole executor, it is always advisable to appoint a substitute or substitute executors, such appointment to operate in the event the first named executor predeceases the testator or is otherwise unable or unwilling to act.

9E   APPOINTMENT OF SPOUSE OR CIVIL PARTNER AS SOLE EXECUTOR AND TRUSTEE WITH SUBSTITUTE OF CHILDREN

I APPOINT my [husband] [wife] [civil partner] to be the sole executor and Trustee of this my will but if [he] [she] is unable or unwilling to act or if [he] [she] dies before proving my will I APPOINT as my Executors and Trustees my children [name] and [name].

Note a substitute appointment as in Precedent 9E does not allow the spouse or civil partner and one or more of the children to act and seek probate together as executors. If the testator considers the surviving spouse or civil partner might require some support in the administration, then a joint appointment, as in Precedent 9B, may be preferable. A joint appointment does not compel the spouse or civil partner (or any other appointed executor) to act and, if unwilling to do so, following the testator's death, they have the option of renouncing (see **9.3**) or having power reserved.

Where it is desired to appoint a firm of solicitors as executors, careful wording should be used. Where a firm of solicitors is appointed, the appointment is of all the individual partners in the firm at the date of the will unless the will contains a contrary intention. Provision should also be made against a change of name or amalgamation with another firm. If the firm is likely to, or may, become a limited liability partnership or incorporated practice, the appointment should be of 'the equity partners, directors or members as appropriate at the date of my death in the firm of …'. This covers all eventualities. In *Re Rogers Deceased* [2006] EWHC 753 (Ch), [2006] 1 WLR 1577, it was held that where a will appoints partners in a firm of solicitors as executors and the firm subsequently converts to a limited liability partnership or incorporated practice, probate should be granted only to those partners who are profit-sharing partners.

As a result of the comments in *Re Rogers Deceased*, the appointment of a 'partner' is to be construed as a profit-sharing partner unless the will provides otherwise. If the testator wishes a non-profit-sharing partner to be an executor then the person can be appointed by name or the definition of partner can be extended in the will to include salaried as well as profit-sharing partners.

9F   APPOINTMENT OF PARTNERS IN A FIRM OF SOLICITORS AS EXECUTORS AND TRUSTEES (OPTION FOR INCLUSION OF SALARIED PARTNERS)

I APPOINT the partners at the date of my death in the firm of [name] [or the firm which at that date has succeeded to and carries on its practice] of [address] to be the Executors and Trustees of this my will [and I DECLARE the expression 'partners' means both the profit-sharing partners and salaried partners in the firm] [and I express the wish that two and only two of them shall prove my will and act initially in its trusts]. [Insert charging clause (see Chapter 22).]

9G   APPOINTMENT AS EXECUTORS OF DIRECTORS OF A FIRM OF SOLICITORS WHICH IS A LIMITED LIABILITY PARTNERSHIP OR LIMITED COMPANY

I APPOINT the profit-sharing directors at the date of my death in the company known as [name] or the profit-sharing members of the limited liability partnership which at that date has succeeded to and carries on its business of [address] to be the Executors and Trustees of this my will and I express the wish that two and only two of such directors or profit-sharing members shall prove my will and act initially in its trusts. [Insert charging clause (see Chapter 22).]

Where a trust corporation is to be appointed as executor, either alone or jointly with others, the corporation's own appointment clause should be used in order to ensure the appointment is accepted.

9H   APPOINTMENT OF A BANK AS EXECUTOR AND TRUSTEE TOGETHER WITH INDIVIDUALS

(a)   I APPOINT the ... Bank plc and [name] of [address] and [name] of [address] (hereinafter called 'my Trustees' which expression shall include the Trustees for the time being hereof) to be the Executors and Trustees of this my will.

(b)   [Add the bank's standard clauses, which normally include a remuneration clause.]

It must be ascertained whether the trustee department of the bank is a separate company; if it is, it must be referred to by that name.

9I   APPOINTMENT OF A BANK AS SOLE EXECUTOR AND TRUSTEE

(a)   I APPOINT ... Bank to be the sole Executor and Trustee of this my will.

(b)   [Clauses required by the bank.]

The Public Trustee may be appointed executor, either alone or jointly with others. Such an appointment is rarely called for but may be necessary where there is difficulty in finding someone who is able and willing to act. The Public Trustee can refuse to act and does not generally act in estates involving the carrying on of a business for an indefinite period, nor may the Public Trustee undertake a trust where the whole of the trust property is devoted to religious or charitable purposes. The Public Trustee Act 1906 also forbids the Public Trustee from acting in certain types of estate. If the Public Trustee is to be appointed as executor, the testator should first obtain the Public Trustee's consent by sending a copy of the will and an explanation of the testator's circumstances to The Public Trustee, Victory House, 30–34 Kingsway, London WC2B 6EX. Even if the request is initially accepted, the Public Trustee may still refuse to act depending on the circumstances at death, for example if the estate is insolvent or there is someone else at that time capable of administering the estate.

9J   APPOINTMENT OF THE PUBLIC TRUSTEE AS SOLE EXECUTOR AND TRUSTEE

I APPOINT the Public Trustee to be the sole Executor and Trustee of this my will.

See the Public Trustee (Fees) Order 2008 (SI 2008/611).

Where an estate includes rights in published or unpublished literary works and it is considered that someone with special experience should deal with this part of the estate, a special literary executor may be appointed. On the other hand, because of the need for a special grant in such a situation, and the added administrative difficulties, the appointment of such an executor as trustee should be avoided if possible. It would not be necessary, for example, simply to collect the royalties from unpublished works.

9K   APPOINTMENT OF LITERARY EXECUTORS

I APPOINT [name] of [address] and [name] of [address] to be the Executors of this my will in respect of my literary estate [and I DIRECT that the expenses of extracting a limited grant of probate in respect of the part of my estate to be administered by them and all taxes payable in respect of that part of my estate shall be borne by and payable out of [my residuary estate] [the part of my estate so given as a first charge thereon.]].

This would be followed by the appointment of general executors in respect of the estate save and except literary estate. See also **12.1.5** as regards dealing with digital assets.

Again, it may be appropriate to appoint special executors to run the testator's business after their death.

9L   APPOINTMENT OF SPECIAL EXECUTORS TO CONTINUE TESTATOR'S BUSINESS

I APPOINT [name] of [address] and [name] of [address] to be the Executors of this my will in respect of my business of [...] called [...] with full authority to do such acts as are necessary to continue the business [until it is sold] [and I DIRECT that the expenses of extracting a limited grant of probate in respect of the part of my estate to be administered by them and all taxes payable in respect of that part of my estate shall be borne by and payable out of [my residuary estate] [the part of my estate so given as a first charge thereon]].

This would be followed by the appointment of general executors in respect of the estate save and except the business.

9.3   RENUNCIATION

Acceptance of the office of executor need not be formal, and may be shown by the executor's taking out a grant of probate, or by acting as executor.

A person named as an executor may renounce that office at any time after, but not before, the testator's death. A named executor may renounce the appointment even after swearing the oath and applying for a grant, provided the grant has not been made at the time of renunciation and provided the person has not acted as an executor at that time in relation to the estate.

Where it is sought to show that an executor has taken up the office as a result of acting as executor (called an executor *de son tort*), all the circumstances of the case are looked at. Merely dealing with assets as the agent of another executor is not sufficient to imply acceptance, neither will it be implied from trivial administrative acts (see *James v Williams* [2000] Ch 1 (CA)).

The renunciation should be in writing and filed in court. It must be signed by a disinterested witness, i.e. a person who has no interest in the estate.

9M   RENUNCIATION OF EXECUTORSHIP

In the High Court of Justice Family Division
The Principal [… District Probate] Registry
In the Estate of [name of deceased] deceased
WHEREAS [deceased's name] of [address], deceased, died on the … day of …, having made and duly executed [his] [her] last will and testament dated the … day of … and thereof appointed [name] [his] [her] sole Executor; now I the said [name] do HEREBY DECLARE that I have not intermeddled in the estate of the said deceased and will not hereafter intermeddle therein with the intent of defrauding creditors, and I HEREBY RENOUNCE all my right and title to the probate and execution of the said will.
[Signature of Executor]
[Signature, address and description of witness]

Once the executor has renounced office, the renunciation is final unless the court allows retraction of the renunciation (see Non-Contentious Probate Rules 1987 (SI 1987/2024), rule 37).

Since the amendments to the Non-Contentious Probate Rules in 1998, a firm, or the partners in a firm, who have been appointed executors may renounce their right and title to probate, and to letters of administration (with will annexed) as residuary legatees and devisees in trust, through any two of the partners. As the appointment is now deemed to be of the profit-sharing partners only (see *Re Rogers Deceased* [2006] EWHC 753 (Ch), [2006] 1 WLR 1577), it is two of the profit-sharing partners who may renounce on behalf of themselves and the other profit-sharing partners.

9N   RENUNCIATION OF PROBATE BY PARTNERS (ON BEHALF OF THEMSELVES AND OTHERS)

[Headings as in Precedent 9M]

WHEREAS [deceased's name] of [last address], deceased, died on the ... day of ... having made and duly executed [his] [her] last will and testament dated the ... day of ... and thereof appointed the partners at the date of [his] [her] death in the firm of [name] [or such firm as at the date of death had succeeded to and carried on its practice] as [his] [her] Executors [and Trustees].

The profit-sharing partners in the firm at the date of death were: [names]. Now we [name] and [name] with the authority of the other said partners do HEREBY DECLARE that neither we nor any of the other said partners have intermeddled in the estate of the said deceased and will not hereafter intermeddle therein with the intent of defrauding creditors, and we HEREBY RENOUNCE all our and their right and title to the probate and execution of the said will [and to letters of administration (with will annexed) as the residuary legatees and devisees in trust of the estate of the said deceased].

[Signatures of Executors]

[Signature(s), address(es) and description(s) of the witness(es)]

9.4   APPOINTMENT OF TRUSTEES

It is usual to appoint the same people as both executors and trustees, although the duties and functions attaching to each office are very different. The trustee's duty is to manage the trusts of the will for as long as they continue, whereas the executor's duty is to gather in and liquidate the assets of the estate and distribute them. Where the executors are to transfer property to the trustees, but both offices are held by the same people, the transfer of personalty to them is notional; in the case of land, an assent must be executed to pass legal title.

The definition of 'trustee' in the Trustee Act 2000 includes a personal representative where the context so admits, and the provisions of that Act therefore apply to both executors and trustees unless otherwise provided.

If there are no specific trusts expressed in the will, the estate is held on trust for the beneficiaries according to their rights and interests under the will. Otherwise the property is held according to the specific trusts expressed.

Where the executors and trustees are different people, the executors first liquidate the estate, paying such debts as there may be. They then vest the property in the trustees, either by delivery, or, in case of realty, by assent.

Where there has been no express provision appointing trustees in the will, or where the appointment has failed to take effect for any reason, or the appointed executors have renounced their office, an intending administrator of the estate must apply for a grant of letters of administration (with will annexed). As from the time of their appointment, such administrators become trustees, but *Re Yerburgh* [1928] WN 208 indicates that they are personal representatives until the estate is cleared, when they become trustees (Administration of Estates Act 1925, section 33). As from 1 January 1997, the trustees under section 33 are not trustees for sale, but rather trustees of land with a power to sell, but not with any duty to sell (Trusts of Land and Appointment of Trustees Act 1996, section 2(6), Schedule 1, paragraph 5). The point at which the transition from personal representative to trustee takes place is important, since, *inter alia*, the beneficiaries' interests during the administration are different; the powers conferred by Administration of Estates Act 1925, section 39, apply to the personal representatives but not to trustees, and the former can act severally whereas the latter cannot.

A person cannot be compelled to act as a trustee, and those appointed may disclaim the office, provided they have not accepted the trust.

9O DEED OF DISCLAIMER BY TRUSTEE NAMED IN A WILL

WHEREAS by a will dated [date] the late [testator] appointed me to be [one of] the Trustee[s] [and Executor] of the said will.
By this deed I [disclaiming Trustee] of [address] HEREBY DISCLAIM all estates and interests in the real and personal estate of the said [testator] devolving to me as Trustee [and Executor] of the said will and the trusts and powers thereby reposed in me whether solely or jointly with some other person or persons ALWAYS PROVIDED THAT this disclaimer shall not operate to disclaim or release any beneficial interest to which I am now or may become entitled under the said will save where such benefit was conferred upon myself solely in consequence of my appointment as Trustee for acting in the said trusts.
IN WITNESS, etc [signature of disclaiming Trustee].

9P CLAUSE TO DEFINE TRUSTEES

I DECLARE that for all purposes of this my will the expression 'my Trustees' shall (where the context admits) be construed and be taken to mean the Trustees for the time being hereof whether original or substituted and if there be no such Trustee shall include such persons as are willing to be bound to exercise and perform any power or trust hereby or by any statute conferred upon my Trustees and who are authorised by statute so to do.

9.5   GUARDIANS

A testator with young children should consider who would care for the minor children after their death. Where there is no parent alive who has parental responsibility for a child, then the court can appoint a guardian (Children Act 1989, section 5(1)(a)). The testator may wish to cater for the possibility that their spouse or civil partner does not survive them, and to appoint a guardian to assume parental responsibility on their death. Such an appointment may be made by two or more persons acting jointly (Children Act 1989, section 5(10)). The appointment may, but need not, be contained in a will or a deed. If it is not contained in a will then it must be made in writing, dated and signed by or at the direction of the person making the appointment, in their presence, and in the presence of two witnesses who each attest the signature.

Any intended guardian should be made aware of the appointment and confirm that they are willing and able to act. The will should also make provision for the maintenance of children. The easiest way to do this is by means of a trust fund. The guardian may be appointed trustee of the trust fund for ease of administration. The trust should contain powers for spending income and capital on the maintenance, education and advancement or other benefit of the child.

9Q   APPOINTMENT OF GUARDIANS CONDITIONAL UPON THE TESTATOR SURVIVING THEIR SPOUSE OR CIVIL PARTNER

[If my [spouse] [civil partner] dies before me] I APPOINT [name] of [address] [and [name] of [address]] to be the guardian[s] of any of my children who have not attained the age of eighteen [and I direct that they shall bring up such children [as members of the Church of England] [in the Roman Catholic faith] [in the Islamic faith]].

9R   APPOINTMENT OF GUARDIAN TO ACT WITH TESTATOR'S SPOUSE OR CIVIL PARTNER DURING THEIR LIFE, AND AFTER THEIR DEATH TO ACT WITH PERSONS TO BE APPOINTED BY THE SPOUSE OR CIVIL PARTNER

I APPOINT [name] of [address] to be guardian of any child or children of mine who may be minors at the date of my death to act jointly with my said [spouse] [civil partner] during [his] [her] life and after [his] [her] death to act either alone or jointly with such persons as my said [spouse] [civil partner] may appoint.

Chapter 10

The Disposal of the Body

10.1 DIRECTIONS AS TO DISPOSAL

A testator may want to express, in their will, their wishes concerning the disposal of their body. The testator should be advised to inform their relatives of their wishes during their lifetime, as well as including them in the will, since the will may not be available until after the testator's funeral.

10A DIRECTION AS TO PLACE OF BURIAL AND TOMBSTONE

> I DIRECT that my body be buried [in my family grave] in the ... Cemetery [in Section ... Grave no ...] AND I FURTHER DIRECT that my Executors shall expend a sum not exceeding £ ... upon the erection of a suitably inscribed tombstone upon the said grave.

A direction as to the burial of the body cannot be legally enforced since at common law a person has no property in their body after death. It is a matter for the executor or proposed administrator to decide the method of disposal of the deceased's body (see *Williams v Williams* (1882) 20 Ch D 659). It follows therefore that directions contained in a will are not binding.

In *University Hospital Lewisham NHS Trust v Hamuth and Others* [2006] EWHC 1609 (Ch), [2007] WTLR 309, there was a dispute about the validity of the will so the executor's right to determine the manner of disposal could not operate. It was held it was for the hospital to decide as the deceased had died there.

In *Borrows v HM Coroner for Preston and Another* [2008] EWHC 1387 (Admin), there was a dispute between the deceased's uncle and his mother over funeral arrangements which came before the court on a judicial review. The deceased had been raised by his uncle as his parents (both drug addicts) had been incapable.

The deceased, who had a history of self-harm, committed suicide aged 15. The deceased had expressed a wish to be cremated. The court held the uncle should make the arrangements. Although, following *Williams*, it would be the person who would be the personal representative, the court had power to pass over the person first entitled if it was necessary or expedient (Senior Courts Act 1981, section 116). Following from this the court said European Convention on Human Rights, Article 8(1) has a bearing in this type of dispute. The case-law of the European Court of Human Rights says that where there is a dispute the deceased's wishes should be taken into account. This principle could be accommodated within UK domestic law since it can be regarded as a 'special circumstance' under section 116 of the Act. It was appropriate that the uncle in *Borrows* should be the replacement personal representative as he had been closer to the deceased and he should make the arrangements.

However, in *Ibuna and Another v Arroyo and Another* [2012] EWHC 428 (Ch), Peter Smith J expressly doubted the applicability of human rights in this context. The established law in England is that the executor has the primary duty to dispose of the body and is entitled to have regard to the expressions of wishes made by the deceased but is not bound by them. Given that principle, there is no room for any post-mortem application of human rights in relation to a body as if it had some independent right to be heard.

In *Hartshorne v Gardner* [2008] EWHC B3 (Ch), the deceased's divorced parents could not agree on the place of burial. The usual rule, that determination rested with the person entitled to the grant of representation, could not be applied as both parents were equally entitled. The court held that in the absence of any known wish of the deceased the decision should reflect, first, the wishes of the majority of those he left behind and, second, where he had most recently lived. Where his father wished him buried was also closest for the deceased's brother and near where the deceased's fiancée lived. The father's wishes were to be followed.

The court has an inherent jurisdiction to determine who is responsible for the burial. In *Anstey v Mundle and Another* [2016] EWHC 1073 (Ch), Klein J was asked to exercise the powers contained in Senior Courts Act 1981, section 116. However, he was concerned that the section was not appropriate because he was not being asked to pass over the person who would otherwise be entitled to a grant. Rather he was being asked to select, for the purposes of the limited grant to arrange the funeral, one of the people who would otherwise be entitled to a grant. He considered, and the parties agreed, that the court has, in appropriate circumstances, an inherent jurisdiction to determine who should be responsible for arranging the disposal of a body. He preferred to rest his decision on the court's inherent jurisdiction. The court's inherent jurisdiction was confirmed by the Chancellor, Sir Geoffrey Vos *in Oldham Metropolitan Borough Council and Another v Makin and Others* [2017] EWHC 2543 (Ch).

In *Ganoun v Joshi and Another* [2020] EWHC 2743 (Ch), a claim was brought by the deceased's mother to be appointed administrator so that she could take charge of the funeral arrangements, or for the court to make directions as to the disposal of her son's body, Robin Vos (sitting as a Judge of the Chancery Division) stated that the principles which the court should apply are not controversial. The court should take into account justice to the claimant, justice to the defendant, whether the declaration would serve a useful purpose and whether there are any other special reasons why or why not the court should grant the declaration. There were insufficient grounds in the case to grant the declaration.

10B   DIRECTION AS TO CREMATION

> I DESIRE that my body be cremated [in the crematorium at ...] and that my ashes be kept at ... [or scattered on consecrated ground at ...].

Cremation must take place at a recognised crematorium.

10C   DIRECTION NOT TO CREMATE A BODY

> I DIRECT that my body shall not be cremated.

It is not unlawful, however, to cremate a body where there is such a direction.

10D   DIRECTION AS TO NECESSARY EXPENSES

> I DESIRE there should be no flowers at my funeral or on my grave and that mourning shall not be worn by my relatives and no expense incurred beyond that which is necessary.

This direction is merely indicative of the testator's desire.

10E   POWER FOR EXECUTORS TO INCUR EXPENSE IN RESPECT OF DIRECTIONS

> [State the directions to the Executors and continue as follows] and I HEREBY AUTHORISE my Executors to spend such sums as they shall in their absolute discretion consider reasonable in carrying out the above directions and their decision as to what is reasonable shall be final and binding upon all Beneficiaries under this my will.

10.2   ANATOMICAL RESEARCH AND ORGAN TRANSPLANTATION

Testators may, if they wish, donate their bodies to a hospital for transplantation purposes or to a medical school for research.

The law in this area is now governed by the Human Tissue Act 2004 (HTA 2004), replacing earlier legislation. Important amendments to the HTA 2004 are made by the Organ Donation (Deemed Consent) Act 2019 (ODDCA 2019), which took effect on 20 May 2020 (see below).

The HTA 2004 covers England, Wales (subject to what is said below) and Northern Ireland, and established the Human Tissue Authority to regulate activities concerning the removal, storage, use and disposal of human tissue (in the HTA 2004 called 'relevant material'). The need for 'appropriate consent' is the fundamental principle underpinning the lawful removal, storage and use of body parts, organs and tissue. Different consent requirements apply when dealing with tissue from the deceased and the living, and the meaning of consent differs depending on whether the tissue is obtained from an adult or a child.

The overriding principle of the HTA 2004, when enacted, was that consent had to be given expressly, so the mere absence of any objection could not be treated as a deemed consent. On 1 December 2015, Wales became the first UK country to introduce a soft opt-out system for organ and tissue donation when the Human Transplantation (Wales) Act 2013 came into effect. If a person has not registered a decision to either opt-in or opt-out of organ donation, they are treated as having no objection to being an organ donor. This is called 'deemed consent' but applies only to persons aged 18 and over who die in Wales and have been voluntarily resident in Wales for more than 12 months.

The increase in consent rates following the introduction of an opt-out system in Wales led to the ODDCA 2019, which, for deaths on or after 20 May 2020 in England, changes the default position away from an option to opt-in to an option to opt-out. ODDCA 2019, section 1 amends the HTA 2004 so that with respect to specific listed transplantation activities carried out in England, in the absence of an express decision on consent, either by the person before their death, or by a person nominated to make that decision for them, deemed consent will apply unless:

- a person in a 'qualifying relationship' to the deceased (as listed in HTA 2004, section 54(9)) provides information that would lead a reasonable person to conclude that the deceased would not have consented; or
- the deceased had not been ordinarily resident in England for a period of at least 12 months immediately before they died (an 'excepted' person); or

- the deceased had, for a significant period before their death, lacked capacity to understand that deemed consent would apply (an 'excepted' person).

The ODDCA 2019 further amends the HTA 2004 by placing a duty on the Human Tissue Authority to give practical guidance on how deemed consent will work in practice, including guidance about the provision of information by a family member or friend of the deceased to override the presumption of consent.

Notwithstanding deemed consent now applying throughout England and Wales, if parts of the body are to be used for transplant purposes, it is better to indicate that intention in an express statement separate from the will, and to notify the relatives, since the organs must be removed shortly after death, before the will is available. The HTA 2004 provides that the deceased's wishes for organ donation take precedence over family objections.

The Human Tissue (Authorisation) (Scotland) Act 2019 provides for a 'deemed authorisation' or 'opt-out' system of organs and tissue donation for trans-plantation. The system came into effect on 26 March 2021.

The opt-out system will apply to adults aged 16 and over who are resident in Scotland (provided they have capacity to understand the deemed authorisation law and have lived in Scotland for 12 months or more before their death).

It is desirable that those wishing their organs to be available for transplant should register their decision on the NHS Organ Donor Register.

If the testator wishes their body to be used for anatomical research, as opposed to organ transplantation, then their consent must be expressed since deemed consent does not apply.

There is no guarantee that bequests of the type suggested below can be carried out. If a *post mortem* has been performed on the body, then it may be impossible to preserve it and so the body would be unsuitable for anatomical examination or transplant purposes.

10F DIRECTION FOR ANATOMICAL EXAMINATION AND USE OF BODY PARTS

(a) I DESIRE that after my death my body may be made available [to …] for such anatomical examination and research or transplantation of any part or parts as may be thought fit provided that such examination is in accordance with the provisions of the Human

Tissue Act 2004 [and I DIRECT that the institution receiving my body shall have it cremated in due course].

(b)   I HEREBY REQUEST that my body or any part thereof as is suitable shall be used for such therapeutic purposes or for the purposes of medical education or research as [institution] thinks fit.

The surviving spouse or nearest relative can require interment without examination of the body. The institution receiving the body is responsible for ensuring that it is decently cremated or buried in consecrated ground or in a public burial ground being used for persons of the religious persuasion of the deceased.

10G   CLAUSE PROVIDING FOR USE OF TESTATOR'S BODY FOR THERAPEUTIC PURPOSES, BUT NOT FOR MEDICAL EDUCATION OR RESEARCH

(a)   I DESIRE that after my death any part or parts of my body which may be suitable for any therapeutic purpose (including corneal grafting in the case of my eyes and transplantation in the case of any other parts of my body) shall be removed in order that they may be used for such purposes.

(b)   For the avoidance of doubt I DECLARE that the foregoing provisions shall not authorise the use of my body or any part of it for medical education or research and I express my desire that neither my body nor any part of it should be used for such purposes.

(c)   I DESIRE that after the removal of such parts of my body as may be removed under the provisions hereinbefore set out the remainder shall be cremated by any hospital or other institution which has custody of my body after such removal has been completed.

Where a deceased person has in their lifetime made a statement in accordance with HTA 2004, section 3, requesting the use of any parts of their body, or a specified part or parts, for one or more uses under that section, then 'the person lawfully in possession of the body' may authorise the removal of such parts for use in accordance with the request unless the request has been withdrawn by the deceased. If the person died in hospital, then the health authority is in possession of the body while it is still on hospital premises (until executors or relatives claim the body), or if there is a dispute as to the identity of the personal representatives (see *University Hospital Lewisham NHS Trust v Hamuth and Others* [2006] EWHC 1609 (Ch), [2007] WTLR 309). A person may nominate another person in relation to consent for the purposes of HTA 2004, section 1. An appointment under this section may be general or limited to consent in relation to such one or more activities as may be specified in the appointment. An appointment may be made orally or in writing but an oral appointment is only valid if made in the presence of at least two witnesses present at the same time.

A written appointment under this section is valid only if:

(i)   it is signed by the person making it in the presence of at least one witness who attests the signature;
(ii) it is signed at the direction of the person making it, in their presence and in the presence of at least one witness who attests the signature; or
(iii) it is contained in a will of the person making it, being a will which is made in accordance with the requirements of:

–   Wills Act 1837, section 9; or
–   Wills and Administration Proceedings (Northern Ireland) Order 1994 (SI 1994/1899) (NI 13), article 5.

The relatives of the deceased, including the next of kin, cannot themselves countermand the deceased's request and cannot prevent the removal or examination of parts of the body in accordance with the request. There is no duty imposed by the HTA 2004, provided they have the deceased person's consent, upon the person lawfully in possession of the body to consult relatives or consider any objections by them, although it is customary for near relatives to be consulted.

If a person positively objects to their body being used for these purposes, they should inform their relatives so that the relatives are aware of the person's view, and the person should sign a written statement of objection which may either be included in their will or kept with it.

Chapter 11

Foreign Property or Domicile

11.1 GENERAL

EU Regulation 650/2012 ('the Succession Regulation') (also known as Brussels IV), which applies from 17 August 2015, has made significant changes to this area in relation to land held by UK nationals in EU states which have adopted the legislation (all except Ireland and Denmark). The Succession Regulation remains important, despite Brexit, and is dealt with below.

Before considering wills involving foreign property, or made by a testator who has a foreign domicile, the classification of property into movables and immovables must be considered. The term 'immovables' roughly corresponds with realty, comprising all estates and interests in freehold land, including those subject to a statutory trust for sale (but see Trusts of Land and Appointment of Trustees Act 1996, section 5), leasehold land, rentcharges and annuities payable out of rents and profits of land. The term 'movables' has a meaning broadly similar to that of 'personalty'.

The United Kingdom applies *lex situs* to the system of law applying to succession to land, but applies the law of domicile to succession to movable property.

Testators may make a declaration of their choice of the law to be applied to their will and its dispositions under the Succession Regulation. The effect of the Succession Regulation (in force from 17 August 2015) is that states that have adopted it will recognise a choice made in a will by nationals of any state that they want the law of their nationality to apply to their succession. If no choice is made, EU states will apply the law of the habitual residence of the deceased at the date of death.

The effect is that UK nationals can avoid forced heirship rules applying in civil law jurisdictions and substitute their national law (see further **11.6**).

11.2   THE CONCEPT OF DOMICILE

Domicile is a particular UK concept and may not exist in the country from where the client originates.

An English person living in France may still be domiciled in England and Wales for these purposes, even though habitually resident in France.

The concept of domicile is derived from the common law and looks at all aspects of a person's life to establish with which country they are most closely associated. Every person has a domicile and cannot have more than one at a particular time or be without one.

There are three types of domicile: origin, dependency and choice.

11.2.1   Domicile of origin

In determining a person's domicile, the first step is to find the domicile of origin, which means the domicile with which the person was born.

Legitimate children born during their father's lifetime have a domicile of origin in the country in which their father was domiciled at the time of their birth. Legitimate children born after their father's death and illegitimate children are domiciled in the country in which their mother was domiciled at the time of their birth. This may well differ from the country in which the children are actually born.

The domicile of origin is always described as 'adhesive' or 'sticky'. A person may be long-term resident in another country without losing their domicile of origin.

11.2.2   Domicile of dependency

Until a person reaches the age of 16 they cannot change their own domicile; it follows that of the person on whom they are legally dependent. Hence, a child will obtain a domicile of dependency if the person on whom they are dependent acquires a domicile of choice.

On ceasing to be dependent (i.e. when attaining the age of 16), a person often continues to be domiciled in the country of their last domicile of dependence. However, they have the normal capacity to change domicile and acquire a domicile of choice.

For married women it is important to check the date of their marriage. If the marriage is on or after 1 January 1974, the woman's domicile is entirely independent of her husband's (Domicile and Matrimonial Proceedings Act 1973, section 1(1)). Thus, a married woman is now capable of acquiring a separate domicile.

However, if the marriage took place before that date, the wife acquired her husband's domicile as a domicile of dependency. This meant it followed her husband's and could not be changed unilaterally while the marriage continued.

Under a transitional provision, a woman already married on 1 January 1974 is treated as retaining her existing domicile (but as a domicile of origin or choice, not dependence) until it is changed by her subsequent acquisition of a new domicile of choice or the revival of her domicile of origin (special rules applied to American wives under the UK–USA double tax treaty).

11.2.3   Domicile of choice

A domicile of choice is acquired by:

(i)   residence in a country, together with,
(ii) an intention of permanent or indefinite residence there.

Residence alone is insufficient to acquire a domicile of choice: there must be an intention of permanent residence. It is possible to reside for decades in a country without acquiring a domicile of choice there if, for example, the person plans to return to their domicile of origin at some point in the future.

Intention alone is not sufficient. There must also be residence. See *Kelly v Pyres* [2018] EWCA Civ 1368, where an Irish woman who worked in Europe but planned to settle in England when she retired was held not to have acquired a domicile of choice in England and Wales as she had spent almost no time there.

A statement or declaration of domicile contained in a will is insufficient to establish the testator's domicile at death; the domicile will be determined by the prevailing facts at the time of death.

To acquire a domicile of choice, it is not necessary to show that the intention to make a new home in the new country is irrevocable. The test is whether the person intends to make their home in the new country until the end of their days, unless and until something happens to change their mind (*IRC v Bullock* [1976] 1 WLR 1178). There needs to be strong evidence that the links with the domicile of origin/dependency have been severed.

The burden of proof is on the person asserting that a change of domicile has occurred. See *Re Clore (Deceased) (No 2)* [1984] STC 609, in which it was held that Charles Clore had a domicile of origin in England and Wales, and that, as he had not formed a settled intention permanently to reside in Monaco, he remained domiciled in England at his death. See also *Civil Engineer v IRC* [2002] STC (SCD) 72, where there was insufficient evidence that the taxpayer had ever relinquished his domicile in England and Wales and acquired a Hong Kong domicile of choice.

In *Agulian and Another v Cyganik* [2006] EWCA Civ 129, the deceased was born in Cyprus, but went to London and ran a restaurant there for several years before his death. He retained property in Cyprus and visited there frequently. It was held the deceased retained his original domicile of Cyprus. In reaching the decision, the Court of Appeal relied heavily on the decision in *In the estate of Fuld Deceased (No 3)* [1968] P 675 that the domicile of origin is more enduring than the domicile of choice. The decision to abandon one's domicile of origin should be clearly and unequivocally proved as it was in *Estate of Haji-Ioannou (Deceased) and Others v Frangos* [2009] EWHC 2310 (QB), discussed below).

If a domicile of choice has been acquired, the next step is to see whether a further domicile of choice has been acquired or whether a domicile of choice has been lost.

A domicile of choice can be lost in the same way that it is acquired. The person must have ceased to reside in the country and have no intention of returning to reside there permanently or indefinitely. The absence of intention must be unequivocal. A person in two minds does not have the necessary absence of intention. See *Morgan v Cilento and Others* [2004] EWHC 188 (Ch), where it was held that the deceased who, shortly before his death, had returned to the United Kingdom from Queensland where he had obtained a domicile of choice, had not yet abandoned that domicile of choice at the date of his death. Had he lived longer following his return, the position might have been different. The abandonment of a domicile of choice is not to be lightly inferred.

In *Haji-Ioannou (Deceased) v Frangos* [2009] EWHC 2310 (QB), it was held the deceased, who had been born in Cyprus and held British nationality, had acquired a domicile of choice in Monaco when he moved there to live permanently in 1990. Although he died in Greece, it was accepted he only went there towards the end of his life when terminally ill to be able to communicate with medical staff in Greek. He died intestate and questions arose as to the applicable law to determine distribution of his estate which varied under Monégasque, Greek and English succession law.

If a domicile of choice is lost and no new domicile of choice acquired, the domicile of origin takes over.

11.2.4   Deemed domicile

Because of the difficulty of establishing the acquisition of a domicile of choice, the United Kingdom has had deemed domicile rules for many years. Initially, deemed domicile rules applied for inheritance tax only, but the Finance (No 2) Act 2017 inserted a new section 835BA into the Income Tax Act 2007, which extended them to capital gains tax and income tax as well as toughening the rules. The corresponding inheritance tax provision is Inheritance Tax Act 1984, section 267, as amended.

The detail of the deemed domicile rules is beyond the scope of this book, but in outline from 6 April 2017 there are two rules.

Rule 1 – Fifteen of the previous 20 years

For income tax and capital gains tax purposes, a person is deemed domiciled if resident in the United Kingdom for at least 15 of the 20 tax years immediately preceding the relevant tax year.

For inheritance tax purposes, an individual is deemed domiciled if resident in the United Kingdom:

(i)   for at least 15 of the 20 tax years immediately preceding the relevant tax year; and
(ii)   for at least 1 of the 4 tax years ending with the relevant tax year.

The effect of point (ii) is to replicate the position on losing domicile under the previous rules where a person had to be resident in the United Kingdom for 17 out of the previous 20 years.

A deemed UK domicile will cease for inheritance tax purposes after 4 tax years of non-residence. Note, however, that if the individual returns to the United Kingdom within 6 tax years, they will immediately become deemed domiciled for inheritance tax because they will fulfil the 15 out of 20 test.

Rule 2 – The formerly domiciled resident

This change is designed to deal with the situation (regarded as abusive) of a UK national who works abroad, acquires a domicile of choice in the new jurisdiction and then returns to the United Kingdom claiming to still be domiciled in the new jurisdiction. Rather inelegantly, such persons are referred to in the legislation as 'formerly domiciled residents' (FDRs).

An individual is now deemed domiciled for income tax and capital gains tax if:

(i)   the individual was born in the United Kingdom;
(ii)   the individual's domicile of origin was in the United Kingdom; and
(iii) the individual is UK resident for the relevant tax year.

FDRs are simply treated as UK domiciled for income tax and capital gains tax purposes where they are UK resident for the tax year in which the relevant time falls (Income Tax Act 2007, section 835BA(2) and (3)).

Therefore, from 6 April 2017, an FDR will acquire a deemed UK domicile for income tax and capital gains tax purposes as soon as they become UK resident (i.e. from the start of the first tax year in which they assume or resume UK residence).

Example

Rufus was born in the United Kingdom in 1975 with a UK domicile of origin. He acquires a domicile of choice in Monaco in 2000, but becomes resident in the United Kingdom on 1 January 2022 (he retains his domicile of choice in Monaco). He is deemed domiciled in the United Kingdom for 2021/22.

It does not matter how many years Rufus spent abroad nor his reasons for resuming UK residence. He loses FDR status in the first year when he becomes non-resident.

For inheritance tax there is an additional requirement:

(iv) the individual was resident in the United Kingdom for at least 1 of the 2 tax years immediately preceding the relevant tax year.

The relaxation for inheritance tax reflects the fact that acquiring domicile for inheritance tax purposes has such serious tax consequences: worldwide assets become subject to inheritance tax.

Example *(continued)*

If Rufus in the previous example dies on 5 April 2022, he would not be deemed domiciled for inheritance tax. If he dies on or after 6 April 2022 (still UK resident) then he is deemed UK domiciled so that his worldwide estate is subject to inheritance tax, including property in trusts set up when he was not UK domiciled.

An amendment was also made to Inheritance Tax Act 1984, section 48, as a result of which any settlement created by the FDR while they were not UK domiciled will cease to be excluded property for any tax year in which the settlor is an FDR (see section 48(3E)).

11.2.5   Election to be UK domiciled

The inheritance tax exemption contained in Inheritance Tax Act 1984, section 18 which normally applies to transfers between spouses or between civil partners is limited to the level of the nil rate band where the donor spouse or civil partner is domiciled in the United Kingdom and the recipient is not. It is possible for the non-domiciled spouse or civil partner to elect to be treated as UK domiciled so securing a full exemption. However, the election carries with it disadvantages in that the worldwide assets of the electing spouse or civil partner become liable to inheritance tax. For a fuller discussion, see **27.7.2**.

11.3   MOVABLES

A will that has been executed in England and Wales by a testator who is domiciled or habitually resident in England and Wales at the date of their will or their death, is governed by English law in all respects, except with regard to the disposition of immovables situated outside England and Wales. If, on the other hand, a testator dies domiciled elsewhere but with movables in England, a grant of representation must be taken out in England and Wales and the estate administered according to English law, but all questions concerning beneficial succession under the will are dealt with according to the law of the testator's domicile at death.

The rules governing testamentary dispositions are best dealt with according to the issue involved.

11.3.1   Capacity

The capacity of a testator to make a will is determined by the law of their domicile. Problems can arise where a testator changes their domicile after making their will and there is an element of disagreement as to whether the governing law is that of the domicile at the date of death or at the time the will was made. The law at the testator's death should govern the situation. The testator must also be aware of, and advised on, making a will in the country where their property is situated, and any system of enforced heirship/reserved portions applicable in that country.

The jurisdiction of the courts in England and Wales is based on the deceased's domicile at the time of their death, although validity of their will may be determined by their domicile or habitual residence at the time of the making of their will or their death. The distribution of their estate may also fall to be determined by the law of the place of domicile or habitual residence.

Whether or not a legatee has capacity to take a gift under a will is determined by either the law of the legatee's domicile, or the law of the testator's domicile (see *Re Schnapper* [1928] Ch 420), whichever is more favourable to the legatee.

11.3.2   Formal validity

It was thought at one time that the formal requirements for validity were those of the law of the country where the testator was domiciled at the date of their death. The Wills Act 1963, which applies to the wills of testators dying after 1 January 1964, provides in section 1 that 'a will shall be treated as properly executed' if its execution conforms to the internal law in force in any one of the following territories:

(i)   the territory where the will was executed (this is so irrespective of the duration of the testator's visit to the territory); or
(ii)   the territory where the testator was domiciled either at the time of making the will or at death; or
(iii) the territory where the testator was habitually resident either at the time of making the will or at death; or
(iv)   the state of which the testator, either at the time of making the will or at death, was a national.

Following the United Kingdom's ratification of the Convention providing a Uniform Law on the Form of an International Will (Washington, 1973), a will is formally valid in all the contracting states if it complies with the formalities provided for by the Convention. The domicile and nationality of the testator are no longer relevant, nor is the place where the will was made, nor the location of the assets of the estate. Under the Convention the will must be made in writing and the main formalities are that it must be signed and acknowledged by the testator in the presence of two witnesses and an 'authorised person'. The 'authorised person' (a solicitor or notary public if the will is made in England) must complete a form of certificate authenticating the will and confirming that it has been properly executed. The certificate is then annexed to the will. This rarely, if ever, happens when a will is made in England and Wales. Administration of Justice Act 1982, sections 27 and 28 dealing with the provisions relating to international wills have yet to be brought into force in the United Kingdom.

11.3.3 Essential validity

Issues of 'essential validity' include whether or not a gift to an attesting witness is valid; whether a gift infringes rules on perpetuity periods; and whether the testator has fulfilled a requirement to leave part of their property to their spouse or civil partner and children. Whether or not a gift or will has 'essential validity' or 'material validity' depends on whether or not the testator has complied with all the requirements of the relevant law.

In respect of movable property, the 'relevant law' is that of the country in which the testator is domiciled at the time of their death (see *Dellar v Zivy and Others* [2007] EWHC 2266 (Ch)).

Mere compliance with the formalities required by the Wills Act 1963 does not necessarily make valid either individual gifts or the whole will. That Act only provides proof that the document in question is a will and therefore admissible to probate. An obvious example of this distinction is where the testator is a British subject who dies domiciled in France, having made a will in England according to English law. Probate will be granted provided the formalities of English law have been complied with when executing the will. But under French law the testator would be required to make provision for their spouse, children and remoter kin from their estate, and if the will does not contain such a provision, some or all of it may be ineffective. The will would take effect subject to the French law, which would apply unless the testator had made a valid choice of national law under the Succession Regulation (see **11.6**), which may result in intestacy. If only part of the estate fails, then the remainder may pass under the will, although any bequest would be reduced *pro rata* (see *Re Groos* [1915] 1 Ch 572, *Re Annesley* [1926] Ch 692 and *Re Ross* [1930] 1 Ch 377).

11.3.4 Construction

In *Curati v Perdoni and Another* [2012] EWCA Civ 1381, Tomlinson LJ said at [16]:

> It is trite that that the construction of a will is governed by the law intended by the testator. In *Halsbury's Laws of England*, Fifth Edition, Volume 19, 2011, at para 750 it is stated:
>
>> 'The construction of a will is governed by the law intended by the testator. In the case of a will of movables, this is presumed to be the law of the testator's domicile at the date of execution of the will, but this presumption is rebutted by any sufficient indication that the testator intended his will to be construed according to the law of another country. The testator's intention may be

> expressed in the will, or it may be implied from circumstances such as his use of
> a particular language, or of expressions known only to a particular law.'

The case turned on the issue of domicile as the Italian testator had executed a second will which did not contain a revocation clause. If Italian law was applicable, the whole of the first will was revoked. If the law of England and Wales applied, the first will was only revoked in so far as it was inconsistent with the second will. It was held that the testator had acquired and not abandoned a domicile of choice in England and Wales, therefore it was presumed that the law of England and Wales applied.

The case is a reminder of the importance of including a governing law clause where there is any doubt as to the testator's domicile. Clear evidence is required to rebut the presumption and there was nothing sufficient.

11A   GOVERNING LAW CLAUSE

> The terms of this will and the trusts that it creates shall be governed by
> and construed in all respects in accordance with the law of England and
> Wales.

In *Dellar v Zivy and Others* [2007] EWHC 2266 (Ch), the court said that evidence to rebut the presumption might arise from the nature of the will or from other matters that the testator had written his will with reference to, and with the intention that it should be interpreted according to, the law of some other country.

11.3.5   Revocation

The rules relating to revocation vary under different legal systems and the choice of law is determined by the method of revocation.

Revocation by a later will

A will purporting to revoke an earlier will is formally valid and effective if it satisfies the requirements of any of the laws by which, under the Wills Act 1963, its formal validity is determinable, or if it complies with the requirements of any one of the laws qualified to govern the formal validity of the earlier will.

Revocation by destruction of the will

The Wills Act 1963 deals only with revocation by a testamentary instrument, and not by destruction. If, when the act of revocation by destruction was performed, the domicile was different from that when the will was executed, the common law principle of domicile operates and the legal effect of the act of destruction falls to be determined at the time of its performance.

Revocation by marriage

The rule of revocation by marriage or formation of a civil partnership under the English legal system is not commonly adopted by other systems. If a person makes a will, marries or forms a civil partnership, and later dies leaving movables in another country, the effect on the will of the marriage or partnership may need to be determined. Whether or not the relevant law is that of the domicile at the date of the marriage or formation of the partnership, or at the date of the death, depends on whether the rule itself is matrimonial or testamentary in nature. If matrimonial, then the domicile at the time of the marriage or formation of civil partnership applies. Otherwise the domicile at death applies. The matter was settled in the case of *Re Martin* [1900] P 211, where it was decided that revocation by marriage was essentially a doctrine connected with the relationship of marriage and therefore matrimonial.

11.4 IMMOVABLES

11.4.1 Capacity

In the case of testamentary succession to immovables, the *lex situs* governs questions of capacity, although there is no English authority on the point.

11.4.2 Formal validity

The Wills Act 1963 has considerably extended the common law position in relation to immovables. Previously, a will relating to immovables was subject to the formal requirements of the *lex situs*. Under the 1963 Act the will is valid if it complies with any one of the laws specified in section 1 (above). The *lex situs* is defined for the purpose of the Act to mean 'the internal law in force in the territory where the property was situated' (section 2(1)(b)), and the doctrine of *renvoi* appears to have been excluded by the reference to the 'internal law' of the *lex situs*.

11.4.3 Essential validity

The material or essential validity of a gift of immovables by will is again governed by the *lex situs*.

11.4.4   Construction

Provisions in a will concerning immovables are construed according to the system of law intended by the testator. This is presumed to be the law of the testator's domicile at the time the will was made, but the presumption may be rebutted by adducing evidence from the language of the will to prove that they made their dispositions with reference to some other legal system. If, however, the interest that arises from such construction is not permitted or not recognised by the *lex situs*, then that law must nevertheless prevail.

In *Curati v Perdoni and Another* [2012] EWCA Civ 138 (discussed at **11.3.4**), Tomlinson LJ at [16] continued the quotation from *Halsbury's Laws of England*, Fifth Edition, Volume 19, 2011, at para 750:

> *Prima facie*, a will of immovables must be construed according to the law of the testator's domicile at the date of execution of the will, but this presumption may be rebutted by any sufficient indication that the testator intended to refer to some other law, as where he uses the technical language of the country where the immovables are situated.

11.4.5   Revocation

Broadly speaking, a will in relation to immovables may be revoked in the same way as one concerning movables. Thus it may be revoked by a later will or a testamentary document showing an intention to revoke. The effect of an act of revocation by destruction or obliteration is determined by reference to the *lex situs*.

In the case of revocation by a subsequent marriage or formation of a civil partnership, reference should be made to the law of the domicile at marriage or formation and not the *lex situs*. This is despite a view to the contrary in *Re Caithness* (1891) 7 TLR 354, since the Australian decision of *Re Micallef's Estate* [1977] 2 NSWLR 929 seems to have found more support.

11.5   POWERS OF APPOINTMENT EXERCISED BY WILL

For a detailed discussion of powers of appointment, see Chapter 18.

11.5.1   Nature of a power

Whether a power of appointment is special or general is a matter of construction to be determined according to the law governing the instrument creating it.

11.5.2 Capacity

Capacity to exercise a testamentary power is determined by the law of the appointor's domicile. The instrument which creates the power (not the one by which the power is exercised) is the governing instrument and the appointee takes under the instrument, and not under the will of the appointor.

It appears that an appointor must have capacity under the law of their domicile in order validly to exercise a general power of appointment. In the case of a special power, however, the appointor is treated as an agent acting under the terms of the governing instrument, and the exercise of that power is valid if the appointor is capable either under the law of their domicile or under the law that governs the instrument of creation.

11.5.3 Formal validity

The situation may well arise in which a testamentary appointment is given, under an English instrument, to a person who either makes their will abroad, or dies while domiciled in another country. In such a case, a will exercising that power of appointment is treated as properly executed in respect of the exercise of that power if it complies with the requirements of one of the specified legal systems under the Wills Act 1963 (see **11.3.2**). The governing law is therefore determined according to the place where the will was executed or the nationality, domicile or habitual residence of the testator or, in the case of immovables, the *lex situs*.

A will exercising a power of appointment is also duly executed for these purposes if its execution is in the manner prescribed by the law governing the essential validity of the instrument creating the power (Wills Act 1963, section 2(1)(d)). Under section 2(2), the testamentary exercise of a power of appointment is not formally invalid by reason only of a failure to observe a formality required by the instrument of creation.

11.5.4 Essential validity

The effect of an appointment under a special power is subject to the law governing the instrument creating the power.

The effect of the exercise of a general power relating to movables depends on the circumstances and is a matter of construction. If the settled property was treated by the donee as their own, the operation and effect of the will exercising the power are determined by the law of the donee's domicile at death. If the settled property, though subject to a general power of appointment, has been kept separate from the donee's own property and the funds remain distinct, then the same law applies to the will making the appointment as would apply in the case of the special power, and that will is governed by the law governing the instrument of creation.

Where there is a general power of appointment in respect of immovables, the *lex situs* governs the essential validity of the will exercising that power.

11.5.5 Construction

Whether or not a power of appointment is special or general, the construction is governed by the legal system in the mind of the appointor when the power was created. If there is no express intention in the instrument of creation, the intended law is presumed to be the law of the domicile where that instrument was executed.

Where the appointor (or testator) specifies the legal system which is to apply, then such an indication is conclusive, even where the nominated legal system does not recognise the concept of powers.

11.5.6 Revocation

The domicile of the donee governs the revocation of a power of appointment over movables.

A power of appointment over movables or immovables may be revoked by a properly executed will (which is valid if it complies with the law governing the legal validity of the power under Wills Act 1963, section 2(1)), provided another power of appointment is drafted in its place.

Where a will is revocable by marriage or formation of a civil partnership under the law of the domicile of the testator at the time of such a marriage or formation, then a power under the will may be revoked. In England and Wales, however, powers of appointment are saved from revocation by marriage or formation of a civil partnership under Wills Act 1837, sections 18(2) and 18B(2) (as inserted by the Civil Partnership Act 2004 with effect from 5 December 2005) 'unless the property so appointed would in default of appointment pass to [the testator's] personal representatives'.

11.6 EU REGULATION 650/2012

11.6.1 Effect of the Regulation

On 4 July 2012, the European Union adopted EU Regulation 650/2012 ('the Succession Regulation'), most of which did not take effect until 17 August 2015.

The United Kingdom was at that time a member of the European Union, but the government exercised its right not to opt-in to the Succession Regulation (as did Ireland and Denmark). Despite the United Kingdom's opt-out (and Brexit), the Succession Regulation is still very significant for UK private client practitioners and anyone resident in the Succession Regulation Zone (all EU member states other than Denmark, Ireland and the United Kingdom).

The Succession Regulation is intended to allow individuals to be certain as to what law will govern succession to their property situated in the EU states that have adopted it.

Article 21(1) introduces a general rule: the law applicable to succession is that of the habitual residence at the time of death, unless, exceptionally, the individual was 'manifestly more closely connected with another state'.

As an alternative, Article 22 provides that a person may choose the law of their nationality as the law to govern their succession as a whole.

Choosing the law of nationality allows a testator to achieve certainty where there is doubt (or may be doubt in the future) about their habitual residence, or whether they are manifestly more closely connected with another state.

Because the law chosen, whether by choice or by default, can be the law of a state that is not a signatory (Article 20), an English client resident in England but owning a property in, for example, Spain, could choose the law of England and Wales to apply to their succession, resulting in the application of the law of England and Wales. This would avoid *lex situs* applying to land. It is, therefore, worth including a choice of national law, but most important that clients take local advice.

The relevant law chosen must apply to the whole of the succession. It is not possible to have different succession laws applying to one estate.

'Succession' is basically what passes under a will. It does not include property passing by survivorship or community of property regimes. If a couple holds assets in a country under a 'community of goods' regime, the assets pass automatically to the survivor (as with our beneficial joint tenancy), so do not form part of the 'succession'.

The Succession Regulation does not affect tax or administrative matters. Any issues relating to tax, for example, are therefore excluded and are still governed by the existing rules.

11.6.2   How is a choice made?

The choice is made in a disposition on death. It can be made expressly or impliedly. An express choice is made in a disposition on death, in other words a will.

An implied choice may be demonstrated by the terms of a will. For example, a choice may be implied if the will refers to specific provisions of the law of the state of the testator's nationality, or otherwise mentions that law. It is clearly preferable to have an express choice.

11.6.3   One will or two?

Some practitioners take the view that because the election must affect the whole succession, only one will is permitted. This does not seem to follow. Provided both wills refer to a choice of national law, there should be no problem.

There are good reasons for having separate wills (and as advice will be needed on the effect of local tax law, there should be no additional expense):

(i)   It is likely to speed up the administration if there are two wills which can be dealt with side by side rather than having to prove one in the United Kingdom and then get it recognised in the other jurisdiction.
(ii)   It may make life easier when dealing with the foreign assets to have a will in a form familiar to the local jurisdiction.
(iii) Tax consequences may flow from the distribution of the estate in accordance with the chosen law. For example, a foreign jurisdiction may tax assets that pass to the testator's children at a lower rate than assets that pass to other relatives or to non-relatives. This may lead to a higher tax burden if forced heirship provisions are displaced by the chosen law.
(iv)   Most civil law jurisdictions do not recognise the office of personal representative and so will regard a will giving assets to executors to distribute to beneficiaries as involving two transfers with, potentially, two charges to tax.
(v)   Similarly, most civil law jurisdictions do not recognise trusts so a simpler form of will is preferable.

11B   CHOICE WHERE THE TESTATOR IS A UK NATIONAL

I choose the law of [England and Wales] [Scotland] [Northern Ireland] to govern succession to the whole of my assets, rights and obligations, including any not disposed of by this will. I am a UK national who is most closely connected with the jurisdiction of [England and Wales] [Scotland] [Northern Ireland].

11C   CHOICE WHERE THE TESTATOR IS A NON-UK NATIONAL

I choose the law of [state] [jurisdiction*] to govern succession to the whole of my assets, rights and obligations as a whole, including any not disposed of by this will. I am a [state] national [who is most closely connected with the jurisdiction of [jurisdiction]].

* If the state is a *single jurisdiction*, refer to the law of the state and omit the optional wording about connection to a jurisdiction. If the state comprises *more than one jurisdiction*, refer to the law of the jurisdiction with which the testator is most closely connected and include the wording confirming the connection at the end of the clause.

11.6.4   Developments in France

The French are very attached to the forced heirship rules contained in Articles 912 *et seq* of the French Civil Code, which give fixed inheritance rights to the deceased's children and, in some cases, the surviving spouse. There was some unhappiness at the way in which the Succession Regulation could erode the rules. Article 35 allows states to refuse to give effect to any part of the Succession Regulation which is 'manifestly incompatible' with the state's public policy. In 2017, the French Cour de Cassation (the Supreme Court) held in relation to the estate of Maurice Jarre (who had been resident in California for many years before his death) that excluding the forced heirship portion, pursuant to the foreign law designated by the conflict-of-law rule, 'was not, in and of itself, contrary to French international public order policy'.

However, a new law, adopted by the French Parliament on 24 August 2021 (Loi no. 2021-1109 du 24 août 2021 confortant les respect des principes de la République), which came into force on 1 November 2021, amends Articles 913 and 921 of the French Civil Code by providing for an increased protection of the rights of protected heirs in situations where the deceased or one of their heirs is either a national of a member state of the European Union or an habitual resident of a member state of the European Union. French notaries will be under an obligation before distributing the estate to inform those forced heirs whose rights may be affected by the provisions of the testator's will of their entitlement under the new law.

> **Example**
>
> A UK national with two children who dies while habitually resident in France would be subject to the forced heirship rules.

This new law conflicts not only with the Succession Regulation, but also with the decision of the Cour de Cassation and so is likely to be challenged in the French courts. Until then, however, it is unclear whether any elections for national law in wills of UK nationals who fall within the terms of Articles 913 and 921 of the French Civil Code will be effective.

Chapter 12

Legacies

There are three types of legacy that may be made in a will:

- a specific legacy;
- a general legacy; or
- a demonstrative legacy.

The category into which any particular gift falls is a question of construction.

12.1 SPECIFIC LEGACIES

A specific legacy is a gift by will of some specified and distinguishable property forming part of the testator's estate at death, for example, 'I give my grandfather clock to X'. Any word of possession or reference to the acquisition of the specified property by the testator indicates that the testator intended to give that property, and not some property of the same kind to be purchased by the executors.

12.1.1 Personal chattels

Where the testator wishes to make a gift of all their personal chattels, the phrase should be defined, usually by reference to Administration of Estates Act 1925, section 55(1)(x) as substituted, to avoid any confusion (see Chapter 24 for a full discussion of the meaning of the term 'personal chattels'). Individual items can be listed, although this makes no allowance for future additions to the property and can be cumbersome. The same problems arise if the will provides for gifts by way of a separate list, schedule or memorandum intended to be incorporated into the will.

It is usually preferable to allow beneficiaries to select items, in which case the personal representatives should be given power to deal with disputes or to give them to a named individual with a request that items are distributed in accordance with a memorandum of wishes left by the deceased. Where the individual complies with the testator's wishes within 2 years of death, the dispositions are treated as though made by the testator for inheritance tax purposes under Inheritance Tax Act 1984, section 143.

Digital assets such as photographs, music and games are increasingly valuable, and it is helpful if a will deals expressly with ownership of such items.

12A   GIFT OF PERSONAL CHATTELS USING DEFINITION IN THE ADMINISTRATION OF ESTATES ACT 1925 [WITH OPTION TO INCLUDE INTANGIBLE DIGITAL ASSETS]

I GIVE to [name] absolutely all my personal chattels as defined in Administration of Estates Act 1925, section 55(1)(x) (as substituted) [and I declare this gift shall include any software, files, documents, pictures, videos, sound recordings and other similar property of an intangible nature which is at the date of my death installed or stored on any of my personal chattels as hereinbefore defined] but there is not included herein any chattels used at my death solely or mainly for business purposes [other than my car] nor money or securities for money nor any chattel held by me at my death solely as an investment and this gift shall take effect subject to any specific disposition in the provisions of this my will or any codicil hereto.

12B   GIFT OF PERSONAL CHATTELS – SHORT FORM

I GIVE to my [spouse] [civil partner] [name] absolutely all articles of personal domestic household or garden use or ornament not otherwise specifically disposed of by the provisions of this my will or by any codicil hereto.

12C   GIFT OF SUCH ARTICLES AS BENEFICIARY MAY SELECT

I GIVE absolutely such of my personal chattels as defined in Administration of Estates Act 1925, section 55(1)(x) (as substituted) other than those specifically disposed of by the provisions of this my will or by any codicil hereto as [name] may select by written notice to my personal representatives within [two] months after my death (the 'Selection Period') and any such articles not so selected within the Selection Period shall fall into my residuary estate [PROVIDED THAT during the Selection Period no beneficiary under this my will or of any codicil hereto shall be entitled to the use or enjoyment of any articles which are subject to this clause and which have not been so selected by [name]].

The beneficiary may select all such articles not specifically bequeathed. If the beneficiary should die within the Selection Period, then the right of selection ceases and cannot be exercised by the beneficiary's personal representatives.

12D GIFT OF PART ONLY OF PERSONAL CHATTELS TO BE SELECTED BY THE BENEFICIARY UP TO A GIVEN VALUE, THE REMAINDER TO BE GIVEN TO CHILDREN

I GIVE to [name] absolutely such of my personal chattels as defined in Administration of Estates Act 1925, section 55(1)(x) (as substituted) save those otherwise specifically disposed of as [name] may within [two] months of my death (the 'Selection Period') select by written notice to my personal representatives up to the value of [£1,000] such value to be determined by my personal representatives in such manner as they think fit and I GIVE the remainder of my said personal chattels not so selected by [name] or the whole of them if [name] shall for any reason not make any selection within the Selection Period to my two children [name] and [name] in equal shares [and I DIRECT that if there is any dispute as between my said children in respect of any articles then my personal representatives shall sell the same and divide the net proceeds of such sale between my said two children equally].

If the will is drafted so the residue passing to the children is defined as that remaining after the beneficiary's selection, it has been held that the gift of residue to the children will fail if the beneficiary predeceases the testator (see *Boyce v Boyce* (1849) 16 Sim 476). It is unlikely that a modern court would reach the same conclusion, but clearly it is preferable to avoid drafting in such a way.

12E POWER TO EXECUTORS TO DISPOSE OF ARTICLES OF LITTLE VALUE

My Executors shall have power to dispose by way of gift to whomsoever they think fit or to any charitable organisation such articles of household or personal use or ornament (save those otherwise specifically disposed of by this my will or any codicil hereto) as in their opinion are of trivial value or for any reason impractical to sell.

If such articles are donated to charity by the executors, or by the beneficiaries otherwise entitled to them, the charity exemption can be claimed by completing HM Revenue & Customs, Schedule IHT408 when submitting Form IHT400. This requires signing by the relevant beneficiaries and so meets the statutory requirements of Inheritance Tax Act 1984 section 142, provided evidence that the charity has received the items is also submitted (see further **27.11**).

12F   GIFT TO BE DISTRIBUTED IN ACCORDANCE WITH LIST LEFT BY TESTATOR – NO TRUST

> I GIVE to [name] absolutely all the contents of my house at [place] and I request that [name] should distribute the same in accordance with a list to be placed with this will and in default of such a list as aforesaid I request [name] to divide the said property between each of my children living at my death as they think fit ALWAYS PROVIDED THAT nothing in this gift shall impose any trust or binding obligation on [name] or confer any interest upon any other person.

For details regarding incorporation, see Chapter 4. The wording of this clause would be insufficient to enable the list to be incorporated with the will and admitted to probate. To achieve incorporation, the reference must be to a list sufficiently identified and existing at the date the will is executed. It cannot, therefore, be altered after the date of the will. Many people prefer to have the ability to change the terms of the document. This can be done but, as here, only by sacrificing certainty.

This is an absolute gift and the testator should be made aware that the named beneficiary may take the property without carrying out the testator's wishes. This form of gift may be useful if the testator wishes to maintain flexibility without constantly changing or replacing the will, provided the testator trusts the named beneficiary.

12.1.2   Furniture

The term 'furniture' generally means only ordinary household and movable furniture; valuable articles such as fixtures, pictures, books or similar articles should be specifically dealt with.

12G   GIFT OF FURNITURE

> I GIVE to [name] absolutely all my furniture except such as is fixed to the premises whether or not the same is in law a fixture [and I DECLARE the cost of delivering any such item to [name] or vesting it shall be a testamentary expense as shall be the upkeep and insurance of the item until delivery or vesting].

Ordinarily, the cost of delivery and vesting falls on the specific beneficiary, but there can be some uncertainty in determining at what point in the administration the beneficiary assumes responsibility for any costs incurred. In expressing all such costs as a testamentary expense, the costs will be paid from the residuary estate.

12H   GIFT TO CHILD OF FURNITURE AND EFFECTS IN THEIR BEDROOM

I GIVE to my [son[[daughter] [name] all articles of household or domestic use furniture pictures and other effects whatsoever ordinarily used by them in their bedroom in such house as I may reside in at my death.

See Chapter 14 for the meaning of the phrase 'as I may reside in at my death'.

12.1.3   Stocks and shares

A gift of stocks and shares may be either specific or general. It is specific if it is, for example, a gift of 'my shares' or 'such shares in X company as I own at the date of my death', and the testator dies owning shares, or such shares.

Alternatively, the gift of shares may be a general legacy if worded in the following manner 'Y [number] of shares in Z Company Plc'. In this case, the executor must purchase that number of shares in the specified company if the testator does not own such shares at the date of their death. In the former case, if there were no shares, or no shares in the specified company, in the estate, the gift would lapse.

Whether a gift is specific or general in nature is a question of construction which depends on the wording of the will. Appropriate provision may be made in anticipation of a change of name of the company, amalgamation or re-naming of the share or stock in question.

12I   GIFT OF SHARES – GENERAL LEGACY

I GIVE to [name] absolutely five hundred ordinary shares in [name of company] and I DECLARE for the avoidance of doubt that this gift is a general legacy and not a specific legacy [and I FURTHER DECLARE that if the said shares are represented by a different holding as a result of a change of name takeover amalgamation or reconstruction of the company or the said shares then this gift shall take effect as a gift of that different holding].

See *Re Compton* [1914] 2 Ch 119. In the case of a general legacy, the beneficiary has the option of taking the cash sum which would have been used to purchase the shares on the basis 'equity does nothing in vain'.

12J   GIFT OF STOCK – SPECIFIC LEGACY

I GIVE to [name] absolutely all my ordinary shares in [name of company] which I own at the date of my death as a specific legacy [and I FURTHER DECLARE that if the said shares are represented by a different holding as a result of a change of name takeover amalgamation or reconstruction of the company or the said shares then this gift shall take effect as a gift of that different holding].

12K   GIFT OF SHARES IN PUBLIC OR PRIVATE COMPANY – PROVISION FOR LESSER NUMBER OF SHARES ONLY BEING AVAILABLE

I GIVE to [name] absolutely [one thousand] of my shares in [X company] [Limited] [plc] ALWAYS PROVIDED THAT if the number of shares in the said [X company] [Limited] [plc] held by me at the time of my death is insufficient to satisfy the provisions of this legacy then I GIVE to the said [name] in lieu of each share by which my holding in the said company falls short a sum equal to the mean market value of such shares at the date of my death [such value to be ascertained by my Trustees by such means as they in their absolute discretion think fit] AND I DIRECT that any charge affecting any shares given hereunder shall be discharged primarily from my residuary estate.

A provision regarding valuation is generally required only if the relevant shares are not officially quoted.

12L   SPECIFIC LEGACY OF SHARES WITH WORDS ADDED NEGATIVING APPORTIONMENT

I GIVE to [name] all my [number] [description] shares in … [plc] [Limited] held by me at the date of my death now standing in my name together with all dividends already accrued due or accruing thereon at my death.

Under the Apportionment Act 1870, dividends and interest due and payable before the death of the testator form part of their residuary estate unless the will provides otherwise. The specific legatee is entitled to dividends and interest accruing after death. Dividends and interest paid after death must be apportioned. In the case of trusts created before 1 October 2013, apportionment of income was required in relation to trusts to ensure that each beneficiary received only income attributable to their period of ownership (see *Re Joel* [1936] 2 All ER 962).

However, in relation to trusts created or arising on or after 1 October 2013, Trusts (Capital and Income) Act 2013, section 1 provides that any entitlement to income is to income as it arises (and, accordingly, Apportionment Act 1870, section 2, which provides for income to accrue from day to day, does not apply). See also Chapter 19 for further details of apportionment.

12.1.4   Copyright, unpublished works and patents

12M   GIFT OF COPYRIGHTS AND UNPUBLISHED WORKS TO LITERARY EXECUTOR

I GIVE to my Literary Executor absolutely all my works manuscripts letters and writings whether published or unpublished and whether in hardcopy or softcopy format together with the copyright and all other rights and privileges in respect thereof for their own absolute use.

12N   GIFT OF COPYRIGHTS AND UNPUBLISHED WORKS TO LITERARY EXECUTORS TO ADMINISTER AND TRANSFER NET PROCEEDS TO GENERAL EXECUTORS AND TRUSTEES

I GIVE to my Literary Executors all my works manuscripts letters and writings whether published or unpublished and whether in hardcopy or softcopy format (except those required for the administration of my general estate) TOGETHER WITH the copyrights and all other rights and privileges in respect thereof with full liberty to publish any unpublished works and to complete and publish any unfinished work SUBJECT to such terms and conditions as my Literary Executors may in their absolute discretion think fit PROVIDED THAT my Literary Executors shall not be liable for any loss sustained in the exercise of such discretion which shall primarily be borne by the literary assets hereby bequeathed and thereafter by my general estate AND I DECLARE THAT my Literary Executors shall collect all payments of every kind made in respect of my works as aforesaid and after paying all administrative and other expenses necessary to carry out the terms of this bequest shall transfer the net proceeds to my Trustees to hold upon the same trusts as are herein declared in respect of my residuary estate.

12O   GIFT OF PATENTS

(a)   I GIVE all patents and interests in patents to which I am entitled to my Trustees with full power to deal with the same as if absolute beneficial owners thereof.

(b)   My Trustees shall hold the said patents [upon the trusts herein declared in respect of my residuary estate] [upon the following trusts].

12.1.5   Digital assets

Modern technology has influenced how people keep information such as that contained in photographs, music and books, as well as popularising the use of online bank accounts, social media and so on. Many testators have so-called 'digital assets' and are often concerned as to how they can be passed on after death. Many assume, perhaps naturally, that digital assets can be dealt with just like anything else they might leave by will. However, some items which the testator regards as theirs, such as downloaded music or films, may only be enjoyed on licence and so are not, strictly speaking, theirs to leave on death.

Digital assets cover a whole range of items. Some, such as social media and email accounts, are not assets in the usual sense because they have no intrinsic value and are usually not transferrable. On the other hand, online bank accounts, investment accounts, accounts used for online betting or auction selling, store cards, etc may have a credit (or debit) balance at death. Somewhere in the middle are online facilities or platforms such as Dropbox, the Cloud, etc which offer file and document storage. These may, or may not, hold something of value to a third party, such as intellectual property rights or commercially sensitive information. Ownership of a domain name or website is yet another form of digital asset which may have a value to someone.

Essentially, a digital asset is no different to any other and so it would fall to the personal representatives to first identify such assets and then take appropriate steps to secure them. While the practices of institutions differ, major banks and financial organisations do not usually require the username or password of the deceased before taking steps to freeze the account on being notified of the death. However, it is vital that personal representatives make a point of asking for information about both conventional and online accounts, not least since these may well be dealt with by different limbs of the same organisation. The personal representatives' task will be easier if the testator keeps a clear record of digital assets, particularly those for which there is no ordinary paper trail. It should be the task of the will drafter to enquire of such assets when taking instructions.

Inevitably, many digital assets are subject to terms and conditions entered into by the testator which often state how access and realisation of the asset is obtained following the testator's death. Depending on the nature of the digital asset, this could present the personal representatives with difficulties, added to which the asset may be operated from overseas, so adding an international dimension with inherent jurisdiction issues for the personal representatives.

The Law Society's Wills and Inheritance Quality Scheme Protocol recommends completion and maintenance of a Personal Assets Log, including digital assets, and says that consideration should be given to ensuring that those dealing with the estate can access those assets when the time comes. On 16 April 2014, the Law Society published a press release urging people to leave clear instructions about their social media, computer games and other online accounts after death, suggesting this is preferable to leaving a list of passwords or PINs because someone accessing an account using this information faces the risk of committing a criminal offence under the Computer Misuse Act 1990.

In terms of what is put into a will, it may be important for the will drafter to distinguish between the electronic data or digital asset and the hardware on which it is held. For many testators, no special provisions need be included in the will since the deceased's digital assets can be left to follow the hardware passing with the general estate. However, care is needed if a specific gift of 'personal chattels', as defined by Administration of Estates Act 1925, section 55(1)(x) (see **24.9.1**) is suggested and the testator intends the beneficiary should acquire (*inter alia*) both their computer and what is saved to its hard drive. For wills made on or after 1 October 2014, devices holding data are not 'personal chattels', if used solely, or mainly, for business purposes at the date of death. Furthermore, data files (documents, pictures, videos, etc) and software programs cannot be 'personal chattels', even if held on a device which is a personal chattel. This is because the new definition of 'personal chattels', inserted into section 55(1)(x) by Inheritance and Trustees' Powers Act 2014, section 3, includes only tangible property.

The following precedent might be used, suitably adapted, for a testator who possesses a considerable amount of data in digital or electronic format, much of it (and probably that which has value) being related to their work, profession or source of income. It also makes provision for such data to be made available to others if there is an interest in it.

12P   SPECIFIC DIRECTIONS FOR AND GIFT OF ELECTRONIC DATA (DIGITAL PROPERTY)

5.1 In this clause 'Digital Property' means such property rights and interests whether existing at the date hereof or at the date of my death consisting of:

5.1.1 my domain name website www… and its contents; and

5.1.2 my Facebook, Twitter and other social media accounts and contents; and

5.1.3 all my published and unpublished works, manuscripts, letters, notes, records and other writings (including digital materials stored electronically on computers, tablets, communications equipment, word processors, discs, memory sticks, devices and accessories, operating systems, software, online storage accounts including but not limited to 'Dropbox' and 'Cloud', access codes and other data and also similar materials not otherwise mentioned herein produced in the course of or otherwise related to my literary work; and

5.1.4 any materials as in 5.1.3 existing as voice, sound, image or visual recordings; and

5.1.5 all my copyrights and intellectual property rights and any other rights and privileges which may exist in any of the foregoing materials; and

5.1.6 the hardware on which any of the foregoing materials are stored.

5.2 To assist them with the directions below concerning my Digital Property I request my Trustees [or my Literary Executors] to instruct my friend [name] who has worked for me and has knowledge of my Digital Property [or any one or more of my employees or agents who I have previously instructed] but if [they are] unwilling or unable to assist my Trustees [or my Literary Executors] may instruct such other person or persons who in their opinion is or are both discreet and who has or have the necessary know-how to help my Trustees [or my Literary Executors] in the tasks below concerning my Digital Property and in all such cases my Trustees [or my Literary Executors] may pay to [name] [such persons] out of my general estate such remuneration as is reasonable.

5.3 I DIRECT my Trustees [or my Literary Executors] to carry out and perform such of the following tasks in respect of my Digital Property as shall be or become necessary as soon as possible after my death:

5.3.1 in so far as possible to access all my digital files and accounts relevant to my Digital Property; and

5.3.2 to identify files within my Digital Property whose contents have, or might have, monetary value and deal with, apply and dispose of them and their contents in accordance with either any agreements made by me in respect of them, or as they think appropriate and in this respect my Trustees [or my Literary Executors] shall have the powers of an absolute beneficial owner including (but without prejudice to the generality of the foregoing words) the power to complete (if necessary) and publish any unfinished Digital Property subject to any terms and conditions as my Trustees [or Literary Executors] think fit including the engagement of any third party to effect such completion or publication as required; and

5.3.3 to destroy irrecoverably all files which I identify for that purpose in writing by file name, whether so identified in hardcopy form left with my will or elsewhere or electronically in softcopy form in one or more of my computer files; and

5.3.4 to insert a notice of my death and subsequently thereafter close any of my social media accounts; and

5.3.5 to insert a notice of my death on the home page of my personal website www... and to take all actions required to transfer title to the domain name to themselves or to such other person or persons as they see fit in order thereafter to maintain the website after my death for so long as is necessary; and

5.3.6 to identify and copy and preserve in one place all files which my Trustees [or Literary Executors] believe could be of interest or use to individuals, organisations or public bodies or any such file where interest has been expressed in my work and enquire of such individuals, organisations or bodies whether they wish to receive copies of some or all of them and to provide copies either in hardcopy or in digital form as may be requested; and

5.3.7 to collect all royalties and payments of every kind made in respect of my Digital Property and after paying all administrative and other expenses necessary to carry out the terms of this bequest to transfer the net proceeds [to my Trustees] to hold on the trusts of clause 5.4; and

5.3.8 to do all other things that are necessary for the performance of the above tasks or ought reasonably to be done in connection with or in addition to them.

5.4 SUBJECT TO clause 5.3 my Trustees [or Literary Executors] shall HOLD my Digital Property TOGETHER WITH all royalties and other income derived from them for the benefit absolutely of such of them my son [name] and my son [name] and my daughter [name] as shall survive me and if more than one in equal shares and it is my WISH but without imposing a binding obligation that together my said sons and daughter will take responsibility for the body of my Digital Property including taking responsibility for the ongoing storage of my archived work and the ongoing maintenance of my website www… so as to preserve my posthumous reputation.

5.5 My Trustees [*or* my Literary Executors] shall not be liable for any loss sustained in the exercise of the above tasks, discretions or duties and any such loss so sustained shall instead be borne by the Digital Property or in case of deficiency of such assets by my general residuary estate.

As to the appointment of literary executors and provision for the cost of obtaining a separate grant, see **9.2** and Precedent 9K.

Cryptocurrencies such as bitcoin can be enormously valuable, but present unique problems for personal representatives and beneficiaries. People owning bitcoin (and similar currencies) do so through a digital wallet. A bitcoin wallet is a device or program that can interact with the bitcoin blockchain. Although it is common to think of these wallets 'storing' bitcoins, a bitcoin wallet actually represents cryptographic control of a blockchain address.

Each bitcoin wallet contains a set of secret numbers, or private keys, corresponding to the user's blockchain address book. These keys are used to sign bitcoin transactions, effectively giving the user control over the bitcoins in that address. The main types are desktop wallets, mobile wallets, web wallets and hardware wallets. Anyone who has the private key can access the wallet, but private keys cannot be recovered once they are lost or forgotten. That means that without those keys, people who are entitled to inherit cryptocurrency cannot access it. Obviously, it is not appropriate to include details of keys in wills. However, those in possession of such assets need to consider how their heirs will get the details.

Options include writing the details of their keys on a piece of paper, and storing it in a safe place. There are platforms which store details and will disclose those details to persons who can prove entitlement. However, these platforms are not popular as they are a consistent target for hackers. There are companies which, essentially, allow people to lock their crypto keys within several layers of other private keys, which can then be dispersed across several different people. While this technology is supposed to make inheriting cryptocurrencies easier, it can also lead to some elaborate procedures.

The only thing that an adviser can do is alert clients to the danger of valuable assets becoming inaccessible after death. Subject to that, any cryptocurrency not specifically given away at death will potentially pass to those entitled to residue, just like any other asset not specifically given in the will. If the testator wishes to leave cryptocurrency to a specific beneficiary, a gift along the lines of Precedent 12Q can be included in a will, as long as the testator remembers to make appropriate plans outside the will to ensure the cryptocurrency can be unlocked by the beneficiary. Such plans may involve entrusting details of the crypto key to more than one person, that may or may not be an executor, and for security it is better if such details are dispersed among several people, none of whom can unlock the cryptocurrency without the co-operation of the others.

12.1.6 Miscellaneous specific legacies

12Q GIFT OF BITCOIN (OR OTHER CRYPTOCURRENCY)

I GIVE to [name] absolutely the balance of my [bitcoin] cryptocurrency account.[*]

[*] See text in **12.1.5** warning of the need to make plans outside the will to ensure the cryptocurrency can be unlocked by the beneficiary.

12R GIFT OF A STAMP COLLECTION

I GIVE to [name] absolutely my collection of stamps together with all albums catalogues accessories loose stamps covers and other materials appertaining thereto [to a value not exceeding £ ...] [AND I DIRECT that if there be a disagreement such value shall be ascertained in such manner as my personal representatives shall determine] [AND I DIRECT that the value to be taken shall be the value agreed with HM Revenue & Customs for probate purposes].

Words in a precedent simply referring to 'value agreed for probate purposes' would in any event mean the valuation ultimately agreed with HM Revenue & Customs (see *Re De Lisle's Will Trusts* [1968] 1 WLR 322).

12S GIFT OF MONEY SECURED BY AN ASSURANCE POLICY ON TESTATOR'S LIFE

I GIVE to [name] absolutely all moneys due under the policy of assurance on my life with policy number ... effected with the ... Life Assurance Society including all bonuses and other sums payable in respect thereof [SUBJECT TO any charge on the said policy as there may be at the date of my death].

The words in brackets are not strictly necessary since Administration of Estates Act 1925, section 35 states that, in the absence of any indication or provision to the contrary, property or an interest in property charged with the payment of money has to bear that charge. An expression of contrary intention may be inserted, but it must state from what property the charge is to be paid, and must show how the charge is to be met between the specific donee and the residuary estate. A direction may be included to pay any charge out of residue. Life policies and shares are frequently used as security for loans and may be subject to such charges (see *Re Turner* [1938] 1 Ch 593). Furthermore, a charge may arise where a testator makes a gift of land contracted to be purchased but dies before completion. In such a case there is a charge on the property in respect of any unpaid purchase moneys.

12T CLAUSE EXONERATING SPECIFIC BEQUESTS FROM CHARGES

I DIRECT that if any property being the subject matter of any specific gift under this my will or any codicil hereto is subject at the date of my death to any charge for the payment of money then such charge shall be discharged primarily out of my residuary estate in exoneration of the property so charged.

12U   GIFT OF PROCEEDS OF PREMIUM SAVINGS BONDS AND PRIZES AWARDED SINCE THE TESTATOR'S DEATH

I DIRECT my Trustees to cash all premium savings bonds in my name at the time of my death and I GIVE the net proceeds thereof together with any prize moneys arising therefrom since the date of my death to [Beneficiary].

Premium bonds are not transferable but remain eligible to win prizes for up to 1 year from the date of the holder's death.

12.2   GENERAL LEGACIES

A general legacy is a gift of money or property to be provided out of the testator's general estate, whether or not the subject matter forms part of that estate at the testator's death. A general legacy is not made specific merely by the fact that the property referred to actually forms part of the testator's estate at death. The executors may, but need not, use the existing property to satisfy the legacy, or they may prefer to purchase other property in the same form out of the residue. A legacy is general unless the subject matter is referred to as belonging to the testator or otherwise defined to exclude the possibility of a replacement fitting the same description.

12V   IMMEDIATE LEGACY CARRYING INTEREST FROM DEATH

I GIVE to [name] the sum of £ ... AND I DIRECT that the said sum shall be paid to [name] as soon as is practicable after my death in priority to all other legacies herein or in any codicil hereto together with interest from the date of my death to the date of payment such interest being paid at the rate of [2]% above the Bank of England rate that had effect at the end of the day on which I died.

12W   LEGACY TO INDIVIDUAL

I GIVE to [name] of [address] the sum of £ ... [free of inheritance tax] [to be paid ... months after my death].

The time for payment does not place any obligation on the executors to pay the legacy within the executor's year, but interest on the legacy runs from the date on which the legacy is due to be paid (see Chapter 19). Unless otherwise specified by the will, the rate of interest payable on a general legacy is that specified by Civil Procedure Rules, Practice Direction 40A, paragraph 15, being the basic rate payable for the time being for funds held in court. At the time of writing, the rate was 1.688%.

12X LEGACIES GIVEN BY REFERENCE TO A SCHEDULE

I GIVE to each person or institution in the schedule following this clause such sum as appears opposite each name in the second column thereof AND I DECLARE that the receipt of the treasurer or other proper officer for the time being of any institution named in the said schedule shall be a sufficient discharge to my Trustees in respect of the legacy herein bequeathed to it.

SCHEDULE	
Name of Legatee	*Amount of Legacy*
....	....

12Y POWER TO TRUSTEES TO POSTPONE PAYMENT OF LEGACIES

I DECLARE THAT my Trustees shall have full power to postpone the payment of any legacy made in this my will or in any codicil hereto for so long as they shall in their absolute discretion think fit but not exceeding [three] years from the date of my death ALWAYS PROVIDED THAT any such postponed legacy shall carry interest from [the date of] [twelve months after] my death until payment at the rate of [2]% above the Bank of England rate at [the time of] [twelve months after] my death.

12Z LEGACY TO INDIVIDUAL LEGATEE WITH SUBSTITUTION CLAUSE IN THE EVENT OF LAPSE

I GIVE the sum of £ ... [free of inheritance tax] to [name] PROVIDED THAT if [name] shall die before me or if this gift shall fail for any reason then I GIVE the said sum to [substitute beneficiary's name].

12AA LEGACY TO MINOR

I GIVE to [minor] the sum of £ ... [free of inheritance tax] PROVIDED THAT:

(a)   If the said [minor] shall at the time when the above legacy is payable have attained the age of sixteen years then the receipt of the said [minor] shall be a full and proper discharge to my Trustees for the payment of the same.

   (b)   If at the time when the above legacy is paid the said [minor] shall not have attained the age of sixteen years then the receipt of their parent or guardian shall be a full and proper discharge to my Trustees for the payment of the same.

When property is given to a minor outside a trust, proper directions should be given for the discharge of the testator's personal representatives.

Where the legacy is small it is easier to allow the minor to sign a receipt for the moneys, provided they are of reasonable age. If the minor is too young or the legacy is large, the minor's parent or guardian can provide a receipt. Under Children Act 1989, section 3, 'parental responsibility' is defined to include, in particular, the right to receive or recover in their own name, for the benefit of the child, property of whatever description and wherever situated which the child is entitled to receive or recover.

Testators may not be happy for a parent to give such a receipt (e.g. where a divorced spouse is leaving property to children of the former marriage). In such a case, it is preferable to provide for trustees to hold the funds. Alternatively, the personal representative may be directed to open a building society account in the name of the minor and to give the pass book to the minor.

As long as the legacy is absolute, if the legacy is a substantial sum and no directions for its payment are given, the personal representatives may:

(i)   if they are the trustees of the will, retain the legacy together with accrued interest upon trust until the minor attains their majority; or

(ii)   pay the money into court under Trustee Act 1925, section 63; or

(iii) appoint trustees to hold the money until the minor's majority under Administration of Estates Act 1925, section 42.

12BB   SUBSTANTIAL VESTED LEGACY TO MINOR WITH PROVISION FOR MAKING CAPITAL AND INCOME AVAILABLE FOR MAINTENANCE, EDUCATION, ADVANCEMENT OR OTHER BENEFIT

      I GIVE to [name] the sum of £ ... [free of inheritance tax] and I DECLARE that if the said [name] shall not have attained the age of eighteen years at the time of my death my Trustees may invest the same as they in their absolute discretion think fit as if beneficially entitled thereto and I DECLARE that my Trustees may advance the whole or any part of the said sum and the whole or any part of the income therefrom in such manner as they shall in their absolute discretion think proper for the maintenance education advancement or other benefit of the said [name] including the provision of an allowance for them during their minority and I FURTHER DECLARE that if all or any part of the said sum together with the income therefrom shall not be applied during the minority of the said [name] as aforesaid then the said sum or so much thereof as shall not have been so applied shall be paid to the said [name] upon their attaining the age of eighteen years ALWAYS PROVIDED THAT if the said [name] shall die before attaining the age of eighteen years the money held by my Trustees under this provision shall be paid to the personal representatives of the said [name].

The declarations to this clause are not strictly necessary because the trustees would, in the absence of contrary intention, be empowered by statute to invest the sum and make both capital and income available as expressed anyway. Likewise, the proviso is also not necessary because, as a vested gift, the proceeds would in any event be payable to the personal representatives in these circumstances.

12CC LEGACY OF A CAPITAL SUM FOR THE EDUCATION OF CHILDREN

I GIVE the sum of £ ... (the 'Fund') [free of inheritance tax] to my Trustees to invest the same in any investments hereby or by statute authorised with full power to vary and transpose the same and to hold such investments and the income thereof upon the following trusts:

(a) UPON TRUST to apply the income from the Fund at the sole discretion of my Trustees for the education of my children who shall be under the age of [twenty-five] years or any one or more of them to the exclusion of the other or others in such manner and in such amounts as my Trustees shall in their absolute discretion think fit.

(b) UPON TRUST in so far as the income of the Fund proves to be insufficient for the purposes of the education of my said children to apply so much of the capital thereof as my Trustees in their absolute discretion think necessary for the education of my children.

(c) For a period of twenty-one years from the date of my death my Trustees may invest any surplus income from the fund in any authorised investments to be held as augmentations to the said Fund and after the expiration of the said twenty-one years all surplus income shall be deemed to be and distributed as part of my residuary estate.

(d) I DECLARE that my Trustees may provide out of the said fund such books of reference of any educational nature and all such instruments and other things as may be reasonably required by my said children in relation to such education and as my Trustees in their absolute discretion think fit AND I FURTHER DIRECT that the term education shall be interpreted for the purposes of the trusts hereunder to include training articles pupillage or apprenticeship in relation to any trade, profession or vocation.

(e)   When all my children shall have attained the age of [twenty-five] years or have died under that age the said Fund or as much thereof as has not been expended in the execution of the foregoing trusts shall fall into and form part of my residuary estate.

Note: As regards paragraph (c), since the coming into force of the Perpetuities and Accumulations Act 2009 on 6 April 2010, there is no particular reason why accumulation of income should be restricted to a maximum of 21 years. See Chapter 23.

12DD LEGACY TO CHILDREN EXPRESSLY INCLUDING AN ILLEGITIMATE CHILD

I GIVE to each of my children (including my child [name]) the sum of £ ... [free of inheritance tax].

The expressions 'child', 'son', 'daughter' and 'issue' now *prima facie* include illegitimate and adopted children, sons, daughters or issue. However, an express provision is advisable, especially where there could be a doubt as to paternity.

12EE   LEGACY CONTINGENT ON ATTAINING THE AGE OF EIGHTEEN OR TWENTY-ONE OR EARLIER MARRIAGE [FORMATION OF CIVIL PARTNERSHIP]

I GIVE the sum of £ ... [free of inheritance tax] to [name] if [he] [she] shall attain the age of [state contingency age] years [or marry under that age and in the latter event the receipt of the said [name] shall be sufficient discharge to my Trustees] [and I DIRECT that such sum shall carry interest at the rate of [5]% per annum from my death until the said [name] attains the age of [state contingency age] years [or marries under that age]] [and I DECLARE that for the purpose of this gift any reference to marriage [includes entering into a civil partnership] [includes only a marriage [or entering into a civil partnership] to [or with] a person of the opposite sex]].

As a result of the changes introduced by the Finance Act 2006, any continuing trust created by a contingent gift is subject to inheritance tax in the form of anniversary and exit charges, unless the beneficiary is the testator's own child and the age selected is no greater than 18. See Chapter 27.

12FF   LEGACIES TO TWO PERSONS CONTINGENTLY ON THEIR ATTAINING THE AGE OF EIGHTEEN OR TWENTY-ONE WITH SURVIVORSHIP PROVISION

I GIVE to each of [name] and [name] the sum of £ ... [free of inheritance tax] contingently on each attaining the age of [eighteen] [twenty-one] years and in the event of either of them dying under the said age the legacy hereby given to the one so dying with all interest accruing thereon shall be paid to the survivor of them on [his] [her] attaining the said age PROVIDED THAT if both of them shall die before attaining the said age then the legacies herein and all interest thereon shall fall into and be distributed as part of my residuary estate.

12GG LEGACIES WITH PROVISION WHERE SOME OF THE LEGATEES CANNOT BE FOUND

I GIVE the sum of £ ... [free of inheritance tax] to each of my [nephews] [names] PROVIDED THAT if the whereabouts of any such [nephew] cannot be ascertained by my Trustees by such means as they in their absolute discretion feel appropriate and such [nephew] does not claim the said legacy within two years of my death then the sum or sums bequeathed to any such [nephew] or those [nephews] shall fall into and form part of my residuary estate and I DECLARE that the extent and nature of the enquiries made or to be made by my Trustees shall not be open to challenge by any Beneficiary or potential Beneficiary hereunder or by any person or body.

Note: See *Hawkes v Baldwin* (1838) 9 Sim 355.

12.2.1 Nil rate band legacy

It is common for parties to a marriage or civil partnership to want to leave the bulk of their estates to the surviving spouse or civil partner, to take advantage of the exemption from inheritance tax for a surviving spouse. They may also want to make use of the unused portion of their inheritance tax nil rate band to give either a pecuniary legacy direct to their children and/or issue, or to make a gift to a discretionary trust for the benefit of the surviving spouse, children and issue, thus allowing the children and issue access to funds in case of need before the death of the surviving spouse or civil partner. Formula clauses are normally used so that the amount passing under the terms of such a gift is an amount equal to the nil rate band at the date of death, reduced to take account of:

(i) lifetime chargeable transfers made by the testator within the 7 years before death;
(ii) gifts to non-exempt beneficiaries made in the will or under the intestacy rules;
(iii) property passing outside the will (e.g. by survivorship or as a result of a nomination);
(iv) property treated as part of the estate under the reservation of benefit rules.

Some precedents set out in detail the matters to be taken into account in determining the size of the gift, but this makes for an unwieldy clause. It is preferable to use a short clause which achieves exactly the same result and is much simpler.

12HH NIL RATE BAND LEGACY

(a)   This clause shall not take effect unless the gift to my [spouse] [civil partner] made in clause [...] takes effect and qualifies in its entirety for exemption under Inheritance Tax Act 1984, section 18 (or any modification or re-enactment of it) (or but for the existence of this clause would do so).

(b)   In this clause the 'Nil Rate Sum' means the largest sum of cash which could be given on the trusts of this clause without any inheritance tax becoming due in respect of the transfer of the value of my estate which I am deemed to make immediately before my death [or the sum of £ ... whichever is the smaller].

(c)   I GIVE the Nil Rate Sum to my Trustees UPON TRUST to invest it in exercise of their powers of investment and to hold it and the property which currently represents it UPON TRUST absolutely for such of my children living at my death as reach the age of [...] and if more than one in equal shares PROVIDED that if any child of mine dies (in my lifetime or after my death) before attaining a vested interest but leaves a child or children alive at or born after my own death [who reach the age of [...] [or marry] [or form a civil partnership] under that age] then such child or children shall take absolutely and if more than one in equal shares the share which that child of mine would have taken on attaining a vested interest.

[(d)   I REQUIRE and DECLARE that my Trustees shall claim the benefit of any unused inheritance tax nil rate band to which my estate may be entitled and that the value of that unused nil rate band shall be taken into account in arriving at the Nil Rate Sum]

Notes:

(1) This form is not normally suitable if there is any possibility that property eligible for inheritance tax business or agricultural relief may be included in the residue of the estate. Inheritance Tax Act 1984, section 39A provides that if it is, the benefit of the relief has to be apportioned over all the gifts made in the will. The effect is that substantially more than was originally intended may pass under the terms of this gift. The surviving spouse may then have inadequate funds available. In a case where such property may be available at death, the solution is either to make a specific gift of the property eligible for relief (in which case the inheritance tax relief attaches only to that property), or to 'cap' the size of the pecuniary legacy by stating that it is not to exceed the value of the nil rate band at the date of death. It should also be kept in mind that a 'cap' might be desirable in a will made by a surviving spouse or civil partner who has the benefit of a transferable nil rate band

because otherwise the amount that passes under the definition of 'Nil Rate Sum' might be anything up to 100% more than the actual nil rate band threshold at the time of the testator's death. As to the use of the transferable nil rate band, see Chapters 27 and 30, and as to the use of the nil rate band to create a discretionary trust, see also Chapter 18 and Precedent 18H and the notes thereto.

(2) If issue are substituted for a deceased child, any continuing trust created by this gift is subject to inheritance tax in the form of anniversary and exit charges.

(3) Since the benefit of any transferred nil rate band has to be claimed, it is sensible to make clear that the testator wants this to be done (see *The Woodland Trust v Loring and Others* [2014] EWCA Civ 1314; [2013] EWHC 4400 (Ch), where the Court of Appeal accepted that the decision whether or not to claim was at the discretion of the executors unless the will provided otherwise).

Formula clauses are also used where a testator wishes to make gifts within the nil rate band to friends or family and to leave the residue to charity. It is important to explain to the testator that the use of the formula imposes a top limit on the amount that can pass. If lifetime gifts have been made, very little or nothing may pass. If gifts of specific assets are made in addition to the formula legacy, the result may be that nothing can pass to the pecuniary legatee. See *Royal Commonwealth Society for the Blind v Beasant and Another* [2021] EWHC 2315 (Ch), where exactly this happened. It is helpful to have a clear explanation in writing of the risks to ensure that the disappointed pecuniary legatee does not allege that the testator misunderstood the effect of the clause.

12.3   DEMONSTRATIVE LEGACIES

A demonstrative legacy is, in essence, similar to a general legacy but in addition contains a direction as to which property or fund is to be used first to satisfy the legacy.

The gift does not adeem merely because the fund or property specified is insufficient to meet the legacy. If there is a shortfall in the specified property then the remainder of the legacy is payable out of the testator's general personal estate, and that remainder has the same priority as other general legacies.

12II   DEMONSTRATIVE LEGACY

I GIVE to [name] the sum of £ ... to be paid primarily out of my [description of account] account [number] with the ... Bank plc PROVIDED THAT if there are insufficient funds in the said account to pay the whole of the legacy herein then any shortfall shall be payable out of my residuary estate.

12.4   GIFTS TO A DEBTOR

Where a testator leaves money to a person who owes a debt to them, the amount of the debt is set off against the legacy and the amount of the legacy actually paid reduced accordingly. This does not apply where the bequest is a specific legacy unless it is of a sum of money.

Any of the following gifts may be subject to set-off:

- a pecuniary legacy;
- a gift of all or part of the residuary personal estate;
- a gift of part or all of the residuary estate where it includes either personalty or the proceeds of sale of realty or both;
- a specific legacy if (and only if) of money;
- a gift of personalty subject to a partial intestacy;
- the proceeds of sale under a trust for sale (although the proceeds of sale of personalty are applied to discharge debts prior to the application of the proceeds of sale of realty).

The debt must be brought into account against all such interests under a will, regardless of how they are acquired. Thus, interests purchased from other beneficiaries and reversionary interests are also subject to the rule of set-off.

Only debts which are due to the testator personally and payable at the time the legacy is payable may be deducted. Debts due from a partnership in which the legatee is a partner are not deductible from the legacy.

Included in the debts which must be brought into account are the following:

- debts which are statute-barred when the testator dies;
- debts of which the testator was an equitable owner only;
- debts due from an estate of which the legatee is an executor.

12JJ   RELEASE TO A DEBTOR OF A DEBT

I FORGIVE AND RELEASE to [debtor] all moneys now owing by them to me as at the date of this my will.

12KK   RELEASE OF DEBTS – INCLUDING FUTURE DEBTS

I RELEASE [debtor] from all debts owed by them to me at the date of my death whether of principal or interest and I DIRECT that any mortgages bonds or other securities in respect of any such debt shall be cancelled and released to [debtor] as soon as practicable after my death and my personal representative shall execute and deliver to [debtor] all necessary receipts reconveyances or reassignments AND I DECLARE that if the said [debtor] shall fail to survive me then this provision shall take effect as if the said [debtor] died immediately after my death and the benefit of the same shall pass to [debtor's] personal representatives accordingly.

A provision forgiving or releasing all debts due to the testator from creditors generally should be avoided because this may give rise to unintended problems in respect of debentures held by the testator, balance(s) at the testator's bank and the effect on secured and unsecured debts.

12LL RELEASE OF MORTGAGE DEBT TO THE MORTGAGOR

I FORGIVE AND RELEASE to [mortgagor] absolutely all sums of principal and interest both due or accruing due at the date of my death and secured on [property] by a mortgage dated … and made between [parties] and I DIRECT my Trustees at the cost to my residuary estate as soon as practicable after my death to execute in favour of the said [mortgagor] a full discharge of the said mortgage and of all claims thereunder and to deliver up to them all title deeds and other documents held by me in respect thereof.

12MM PROVISION FOR ACCOUNT IN RESPECT OF RELEASE OF DEBT

I DIRECT that where any debts or other sums of money due or accruing due to my estate from the said [debtor] have been released by the provisions of this my will or any codicil hereto the said sums together with interest thereon from the date of my death [to the date of final distribution of my residuary estate] at the rate of […]% per annum shall be brought into account as against the share of my residuary estate [hereby given to [debtor]] [in which the said [debtor] takes a life interest hereunder].

12NN DECLARATION THAT GIFTS SHOULD NOT BE BROUGHT INTO ACCOUNT

I DECLARE that [name] shall not be liable to repay or bring into account any sums given to [him] [her] during my lifetime and my personal representatives shall make no claim against the said [name] or [his] [her] estate.

12.5   GIFTS TO AN EXECUTOR

There is a presumption that any gift made by will to a person appointed as an executor is given to that person by reason of that office. The presumption may be rebutted, for example, by a statement in the gift that it is given to the executor as a relative or friend. The type of gift, for example, a gift of residue or a gift over after the death of a tenant for life, may also be sufficient to rebut the presumption.

Where a legacy is given to a person as executor, there is a rebuttable presumption that they are not entitled to the benefit of the gift unless they take up the office.

Legacies attached to the office of executor rank equally with other ordinary legacies and are therefore subject to abatement and tax.

Where a testator has sought to make a lifetime gift to a person and the gift has failed for technical reasons, the appointment of that person as executor or trustee of the will may perfect the gift, provided it can be shown that the testator had a continuing intention to make the gift (see *Strong v Bird* (1874) LR 18 Eq 315, and *Re Ralli's Marriage Settlement* [1964] Ch 288).

A trustee who acts in a professional capacity or a trust corporation may receive 'reasonable remuneration' if the co-trustee(s) consent(s) in writing, even if there is no charging clause (Trustee Act 2000, section 29).

12OO LEGACY TO EXECUTOR AND TRUSTEE

> I GIVE to each of my Trustees [names] [free of inheritance tax] the sum of [amount] [provided that they prove my will and act in the trusts thereof] [whether or not they prove my will and act in the trust hereof].

12.6   GIFTS TO EMPLOYEES

Where the legatees are described in the will by reference to their employment, then, *prima facie*, those fitting the description at the date of the will, and not the date of the testator's death, take the gift.

Where a testator makes a gift to their employees as a class, rather than as named individuals, the members of that class are ascertained as at the time of the will, rather than at the testator's death, unless the gift provides otherwise.

12PP LEGACY TO HOUSEKEEPER OR CARER

I GIVE to my [housekeeper] [carer] [name] if in my service at the time of my death [and not under notice to leave whether given by them or by me or on my behalf] the sum of £ ... [free of inheritance tax] in addition to any sums then owing to them for wages or otherwise.

The words 'at the time of my death' exclude a person who leaves the testator's service between the making of the will and the testator's death.

12.7 GIFTS OF UNDIVIDED SHARES OF PERSONALTY

The rules relating to the co-ownership of personalty differ significantly from those governing realty. Law of Property Act 1925, sections 34 to 36 and Settled Land Act 1925, section 36 have no application to personalty. The result is that legal joint tenancies and tenancies in common can co-exist, although a *chose in action* is an exception to the general rule and cannot be held under a legal tenancy in common.

12QQ BEQUEST OF UNDIVIDED SHARE IN PERSONAL PROPERTY

I GIVE to [name] all my share and interest in any [racehorse, boat, etc] owned by me at the date of my death as tenant in common with [co-owner] [or with any other person].

Chapter 13

Gifts of Businesses

A small business may be run through the medium of a private company, or as an unincorporated business either in partnership or by person. When planning how best to deal with the business on death, you need to consider a number of matters with the client.

13.1   BUSINESS PROPERTY RELIEF

Whichever business medium the owner of the business adopts, inheritance tax business property relief is normally available at 100% on the value of the deceased's interest at death, so long as the requirements of Inheritance Tax Act 1984, sections 103 to 144 are met.

Inheritance tax relief is available at 100% on the following:

- a business (Inheritance Tax Act 1984, section 105(1)(a));
- an interest in a business (section 105(1)(a));
- unquoted shares which gave the transferor control of the company (section 105(1)(ba)); unquoted shares include those dealt in on the Alternative Investment Market;
- any unquoted shares in a company (section 105(1)(bb)).

It is available at 50% on:

- listed shares or securities which gave the transferor control of the company (section 105(1)(cc));
- any land or buildings, plant or machinery which immediately before the transfer was used by a partnership or by a company of which the deceased had control (section 105(1)(d)).

Relief is given on the net value of the business, which is stated in Inheritance Tax Act 1984, section 110(b) to be:

> the value of the assets used in the business (including goodwill) reduced by the aggregate amount of any liabilities incurred for the purposes of the business.

The value qualifying for relief cannot be increased by charging business debts on non-business property. Inheritance tax relief is not available on 'excepted assets'. An excepted asset is defined by section 112 as one which was neither:

(a)   used wholly or mainly for the purposes of the business concerned throughout the whole of the last two years [before death], nor

(b)   required at the time of the transfer for future use for those purposes.

This means that non-business assets (e.g. those appearing on the balance sheet but used personally by the deceased and the family) or excessive amounts of cash held within the business do not attract relief. Having said that, an active business must have cash, so having a positive bank account is not in itself an issue as long as it satisfies the section 112 test. However, cash in a business bank account may not belong to the business. For example, in the case of a company, it may represent money due to a director/shareholder as dividends declared but not yet paid, or salary, fees and bonus payments due to a director but not yet withdrawn. Similarly, cash may represent what is due to the director by way of money lent to the company. Such sums typically appear in a director's loan account as a current liability payable by the company, so reducing its net asset value upon which relief is *prima facie* given. Of course, the other side of the coin is that amounts due to a director, shown in the balance sheet but not yet paid, are treated as part of the director's personal estate.

There is an ownership requirement. Briefly, the deceased must have owned the assets for at least 2 years (section 106). Assets owned for less than 2 years do not normally qualify for relief, although there are special 'succession' provisions where a surviving spouse inherits business assets from a deceased spouse (section 108).

Section 105(3) provides that relief is not available if:

> the business ... consists wholly or mainly of one or more of the following, that is to say, dealing in stocks or shares, land or buildings or the making or holding of investments.

The question of whether a business is 'wholly or mainly' an investment business is one of fact to be decided by an intelligent business owner who would consider the use to which the asset was being put and the way it was being turned to account (see *Brander v RCC* [2009] UKFTT 101 (TC), [2009] SFTD 374, aff'd *RCC v Brander* [2010] UKUT 300 (TCC), [2010] STC 2666).

A series of cases has decided that taking an income from land is an investment activity. Holiday lettings, buy-to-let residential landlords, landlords of commercial properties, marinas, caravan sites, land let on grazing licences, do-it-yourself livery stables are all examples of businesses that are likely to fall foul of section 105(3).

Such businesses often offer additional services but the level of services will have to be very high to prevent the business being regarded as 'mainly' an investment business (e.g. *George and Another v IRC* [2003] EWCA Civ 1763, *McCall and Another v RCC* [2009] NICA 12, [2009] STC 990, *RCC v Lockyer and Another* [2013] UKUT 50 (TCC), *The Trustees of David Zetland Settlement v RCC* [2013] UKFTT 284 (TC) and *Executors of the Late Sheriff Graham Loudon Cox v RCC* [2020] UKFTT 442 (TC). Unusually in *The Personal Representatives of Graham (Deceased) v RCC* [2018] UKFTT 306 (TC), the services provided by a self-catering holiday business were accepted as being so truly exceptional that relief was available).

In *The Personal Representatives of Vigne (Deceased) v RCC* [2017] UKFTT 632 (TC), aff'd [2018] UKUT 0357 (TC), the taxpayer succeeded in claiming relief on a do-it-yourself livery stables which provided more services than is usual for such businesses. The First-tier Tribunal said it had no doubt that business offered significantly more than the mere right to occupy a particular parcel of land. Any objective observer who visited the site would have concluded that a business was being run from the land which provided services to those who kept their horses there. No properly informed observer could or would have said that the deceased was in the business of 'holding investments'. That would have been a wholly artificial analysis.

Because of the level of services provided, hotels and bed and breakfast establishments are not normally regarded as 'mainly' investment businesses. However, budget hotels providing very little in the way of services beyond the provision of a bedroom may be at risk as may 'hotels' providing accommodation for various groups, such as asylum seekers or vulnerable adults. The range of services provided in these businesses can vary enormously, and HM Revenue & Customs will examine them in detail to establish where they sit on the trading/investment spectrum (see HM Revenue & Customs, *Inheritance Tax Manual* at IHTM25277, available at www.hmrc.gov.uk/manuals/ihtmanual).

If a mixed business consists 'mainly' of one of the prohibited activities, no relief at all is available, not even on those parts which do not consist of prohibited activities.

By the same token, however, if the business consists 'mainly' of non-prohibited activities, relief is available on the whole business including those parts which comprise prohibited activities.

As a planning matter, it is sensible for taxpayers with 'mixed' businesses which are approaching the point at which they will consist mainly of prohibited activities to consider dividing activities into separate businesses. The businesses which consist of prohibited activities will not attract relief but they will not taint the safe businesses which will continue to attract relief.

The decision in *Trustees of the Nelson Dance Family Settlement v RCC* [2008] UKSPC SPC00682, [2008] STC (SCD) 792, confirmed in *RCC v Trustees of the Nelson Dance Family Settlement* [2009] EWHC 71 (Ch), is helpful here. It had been thought that business property relief was only available on the transfer of *a business* (including a part of a business capable of being a separate business), and not on transfers of mere business assets. However, the court held that relief was not restricted to transfers of whole businesses. It is possible to obtain relief on transfers of business assets. Hence where a business is approaching a point where it consists mainly of prohibited activities but has not yet reached that point, it will be possible to transfer assets out and obtain relief.

At the time of drafting a will it is not possible to know for certain whether a business which qualifies for relief at that time will still do so by the date of death: the rules may change; the nature of the business may change; the business may build up cash reserves which are not required for business purposes and which are therefore excepted assets not qualifying for relief under section 112. A client may wish to leave the business to issue if it qualifies for relief but to a spouse or civil partner if it does not. In such cases it is sensible to consider leaving the business to a discretionary trust. The trustees can assess the position at the date of death and make an appointment to spouse or civil partner or to issue depending on the availability of relief. Provided the appointment complies with the requirements of Inheritance Tax Act 1984, section 144, it will be read back into the will and treated as the deceased's disposition for inheritance tax purposes. If the value of the business is not certain to exceed the nil rate band, a pecuniary legacy should be left which is equal to the nil rate band to the discretionary trust in addition to the business to ensure that HM Revenue & Customs will rule on the availability of relief. It will not do so if no tax is at stake.

13.2   SUCCESSION PLANNING

When taking instructions for a will from someone who owns a business or an interest in a business, it is important to discuss the client's plans for dealing with the business after their death (and also a lasting power of attorney in case of sudden incapacity).

In the case of a sole trader, there may be an heir apparent to whom the business can be left; it is normally convenient to make the donee of the business a special executor of that part of the estate. If the donee is one of the testator's children, there may be difficulties achieving a distribution which satisfies all the children. Where the other assets are limited, it may be possible to make some provision for the others by giving one child an option to purchase the business at a reduced price, and using the proceeds to fund legacies for the other children. Alternatively, the business could be left to one child with a condition that a certain sum is paid to the other children within a stated period.

Where the testator is a partner in a business, any partnership deed or agreement must be consulted before drafting a gift concerning the business. It is also advisable to check that the partners are clear as to the ownership of assets used by the partnership. Are they partnership assets or are they owned by a partner personally? See *Ham v Bell and Others* [2016] EWHC 1791 (Ch) for an unfortunate example of a mistake as to who owned what.

The partnership agreement may provide that on the death of any partner, the surviving partners may buy the testator's interest in the partnership from their estate. From an inheritance tax perspective it is important that the deceased cannot be regarded as dying with a contract in place to sell the partnership interest to the surviving partners. This would lead to a loss of business property relief as the testator would be treated as dying entitled to the proceeds of sale rather than the business. HM Revenue & Customs has accepted that options and automatic accruer clauses do not constitute binding contracts for sale (see *Law Society Gazette*, 4 September 1996). To avoid argument after the death, the partnership agreement should deal with the basis of valuation of partnership assets. This may be the current market value at the date of the death (likely to be the most beneficial for the deceased's estate), or the historic value at which assets are carried in the partnership's accounts (likely to benefit the continuing partners). There is no presumption as to the basis. It is simply a matter of evidence of intention (see *White v Minnis and Another* [2000] EWCA Civ 149, [2001] Ch 393).

Where there is no deed or agreement, or where there is such a document but it contains no provisions for the death of a partner, then the death of any partner causes the dissolution of the partnership, and the amount due to the deceased partner for their interest must be paid to their personal representatives. This is not normally what the parties would want.

If the business in question is incorporated, the testator can leave their shareholding to whomever they choose, subject to any pre-emption rights contained in the articles of association. It is important to consider the articles when taking instructions for the will. If the client does not want to comply with the pre-emption rights, it may be possible to alter the articles. This requires a 75% majority. If the testator has a sufficiently large shareholding, they can do this alone. In other cases, the testator needs the support of other shareholders. Failure to alter the articles would mean that the testator's beneficiary would take the shares subject to the pre-emption rights (see *Cottrell v King and Another* [2004] EWHC 397 (Ch), [2005] WTLR 63).

'One-man' companies can cause severe difficulties when the only shareholder and director dies, unless the articles of association make suitable provision.

Companies with articles of association contained in Companies (Model Articles) Regulations 2008 (SI 2008/3229), Schedule 1, which came into effect on 1 October 2009, do not have a problem because the current article 17(2) says:

> In any case where, as a result of death, the company has no shareholders and no directors, the personal representatives of the last shareholder to have died have the right, by notice in writing, to appoint a person to be a director.

Companies with earlier articles have a problem unless an express article authorising appointment of directors was included. Without such an article there is no one to deal with the company's affairs until new shareholders are registered as members and can appoint new directors. For an example of the problems this can cause, see *Williams and Others v Russell Price Farm Services Ltd* [2020] EWHC 1088 (Ch).

It may be that the articles provide for the appointment by will of a permanent director to succeed the testator if the testator was a permanent director.

The following clauses need to be considered in the light of the trustees' powers to appoint agents and nominees under Trustee Act 2000, section 11.

13A   GIFT OF A SMALL BUSINESS

(a)   I GIVE to [name] all my business of … trading as [name of business] from the premises at [address[es]] to include [the said premises and] all plant machinery stocks vehicles tools computer and technology systems (together with all software and other intangible property including the rights to any domain name) and all other things employed or used in carrying on the said business together with the goodwill of the same and the benefits of all contracts entered into and all book debts due to the said business and together also with any cash at bank and cash in hand employed or used in carrying on the said business but subject in all respects to the liabilities of the said business.

(b)   In the event of any premises from which my business trades being held under a lease or tenancy agreement at the time of my death then the said [name] shall pay the rent due from time to time in respect of those premises and shall observe and perform the lessee's covenants under the said lease or tenancy agreement and shall keep my personal representatives and estate indemnified against all liability under the said lease or tenancy including any liability that may have arisen in my lifetime or from acts or omissions done or arising in my lifetime.

(c)   I APPOINT the said [name] as Special Executor of this my will to act only in respect of the said business and other property bequeathed to [name] by this clause and I direct that the inheritance tax attributed to the above gift (allowing for any reduction in value for inheritance tax purposes) and the expenses of obtaining a grant limited to such property shall be paid by the said [name].

Note: Where a gift is of a 'business', it is normally taken to include all the testator's interest in all the assets of the business, including business premises (see *Re Rhagg* [1938] Ch 828). See Appendix A1C for a complete will disposing of a business.

13B   GIFT TO TRUSTEES OF A BUSINESS UPON TRUST TO CARRY ON FOR A LIMITED PERIOD

I GIVE to my Trustees all my business of … trading as [name of business] from the premises at [address[es]] to include [the said premises and] all plant machinery stocks vehicles tools computer and technology systems (together with all software and other intangible property including the rights to any domain name) and all other things employed or used in carrying on the said business together with the goodwill of the same and the benefits of all contracts entered into and all book debts due to the said business and together with any cash at bank and cash in hand employed or used in carrying on the said business but subject in all respects to the liabilities of the said business upon the following trusts:

(a)   TO CARRY ON the said business and/or any other business on the said premises or any other suitable premises for so long and in such manner and on such terms as they in their sole discretion may think fit and subject thereto without being liable to my estate for any loss arising therefrom.

(b)   UPON TRUST to sell the said business including any premises used in connection with the said business as a going concern together with the goodwill thereof and all the then existing assets thereof or such of them as my Trustees think fit but subject to the liabilities thereof or such of them as my Trustees think fit upon such terms as they may in their sole discretion think proper [and thereafter the proceeds of sale of the said business shall fall into and become part of my residuary estate].

13C   TRUSTS OF NET PROFITS UNTIL SALE OF BUSINESS AND PROCEEDS OF SALE

I DECLARE that my Trustees shall stand possessed of the said business and the net annual profits thereof after payment of all the expenses and liabilities of the same until sale of the said business as aforesaid and after the said sale shall also stand possessed of the net proceeds of sale thereof and of any other moneys arising therefrom or in connection therewith and of the income of such proceeds of sale and other moneys UPON TRUST to pay such annual profits or income as the case may be to my [spouse] [civil partner] during [his] [her] life and after [his] [her] death as to the said business and the said annual profits or (as the case may be) the said proceeds of sale and other moneys and the income thereof respectively UPON TRUST, etc.

13D   PROVISION FOR CHILD OF TESTATOR TO TAKE ON BUSINESS ON PAYMENT TO TRUSTEES

(a)   I DECLARE that if any child of mine shall give notice to my Trustees within [three] months of my death of his or her wish to carry on my said business and shall pay to my Trustees the sum of £ ... such sum if not paid at once to be paid within a period not exceeding [two] years from the date of my death and to bear interest at the rate of [...]% per annum then my Trustees shall transfer the business as aforesaid including any premises but subject to all liabilities of the business to my said child and my Trustees shall stand possessed of the said sum of £ ... and any interest thereon as and when the same shall be received upon the following trusts ...

(b)   I FURTHER DECLARE that where more than one of my children wish to carry on my business and give notice to my Trustees as hereinbefore prescribed then in the absence of any agreement between or among my children the eldest of such children shall be entitled to the transfer of the business to his or her name on the making of the payments as aforesaid and in priority to and to the exclusion of my other children.

13E   POWER TO TRUSTEES TO CARRY ON BUSINESS WHERE THERE IS A TRUST FOR SALE

I DECLARE that my Trustees shall have full power to carry on my business of ... at ... and to postpone the sale and conversion thereof into money for so long as they shall think fit until such time as the same may be sold either as a going concern or otherwise and that during any period when the business is being carried on by my Trustees they shall be free from control or interference from any person or persons beneficially entitled to the said business or the proceeds of sale thereof under this my will.

13F   POWER FOR WILLING TRUSTEES TO CARRY ON TESTATOR'S BUSINESS WHERE OTHER TRUSTEES REFUSE

I DECLARE that should any one or more of my Trustees be unwilling to carry on my business then the other or others of my Trustees may carry on such business and may exercise alone all powers authorities and discretions hereby conferred on my Trustees in relation to carrying on the said business or the winding up or sale of the said business.

13G   PROVISION OF SALARY FOR TRUSTEES MANAGING BUSINESS

I DECLARE that any one or more of my Trustees who act as manager or manageress of my business aforesaid shall be entitled to [a salary of £ ... per annum] [such salary as may be agreed upon by my Trustees for the time being] throughout the period during which he she or they shall so act without being liable to account to my estate in respect thereof.

13H   PROVISION FOR EXERCISE OF POWERS THOUGH TRUSTEES INTERESTED IN BUSINESS

All or any of the above powers hereinbefore granted to my Trustees shall be exercisable and may be exercised by any of my Trustees notwithstanding that he or she may be interested as a partner in the said business or as a Beneficiary under this my will.

13I   INDEMNITY TO TRUSTEES CARRYING ON BUSINESS

I DIRECT that each and every one of my Trustees concerned in the running of my business shall be fully and effectively indemnified from my estate in respect of any personal loss or liability arising from the carrying on of the said business and I DECLARE that none of my Trustees shall be liable to my estate or any part thereof for any loss arising from the carrying on of the said business.

Chapter 14

Gifts of Land

14.1 GENERAL

Before drafting any provision dealing with land, the will drafter must check the exact nature of the testator's interest in the property by reference to the title deeds and/or official copy entries. It is also important to ascertain whether the testator has power to dispose of the land.

The Trusts of Land and Appointment of Trustees Act 1996 came into force on 1 January 1997. The Act does not abolish strict settlements, but no new settlements can be created on or after 1 January 1997. Settlements which were in existence at the commencement of the Act continue to be governed by the Settled Land Act 1925. Trusts for sale of land became trusts of land, whether they were created before or after the commencement of the Act. Trusts for sale are not abolished by the Act and they may still be appropriate where, for example, a testator wants an early sale or where land is intended to be used as an investment, and not for occupation by the beneficiaries.

The Act introduces a single system of trusts of land, which replaces the strict settlement and trust for sale.

Section 4 of the Act provides that where a will contains an express trust for the sale of land there is an implied power for trustees to postpone sale.

14A   ABSOLUTE GENERAL GIFT OF ALL FREEHOLD PROPERTY

I DEVISE all my estate or interest in all my freehold property where ever situate including any property over which I may have any general power of disposition by will to [name] absolutely.

Where the subject matter of the gift is referred to as 'my land' or by some other generic term the gift is construed to include leasehold estates, unless a contrary intention appears (see Chapter 24).

If there is no direction as to the payment of tax, then inheritance tax on the land is a testamentary expense and payable from the residuary estate. This general rule can be stated expressly for clarity as follows.

14B   SPECIFIC GIFT OF FREEHOLD LAND (FREE FROM INHERITANCE TAX)

I GIVE to [name] in fee simple absolutely my freehold property situate at and known as … in the county of … [or my freehold property registered at the Land Registry under Title No … and known as …] and I DIRECT that any inheritance tax payable on my death in respect of the property shall be payable out of my residuary estate in exoneration of the said property.

If the testator wishes to vary the statutory rule, the following clause can be used to throw the burden of tax onto the beneficiary.

14C   SPECIFIC GIFT OF FREEHOLD LAND (SUBJECT TO INHERITANCE TAX)

I DEVISE to [name] in fee simple my freehold property situate and known as … in the county of … [or my freehold property registered at the Land Registry under Title No … and known as …] and I direct that any inheritance tax payable on my death in respect of such property shall be borne by the property and not by my residuary estate.

14D   DECLARATION AS TO VESTING COSTS

I DECLARE that all costs and fees relating to the vesting transfer and the registration of title to this gift in the name of [name] shall be payable out of my residuary estate.

Unless a will states otherwise, the costs of assenting land to a specific beneficiary are a testamentary expense payable from the residuary estate (although this is not the case for settled land). All assents of property with an unregistered title following a death are now subject to compulsory registration at the Land Registry. Who is liable for the fees payable on compulsory first registration in the absence of an express direction?

The general principle established by *Sharp v Lush* (1879) 10 ChD 468 is that the estate must bear expenses that are incidental to the proper performance of the duties of the personal representatives.

The obligation to apply for first registration following the assent falls on the specific legatee as the transferee. In *Re Grosvenor, Grosvenor v Grosvenor* [1916] 2 Ch 375, it was held that after the executors had assented to a specific gift, any further costs were to be borne by the specific beneficiary even though they were the costs of vesting the property in him. In that case, the asset to be transferred was shares which had to be vested in the beneficiary by a transfer.

Applying the above, it would seem that the fees payable on compulsory first registration are not incidental to the proper performance of the duties of the personal representatives and should be borne by the beneficiary.

Unless the will states otherwise, a specific beneficiary will be liable for outgoings, such as utility bills, that arise between the testator's date of death and the assent of the property to the beneficiary (*Re Rooke* [1933] Ch 970). The beneficiary will also usually be entitled to any rents or profits from the property from the date of death.

Outgoings arising prior to the testator's death will usually be a liability of the estate.

14E   GIFT TO JOINT TENANTS OR TENANTS IN COMMON

I GIVE my freehold house and premises situate at and known as ... [or my freehold property registered at the Land Registry under Title No ... and known as ...] to my children [names] as joint tenants [or as tenants in common in equal shares].

14F   SPECIFIC GIFT OF PROPERTY WITH PROVISION AGAINST APPORTIONMENT

I GIVE to [name] my freehold property situate at and known as ... in the county of ... [or my freehold property registered at the Land Registry under Title No ... and known as ...] together with all the rents and profits due or accruing in respect thereof whether before or after my death but subject to the payment by the said [name] of all outgoings and expenses whether before or after my death usually chargeable against the income of such property.

As to outgoings usually chargeable against income, see *Eccles v Mills* [1898] AC 360 and *Re Hughes* [1913] 2 Ch 491.

14G   GIFT SUBJECT TO A MORTGAGE

> I GIVE my freehold land situate at and known as ... [or my freehold property registered at the Land Registry under Title No ... and known as ...] subject to and charged with the payment of all principal sums and interest secured thereon by way of mortgage or otherwise at my death to [name] absolutely.

In the absence of an express contrary intention, a beneficiary of any property or interest in property is primarily liable for the payment of any money charged on that property at the time of the deceased's death (see Administration of Estates Act 1925, section 35, and the definition of property in section 55(1)(xvii)). The fact that the mortgage debt attributable to the property exceeds the value of the property itself does not amount to a contrary intention for these purposes. If it is intended that the gift be subject to outstanding charges it is in the interests of certainty expressly to state that fact.

Where other property forming part of the residuary estate is also subject to the mortgage or charge affecting the specific gift, then the debt is apportioned between the different properties according to value (see *Re Neeld* [1962] Ch 643 (CA)).

In *Ross v Perrin-Hughes* [2004] EWHC 2559 (Ch), [2005] WTLR 191, the testator had bought the lease of a flat and the freehold of the two maisonettes which formed the premises, in separate but contemporaneous transactions. The flat was subject to a mortgage with an endowment policy assigned to the building society. In his will the testator devised 'my apartment' to the defendant. The executor sought the court's determination as to whether the bequest was of all the premises and free from mortgage. It was held that the word 'apartment' was ambiguous in the context of the premises in question, but there was evidence to show that the deceased had drawn no distinction between the flat and the premises as a whole; as he had assigned the endowment policy to the building society, this showed an intention that the gift of the apartment was to be mortgage-free.

14H   GIFT OF LAND FREE FROM A MORTGAGE DEBT

> I GIVE my freehold property [etc] to [name] absolutely free and discharged from all sums secured thereon by way of mortgage or otherwise at my death and I DIRECT that such sums including all interest in respect thereof and also the costs and expenses relating to the discharge of the said mortgage or charge [and of the registration of the absolute title of [name]] shall be paid out of my residuary estate.

14I   GIFT OF FREEHOLDS SUBJECT TO THE PAYMENT OF A LEGACY

I GIVE my lands situate [etc] to [name of devisee] subject to and charged with the payment of [the clear sum of] £ ... to [name of legatee] and the said [name of devisee] accepting this devise shall [not] be personally liable for such payment. [Or I CHARGE my lands situate [etc] with the payment of [the clear sum of] £ ... to [legatee] and subject to such charge give the same to [name of devisee].]

This type of provision may be useful for a testator who wants land to pass to one beneficiary *in specie* but at the same time give another a cash legacy and the estate is not sufficiently cash rich to achieve both aims. If a gift of land is made upon the condition of certain payments by the devisee to another, those payments are usually construed as a charge upon the land.

14J   GIFT SUBJECT TO THE PAYMENT OF DEBTS, FUNERAL AND TESTAMENTARY EXPENSES

I GIVE my freehold lands situate [etc] but subject to and charged [in exoneration of my personal estate] with the payment of my debts funeral and testamentary expenses and the legacies given by my will and any codicil hereto and the inheritance tax on any legacy bequeathed free of inheritance tax to [name] absolutely.

14K   DEVISE IN EXERCISE OF A SPECIAL POWER OF APPOINTMENT

In accordance with the will of [name] deceased dated ... which will was proved in the [Principal] [... District Probate] Registry of the Family Division on ... [and in exercise of the power therein contained] and of every or any other power enabling me in this behalf I DEVISE AND APPOINT such freehold property and such capital moneys and investments which may at my death be subject to such power of appointment to [name[s]] [in equal shares as tenants in common absolutely].

14L   GIFT BY REFERENCE TO A PRIOR SETTLEMENT ON TRUST FOR SALE

I GIVE all my [freehold land] to my Trustees UPON TRUST to vest the same in the Trustees for the time being of a conveyance dated ... and made between [parties] UPON TRUST for sale and to hold the rents profits and other income thereof until sale and net proceeds of sale and

> the income thereof upon the trusts declared by the trust instrument referred to in the said conveyance in so far as the same are for the time being subsisting and capable of taking effect and so that the property hereby devised shall be dealt with and treated as if the same had formed part of the property conveyed in the said conveyance.

Adding property to an existing settlement should be avoided if possible since it may be unclear how the original trusts and powers apply to the new property, and because it can be disadvantageous for inheritance tax purposes if the testator is the settlor of the settlement, especially if the original settlement is a discretionary settlement created before 27 March 1974. See also Trusts of Land and Appointment of Trustees Act 1996, Part 1. (For the use of pilot trusts, see Chapter 16.)

14M   GIFT OF PROPERTY TO TESTATOR'S ELDEST CHILD WITH A GIFT OVER TO YOUNGER CHILD

> I GIVE all my [describe property] to my eldest child [name] in fee simple but if [name] shall die in my lifetime or if this gift fails for any reason I GIVE the same to my second child [name] in fee simple but if my said second child [name[dies in my lifetime or if this gift fails for any reason I DECLARE that all my said [property] shall fall into and form part of my residuary estate.

But for the express gift over to the second child, Wills Act 1837, section 33, as substituted by Administration of Justice Act 1982, section 19, would come into operation and confer an interest on the issue of the eldest child by substitution in the event of that child having predeceased the testator. Likewise, the section similarly operates in the event of the second child also having predeceased were it not for the express gift over to the residuary estate. The section applies to gifts to 'issue' of the testator, i.e. lineal descendants.

Wills Act 1837, section 33 applies unless contrary intention appears in the will. A gift 'to such of my children as are living at my death, equally if more than one' was held not to amount to contrary intention in *Ling v Ling* [2002] WTLR 553, [2001] All ER (D) 322 (Nov). However, *Rainbird v Smith* [2012] EWHC 4276 (Ch), reached the opposite conclusion. In *Hives v Machin* [2017] EWHC 1414 (Ch), the judge reviewed both cases and preferred *Ling v Ling*. He considered that the 'default setting' was that the provision applied. If it is to be excluded, clear words must be included in the will (in the absence of admissible extrinsic evidence) to show the testator did not wish the issue of a deceased child to benefit. It is therefore desirable to include in the will a clause dealing expressly with the destination of the share of a child who predeceases. This is the case for all gifts to the testator's issue, not just gifts of land (see **5.2.2** and **17.9**).

Where the primary gift is subject to a contingency or condition, the substituted descendant takes subject to the same contingency or condition (see *Ling v Ling* [2002] WTLR 553, [2001] All ER (D) 322 (Nov) and *Naylor and Another v Barlow and Others* [2019] EWHC 1565 (Ch)). The substituted beneficiary 'steps into the shoes of the original deceased beneficiary for all purposes', *per* HHJ Hodge QC (sitting as a Judge of the High Court) in *Naylor and Another v Barlow and Others* [2019] EWHC 1565 (Ch), [16].

In the case of gifts to non-lineal descendants who predecease, there is no automatic substitution of the beneficiary's issue under section 33. So an express provision saving the gift from lapse and substituting the beneficiary's children is necessary if this is what is required.

14N   GIFT WITH PROVISIONS AGAINST LAPSE

I DEVISE all my freehold property [describe property] to my [nephew] [name] absolutely and if my said [nephew] shall fail to survive me or if this gift fails for any reason then to such of his children as shall be living at my death and if more than one then in equal shares as tenants in common.

14.2   GIFTS TO MINORS

A minor cannot hold a legal estate in land, but if land is devised to a minor under the will of a testator dying on or after 1 January 1997, it is held in trust for the minor during their minority, and the Settled Land Act 1925 does not apply to it (Law of Property Act 1925, section 1(6), and Settled Land Act 1925, section 1(1)(ii)(d)).

14O   GIFT TO MINOR WITHOUT TRUST FOR SALE

(a)   I GIVE all my freehold property situate at and known as ... to [minor] absolutely.

(b)   If the said [minor] shall fail to survive me or shall die under the age of [eighteen] years without leaving children living at their death then I GIVE the said property to ... [substitute beneficiary] PROVIDED that if the said [minor] shall either predecease me or shall die under the age of eighteen years and in either case leave children living at the date of my death or born thereafter then I GIVE the said property to such children and if more than one as tenants in common in equal shares.

14.3   DIRECTIONS AS TO INHERITANCE TAX

Inheritance tax on a specific devise of land is a testamentary expense payable out of the residue, provided no contrary intention is expressed in the will (Inheritance Tax Act 1984, section 211). This section does not, however, treat the inheritance tax attributable to property comprised in a settlement immediately before the testator's death as a testamentary expense. A settlement for inheritance tax purposes includes entailed property (Inheritance Tax Act 1984, section 43(2)) and therefore any property disposed of by means of a special or general power of appointment of settled property, or by means of Law of Property Act 1925, section 176, bears its own inheritance tax unless the will demonstrates a contrary intention.

14P   DECLARATION AS TO PAYMENT OF INHERITANCE TAX ON SPECIFIC DEVISES

I DECLARE that any inheritance tax payable on my death in respect of [property] hereinbefore given to [name] [and any inheritance tax payable on my death in respect of [property] given to my Trustees in trust for [name]] shall be a charge on such specifically devised property in exoneration of my residuary [personal] estate.

14Q   SPECIFIC DEVISE SUBJECT TO INHERITANCE TAX

I GIVE to [name] my freehold property situate at … subject to all inheritance tax (if any) attributable thereto and payable on my death.

14.4   IMPACT OF THE RESIDENCE NIL RATE BAND

The Finance (No 2) Act 2015 inserts new sections 8D to 8M into the Inheritance Tax Act 1984. The effect of the new legislation (discussed in more detail in Chapter 27) is to provide an additional nil rate band available for deaths on or after 6 April 2017 when a residence is inherited by a deceased's children or remoter issue or spouses or civil partners of such children or issue. There are also provisions inserted by the Finance Act 2016 which introduce a downsizing allowance where a person disposes of a residence or interest in a residence on or after 8 July 2015 and, as a result, loses some or all of the residence nil rate band (RNRB) they would otherwise have been entitled to. Where a person dies without using all or part of their RNRB (e.g. because they died before its introduction), the unused proportion can be transferred to a surviving spouse or civil partner.

Property left to certain sorts of settlement for the benefit of lineal descendants is treated as 'inherited' for this purpose under Inheritance Tax Act 1984, section 8J(4). The settled property must be held on trusts creating one of the following:

- an immediate post-death interest under section 49A; or
- a disabled person's interest under section 89; or
- a bereaved minor or bereaved young person trust (section 71A or section 71D).

Very few settlements qualify. A discretionary settlement is not included even if all the beneficiaries are lineal descendants. A typical grandparental settlement, 'to such of my grandchildren as reach 21' will not qualify because the trust created is a relevant property trust and so not one of the 'permitted' trusts. However, an appointment from a discretionary trust or advancement of capital to a beneficiary with a contingent interest made within 2 years of death to the lineal descendants would be read back into the will under Inheritance Tax Act 1984, section 144 and so trustees could retrospectively secure the RNRB for the estate.

Testators wishing to leave residential property to adult children with a substitutional gift to children of a deceased child will, therefore, need to consider the form of the substitutional gift carefully if they want to secure the RNRB in relation to that gift. The possible options are a bare trust where the grandchildren will become absolutely entitled at 18 or an immediate post-death interest.

The latter may be attractive as the trustees can be given overriding powers to appoint capital as they see fit. It is necessary to vary Trustee Act 1925, section 31 to provide that any accumulated income (e.g. where the residence has been sold after death and the proceeds invested) is held on a bare trust for the beneficiary. If this is not done, section 31(2)(ii) provides that any accumulated income is held as an accretion to capital where a minor beneficiary dies before reaching 18. This has a divesting effect and the settlement will not create an immediate post-death interest.

For further consideration of the RNRB, see **14.6**.

14.5 GIFTS OF UNDIVIDED SHARES AND CLAUSES DEALING WITH JOINT PROPERTY

Where property is given to several persons concurrently, the gift may be of a joint tenancy or of a tenancy in common. *Prima facie* the persons take under a joint tenancy but anything indicating an intention to divide the property negatives the presumption. Any words indicating an intention to divide property creates a tenancy in common and the following words have been held to be sufficient:

'between', 'divided', 'equally', 'equal proportions', 'equal shares', 'equally to be divided', 'share and share alike' and 'among'.

14R   GIFT OF UNDIVIDED BENEFICIAL SHARE IN EQUITY OF LAND HELD IN TENANCY IN COMMON

I GIVE to [name] all my share of and interest in [property] and all my share and interest in the proceeds of sale thereof and any income arising from the property whether before or after the sale absolutely.

14S   CLAUSE DEALING WITH PROPERTY HELD IN JOINT TENANCY

WHEREAS I am beneficial joint tenant of [property] together with [name A] in fee simple in possession I DECLARE that:

(a)   should the said joint tenancy be severed in my lifetime then I GIVE all my interest in the said property and the proceeds of sale thereof to [name B].

(b)   should there be no such severance and if the said [name A] shall die in my lifetime then I GIVE the said property to [name B].

A testator cannot sever an equitable joint tenancy by will – although a retrospective severance can be achieved if the surviving joint tenant makes a post-death variation (see **27.13** and Appendix 1, Precedent A1K). The testator may, however, wish to sever the joint tenancy in their lifetime (most easily done by notice as provided by Law of Property Act 1925, section 36(2)), and dispose of the severed share by will. When taking instructions for a will to leave an interest in a property, it is important for the person taking instructions to advise on the need to sever a joint tenancy if the will is to be effective. Failure to do so is likely to lead to liability in negligence to the disappointed beneficiary of the will. According to *Carr-Glynn v Frearson* [1998] 4 All ER 225, it is necessary to go even further and to advise on the possibility of serving a precautionary notice of severance where the testator is uncertain of the nature of the co-ownership.

14.6   RIGHT TO OCCUPY A PERSONAL RESIDENCE

The testator may wish their personal residence to be retained after their death to provide a residence for a beneficiary. Since 1 January 1997 and the coming into force of the Trusts of Land and Appointment of Trustees Act 1996, this can be achieved without the risk of creating a strict settlement. Typically, a testator may wish to give a surviving spouse or civil partner a right of occupation for life or until remarriage or entering into a further civil partnership followed by a gift over. In such a case, the title to the property is vested in the trustees of land, who have powers to manage the property. The trustees may, however, by section 9 of the 1996 Act, delegate their functions as trustees which relate to the land to the occupier as the person entitled to possession.

The trustees of land have all the powers of the absolute owner of the land (Trusts of Land and Appointment of Trustees Act 1996, section 6(1)). They have a power of sale and a power to acquire land under Trustee Act 2000, section 8, which specifically allows land to be acquired for occupation by a beneficiary. Hence the house may be sold and an alternative property purchased if the circumstances of the case so dictate.

14T   CLAUSE CREATING TRUST TO PROVIDE A RESIDENCE FOR A SPOUSE OR CIVIL PARTNER

> I GIVE my freehold property situate at ... to my Trustees UPON TRUST to sell the same with power to postpone the sale so long as they see fit and to use the proceeds of such sale for the purpose of acquiring a freehold property to be held on trust with power to grant my [spouse] [civil partner] [name] a right to occupy the said property or any other property acquired in substitution therefor during [his] [her] lifetime [or until [he] [she] shall remarry or enter into a further civil partnership].

Granting a right to occupy creates an immediate post-death interest for inheritance tax purposes; this may be undesirable. However, if the occupant is the deceased's spouse or civil partner, the transfer of the right will attract the spouse exemption. The value of the property will be included in the surviving spouse's or civil partner's estate for inheritance tax purposes. The introduction of the transferable nil rate band in October 2007 meant that this ceased to be a problem. However, the introduction of the new RNRB as from 6 April 2017 means that testators may have to reconsider their strategy. The RNRB is £175,000 until 2025–26, but is withdrawn by £1 for every £2 that an estate exceeds the taper threshold. The taper threshold is £2 million until the end of 2025–26 when it will rise in line with the Consumer Price Index. So, if a married couple each have assets of £1.35 million and the first to die leaves everything to the survivor (absolutely or as an immediate post-death interest), the survivor's estate has reached the taper threshold and no RNRB will be available on the second death.

Testators should consider whether the right of occupation is to be limited to the original property or whether, as will normally be preferable, trustees are to have power to sell the original and purchase a substitute property for occupation by the beneficiary (see Precedent 14U) As the substitute property may be cheaper than the original property, it may be helpful to provide expressly for the treatment of surplus funds.

Testators should also be aware that if surviving spouses or civil partners are unhappy with the level of provision made for them, they can bring an application for reasonable financial provision under the Inheritance (Provision for Family and Dependants) Act 1975 (see Chapter 26). Awards to surviving spouses and civil partners are not limited to provision for maintenance, and the court is required to consider what the survivor would have received had the marriage or civil partnership ended in divorce or dissolution rather than death. Since *White v White* [2000] UKHL 54, [2001] 1 AC 596, the court is likely to start by asking why the parties should not share the assets equally. A will giving limited rights to a surviving spouse or civil partner may mean that the survivor initiates a claim under the Act. See, for example, *Cowan v Foreman and Others* [2019] EWCA Civ 1336, [2020] Fam 129, where the Court of Appeal considered that a widow should be granted leave to make a claim out of time, in part because her claim stood real prospect of success. Her wealthy husband had left his entire estate on trust. Asplin LJ said at [59] that the widow had 'received only the chattels outright, which it is accepted were of nominal value, she has no autonomy and no security and has no direct interest, even in the Montecito property which has been her home for more than 20 years'. It is preferable for the parties to discuss the level of provision before death and try to agree a mutually satisfactory arrangement. In *Grattan v McNaughton* [2001] WTLR 1305, the court doubted whether it was appropriate in modern conditions to limit a life interest 'until remarriage'.

If the testator, for inheritance tax reasons, does not wish to create a right to occupy the dwelling house, then the property may be given to trustees upon discretionary trusts for a class of persons. No one individual has a right to occupy under the trust, but the trustees could grant a licence to occupy. This would not create an immediate post-death interest.

If trustees later want to give a beneficiary a right to occupy, they can do so without inheritance tax consequences once 2 years has elapsed from death. If they grant such a right within 2 years of death, the writing back effect of Inheritance Tax Act 1984, section 144 (see **29.3**) will produce an immediate post-death interest which may not be what they want. Once 2 years has elapsed, no writing back can take effect so granting a right to occupy or a right to income has no inheritance tax consequences.

14U CLAUSE CREATING TRUST FOR SPOUSE OR CIVIL PARTNER OF THE TESTATOR'S SHARE AS TENANT IN COMMON OF RESIDENCE, WITH A FULL LIFE INTEREST FOR THE SPOUSE OR CIVIL PARTNER AND A PROVISION FOR A SUBSTITUTE DWELLING

> I GIVE to my Trustees UPON TRUST my share held as tenant in common with my [spouse] [civil partner] [name] in the freehold property situate at ... for [his] [her] lifetime with power to sell the said share with the consent

of my said [spouse] [civil partner] and with power to use the said proceeds of the sale of my said share in or towards the purchase of a further property my share in which or the proceeds of sale (or balance thereof) to be held UPON TRUST by my Trustees for my said [spouse] [civil partner] during [his] [her] lifetime.

Note: This clause is likely to create an immediate post-death interest. It may be used in the case of couples who are neither married nor in a civil partnership but, of course, the spouse exemption will not apply.

14V GIFT OF PART INTEREST ONLY IN RESIDENCE TO CHILDREN TO USE RESIDENCE NIL RATE BAND WITH REMAINING INTEREST TO ANOTHER

1.1   In this clause:
   1.1.1   'the Property' means any property whether leasehold or freehold which I occupy as my principal residence at the date of my death and own or in which I have a beneficial interest, but if I have more than one residence at the date of my death, my Trustees shall decide which residence is my principal residence provided that if I have no principal residence at the date of my death then 'the Property' means:
   (a)   the last property which I occupied as my principal residence before my death and own or have a beneficial interest in at the date of my death, or
   (b)   such cash amount as is equivalent in value to the net proceeds of sale (or its open market value with vacant possession) of the last property which was my principal residence at any time before its sale or other disposal;
   1.1.2   'the Residential Nil Rate Amount' means the total amount or allowance in respect of the increased nil rate band for inheritance tax to which I may be entitled at the date of my death under sections 8D to 8M of the Inheritance Tax Act 1984 as amended (or any re-enactment thereof at the date of my death) including any amount brought forward under section 8F and any downsizing addition under sections 8FA to 8FE (or any re-enactment thereof at the date of my death).
1.2   I DIRECT my personal representatives to make such claim or claims as may be required to secure the Residential Nil Rate Amount as soon as practicable after my death and in any event within the maximum statutory period as may be prescribed.
1.3   I GIVE free of tax such interest in the Property as shall be equal in value at the date of my death to the amount of the Residential Nil Rate Amount to hold on trust for such of them my daughter [name] and my son [name] as shall be living at the date of my death and if both shall be living in equal shares provided that if either of my children shall die before attaining a vested interest leaving issue

who are living at the date of my death then such issue shall take by substitution and if there shall be more than one of such issue they shall take in equal shares *per stirpes* the share which such child would otherwise have taken had he or she attained a vested interest but so that no issue shall take whose parent is alive and so capable of taking; and subject thereto

1.4   I GIVE the balance of my interest in the Property to my [spouse] [civil partner] [parent] [etc] absolutely.

Notes:

(1) This form might be used if the testator wishes to ensure that RNRB is utilised on their death but at the same time pass an interest in the property to their surviving spouse, civil partner or another relative to secure their continued occupancy (although the testator needs to be confident that the survivor's occupancy will not be disturbed by the children). The form assumes that the value of the house will be sufficient to leave an interest for the survivor; if the RNRB is likely to exceed the value of the residence, then a limitation might be considered to restrict its value so as to leave the survivor, say, a 10% interest in the property.

(2) The reason for using RNRB on the first death of a married couple/civil partners might be that RNRB will not be available on the second death due to the taper threshold being reached as a result of aggregation. Also, if the testator already has the benefit of a carry forward allowance from a previous marriage/civil partnership, it might be wasted if not used on the testator's death because the survivor, if also previously married/in a civil partnership, might already have a carry forward allowance of their own.

(3) The gift over to the grandchildren is vested since imposing a contingency would not allow RNRB to be claimed on the share attributable to their entitlement.

(4) As an alternative, the house could be left to trustees with the RNRB element being held for the children absolutely (or by way of an immediate post-death interest) and the balance of the interest in the house left on an immediate post-death interest trust, for example to the testator's widowed mother. A letter of wishes to the trustees could ask that the trustees allow exclusive occupation for the mother by restricting the children's right to occupy under Trusts of Land and Appointment of Trustees Act 1996, sections 12 and 13. On the mother's death, her equitable share could be given so as to pass to her grandchildren and so attract RNRB (together, possibly, with any carry-forward allowance from the death of her husband). If the house is sold by the trustees prior to the mother's death, either through downsizing or because the mother moves into care, the disposal by the trustees is treated as a disposal by the person with the interest in possession. So, it is the mother's qualifying former residential interest for the purpose of the RNRB (see Inheritance Tax Act 1984, sections 8FA to 8FE and section 8HA).

14W   CLAUSE TO MAKE GIFT OF RESIDENCE TO TRUSTEES AND ALLOWING THEM TO GRANT A LEASE TO THE SURVIVING SPOUSE OR CIVIL PARTNER

I GIVE my [freehold] property situate at … to my Trustees to be held UPON TRUST with power to grant to my [spouse] [civil partner] [name] a lease to occupy the said property upon such terms as my Trustees shall in their absolute discretion deem fit and provided that [he] [she] shall pay any rent due in respect of the same and shall observe and perform the lessee's covenants and conditions reserved by and contained in the lease of the said property throughout [his] [her] period of occupation.

14X   GIFT OF RESIDENCE ON TRUST WITH DIRECTION TO TRUSTEES TO ALLOW UNMARRIED DAUGHTER TO LIVE THERE

I GIVE my freehold residence situate at [etc] [free of inheritance tax] [and free of all moneys secured thereon at my death (which moneys shall be paid out of my residuary estate)] to my Trustees UPON TRUST AND I DIRECT that my Trustees shall permit my daughter [name] if she shall be unmarried at my death to reside there rent free for so long as she shall remain unmarried she keeping the same in good repair and insured to the satisfaction of my Trustees throughout the period of her residence and I DECLARE that upon her death or marriage or entering into a civil partnership or if after my death she ceases to reside therein my Trustees shall determine my daughter's interest therein to have ended and shall stand possessed of the said property upon the following trusts ...

Note: This clause is likely to create an immediate post-death interest and as such is 'inherited' for the purpose of the RNRB.

14.7   GIFTS OF TESTAMENTARY OPTIONS

An option to purchase can provide useful flexibility if a testator wants one person to benefit from a particular asset and also wants to make provision for others but may not have adequate funds to do both.

See Chapter 21 for a consideration of the issues in granting testamentary options.

14.8   GIFTS OF LEASEHOLDS

Although leaseholds are personalty, they nevertheless relate to land and any gift of 'land' should distinguish between freehold and leasehold land if the two are to be dealt with separately by the testator. A beneficiary takes leasehold property subject to the rent payable and any other covenants under the lease.

An ordinary covenant against the assignment of a leasehold interest without consent does not apply to a specific or general bequest of the leasehold (see *Doe d. Goodbehere v Bevan* (1815) 3 M&S 353).

14Y   GIFT OF LEASEHOLDS

I GIVE to [name] my leasehold property situate at [etc] for all the residue [that shall at my death be unexpired of the term or terms upon which the same is held] [of the term created by the lease dated … and made between [parties]] and subject to the rent and covenants and conditions therein reserved and contained.

14Z   GIFT OF LEASEHOLD HOUSE FREE FROM MORTGAGE

I GIVE my leasehold residence and premises situate at [etc] to [name] absolutely free from any incumbrances and I DIRECT that [name] shall be kept indemnified in respect of any mortgage debt or other charge in relation to the property which shall be paid out of my residuary [personal] estate but provided that [name] shall take the said residue and premises subject to any rent from time to time payable and subject to the covenants and conditions contained in the lease under which the said property is or may be held.

14AA   GIFT OF LEASEHOLDS – LEGATEE TO PAY ALL ARREARS OF RENT AND COST OF DILAPIDATIONS

I GIVE my leasehold residence and premises at … to [name] absolutely PROVIDED THAT [name] shall pay any rent payable in respect thereof and perform and observe the covenants and conditions contained in the lease under which the same is held and on the lessee's part to be performed and observed and I DECLARE that the rent in respect thereof owing or accruing at my death and the costs and expenses of putting the said premises into repair in compliance with the provisions of the said lease shall be borne and paid by the said [name] in exoneration of my residuary estate.

Chapter 15

Conditions Attached to Gifts

15.1 CONDITIONS PRECEDENT AND SUBSEQUENT

A condition may be a condition precedent or a condition subsequent, depending on the wording of the will and the construction of that wording.

If a gift is not intended to take effect until the condition has been fulfilled, the condition is a condition precedent. Conditions precedent are valid if expressed to allow a particular individual to come with evidence to the court and show that the individual does or does not satisfy that condition (see *Re Tepper's Will Trusts* [1987] Ch 358). A condition is a condition subsequent if the gift is already vested and the object of the condition is to put an end to the gift if its terms are fulfilled.

In the case of a condition precedent, if the condition is void the whole gift fails, but in the case of a condition subsequent the gift takes effect free from a void condition.

If a condition attached to a testamentary gift is capable of being construed either as a condition precedent or a condition subsequent, the court will prefer the latter construction (see the Court of Appeal in *Re Greenwood* [1903] 1 Ch 749).

15.2 GENERAL

A testator may attach any condition they wish to the gifts they make in their will, but such conditions may be void if they are:

- against public policy or illegal;
- repugnant to the interest given to the beneficiary or other gifts or provisions in the will;
- too uncertain to be enforced;

- impossible to perform;
- made against the beneficiary '*in terrorem*'.

15.2.1 Public policy

A condition is void as against public policy if it is in the interest of the state that it should not be performed. What has been held to be void under this category has varied from time to time, but has included the following:

(i)   a condition inciting a beneficiary to commit a crime;
(ii) a condition requiring a beneficiary to exert their influence in a political manner;
(iii) a condition tending to induce the future separation of a husband and wife;
(iv) a condition in total or virtual restraint of marriage. Partial restraints, for example a condition prohibiting a person's marriage with a papist or a Scotsman, have been allowed. If the purpose of the condition is not to restrain marriage, but to provide for the donee until marriage, then the condition is allowed.

15.2.2 Repugnant conditions

Repugnant conditions are those in which it is sought to make a beneficiary's enjoyment of a vested interest contrary to the basic principles of the law affecting such gifts. An example is a gift of capital to an adult, subject to a condition that it is not to be paid to them until they reach an age which is greater than 18. Such an object cannot be achieved unless the income is given to another person until the primary beneficiary attains the specified age. A way of achieving this is to make a gift by means of a discretionary trust. If the gift is worded in such a way as clearly to take the income from the legatee, the court will declare there to be an intestacy of that income.

A further example of a condition which is void for repugnancy is a condition limiting the power of absolute alienation of property, since one of the primary rights of ownership of property is the right to sell, give or otherwise dispose of it. Partial restraints are valid, so that a devise to a beneficiary on condition that they never sell the property to a person who is not a member of the family is not void.

In *Nathan v Leonard* [2002] EWHC 1701 (Ch), [2003] 1 WLR 827, [2002] WTLR 1061, a will contained a clause depriving all beneficiaries of their entitlement if any one of them challenged the will. The court held that the condition was not repugnant. A condition is only repugnant if it purports to limit or remove the incidents of ownership which necessarily attach to the gift, as where the condition operates if the donee wishes to sell the property given to them. Having given the property absolutely, the testator cannot control what the donee does with it. This condition attacked the whole gift, rather than merely the incidents of the gift and, therefore, did not have the same inconsistency. The fact that other gifts might be divested too made no difference.

A condition may be repugnant where it is impossible to perform.

15.2.3 Uncertainty

The test whether a condition is void for uncertainty differs depending on whether the condition is a condition precedent or a condition subsequent. Where there is a condition subsequent, it must be drafted so that the court or persons affected by it understand from the outset exactly the event upon the occurrence of which the preceding vested interest is to determine. In the case of a condition precedent no such test is needed (see *Tuck's Settlement Trusts* [1978] Ch 49 (CA) and *Re Barlow's Will Trusts* [1979] 1 WLR 278). In *Re Tepper's Will Trusts* [1987] Ch 358, a condition subsequent forfeiting the interests of beneficiaries who remained outside the Jewish faith was held to be void for uncertainty, in the absence of admissible evidence as to the nature of the Jewish faith practised by the testator and family.

15.2.4 Impossibility

Impossibility is a state of affairs which does not or cannot exist (see *Re Jones* [1948] Ch 67).

If the performance of a condition is highly improbable or is out of the power of the donee, this does not mean that the condition is impossible.

Where a condition is a condition precedent and is either impossible or becomes impossible by operation of law before the date of the will, the gift remains intact and the condition is void. Where the condition is intended to be operative in any event, and performance is possible at the date of the will, but afterwards becomes impossible by an act of God or circumstances over which neither the legatee nor the testator had any control, the gift does not vest.

Where a condition subsequent is impossible, the gift always takes effect free from the condition. However, the question of whether or not the condition is impossible is not always easy to decide.

In *Re Jones* [1948] Ch 67, non-compliance with a condition subsequent requiring a village hall to be completed within a certain period of time was due to assets not being saleable due to war conditions, making it impossible to build the hall. In *Re Berens* [1926] Ch 596, performance of the condition to assume and use the surname and arms of Dowdeswell was 'impossible of fulfilment' because the arms in question had already been granted to another. The condition was therefore held not to be binding on the beneficiary. Similarly in *Watson v The National Children's Home Co* [2001] WTLR 1375, where the subject matter of the condition (a dog) no longer existed, the condition was spent and the gift took effect free from the condition.

However, failing to comply with a time limit because you have not been informed of the requirement is not a case of impossibility. A number of decisions make this point. In *Astley v Earl of Essex* (1874) LR 18 Eq 290, 297, Sir George Jessel MR said:

> The principle is, that a person who takes by gift under a will cannot plead want of knowledge of the contents of the will as an excuse for not complying with its provisions.

Similarly, the decision of Sir John Wickens V-C in *Re Hodges' Legacy* (1873) LR 16 Eq 92 is authority for the further limitation that 'a legatee is not entitled to notice of the condition, unless the terms of the condition expressly provide that an interested party is to give him notice thereof'.

These cases were cited in *Naylor and Another v Barlow and Others* [2019] EWHC 1565 (Ch), where a legacy was conditional on the testator's son paying a stated sum to his two siblings within 9 months of the death. The son predeceased his father but was survived by his two daughters. No one realised that the daughters were entitled to take their father's place until more than 9 months had elapsed.

HHJ Hodge QC (sitting as a Judge of the High Court) held that the law distinguishes between the situation where a beneficiary fails to fulfil a condition (otherwise capable of fulfilment) simply because he does not know about it in sufficient time to do so and the different situation where it is physically impossible for him to fulfil the condition, as where the College of Heralds will not award him the stipulated arms or an animal charity cannot look after the testator's dog because he was no longer in possession of any dog at the time of his death. This is because in the latter situation, neither the testator nor the beneficiary has any control over whether or not the condition can be fulfilled, while in the former situation, it was within the testator's power to make fulfilment of the condition contingent upon it having been notified to the beneficiary in sufficient time to enable compliance. In making this distinction, the law is seeking to draw what it considers to be an appropriate compromise between the competing interests of the primary beneficiary and those who would take in default of fulfilment of the condition.

The case is a stark example of the importance of drafting time limits to run from the date the beneficiary is informed and to impose a duty on the executors to do so. HHJ Hodge QC said at [20]:

> If any lessons are to be learned from the present case, it is that the draftsman of a will incorporating a condition along the lines of clause 3 should consider expressly making the time for compliance run only from the time of notification of the condition to the relevant beneficiary.

15.2.5 Conditions 'in terrorem'

Certain conditions may be void against the legatee if made as a 'threat' to induce them to comply with the condition.

This rule does not apply to freeholds, or to legacies charged on freeholds, or to personalty directed to be paid out in the purchase of land.

The court may, however, avoid the question of the validity of such words by construing them not as a condition but as a limitation or a trust (see *Page v Hayward* (1705) 11 Mod Rep 61). Examples of such a construction include:

- a gift to a person so long as that person remains unmarried (see *Webb v Grace* (1848) 2 Ph 701);
- a gift subject to marriage with consent (see *Fry v Porter* (1670) 1 Mod Rep 300);
- a reduction of an annuity on marriage (see *Brown v Cutter* (1683) 2 Show 152);
- a proviso against alienation (see *Newis v Lark* (1571) 2 Plowd 408).

The court held that the forfeiture clause in *Nathan v Leonard* [2002] EWHC 1701 (Ch), [2003] 1 WLR 827, [2002] WTLR 1061 which would take effect if the will was challenged was not contrary to public policy. The argument was advanced that the condition could not stand because its effect was to deter an applicant from making a claim under the Inheritance (Provision for Family and Dependants) Act 1975 for fear of losing the benefits given to him by the will. However, while the court agreed that the effect of the clause was to make such a claim less likely, it did not prevent an applicant making his claim. The applicant remained free to do so and, if he did, the court would take the lack of provision in the will into account when determining whether or not to make an award.

15.2.6 Provision terminating 'on marriage' or 'on formation of a civil partnership'

A testator wishing to limit a gift to a surviving spouse until remarriage should understand that if the spouse chooses to bring an application under the Inheritance (Provision for Family and Dependants) Act 1975, the court may strike out the limitation as it did in *Grattan v McNaughton* [2001] WTLR 1305. If including such a provision the testator should consider whether the formation of a civil partnership, as well as marriage, should be mentioned.

15A   INTEREST TO SPOUSE OR CIVIL PARTNER FOR LIFE OR UNTIL REMARRIAGE OR ENTRY INTO CIVIL PARTNERSHIP

My Trustees shall pay any and all income arising from my residuary estate or any part thereof to my [spouse] [civil partner] so long as [he] [she] shall live [or until [his] [her] remarriage or entry into a civil partnership whichever shall be the shorter period].

15B   INTEREST TO SPOUSE OR CIVIL PARTNER FOR LIFE TO BE REDUCED ON REMARRIAGE OR ENTRY INTO CIVIL PARTNERSHIP

My Trustees shall pay the income of my residuary estate to my [spouse] [civil partner] so long as [he] [she] shall live and remain single PROVIDED THAT if [he] [she] shall remarry or enter into a civil partnership then my Trustees shall pay [him] [her] [one half only] of the income of my residuary estate and the remainder of such income therefrom shall be paid to [name] [accrue to and form part of my residuary estate].

15C   LIFE INTEREST TRUST FOR SPOUSE OR CIVIL PARTNER SUBJECT TO AN OBLIGATION TO MAINTAIN CHILDREN

My Trustees shall pay the income of my residuary estate to my [spouse] [civil partner] so long as [he] [she] shall remain single PROVIDED THAT [he] [she] shall maintain and educate our children while under the age of twenty-five years to the satisfaction of my Trustees.

15D LIFE INTEREST TRUST FOR SPOUSE OR CIVIL PARTNER WITH REQUEST TO MAINTAIN CHILDREN; NO BINDING LEGAL OBLIGATION

My Trustees shall pay the income of my residuary estate to my [spouse] [civil partner] so long as [he] [she] shall live and remain single and I REQUEST that [he] [she] shall maintain and educate our children ALWAYS PROVIDED THAT nothing in this provision shall be construed as to impose any condition or legal obligation whatsoever upon my said [spouse] [civil partner].

15E LIFE INTEREST TRUST FOR SPOUSE OR CIVIL PARTNER WHILE SINGLE WITH GIFT OVER TO CHILDREN IN EQUAL SHARES

(1) My Trustees shall pay the income from my residuary estate to my said [spouse] [civil partner] until [his] [her] death [or remarriage or entry into a civil partnership].

(2) Upon the death [or remarriage or entry into a civil partnership] of my said [spouse] [civil partner] my Trustees shall hold my residuary estate together with any interest accruing thereon after [his] [her] death [or remarriage or entry into a civil partnership] for all my children who attain the age of [eighteen] years or marry or enter into a civil partnership under that age in equal shares if more than one PROVIDED THAT if any child of mine shall fail to survive me and dies leaving issue alive at the date of my death such issue if and when they attain the age of [eighteen] years or marry or enter into a civil partnership under that age shall take by substitution and if more than one in equal shares *per stirpes* the same share of my residuary estate that such deceased child of mine would have taken had he or she survived me but so that no issue shall take whose parent is alive at my death and so capable of taking.

15.3 EFFECT OF INVALIDITY

In a condition precedent, if the condition is void the gift fails, whereas if a condition subsequent is void, the gift takes effect free from the condition. In the case of voidable conditions avoided by the donee, or a condition repugnant to the gift to which it is attached, then the gift takes effect free from the condition, irrespective of whether the condition is precedent or subsequent.

Where a condition precedent is invalid as *malum in se* (wrong in itself), both the gift and the condition are void and the gift fails. But where such a condition is invalid as *malum prohibitum* (prohibited by law), the condition only is void and the gift becomes absolute.

15F   FORFEITURE OF GIFT – CONDITION SUBSEQUENT – MARRIAGE TO A PERSON NOT OF A SPECIFIED RELIGION

I DIRECT that if any child or children of mine has or have married or shall have married at the date of my death or shall marry at any time any person who did not at the time of such marriage profess the ... religion such child or children shall from the date of that marriage absolutely forfeit and lose all [his] [her] [their] interest in and right to the capital or income given to [him] [her] [them] under the provisions hereof [and the gift so forfeited shall fall into and form part of my residuary estate] PROVIDED ALWAYS THAT this provision shall not operate in respect of any marriage for which I have given my approval or forgiveness AND I DIRECT that the decision of my Trustees both as to whether or not I have given my approval or forgiveness as aforesaid and as to whether or not any person professed the ... religion at the time of any marriage shall be absolute and binding upon all Beneficiaries claiming under this will.

15G   FORFEITURE OF GIFT – CONDITION PRECEDENT – MARRIAGE TO A PERSON PROFESSING A SPECIFIED RELIGION

I DECLARE that the share of any child of mine in my residuary estate shall not be paid or transferred to that child immediately upon my death but shall be retained by my Trustees and held by them upon the following trusts:
(a)
    (i)   In the case of any child married at the time of my death to a person of the ... religion then UPON TRUST as to both capital and income for that child absolutely.
    (ii) In the case of any child of mine married at the date of my death to a person not of the ... religion the share given to that child shall be forfeit and shall be applied as if my said child had predeceased me without issue unless my Trustees are of the opinion that at the date of my death I had approved or forgiven the said marriage and if so my Trustees shall hold the said share UPON TRUST as to both capital and income for that child absolutely.
(b)   In the case of any child of mine unmarried or divorced at the date of my death UPON TRUST to pay the income thereof to the said child during his or her lifetime or until the said child shall marry or marry again, and

(i) if the said marriage be to a person of the ... religion then UPON TRUST as to both capital and income for such child absolutely, but

(ii) if the said marriage be to a person not of the ... religion the share given to that child shall be forfeit and shall be applied as if my child had predeceased me without issue.

15.4 DETERMINABLE INTERESTS

A condition or proviso against alienation or forfeiture on bankruptcy is void, but a limitation until bankruptcy or until an attempted alienation is valid. In the former case the beneficiary is given, for example, a complete life interest, whereas in the latter case he is given a limited life interest, that is, a life interest until the attempted alienation. The limitation in the determinable interest marks the bounds of the interest, whereas the condition in the conditional interest is intended to defeat the interest before it attains its boundary.

15H DETERMINABLE LIFE INTEREST

(a) Until the death of my son [name] my Trustees shall pay the income of [my residuary estate] to him PROVIDED THAT no act or thing shall have been done permitted or suffered by my said son or shall have been attempted to have been done and no event shall have happened (other than a consent to any advancement under any statutory or express power) whereby the income of [my residuary estate] or some part thereof would or might if belonging absolutely to my said son become vested in or charged in favour of some other persons or a corporation or my said son would or might be deprived of the right to receive the same or any part thereof and my Trustees shall continue to pay the said income to my said son during his life until some such event as aforesaid shall happen.

(b) After the death or earlier failure or determination of the trust hereinbefore contained my Trustees shall stand possessed of [my residuary estate] and the income thereof in trust, etc.

Chapter 16

Pilot Trusts

16.1 BACKGROUND

When taking instructions for a will, it is often helpful to consider other steps which may be necessary or useful, for example severing a joint tenancy or preparing a lasting power of attorney.

One common step has been the creation of one or more lifetime discretionary settlements to which the client transfers a nominal amount of cash, typically £10. The intention is that the client will leave further assets to the trust(s) by will. The original settlements are normally referred to as 'pilot trusts'.

Pilot trusts have been used when a client wants to settle funds in excess of the nil rate band, but avoid the trust having to pay inheritance tax on 10-year anniversaries and on appointments of capital from the trust. Changes introduced by the Finance (No 2) Act 2015 have substantially limited the usefulness of pilot trust planning, but there are still circumstances where pilot trust planning continues to be useful.

16.2 TRADITIONAL PILOT TRUST PLANNING BEFORE THE 2015 CHANGES

Tax on relevant property settlements is charged on three occasions:

- when property is transferred to the settlement (pilot trust planning does not assist with this);
- an anniversary charge at 10-yearly intervals following creation;
- an exit charge when property ceases to be held on relevant property trusts (this is calculated on a time basis using the previous anniversary rate).

For anniversary charges, the tax is calculated on the value of the settled property on that date.

The rate of tax to be charged is calculated by working out the tax that would be charged on a 'hypothetical chargeable transfer', turning it into an average rate and then applying 30% of the average rate to the value of the relevant property in the settlement.

Exit charges use the rate calculated on the previous anniversary.

Before the changes, the 'hypothetical chargeable transfer' was:

(i)   the value of property contained in the settlement immediately before the anniversary; and
(ii) the value, immediately after creation, of property in any 'related settlements'; and
(iii) the value at the date the settlement was created of any non-relevant property which has not subsequently become relevant property

'Related settlements' are settlements which have the same settlor and which commence on the same day (Inheritance Tax Act 1984, section 62).

Tax is calculated on the hypothetical chargeable transfer using lifetime rates, so it is 20% on any part of the 'hypothetical chargeable transfer in excess of the available nil rate band'.

The table of rates is joined at the point reached by the settlor's chargeable transfers in the 7 years before death. Hence if the settlor has a full nil rate band immediately before creation, the settlement inherits that nil rate band, although if the settlor adds property at a time when they have used more of their nil rate band, the settlement's nil rate band is similarly reduced. Transfers made from the settlement in the 10 years preceding the anniversary charge will also reduce the available nil rate band.

Once the tax is calculated, it is turned into an average rate and 30% of it is then applied to the value of the settled property. This means that the highest rate possible is 6% (30% of 20%), but wherever any nil rate band is available the rate will be lower.

If a testator wanted to settle £1 million of assets for the benefit of their grandchildren and did so using one will trust, there would be substantial inheritance tax anniversary and exit charges. If the testator divided the £1 million between several will trusts on the same day, they would all be related settlements and anniversary and exit charges would again be high.

However, if the testator creates several pilot trusts on different days, the settlements are not related to each other. If the testator transfers only a nominal amount to each settlement at the time of creation, their cumulative total will be virtually nil for each (or actually nil if the transfers are covered by the annual exemption).

Provided later funds are added on the same day (normally the date of death, although it could also be done by a lifetime transfer), the settlor's cumulative total is not increased as transfers made on the same day do not affect the cumulative total (Inheritance Tax Act 1984, section 66(5)(a)).

The associated operations rules do not apply (see *IRC v Rysaffe Trustee Company (CI) Ltd* [2003] EWCA Civ 356, [2003] STC 536).

16.3   THE NEW RULES INTRODUCED BY THE FINANCE (NO 2) ACT 2015

When calculating the hypothetical chargeable transfer on or after 18 November 2015, a new section 62A(1) inserted into the Inheritance Tax Act 1984 provides that the value of any 'same day addition' must be included.

There is a 'same day addition' if a person who has created two or more relevant property settlements:

(i)   makes a transfer of value as a result of which the value of the property comprised in one settlement ('Settlement A') increases; and
(ii) on the same day, as a result of the same, or another, transfer of value, the value immediately afterwards of the property comprised in another settlement ('Settlement B') increases.

The hypothetical chargeable transfer after the changes is now as follows:

(i)   the value of property contained in the settlement immediately before the anniversary; and
(ii) the value, immediately after creation, of relevant property in any 'related settlements'; and
(iii) the value at the date of the addition of any 'same day addition', and the initial value added to the other settlement if it was not a related settlement.

Note that it is no longer necessary to include the value of non-relevant property in related settlements. This is a genuine simplification.

Section 62A does not apply to settlements created and added to *before* 10 December 2014 (the date that original draft legislation introducing changes was announced). The result is that those who have completed their pilot trust planning by adding to their pilot trusts before 10 December 2014 will continue to benefit from multiple nil rate bands.

There was, in addition, a transitional protection period which applied where death occurs before 6 April 2017, and additions are made to existing trusts under 'provisions of the settlor's will that at the settlor's death are, in substance, the same as they were immediately before 10 December 2014'.

If clients die on or after that date without changing their wills, the trustees can appoint out of the trusts and get it read back into the will under Inheritance Tax Act 1984, section 144 as the property is 'settled by will'.

16.4   ADDITIONAL POINTS ON THE NEW RULES

The first is that the *same day addition* can be an increase in value as opposed to a transfer of property; for example a settlor releasing their loan to a settlement or paying a 10-year anniversary charge when the trust is 'dry'. In the latter case, it is preferable to lend the cash to the settlement on a demand loan.

The second is that if the value of an addition is £5,000 or less, the same day addition rule does not apply. There are anti-fragmentation provisions to prevent individuals avoiding the same day addition rules by transferring amounts in excess of £5,000 to settlements in multiples of £5,000.

16.5   IS THERE ANY PLACE FOR FUTURE PILOT TRUSTS PLANNING?

First, where asset values are expected to rise, there is a benefit to splitting them between two settlements. A same day addition is included at its value at the date of addition, so subsequent increases in value are ignored. This will result in a lower rate of tax being applied to the settled property than if all the assets were comprised in one settlement.

Example

In January 2014, Sam created three pilot trusts on consecutive days, each receiving £10. Sam had a full nil rate band available. At the same time, he made a will leaving £250,000 to each settlement.

- Assume that Sam dies in January 2017 with his will unchanged and £250,000 is transferred to each settlement. In January 2024, the first anniversary charge has to be calculated.

  - Assume the value of the settled property in each settlement at that date is £325,000 and the nil rate band has remained at £325,000.
  - The same day addition rule will not apply as death is within the transitional period. Hence the hypothetical chargeable transfer for each settlement is £325,000. All three settlements have a full nil rate band available, so the anniversary rate of tax on each is nil.

- If, instead, Sam died in January 2022, the same day addition rule will apply, so in 2024 the hypothetical chargeable transfer for each settlement is £325,000 + £250,000 + £250,000 (ignoring the initial £10 settled to keep the calculation simple).

  - All three settlements have a full nil rate band available. The anniversary rate is calculated on a hypothetical chargeable transfer of £825,000.
  - There is a full nil rate band available to each settlement, so 20% is charged on £500,000 = £100,000.
  - This is an average rate of £100,000/£825,000 x 100 = 12.12%.
  - The rate actually charged on the funds in each settlement is 30% of that, so 3.6%.

Note that, where asset values rise, there is still a benefit to using three settlements rather than putting the whole lot into one big settlement. If Sam had used one settlement, the rate of tax would have been calculated on a hypothetical chargeable transfer of £975,000. One nil rate band would have been available, so tax at 20% would be charged on £650,000 = £130,000.

This is an average rate of £130,000/£975,000 x 100 = 13.33%. The rate actually charged is 30% of that, so 3.9%.

Second, death benefits paid to a lifetime trust from a pension scheme operated via a trust remain in the original trust for inheritance tax purposes as a result of Inheritance Tax Act 1984, section 81. Hence, a testator can settle property into one will trust and direct that a death benefit be paid into a separate trust without triggering the same day additions rules.

Third, property added on different days is obviously not subject to the 'same day additions' rule. Hence, every 7 years a settlor could create a settlement with a full nil rate band.

Fourth, if property is exempt or attracts 100% relief, it does not affect the settlor's cumulative total, so multiple settlements can be created using the normal expenditure from income, all of which will have a full nil rate band available.

16.6   NON-RELATED SETTLEMENTS

There are two occasions when settlements created on the same day are not related to each other:

(i)   When the property settled in one settlement is settled for charitable purposes without limit of time (Inheritance Tax Act 1984, section 62).

(ii) When a will creates a settlement for a *spouse* (and this term includes a civil partner) for life, that settlement is not related to any other settlement created in the will. This is because Inheritance Tax Act 1984, section 80 provides that a settlement for a spouse for life is treated as created when the spouse's interest comes to an end. The effect of this useful provision is that a will can create both a life interest trust for a spouse and a discretionary trust for children which will not be related to each other.

16A   CLAUSE IN A WILL LEAVING PROPERTY TO AN EXISTING PILOT SETTLEMENT

I GIVE the sum of £ ... to the Trustees for the time being of the [name] Discretionary Settlement to be held by those Trustees as an accretion to the funds held on the trusts set out in the deed of settlement dated [insert date] and made by me as settlor of the one part and [name Trustee 1] and [name Trustee 2] (therein together called 'the Original Trustees' [*or as the case may be*]) of the other part.

Notes:

(1) It is imperative that the pilot settlement is in existence at the time when the will is executed and it should be clearly identified in the will by reference to the name, date and parties.

(2) Also, since the settlement will not be constituted until the first trustees have received the nominal pilot amount, it is necessary to ensure that the stated sum in the pilot settlement is actually handed over to the trustees before execution of the will, or at least held by the practitioner setting up the trust on behalf of the trustees.

(3) Once set up, the terms of the settlement must not be changed between the date of the will and the testator's death, e.g. by the trustees adding a beneficiary even if they have express power to do so.

Chapter 17

Gifts of Residue

17.1 GENERAL

Every will should contain a residuary gift, to ensure that the residue of the estate devolves to the beneficiaries chosen by the testator rather than on intestacy. A residuary gift has the effect of passing the property not otherwise disposed of. The residuary gift may be limited (but is generally not), or it can pass all property not otherwise disposed of.

An unlimited residuary gift exercises any general power of appointment the testator may have over trust property (Wills Act 1837, section 27) and so any default provision in the trust is prevented from taking effect (see Chapter 18). It is, however, preferable to make express reference to the power rather than relying on section 27, so that there is no risk of argument that the testator was unaware that the gift of residue included property subject to the power. In *Gibbons v Nelson* [2000] Lloyd's Rep PN 603, a case involving the exercise of a power of appointment by section 27, Blackburne J criticised the solicitor concerned for failing to establish the client's intentions with regard to the destination of trust property.

The will should be drafted so as to deal with the payment of debts, inheritance tax, testamentary expenses and legacies in a manner which complies with the testator's wishes. Usually, this means that they are payable out of the residuary estate. It is important to state this expressly, to avoid any possible disputes after death. Testators who make substantial non-residuary gifts should be warned to consider carefully whether the amount of residue likely to remain after provision for legacies and other liabilities will be sufficient for the residuary beneficiary.

It is desirable to include substitutional gifts and a survivorship condition.

17.2   THE NECESSITY FOR A TRUST

If the testator wishes to create a continuing trust of residue, it is necessary to create express trusts of residue. It is important to remember that a trust may arise by substitution where adult beneficiaries predecease the testator and are replaced by their children contingent on reaching a stated age. Therefore, in all but the simplest cases, for example where residue is passing outright to a charity or to adult beneficiaries with no possibility of contingent interests arising by substitution, a trust is required.

If a trust is not created, the will should include a simple direction that debts and the like be paid from residue.

17A   RESIDUARY GIFT TO ONE PERSON WITHOUT A TRUST

Subject to the payment of my debts funeral and testamentary expenses legacies and all tax payable from my estate* I GIVE all my property not otherwise disposed of (including any property over which I may have a general power of appointment or disposition by will) to [name] absolutely.

* For the rules on the burden of inheritance tax, see **17.7**.

17B   RESIDUARY GIFT TO A CLASS WITHOUT A TRUST

I GIVE all my property not otherwise disposed of (including any property over which I may have a general power of appointment or disposition by will) to my Trustees for the payment of my debts funeral and testamentary expenses legacies and all tax payable from my estate* and subject thereto to be divided between all [my children] in equal shares absolutely.

* See **17.7** for a discussion of the rules on the burden of inheritance tax; and see **24.13** on class closing rules, the effect of which should be explained to the testator.

17C   GIFT OF RESIDUARY ESTATE TO NAMED PERSONS ON TRUST WITH SUBSTITUTION PROVISIONS

Subject to the payment of my debts funeral and testamentary expenses legacies and all tax payable from my estate my Trustees shall hold my residuary estate IN TRUST for such of them [names] as shall survive me and if more than one as tenants in common in equal shares PROVIDED THAT if any one or more of them shall die in my lifetime leaving issue the share of each so dying shall be held in trust for [his] [her] respective issue living at my death and attaining the age of [eighteen] years or marrying or entering into a civil partnership under that age in equal shares *per stirpes* but so that no issue shall take whose parent is alive at my death and so capable of taking and further provided that if any of the said [names] shall die in my lifetime without issue who attain a vested interest the share of anyone so dying shall be held for the other person[s] entitled to my residuary estate under this clause as if the one or more so dying had never been named or included in this gift.

17.3 TRUST FOR SALE OR POWER TO SELL

The Trusts of Land and Appointment of Trustees Act 1996 significantly affects the drafting of wills. It introduces the 'trust of land' as the vehicle for all new settlements of land. It is no longer possible to create new Settled Land Act 1925 settlements, and the doctrine of conversion in relation to trusts for sale of land is abolished. The result is that it is no longer necessary to impose a trust for sale to avoid creating a Settled Land Act 1925 settlement where land is held for persons in succession or under a contingency.

Residue can continue to be left on trust for sale, although in relation to land this achieves little; the trust is still a trust of land. The trust for sale may be helpful in relation to personalty where, once the administration is completed, trustees have no general power to sell personalty (Administration of Estates Act 1925, section 39 applies only during the administration). If imposing a trust for sale, it is important to include a power to postpone sale as there is no implied power to postpone sale of personalty. There are some situations in which a trust for sale is advisable:

(i)   to emphasise the testator's intention where an early sale is desired;
(ii)   to emphasise the testator's intention where land is intended to be held as an investment rather than for occupation by beneficiaries;
(iii) where land is left to several people who may disagree about whether or not to sell, a direction for sale may assist those in favour of sale. The court's power to order a sale under Trusts of Land and Appointment of Trustees Act 1996, section 14 is discretionary, so a beneficiary applying for an order for sale has no certainty as to the outcome;
(iv)   where the gift of residue is into immediate fractional shares.

In other cases, the better course may be to leave the residue on trust with a power to sell. It is always appropriate to include a power of sale as there is no implied general power to sell personalty (see above). A power to sell is likely to accord better with the wishes of clients than a trust.

Irrespective of whether a trust or power is used, it is desirable to consider whether any directions as to the burden of inheritance tax are required to vary the statutory position.

17D   ADMINISTRATION TRUST WITHOUT A TRUST FOR SALE

(a)   I GIVE all my property not otherwise effectively disposed of [(including any property over which I may have a general power of appointment or disposition by will)] to my Trustees UPON TRUST with power at their discretion to sell all or any of it when they think fit.

(b)   My Trustees shall pay my funeral and testamentary expenses my debts [all inheritance tax payable from my estate*] and any legacies given by this will or any codicil to it out of such property or its proceeds of sale.

(c)   My Trustees shall have a discretion as to how such payments shall be borne as between capital and income.**

(d)   None of the equitable rules of apportionment between capital and income shall apply in any circumstances whatever.***

(e)   Subject as aforesaid my Trustees shall invest all money comprised in such property or arising from its sale in any of the investments authorised by this will with power to change such investments into any others so authorised and the said property and the assets from time to time representing it (hereinafter called 'my Residuary Trust Fund') shall be held on the trusts declared below.

(f)   All income of my Residuary Trust Fund shall be treated as accruing on the date on which it becomes payable and there shall be no statutory apportionment of it to any other time or period.***

* See **17.7** for a discussion of the rules on the burden of inheritance tax.

** This clause gives the trustees a discretion as to how they allocate the burden of debts between capital and income.

*** These clauses may be included for clarity, but are no longer necessary in a will made on or after 1 October 2013 since the Trusts (Capital and Income) Act 2013 automatically disapplies the equitable apportionment rules in relation to trusts created or arising on or after that date unless it provides otherwise. Similarly, the need to apportion income under the Apportionment Act 1870 is disapplied for such trusts.

17.4   DIFFERENT PERSONS AS EXECUTORS AND TRUSTEES

Often, the executors and trustees will be the same people, but this is not always the case. There may be cases where it is appropriate to appoint different people.

17E   GIFT OF RESIDUE TO TRUSTEES WHO ARE DIFFERENT PERSONS FROM THE EXECUTORS

My Executors after paying or satisfying my debts funeral and testamentary expenses inheritance tax and the aforesaid pecuniary and specific legacies shall transfer all the residue of my estate (including all property over which I have a power of appointment or disposition by will) to [...] and [...] (hereinafter called 'my Trustees') to hold the same upon the following trusts: ... .

17.5 TRUSTS OF FRACTIONAL SHARES OF RESIDUE

Testators often want the residue to be divided into unequal shares. This can be done by dividing it into fractions, ensuring they total 100%. In a surprising number of cases they add up to something different. See for example, *Clarke v Brothwood and Others* [2006] EWHC 2939 (Ch), where the effect of a gift of fractions was to leave 60% of the testatrix's estate undisposed of.

Always consider the impact of inheritance tax (see **17.7**) when deciding on the appropriate size of share.

17F **CLAUSE DISPOSING OF RESIDUE IN UNEQUAL FRACTIONAL SHARES, THE INTEREST OF ONE OF THE BENEFICIARIES BEING CONTINGENT, WITH SUBSTITUTIONAL GIFTS AND ACCRUER PROVISIONS**

My Trustees shall hold my Residuary Trust Fund UPON TRUST to divide it or to treat it as being divided into fifteen shares of equal value and shall hold them upon the following trusts and subject to the following provisions:

(a) My Trustees shall hold such fifteen shares UPON TRUST absolutely:
  (i) As to three of them for [name].
  (ii) As to four of them for [name].
  (iii) As to one of them for such of my friends [names] as survive me and if more than one in equal shares.
  (iv) As to one of them for [name] but if [name] predeceases me then for their wife [name].
  (v) As to two of them for [name].
  (vi) As to four of them for [name] [contingently upon reaching the age of [twenty-one] [eighteen] or marrying or entering into a civil partnership under that age].*

(b) PROVIDED THAT if any of the persons named in paragraphs (i), (ii) and (v) or if both of those named in paragraph (iv) of subclause (a) of this clause predecease me leaving a child or children living at my death [who reach the age of [eighteen] or marry or enter into a civil partnership under that age]* then such child or children shall take absolutely and if more than one equally between them the share or shares of my Residuary Trust Fund which his, her or their parent would have taken if such parent had survived me.

(c)   PROVIDED ALSO that if at any time the trusts declared by subclause (a) read in conjunction with subclause (b) of this clause in respect of any share or shares of my Residuary Trust Fund lapse or fail then from the date of such lapse or failure such share or shares (and any further share or shares or part thereof which may have accrued thereto by virtue of this provision) shall accrue to the other share or shares (and equally if more than one [and if more than one in the proportions which they bear to each other]) the trusts of which have not at that date lapsed or failed and be held upon the trusts and with and subject to the powers and provisions from time to time affecting such other share or shares.

* Since the changes introduced by the Finance Act 2006, the inclusion of an age contingency normally creates a 'relevant property trust' if the contingency is unfulfilled at the testator's death. Relevant property trusts are subject to anniversary and exit charges. Where the beneficiaries are the testator's own children, the trusts may qualify for privileged treatment under Inheritance Tax Act 1984, section 71A or section 71D. When drafting, therefore, it is important to consider whether the value of the estate is such that inheritance tax is likely to be an issue and, if so, whether the testator wants to avoid paying anniversary and exit charges. To avoid them, the gifts must be made absolute or the beneficiaries given an immediate post-death interest. See Chapter 29.

17G   CLAUSE DISPOSING OF RESIDUE IN PERCENTAGE SHARES

My Trustees shall hold my Residuary Trust Fund UPON TRUST to hold the same upon the following trusts and subject to the following provisions:

(a)

(i)   As to [40]% for [name].

(ii)   As to [15]% for [name].

(iii)   As to [15]% for such of [names] as survive me and if more than one in equal shares.

(iv)   As to [10]% for [name].

(v)   As to [20]% for [name].

[(b)   PROVIDED THAT if any of the persons named in paragraphs (i), (ii), (iv) and (v) or if both of those named in paragraph (iii) of subclause (a) of this clause predecease me leaving a child or children living at my death [who reach the age of [eighteen] [twenty-one] or marry or enter into a civil partnership under that age]* then such child or children shall take absolutely and if more than one equally between them the share or shares of my Residuary Trust Fund which his, her or their parent would have taken if such parent had survived me.]

(c)   PROVIDED ALSO that if at any time the trusts declared by subclause (a) read in conjunction with subclause (b) of this clause in respect of any share or shares of my residuary estate lapse or fail then from the date of such lapse or failure such share or shares (and any further share or shares or part thereof which may have accrued thereto by virtue of this provision) shall accrue to the other share or shares (and equally if more than one [and if more than one in the proportions which they bear to each other]) the trusts of which have not at that date lapsed or failed and be held upon the trusts and with and subject to the powers and provisions from time to time affecting such other share or shares.

* See note to Precedent 17F.

17.6   PROVIDING FOR SPOUSES AND CIVIL PARTNERS

The introduction of the transferable nil rate band (Inheritance Tax Act 1984, sections 8A to 8C) means that there are often strong inheritance tax reasons for leaving the whole estate to a surviving spouse or civil partner so that on their death, a whole additional nil rate band is available.

There are advantages in leaving residue to a surviving spouse or civil partner for life rather than absolutely. The spouse exemption will be available, but the capital will be preserved for issue and there will be protection against exposure to care home fees.

However, it will normally be beneficial to include flexibility to allow the trustees to terminate the life interest by appointing capital to the spouse or to the remainder beneficiaries. It is often easier to draft such gifts as a discretionary trust with a right to income for the spouse until the trustees choose to exercise their discretionary powers (see Precedent 18F).

17H   TRUST OF RESIDUE FOR SPOUSE OR CIVIL PARTNER FOR LIFE WITH PROVISION FOR APPLICATION OF CAPITAL; REMAINDER TO CHILDREN WITH SUBSTITUTION FOR ISSUE

(a)   My Trustees shall pay the income of my Residuary Trust Fund to my [spouse] [civil partner] during [his] [her] lifetime ('the Trust Period') provided that my Trustees may at any time during the Trust Period in their discretion pay [or apply] the whole or any part of my Residuary Trust Fund in which my said [spouse] [civil partner] is then entitled to an interest in possession to [him] [her] or for [his] [her] advancement or otherwise for [his] [her] benefit and subject thereto.

(b)   My Trustees shall hold the capital and income of my Residuary Trust Fund for such of my children as shall survive me [and shall reach the age of [eighteen] [twenty-five] or marry or enter into a civil partnership under that age]* and if more than one in equal shares absolutely PROVIDED THAT if any child is already dead or predeceases me the share of my Residuary Trust Fund to which such child would have been entitled if he or she had survived me shall be held in trust for such of his or her children and remoter issue (if any) as shall be living at my death [and shall reach the age of [eighteen] years or marry or enter into a civil partnership under that age]** such issue to take through all degrees according to their stocks if more than one in equal shares and so that no issue shall take whose parent is living at my death and so capable of taking.

* In relation to the remainder interest, the gift is to the testator's *own* child and so may qualify for privileged treatment under the Inheritance Tax Act 1984. If age eighteen is selected and the child is under that age at the date of death of the testator or surviving spouse or civil partner, the trust may qualify as a bereaved minor's trust under section 71A, in which case it would not be subject to anniversary and exit charges. If age twenty-five is selected and the child is under that age at the date of death of the testator or surviving spouse or civil partner, the trust may qualify for special treatment under section 71D. In this case, there would be no anniversary and exit charges while the child is under eighteen, but if the trust continues beyond that age, there would be an exit charge calculated on the time which has elapsed since the child's eighteenth birthday. See Chapter 29.

** The substitutional gift to issue will not attract privileged tax treatment.

The following gift of residue to a spouse absolutely does not include a survivorship clause. See **17.8** for a discussion of survivorship clauses.

171   RESIDUE TO SPOUSE OR CIVIL PARTNER ABSOLUTELY WITH SUBSTITUTIONAL GIFT TO CHILDREN OR ISSUE

(a)   My Trustees shall pay my Residuary Trust Fund to my [spouse] [civil partner] [name] absolutely provided that

(b)   If my [spouse] [civil partner] [name] fails to survive me or if the gift fails for any other reason my Trustees shall hold the capital and income of my Residuary Trust Fund for such of my children as shall survive me and if more than one in equal shares absolutely PROVIDED THAT if any child is already dead or predeceases me or otherwise fails to take a vested interest the share of my Residuary Trust Fund to which such child would have been entitled if [he] [she] had survived me shall be held in trust for such of [his] [her] children and remoter issue (if any) as shall be living at my death and shall reach the age of eighteen [18] years or marry or enter into a civil partnership under that age such issue to take through all degrees according to their stocks if more than one in equal shares and so that no issue shall take whose parent is living at my death and so capable of taking.

17.7 BURDEN OF INHERITANCE TAX

Unless the will provides otherwise, Inheritance Tax Act 1984, section 211 provides that inheritance tax payable on death is a testamentary expense to be paid from the same property as other debts (normally residue), unless the tax, or the property in question, falls into one of the following categories:

(i)   foreign property;
(ii) property passing by survivorship, *donatio mortis causa* or nomination (that is, property which does not vest in the personal representatives);
(iii) property comprised in a settlement immediately before the testator's death;
(iv) additional inheritance tax on lifetime gifts chargeable as a result of the testator's death;
(v)   property treated as part of the testator's estate as a result of the reservation of benefit rules (as in category (ii) above, the property does not vest in the personal representatives);
(vi) works of art and the like, where tax becomes payable as a result of sale or breach of an undertaking.

The burden of tax payable on property falling within categories (i) to (vi) above, therefore, falls on the donee. The personal representatives have a right under section 211(3) to recover from the donees any tax they pay which is not a testamentary expense.

A gift of residue usually includes an express direction that inheritance tax is to be paid from residue. It is important to consider whether the testator wishes merely to restate the statutory position for the avoidance of doubt, or to change it so that the tax payable in all or any of categories (i) to (vi) above becomes payable from residue. For example, a direction that 'inheritance tax payable on property passing under my will' is to be paid from residue merely restates the statutory position, whereas a direction to pay 'all inheritance tax resulting from my death' is much wider and throws the burden of tax in categories (i) to (vi) above onto residue.

17J   SEPARATE DIRECTIONS AS TO INHERITANCE TAX

My Trustees shall pay my funeral and testamentary expenses and my debts together with inheritance tax payable [and any death duties payable outside the United Kingdom] [in respect of any property passing under this will] [in respect of any property passing as a result of my death] [and in respect of any gift or other transaction given or effected in my lifetime giving rise to a claim for inheritance tax or additional inheritance tax] and any legacies given by this will or any codicil to it out of such property or its proceeds of sale.

17.7.1 Residue divided between exempt and non-exempt beneficiaries

Inheritance Tax Act 1984, section 41 provides that, where part of an estate passes to non-exempt beneficiaries and part to exempt beneficiaries (e.g. a spouse or charity), the exempt share of the estate cannot be made to bear any part of the tax on the non-exempt part. Thus, if residue is to be divided into a number of equal shares, the shares of non-exempt beneficiaries are reduced by the inheritance tax attributable to their shares. The shares of exempt beneficiaries have no liability to tax and are not reduced. The two classes of beneficiary, therefore, receive different amounts. Although it is not possible to vary the statutory position by directing that an exempt share of residue bears the tax attributable to a non-exempt share, it is possible to direct that the residue be divided into unequal shares so that each beneficiary ultimately receives the same amount (see *Re Benham's Will Trusts* [1995] STC 210). However, the calculation is complex and drafting in this way is not recommended. It is preferable to avoid any doubt by including a statement that the residue is to be divided equally and that each share is to bear its own tax.

17K DECLARATION CONCERNING PARTIALLY EXEMPT RESIDUE

The entitlement of the [charities and] persons interested in [my Residuary Trust Fund] shall be determined by dividing [my Residuary Trust Fund] into the fractional shares set out above without making any deduction or allowance for the inheritance tax payable by reason of my death and attributable to [my Residuary Trust Fund] and then reducing such shares as are not exempt from inheritance tax by the inheritance tax attributable thereto.

17.7.2 Property eligible for business or agricultural property relief

If property eligible for business or agricultural relief is specifically given, the specific legatee alone benefits from the relief. If such property is left to an exempt beneficiary, the relief is wasted. It is, therefore, tax-efficient to leave property eligible for relief to non-exempt beneficiaries. The testator may particularly wish a spouse to receive property eligible for relief; in this case, it may be appropriate to leave the property to the non-exempt beneficiary subject to an option to purchase in favour of the spouse. When the option is exercised, the spouse will acquire the business or agricultural property, the non-exempt beneficiary will receive a sum of cash, and the estate will benefit from a reduced tax liability.

Where the property eligible for relief is not specifically given, the benefit of the relief is apportioned among the different gifts, using the formula set out in Inheritance Tax Act 1984, section 39A. This means that the inheritance tax value of a specific or pecuniary legacy is reduced by a proportion of the relief available on property comprised in the residue.

This can lead to a loss of relief as shown by the following example:

Example

Ted leaves his £1 million estate as follows:

- £200,000 to charity;
- £300,000 to his wife;
- the residue (£500,000) to his son. Half of the residue consists of a business eligible for 100% business property relief.

The benefit of the relief must be apportioned through the estate. So 2/10ths is allocated to the charitable legacy, 3/10ths to the gift to his wife and only 5/10ths to the gift to the son. Effectively, half of the relief is wasted. Had the business been left specifically to the son, the whole of the relief would have been available to the son's gift.

Similar problems arise where a will leaves a nil rate band legacy and the residue contains property eligible for relief. A legacy expressed to pass 'the greatest sum possible without attracting the payment of inheritance tax' will pass more than the value of the nil rate band if there is apportionment of relief under section 39A. This is because the inheritance tax value of the pecuniary legacy is reduced by the proportion of business relief allocated to it. If the testator is anxious to avoid passing too much to the pecuniary legatee, the legacy should be made subject to a maximum figure (typically the value of the nil rate band at death).

A testator may be uncertain whether or not property qualifies for relief. This may be because of the possibility that the business consists wholly or mainly of dealing in securities, stocks or shares, land or buildings, or making or holding investments (caravan sites often cause problems). Alternatively, there may be large amounts of cash held in the business which HM Revenue & Customs may argue are excepted assets. Such a client may want the will drafted to give the property to a non-exempt beneficiary if it qualifies for relief, and to a spouse or civil partner if it does not. It is not, however, desirable to draft the will in this form. HM Revenue & Customs will refuse to rule on whether or not the property attracts relief as it does not stand to collect tax in either event. As a result there would be uncertainty in the administration. The best solution is to leave the property to a discretionary trust. If an appointment out is made within 2 years, it can be read back into the will under Inheritance Tax Act 1984, section 144 (see **29.3**). The trustees can therefore decide on the appointee once they know whether or not assets qualify for relief.

17.8   SURVIVORSHIP CLAUSES

Survivorship clauses are most commonly used to ensure that property does not pass through two estates in close succession. This would occur when a beneficiary under a will dies shortly after the testator. Such a clause may also help to avoid a double charge to inheritance tax. Rather than adding a separate survivorship condition to each gift, it is often preferable to include a declaration that any person not surviving for a specified period is to be treated as having predeceased.

Where a survivorship clause is used, the estate cannot be distributed until after the expiry of the survivorship period, unless the beneficiary to whom the clause relates dies before the period ends. A survivorship period should not exceed 6 months since, if it does, a settlement is created for inheritance tax purposes. This may lead to a double charge to tax.

It may be desirable not to include a survivorship clause for spouses or civil partners for two inheritance tax reasons – impact of the transferable nil rate band and *commorientes*.

17.8.1   Impact of the transferable nil rate band

Where the transferable nil rate band is available and both spouses/civil partners have the same default beneficiaries, there is arguably no advantage to including a survivorship clause. If one dies shortly after the other having inherited the estate of the first to die, there is no increased inheritance tax as two nil rate bands will be available to the estate of the survivor.

Indeed, in certain situations the inclusion of a survivorship clause can have adverse tax consequences. For example, if one estate is below the level of the nil rate band and one is above, it is preferable for the larger estate to pass to the survivor attracting the spouse exemption.

> **Example**
>
> Assume Fred has £400,000 and his wife, Martha, has £200,000. Their wills leave everything to the other subject to a 28-day survivorship period and in default to their children.
>
> Fred dies on 20 March 2022 and Martha dies 11 days later, on 31 March.
>
> The nil rate band is £325,000. Fred's estate will pass to the children with a charge to inheritance tax on £75,000. Martha's estate will pass to the children without any charge to tax.
>
> However, without a survivorship clause, Fred's estate would have passed to Martha without tax. Martha's estate of £600,000 would have benefited from a nil rate band transferred from Fred and the couple's wealth would have escaped tax.
>
> (If the children are adults, they could vary the disposition of Fred's estate to leave it all to Martha absolutely, but if they are minors, an application to court may have to be made as HM Revenue & Customs will not accept a variation on behalf of minors which is 'adverse' to their interests.
>
> See HM Revenue & Customs, *Inheritance Tax Manual* at IHTM35045 (available at www.hmrc.gov.uk/manuals/ihtmanual).
>
> Query whether a variation in such circumstances can properly be regarded as 'adverse'.)

A survivorship clause will obviously be required if the spouses/civil partners want different default beneficiaries.

For administrative simplicity a survivorship clause may be included where it is clear that both estates are above (or below) the nil rate band.

17.8.2 Commorientes

Even if a survivorship clause is to be included for spouses/civil partners, there can be a tax saving if the survivorship condition is drafted so as not to apply where the order of deaths is uncertain. This is because Inheritance Tax Act 1984, section 4(2) provides that where persons have died in circumstances where it is uncertain which died first, they are to be treated for the purposes of inheritance tax as having died at the same moment. If the older spouse or civil partner leaves everything to the younger, the gift takes effect as a result of Law of Property Act

1925, section 184, so there is no tax on the estate of the first to die because it benefits from the spouse exemption. The younger spouse or civil partner is treated as having died at the same moment as the first but inheritance tax is assessed on assets owned immediately before death. Tax is, therefore, not charged on property inherited from the older.

There can be a non-tax reason for not including a survivorship clause, as illustrated by *Jump and Another v Lister and Another* [2016] EWHC 2160 (Ch), [2017] WTLR 61. A problem can arise if the parties have made mirror wills and there is uncertainty as to the order of deaths.

In *Jump and Another v Lister and Another*, a husband and wife left everything to the other, and if the other failed to survive, each will contained a series of specific and pecuniary legacies and gave the residue to nieces. Each will contained a general survivorship clause requiring anyone named in the will to survive the testator by 28 days in order to take under the will.

The wife was older than her husband so, as there was uncertainty as to the date of death, she was deemed to die first. Her estate did not pass to him because he had failed to survive for the appropriate period. The various legacies were paid.

The husband, being younger, was deemed to survive his wife so the gift to her failed and the various legacies were paid again. The nieces were not happy as their share of the estate was significantly reduced by the double payment of legacies.

17L   SURVIVORSHIP CLAUSE FOR GIFT TO SPOUSE OR CIVIL PARTNER WITH OPTIONAL PROVISO AS TO COMMORIENTES FOR THE WILL OF THE OLDER SPOUSE OR CIVIL PARTNER

(a)   IF my [spouse] [civil partner] fails to survive me by [twenty-eight days] or if the gift to my [spouse] [civil partner] fails for any other reason (but not otherwise) I GIVE my Residuary Trust Fund to my Trustees to hold the same on trust to sell call in and convert the same into money with full power to postpone the said sale calling in and conversion thereof so long as they shall in their absolute discretion think fit without being liable for any loss UPON TRUST to hold the proceeds of the said sale calling in and conversion and any property for the time being remaining unsold and unconverted UPON the trusts set out in clause [number of clause setting out the terms of the gift over].

[(b)   PROVIDED THAT if my [spouse] [civil partner] and I shall die in circumstances where it cannot be known which of us survived the other then the foregoing survival condition shall not apply and all gifts in my [spouse's] [civil partner's] favour [other than ...] shall take effect.]

Note: The proviso should be included only in the will of the older spouse or civil partner.

17M   GENERAL SURVIVORSHIP CONDITION

Every person who would otherwise benefit under this will but who fails to survive me for [twenty-eight days] shall be treated for all purposes connected with the devolution of my estate [[including] [but not including] Wills Act 1837, section 33*] as having predeceased me and my estate together with any intermediate income produced shall devolve accordingly.

* See **17.9**.

17.9   SUBSTITUTIONAL GIFTS

In most cases a testator wishes to provide a substitutional gift to apply where intended beneficiaries predecease or die before the expiry of any stated survivorship period. This is particularly important in the case of gifts of residue, as it is usually desirable to avoid a partial or total intestacy.

Wills Act 1837, section 33 provides a statutory substitutional gift in the case of gifts to the testator's children or issue, where the will contains no provision for the death of the beneficiary. Where the primary beneficiary predeceases the testator, leaving issue, the issue of the primary beneficiary take the share of their parent (see **5.2.2**). An express provision is, however, preferable, to show the testator's intention and is essential in the case of beneficiaries who are not children or issue of testator as section 33 does not apply to them. Frequently, the substitutional gift is made to the children or issue of the original beneficiary should that beneficiary fail to survive.

It is wise not to restrict the substitution to cases of death or failure to survive, but to allow the substitution to take effect if the gift should fail for *any* reason. For example, a gift to an individual will be forfeited if they kill the testator and a gift to a person who witnesses the will cannot take effect. A substitutional gift drafted to apply only in the event of the *death* of such individuals could not take effect.

The Estates of Deceased Persons (Forfeiture Rule and Law of Succession) Act 2011 amends the Wills Act 1837 for deaths on or after 1 February 2012 to provide that for the purposes of the 'Act' a person who disclaims an entitlement under a will or who is deprived of it by the operation of the forfeiture rule is to be treated as having died immediately before the testator. The amendment appears to be limited to children and issue of the testator, so express provision will still be required to deal with forfeiture or disclaimer by any other person.

17N   TRUST FOR TESTATOR'S CHILDREN AT A STATED AGE WITH SUBSTITUTION OF ISSUE IF A CHILD PREDECEASES OR DIES AFTER THE TESTATOR'S DEATH WITHOUT ATTAINING A VESTED INTEREST

(a)   My Trustees shall hold [my Residuary Trust Fund] IN TRUST for such of my children as shall be living at or after my death [and attain the age of [eighteen] years]* and if more than one in equal shares

(b)   PROVIDED THAT
  (i)   if any of my children is already dead or dies during my lifetime, or dies after my death without attaining the age of [eighteen] years,** or
  (ii)   the gift to any of my children shall fail for any reason
  the share of [my Residuary Trust Fund] to which such child would be entitled if he or she survived me and attained a vested interest shall be held IN TRUST for such of his or her children and remoter issue (if any) as shall be living at my death [and attain the age of [eighteen] years]** in equal shares *per stirpes* but so that no issue shall take whose parent is living at my death and capable of taking AND FURTHER PROVIDED THAT if any child of mine or any remoter issue of mine presumptively entitled under the foregoing proviso survives me but dies without attaining a vested interest under the foregoing trusts the share of [the Residuary Trust Fund] to which such child or issue of mine would be entitled if he or she lived to attain such a vested interest shall be held in trust for such of his or her children (if any) as attain the age of [eighteen] years or marry under that age if more than one in equal shares.

* See the first note to Precedent 17H.

** Clause (b(i)) goes further than the statutory substitution under Wills Act 1837, section 33 by contemplating the failure of the primary gift *after* the testator's death as well as before.

Testators concerned about inheritance tax, who wish to make gifts to young people but do not wish them to have access to capital at too early an age, may wish to leave property on trust for the young people for life with power for the trustees to advance capital – an immediate post-death interest. See Chapter 29. This has the advantage of deferring entitlement to capital without incurring anniversary or exit charges. However, there are tax considerations. Should the child die before the capital is advanced, the value of the trust property is aggregated with their own assets for inheritance tax purposes. Also, capital gains tax holdover relief will not be available when the child becomes absolutely entitled.

17O RESIDUE TO YOUNG PEOPLE FOR LIFE WITH POWER TO ADVANCE CAPITAL

1. Definitions
In this clause the following expressions shall have the following meanings:
(1)   The 'Beneficiaries' means and includes:
    (a)   all my children and remoter issue who may be born before the end of the Trust Period;
    (b)   any spouse, widow or widower of any of my children or remoter issue of [...] [including] [not including] a widow or widower who has remarried;
    (c)   any civil partner or surviving civil partner of any of my children or remoter issue of [...] and [...] [including] [not including] a civil partner or surviving civil partner who has formed a new civil partnership;
    (d)   [any other family members to be included].
(2)   The 'Principal Beneficiaries' means all my children.
(3)   The 'Trust Period' means [as in Precedent 18F].

2. Gift of residue to Trustees
[as in Precedent 18F, clause 3].
3. Power to appoint capital at Trustees' discretion
[as in Precedent 18F, clause 4].
4. Life interest trusts in default of appointment
The provisions of this clause shall apply until, subject to and in default of any appointment under clause 3.
(1)   My Trustees shall hold my Residuary Trust Fund upon trust, subject to the provisions of my will for the Principal Beneficiaries in equal shares.
(2)   The provisions of sub-clauses 4(3) and 4(4) shall apply to the share of my Residuary Trust Fund held upon trust for any one of my Principal Beneficiaries under sub-clause 4(1). In those provisions, such share is called 'the Share' and that one of the Principal Beneficiaries who is primarily interested in the Share is called 'the Life Tenant'.
(3)   The income of the Share shall be paid to the Life Tenant during their lifetime. [If and so long as the Life Tenant is under the age of eighteen, the Trustees may pay or apply any income of the Share to them or for their maintenance or education or otherwise for their benefit as the Trustees shall in their discretion think fit. Any balance

of the income shall be retained by my Trustees upon trust for the Life Tenant absolutely. Any such retained income may at any time be paid or applied as if it was income arising in the then current year. Trustee Act 1925, section 31 shall not apply to the Share so long as the Life Tenant is under the age of eighteen.]

(4)   My Trustees may at any time during the Trust Period pay or apply the whole or any part of the Share in which the Life Tenant is then entitled to an interest in possession to them or for their advancement or otherwise for their benefit in such manner as my Trustees shall in their discretion think fit. In exercising the powers conferred by this sub-clause my Trustees shall be entitled to have regard solely to the interests of the Life Tenant and to disregard all other interests or potential interests under this will.

(5)   Subject as above the capital and income of the Share shall be held upon trust for such of the children of the Life Tenant as attain the age of [twenty-five] before the end of the Trust Period or are living and are under that age at the end of the Trust Period and if more than one in equal shares absolutely.

(6)   Subject as above the Share together with any accrual to it shall accrue to the other Shares the trusts of which shall not previously have failed or determined (otherwise than by absolute vesting) and if more than one equally between them. Each such accrual shall be held upon, with and subject to the same trusts, powers and provisions as the Share to which it accrues.

5. Ultimate default clause

In the event of the failure or determination of the above trusts the capital and income of my Residuary Trust Fund shall be held upon trust for [...] absolutely.

6. Manner of exercise of powers of appointment.

Any exercise of the power of appointment conferred by clause 3 shall:

(1)   be subject to the application of the rule against perpetuities; and

(2)   be by deed, revocable during the Trust Period, or irrevocable, executed during the Trust Period.

Chapter 18

Powers and Discretionary Trusts

18.1 NATURE AND CLASSIFICATION OF POWERS

Powers of appointment are classified as general, special or hybrid. A power is a discretion given to a person to deal with or dispose of property of which they are not the owner. Powers may be administrative (see Chapter 22), for example, where a power is given to trustees to insure trust property; or may be powers of appointment, for example:

> I devise Blackacre to my wife Sarah [who is the donee and appointor of the power] for life and declare that at her death she may appoint whichever one of our children as she wishes to be the absolute owner of Blackacre.

The donor may specify that an appointment is to be made in a particular way, for example by will or by deed. If the appointment is not made in such a manner it is void (see *Pitt and Holt v RCC* [2013] UKSC 26).

Powers of appointment can be distinguished from trusts because the donee of a power of appointment can choose whether or not to make the appointment. If the donee chooses not to make the appointment, any gift over takes effect. If there is no gift over, a resulting trust in favour of the testator's estate arises in respect of the property.

18.1.1 General powers

Under a general power, the donee of the power is free to exercise it in favour of anyone they choose, including themselves. Title is derived not from the appointment itself, but from the instrument conferring the power. All property appointed by will under such a power passes to the appointor's personal representatives, and may be applied to the payment of the appointor's debts, although first recourse must always be made to the appointor's own property.

Interests given in default of appointment may be defeated by the exercise of the power at any time, and any assignment of such an interest before the exercise of the power, in effect, passes nothing.

If, for any reason, an appointment is ineffectual, the property devolves as part of the testator's estate. Where no appointment is made, the property passes according to the intention of the donor as expressed in the deed of appointment. Any exercise of a power must be in accordance with any prescribed conditions.

A general power of appointment can be very useful as it allows a person with an immediate post-death interest to create a subsequent immediate post-death interest in the same property. The creation of successive immediate post-death interests is not normally possible since the changes to the taxation of trusts introduced by the Finance Act 2006. However, because a person with a general power is treated as beneficially owning the property, they can create an immediate post-death interest in the property subject to the power.

Example

Freda's father created a will trust giving Freda an immediate post-death interest, remainder to her children.

Normally, on Freda's death there would be a charge to inheritance tax on the settled property as part of her estate. However, if Freda has a general power of appointment over the settled property which she exercises to create a flexible life interest for her surviving spouse, Sam, she will create an immediate post-death interest. That part of her estate is spouse exempt.

The trustees can terminate Sam's interest at any point, so accelerating the remainder interests, and he will be treated as making a potentially exempt transfer.

18.1.2   Special powers

A special power restricts the appointor as to the class of possible appointee, for example by reference to the relationship of the potential appointees to the donor. This does not, however, prevent the appointor themselves from being appointed if they are a member of the restricted group.

18.1.3   Hybrid powers

A 'hybrid' or 'intermediate' power does not fit into either of the two categories above; it permits the donee to appoint anyone as appointee, except a certain person or class of people. Intermediate powers are treated as special powers for the purpose of Wills Act 1837, section 27 and for perpetuity purposes (see Chapter 23).

A power which is exercisable by will only, whether general or special, is known as a testamentary power.

18.2 WILLS ACT 1837, SECTION 27

Wills Act 1837, section 27 provides that, in the absence of an expressed contrary intention, a general devise or bequest operates as an execution of 'a power to appoint in any manner [the appointor] may think proper', whether that power relates to real or personal property. For example, if A has a general power of appointment over Blackacre but fails to mention the power over Blackacre in his will, a general gift of 'all my realty' would successfully dispose of Blackacre. The provision does not apply to special or hybrid powers which in any way restrict the choice of appointee, but it does apply even if a will is executed before the power is created. To satisfy section 27, the general gift may be of the whole or any part of the testator's estate, provided any part is sufficiently well described to include the property to which the power relates.

As noted in Chapter 17, it is preferable to make express reference to the power rather than relying on section 27, to avoid any argument, by those entitled in default of appointment, that the testator was unaware that the residuary gift would pass the property subject to the power. In *Gibbons v Nelson* [2000] Lloyd's Rep PN 603, a case involving the exercise of a power of appointment by section 27, Blackburne J criticised the solicitor concerned for failing to establish the client's intentions with regard to the destination of trust property.

Any power to which section 27 does not apply can be exercised by will only if the disposition is expressed to be in exercise of such a power.

18.3 PERPETUITIES AND ACCUMULATIONS ACT 2009

See Chapter 23 for a discussion of this important topic.

The Perpetuities and Accumulations Act 2009 applies to trusts created and wills executed on or after the date on which it came into effect (6 April 2010).

If a trust created before that date includes a power of appointment which is used after that date to create a new trust interest, does the new trust interest benefit from the new rules?

It does not if the power was a special power as defined in section 11 of the Act. A special power of appointment for the purposes of the Act is any power other than one that can be exercised by a single appointee to transfer to themselves or their personal representatives the whole of the interest governed by the power without the consent of any other person or compliance with any other condition.

In the case of an appointment made under a special power of appointment (as defined in section 11) on or after the Act comes into force, the perpetuity period starts when the instrument creating the power took effect (section 6(2)) and will be subject to the same accumulation period as the original instrument (section 15(1)(b)).

Example

A trust is created on 1 July 1980 with an 80-year perpetuity period from that date. The trust includes a special power of appointment which is exercised after the Act comes into force. The perpetuity period for any trust created by the power will be 80 years starting on 1 July 1980 and the accumulation period will be that applying to the original instrument.

At the time of writing, there is some uncertainty as to the position in relation to pension schemes created before 6 April 2010 which make a discretionary payment to a trust on behalf of a scheme member who joins on or after that date. See Chapter 23.

18.4 DELEGATION OF POWERS

The general rule is that a power involving the exercise of personal discretion by the donee cannot be delegated; any attempt to do so is a nullity, although it in no way affects the validity of the interests limited in default of execution of the power. A special power can never be delegated, since by the terms of its creation the obligation on the donee is to exercise personal discretion. Conversely, in a general power the obligation to exercise the donee's personal discretion is never an inherent part of the power.

The donee of any power may delegate the performance of any administrative act, provided it involves no act of personal discretion (e.g. the execution of a document already approved may be delegated).

The Trustee Act 2000 confers limited implied powers to delegate certain functions.

18.5   CONSENT TO EXERCISE POWER

Where a power is exercisable only with the consent of another person, that consent must be given during the donee's lifetime. If the person whose consent is required dies, the power cannot be exercised.

18.6   RELEASE OF POWERS

A power involving a duty or a power in the nature of a trust cannot be released, but other powers may be released by deed. Powers must generally be exercised in good faith in order to carry out the intention of the donor of the power. This does not, however, prevent the release of a special power or the release of a power of revocation contained in the instrument exercising the power. The donee may release the power either wholly or in part, and any dealing with the property which is inconsistent with the exercise of the power operates as a release. An absolute release of a power is irrevocable and any attempt to exercise the power after the release is void.

Where it is provided that in default of appointment a trust (either express or implied) arises in favour of the members of a class of objects, the donee of the power cannot defeat the interest of the members of the class of objects, by either attempting to release the power or failing to appoint. The donee is under a duty to exercise the power and it cannot, therefore, be released. The court cannot, though, compel the appointor to exercise the power, but can only execute the trust in default of the appointment.

A power conferred on trustees by virtue of their office in relation to their trust property cannot be released unless such release is authorised in the trust deed (see *Muir v IRC* [1966] 1 WLR 1269). This is also the case where the power is conferred on named persons chosen by reason of their office as trustees of the settlement.

Provided the donee of a power is not a trustee of the property to which it relates or, if they are such a trustee, the power is not conferred on them in that capacity, then, in the absence of a trust in favour of the objects of the power in default of appointment, the donee of such a power can release it.

18.7   FRAUDULENT APPOINTMENTS

A person with a limited power of appointment must exercise it *bona fide* for the purpose for which it was created. If the power is exercised for any other reason, the appointment is void. The reason may be to benefit the appointor, but it is equally objectionable if the appointor intends to benefit anyone who is not an object of the power.

An appointment made in pursuance of an agreement on the part of the appointee to benefit a non-object is clearly void. The fact that the appointor knows that the appointee intends to benefit a non-object is not enough to vitiate the appointment unless the appointment would not otherwise have been made. The question is always whether the appointment was made for the benefit of the appointee. If it was not, the appointment is void (see *Cooper v Cooper* (1869) LR 8 Eq 312).

Trustees can find themselves having to think carefully about the purpose for which they are exercising a power. However, where a power has to be exercised for the 'benefit' of an appointee, case-law makes it clear that 'benefit' has a wide meaning. In *Re Clore's Settlement Trusts* [1966] 1 WLR 955, the court held that benefit is not confined to a person's direct financial situation but can include the discharge of certain moral or social obligations, particularly in relation to provision for family and dependants. In *Re Hampden Settlement Trusts* [1977] TR 177, the court allowed a settlement on the beneficiary's children relieving him of the 'considerable obligation in respect of making provision for their future' which he would otherwise have owed. However, in *X v A and Others* [2005] EWHC 2706 (Ch), the court refused to authorise trustees to release the bulk of a substantial fund to the wife of the settlor who, being opposed to inherited wealth, wished to donate the fund to charity rather than have it used for the beneficiaries. Similarly, in *Smith and Another v Michelmores Trust Corporation Ltd and Others* [2021] EWHC 1425 (Ch), the court refused to authorise the use of a power to appoint trust property to a bankrupt beneficiary just before his discharge from bankruptcy. The use of the power was clearly intended to benefit the beneficiary's creditors rather than the beneficiary.

18A   POWERS EXERCISABLE IN FAVOUR OF A BENEFICIARY WHO IS ALSO A TRUSTEE

I DECLARE that the powers and discretions hereinbefore contained or otherwise vested in my Trustees may be exercised in favour of a Beneficiary notwithstanding that he or she may be one of my Trustees ALWAYS PROVIDED that such power or discretion shall not be so exercised unless my Trustees for the time being include at least one other person who is not such a Beneficiary or the spouse or child of such a Beneficiary.

18B POWER TO RELEASE POWERS

I HEREBY AUTHORISE my Trustees at any time to release by deed or otherwise restrict in any manner the future exercise of any powers or discretions hereinbefore or otherwise conferred on them so as to bind their successors as Trustees hereof whether or not such power or discretion shall be vested in them in a fiduciary capacity ALWAYS PROVIDED that no such release or restriction shall prejudice or affect the exercise of any such powers or discretions made before any such release or restriction.

18C POWER TO TRUSTEES TO SETTLE CHILDREN'S SHARE IN CASE OF MARRIAGE OR ENTERING INTO A CIVIL PARTNERSHIP BEFORE ENTITLEMENT

I HEREBY DECLARE that if any one or more of my children shall marry or enter into a civil partnership before attaining the prescribed age to become entitled to any gift contained in this my will or any codicil hereto then my Trustees shall hereby be empowered at any time before each such child has attained the prescribed age to appoint by deed or deeds to settle the whole or any part of the [share of residue] [property] hereinbefore bequeathed to such child or any specific property appropriated to the said share UPON SUCH TRUSTS for the benefit of such child and [his] [her] [spouse] [civil partner] and their children or issue or any of them and in such manner and form as my Trustees shall in their absolute discretion think fit and this power shall extend to any appointment deed or settlement contingent or dependent upon the future marriage or civil partnership of any such child while under the prescribed age as aforesaid and my Trustees shall have power to execute such a deed accordingly should they in their absolute discretion see fit to do so ALWAYS PROVIDED that the foregoing powers if exercised shall be exercised at all times to ensure that such child becomes entitled to the said share or to an interest in possession therein on or before attaining the age of [...] and so as to ensure that the income of the said share insofar as the same shall not be applied for such child's maintenance education or benefit shall be accumulated until such child becomes entitled.

Note: This will be a relevant property trust (see Chapter 29).

18D CLAUSE CREATING PROTECTIVE TRUST AND CONFERRING A POWER TO RAISE AND PAY CAPITAL

I GIVE to my Trustees [the Residuary Trust Fund] as to the income thereof upon protective trusts* for the benefit of [name] during their life and I HEREBY DECLARE that my Trustees shall have power at their absolute discretion and at any time or times before the failure or determination of the said trust of income and without being liable in any way to account for the exercise of such discretion to raise and pay to the said [name] for their own absolute use and benefit [the whole or any part or parts of] the capital of [the Residuary Trust Fund] and my Trustees shall hold any part not so transferred to [name] during their lifetime as the said [name] shall by will or codicil appoint and in default of and subject to any such appointment upon the following trusts [...] AND I DIRECT that my Trustees shall on no account be liable or responsible for making any such payments whether of income or capital to the said [name] after the failure or determination of their said determinable life interest unless or until my Trustees shall have received express notice of the act or event causing such failure or determination.

* As to protective trusts, see **18.11**.

18E   TRUST FOR SPOUSE OR CIVIL PARTNER FOR LIFE AND THEN TO SUCH CHILDREN AS HE OR SHE SHALL APPOINT

[Commence with gift of property to Trustees ...]
(a)   UPON TRUST to pay the income thereof to my [spouse] [civil partner] for [his] [her] life and after [his] [her] death
(b)   UPON TRUST as to both capital and income for all or any one or more of my children and remoter issue in such shares and subject to such powers provisions and generally in such manner as my said [spouse] [civil partner] shall by deed or will appoint and subject to any such appointment or in default of the same UPON TRUST for all my children living at my death if more than one in equal shares as tenants in common.

18.8 DISCRETIONARY TRUSTS

A discretionary trust is one under which the trustees are given a discretion to pay or apply the income or capital, or both, for the benefit of all or any one or more of the beneficiaries. The beneficiary is given no right to any part of the income or capital of the trust property and has no way of knowing whether any discretion will be exercised in their favour. A discretionary trust can be either exhaustive or non-exhaustive. In the former case, the trustees are under a duty to distribute the whole of the income but have a discretion as to whom to distribute it. In the latter case, the trustees are given a discretion to determine not only to whom the income should be distributed, but also whether and to what extent it should be distributed, if at all. The trustees must exercise the discretion as and when necessary, but failure to do so does not extinguish the discretion.

There are many reasons for creating a discretionary trust by will. Some are non-tax reasons and some are tax reasons.

Before considering the reasons which remain for using a discretionary trust, it is important to consider one which no longer exists. Before the introduction of the transferable nil rate band for surviving spouses and civil partners dying on or after 9 October 2007, couples of middling wealth who wanted to make tax-efficient wills providing for close family members had only one real option: the nil rate band discretionary trust.

The problem for such couples was that if the first spouse or civil partner left everything to the survivor, the nil rate band of the first to die was wasted; the couple's combined wealth was concentrated in the estate of the survivor and on the survivor's death only one nil rate band was available.

If the couple had sufficient assets to allow the first to die to leave assets equal to the nil rate band away from the survivor, there was no problem, but for many couples this was impossible. The solution that developed was for the first to die to leave a legacy equal to their nil rate band to a discretionary trust for the benefit of the surviving spouse or civil partner and other close family members and the residue to the surviving spouse or civil partner.

A refinement of this arrangement was for the will to authorise the trustees of the nil rate band discretionary trust to accept a debt or charge over the assets for the value of the legacy. All the assets would then be transferred to the surviving spouse or civil partner who would have the benefit of the assets, but whose estate would be reduced at death by the value of the debt.

The introduction of the transferable nil rate band means that couples can benefit from a combined nil rate band without having to create a trust. They may still choose to use a trust for other reasons, but most people prefer a simpler option. See **18.9** for one situation where there is still a compelling reason for using a nil rate band discretionary trust (where a person with the benefit of a transferred nil rate band has remarried or formed a civil partnership). Also, the use of a discretionary trust to hold other assets on the death of a spouse or civil partner will help to keep the estate of the surviving spouse or civil partner below the taper threshold and, thus, preserve the RNRB on the second death.

Note that the use of a discretionary trust to hold a residence or interest in a residence will mean that the RNRB is not available on the property held in the trust. Residential property must be inherited by children or issue if the RNRB is to be available. Property held on discretionary trusts is not treated as inherited even if all the beneficiaries are children and issue. See **14.4**.

However, an appointment from the trust within 2 years of death can be read back into the will under Inheritance Tax Act 1984, section 144, and so it is possible to secure the RNRB retrospectively. See **14.4**.

18.8.1   Non-tax reasons for using a discretionary trust

(i)   A discretionary trust gives flexibility. Trustees can adapt the amounts paid to the changing needs of beneficiaries.

(ii)   Beneficiaries can be protected from their own improvidence.

(iii)   A testator is able to defer entitlement so that young beneficiaries do not have too much at too early an age.

(iv)   Assets are protected from creditors in the event of a beneficiary's bankruptcy.

(v)   Assets are protected from care home fees.

(vi)   A discretionary trust avoids the statutory rights of occupation conferred on beneficiaries with an interest in possession by the Trusts of Land and Appointment of Trustees Act 1996.

(vii)   Testators can provide for beneficiaries who are disabled and unable to manage their own property (although in this case it will normally be preferable to ensure that the requirements of Inheritance Tax Act 1984, section 89 are satisfied so that the trust will receive beneficial inheritance tax treatment as a trust for the disabled).

(viii) A discretionary trust may afford a mechanism for providing for a beneficiary's needs without prejudicing means-tested benefits.

18.8.2   Tax reasons for using a discretionary trust

(i)   The property in a discretionary trust is not treated as 'owned' by any beneficiary. This is unlike an immediate post-death interest in possession trust, where the trust property is treated as part of the estate of the beneficiary with an interest in possession.

(ii)   Holding assets outside the estates of beneficiaries helps to keep estates below the taper threshold for the RNRB.

(iii)   The trust is treated as a separate entity for tax purposes.

(iv)   Tax is paid periodically (every 10 years, and when property leaves the trust between 10-year anniversaries) rather than in a single sum.

(v)   The rates of tax are currently moderate and, where the extent of the trust property is within the testator's nil rate band, no tax at all is payable for the first 10 years.

(vi)   An appointment from a discretionary trust created by will before the expiry of 2 years is 'read back' into the will under Inheritance Tax Act 1984, section 144 (see **29.3**). The effect is that the estate is treated, for inheritance tax purposes, as if the deceased had left the property in accordance with the terms of the appointment. This results in an additional 2 years of flexibility for an estate.

As with powers, it is important that the will should, where appropriate, give the person with the discretion express authority to exercise it in their own favour. Failure to do so will lead to uncertainty as to the testator's intentions.

A popular form of discretionary trust allows testators to combine the flexibility of the discretionary trust with the immediate benefit of the spouse exemption. To achieve this, the trust is drafted as discretionary in form but the surviving spouse or civil partner is given a right to income unless and until the trustees exercise a power of appointment to terminate the right to income. The effect is that the spouse or civil partner has an immediate post-death interest which qualifies for the spouse exemption. If the trustees choose to terminate the interest at a future date, the spouse or civil partner will be deemed to make a potentially exempt transfer of the value of the assets in which the interest has terminated (see Precedent 18G).

If on the death of the surviving spouse or civil partner, the trust property includes a residence or interest in a residence, the RNRB will be available to the survivor's estate, provided a lineal descendant becomes beneficially entitled. See Chapter 27.

18.9 NIL RATE BAND DISCRETIONARY TRUSTS

As explained at **18.8**, before the introduction of the transferable nil rate band, it was common for married couples or civil partners of moderate means to include a nil rate band discretionary trust to allow the first spouse or civil partner to die to make use of their nil rate band while allowing the survivor to have access to the combined assets of the couple. The introduction of the transferable nil rate band has reduced the frequency with which such trusts are used.

However, a nil rate band discretionary trust is still useful where testators wish to protect capital but to retain flexibility.

In addition, there remains one situation where a nil rate band discretionary trust is uniquely useful in inheritance tax planning. Where a surviving spouse or civil partner, who has the benefit of a nil rate band transferred from the dead spouse or civil partner, marries again or forms a new civil partnership, a discretionary trust is extremely useful. Inheritance Tax Act 1984, section 8A provides that no one can benefit from more than one additional nil rate band. Hence, if the person with the 'double' nil rate band dies and leaves everything to the new spouse or civil partner, only one nil rate band can be transferred and the other will be wasted. If the person with the double nil rate band wants the surviving spouse or civil partner to have access to all the assets, the best solution is to leave assets equal to the value of at least one nil rate band to a discretionary trust for the benefit of the survivor and close family members; the rest of the assets can be left to the surviving spouse or civil partner. On the death of the survivor, Inheritance Tax Act 1984, section 8C allows their personal representatives to claim the unused nil rate band.

Before the introduction of the transferable nil rate band it was common to include in wills a power to constitute the discretionary trust fund with a debt or charge, rather than with assets. This was advantageous because the surviving spouse or civil partner becomes the owner of all the deceased's assets (and, therefore, the principal private dwelling house exemption was available), but on death, the deceased's estate would be reduced by the debt owed to the estate of the first spouse or civil partner. Although such arrangements for married couples and civil partnerships will be created less commonly, there are still numerous trusts of debts and charges in existence. Such provisions may still be included where a spouse or civil partner has a double nil rate band and, as explained above, needs to make use of a nil rate band discretionary trust to achieve an inheritance tax-efficient result. Appendix 2 explains how such trusts should be constituted and what paperwork should be available.

Some spouses and civil partners may wish to make use of nil rate band discretionary trusts because the value of their combined estates will exceed the taper threshold at which point the RNRB starts to be withdrawn. See **14.4**.

For further guidance on the conveyancing aspects and Land Registry requirements where a house is included in the property subject to a nil rate trust, see Land Registry Practice Guide 70 (June 2015), *Nil Rate Band Discretionary Trusts*, available at www.gov.uk/government/publications/nil-rate-band-discretionary-trusts/practice-guide-70-nil-rate-band-discretionary-trusts.

18F   DISCRETIONARY TRUST OF RESIDUE FOR THE TESTATOR'S FAMILY

1. In this clause the following expressions shall have the following meanings:
   (1) 'The Trust Period' means the period starting with the date of my death and ending one hundred and twenty five years* afterwards (and that period shall be the perpetuity period applicable hereto) PROVIDED THAT my Trustees may declare by irrevocable deed that the Trust Period (but not the perpetuity period) shall terminate on such earlier date as they may specify.
   (2) 'The Beneficiaries' means:
       (a)   my [spouse] [civil partner] [name];

(b)   all my children and remoter issue who may be born before the end of the Trust Period;

(c)   any spouse** widow or widower of any such children or remoter issue ([including] [not including] a widow or widower who has remarried or formed a civil partnership);

(d)   any civil partner** or surviving civil partner of any such children or remoter issue ([including] [not including] a surviving civil partner who has formed a new civil partnership or married);

(e)   [any other family members to be included].

2.

(1)   My Trustees (being not less than two in number or a trust†† corporation) shall have power by any deed or deeds revocable (during the Trust Period) or irrevocable executed during the Trust Period to declare that:

(a)   any individual or individuals whether or not then born or ascertained or any charity or charities (other than any individual or charity previously excluded under the power set out in sub-clause (b) below) shall from such time and (subject to any future exercise of the power set out in sub-clause (b) below) either permanently or for such period or periods as shall be specified in any such deed or deeds be included in the class of Beneficiaries defined in clause 1(2) above;*** and

(b)   any individual or individuals whether or not then born or ascertained or any charity or charities who or which is or are a member or members (or eligible to be added as a member or members) of the class of Beneficiaries immediately prior to the execution of such deed or deeds shall from such time and either permanently or for such period or periods as shall be specified in any such deed or deeds cease to be a member† or members (or eligible to become a member or members) of such class.

(2)   PROVIDED always that no such deed made in exercise of either of the powers conferred by sub-clauses 2(1)(a) and (b) shall affect the validity or effect of:

(a)   any distribution previously made to or for the benefit of any of the Beneficiaries under or pursuant to any power or discretion;

(b)   any transmissible interest (whether vested or contingent) previously conferred on any of the Beneficiaries;

(c)   any future distribution to any of the Beneficiaries consequent on the absolute vesting in possession of any such interest.

(3)   My Trustees (being not less than two in number or a trust†† corporation) may at any time or times during the Trust Period by deed or deeds extinguish (or restrict the future exercise of) both or either of the powers (but not any of the restrictions applicable to them) conferred by sub-clauses 2(1)(a) and (b).

3. I GIVE all my property of whatever nature and wheresoever situated except property otherwise disposed of by this will or by any codicil hereto to my Trustees UPON TRUST to sell call in and convert the same into money (so far as not already consisting of money) with power to postpone the sale calling in and conversion thereof (even as regards property of a terminable hazardous or wasting nature) in the absolute and uncontrolled discretion of my Trustees without being liable for loss and to hold the net proceeds and my ready money upon the following trusts:

(1)   to pay (in exoneration of any property which would otherwise be liable for payment of the same) all my funeral and testamentary expenses and debts and any general legacies given by this will or any codicil hereto and any tax or duty arising in respect of my death (even if not a testamentary expense) on all gifts in this will and any codicil hereto given free of such tax or duty;

(2)   if necessary to invest the remainder after such payment in or upon any investments hereinafter authorised for the investment of trust funds with power to vary and transpose the same;

(3)   to stand possessed of such investments and such of my estate as remains for the time being unsold and my ready money and all property from time to time respectively representing the same (together called 'my Residuary Trust Fund') and the income from it upon the following trusts.

4.

(1)   During the Trust Period my Trustees shall hold the capital and income of my Residuary Trust Fund UPON TRUST for all or such one or more of the Beneficiaries at such ages or times in such shares and upon such trusts for the benefit of all or any one or more of the Beneficiaries as my Trustees (being at least two in number or a [trust][††] corporation) may by deed or deeds revocable or irrevocable at any time or times during the Trust Period appoint.

(2)   In making any such appointment my Trustees shall have powers as full as those which they could possess if they were the absolute beneficial owner of my Residuary Trust Fund and in particular (but without prejudice to the generality of the foregoing words) may:

(a)   appoint new Trustees of the whole or any part or parts of my Residuary Trust Fund and provide for the remuneration of any who may be professional or corporate Trustees;

(b)   create or delegate powers and discretions over capital or income (including powers of further delegation) whether of a dispositive or administrative nature.

(3)   PROVIDED THAT:

(a)   no appointment shall be capable of being made and no revocable appointment shall be capable of being revoked after the expiration of the Trust Period;

(b)   no appointment shall prejudice or affect any prior payment transfer or application of income or capital hereunder;

(c) any appointment under the foregoing power may be made subject and without prejudice to any existing interests trusts or powers;

(d) any such appointment may be made of income without any appointment of capital; and

(e) my Trustees (being at least two in number or a [trust][††] corporation) may at any time or times by deed or deeds extinguish release or restrict the foregoing power in any manner and to any extent.

5. In default of and subject to any exercise of the powers given them by the preceding provisions:

(1) during the Trust Period my Trustees shall pay or apply the income of my Residuary Trust Fund to or for the maintenance education support or otherwise for the benefit of such one or more of the Beneficiaries as my Trustees may in their absolute discretion think fit but with power to accumulate such income or any part or parts of it (with power to apply the accumulations of past years as if they were income of the current year) and with power (during the Trust Period) to resolve to hold the whole or any part or parts of such income as income on trust for any of the Beneficiaries absolutely; and

(2) on the expiry of the Trust Period my Trustees shall hold my Residuary Trust Fund as to both capital and income on trust absolutely for [insert name of desired default Beneficiaries, for example such of my issue as are living at the end of the Trust Period and if more than one in equal shares through all degrees according to their stocks and so that no issue shall take whose parent is alive and so capable of taking].

6. Any power or discretion hereby or by law vested in my Trustees may be exercised in favour of a person who is an object of such power or discretion notwithstanding that he or she is one of my Trustees[†††] provided that any such exercise of such a power or discretion is made by at least one of my Trustees who does not have a personal interest in the mode or result of exercising the same.

* Where a fixed perpetuity period is chosen, any appointments made under the trust are subject to that perpetuity period. Thus, if an appointment is made on new trusts, all interests in the new trust must vest within one hundred and twenty five years of creation of the original trust.

** A common reason for including spouses and civil partners of children and issue as beneficiaries was that the trustees were able to make use of the spouse exemption by creating and terminating interests in possession. This gave additional flexibility when managing the trust funds. Since the Finance Act 2006, this advantage has largely disappeared, although there are still non-tax reasons for including a spouse or civil partner among the class of potential beneficiaries.

*** It is in the interests of flexibility to give trustees power to add members to a class.

† It is equally helpful to be able to exclude class members, for example where a class member is a party to divorce proceedings and the trustees wish to avoid the possibility that a court might take into account funds potentially available from the trust.

†† Delete the word 'trust' if a foreign corporation may be appointed.

††† This provision is required where a beneficiary is or may become one of the trustees.

18G   FLEXIBLE LIFE INTEREST FOR SURVIVING SPOUSE OR CIVIL PARTNER

[Clauses 1 to 3 as Precedent 18F.]

4. Until subject to and in default of any appointment under clause 5(1):
(1)   my Trustees shall pay the income of my Residuary Trust Fund to my [spouse] [civil partner] during [his] [her] lifetime;
(2)   my Trustees (being not less than two in number or a trust corporation) may at any time during the Trust Period pay or apply the whole or any part of my Residuary Trust Fund in which my said [spouse] [civil partner] is then entitled to an interest in possession to [him] [her] or for [his] [her] advancement or otherwise for [his] [her] benefit in such manner as my Trustees shall in their discretion think fit; and subject thereto
(3)   my Trustees shall hold the capital and income of my Residuary Trust Fund for such of my children as shall survive me [and shall reach the age of [eighteen] [twenty-five] or marry or enter into a civil partnership under that age]* and if more than one in equal shares absolutely PROVIDED THAT if any child is already dead or predeceases me the share of my Residuary Trust Fund to which such child would have been entitled if he or she had survived me shall be held in trust for such of his or her children and remoter issue (if any) as shall be living at my death [and shall reach the age of [eighteen] years or marry or enter into a civil partnership under that age] such issue to take through all degrees according to their stocks if more than one in equal shares and so that no issue shall take whose parent is living at my death and so capable of taking.

5.
(1)   **My Trustees (being not less than two in number or a trust corporation) shall have power to appoint the whole or any part of the capital and/or income of my Residuary Trust Fund UPON TRUST for or for the benefit of such of the Beneficiaries at such ages or times in such shares and upon such trusts which may include discretionary or protective powers or trusts and in such manner generally as my Trustees shall in their discretion think fit.
(2)   [As Precedent 18F, clause 4(2).]
(3)   [As Precedent 18F, clause 4(3).]

6. [As Precedent 18F, clause 6.]

* See the first note to Precedent 17H.

** If the settled property includes a residence or an interest in a residence and it is desired that the RNRB be available, it is necessary for lineal descendants of the spouse to become 'beneficially entitled' on the surviving spouse's death: see Chapter 27. The existence of the overriding powers contained in this clause at the death of the surviving spouse will prevent such an entitlement. Therefore, the overriding powers should be limited to the surviving spouse's lifetime by the addition of the words [during the lifetime of my spouse or civil partner] or the trustees should release their powers, at least in relation to any residence or interest in a residence contained in the settlement during the lifetime of the survivor.

18H DISCRETIONARY TRUST OF AMOUNT EQUAL TO UNEXHAUSTED PORTION OF TESTATOR'S 'NIL RATE BAND'

1. In this clause the following expressions shall have the following meanings:
(1) 'the Beneficiaries' means and includes:
    (a) [my [spouse] [civil partner] [name]] and
    (b) all my children and remoter issue;
(2) 'the Trust Period' means the period of one hundred and twenty five years commencing on my death;
(3) 'my Legacy Fund Trustees'* means [name] of [address] and [name] of [address] or other the Trustee or Trustees for the time being of the Legacy Fund];
(4) 'the Nil Rate Sum' means whichever is the lesser of:
    (a) the largest sum of cash which could be given on the trusts of this clause without any inheritance tax becoming due in respect of the transfer of the value of my estate which I am deemed to make immediately before my death, or
    (b) such sum as is equal to [twice] the upper limit of the nil percentage band in the table of rates of tax (applicable on my death) in Inheritance Tax Act 1984, Schedule 1];**
(5) 'the Legacy Fund' means the Nil Rate Sum and the assets for the time being representing the same.
[2. I DIRECT that my personal representatives shall as soon as practicable after my death make any claim which may be required under Inheritance Tax Act 1984, section 8A to claim any available transferrable nil rate band].
3. [As Precedent 18F, clause 2 (power to add and exclude Beneficiaries).]
4. I GIVE*** the Nil Rate Sum to my Legacy Fund Trustees UPON TRUST to invest it in exercise of the powers of investment given them by my will and by law and to hold the Legacy Fund on the trusts and with and subject to the powers and provisions set out in this clause.†
5. My Legacy Fund Trustees shall hold the Legacy Fund and the income thereof upon such trusts for the benefit of all or any one or more exclusively of the others or other of the Beneficiaries and if more than one in such shares and with such trusts and powers [(including trusts and

powers conferring a discretion as to the distribution of capital or income exercisable by my Legacy Fund Trustees or by any other person or persons)] and with such provisions generally as my Legacy Fund Trustees (not being fewer than two in number or being a corporation) shall by any deed or deeds revocable or irrevocable appoint provided that no appointment shall be made and no revocable appointment shall be revoked after the expiration of the Trust Period.

[6. At any time or times during the Trust Period my Legacy Fund Trustees (not being fewer than two in number or being a trust corporation) may raise the whole or any part or parts of the Legacy Fund and pay or apply the same to or for the advancement or benefit of any of the Beneficiaries for the time being living in such manner as they think fit.]

7. Subject to any exercise of the foregoing power[s] my Legacy Fund Trustees shall during the Trust Period hold the Legacy Fund UPON TRUST to pay or apply the income thereof to or for the maintenance education or benefit of all or any one or more of the Beneficiaries for the time being living in such shares if more than one and generally in such manner as they think fit provided that my Legacy Fund Trustees may accumulate the whole or any part of the income of the Legacy Fund by investing the same and the resulting income thereof in any of the investments hereby authorised and any accumulations of income so made shall form part of the capital of the Legacy Fund for all purposes.

8. Subject to any exercise of the foregoing powers the Legacy Fund and the income thereof shall be held at the expiration of the Trust Period in trust absolutely for such of my children and remoter issue as shall then be living in equal shares *per stirpes*.

9. Any of my Trustees or my Legacy Fund Trustees may exercise any power or discretion hereby or by law conferred notwithstanding that he or she has a direct or indirect personal interest in the mode or result of such exercise.

10. My Legacy Fund Trustees may lend money currently held by them to my [spouse] [civil partner].

* The legacy fund trustees may have to be different from the personal representatives if the provisions allowing the fund to be constituted by using a debt or charge are included. See † below.

** The words in (b) limit the maximum amount passing under the Nil Rate Sum to either a single or two nil rate bands as required. If it is intended that any transferrable nil rate band is included, the direction in clause 2 should be added. Note that if property attracting 100% business or agricultural relief is passing as part of the residue of the estate, the benefit of the relief is apportioned, and results in a larger pecuniary legacy being payable without attracting inheritance tax than would otherwise be the case. If the testator is concerned about too much property being diverted from the surviving spouse or civil partner, the amount can be restricted by including the words in (b). See also Chapter 30.

*** This gift should not be made conditional on the survival of the spouse or civil partner to take the residue. This is because Inheritance Tax Act 1984, section 92 (which provides that the disposition of property under a survivorship clause not exceeding six months is not to be treated as a settlement) would not apply because the condition is not the survival of the beneficiary of the clause.

† The trust could include provisions allowing the trust to be constituted by a debt or charge (see **18.9**) but these will now rarely be required. See Chapter 30 and Appendix 2 for additional precedent clauses.

18.10 TRUSTS FOR THE DISABLED

The inheritance tax legislation has always included special provision for trusts for a disabled beneficiary. The definition of a disabled beneficiary is now contained in Finance Act 2005, Schedule 1A, paragraph 1 of which states that:

'Disabled person' means—

(a) a person who by reason of mental disorder within the meaning of the Mental Health Act 1983 is incapable of administering his or her property or managing his or her affairs,
(b) a person in receipt of attendance allowance,
[(c) a person in receipt of a disability living allowance by virtue of entitlement to—

   (i) the care component at the highest or middle rate, or
   (ii) the mobility component at the higher rate,]

(d) a person in receipt of personal independence payment ...,
(e) a person in receipt of an increased disablement pension,
(f) a person in receipt of constant attendance allowance, or
(g) a person in receipt of armed forces independence payment.

Later paragraphs extend the definition to those who would be entitled to allowances were it not for the fact that they live outside the United Kingdom, or are provided with certain types of residential accommodation. Disability is assessed at the time the settlement is created. Later recovery does not affect the status of the settlement.

The conditions set out in the original Inheritance Tax Act 1984, section 89 were amended by the Finance Act 2013 for trusts created on or after 8 April 2013. The conditions are now as follows:

(i) during the lifetime of the disabled person there must be no entitlement to income; and
(ii) the trusts must secure that, if any of the settled property or income arising from it is applied during the disabled person's life for the benefit of a beneficiary, it is applied for the benefit of the disabled person.

A trust which satisfies the requirements is discretionary. The trustees are not required to distribute anything. The only constraint is anything that is distributed must be distributed to a disabled beneficiary. Because the disabled beneficiary has no entitlement to benefit, the trust property is not taken into account for means-tested benefits. However, trusts which satisfy the requirements of section 89 are treated for inheritance tax purposes as trusts with a qualifying interest in possession, thus avoiding the anniversary and exit charges which would otherwise apply. The settled property is treated as part of the disabled person's estate at death but many people feel that the advantages of:

- no impact on means-tested benefits, and
- no anniversary or exit charges,

outweigh the disadvantage of a possible charge to tax on death.

The Finance Act 2006 added a new section 89A which extends the special treatment to lifetime self-settlements by a person with a condition expected to lead to disability.

In the case of trusts for the disabled created by lifetime transfer, there is a further advantage to section 89 status. The initial lifetime transfer is treated as a potentially exempt transfer rather than an immediately chargeable transfer. In *Phelps v Stewarts (A Firm) and Another* [2007] EWHC 1561 (Ch) and *Pitt and Holt v RCC* [2013] UKSC 26, very substantial personal injury damages were transferred to an ordinary discretionary trust which failed to comply with the section 89 requirements giving rise to an immediate charge to inheritance tax and anniversary and exit charges. In *Phelps*, the will drafter was held to be liable for the unnecessary inheritance tax liability. In *Pitt and Holt v RCC*, the Supreme Court held that it could set aside the discretionary trust under the equitable doctrine of rescission for mistake.

The section 89 trust can be set out in the will, but it is often administratively more convenient to create a lifetime settlement in pilot form and leave assets to the settlement by will. This means that the trustees have a dedicated trust instrument which deals only with the trust. It also has the important incidental benefit that the trust is in existence immediately, allowing other family members to make gifts to it if they so wish.

During consultation on changes to section 89, many people expressed the view that a disabled beneficiary should be able to ask the trustees to make small gifts on their behalf and also that trustees should be able to make small payments to third parties which might not obviously be for the benefit of the disabled beneficiary; for example a holiday for caring parents. As a result, section 89(3A) provides that a trust will not be treated as failing to fulfil the section 89 requirements by reason only that the trustees have power to make payments to third parties within the 'annual limit'. The 'annual limit' is defined as whichever is the lower of: (i) £3,000; and (ii) 3% of the maximum value of the settled property during the relevant tax year. Such a power must be included in the trust instrument, and it is desirable for the settlor to leave an expression of wishes to help the trustees in the exercise of their discretion.

The following precedent is designed to satisfy the requirements of Inheritance Tax Act 1984, section 89, so that the trust, while discretionary, is treated for inheritance tax purposes as a trust with an interest in possession.

It is irrelevant what provisions are included to provide for the position after the death of the disabled beneficiary. The remaining property could be left to beneficiaries absolutely or could be left on continuing discretionary trusts. This is entirely a matter for the testator and has no implications for the status of the settlement during the lifetime of the disabled beneficiary.

181 TRUST FOR A PERSON UNDER A DISABILITY

1. Definitions and interpretation
In this settlement the following expressions have where the context permits the following meanings:
1.1 'the Trustees' means the Original Trustees or other the trustees or trustee for the time being of this settlement and 'Trustee' means each and any of the Trustees;
1.2 'the Trust Fund' means the assets described in the schedule all assets at any time added to it by way of further settlement (whether by the Settlor or any other person) accumulation of income capital accretion or otherwise and all property from time to time representing the same;
1.3 'the Principal Beneficiary' means (disabled person);
1.4 'the Discretionary Beneficiaries' means (set out class including those able to benefit under exercise of the power in 2.3);
1.5 'Section 89' means Inheritance Tax Act 1984, section 89;
1.6 'interest in possession' means an interest in possession within the meaning of section 89(1)(a);
1.7 'the Trust Period' means the period of one hundred and twenty-five years from the date hereof.

2. Beneficial trusts during the lifetime of the Principal Beneficiary
During the lifetime of the Principal Beneficiary:
2.1 The Trustees may from time to time pay or apply the income of the Trust Fund to or for the benefit of the Principal Beneficiary PROVIDED that:

2.1.1   such payment or application shall from time to time be made in such manner and upon such terms and conditions (if any) as the Trustees in their discretion shall from time to time think proper;

2.1.2   the Trustees shall accumulate the whole or any part of the income of the Trust Fund that is not paid out under clause 2.1.1 by investing the same and the resulting income of it in any investments by this settlement authorised and adding the accumulations to the capital of the Trust Fund.

2.2   The Trustees shall have power in their absolute discretion to pay transfer or apply in any manner to or for the benefit of the Principal Beneficiary the whole or any part or parts of the capital of the Trust Fund.

[2.3   The Trustees shall have power to apply for the benefit of the Discretionary Beneficiaries amounts (whether consisting of income or capital, or both) not exceeding the annual limit as defined in Inheritance Tax Act 1984, section 89(3A).]

* This clause is designed to meet the revised requirements of Inheritance Tax Act 1984, section 89(1) which are that during the life of the disabled person there is no interest in possession in the property and that no other person can benefit from income or capital.

Note: Consideration should be given to providing the trustees with a letter of wishes explaining the testator's intentions as regards the welfare of the person under disability. See Appendix A1l for a suggested precedent.

18.11   PROTECTIVE TRUSTS

The basis of a protective trust is a determinable interest, given to the principal beneficiary, but determinable on, for example, bankruptcy or an attempted alienation of the property. On determination, a discretionary trust arises in favour of the principal beneficiary and others.

The term of a protective trust is normally the life of the principal beneficiary, but a shorter period may be used.

Trustee Act 1925, section 33 operates to imply into trusts certain terms concerning income which is directed to be held 'on protective trusts' for someone's benefit. The statutory implied terms are subject to any contrary intention in the will, although they may be expressly incorporated into the will. Section 33 provides for the income to be held during the trust period:

(i)   Upon trust for the principal beneficiary ... until he, whether before or after the termination of any prior interest, does or attempts to do or suffers any act or thing, or until any event happens, other than an advance under any statutory or express power, whereby, if the said income were payable during the trust period

... he would be deprived of the right to receive the same or any part thereof ... [and thereafter] ...;

(ii)   ... upon trust for the application thereof for the maintenance or support, or otherwise for the benefit, of all or any one or more ... of the following persons ...;

    (a)   the principal beneficiary and his or her spouse or civil partner, if any, and his or her children or more remote issue, if any; or

    (b)   if there is no spouse or civil partner or issue of the principal beneficiary in existence, the principal beneficiary and the persons who would, if he were actually dead, be entitled to the trust property or the income thereof or to the annuity fund, if any, or arrears of the annuity, as the case may be;

as the trustees in their absolute discretion ... think fit.

This section does not validate any trust which would otherwise be invalid, such as a settlement by a person of their own property on themselves until bankruptcy.

Protective trusts attract special treatment for inheritance tax purposes in certain circumstances. Inheritance Tax Act 1984, section 88 provides that in the case of a trust created before 22 March 2006, the termination of a life interest under Trustee Act 1925, section 33, or an express provision of 'like effect', is not a transfer of value, and the former life tenant is treated as continuing to enjoy an interest in possession. HM Revenue & Customs has indicated that it does not regard a trust, where the class of discretionary objects is wider than that contained in the statutory trust, as of 'like effect', but it does accept a power to pay capital to the principal beneficiary. Express trusts which differ from the statutory trust do not attract the privileged tax treatment.

In the case of protective trusts created on or after 22 March 2006, the special treatment applies only if the interest of the principal beneficiary is:

- an immediate post-death interest; or
- a disabled person's interest within section 89B(1)(c) or (d); or
- a transitional serial interest.

18J   PROTECTIVE LIFE INTEREST WITH A POWER TO RAISE AND PAY CAPITAL

    (a)   I GIVE to my Trustees the sum of £ ... free of inheritance tax payable on my death [or the residue of my property both real and personal wherever situate being or arising] as to the income thereof upon protective trusts for the benefit of A during their life.

    (b)   My Trustees shall until the failure or determination of the trust of income in favour of the said A have the further power at their absolute discretion and without being liable in any way to account for the exercise of such discretion to raise and pay to the said A for their own absolute use and benefit at any time or times as my Trustees shall determine [the whole or any part or parts of] [any sum or sums not exceeding on any one occasion £ ... clear of expenses out of] the capital of the said fund [or residue].

(c)   My Trustees shall hold any part of the said fund [residue] not so transferred to the said A during their lifetime as the said A shall by will or codicil appoint and in default of and subject to any such appointment [set out trusts in remainder].

(d)   I DIRECT that my Trustees shall on no account be liable or responsible for making any such payment whether of income or capital to the said A after the failure or determination of A's said determinable life interest unless or until my Trustees shall have received express notice of the act or event causing such failure or determination.

The following trusts would probably not attract privileged treatment under Inheritance Tax Act 1984, section 88, as HM Revenue & Customs does not accept that they are of 'like effect'.

18K   PROTECTIVE INCOME TRUSTS GIVING LIFE TENANT POWER TO ASSIGN INCOME TO CHILDREN

(a)   My Trustees shall hold the income of my residuary estate [the fund] upon protective trusts for the benefit of [A] during their life.

(b)   Provided that the discretionary trusts by statute implied to arise after the failure or determination of the trust to pay such income to the said A during their life shall be varied as follows.

   (i)   My Trustees may in their discretion apply any income accrued but unapplied in any year for the purpose of such discretionary trusts in any subsequent year.

   (ii) Notwithstanding the protective trusts hereinbefore declared and without determining A's life interest thereunder the said A may by deed or deeds but only with the consent of my Trustees therein expressed (which consent my Trustees shall have absolute power to give or withhold) assign any part or parts not exceeding in total one half of the income of the fund to any child or children or issue of the said A who shall at the date of such assignment have attained the age of [eighteen] [twenty-one] years or have married or entered into a civil partnership.

18L STATUTORY PROTECTIVE TRUSTS, VARIED BY ALLOWING ACCUMULATION*

(a) I DECLARE that the income hereinbefore directed to be held UPON TRUST for or to be paid to the said [name] for life shall not vest absolutely in [him] [her] but shall be held by my Trustees upon the statutory protective trusts save insofar as the same are hereinafter varied for the benefit of the said [name] for the period of [his] [her] life.

(b) PROVIDED HOWEVER that in each year prior to the death of the said [name] my Trustees shall from time to time exercise their absolute discretion to determine how much if any of the income of the then current year they will apply under the statutory trusts and the said trusts shall apply to the amount so determined and my Trustees shall accumulate any income above that amount by investing the same and the resulting income thereof but my Trustees shall have power at any time or times to declare that any whole or part of the past accumulations shall be income of the current year and be applicable accordingly at the discretion of my Trustees.

(c) I DECLARE that after the death of the said [name] the said accumulations or the balance thereof shall be deemed to be and treated as an accretion to the capital of the property from which such accumulations arose and be one fund with such capital for all purposes and shall be held by my Trustees UPON TRUST accordingly.

* Trustee Act 1925, section 33 does not allow for the accumulation of income. It provides for the whole of the yearly income to be applied each year.

Chapter 19

Income and Interest

19.1   IMMEDIATE SPECIFIC GIFTS AND DEVISES

Beneficiaries who have been left immediate specific legacies or devises are entitled to any income or profits produced by the assets as from the date of death.

Where income (or profits) is paid after the date of death but has arisen partly before and partly after death, then, in the absence of express words excluding the apportionment rules, the income must normally be apportioned according to Apportionment Act 1870, section 2. That section states:

> All rents, annuities, dividends, and other periodical payments in the nature of income … shall, like interest on money lent, be considered as accruing from day to day, and shall be apportionable in respect of time accordingly.

Rent, profits, interest, dividends on company shares or other income accruing before the testator's death fall into the testator's residuary estate.

It has long been usual to exclude the Apportionment Act 1870, as the cost and trouble of apportionment is disproportionate to any benefit derived. However, for trusts created or arising on or after 1 October 2013, the requirement to apportion is disapplied in the absence of contrary intention. It is still desirable to include a direction as to the treatment of post-death income.

19A   DIRECTION AS TO INCOME

> All income of my estate which is received after my death but which relates to a period wholly or partly before my death shall be treated as if it had accrued wholly after my death and shall not be subject to any apportionment.

The Apportionment Act 1870 does not apply to the profits of the testator's business if the testator was a sole proprietor or in private partnership. No apportionment is necessary in such a case, as the profits are treated as accruing on the last day of the period in respect of which they are declared.

A beneficiary must normally take the gift subject to any liabilities outstanding at the testator's death. There are, however, two exceptions to this general rule. The first is where the testator has before death entered into a leasehold covenant as a landlord. In such a case, the testator's estate, rather than the beneficiary, bears the burden of that covenant.

The second is where a testator has entered into a contract to have building work done to property devised to a beneficiary. The estate then bears the expense of that building work (see *Re Rushbrook's Will Trusts* [1948] Ch 421).

19.2   CONTINGENT OR DEFERRED SPECIFIC GIFTS

Contingent and deferred specific gifts are governed by Law of Property Act 1925, section 175, which states:

(1)   A contingent or future specific devise or bequest of property, whether real or personal, and a contingent residuary devise of freehold land, and a specific or residuary devise of freehold land to trustees upon trust for persons whose interests are contingent or executory shall, subject to the statutory provisions relating to accumulations, carry the intermediate income of that property from the death of the testator, except so far as such income, or any part thereof, may be otherwise expressly disposed of.

(2)   This section applies only to wills coming into operation after the commencement of this Act.

The effect of this section is that any contingent or deferred specific gift of property to which the section relates carries the intermediate income of that property unless it is expressly left elsewhere. A gift of residue is not regarded as an express disposition for this purpose.

The intermediate income can be accumulated. There are now no statutory limitations on the period for which income can be accumulated (see Chapter 23). The terms of the instrument may contain a limitation but this would be unusual.

19.3   GENERAL AND DEMONSTRATIVE GIFTS

A general gift (e.g. a pecuniary legacy), subject to contrary intention, carries interest from the time it is payable. The time at which the gift is payable depends on the express provisions of the will or rules of law. Immediate gifts are payable

1 year after the testator's death unless the will provides otherwise. The rule applies even though it may be impracticable for the personal representatives to pay the legacy at the end of the executor's year.

The same rule applies to a general legacy held on trust for the first beneficiary for life with the remainder to a second beneficiary absolutely. The legacy carries interest from the end of the executor's year and the first beneficiary would not be entitled to any interest in respect of the executor's year itself.

Interest on legacies used to be at the rate of 6% per annum. This was by analogy with Rules of the Supreme Court, Order 44, rule 10, which stated that if, in an action, the court ordered an account of legacies, the rate would be 6%.

Order 44 was replaced by Civil Procedure Rules, Practice Direction 40 (now 40A) paragraph 15, which provides that the rate is the basic rate payable for the time being on funds in court, unless the will provided otherwise or the court specifically ordered otherwise. At the time of writing, the rate was 1.688%.

Interest is normally simple, unless there are particular reasons for awarding it at compound rates (see *Evans v Westcombe* [1999] 2 All ER 777).

If a testator fixes a time for payment, then interest is payable from that time. Thus a gift expressed to be payable 'immediately after my death' carries interest from the date of death.

A general legacy which is contingent or deferred carries interest from the time at which it becomes payable. For example, a gift to a beneficiary on attaining the age of 21 becomes payable on the beneficiary's 21st birthday and bears interest from that birthday until payment.

A legacy may contain a direction that the subject matter be severed from the testator's general estate, in which case it may carry interest from the end of the executor's year even though the beneficiary's interest in the legacy is contingent or deferred. If the purpose of the severance was merely to simplify the administration of the testator's estate, then the legacy carries interest only from the time of absolute vesting. If, on the other hand, the severed property is to be invested by the trustee and held, together with any investments representing that legacy, on trust for the beneficiary until the latter attains a given age, then the legacy carries interest as from the end of the executor's year. This is also the case where property is severed to be held for the beneficiary if they attain a certain age.

There are four exceptional rules under which a general legacy carries interest from the date of the testator's death.

19.3.1   Satisfaction of a debt

Subject to contrary intention, any legacy made in satisfaction of a debt bears interest from the date of the testator's death and not from the end of the executor's year.

19.3.2   Legacy charged only on realty

Subject to contrary intention, if a legacy is vested and charged on realty, interest runs from the date of the testator's death. The rule does not apply to a legacy directed to be paid out of the proceeds of sale of realty devised on trust for sale. In that case the legacy carries interest from 1 year after the testator's death, on the basis that the sale should reasonably have taken place during that period.

19.3.3   Testator's minor child

A legacy given either to the testator's own minor child, or to a minor to whom the testator stands *in loco parentis*, generally carries interest from the date of the testator's death. This is because it is presumed to be given to discharge the obligation of parents to maintain their children. If the contingency is to attain an age in excess of 18, a court is less likely to find that the legacy was intended to carry interest.

The rule does not apply where:

(i)   the testator has made other provisions for the maintenance of the child in their will; or
(ii) the testator gives the legacy to trustees upon trust for the child.

Trustee Act 1925, section 31(3) provides that interest on such a legacy should be paid at the rate of 5% per annum as long as the income available is sufficient. The interest may be applied for the child's maintenance either under the statutory powers of maintenance or pursuant to an order of the court. Any surplus interest is accumulated and added to the capital of the legacy.

19.3.4   Intention to provide for maintenance of minor

If a testator gives a legacy to any minor, indicating in the will that the legacy is intended to provide for the minor's maintenance then, unless the testator has made some other provision for that child's maintenance in their will, the legacy carries interest from the date of the testator's death. The legatee need not be the testator's own child.

In the case of a contingent legacy where the contingency has no reference to the legatee's minority, the legacy generally carries interest only from the time at which the contingency is satisfied (see **19.3.3**). There are, however, two exceptions to the general rule:

(i)   if the testator directs that the subject matter of the legacy is to be severed from the general estate for some purpose connected with the legacy (other than administrative ease), then interest is payable from the end of the executor's year;

(ii) if the testator shows in their will their intention to provide for the minor's maintenance, then interest accrues from the date of the death of the testator.

When drafting a general legacy to a minor, it is preferable to make express directions as to the payment of interest rather than relying on these rather esoteric rules. A grandparent leaving a substantial pecuniary legacy to a grandchild contingent on reaching a specified age would probably be rather startled to discover that the statutory rule is that the child will receive no benefit from the sum until the specified age is reached. In the case of a substantial pecuniary legacy it will normally be preferable to leave the legacy to trustees to hold and give the trustees appropriate powers to deal with the capital and the income produced from its investment.

19B   GENERAL LEGACY INCLUDING DIRECTION AS TO INTEREST

I GIVE the sum of £ ... free of inheritance tax to [name] contingent on attaining the age of [...] [or marrying or forming a civil partnership under that age in which case [his] [her] receipt shall be a sufficient discharge to my Trustees] and I DIRECT that such sum [shall carry interest at the rate of [...]% per annum from my death until [name] attains the age of [...] [or marries or forms a civil partnership under that age]] [shall not carry interest].

19.4   RESIDUARY GIFTS

Where any residuary gift, either of personalty or realty, is to have immediate effect, all the income or profits arising after the testator's death pass with the gift.

In the case of contingent or deferred residuary gifts, there is a difference in treatment of residuary bequests (of personalty) and residuary devises (of realty).

19.4.1   Contingent or deferred residuary bequests

Where a residuary bequest of personalty is contingent, any intermediate income of that personalty passes with the residuary gift unless otherwise disposed of by the will. Therefore, until the contingency is satisfied (and the gift vests), unless the will provides otherwise, any intermediate income from a residuary bequest is either:

(i) dealt with under Trustee Act 1925, section 31 (see **22.19.2**) where there is a beneficiary living who is contingently entitled; or

(ii) accumulated during the statutory accumulation period as an addition to the capital; once the accumulation period has expired any further income passes as under the testator's intestacy.

Where the residuary bequest is deferred to a future date, it does not carry with it any intermediate income, which should be disposed of separately under the will. Any such income not dealt with under the provisions of the will passes as on the testator's intestacy.

19.4.2   Contingent or deferred residuary devises

Law of Property Act 1925, section 175, which applies to real property only, provides that:

> a contingent residuary devise of freehold land, and a … residuary devise of freehold land to trustees upon trust for persons whose interests are contingent or executory shall, subject to the statutory provisions relating to accumulations, carry the intermediate income of that property from the death of the testator, except so far as such income, or any part thereof, may be otherwise expressly disposed of.

Thus a contingent residuary devise of realty falls within section 175, unless it is also deferred to some future date. This is so even if made to trustees upon trust for a beneficiary whose interest is contingent. Subject to contrary provision in the will, the devise carries with it any intermediate income. The intermediate income is either:

(i) subject to Trustee Act 1925, section 31 (if there is a beneficiary living who is contingently entitled); or

(ii) accumulated during the statutory accumulation period as an addition to the capital.

Section 175 does not, apparently, cover all deferred residuary devises, but does cover devises made to trustees upon trust for persons whose interests are 'executory'. In those circumstances a deferred residuary devise carries intermediate income during the statutory accumulation period, subject to contrary provision in the will.

Chapter 20

Abatement, Ademption, Election, Satisfaction and Conversion

20.1 ABATEMENT

General legacies normally rank equally with each other, unless a direction is given that a particular legacy should have priority over another. There is no presumed priority in respect of a legacy given to the testator's widow or any other person. If a particular beneficiary claims to have priority, the onus is on the beneficiary to prove that that was the testator's intention.

If the estate, after payment of tax, funeral and testamentary expenses and priority legacies, is insufficient to discharge the general legacies in full then each general legacy is subject to abatement. This means that each legacy is reduced in proportion to the overall shortfall in moneys required to satisfy the general legacies.

The benefit of a charging clause is no longer treated as a legacy (Trustee Act 2000, section 28); instead, it is regarded as remuneration. Charges are, therefore, to be paid in full even if there are insufficient funds to pay pecuniary legacies in full.

Where legacies are given in satisfaction of a debt, they abate, together with other pecuniary legacies, if the legatee has elected to accept the legacy in the will and the legacy is 'far in excess' of their debt (see *Re Whitehead* [1913] 2 Ch 56).

This may not be the case, however, where creditors are seeking only the amount of their debts. Here, creditors may have priority over legatees who are volunteers (see *Beyfus v Lawley* [1903] AC 411).

A demonstrative legacy does not abate with the general legacies provided the fund from which it is to be paid is sufficient to satisfy that legacy. To that extent it is a specific legacy and is paid in priority to any general legacies. In so far as the fund is insufficient, the balance ranks equally with general legacies and abates accordingly.

Similarly, a specific legacy does not abate with general legacies but may be subject to abatement *pro rata* with other specific legacies where the general estate is insufficient to pay all the debts. Where specific gifts are made out of a particular fund and the balance is disposed of as residue, if there are insufficient funds in the general estate to satisfy the debts, then first recourse must be had to the residue before the specific gifts abate.

20.2   REFUNDS

It has been held that, once executors have voluntarily paid a legacy to the legatee, they have no right to ask for that legacy to be refunded. However, the case-law is extremely elderly (see *Hilliard v Fulford* (1876) 4 Ch D 389 and *Herbert v Badgery* (1894) 15 NSWLR 236). Similarly, in the case of residue, if the executors had notice of a debt before parting with the residuary estate to the residuary legatee then case-law authority states that they cannot call upon the residuary legatee to refund any part of that money or property merely because there is a deficiency of assets to discharge the liabilities (see *Jervis v Wolferstan* (1874) LR 18 Eq 18, 25). If, however, the executors receive notice of a debt after making a distribution to the residuary legatee, they are entitled to demand a refund of so much of the capital so paid as is necessary to satisfy the debt. The residuary legatee cannot be forced to refund any interest paid on capital.

It is likely that these cases would not be followed today. The doctrine of unjust enrichment is likely to mean that the overpaid beneficiary would be required to repay unless a defence was available.

In *Fea v Roberts* [2005] EWHC 2186 (Ch), [2006] WTLR 255, a legacy paid by mistake to the wrong person was recoverable as money paid under a mistake of fact. The 'beneficiary' was unsuccessful in claiming the change of position defence. The defence is not available to a defendant who has changed their position in bad faith, as where he has paid away the money with knowledge of the facts entitling the claimant to restitution (see *Niru Battery Manufacturing Company and Another v Milestone Trading Ltd and Others* [2003] EWCA Civ 1446). In *Fea v Roberts*, the defendant had appreciated the inexplicable features of the gift he was apparently being offered, and that that the gift might well not be intended for him. However, this defence might well be available to legatees who are entitled but receive too much.

20.3   ADEMPTION

Where property, identifiable at some time before the testator's death, and made the subject of a specific gift in the testator's will, does not form part of the testator's estate at the time of their death, that specific gift adeems and thereby fails.

Ademption does not affect demonstrative or general legacies, nor does it affect gifts of property referred to as existing 'at the time of my death' although, naturally, such gifts may fail if there are insufficient funds, or if the property referred to does not form part of the testator's estate at their death.

A change in substance in the subject matter of a specific gift causes that gift to adeem but a mere change in name or form does not. For example, if the testator makes a specific legacy of ordinary shares in a particular company owned at the date of the will and the shares are in some way altered, due to an amalgamation or reconstruction of the company during the testator's lifetime, but represent the same stock in the same company, then the gift does not adeem (see *Re Clifford* [1912] 1 Ch 29 and *Re Leeming* [1912] 1 Ch 828). If, on the other hand, the original company is acquired by another and the shareholders are given shares in the new company as payment or compensation for their shares in the old company, then the substance of the subject matter changes and the gift then adeems (see *Re Slater* [1907] 1 Ch 665).

In *Re Dorman Deceased* [1994] 1 WLR 282 (a case concerning an attorney acting under an enduring power of attorney), there was held to be no ademption because the new asset (a high earning deposit bank account) was 'substantially the same thing' as the original asset (a lower earning deposit account).

A sale by an attorney under an enduring or lasting power of attorney will cause ademption (see *Banks v National Westminster Bank* [2005] EWHC 3479 (Ch)). If the attorney is aware of the problem, it may be appropriate to apply to the Court of Protection for a statutory will to make provision for the disappointed beneficiary. A sale by a deputy may not deprive a beneficiary of entitlement as Mental Capacity Act 2005, Schedule 2 contains provisions to ensure as far as possible that ademption does not occur. Schedule 2, paragraph 8 provides that testamentary beneficiaries are to take the same interest, if and so far as circumstances allow, in the property representing the property disposed of that they would have taken in the original property.

A binding contract for the sale of property which has been made the subject of a specific gift causes the gift to adeem even if the testator dies before completion. The beneficiary is not entitled to the purchase price payable by the purchaser, although the beneficiary is entitled to enjoy the property or its rents and profits until completion of the contract.

If the testator makes a specific gift of property after entering into a binding contract for the sale of that property to a third party then, in the absence of contrary intention appearing in the will, the beneficiary is presumed to be entitled to the purchase price payable by the purchaser.

20.4 OPTIONS TO PURCHASE AND ADEMPTION

Where a testator makes a specific gift of property in their will and subsequently grants an option to purchase that property to a third party, then the beneficiary is not entitled to the property itself while the option remains in force. It is open to the third party to exercise their option at any time during the operational period of that option, whether or not it is after the testator's death. From the testator's death until the option is exercised or the option period expires, the beneficiary is entitled only to the rents and profits arising from the property (see *Lawes v Bennett* (1785) 1 Cox Eq Cas 167).

Where, on the other hand, property is already subject to an option and the testator then makes a specific gift of the property, the beneficiary stands in the place of the testator on the testator's death and, if the option is exercised, the beneficiary is entitled to the purchase price.

Conditional contracts for the sale of real property are similarly subject to the rule in *Lawes v Bennett* (1785) 1 Cox Eq Cas 167. See, for example, *Re Sweeting* [1988] 1 All ER 1016, where it was held that the fulfilment of a conditional contract for the sale of land after the testator's death effectively converted the land into personal property. The result is that any specific gifts of the land adeem and the proceeds of sale fall into residue.

In *Pennington v Waine (No 2)* [2003] WTLR 1011, the court found that the fact that shares were subject to pre-emption rights did not mean that the exercise of those rights would cause retrospective conversion and ademption. In *Lawes v Bennett* (1785) 1 Cox Eq Cas 167 (and subsequent cases following it), testators had themselves granted options to purchase or conditional contracts, the exercise of which had led to conversion. In effect, they had given the grantees of the options the right to control the destiny of the property. Pre-emption rights are different. They are triggered only when, and if, the property owner decides to sell. The court held that the shares subject to the pre-emption rights would devolve under the will in their unconverted form and be unaffected by subsequent events.

20.5 REPUBLICATION AND ADEMPTION

In general, the republication of a will does not necessarily restore any gift that has already adeemed. However, republication may alter the construction of a will with regard to the subject matter of a specific gift. This can often have the effect of saving the specific gift. See, for example, *Re Reeves* [1928] Ch 351, where a testator, by his will executed in 1921, gave 'all my interest in my present house' to his daughter. At the date of execution the testator had a 5-year lease which had been granted in 1917. He then took a new 12-year lease, and, in a codicil executed in 1926, confirmed his earlier will. The court held that the daughter was entitled to the fresh lease. The effect of the codicil was to republish his earlier will which was reaffirmed at the date of the codicil, not the date of the original will.

Ademption may be avoided by an express provision in the will.

20A CLAUSE AVOIDING ADEMPTION

I DEVISE all my freehold land situate at [etc] to [name] absolutely PROVIDED THAT if any part or all of the said land shall in my lifetime be sold or contracted to be sold or made subject to an option to purchase which is exercisable either before or after my death then I GIVE to the said [name] free of inheritance tax a sum equal in amount to the sum received by way of sale proceeds in respect of such land after the deduction of all expenses of such sale AND I DIRECT that the legacy hereby given shall be subject to abatement as if it were property specifically devised or bequeathed.

20.6 ELECTION

The question of election arises rarely in practice. If a testator makes a gift by will to a beneficiary (Ada), of property which actually belongs to another person (Ben), and if Ben is also a beneficiary under the will then Ben is 'put to his election' as to whether he will:

(i)   take the benefit given to him under the will and give effect to the testator's gift to Ada; or
(ii) forgo the gift under the will to himself but retain his own property that was the subject of the gift to Ada; or
(iii) accept the gift under the will *and* retain his own property but compensate Ada for the gift which she will not receive.

In point (ii) above, both gifts would fail, as the testator has no interest in the subject property to pass to Ada. For modern examples of the doctrine of election in operation, see *Frear v Frear and Another* [2008] EWCA Civ 1320 and *Scarfe v Matthews* [2012] EWHC 3071 (Ch).

20.7 SATISFACTION

20.7.1 Satisfaction of a debt by a legacy

Where a testator makes a will containing a pecuniary legacy to someone to whom the testator owes a sum equal to or in excess of the amount of that legacy, then an equitable presumption arises that the legacy is intended to discharge the debt. If the testator then discharges the debt after the date of their will, the legacy is adeemed. If the debt remains outstanding at the time of the testator's death, the legatee must choose whether to accept the legacy and forgo the debt, or *vice versa*. He is not entitled to both.

No presumption arises if the legacy is for less than the amount of the debt outstanding.

The presumption arises in respect of pecuniary legacies only, and not devises of land or gifts of residue.

If the debt is secured (but the legacy is unsecured), the presumption of satisfaction does not arise. Again, the presumption has no effect if the debt is due immediately and the legacy is due at some time in the future.

The presumption may be rebutted either by an expression of contrary intention in the will, or by extrinsic evidence showing that it was the testator's intention to give a legacy in addition to the debt.

20.7.2 Satisfaction of a legacy by another legacy

If a testator makes two general legacies to the same legatee of the same amount then, in the absence of any expressed intention, certain rebuttable presumptions arise:

(i)   where both legacies are contained in the same will or codicil it is presumed that they are intended to be substitutional, although the presumption may be rebutted by extrinsic evidence;

(ii) where each legacy is contained in a different instrument but the motive expressed for each gift is the same, they are presumed to be substitutional. Again, extrinsic evidence may be admitted to rebut the presumption;

(iii) in other cases where each legacy is contained in a different instrument then, as a matter of construction, the legacies are presumed to be cumulative.

20.7.3 Equity leans against double portions

The equitable principle against 'double portions' is based on the assumption that a parent would wish to treat their children fairly and would not wish to make provision for one of their children twice, at the expense of their other children.

There is, therefore, a presumption that if, after making a will leaving a legacy to a child, a parent gives a portion to that child, the legacy fails. The presumption can be rebutted by evidence that the testator intended a double benefit.

The presumption does not arise at all unless the lifetime gift amounts to a portion. A 'portion is ... very broadly speaking, a gift intended to set up a child in life or to make substantial provision for him or her ...', *per* Lindsay J in *Re Cameron Deceased* [1999] Ch 386.

At one time, the presumption arose only in relation to fathers (and persons who could be shown to be *in loco parentis*). In *Re Cameron*, it was held that it was irrelevant whether the gift was made by the father or the mother (or someone else *in loco parentis*). In *Race v Race* [2002] EWHC 1868 (Ch), [2002] WTLR 1193, the court held that while the rule against double portions used to apply only to gifts of personalty, it can now apply to gifts of land.

The child does not have to be young. In *Casimir v Alexander* [2001] WTLR 939, the court considered the rule in relation to a daughter who was a pensioner. In *Re Clapham* [2005] EWHC 3387 (Ch), [2006] WTLR 203, a daughter was ordered to bring into account £20,000 given to her by her father to help her fund a divorce settlement.

Satisfaction of a portion-debt legacy

If a testator is under a legal obligation to provide a portion for a child, and then makes a will giving either a legacy or a share of residue to that child, it is presumed in equity that the legacy or share of residue so provided for was intended to be given in satisfaction (or partial satisfaction) of the portion-debt. The child must elect whether or not to take the gift in the will in satisfaction of the portion-debt.

Ademption of a legacy by a portion

If a testator falls under a legal obligation to provide a portion for a child after they have made a will or codicil providing for that child to have a legacy or share of residue, then a portion provided after the making of the will is presumed to adeem the testamentary gift either in whole or in part, unless a contrary intention on the part of the testator can be shown.

These equitable doctrines relating to double portions apply only between a child and parent (or other person acting *in loco parentis*), and must not be applied to benefit a stranger.

It is possible to include a statement in a will that the testator did not intend the presumptions to arise. Such statements are not necessarily conclusive, as the intention at the time of the later gift is more important.

20B   PROVISION AGAINST SATISFACTION AND ADEMPTION

> I DIRECT AND DECLARE that no child or issue of mine receiving any share interest or benefit hereunder or under the trusts hereof or under any codicil hereto shall be liable to bring into account any other sum of money or any other property or interest paid transferred or settled or covenanted to be paid transferred or settled upon him or her or them either before or after the date of this my will.

20.8   CONVERSION

The doctrine of conversion arises where land is devised upon trust for sale or where money is bequeathed with a direction to purchase realty, provided the direction is mandatory and not merely a discretion or power. For example, where the will creates a trust for sale of land, equity notionally regards the land as money from the date of death of the testator. The direction may be express or implied.

The effect of conversion is to include realty in a residuary bequest of personalty, and personalty in a residuary devise of realty, irrespective of the actual time of sale, since conversion takes effect from the testator's death notwithstanding any postponement of the sale. If the sale is contingent upon a future event then conversion does not take place until that event occurs.

In the event of postponement, any immediate income passes with the proceeds of sale. If the ultimate beneficiary elects to take the land rather than the proceeds of sale, then such election has the effect of a re-conversion.

Trusts of Land and Appointment of Trustees Act 1996, section 3 is headed 'Abolition of doctrine of conversion'. It provides that where land is held by trustees subject to a trust for sale, the land is not to be regarded as converted into personalty and where personalty is subject to a trust for sale in order that the trustees may acquire land, the personalty is not to be regarded as land.

The section does not apply to a trust created by a will if the testator died before the commencement of this Act.

Despite the heading to the section, conversion remains in the following cases:

(i)   under an order of the court;
(ii) under a contract for the sale of land;
(iii) under an option to purchase;
(iv) in relation to a trust created by a will if the testator died before 1 January 1997 (section 3);
(v)   where land is held by personal representatives, rather than trustees, if the relevant death occurred before 1 January 1997 (sections 18 and 25);
(vi) possibly in the case of partnership property (the relevant provision of the Partnership Act 1890 was repealed by Trusts of Land and Appointment of Trustees Act 1996, section 25, except in so far as it applied in any circumstances involving the personal representatives of a partner who died before 1 January 1997, but it is not clear whether the effect is that there is no conversion, or that the equitable rule is restored).

Chapter 21

Testamentary Options to Purchase

21.1 INTRODUCTION

Testamentary options to purchase provide useful flexibility in cases where a testator wants one individual to have a particular asset and also wants to make provision for others, but may not have adequate funds. The will can grant one person an option to purchase the property at an undervalue and the resulting funds can be used to make provision for the remaining beneficiaries. Where the option price is less than the full value, there is a legacy to the option holder of the difference between the price payable and the value of the property. The burden of inheritance tax on the property subject to the option will fall on the residue of the estate unless the will provides otherwise.

21.2 TERMS

The terms of the option should make clear whether the option is personal to the donee or can be exercised by the donee's personal representatives after their death.

The testator may fix the price in the will, or direct the trustees to fix it, or provide that it be fixed by a valuer. If the valuation is to be by a named person or is to be carried out in some other specified way, it is a matter of construction whether or not the method is of the essence. If it is of the essence and proves impossible (e.g. because the named valuer is dead), the option cannot take effect. If it is not of the essence, the court would order an appropriate method (see *Sudbrook Trading Estate Ltd v Eggleton* [1983] 1 AC 444 (HL)).

Similar problems in construction arise where the will lays down a time within which the option must be exercised. Such a time limit must be complied with strictly if the time is intended to be one of the terms of the offer (see *Allardyce v*

Roebuck and Others [2004] EWHC 1538 (Ch)). If a time limit is included, it should be carefully worded to ensure that the person with the benefit of the option is not placed in a position where it is impossible to meet the time limit because of factors outside their control. If time is intended to be a term of the offer, the court will not extend the time simply because of difficulty in complying with it. If the will contains no prescribed consequences for failure to act in time, it is unlikely that it is intended to be a term (see *Re the Estate of Bowles Deceased; Hayward v Jackson* [2003] EWHC 253 (Ch), [2003] Ch 422).

When drafting, it may be helpful to separate acceptance of the option in principle, for which it may be appropriate to impose a strict time limit, from the mechanics of the conveyancing process, for which it is less likely to be appropriate. If the will does not provide a specific time limit then the option must be exercised within a reasonable time. If the price has to be fixed, the time cannot run until the price has been communicated to the grantee.

If the testator has directed that a valuation be made after their death, the will should state the method of valuation. Unless the will provides otherwise, the valuation will be an open market valuation at the date of death. 'Market value' is not necessarily the same as the probate valuation because, for example, a probate valuation will not take account of rights of occupation conferred by the will but a market valuation will. Because the market valuation is made as at the date of death it will not take into account subsequent events unless the will so directs. In *Re the Estate of Bliss* [2001] 1 WLR 1973, the testatrix granted a married couple an option to purchase her house subject to the right of her 90-year-old husband to live there. The husband vacated the property 6 months after the death of the testatrix and moved into a nursing home. The court held that the house should be valued at the date of death, which meant subject to the husband's right of occupation and without reflecting the fact that the husband had vacated the property.

When drafting an option, it is important to consider whether or not the testator wants a valuer to disregard matters which have affected the value of the property.

Before the coming into force of the Perpetuities and Accumulations Act 2009 (6 April 2010), the date for the exercise of an option had to be within the period allowed by the perpetuity rule (Perpetuities and Accumulations Act 1964, section 9(2)). This is still the position for options created before 6 April 2010. It was generally advisable expressly to limit the period during which the option remains exercisable.

In the case of options created after the 2009 Act came into force, the perpetuity rule no longer applies. Section 1 of the Act defines the circumstances in which the rule against perpetuities applies. The rule only applies to the estates, interests, powers and rights mentioned in section 1 (broadly trust interests). The rule does not apply, for example, to most future easements, options and rights of preemption, which will fall outside these categories. It is, therefore, for testators to include such limitations as they see fit as to the period within which the option can be exercised.

Where an option to purchase given to a grantee is to be exercised after the death of a tenant for life then, if the property has been sold during the life of the life tenant, the grantee is entitled to the proceeds of sale after the life tenant's death if they exercise their option and pay any price fixed in relation to the property. For this situation to arise an actual option to purchase must have been granted to the grantee; a power granted to the trustees to sell the property at a fixed price to a particular person does not suffice. In the latter case, the trustees are not under an obligation to sell the property to any particular person or for less than market value.

In all cases where it is intended to grant an option to purchase to a beneficiary, it is useful to provide expressly for the trustees to give notice of the option to the beneficiary; this will avoid the possibility of the intended grantee failing to exercise the option through ignorance of its existence.

21A   OPTION TO PURCHASE LAND

(a) I DIRECT my Trustees to offer my freehold property situate at [etc] to [name] at the purchase price of £ ... such offer to be made in writing within six months of the date of the grant of probate or administration to my estate and to be accepted by [name] in writing within one year from the date on which such offer is made by my Trustees whereupon the right of the said [name] to exercise the option by accepting such offer shall absolutely cease and I DIRECT that my Trustees shall take such steps as may reasonably be required to bring the said offer to the attention of the said [name] as soon as may be practicable.

(b) I FURTHER DIRECT that:
  (i) the option is personal to [name] and may not be exercised by any person save for [name] and is not transmissible to their personal representative or otherwise;
  (ii) following the payment of the price as aforesaid the said [name] shall be indemnified out of my residuary estate from and against any inheritance tax and any foreign death duties payable in respect of the said property on or by reason of my death or in the administration of my estate;
  (iii) my Trustees may in their absolute and uncontrolled discretion accept payment of the said purchase price in instalments or otherwise and may accept such security as they in their

absolute discretion think fit in respect of any sum remaining unpaid and may charge interest on any outstanding sum at such rate as they shall in their absolute discretion determine;

(iv)   upon the said [name] exercising the said option my Trustees shall forthwith convey to [name] the fee simple of the said property free from incumbrances save any mortgage or other security in respect of part or all of the said purchase price for the time being remaining outstanding and any interest due in respect of the same;

(c)   I DECLARE that if the said option is not exercised within the said period then at any time after the expiration of the said period my Trustees shall deal with the property in accordance with the trusts hereof and in any deed relating to the said property executed by my Trustees any recital or other statement in writing to the effect that the offer to sell the property to [name] hereunder has not been accepted shall be conclusive evidence of the same to anyone dealing with my Trustees for money or money's worth; and

(d)   MY TRUSTEES SHALL accumulate the income of the said property until the exercise of the said option or the expiry of the time for its exercise whichever is the sooner and hold such accumulations as part of my residuary estate.

21B   CLAUSE GRANTING OPTION TO PURCHASE SHARES IN FAMILY COMPANY

I DIRECT my Trustees as soon as conveniently may be after my death to give in writing to my son [name] if living at my death the option to purchase ... shares in ... Limited at a price to be determined by an accountant chosen by my Trustees and I DECLARE that my son shall have [six] months from the date of the receipt of such notice in which to exercise the same by giving notice in writing to my Trustees ALWAYS PROVIDED THAT this option shall absolutely cease to be exercisable on the expiry of one year from the date of my death and no purchaser of the said shares shall be in any way affected by the terms of this clause whether or not the same have been purchased prior to the expiry of the said period of one year and I DIRECT ... [continue as in Precedent 21A by adapting provisions required].

Chapter 22

Administrative Provisions

22.1   INTRODUCTION

In the absence of detailed provisions in the will, the personal representatives and trustees may rely on various statutory powers to aid them in the administration of the estate. The main body of these powers is contained in the Trustee Act 2000. For the purposes of the legislation, the term 'trustee' includes a personal representative. Although the statutory powers are of great use, they are not ideal for all situations. Some are subject to limitations which the testator may wish to remove or extend in order to give greater freedom to the trustees. Trustees and personal representatives require different administrative provisions; although they may be, and frequently are, the same people, their roles are very different (see Chapter 9). Thus the objects of the gifts in the will should be considered when the administrative provisions are drafted.

Personal representatives are in a fiduciary position, and, in the absence of express provision in the will, are subject to a number of restrictions and obligations.

22.2   APPROPRIATION OF ASSETS

Under Administration of Estates Act 1925, section 41, personal representatives may, with the relevant consents, appropriate assets in order to satisfy a general or residuary legacy in the will, either in whole or in part.

If the beneficiary is absolutely and beneficially entitled, is an adult, and has full mental capacity, then their consent alone is all that is required for such an appropriation. If the beneficiary, though absolutely and beneficially entitled, is a minor or is mentally incapable of dealing with their own affairs, then the consent of their parent, guardian, attorney, deputy or receiver, as appropriate, must be obtained.

In the case of a settled legacy, the consent of the trustees of the settlement is required unless those trustees are also the personal representatives of the estate, in which case the consent of the person for the time being entitled to the income of the settlement (provided that person is of full age and has full mental capacity) is required. But if there is no such person, no consent is required, provided the appropriation is of an investment authorised by law or by the will.

The requirement for consent is frequently varied by will to allow the personal representatives to appropriate without a formal consent. This is administratively convenient but does contain a possible inheritance tax downside in relation to claims for loss relief. Where personal representatives sell land or quoted shares within certain periods after death (12 months for quoted shares and 4 years for land) for less than their value at the date of death, they can substitute the sale proceeds for the death value, thereby reducing the inheritance tax payable on the estate. HM Revenue & Customs regards an appropriation made under section 41 with consent as a sale for this purpose. However, it does not regard an appropriation as a sale if the will has removed the need for consent (see HM Revenue & Customs, *Inheritance Tax Manual* at IHTM34153, available at www.hmrc.gov.uk/manuals/ihtmanual).

Personal representatives are authorised (section 41(3)) to employ a valuer, if they see fit, to determine the value of assets.

The value of the asset(s) being appropriated is determined at the date of the appropriation, not at the date of death (see *Re Collins* [1975] 1 WLR 309). This can make a great difference to the amount a legatee takes. A will may give the personal representatives a discretion as to whether they appropriate assets at the death value rather than at the later value. This may be useful as it could allow them, for example, to channel more assets to a non-exempt beneficiary in satisfaction of a nil rate band legacy. HM Revenue & Customs is said to have accepted appropriations on such a basis, but the inheritance tax position is not entirely clear at the time of writing. However, including such a power would allow for the possibility of making such an appropriation if circumstances after the date of death warranted it. The *STEP Standard Provisions* (Society of Trust and Estate Practitioners, 2nd edn, 2013) includes such a power as an option.

If the personal representative is also a legatee, the will must authorise the personal representative to appropriate assets to themselves if this is desired. In *Kane v Radley-Kane* [1999] Ch 274, the rule against self-dealing was held to apply to appropriations under section 41, with the result that an appropriation of unquoted shares in satisfaction of the statutory legacy on intestacy was voidable by the other beneficiaries (the case does, however, state that appropriations of assets which are equivalent to cash, such as quoted shares, are not voidable).

Section 41 does not apply to trusts. It is common to include an express power for trustees to appropriate assets. Such a power is often used to facilitate accounting. For example, a trust fund is settled on four minor grandchildren contingent on them reaching the age of 25. The trustees expect to apply income and advance capital to the grandchildren during the life of the trust. It may make life easier if they allocate the assets into four 'shares' or 'sub-funds'.

In the case of large family trusts, certain assets may be particularly suitable for certain beneficiaries; for example, shares in the family company for a beneficiary who is involved in the running of the company.

Although appropriations are useful, circumstances may change and the trustees may want to switch the assets back. It is helpful to include a power to re-appropriate. See *Cotterell and Another v Ismay Fourth Viscount Allendale and Another* [2020] EWHC 2234 (Ch), where trustees applied to court under Trustee Act 1925, section 57 for an order giving them a power to re-appropriate assets held in one sub-fund to another sub-fund, in exchange for assets of equivalent value from the other sub-fund. It was not considered that the power to appropriate contained in the trust instrument could be construed to include a power to re-appropriate.

Chief Master Marsh had no difficulty in granting the desired power, saying at [21]:

> A general power to re-appropriate is clearly a sensible addition to the power of appropriation because as times change there may be good reasons to make suitable adjustments that are in the interests of the beneficiaries.

22A POWER OF APPROPRIATION TO BE EXERCISED BY PERSONAL REPRESENTATIVES OR TRUSTEES

> I DECLARE that my Trustees may appropriate any real or personal property forming part of my estate to or towards the interest or share of any person or persons in the proceeds of sale thereof PROVIDED THAT the powers conferred hereunder are in addition to any power of appropriation or partition conferred upon my Trustees by statute [and FURTHER PROVIDED THAT in every case my Trustees shall not be required to obtain the consent of any person to any such appropriation].

22B   APPROPRIATION WHERE PERSONAL REPRESENTATIVES BENEFICIALLY INTERESTED

I DECLARE that the power of appropriation hereinbefore contained shall be exercisable by my Trustees notwithstanding the fact that one or more of such Trustees may be beneficially interested in any property appropriated or partitioned thereunder.

22C   POWER OF APPROPRIATION WITH CONSENT OF BENEFICIARIES OF FULL AGE

I DECLARE that my Trustees may at any time or times with the consent in writing of all other persons for the time being entitled to share in my residuary estate who are of full age and capacity appropriate any part of my residuary estate in its then actual condition or state of investment in or towards satisfaction of the share of any Beneficiary in my residuary estate PROVIDED THAT my Trustees shall be required only to give notice of such appropriation to the last known address of each such person and if no objection to the intended appropriation is received within [three] months of the date of posting of such notice my Trustees shall assume that such consent has been given and be entitled to proceed with such appropriation without such consent in writing AND I DECLARE that the powers conferred hereunder are in addition to any powers of appropriation and partition conferred on my Trustees by statute.

22D   POWER FOR TRUSTEES TO APPROPRIATE (FULL FORM)

I DECLARE that [notwithstanding the trust for sale hereinbefore contained] my Trustees (whether acting as personal representatives or as Trustees) may appropriate any real or personal property forming part of [my residuary estate and which is not the subject of a specific gift or option whilst it remains capable of being exercised] to or towards the share or interest whether settled or not of any person or persons in the proceeds of sale thereof under the trusts hereinbefore contained and for the purposes aforesaid shall have and may at any time exercise all such powers of appropriation and other powers conferred upon personal representatives by Administration of Estates Act 1925, section 41 and with the same effect as set out in such section PROVIDED ALWAYS that the power hereby conferred shall be additional to any power of appropriation or partition conferred upon my Trustees by statute, any such appropriation shall be valid and binding without the consent of the Beneficiary or of any other person and any such appropriation shall be valid and binding notwithstanding that one of more of my Trustees may be beneficially interested in the exercise of the said power [PROVIDED ALSO that in making any appropriation of property as aforesaid my Trustees may (but only if it is reasonable for them to do so) take the probate value of such property being its ascertained value at the date of my death as the value to be appropriated rather than having the value of the property determined as at the date of the appropriation].

Note: As explained in the main text, it is possible to give personal representatives power to make an appropriation by valuing the property for that purpose at the date of death, as opposed to the date of appropriation itself. However, care is needed in deciding whether or not to include this power because its exercise might be open to abuse or allegations of unfairness amongst beneficiaries. Also, there might be inheritance tax implications if its exercise gives rise to a change in the values of the respective entitlements taken under the will, particularly those affecting exempt and non-exempt beneficiaries.

22DA CLAUSE ALLOWING RE-APPROPRIATION

Where the Trustees have appointed, appropriated or allocated any assets comprised in the Trust Fund to be held on trusts distinct from any other part of the Trust Fund, the Trustees may at any time or times during the Trust Period transfer any assets comprised in or forming part of the capital of any such fund to any other fund which forms part of the Trust Fund (including that part of the Trust Fund containing assets which have not been appointed, appropriated or allocated to a distinct fund) in exchange for assets which have a value equal to the open market value of the assets or part so transferred, and for this purpose they shall have power to have assets valued as they shall in their discretion think fit.

22.3 POWER TO ACT THOUGH PERSONALLY INTERESTED AND TO PURCHASE TRUST PROPERTY ('SELF-DEALING')

Because of the fiduciary nature of the trustees' position they cannot act when they have a personal interest unless authorised to do so. This is because equity does not allow a person, who is in a position of trust, to carry out a transaction where there is a conflict, or possible conflict between their duty and their interest, unless they are authorised to do so (see *Wright v Morgan* [1926] AC 788).

The rule has two aspects.

First, there may be circumstances in which they are unable to exercise a discretion and this may work to the detriment of the estate or trust.

Second, trustees are generally prohibited from purchasing trust property, although there are some circumstances in which a court may authorise such a purchase (see *Holder v Holder* [1968] Ch 353 (CA) and *Ex parte Lacey* (1802) 6 Ves 625). It is often appropriate to authorise trustees or personal representatives to buy trust or estate property. Trustees or personal representatives may have beneficial interests, or may have particular reasons for wanting to buy assets, for example, where they are the surviving partners or co-shareholders of the deceased. A testator may give the trustees a power to purchase specific items of trust property from the estate. It may be necessary to include in the will provisions to govern the method of ascertaining an appropriate purchase price.

Although there is case-law authority suggesting that a settlor who appoints a beneficiary as a trustee may be taken to be impliedly authorising self-dealing to some extent (see *Sargeant v National Westminster Bank* (1990) 61 P& CR 518, *The Woodland Trust v Loring and Others* [2014] EWCA Civ 1314 and *Brudenell-Bruce v Moore and Another* [2012] EWHC 1024 (Ch)), it is clearly preferable to provide for this expressly. Safeguards can be included, for example requiring there to be an independent trustee. There is also a lack of clarity as to the exact limits of the implied authorisation. In *Caldicott and Others v Richards and Another* [2020] EWHC 767 (Ch), the settlor had appointed a beneficiary as a trustee. The court held that, although this would impliedly authorise the trustee to exercise powers in her own favour, it did not do so in relation to the administrative power of sale. That conflict arose because of the trustee's decision to purchase trust property.

22E   POWER TO ACT THOUGH PERSONALLY INTERESTED AND TO PURCHASE TRUST PROPERTY

I DECLARE that any of my Trustees acting in good faith may exercise or concur in exercising all powers and discretions given to them by this will or by law notwithstanding that they have a direct or other personal interest in the mode or result of any such exercise [and that any of my Trustees shall be free to purchase any part of my estate not specifically disposed of whether real or personal either by private treaty or by public auction for their own account [PROVIDED ALWAYS that in any such case there shall be at least one other Trustee to whom any such personal interest shall first have been disclosed] [and who has no personal interest in the particular transaction] [AND PROVIDED that in the case of a purchase by private treaty the price paid shall be not less than the amount of a valuation made for the purpose by a suitably qualified independent valuer to be paid for by the prospective purchaser] [or in the case of quoted securities not less than the market price at the time of execution of the transfer]].

22F   POWER TO TRUSTEES TO PURCHASE TRUST PROPERTY

I DECLARE that the said [name] shall have power to purchase [specific property] [any part of my estate not otherwise specifically disposed of whether real or personal] either by private treaty or by public auction notwithstanding that the said [name] is one of my Trustees of this my will [and in the event of a sale by private treaty the purchase price shall be the price agreed between the said [name] and my other Trustees for the time being] [PROVIDED that any price agreed in respect of quoted securities shall not be less than the market price thereof at the time of the execution of the transfer] [AND FURTHER PROVIDED that my Trustees other than [name] shall obtain a valuation of the property by an independent surveyor or valuer [to be paid for by the said [name] and the purchase price shall not be less than the said valuation].

22.4   RETENTION OF DIRECTORS' REMUNERATION

In the absence of a contrary provision, a trustee would be liable to account for all director's fees received by them, and an ordinary charging clause is not a sufficient contrary provision to give a trustee-director power to retain such remuneration.

22G   POWER FOR TRUSTEES TO BECOME DIRECTORS AND TO RETAIN REMUNERATION

I DECLARE that any one or more of my Trustees may act as a director or other officer or employee of [the said ... Company Limited] [any company] without being liable to account to my estate or the persons beneficially interested therein for any remuneration paid to such of my Trustees for so acting [and any of my Trustees may become qualified as a director (if the articles of association of the said company so allow) by holding in their own name shares belonging to my estate provided that they execute a declaration of trust thereof in favour of my Trustees generally accompanied by the certificates of such shares and ALSO PROVIDED that they account to my estate for all dividends and bonuses payable in respect thereof].

22.5   POWER TO ACT BY MAJORITY

Trustees, other than trustees of a charity, must act unanimously unless a special provision permits them to act by a majority.

22H   DIRECTION TO TRUSTEES TO ACT BY MAJORITY

I DECLARE that in all matters relating to the execution of the trusts of this my will or any codicil hereto the opinion of the majority of the Trustees for the time being thereof shall be decisive.

22.6   POWER TO EMPLOY AGENTS

Under Trustee Act 2000, section 11 a personal representative or trustee may employ an agent to exercise any or all of their 'delegable functions'. These are all functions except those relating to:

(i)   whether or how trust assets are to be distributed;
(ii)   whether fees or payments should be made out of capital or income;
(iii)   the appointment of trustees;
(iv)   any power (statutory or express) to delegate or appoint nominees or custodians.

They can also appoint nominees or custodians to hold trust assets (sections 16 and 17). When appointing agents, etc trustees are subject to the statutory duty of care in Trustee Act 2000, section 1 unless the will excludes it.

It is increasingly common for trustees to delegate certain functions, such as the investment of funds to a fund manager who makes investment decisions without reference to the trustees but in accordance with an investment policy chosen by the trustees and periodically reviewed by them. Trustee Act 2000, sections 11 to 27 allow trustees and personal representatives to delegate investment functions to such managers and to vest trust assets in nominees. The statutory powers are extensive. There are, however, the following weaknesses which, if desired, can be addressed by express provisions:

(i)   trustees cannot delegate to a beneficiary (Trustee Act 2000, section 12);
(ii)   sections 14 and 20 provide that, unless it is reasonably necessary, the terms on which delegates or nominees are appointed cannot include:

   –   power for the agent/nominee to appoint a substitute;
   –   restrictions on the liability of an agent/nominee; or
   –   power for the agent/nominee to act in circumstances capable of giving rise to a conflict of interest;

(iii)   section 15 requires trustees who are delegating asset management functions to comply with detailed requirements. While generally sensible, there might be occasions where the detailed requirements would be unduly burdensome;
(iv)   section 19 limits the persons who can hold assets as nominees or custodians;
(v)   while agents, nominees and custodians are acting, section 22 requires trustees to keep the arrangements under which they act under review, consider whether there is a need to intervene and, if they conclude that there is, to do so. While generally sensible, there might be occasions where these requirements would be unduly burdensome.

The restrictions set out at points (i) to (v) above can largely be avoided by including express powers which replace them, although there is some doubt at the time of writing whether sections 14 and 15 can be excluded.

The exercise of any trust, power or discretion vested in a trustee may be delegated to a third party by a power of attorney, for a period up to but not exceeding 1 year (Trustee Act 1925, section 25, as substituted by Trustee Delegation Act 1999, section 5).

221 POWER TO DELEGATE INVESTMENT POWERS AND VEST ASSETS IN NOMINEES

(a) My Trustees may delegate with respect to the whole or any part of [my residuary estate] their powers hereunder of investing trust moneys and changing trust investments and any other of my Trustees' powers hereby or by law conferred relating to the management or administration of trust moneys or other trust assets to any person carrying on the business of management of investments to any extent for any period on any terms (which may include authorising self-dealing or limiting the liability of the person to whom such powers are delegated) and in any manner and may remunerate such person and Trustee Act 2000, section 22 shall not apply.

(b) My Trustees shall have power to vest or register any property in any person or persons whether individual or corporate and whether or not an investment manager to whom powers have been delegated under the foregoing power (and who may be or include one or more of my Trustees or the Beneficiaries hereunder) as nominee or nominees for my Trustees upon such terms as to remuneration or otherwise (including terms authorising self-dealing or providing for the limitation of the liability of the nominee) as my Trustees think fit and Trustee Act 2000, section 22 shall not apply.

22.7 APPOINTMENT OF NEW TRUSTEES

The number of executors who may take a grant in respect of any particular part of any estate is limited to four (Senior Courts Act 1981, section 114(1)).

It is not usual, therefore, to appoint more than four trustees in a private trust. Where only one trustee is appointed, they are able to perform most acts of joint trustees, except that a single trustee cannot give a valid receipt for capital moneys arising on the disposition of land unless the trustee is a trust corporation. Trustee Act 1925, sections 36(1) and (2) and 41, detail the circumstances in which new trustees may be appointed either by the persons specified in the Act (section 36, the person nominated in the instrument, the continuing trustees or the personal representatives of the last trustee) or by the court (section 41). Errors in the appointment of new trustees are common. People do not always look at the trust instrument to check who has the power to make new appointments. Once an error has been made, all subsequent decisions made are potentially invalid. For illustrations of the problems that can arise from faulty appointments, see *Jasmine Trustees Ltd v Wells & Hind (A Firm) and Another* [2007] EWHC 38 (Ch), [2008] Ch 194 and *Yudt v Ross and Another* [1998] All ER (D) 375.

22J POWER OF APPOINTMENT OF NEW TRUSTEES CONFERRED BY THE TRUSTEE ACT 1925

I DECLARE that my [spouse] [civil partner] shall have vested in [him] [her] the statutory power of appointment of new Trustees of the trusts hereof and upon [his] [her] death or in the event [he] [she] becomes unable to exercise such appointment due to lacking the capacity to so exercise if sooner the same shall vest in such person of full age as shall for the time being have an interest in possession in the trust property in respect whereof a new Trustee is to be appointed.

22K DIRECTION AS TO NUMBER OF TRUSTEES

I DIRECT that there shall at all times be [four] Trustees of this my will and that any vacancy shall be filled as soon as reasonably practicable always provided that the Trustees hereof for the time being shall during any vacancy have the same powers authorities and discretions and may act in all respects as if there were [four] Trustees hereof.

22.8 POWER TO ACT ON COUNSEL'S OPINION

Legal issues may arise concerning the interpretation of the will, the terms of its trusts, or the estate itself. The trustees may apply to the court for directions in any such case, but this would be an expense to the estate.

The High Court has power under Administration of Justice Act 1985, section 48 without hearing argument to authorise trustees to take action in reliance on counsel's opinion in relation to any question of construction of the terms of a will or a trust. Counsel must have at least 10 years' High Court qualification. The court cannot make the appointment without hearing argument if it considers that a dispute exists which would make it inappropriate to make the order without hearing argument.

It is beneficial for trustees to have a power to rely on counsel's opinion, without having to apply to court and in relation to general administration problems as opposed simply to matters of construction. The trustees or the beneficiaries may still apply to the court if they think fit. It may also be helpful for the power to authorise trustees to use counsel with less than 10 years' qualification as this will reduce costs.

Re BCA Pension Trustees Ltd [2015] EWHC 3492 (Ch) is an illustration of the problems that can ensue in relation to a section 48 application. In an application relating to amendments to a pension deed which had been made incorrectly resulting in uncertainty, the court decided that the issue was one that required a hearing. It then had to decide whether the matter was actually one of construction at all or whether it was actually a matter requiring rectification. The judge decided it was a matter of construction.

22L   POWER TO ACT ON COUNSEL'S OPINION

My Trustees shall have power to seek and act upon the advice of any barrister who has been admitted for not less than five years practising in the Chancery Division of the High Court of Justice in relation to any question of interpretation or administration arising under this my will or any codicil hereto or the trusts hereof and my Trustees shall not be liable to any of the persons beneficially interested in respect of any act or omission done or made in accordance with such advice or opinion.

22.9   INDEMNITY CLAUSES

Trustee 'indemnity' clauses are clauses which are intended to absolve trustees or executors from liability in the event of their own negligence or the negligence or fraud of their co-trustees or agents. It is clearly appropriate to include such a clause where the trustees are friends or family who take office as a favour and are unprotected by insurance. It is less appropriate in the case of professionally paid trustees who have the benefit of professional negligence policies. Nevertheless, liability can be excluded in such cases (see *Armitage v Nurse and Others* [1998] Ch 241). The existence and effect of such a clause should be drawn to the attention of the testator. On 19 July 2006, the Law Commission published the report, *Trustee Exemption Clauses* (Law Com No 301), arguing for a non-legislative solution. It recommended that professional and regulatory bodies should adopt rules or guidance to the effect that any paid trustee who causes a settlor to include a trustee exemption clause in a trust instrument, which has the effect of excluding or limiting liability for negligence, must, before the creation of the trust, take steps to ensure that the settlor is aware of the meaning and effect of the clause. Both the Society of Trust and Estate Practitioners (STEP) and the SRA took that approach.

Those regulated by the SRA are subject to special rules of conduct set out in the SRA Standards and Regulations (which replaced the SRA Code of Conduct 2011 on 25 November 2019). There is no express reference to indemnity clauses. However, Principles 5 and 7 of the SRA Principles require those regulated by the SRA to act with integrity and in each client's best interests. The SRA Code of Conduct for Solicitors, Registered European Lawyers and Registered Foreign Lawyers describes the standards of professionalism expected of those authorised to provide legal services. Under the heading 'Maintaining trust and acting fairly' it states at 1.2, 'You do not abuse your position by taking unfair advantage of *clients* or others' (original emphasis).

It is possible to exclude the statutory duty of care contained in Trustee Act 2000, section 1 (a trustee must exercise such care and skill as is reasonable in the circumstances), and it may be appropriate to do so where unpaid non-professional trustees are acting.

22M   GENERAL INDEMNITY CLAUSE

I DECLARE that none of my Trustees shall be liable for any act or omission of theirs or for any act or omission of any agent employed in the administration of my estate or in the execution of the trusts hereunder nor for any act or omission of any co-Trustee or any co-personal representative save and except for any act or omission involving wilful fraud or dishonesty committed by the Trustee or personal representative sought to be made liable.

22N   GENERAL INDEMNITY CLAUSE WITH PROVISO EXCLUDING PROFESSIONAL AND CORPORATE TRUSTEES

In the professed administration of my estate and the professed execution of the trusts, powers or provisions of this will or any codicil hereto none of my Trustees shall be liable (whether for breach of the duty of care under the Trustee Act 2000 or otherwise) for any act or omission of theirs or for any act or omission of any co-personal representative or co-Trustee of theirs or of any agent, nominee or custodian employed in the administration of my estate or the execution of the said trusts powers and provisions save for any act or omission involving wilful fraud or dishonesty committed by the personal representative or Trustee sought to be made liable. And in particular but without prejudice to the generality of the foregoing provision none of my Trustees shall be bound to take any proceedings against a co-Trustee or past Trustee or their personal representatives for any breach or alleged breach of trust committed or suffered by such co-Trustee. [PROVIDED THAT this clause shall not apply to a corporation and shall not apply to an individual authorised hereby or by law to charge for acting as a personal representative or Trustee [unless they have elected in writing not to charge for so acting at or before the time of their obtaining a grant of representation or (not having obtained such a grant) their being first appointed as Trustee]].

22O CLAUSE EXCLUDING THE STATUTORY DUTY OF CARE

The duty of care contained in Trustee Act 2000, section 1 shall not apply in relation to [any of] my Trustees [who does not act as Trustee in the course of a business or profession].

22P EXCLUSION OF LIABILITY FOR ACTS OF ATTORNEYS

Notwithstanding any statutory provisions to the contrary none of my Trustees or personal representatives who grants a power of attorney to any third party shall be liable for the acts or omissions of the donee of such power provided that the donor acts in good faith and the power so given does not endure for longer than twelve months.

22Q CLAUSE DEALING WITH MISSING BENEFICIARIES

I DECLARE that if after employing all reasonable diligence my Trustees are unable to trace any beneficiary under my estate within one year from the date when the gift to him or her becomes payable or one year from the date of the first grant of representation to my estate if later then my Trustees may distribute my estate as if all such unfound beneficiaries, if any, had predeceased me without leaving issue and the interest of any such beneficiary or their issue in my estate shall wholly and irrevocably cease.

22.10 CHARGING CLAUSES

Before the coming into force of the Trustee Act 2000, on 1 February 2001, a professional trustee could not charge for acting as a personal representative or trustee unless expressly authorised. Trustee Act 2000, section 29(2) gives limited powers to charge to trust corporations and to those acting 'in a professional capacity' in relation to services provided, no matter when the trust was created. Where the section applies, trustees and personal representatives can receive reasonable remuneration for any services provided (including services capable of being provided by a lay person, but only with the written agreement of a co-trustee).

Trustee Act 2000, section 39 provides that 'trust corporation' has the same meaning as in the Trustee Act 1925. Section 28(5) of the 2000 Act defines 'acting in a professional capacity'. To satisfy the definition, a trustee or personal representative must act in the course of a profession or business which consists of or includes the provision of services in connection with:

(i) the management or administration of trusts generally or a particular kind of trust; or
(ii) any particular aspect of the management or administration of trusts generally, or a particular kind of trust.

Express provision is still required to authorise charging by a person who is not within the definition.

Even where a trustee or personal representative comes within the definition, it is preferable to include an express power rather than to rely on section 29, because:

(i) the statutory provision does not allow a sole trustee to charge; and
(ii) the professional trustee requires the written agreement of co-trustees in order to charge.

When including or construing an express power for a professional person to charge, it is important to consider whether the wording authorises the professional person to charge for *any* services provided, or only for *professional* services provided.

It should also be kept in mind that, once a professional person has retired, they are not able to benefit under a standard charging clause which authorises a person 'engaged in a profession' to charge. According to *Glenister v Moody* [2003] EWHC 3155 (Ch), [2005] WTLR 1205, however, a professional trustee who is winding down his practice is still engaged in a profession while finalising the last few trusts. There is a distinction between such a case and a case where a professional trustee has wound up all his trusts but keeps on the administration of a single trust.

Trustee Act 2000, section 28 makes two other important changes to the law relating to remuneration. A trust corporation or trustee or personal representative acting in a professional capacity (as defined above), charging under an express provision contained in the will or trust instrument:

(i) can charge for *any* services provided, even if those services could have been provided by a lay person (section 28(2)). This means that a charging clause can be shorter, as it does not need to provide expressly for payment for such services. But if a professional person who does not come within the definition is (or may be) appointed as trustee or personal representative, the clause must make express provision for payment for non-professional services if the trustee is to be able to charge for them;

(ii)   is treated as receiving *remuneration* and not a legacy for the purposes of Wills Act 1837, section 15, and Administration of Estates Act 1925, section 34(3) (section 28(4)). This means that the benefit of a charging clause is not lost if the professional person or a partner in the relevant firm witnesses the will. It also means that the charges would not abate with the pecuniary legacies if there are insufficient funds to meet the pecuniary legacies in full. This provision applies only in relation to deaths occurring on or after 1 February 2001 (section 33(2)).

Both these provisions are subject to contrary provision in the will or trust instrument.

Company directors are employees and there is some doubt whether they are 'engaged in a profession or business'. In *Da Silva v Heselton* [2022] EWCA Civ 880, Nugee LJ suggested (*obiter*) that a director running a business through a company might be in a different position to a mere employee. To avoid argument, it may be preferable to provide expressly for company directors, or to authorise those acting in a purely personal capacity to charge. In *Da Silva*, the Court of Appeal considered an express charging clause which allowed a person engaged in a profession or business to charge 'usual' fees, and concluded that such a clause only permitted charges to be made for the type of services provided in the profession or business.

There is also a difficulty in fixing the level of remuneration; if the power is to charge a 'reasonable' rate, how is what is reasonable to be ascertained and what can be done if charges are unreasonable? The decision in *Pullan v Wilson and Others* [2014] EWHC 126 (Ch) made the point that a trustee's normal charge out rate is not necessarily 'reasonable'. An objective test must be used looking at what work was done and what the 'going rate' for such work would be. To avoid argument, it is desirable to get the beneficiaries to confirm the rate in advance.

Those regulated by the SRA Standards and Regulations must ensure that they comply with Principles 5 and 7 (acting with integrity and in the best interests of clients). The SRA Code of Conduct for Solicitors, Registered European Lawyers and Registered Foreign Lawyers requires those regulated by the SRA not to abuse their position by taking unfair advantage of clients or others. If appointing members of the firm as executors with the benefit of a charging clause, it is necessary to draw the client's attention to the clause.

If discussing the appointment of firm members as executors, regard must be had to the SRA's *Guidance on Drafting and Preparation of Wills* published on 6 May 2014 (updated 25 November 2019) and Law Society Practice Note, *Appointment of a Professional Executor* published on 3 September 2020. It should be ensured that the client understands that it is possible to appoint a lay executor and that a professional will charge.

**22R	CONCISE CHARGING CLAUSE FOR USE BY PROFESSIONAL TRUSTEES AS DEFINED IN TRUSTEE ACT 2000, SECTION 28(5) ONLY**

Any of my Trustees who acts in a professional capacity as defined by Trustee Act 2000, section 28(5) may be paid reasonable remuneration for services provided by them in connection with the administration of my estate or any trust of this will or of any codicil hereto [including acts which a Trustee could have done personally].

**22S	CHARGING CLAUSE AUTHORISING PROFESSIONAL TRUSTEES NOT WITHIN TRUSTEE ACT 2000, SECTION 28(5) TO CHARGE FOR PROFESSIONAL SERVICES PROVIDED**

Any of my Trustees being engaged in a profession or business whether or not they are acting in a professional capacity as defined by Trustee Act 2000, section 28(5) may charge and be paid reasonable remuneration for professional services provided by them in connection with the administration of my estate or any trust of this will or of any codicil hereto.

Note: As in Precedent 22R, professional trustees within the definition in section 28(5) would be able to charge for all services provided.

**22T	CHARGING CLAUSE AUTHORISING TRUSTEES ENGAGED IN A PROFESSION OR BUSINESS OR ACTING IN A PERSONAL CAPCITY TO CHARGE FOR ALL SERVICES AND TIME SPENT**

Any of my Trustees being engaged in a profession or business or merely acting in a personal capacity may charge and be paid reasonable remuneration for business transacted, acts done, advice given and time spent by them or their firm in connection with the administration of my estate or in connection with the trusts hereof including acts which a personal representative or Trustee not being in any profession or business could have done personally.

**22U	PROVISION FOR APPOINTMENT OF TRUST CORPORATION**

My Trustees in exercising the power of appointment vested in them by statute may appoint a trust corporation to act alone or with another or other Trustees and in the event of a trust corporation being so appointed I hereby authorise such trust corporation to charge and my Trustees to pay such fees and remuneration [as is agreed upon between my Trustees and the said trust corporation at the time of such appointment] [as is chargeable according to the scale of fees charged by such trust corporation from time to time].

22.11 POWER TO INVEST

The statutory powers of investment are contained in the Trustee Act 2000, which came into force on 1 February 2001. The general power of investment is contained in section 3, and authorises trustees to make any kind of investment that they could make if they were absolutely entitled to the trust assets. It does not authorise trustees to invest in land, which is dealt with expressly under section 8. They can, however, invest in loans secured on land.

The statutory power is in addition to any contained in the will or trust instrument, but subject to any restrictions imposed. It applies to trusts and wills whenever created. The statutory power of investment is adequate, but practitioners may want to replicate it in the will so that all powers are in the same place.

The trustees must have regard to the 'standard investment criteria' when exercising any power of investment (express or statutory). They must also review the trust investments from time to time and decide whether, in the light of those criteria, the investments should be varied. The criteria are:

(i)   the suitability to the trust of investments of the kind proposed and the suitability of the particular investment as an example of that type;
(ii) the need for diversification of investments of the trust, in so far as is appropriate to the circumstances of the trust.

The duty to consider the criteria cannot be excluded. However, in cases where a settlor intends the trust to be a vehicle for holding a particular asset, such as land or shares in a family business, the settlor should leave a statement of wishes by way of guidance on the extent to which diversification is appropriate. In *Gregson v HAE Trustees Ltd and Others* [2008] EWHC 1006 (Ch), [2009] 1 All ER (Comm) 457, the court pointed out that the qualification in section 4(3)(b) that the trustees must consider diversification 'in so far as is appropriate to the circumstances of the trust' means that the trustees can properly take into account matters such as the nature and purposes of the settlement, its provisions, any letter of wishes, and the feelings of beneficiaries at this point. The court also stated that a trust instrument can provide that the original trust investments are not to be sold although the particular instrument under consideration in *Gregson* had not done so. It is difficult to imagine circumstances in which an absolute prohibition on sale would be appropriate. Even if such a prohibition were to be included, it would be open to the trustees in appropriate circumstances to apply to the court under Trustee Act 1925, section 57 for an order authorising them to sell (see *Alexander v Alexander and Others* [2011] EWHC 2721 (Ch)).

Before investing, or when reviewing investments, the trustees must also obtain and consider 'proper advice'. Proper advice is the advice of a person reasonably believed by the trustee to be qualified to advise, by reason of their ability in and practical experience of financial and other matters relating to the proposed investment. The trustee is relieved of the obligation to take advice if 'he reasonably concludes that in all the circumstances it is unnecessary or inappropriate to do so'. Matters which might justify a decision not to take advice are:

(i)   the expertise of individual trustees;
(ii)   the fact that the amount to be invested is small in relation to the trust as a whole.

When exercising duties in relation to investment, trustees must exercise such care and skill as is reasonable in the circumstances, having regard in particular:

(i)   to any special knowledge or experience the trustee has or holds themselves out as having; or
(ii)   if the trustee acts as a trustee in the course of a business or profession, to any special knowledge or experience that it is reasonable to expect of a person acting in the course of such a business or profession.

Express provision is also required in the following cases:

- to permit an ethical investment policy;
- to permit borrowing for the purposes of investment; or
- to permit the retention of non-income producing assets.

22.12   'ANTI-BARTLETT' CLAUSES

Where trustees hold a significant shareholding in a private company, it is not enough to leave the conduct of the business to the directors.

Both *Re Lucking's Will Trusts* [1967] 3 All ER 726 and *Bartlett v Barclays Bank* [1980] Ch 515 dealt with the fact that a shareholding in a private company large enough to confer some measure of control brings special responsibilities. Trustees are under a duty to keep themselves informed about the company's affairs and the directors' plans. They must be willing to act on the information and may be liable for a breach of fiduciary duty if they fail to take steps to prevent the dissipation of the company's assets in a speculative and ill-considered venture. However, unless specially chosen for their expertise, trustees will not normally have the expertise to satisfy themselves that a trading company is being managed prudently.

It is, therefore, common to include so-called anti-*Bartlett* clauses. The protection afforded by such clauses will vary depending on their terms.

The clause may give trustees power to leave the conduct of the company's affairs to the directors. Given directors who know their business, it is common for the benefit of the beneficiaries to allow the directors to manage the company, but such a clause will not relieve a trustee who gives no thought to whether or not to exercise any control. Such a power must be consciously exercised and the trustee may be attacked if they have no rational basis for their decision.

More usually, the clause will exclude the trustee's duty to enquire and supervise. The protection is limited to excluding the preliminary duty of keeping abreast of what is going on. If the trustee does become aware of circumstances which call for enquiry and fails to do so, no protection is available.

More sweeping clauses may impose a duty on the trustees not to interfere in the management of the company, sometimes adding in the absence of knowledge of dishonesty on the part of the directors. Such clauses will typically be accompanied by clauses allowing the settlor/protector to give binding directions to the trustees on the exercise of their shareholder rights. If that power is fiduciary, as it normally will be, and the powers are abused, the trustees may have a duty to bring the matter before the court if they have knowledge of circumstances which call for enquiry.

Of course, it is often the case that one or more of the trustees may have a seat on the board of the company anyway. While this type of clause may purport to give protection to such person while wearing their 'trustee' hat, it does not relieve that person from their fiduciary obligations owed to shareholders (i.e. the trust beneficiaries) as a director.

22V ANTI-BARTLETT CLAUSE

> The Trustees shall not be bound to inquire into or be involved in the management of any company in which the Trust Fund is invested unless they have knowledge of circumstances which call for inquiry and so long as the Trustees have no actual notice of any act of dishonesty or misappropriation by any director or other authorised officer, the Trustees may leave the conduct of the company's business (including the payment and non-payment of dividends) wholly to the directors and authorised officers.

22.13   POWER TO ACQUIRE LAND

Trustee Act 2000, section 8 gives trustees power to acquire freehold or leasehold land in the United Kingdom:

- as an investment;
- for occupation by a beneficiary;
- for any other reason.

If they are acquiring for investment, they must have regard to the standard investment criteria (above) and to acquire and consider proper investment advice. They must also have regard to the statutory duty of care unless amended by the will or trust instrument. If they are acquiring land for non-investment purposes (e.g. as a residence for a beneficiary), however, the standard investment criteria and need for proper investment advice are not relevant.

Section 8 does not give trustees power to acquire property outside the United Kingdom or to acquire an interest in land as opposed to a legal estate. It is often beneficial for trustees to have power to acquire property abroad or to invest jointly with a beneficiary, but these powers must be conferred expressly.

It is no longer necessary to provide that land acquired by trustees is to be held on trust for sale. All land held on trust, in a trust created after 1 January 1997, is subject to the provisions of the Trusts of Land and Appointment of Trustees Act 1996. The provisions of the 1996 Act apply to trusts for sale of land created before that date but not to strict settlements created before that date; these continue to be governed by the Settled Land Act 1925.

The purpose of the Trusts of Land and Appointment of Trustees Act 1996 is to create a set of rules under which it makes no practical difference whether or not there is a trust for sale. This raises the question whether there is now any need to include a trust for or power of sale. There is no need for a trust for sale in relation to land, but it is uncertain whether trustees who do not hold land have a general power of sale. Personal representatives have a statutory power of sale (Administration of Estates Act 1925, section 39). It may be sensible to include a power of sale, against the possibility that a continuing trust of personalty arises in a will.

22W   POWER TO INVEST AND APPLY MONEY TO ACQUIRE LAND

My Trustees may:

(a)   make any kind of investment they could make if they were sole beneficial owners of the assets of the trust;

(b)   apply trust moneys in any property of whatever description or location whether within the United Kingdom or elsewhere including land buildings and interests in land or buildings unsecured personal loans non-income yielding property and land or buildings or interests in land or buildings for occupation or use by Beneficiaries as if they were sole beneficial owners of such moneys.

22X POWER TO RETAIN SHARES IN FAMILY BUSINESS

It is my wish that my Trustees shall retain any shares or securities in the [name] Company Limited (whether or not it has undergone any change of name) or in any company which as a result of any reconstruction amalgamation demerger or sale shall be a successor to any business of the said company or of any subsidiary of it [if and so long as any of my children or remoter issue are employed in any of such businesses and if and when none of them are so employed] unless and until it is in their opinion necessary in the interests of the Beneficiaries to sell or otherwise dispose of such shares or securities or any of them and I DECLARE that my Trustees shall not be liable for any loss arising from investment in or retention of any shares or securities of the foregoing kinds.

22Y POWERS TO PERMIT ENJOYMENT OF ASSETS IN KIND

My Trustees may permit any Beneficiary for the time being to have the use or enjoyment in kind of any land building chattel or other property which or the proceeds of sale of which or a share of which is comprised in such whole or part of [my residuary estate] upon such conditions as to payment by such Beneficiary for outgoings insurance and repair as my Trustees think fit (and my Trustees shall not be liable for any failure to pay outgoings or insure or repair such property if a Beneficiary is responsible for the same under the terms of such use or enjoyment).

22Z POWER TO APPLY TRUST MONEY IN THE PURCHASE OF PROPERTY AS A RESIDENCE

My Trustees may apply trust money in the purchase or improvement of any freehold or leasehold dwelling house and may permit such dwelling house to be used as a residence by any Beneficiary upon such terms and conditions as my Trustees think fit.

22AA POWER TO SELL

My Trustees shall have power to sell, mortgage or charge any asset of my estate as if they were sole beneficial owner.

22.14   POWERS TO MANAGE LAND

Trustees and personal representatives have wide statutory powers to manage land in the United Kingdom as a result of Trusts of Land and Appointment of Trustees Act 1996, section 6. (Where they acquire land under Trustee Act 2000, section 8(3) gives them the same powers.) Hence they have the widest discretion in relation to such matters as sale, insurance, repair, improvement, mortgaging and leasing.

The powers are, though, restricted to 'land' as defined. Express powers are needed to deal with foreign land or with interests in land such as arise through co-ownership. It is therefore wise to follow the wording of the statutory power, and it is advisable to include an express power to apply trust capital on the improvement of land.

Trusts of Land and Appointment of Trustees Act 1996, section 6 gives trustees of land the powers of an absolute owner in relation to land. Section 1 defines a trust of land as one which consists of or includes land. The trustees are required by section 6(5) to have regard to the rights of the beneficiaries when exercising their powers.

It may be desirable to extend the trustees' powers to pay for repairs out of capital.

It was necessary to avoid such a power when drafting an accumulation and maintenance trust. Repairs are properly payable from income, and power to pay for them out of capital might have resulted in an argument that capital could be diverted from the beneficiaries of the accumulation and maintenance trust. No new accumulation and maintenance trusts can be drafted after 22 March 2006. Does a similar risk exist in relation to trusts for bereaved minors and trusts for bereaved young people qualifying for privileged inheritance tax treatment under Inheritance Tax Act 1984, section 71A or section 71D?

The conditions for such trusts require that the bereaved minor or young person must become entitled to the settled property at the required age and that if any of the settled property is applied for the benefit of a beneficiary, it is applied for the benefit of the bereaved minor or young person. So long as there is no possibility of settled property being applied for the benefit of a beneficiary who is not the bereaved minor or young person, the conditions are satisfied.

Where a qualifying interest in possession is wanted, it is important that no power prevents the beneficiary from being entitled to income as it arises. The payment of expenses normally attributable to income will not cause problems, but the trustees should not be given power to pay capital expenses from income.

22BB POWER OF MANAGEMENT IN RELATION TO LAND IN ANY LOCATION

My Trustees shall have all the powers of an absolute owner in relation to any land held by them (wherever situated) and for this purpose 'land' includes buildings and estates interests or rights of any kind in or over land.

22CC POWER TO APPLY TRUST CAPITAL IN IMPROVING/MAINTAINING LAND

My Trustees whether acting as Trustees or personal representatives shall have power to apply capital held on the same trusts as any land or interest in land (or which would be so held if the administration of my estate had been completed) in the improvement of such land and to apply such capital or the income of such capital on the repair or maintenance of such land.

22DD POWER TO APPLY RESIDUARY FUNDS IN REPAIRING LAND COMPRISED IN RESIDUE

I DIRECT that my Trustees may repair any building structure chattel or other property forming part of my [residuary] estate or the proceeds of sale which form part of my [residuary] estate whatsoever and wheresoever situate and may pay the costs of such repairs from such of the income or capital of any part of my [residuary] estate as they think fit to be held on the same trusts as the property repaired.

22.15 INSURANCE

The Trustee Act 2000 has substituted a new section 19 in the Trustee Act 1925. It applies to all trusts, whenever created, and allows trustees and personal representatives to insure trust property against all risks, and to pay premiums out of trust funds. The new provision is adequate and it is no longer necessary to make express provision. However, many practitioners prefer not to rely on implied powers, but to include a comprehensive list of powers in the will or trust instrument.

22EE POWER TO INSURE

I DIRECT that my Trustees may insure any asset of my estate on such terms as they think fit and to pay the premiums at their discretion out of income or capital and to use any insurance money received either to restore assets or as if it were the proceeds of sale.

22.16   DEBTS

22FF   POWER TO DEFER PAYMENT OF DEBTS

> My Trustees may defer the calling in or collection of any debt or debts which may be owing to me from [name] at the date of my death for any period not exceeding [three] years provided any interest due thereon be regularly paid and I DECLARE that they shall not be liable for any loss occasioned thereby.

22.17   POWER TO CARRY ON A BUSINESS

Where the testator was running a business as a sole trader, their personal representatives have an implied power (in the absence of any express provision) to continue the business in order to sell it as a going concern. That power is limited to realising the value of the business and does not continue indefinitely. In case market conditions are unfavourable, it is wise to give the personal representatives power to carry on any business for so long as they think fit, or for a long but specified period. Unless otherwise provided, the personal representatives may employ only those assets already used in the business at the date of the testator's death.

Personal representatives running the business are liable for any debts they incur. If the business is being carried on only for the purposes of realisation, then the personal representatives have a right to an indemnity from the estate in priority to the testator's creditors and to the beneficiaries. If, however, the personal representatives are given express authority to carry on the business, their indemnity gives them priority over the beneficiaries only, not the creditors.

It is often appropriate to appoint separate personal representatives to deal with the running of the business after the death of a sole trader.

In the case of partnerships or limited companies, the personal representatives cannot normally take over any management functions on behalf of the testator. Unless the partnership deed states otherwise, the death of one partner terminates a partnership.

In the case of companies, the articles of association should be consulted for the position on the death of a shareholder. It is usually possible to sell the shares, and it may be possible to transfer the shares to a beneficiary, subject to the company's agreement to register the transfer. It is important that any relevant partnership agreement, or the articles of association of any relevant company, are available to and considered by the will drafter preparing a will. (See also Chapter 13.)

22GG POWER TO CARRY ON A BUSINESS

My Trustees may carry on any business of which I am a proprietor or partner at the time of my death and may act either alone or in partnership for so long as my Trustees shall in their absolute discretion consider expedient and my Trustees shall have power to employ any of the capital of my [residuary] estate in order to carry on such business and shall be fully indemnified in respect of any liabilities arising from that business and none of my Trustees shall be liable to any of the Beneficiaries under this my will or any codicil hereto for any loss sustained as a result of the conduct of the business by my Trustees unless such loss arises from fraud or wrongdoing on the part of that Trustee personally.

22.18 POWER TO BORROW

Personal representatives have power to borrow on the security of the personal estate for the purposes of the administration (Administration of Estates Act 1925, section 39).

Trustees and personal representatives have power to borrow under Trustee Act 1925, section 16, Trusts of Land and Appointment of Trustees Act 1996, section 6(1) and Trustee Act 2000, section 8(3). Section 16 of the 1925 Act allows trustees to borrow and mortgage property in order to raise money for an authorised payment or application of capital money. Unsecured borrowing is not permitted. The money cannot be used to finance other investments. The latter provisions give trustees and personal representatives the powers of an absolute owner in relation to land.

Testators often wish to extend the trustees' powers of borrowing, for example to allow unsecured borrowing or borrowing on the security of land to finance the purchase of other investments.

22HH POWER TO BORROW

My Trustees shall have full power to borrow money upon such terms as they in their absolute discretion think fit with or without giving security and may apply any moneys so borrowed for any purpose connected with the trusts of my estate.

22.19   POWERS IN RELATION TO PARTICULAR BENEFICIARIES

22.19.1   Legacies to minors

As a result of Children Act 1989, section 3(2) and (3), a person with parental responsibility for a minor can receive in their own name a legacy on behalf of the minor. In the case of a small legacy a testator may prefer to provide that the personal representatives can accept the receipt of the minor. Alternatively, the testator may consider appointing trustees to take the legacy on behalf of the minor, in which case it is normally appropriate to make the legacy contingent on reaching a specified age. It is advisable to provide expressly whether or not the legacy carries intermediate income.

22II   RECEIPT BY OR ON BEHALF OF MINORS

Where my Trustees are to pay any money whether capital or income to a minor or apply it for [his] [her] benefit under any obligation or discretion my Trustees may pay the said money to any parent or guardian of that minor or to the minor [himself] [herself] if over sixteen years of age and their respective receipts shall be good discharge to my Trustees who shall not be bound to enquire as to the application of such moneys.

Note: If this clause is omitted the trustees would have only the powers conferred on them by statute (e.g. Trustee Act 1925, sections 31 and 32 (see below)) and the power to accept a receipt from a parent or guardian under the Children Act 1989 (see above). No doubt this particular clause may only be suitable for relatively small legacies.

22.19.2   Power to maintain minors

Trustees and personal representatives are given statutory powers of accumulation and maintenance under Trustee Act 1925, section 31. Under that section they can apply any available income towards the maintenance, education or benefit of any minor beneficiary, and that power extends to beneficiaries whose interests are contingent only. Any income that is not applied under that section must be accumulated.

The statute originally required trustees, in the exercise of their discretion, to consider various factors, such as the age and requirements of the minor, the general circumstances of the case and, more particularly, whether any other income is available to be applied for the same power. Where the income of more than one trust fund is available for the same purposes, as originally drafted, the statute required the trustees to apply the income of each fund proportionately to satisfy the purpose, any excess income being accumulated in its respective fund.

The Inheritance and Trustees' Powers Act 2014 has amended section 31 for trusts created or arising on or after 1 October 2014 to remove these restrictions and give the trustees a wholly unfettered discretion. Hence, where there are separate funds available to maintain a person, one fund paying all (or most) has no claim against the other for contribution.

Any income that has been accumulated may be applied during the minority of the beneficiary as if it were the income of the current year. This power thus enables the trustees to make up for any deficiency in income in current years from any unrequired income of previous years.

Once a minor beneficiary attains the age of 18 then, if the gift remains contingent, the trustees must pay to the beneficiary the income of the trust fund until the contingency is met or the gift fails (Trustee Act 1925, section 31(1)).

Any accumulations arising during the minority of the beneficiary are normally added to the capital of the fund when the minor becomes 18. If, however, the beneficiary has only a life interest in the fund, then that beneficiary is entitled to all the accumulated income when they attain the age of majority. If the beneficiary dies under the age of 18, the accumulations are added to capital and devolve accordingly (Trustee Act 1925, section 31(2)).

If a gift is contingent upon the beneficiary's attaining an age greater than 18 years then, unless the statutory right to receive the income at 18 is removed by an express provision to the contrary, the beneficiary obtains a right to income at 18 for income tax purposes.

For inheritance tax purposes, a beneficiary who dies with a contingent interest in capital may have an immediate post-death interest depending on their age at the date of death. For example, if the interest is contingent on reaching 25 and the beneficiary was 18 at the date of death, they will have an immediate post-death interest unless the right to income has been varied. Similarly, if the beneficiary reaches 18 within 2 years of death, the reading back effect of Inheritance Tax Act 1984, section 144 will give them an immediate post-death interest unless the right to income at 18 has been varied (see Chapter 29).

22JJ   EXPRESS CLAUSE FOR MAINTENANCE

(a)   My Trustees shall have power to apply any part or all of the income of the expectant or presumptive share of any child [or grandchild] [of mine] entitled under the trusts hereof during the minority of such child [or grandchild] and subject to payment of any prior charge or interest affecting the said income as they shall in their absolute discretion think fit for or towards the maintenance education or benefit of such child or grandchild and I DIRECT that my Trustees may pay the same to any parent or guardian for the time being of any such minor for the purposes aforesaid without being liable to enquire as to the application of the same.

(b)   My Trustees may exercise the power aforesaid notwithstanding the fact that there may be another fund or other funds or income available for any of the aforesaid purposes and whether or not there is any person bound by law to provide for such maintenance or education.

(c)   Any income not applied towards the purposes aforesaid shall be accumulated by investing the same and the resulting income thereof in any investments authorised under the trusts hereof and by the general law and such accumulations shall be added to the property or to the share therein from which the same was derived and shall devolve therewith so as to follow the destination of such property or share but my Trustees shall be entitled at any time to apply any part of such accumulations for any of the purposes aforesaid as if the same were income arising in the then current year.

[(d)   Trustee Act 1925, section 31 shall be varied to exclude the right to income at eighteen conferred by section 31(1)(ii) and instead the Trustees' discretion under section 31(1)(i) shall continue until the beneficiaries attain a right to capital or the interest fails.]

Note: This clause largely replicates Trustee Act 1925, section 31 (as amended), but is probably easier to follow.

Sub-clause (d) will prevent the creation of an immediate post-death interest if the beneficiary is eighteen at the date of death or within the following two years.

22.20   POWER TO ADVANCE CAPITAL

Subject to certain statutory limitations, trustees and personal representatives have an absolute discretion to apply capital for the advancement or benefit of any person who has either a vested or a contingent interest in capital (Trustee Act 1925, section 32). The power does not extend to capital money or land under a Settled Land Act 1925 settlement.

The statutory power is wide enough to allow property to be advanced to new trustees under new trusts which may contain powers and discretions not given under the original trust instrument.

Any advance given to a contingently interested beneficiary cannot be recovered from that beneficiary's estate should they die before the contingency is met.

There are two limitations on the power, as follows:

(i) any advance made must be brought into account when the beneficiary becomes absolutely entitled;
(ii) any person with a prior interest must consent to the advance.

As originally drawn, there was a third limitation, the trustees could advance up to one half only of the beneficiary's vested or presumptive share. However, this limitation has been removed by the Inheritance and Trustees' Powers Act 2014 for trusts created or arising on or after 1 October 2014, so trustees can advance up to the whole of a beneficiary's vested or presumptive share.

A testator may wish to remove or amend one or more of the remaining statutory limitations and leave the exercise of the power to the trustees' discretion.

Note that the statutory power is limited to advancing capital to a beneficiary with an interest in capital. It is commonly the case that a testator will wish trustees to have power to apply capital for the benefit of an income beneficiary. If so, it is necessary to include an express power allowing this.

22KK VARIATION OF STATUTORY POWER OF ADVANCEMENT

I DECLARE that the statutory power of advancement conferred on my Trustees by Trustee Act 1925, section 32 (as amended) shall apply to the trusts hereof as if incorporated herein save that my Trustees shall be permitted to advance up to only [[half] [three-quarters] of the value of any Beneficiary's vested or presumptive share] [the sum of £ ...].

22LL EXPRESS POWER OF ADVANCEMENT

My Trustees shall have power to raise any sum or sums out of the then presumptive contingent expectant or vested share of any [child] of mine [not exceeding altogether one-third of that share] and may pay or advance the same as my Trustees think fit for the advancement or benefit of such child without obtaining the consent of any person entitled to any prior interest whether vested or contingent in the money so to be paid or advanced and my Trustees shall have an unfettered discretion as to whether an advance shall be brought into account at distribution.

22MM EXTENSION OF POWER OF ADVANCEMENT TO LIFE TENANT

I DECLARE that my Trustees shall have a power to pay or advance capital out of or raised from the trust property or a share thereof in favour of any person who may be entitled to a life interest therein whether or not in so doing they shall exhaust such trust property.

Note: The inclusion of such a power allows trustees to make important decisions as to the destination of trust funds. It will assist the trustees if the testator leaves a letter of wishes setting out the circumstances in which he envisages the power being exercised.

22NN POWER TO MAKE LOANS

My Trustees may lend money or assets comprised in the [trust fund] [Residuary Trust Fund] to any person beneficially interested in the [trust fund] [Residuary Trust Fund] on such terms (whether or not including provision for the payment of interest) as my Trustees see fit.

Chapter 23

Perpetuities and Accumulation

23.1 THE GENERAL PERPETUITY RULE

A gift in a will must comply with the rule against perpetuities.

The rule restricts the time within which future interests in property created by a disposition must either vest or take effect. Despite its name, the rule against perpetuities is concerned with the *commencement* of interests rather than with their duration, although by restricting the time within which future interests may be created, the rule may (and commonly will) have the effect of limiting the life of a trust.

Why does the rule exist? According to the Law Commission in its 1998 Report, *Rules against Perpetuities and Excessive Accumulations*, the most convincing modern explanation of the functions of the rule against perpetuities is the so-called 'dead hand rationale'. This suggests that the rule is necessary in order to strike a balance between, on the one hand, the freedom of the present generation and, on the other hand, that of future generations to deal as they wish with the property in which they have interests.

The rule against perpetuities grew up in relation to the devolution of estates and interests under family settlements. It was then extended piecemeal to a wide range of rights over property unconnected with family arrangements, including options, rights of pre-emption and easements. Such extensions were not necessarily made with a proper consideration of their appropriateness. They caused difficulty in the context of commercial transactions, placing restrictions on the creation of future options and easements, for example, that were a significant obstacle to properly planned developments. This was a main reason for the significant limitation to the extent of the rule introduced by the Perpetuities and Accumulations Act 2009.

The original common law rule has been amended by the Law of Property Act 1925, the Perpetuities and Accumulations Act 1964 and the Perpetuities and Accumulations Act 2009. Neither the 1964 Act nor the 2009 Act was retrospective.

The 1964 Act applies only to gifts made in instruments taking effect on or after 16 July 1964.

The 2009 Act applies only to trusts taking effect and wills executed on or after 6 April 2010 (section 15).

In relation to perpetuities and accumulations there are three separate matters to consider:

(i)   the rule against vesting outside the perpetuity period;
(ii)   the rule against perpetual trusts;
(iii)   the rule against accumulations.

23.2   THE RULE AGAINST VESTING OUTSIDE THE PERPETUITY PERIOD

23.2.1   The common law rule

The common law rule against vesting outside the perpetuity period is to the effect that any future interest in any property is void *ab initio* if at the time of its creation (which, in the case of a will, is the date of death of the testator) there is a remote possibility that the gift may vest outside the perpetuity period.

23.2.2   Application of the rule

The rule applies to future interests, that is, interests which do not give rise to a present enjoyment of the property, but it does not apply to *all* future interests, only to those which are contingent as opposed to vested. An interest is vested for the purposes of the perpetuity rule if certain criteria are satisfied:

(i)   the person or persons entitled is ascertained;
(ii)   there is no condition attached to the gift;
(iii)   the size of the beneficiary's interest is known (particularly in relation to class gifts).

If there is any possibility, however remote, that a person's share of the property may vest outside the perpetuity period, the gift is void.

A future interest is still vested if the above criteria are fulfilled and the person entitled to the interest is being kept out of enjoyment, not because any condition is unmet for the time being, but by a prior interest which has been granted. For example, where Blackacre is left to A for life then to B absolutely, A has a vested interest which is in possession and B has a future interest, but that future interest is vested since A must die at some time.

The rule applies to all types of proprietary interest, except charitable gifts and devises, and it is irrelevant that a gift may never vest at all. The rule is concerned only with the fact that if the interest is going to vest, it must do so within the perpetuity period.

A gift which would in normal circumstances be void for perpetuity at common law may be saved by the insertion of an express clause confirming that the gift will vest within a valid period. Such a clause must be explicit. The phrase 'within the limitations prescribed by law' has in the past been held to save a gift (see *Re Vaux* [1939] Ch 465), but the phrase 'so far as the rules of law and equity will permit' has not (see *Portman v Viscount Portman* [1922] 2 AC 473).

23.2.3   The period allowed by the rule

The common law perpetuity period is a life or lives in being at the date of the gift plus a period of 21 years after the termination of the last of those lives. The expression 'life in being' includes a person *en ventre sa mère* at the date the gift comes into effect and born alive later. A testator may choose any person or persons to be the life or lives in being for the purposes of the perpetuity rule, provided that such a person is alive or *en ventre sa mère* at the date of the death of the testator (i.e. the date of the gift). Such a person can expressly or implicitly be referred to in the gift, or can be a person whose life or lives have some connection with the vesting contingency, although they need not be entitled to any benefit under the gift. Any number of people may be lives in being at any one time as long as it is reasonably possible to ascertain them (see *Thelluson v Woodford* (1805) 11 Ves 112).

This is the basis of the so-called 'royal lives clause', which is a period of restriction ending at the expiration of, for example, 20 years from the day of the death of the last survivor of all the lineal descendants of Queen Victoria who shall be living at the time of the testator's death (see *Re Villar* [1929] 1 Ch 243). Such a clause is always valid provided that it is workable and practicable. Where there are no lives in being, the perpetuity period is 21 years only (see also Chapter 5).

23.2.4   Future parenthood at common law

Under the common law rule, if there is a remote possibility that the interest could vest outside the perpetuity period then the gift is void *ab initio*. This has led to some bizarre results, particularly in the area of 'future parenthood', as is illustrated by the case of in *Re Dawson* (1888) 39 Ch D 155, where the court said that a woman over the age of 70 may give birth to a child, although the court accepted that such an occurrence was all but physically impossible.

Legal impossibilities are recognised at common law, as illustrated by the case of *In Re Gaite's Will Trusts* [1949] 1 All ER 459, where the court accepted that it was legally impossible for a person under the age of 16 to give birth to a legitimate child.

23.2.5   Class gifts at common law

Special rules apply to gifts which are 'class gifts'. A class gift is a gift of property 'to a class, consisting of persons who are included and comprehended under some general description and … it may be nonetheless a class because some of the individuals of the class are named', *per* Lord Davey in *Kingsbury v Walter* [1901] AC 187, 192. The object of the special rule is to facilitate the distribution of the estate or fund at the earliest possible date. Where a class gift is made, the composition of the class and the size of the share that each member of that class is to take must be described in the will.

Originally, to comply with the vesting requirement at common law, it had to be possible to say at the outset, that is, at the time the instrument creating the gift took effect, that by the end of the perpetuity period all the members of the class would be known. If this could not be done the gift would fail, even in relation to those beneficiaries who were in being and otherwise satisfying the contingency within the period.

This general rule was modified by the rules of construction known as the 'class closing rules'. *Viner v Francis* (1789) 2 Bro CC 658 established that where there is an unconditional class gift, and there is at least one person who satisfies the class description who is alive when the instrument takes effect, the class closes at that point. All those who are born afterwards are excluded. If there is no one who satisfies the class description when the instrument takes effect, the rule does not apply and the class remains open.

The rule in *Andrews v Partington* (1791) 3 Bro CC 401 applies to conditional class gifts. It provides that a class can be closed when the first member becomes entitled to claim their share. The effect is that no one born after the class has closed can become a member of the class, but any potential members who are already born are included, provided they ultimately satisfy the contingency. Where a class gift is preceded by a life interest, the class cannot close until the death of the tenant for life at the earliest, since only then is the interest vested in possession. Where members of a class are to take an interest at birth, and no member exists at the time of distribution, the class remains open indefinitely.

The class closing rules can be excluded by a contrary intention. In *Re Edmondson's Will Trusts* [1972] 1 WLR 183 and *Re Tom's Settlement* [1987] 1 WLR 1021, the rules were held to have been excluded by express language in the deed, showing an unequivocal intention that the class was to remain open until a defined date.

23.2.6 Age-reduction provisions

Where a gift is made contingent upon the beneficiary's attaining an age greater than 21, then that gift is *prima facie* void at common law. If, however, the age contingency is the only reason that the gift is void, then the gift is saved by Law of Property Act 1925, section 163(1), which allows for the substitution of the age of 21 years for the offending age provided for in the gift.

23.2.7 Dependent gifts

A dependent gift is one that is expressed to take effect only if a prior gift takes effect or fails to take effect.

The prior gift would not be void merely because the second dependent gift is void, but if a gift is made to take effect subsequent to and dependent upon a prior gift which is itself void then the subsequent gift fails at common law.

23.2.8 The unborn spouse trap

Some gifts at common law used to be caught by what was known as the 'unborn spouse trap'. This would occur in the case of a gift to A (a bachelor who is alive at the testator's death) for life; remainder to any wife A might marry; remainder to the children of A living at the death of the survivor of A and such wife. The gift to A and any wife he may marry is a valid gift, but there is a remote possibility that A might marry someone not born at the date of the gift. Therefore, she would not be a life in being, and if she survived A by more than 21 years, the gift to the children would be postponed beyond the perpetuity period. The gift to the children is void at common law.

23.2.9   Powers and the perpetuity rule

To determine the application of the common law rule of perpetuity to powers of appointment, it is necessary to establish whether the power is general or special. For perpetuity purposes a power of appointment is regarded as special unless it was equivalent to absolute ownership of the property by the donee. If, therefore, a power allowed the donee to appoint anyone in the world, including themselves, or was limited to a class of which the donee was a member, so that they could appoint themselves, then the power would be general. An unrestricted power to appoint by will only is treated as a special power for the purpose of ascertaining the validity of the power, but as a general power for ascertaining the validity of the appointment.

The common law rule could affect a power of appointment in one of two ways:

(i)   by affecting the validity of the power itself. If the power was general, it was valid if it was bound to become exercisable within the perpetuity period, although the fact that it could also be exercised outside the perpetuity period was of no consequence. If, however, the power was special, it was void if there was a possibility that it would be exercised outside the perpetuity period;

(ii) by affecting the validity of the appointment made under the power. Just because a power has been validly created does not mean that an appointment made under the power is also valid. The appointment itself must comply with the perpetuity rules. In the case of a general power the perpetuity period begins at the date the instrument exercising the power comes into effect. In the case of a special power, the period begins not at the date of the appointment but at the date of the instrument creating the power, that is, the appointment is 'taken back' to the instrument creating the power (see *Re Pilkington* [1964] AC 612).

23.2.10   The Perpetuities and Accumulations Act 1964

The Perpetuities and Accumulations Act 1964 provides an alternative to the common law perpetuity period of a life in being plus 21 years. Under section 1, a gift may expressly include a fixed perpetuity period of up to 80 years and, in certain circumstances, a fixed period is implied.

Section 2 of the Act creates presumptions in relation to childbearing, overcoming the common law difficulties which often rendered gifts void because of the possibility of further children being born, even when such births were a virtual physical impossibility. The presumptions, which are rebuttable, are that:

(i)   a male cannot father a child until he is 14 years old; and
(ii) a woman is capable of bearing children only between the ages of 12 and 55.

In general, the aim of the Act is to ensure that any gift which will in fact vest within the perpetuity period is valid.

Under the common law, the test to determine whether or not a gift would vest during the perpetuity period applied as at the date of creation of the gift. This meant that many gifts were rendered void as they could possibly vest outside the perpetuity period. Perpetuities and Accumulations Act 1964, section 3 provides that a gift fails only if and when 'it becomes established that the vesting must occur, if at all, after the end of the perpetuity period'. Until such time the gift is treated as if the common law rule does not apply. Section 3 is normally referred to as the 'wait and see' rule. It applies only where:

(i)   the gift is void at common law;
(ii) the instrument creating the gift takes effect after 15 July 1964; and
(iii) section 15(4) of the Act does not apply to the gift.

For the purposes of the 'wait and see' rule, a statutory category of lives in being is provided. The categories are (section 3(5)):

(a)   the person by whom the disposition was made;
(b)   a person to whom or in whose favour the disposition was made, that is to say:

    (i)   in the case of a disposition to a class of persons, any member or potential member of the class,
    (ii) in the case of an individual disposition to a person taking only on certain conditions being satisfied, any person as to whom some of the conditions are satisfied and the remainder may in time be satisfied,
    (iii) in the case of a special power of appointment exercisable in favour of members of a class, any member or potential member of the class,
    (iv) in the case of a special power of appointment exercisable in favour of one person only, that person or, where the object of the power is ascertainable only on certain conditions being satisfied, any person as to whom some of the conditions are satisfied and the remainder may in time be satisfied,
    (v)   in the case of any power, option or other right, the person on whom the right is conferred;

(c)   a person having a child or grandchild within sub-paragraphs (i) to (iv) of paragraph (b) above, or any of whose children or grandchildren, if subsequently born, would by virtue of his or her descent fall within those sub-paragraphs;
(d)   any person on the failure or determination of whose prior interest the disposition is limited to take effect.

As well as falling within this list, the lives in being:

(i)   must be alive and ascertainable at the date of the gift; and
(ii)   in the case of a class or description, must not be so numerous as to render it impracticable to ascertain the death of the survivor.

Where there are no lives in being, as in trusts of imperfect obligation for animals, the period is 21 years (see Chapter 5).

Section 4 of the 1964 Act affects gifts made after 15 July 1964 and comes into operation where a gift is void at common law because of an age contingency greater than 21, and is not covered by the 'wait and see' rule in section 3. The section replaces Law of Property Act 1925, section 163 in relation to such gifts. Where the age contingency is greater than 21, then that age is replaced by section 4(1) with 'that age which would, if specified instead, have prevented the disposition from being so void'.

The age is not necessarily 21, but may vary according to the ages of the potential beneficiaries. For example, if a gift is expressed to be 'to all my children who attain the age of thirty', and if the testator's two children are aged 1 and 2 at the date of their death, then section 4(1) substitutes the age of 22 for the offending age in the gift to ensure that the gift vests in all the beneficiaries within the perpetuity period. Section 4(1) is open to alternative interpretation, namely that the age contingency in the case of each child would be reduced to 22 and 23, respectively.

Subsections 4(3) and 4(4) apply only to class gifts. They provide that, where under the pre-1964 law a class gift would be void for remoteness because of the possibility that more members may be added to the class outside the perpetuity period, and it is not saved by section 3, or by the reduction in the age of vesting under section 4(1), the possible additional members are treated as excluded from the class.

Section 5 deals with the 'unborn spouse trap' of common law (see above) by applying a variation of the 'wait and see' principle. If, for example, a gift were made to a bachelor (B) for life with a gift over to any wife B may have at his death, and a remainder to such of the children of B and his wife as survive them both, the gift of remainder to the children would be void at common law. Section 5 applies the 'wait and see' principle to save the gift if it vests within the perpetuity period. If, at the end of the perpetuity period, the gift has not vested, then under section 5 the gift is 'converted' into a gift to the children of B and his wife living at the expiry of the perpetuity period, and the gift takes effect as if B's wife predeceased those children.

Section 6 of the Act overcomes the common law rule of dependent gifts (**23.2.7**) and provides that a disposition is not void for remoteness only because it is 'ulterior to and dependent upon' a prior void gift. In such a case the perpetuity period is applied to the subsequent gift independently of the prior gift, and both gifts are dealt with as if distinct and unrelated.

Section 12 of the Act provides that, if an estate (in land) arising under a right of reverter or an interest (in property other than land) arising under a resulting trust on the determination of a determinable interest is void under the rule, the determinable estate or interest becomes absolute.

23.2.11   The Perpetuities and Accumulations Act 2009

Circumstances in which the rule against remoteness of vesting
now applies

Although, in general, for the purposes of the 2009 Act a will is treated as coming into effect when the testator dies, the Act does not apply to a will which is executed before the rules come into force, even where the testator dies after that date. The 2009 Act applies only to trusts taking effect and wills executed on or after 6 April 2010 (section 15).

It is unclear to what extent the Act will apply where a will executed before commencement is republished after commencement by a codicil. It must apply to the contents of the codicil document itself, but it is not clear whether it will apply to the contents of the original will document if these are not expressly restated in the codicil. *In Re Heath's Will Trusts* [1949] Ch 170, which concerns a statute using similar language, suggests that it may not.

Testators who want to be sure that the Act will apply to any trusts in their wills should either execute a new will after commencement or execute, after commencement, a codicil that restates in full the trusts contained in a will executed before commencement.

The scope of the rule against perpetuities is significantly narrowed. It now applies only to the estates, interests, powers and rights mentioned in section 1 (broadly trust interests). The rule does not apply to most future easements, options and rights of pre-emption, which will fall outside these categories. The parties negotiating the terms of an option are free to negotiate such limitations as they see fit as to the period within which the option can be exercised.

Section 2 specifies certain exceptions to the rule against perpetuities. Section 2(2) and (3) replicate pre-Act exceptions to the rule against perpetuities so that the rule does not apply in certain circumstances where property passes from one charity to another; for example, where property is vested in one charity and on the happening of an event it will become vested in another charity (see *Christ's Hospital v Grainger* (1845) 1 Mac & G 460).

Section 2(4) provides that the rule does not apply to interests arising under relevant pension schemes. However, section 2(5) removes from the exception interests and rights arising under two types of private trust created in respect of property subject to a pension scheme. These are defined as interests and rights arising under an instrument: (i) nominating benefits under the pension scheme; or (ii) made in the exercise of a power of advancement arising under the scheme. By way of example of the first, a member may make a nomination binding on the pension scheme trustees for a trust to be created with certain pension benefits in favour of a nominated person (typically death in service benefits). The interests under that trust are subject to the rule against perpetuities. An example of the second is where pension scheme trustees exercise a power of advancement to make capital payments to trustees in favour of relatives of a member before any entitlement to a pension arises. This capital sum may be settled in such a way that it creates successive interests. These interests are also subject to the rule against perpetuities.

The new perpetuity period

Where the Act applies there will be one perpetuity period of 125 years which will apply to all trust interests created by a trust or will executed after 6 April 2010 irrespective of whether the instrument specifies any other period (section 5).

In general, the 2009 Act applies only to trusts created and wills executed after 6 April 2010. However, section 12 allows trustees of pre-Act trusts which have perpetuity periods calculated by reference to lives in being to execute a deed stating that they believe that it is difficult or not reasonably practicable for them to ascertain whether the lives have ended and therefore whether the perpetuity period has ended. The instrument will then automatically have effect as if it had specified a perpetuity period of 100 years from the date when the instrument took effect.

The position in relation to interests created under a special power of appointment is a little surprising.

Section 15(1) provides that the main provisions of the Act apply to instruments 'taking effect' on or after 6 April 2010, but section 15(1)(b) excludes from this an instrument made in exercise of a special power of appointment if the instrument creating the power 'took effect' before that day.

Section 20(6) provides that a will 'takes effect' at the testator's death. While section 15(1)(a) expressly excludes from the Act wills executed before 6 April 2010 by persons dying on or after that date, there is no such exclusion for exercises of powers created by wills made before that date by persons dying on or after it. Hence, the new statutory perpetuity period will apply to an exercise of a special power of appointment created by a will made before 6 April 2010, where the testator dies on or after that date (the perpetuity period running from the date of the testator's death).

Section 11 defines when a power of appointment is a 'special power of appointment' for the purposes of the Act. The definition has substantially the same effect as section 7 of the 1964 Act. Powers of appointment not falling within the section 11 definition are classed as general powers; these are tantamount to outright ownership.

Although section 2(4) of the Act provides that the perpetuity rule does not apply to an interest or right arising under a relevant pension scheme, section 2(5) creates an exception for interests or rights arising as a result of a nomination of death benefits or the exercise of a power of advancement. So, for example, where a member has nominated their interest to pass to a trust created in their lifetime, the perpetuity rule applies to the trust. Whether the new or old rule applies is not always obvious. Clearly, if the scheme was created on or after 6 April 2010, the new rules apply (see below). If the scheme was created before that date, the position appears to depend on the date the member joined the scheme.

It is generally accepted that, for the purposes of perpetuity, a pension scheme consists of a series of trusts, and that a new trust is created each time a member joins the scheme (see *Air Jamaica Ltd v Charlton and Others (Jamaica)* [1999] UKPC 20). Section 19 provides that if a provision is made otherwise than by instrument, the Act applies as if the provision were contained in an instrument taking effect on the making of the provision. Hence, on the date a member joins a pension scheme an instrument is deemed to have been made under section 19.

The result is that if a member joins a pre-6 April 2010 scheme before that date, the old rules apply. The perpetuity period of the death benefit trust is normally restricted to 21 years from the death of the scheme member and the accumulation period will be similarly limited. For accumulation rules generally, see **23.4**.

If the member joins a pre-6 April 2010 scheme *on or after* that date, although the position is not entirely free from doubt, it appears that the new rules do apply. Hence, the perpetuity period of the death benefit trust will be 125 years beginning on the date the member joined the scheme (section 6(3)); and there will be no statutory restrictions on accumulation, although the trust document may contain restrictions.

Difficulties will arise when payments governed by the old rules are made to a pilot trust created on or after 6 April 2010. The new trust will automatically have a perpetuity period of 125 years but the property added will not.

The position is not catastrophic. The wait and see rules will apply and may mean that there is in fact no difficulty. It will be sensible, however, to deal with the problem when the pilot trust is drafted.

It is not possible to alter the perpetuity period of a settlement created on or after 6 April 2010.

However, it is possible to select a trust period (the period within which trust powers have to be exercised) of a different length.

Therefore, the terms of the pilot trust should either limit its trust period to the perpetuity period of the pension scheme or give the trustees power to reduce the trust period at a later stage to ensure that all interests will vest before the perpetuity period allowed to the appointed property expires.

Wait and see and other rules introduced by the 1964 Act

Section 7 of the 2009 Act applies the principle of 'wait and see' to instruments to which the Act applies. If, after applying the principle, it becomes clear that the interest is void for perpetuity, subsections 7(2)(b) and 7(4)(b) preserve the validity of things already done in relation to the estate or interest, or by way of exercise of the right or power, during the 'wait and see' period.

Section 8 replicates the effect of section 4(4) of the 1964 Act allowing the exclusion of any class members who have not qualified during the perpetuity period.

Section 9 replicates the effect of section 6 of the 1964 Act so that a disposition is not void for remoteness only because it is 'ulterior to and dependent upon' a prior void gift.

Section 10 replicates the effect of section 12 of the 1964 Act to allow a determinable estate or interest to become absolute if an interest arising on its determination is void under the rule.

23.3   THE RULE AGAINST PERPETUAL TRUSTS

The rule against perpetual trusts is that a gift which requires capital to be retained beyond the perpetuity period is void. This rule cannot be avoided simply by giving a power to change the property and investments if the proceeds of sale are required to be re-invested and the capital fund has to be retained in perpetuity. This rule does not apply to charitable bequests and devises.

Whereas both the 1964 and 2009 Acts provide 'wait and see' in relation to the rule against perpetuities, they do not do so for the rule against perpetual trusts, which is excluded from the scope of both Acts (see section 15(4) of the 1964 Act and section 18 of the 2009 Act). A legacy to a perpetual non-charitable institution is valid if, when paid, it will not become subject to any trust preventing the members from spending it as they please (see *Cocks v Manners* (1871) LR 12 Eq).

23.4   THE RULE AGAINST ACCUMULATIONS

23.4.1   The common law rule

The rules relating to the restriction of accumulation of income were developed to prevent a testator from inflicting compulsory 'hoarding' of capital on the beneficiaries by compelling the personal representatives or trustees, by directions in the will, to accumulate income.

At common law, if the period for which an accumulation is directed may possibly exceed the common law perpetuity period, the direction to accumulate is totally void.

For dispositions taking effect before 16 July 1964, Law of Property Act 1925, sections 164 to 166 require that the accumulation of income may not be directed for longer than one of the following periods:

(i)   the life of the settlor;
(ii)   21 years from the death of the settlor or testator;
(iii) the minority or minorities of any person or persons living or *en ventre sa mère* at the death of the testator;
(iv)   the minority or minorities of any person or persons who under the limitations of the instrument directing the accumulation would for the time being, if of full age, be entitled to the income directed to be accumulated.

23.4.2   Accumulation periods under the 1964 Act

Two further periods were added by section 13 of the 1964 Act for dispositions taking effect after 15 July 1964:

(i)   21 years from the making of the disposition;
(ii)   the minority or minorities of any person or persons in being at that date.

If the period for which the accumulation is directed could exceed the perpetuity period at common law the accumulation direction is void *ab initio*.

If the period for which the accumulation is directed cannot exceed the perpetuity period at common law but exceeds the relevant accumulation period, the direction to accumulate is good *pro tanto*. Only the excess over the appropriate accumulation period is void. In ascertaining the appropriate period, the courts endeavour to reflect the testator's intentions as far as possible.

If a direction to accumulate income is void, wholly or partially, the income so released passes to the persons who would have been entitled had no such accumulation been directed.

23.4.3   Accumulation under the 2009 Act

Perpetuities and Accumulations Act 2009, section 13 abolishes the pre-Act rule against excessive accumulations. Because that rule was entirely statutory, the repeal of the relevant statutory provisions necessarily abrogates it. The repeals apply only to trusts created and wills executed after 6 April 2010.

The removal of the statutory restrictions on accumulations does not mean that it is possible to accumulate income in perpetuity. This is because the rule against perpetuities, in effect, limits the life of a trust and so provides an upper limit on any accumulation.

It is possible for the trust instrument to limit the powers of the trustees to accumulate income by stating an accumulation period. It is difficult to imagine circumstances in which this would be desirable.

Section 14 makes specific provision for accumulation in relation to charitable trusts. The section provides that any power or duty to accumulate is normally subject to a maximum period of 21 years which starts from the first day when the power or duty must or may be exercised.

If a trust instrument provides for an accumulation period longer than 21 years, then the power or duty to accumulate normally ceases to have effect after 21 years. In such a case, section 14(6) provides that the income which would otherwise have been accumulated must either:

(i)   go to the person who would have been entitled to it if there had been no duty or power to accumulate, or

(ii) be applied for the purposes for which it would have had to be applied if there had been no such duty or power.

Chapter 24

Construction

24.1 GENERAL PRINCIPLES

The overriding aim of the rules of construction of a will is to discover as nearly as possible the meaning the testator intended in any particular words. The will is to be looked at as a whole and extrinsic evidence is sometimes admissible to aid interpretation. Generally, the court relies only on the words written by the testator and does not seek to make more sense of those words by adding to them, altering them or assuming they are mistaken. All cases on construction now refer to the important statement of principle set out by Lord Neuberger in *Marley v Rawlings and Another* [2014] UKSC 2, [2015] AC 129.

24.2 THE MODERN APPROACH TO CONSTRUCTION

This is a mixture of common law principles as set out by Lord Neuberger in *Marley v Rawlings and Another* [2014] UKSC 2, [2015] AC 129, and two important statutory provisions contained in the Administration of Justice Act 1982: section 21 allowing the admission of extrinsic evidence and section 20 allowing rectification of a will failing to carry out the testator's intentions.

24.2.1 At common law

Lord Neuberger in *Marley v Rawlings and Another* [2014] UKSC 2, [2015] AC 129 said at [23] that subject to any statutory provision to the contrary, the correct approach to the interpretation of wills is that laid down over the last 40 years by the Supreme Court and House of Lords to the construction of contracts and unilateral documents.

When interpreting a contract, the court is concerned to find the intention of the party or parties, and it does this by identifying the meaning of the relevant words:

(i)   in the light of:

        –   the natural and ordinary meaning of those words;
        –   the overall purpose of the document;
        –   any other provisions of the document;
        –   the facts known or assumed by the parties at the time that the document was executed; and
        –   common sense; but

(ii)   ignoring subjective evidence of any party's intentions.

Whether the document in question is a commercial contract or a will, the aim is to identify the intention of the party or parties to the document by interpreting the words used in their documentary, factual and commercial context.

Lord Neuberger did not consider this to be a particularly revolutionary conclusion. The well-known suggestion of James LJ in *Boyes v Cook* (1880) 14 Ch D 53, 56, that, when interpreting a will, the court should 'place [itself] in [the testator's] arm-chair', was consistent with the approach of interpretation by reference to the factual context.

Courts have seized on this passage and have in a number of cases managed to interpret words in an unusual way because of the general context.

See, for example, *Reading v Reading* [2015] EWHC 946 (Ch), where Asplin J (as she then was) felt able to construe the expression 'issue' as including step-children where there were indications in the will as a whole and the factual background that this was the testator's intention.

In *Bracey v Curley and Another* [2022] EWHC 359 (Ch), the testator wanted to leave his wife (who was seriously ill) the right to occupy the matrimonial home, 'Briardale' for as long as she wished and then to his son absolutely. The residue of the estate was to be divided equally between his son and his daughter. As drafted, the will gave the testator's wife (defined as the 'Beneficiary') the right to occupy Briardale during the 'Trust Period' and to enjoy the proceeds of sale if it was sold. The 'Trust Period' was defined as 'the period between my death and the death or earlier remarriage of the Beneficiary'. At the end of the 'Trust Period' the Trustees were directed to hold 'any property then the subject of this clause upon trust for my said son'.

Unfortunately, the testator's wife predeceased him. As a result, the daughter argued that there was no trust period created and therefore no trust period to end.

Briardale would, therefore, not pass under the terms of 'this clause' and would fall into residue to be divided equally between the siblings.

Philip Mott QC (sitting as a Deputy High Court Judge) said that it was necessary to apply the principles of construction set out by Lord Neuberger in *Marley v Rawlings and Another* [2014] UKSC 2, [2015] AC 129: to arrive at the intention of the testator by interpreting the words used in their documentary, factual and commercial context.

He concluded that the natural and ordinary meaning of 'when the Trust Period ends' was that it that it referred to the later of the testator's death and the death or earlier remarriage of his wife. The testator's death was the later date, so the trust imposed by the clause arose at that point.

In *Wales and Another v Dixon and Others* [2020] EWHC 1979 (Ch), considered in Chapter 6, a testator who had made a series of wills giving equal benefits to his own nephews and nieces made a will shortly after his wife's death which referred to 'my' nephews and nieces. The term 'nephew' and 'niece' is normally limited to the nephews and nieces of the testator and will not include those of a spouse. However, the context and circumstances of the case can extend the meaning.

Master Teverson considered that 'the context and circumstances of the case' is not limited to the other provisions in the will. The court is obliged to look at the background facts known to the testator alongside the terms used in the will to establish their intended meaning, as required by Lord Neuberger in *Marley v Rawlings and Another* [2014] UKSC 2, [2015] AC 129.

In his view, the prior wills made by the deceased and his wife were part of the surrounding circumstances and background facts. They showed that throughout their marriage, and especially after it became clear they were not to have children, both the deceased and his wife made mirror-like wills by which, whichever of them was the survivor left a bequest or share of residue to members of both their family and their spouse's family. Looking at the surrounding circumstances, it was clear that the deceased had intended to include nephews and nieces by affinity as well as by consanguinity, and the will should be construed in that way.

Master Teverson was fiercely critical of the way that the testator's instructions for the will had been taken, saying at [28] and [29]:

> The manner in which the Deceased's instructions were taken for the Will greatly increases the likelihood that the Deceased's intention with regard to residue was not understood. His instructions were taken by telephone. The draft will was prepared and sent out on the same day.

The striking feature of the communications between the Deceased and [the will drafter] is ... the complete lack of any attempt to establish by name or parent who was intended to receive a share of residue. This illustrates graphically the dangers of taking instructions by telephone from an elderly widower without sight of his prior will or knowledge of his family tree. Clause 7 of the Will is badly drafted. It contains grammatical and punctuation errors. It fails to identify by name or parent or family the intended recipients of the gift. The manner in which the Deceased's instructions were taken and the poor quality of clause 7 enhances the scope for giving the words an extended meaning when interpreted against the surrounding circumstances known to the Deceased.

However, if the will makes sense and is not ambiguous on its face, there is no scope for interpreting the words as having a different meaning. See, for example, *Gledhill and Another v Arnold* [2015] EWHC 2939 (Ch), where a testator left his interest in the house he shared with his sister-in-law to her for life, or until she moved out and then on the trusts of residue. The residue was then left to the sister-in-law absolutely with a substitutional gift to her children should she predecease. The deceased's earlier will had specifically left the interest in the house to the children after the sister-in-law's interest came to an end and the instructing solicitor gave evidence that the intention had been to do the same in the final will. Proudman J refused to interpret the will to give effect to the testator's intention in this way on the basis that there was no ambiguity in the will to justify departing from the normal meaning. (However, she did agree to rectify it under Administration of Justice Act 1982, section 20. See **24.2.3**.)

Royal Commonwealth Society for the Blind v Beasant and Another [2021] EWHC 2315 (Ch) is another example of the court refusing to depart from the clear meaning of the will. The testatrix had left her executor (an old friend) a legacy equal to 'the largest sum of cash which could be given on the trusts of this clause without any inheritance tax becoming due'. The will made further specific and pecuniary gifts to non-exempt beneficiaries. The residue was left to charity. Unfortunately for the executor, the specific gifts exceeded the testatrix's nil rate band, with the result that nothing could pass under the terms of the pecuniary legacy. The executor contended that the clause should be construed as a tax-free gift of an amount of the nil rate limit in force at the deceased's death, without reference to the other gifts of the will allowing £325,000 to be paid. Master Shuman did not agree. He considered that it would do considerable violence to the language of the will to read the clause as meaning a sum which equates to the nil rate band at the date of death of the deceased. If the deceased had intended to gift the nil rate band to the executor, the will could simply have said that.

24.2.2   Admissibility of extrinsic evidence of intention

Administration of Justice Act 1982, section 21(1) applies to a will:

(a)   in so far as any part of it is meaningless;

(b)   in so far as the language used in any part of it is ambiguous on the face of it;

(c)   in so far as evidence, other than evidence of the testator's intention, shows that the language used in any part of it is ambiguous in the light of surrounding circumstances.

Where section 21(1) applies to a will, section 21(2) allows extrinsic evidence, including evidence of the testator's intention, to be admitted to assist in its interpretation.

Lord Neuberger considered that section 21(1) confirms that a will should be interpreted in the same way as a contract or unilateral document. In particular, section 21(1)(c) shows that 'evidence' is admissible when construing a will, and that that includes the 'surrounding circumstances'. However, section 21(2) goes rather further. It indicates that, if one or more of the three requirements set out in section 21(1) is satisfied, then direct evidence of the testator's intention is admissible, in order to interpret the will in question.

Hence, although the general approach to interpretation of a will is the same as for any other document, section 21 provides an additional aid to interpretation by allowing reference to evidence of the testator's actual intention (e.g. what they told the drafter of the will, or another person, or by what was in any notes they made or earlier drafts of the will which they may have approved or caused to be prepared).

Section 21 is considered further at **24.4**.

24.2.3   Rectification of wills

The remedy of equitable rectification allowing courts to correct a written instrument which, by a mistake in verbal expression, does not accurately reflect the parties' true agreement, has a long history. It allows the correction of bilateral or multilateral arrangements such as contracts, and also unilateral documents, such as settlements. However, it has always been assumed that the courts had no such power to rectify a will. In *Marley v Rawlings and Another* [2014] UKSC 2, [2015] AC 129, Lord Neuberger said at [28] that, had it been necessary, he would have held that it was, as a matter of common law, open to a judge to rectify a will in the same way as any other document: no convincing reason for the absence of such a power having been advanced.

However, it was unnecessary to consider that point, as Administration of Justice Act 1982, section 20 provided a statutory power to rectify wills.

Section 20(1) provides as follows:

> If a court is satisfied that a will is so expressed that it fails to carry out the testator's intentions, in consequence:
>
> (a)   of a clerical error; or
> (b)   of a failure to understand his instructions,
>
> it may order that the will shall be rectified so as to carry out his intentions.

Section 20(2) provides that, save with the court's permission, no application for rectification under section 20(1) can be made more than 6 months after the grant of probate.

Section 20(3) protects executors who distribute in accordance with the terms of a will before it is rectified after the 6-month period referred to in section 20(2).

In *Marley v Rawlings and Another* [2014] UKSC 2, [2015] AC 129, Lord Neuberger said that clerical error was not confined to mistakes involved in copying or writing out a document. It can carry a wider meaning, namely a mistake arising out of office work of a relatively routine nature, such as preparing, filing, sending or organising the execution of a document (save, possibly, to the extent that the activity involves some special expertise).

Section 20 is considered further at **24.5**.

24.3   PRESUMPTIONS

It is probably the case that since Lord Neuberger's guidance in *Marley v Rawlings and Another* [2014] UKSC 2, [2015] AC 129, the courts pay less regard to these presumptions.

24.3.1   Ordinary meaning

In the absence of any indication to the contrary, the words used in a will are presumed to bear their 'ordinary meaning'. Where one word has several possible 'ordinary' meanings, the court must consider the will as a whole and any available extrinsic evidence to determine the meaning intended by the testator.

If, having examined all the other provisions of the will and having construed those provisions with the aid of any extrinsic evidence, it is apparent that the testator intended a word or phrase to convey a meaning other than its ordinary meaning, then the word or phrase is construed in that different sense. If a testator intends a sense other than the ordinary meaning of a word or phrase, a definition clause, setting out the intended meaning, should be included in the will.

If a word or phrase has an ordinary meaning and a secondary meaning, and if the word or phrase as used makes sense only if construed as having its secondary meaning, then that secondary meaning is applied.

24.3.2   Technical or legal words and expressions

Technical or legal words and expressions are, *prima facie*, construed in accordance with their technical meanings. Again, this presumption may be expressly or impliedly rebutted by the will or the surrounding circumstances. Any secondary meaning may be applied if the technical meaning fails to make sense in the context.

24.3.3   Later codicil

A gift clearly expressed in a will or codicil is not revoked by a later codicil unless the intention to revoke is as clear as the original intention to give.

24.3.4   Presumption against intestacy

Where the construction of a will is in doubt, the court presumes that the testator did not intend to die either wholly or partly intestate. The presumption depends on the context of the words being construed and on the surrounding circumstances. An intestacy cannot be defeated merely by showing an intention on the part of the testator to make a disposition by will. The wording of the will must be sufficient to constitute a gift, either expressly or by necessary implication, in favour of a particular beneficiary. Thus the rights of those entitled on intestacy are protected.

24.3.5   Unambiguous words

Unambiguous words must be interpreted according to their clear meaning even if it is difficult or inconvenient to carry out the testator's intention, and even if the testator is being deliberately capricious. Where the words are ambiguous, however, it is presumed that the testator did not intend to be capricious.

24.3.6 Accidental creation of life interest

A problem of unprofessionally drafted wills used to be the accidental creation of life interests in favour of spouses, where the actual intention of the testator was to make an absolute gift to their spouse. Phrases such as 'I leave everything to my wife and then to my children' *prima facie* give rise to a life interest in favour of the spouse with remainder to the children.

Administration of Justice Act 1982, section 22, which affects the construction of the wills of testators dying after 31 December 1982, provides for a statutory presumption against such life interests. Thus, in the absence of a contrary intention it is presumed that if a testator devises or bequeaths property to their spouse in terms which, in themselves, would give an absolute interest to the spouse, but by the same instrument purports to give the testator's issue an interest in the same property, then the gift to the spouse is absolute regardless of the purported gift to the issue.

24.4 ADMISSIBILITY OF EXTRINSIC EVIDENCE

Once proved, the will admitted to probate or annexed to a grant of letters of administration is conclusive as to the contents of the will. A court of construction is not entitled to alter the wording of the will to correct any alleged error. Neither can a court of construction admit extrinsic evidence to complete any blanks or omissions in the will.

The court of construction may consider the format and punctuation of the original will and the existence of blanks and erasures, all of which may assist in determining the testator's intention.

Where two testamentary documents have been admitted to probate the court may decide, as a matter of construction, that part or all of the earlier document has been revoked or replaced by the later document.

Extrinsic evidence is admissible to prove the existence and identity of any person described in the will. There are two types of extrinsic evidence: circumstantial and direct. If a testator leaves a legacy to 'Mrs G' and there is evidence that he knew a Mrs G and was in the habit of referring to her as Mrs G, this is circumstantial evidence of the testator's meaning. But a statement by the testator that he had left a legacy of £1,000 to Mrs Greggs is direct evidence of the testator's intention.

Where the testator died before 1 January 1983, the common law rules applied and direct evidence was admissible only in very limited circumstances. In the case of deaths on or after that date, Administration of Justice Act 1982, section 21 makes it possible to admit direct evidence in a wider range of cases.

24.4.1   Deaths before 1 January 1983

Circumstantial evidence was admissible where:

(i)   there was a patent ambiguity;
(ii)   under the armchair principle where, in cases of uncertainty or ambiguity, the court is permitted to place itself in the testator's position and consider the surrounding circumstances when the will was made. For example, in *Thorn v Dickens* [1906] WN 54, the testator left 'all to mother'. His mother was dead, but there was evidence that he habitually referred to his wife as 'mother'.

Direct extrinsic evidence was admissible:

(i)   in cases of equivocation. Equivocation (or latent ambiguity) arises where a given description may be applied to two or more different objects ('the manor of Dale' and there are two manors, North Dale and South Dale), or people 'my nephew, Arthur Murphy' and there is more than one nephew of that name;
(ii)   to rebut equitable presumptions such as the equitable presumptions of the satisfaction of a debt by a legacy, the satisfaction of a legacy by a legacy, and the satisfaction of a portion-debt by a legacy (see Chapter 20). Extrinsic evidence is also admitted to show a contrary intention to rebut other equitable presumptions. Generally, no other extrinsic evidence is admitted.

24.4.2   Testator who dies after 31 December 1982

The effect of Administration of Justice Act 1982, section 21 is to make both direct and circumstantial extrinsic evidence of the testator's intention admissible to assist in interpretation in three situations:

(i)   to construe any part of a will which is meaningless;
(ii)   to construe words which appear ambiguous;

(iii) where evidence, other than evidence of the testator's intention, shows that the language used in any part of the will is ambiguous in the light of the surrounding circumstances, to construe the testator's intended meaning. This is so whether or not it is a case of equivocation.

In *Ross v Perrin-Hughes* [2004] EWHC 2559 (Ch), [2005] WTLR 191, the question was whether a gift of 'my apartment' passed the freehold reversion as well as the lease. The expression was ambiguous and the court was, therefore, able to admit extrinsic evidence. It considered a witness statement made by one of the parties relating to the testator's intentions and decided that the reversion was included. *Re Fleming's Will Trusts* [1974] 1 WLR 1552 was also relevant. In this case, Templeman J had held that a devise of property should normally be construed as a gift of whatever interest in the property the donor has at the date of death.

Reading v Reading [2015] EWHC 946 (Ch), referred to at **24.2.1**, is a good example of the circumstances that will justify the admission of extrinsic evidence of the testator's intention to be admitted. The language used was not 'meaningless' and the term 'issue' was not ambiguous on the face of it, so section 21(1)(a) and (b) was not engaged. However, had it been necessary, extrinsic evidence could have been admitted under section 21(1)(c). There was sufficient evidence to show that the language used was ambiguous in the light of the surrounding circumstances, and therefore extrinsic evidence of the testator's intentions would have been admissible. Once that evidence was admitted, there could be no doubt that 'issue' should be interpreted to include both the testator's children and step-children.

Similarly, in *Bracey v Curley and Another* [2022] EWHC 359 (Ch), referred to at **24.2.1**, Philip Mott QC (sitting as a Deputy High Court Judge) said that, had it been necessary, he would have admitted extrinsic evidence under Administration of Justice Act 1982, section 21 to clarify the meaning of 'when the Trust Period ends' as the words used were undoubtedly ambiguous.

In *The Royal Society v Robinson and Others* [2015] EWHC 3442 (Ch), extrinsic evidence was admitted under section 21(1)(c). Nugee J had to consider a will which was expressed to be limited to the testator's assets in the United Kingdom. This was unfortunate as the testator had bank accounts holding significant amounts in the Channel Islands and the Isle of Man (neither of which is part of the United Kingdom). Nugee J considered that the will came within section 21(1)(c) because evidence, not including evidence of the testator's intention, showed that the language used was ambiguous. It was inherently unlikely that a person who went to the trouble of obtaining a professionally drafted will which dealt with matters such as age contingencies for minor beneficiaries would choose to allow valuable assets to pass under the intestacy rules. Looking at the facts other than the facts relating to the testator's intention, a real question was raised as to whether, by using the words confining the will to the United Kingdom, the testator intended to cut out any reference to his offshore bank accounts. Having admitted extrinsic evidence, it was clear that he had not so intended.

24.5   RECTIFICATION

The court had limited common law powers to add or omit words in certain circumstances. These have been supplemented by Administration of Justice Act 1982, section 20.

24.5.1   At common law

A probate court can omit words that have been included in the will without the testator's knowledge and approval (see *Re Morris* [1971] P 62). Further, if it is clear to the court that certain words have been accidentally omitted and if no sensible literal construction of the words is possible as they are written, then the court may read additional words into the will in order to construe it sensibly.

Similarly, a court may change a word when it is apparent from the context that the word was used incorrectly in place of another word, the most common examples being the use of the word 'or' instead of 'and' and *vice versa*.

24.5.2   Under the Administration of Justice Act 1982

Administration of Justice Act 1982, section 20 is set out at **24.2.3**. It gives the court power to order that a will be rectified to carry out the testator's intentions if it is satisfied that the will fails to do so in consequence of a:

(a)   clerical error; or
(b)   failure to understand his instructions.

Marley v Rawlings and Another

In *Marley v Rawlings and Another* [2014] UKSC 2, [2015] AC 129, the Supreme Court had to decide whether a clerical error extended to a husband signing his wife's will and *vice versa*. Lord Neuberger giving the judgment of the court held that it did. He made the following points:

(1)   If, as a result of a slip of the pen or mistyping, a solicitor (or a clerk or indeed the testator himself) inserts the wrong word, figure or name into a clause of a

will, and it is clear what word, figure or name the testator had intended, that would undoubtedly be a clerical error which could be rectified under s 20(1)(a). It is hard to see why there should be a different outcome where the mistake is, say, the insertion of a wrong clause because the solicitor cut and pasted a different provision from that which he intended.

(2) Equally, if the solicitor had cut and pasted a series of clauses from a different standard form from that which he had intended, it is difficult to see why that should not give rise to a right to rectify under s 20(1)(a), provided of course the testator's intention was clear. The volume of amendment that is required is not significant.

(3) The expression 'clerical error' can have a narrow meaning, which would be limited to mistakes involved in copying or writing out a document, and would not include a mistake of the type that occurred in this case. However, the expression is not one with a precise or well-established, let alone a technical, meaning. The expression can carry a wider meaning, namely a mistake arising out of office work of a relatively routine nature, such as preparing, filing, sending, or organising the execution of a document (save, possibly, to the extent that the activity involves some special expertise). Those are activities which are properly to be described as 'clerical', and a mistake in connection with those activities, such as wrongly filing a document or putting the wrong document in an envelope, can properly be called 'a clerical error'.

(4) The term must be interpreted in its context, and, in particular on the assumption that the section is intended to represent a rational and coherent basis for rectifying wills. The expression should be given a wide, rather than a narrow, meaning for the following reasons:

(i) Rectification of other documents (including unilateral documents) is not limited to cases of clerical error. Accordingly, given that there is no apparent reason for a different rule for wills, it would appear appropriate that the grounds for rectification is as wide for wills as the words of s 20(1) can properly allow.

(ii) There is no apparent limit on the applicability of s 20(1)(b), (failure to understand the testator's instructions) which supports the notion that s 20(1)(a) should not be treated as being of limited application.

(iii) The 1982 Act as a whole is aimed at making the law on wills more flexible and rendering it easier to validate or 'save' a will than previously. The whole thrust of the provisions is in favour of a broad interpretation of a provision such as s 20(1)(a).

(iv) The law would be incoherent if subtle distinctions led to very different results in cases where the ultimate nature of the mistake is the same. If a solicitor is drafting two wills, and accidentally cuts and pastes the contents of B's draft will onto what he thinks is A's draft will, and hands it to A, who then executes it as his will, that will would be rectifiable under s 20(1)(a), as the solicitor's mistake would, on any view, be a clerical error. On the other hand, if the solicitor accidentally gives B's will to A to execute, and A executes it, that would not, on the respondents' case, be a clerical error and therefore rectification would not be available.

A distinction of this sort would be capricious or arbitrary. The position is essentially the same in the two cases. In each case, it was because his solicitor accidentally handed A a document which contained B's will rather than A's will, that A executed B's will thinking that it was his will. In each case, the reason that the will which A executed did not represent his intentions was a silly mistake by the solicitor in the mechanics of faithfully carrying out his instructions. In neither case did the mistake involve the solicitor misunderstanding or mischaracterising the testator's intention or instructions, or making any error of law or other expertise, so the error may fairly be characterised as 'clerical'.

(5)   The term 'clerical error' can, as a matter of ordinary language, quite properly encompass the error involved in this case. There was an error, and it can be fairly characterised as clerical, because it arose in connection with office work of a routine nature. Accordingly, given that the present type of case can, as a matter of ordinary language, be said to involve a clerical error, it would seem to follow that it is susceptible to rectification.

Lord Neuberger's reference at [72] to an error by 'a solicitor (or a clerk or indeed the testator himself)' means that the error can be made by the testator themselves so long as it is of a mundane and mechanical nature.

However, rectification does not extend to the situation where the will drafter or testator writes a will using inappropriate language because they are mistaken as to its effect.

In *Reading v Reading* [2015] EWHC 946 (Ch), referred to **24.2.1**, Asplin J (as she then was), would not have allowed rectification. Although the solicitor said that when using a precedent to draft the will, he had simply overlooked the fact that 'issue' would not include step-children, this did not, in her opinion, fall within the ambit of 'clerical error'. It fell within Lord Neuberger's caveat in relation to activities involving special expertise. In carrying out his professional duty and judgment as a drafter of the will, he failed to use an apposite term.

In *Bracey v Curley and Another* [2022] EWHC 359 (Ch), referred to at **24.2.1**, Philip Mott QC (sitting as a Deputy High Court Judge) said that, had it been necessary, he would have rectified the will under Administration of Justice Act 1982, section 21 on the basis of a clerical error having been made. If his construction of the will was wrong and there was a mistake it was to use Lord Neuberger's words 'a silly mistake by the solicitor in the mechanics of faithfully carrying out his [the testator's] instructions'. It resulted from a failure to appreciate that, if the beneficiary did not survive the testator, there would be no trust period to end. That led to the omission of an alternative condition to the end of the trust period of 'if the Beneficiary fails to survive me'.

Philip Mott QC acknowledged that in *Reading v Reading* [2015] EWHC 946 (Ch), Asplin J (as she then was), had concluded that the choice of the word 'issue' was not a 'clerical error', but related to the professional judgment and expertise of the solicitor who drafted the will. He said that he some doubts about this, both in the context of the old law, and particularly in the light of Lord Neuberger's wide interpretation of the phrase in *Marley v Rawlings and Another* [2014] UKSC 2, [2015] AC 129. However, he did not have to decline to follow that decision as he considered the concepts in the two cases to be different. *Reading v Reading* involved a positive choice of a word which had an established legal meaning, whereas this case involved the omission of words to make clear what conditions apply to a disposition.

Other points on section 20

An application for rectification must generally be made within 6 months of the grant of probate or letters of administration with the will annexed. It is possible to seek leave to apply out of time. The court accepts that the principles which govern applications under the Inheritance (Provision for Family and Dependants) Act 1975 apply equally to rectification cases (see *Re Chittock* [2000] WTLR 643). If unopposed, the matter can be dealt with at a probate registry under Non-Contentious Probate Rules 1987 (SI 1987/2024), rule 55(1). In other cases, a court hearing is required.

In *Grattan v McNaughton* [2001] WTLR 1305, Behrens J made the point that rectification is a discretionary remedy and will not necessarily be granted. Lord Neuberger made the same point in *Marley v Rawlings and Another* [2014] UKSC 2, [2015] AC 129 when comparing the two remedies of interpretation and rectification at [40]:

> At first sight, it might seem to be a rather dry question whether a particular approach is one of interpretation or rectification. However, it is by no means simply an academic issue of categorisation. If it is a question of interpretation, then the document in question has, and has always had, the meaning and effect as determined by the court, and that is the end of the matter. On the other hand, if it is a question of rectification, then the document, as rectified, has a different meaning from that which it appears to have on its face, and the court would have jurisdiction to refuse rectification or to grant it on terms (eg if there had been delay, change of position, or third party reliance).

Virtually all cases on rectification make the point that compelling evidence is needed. This is because it is difficult for the court to accept that a rational adult would sign a formal document which did not set out their wishes. See, for example, Chadwick J (as he then was) in *Re Segelman* [1996] Ch 171 (quoted with approval by Sir Christopher Slade in *Walker v Medlicott* [1999] 1 WLR 727):

... although the standard of proof required in a claim for rectification made under section 20(1) of the 1982 Act is that the court should be satisfied on the balance of probabilities, the probability that a will which the testator has executed in circumstances of some formality reflects his intentions is usually of such weight that convincing evidence to the contrary is necessary.

However, the statement of Lord Neuberger in *Marley v Rawlings and Another* [2014] UKSC 2, [2015] AC 129 at [79] that the changes introduced by Administration of Justice Act 1982, sections 17 to 21 were 'aimed at making the law on wills more flexible and rendering it easier to validate or "save" a will than previously' may mean that the courts take a less stringent approach.

Where a disappointed beneficiary alleges negligence by the will drafter leading to loss, the court expects the beneficiary to mitigate their damage by bringing rectification proceedings (see *Walker v Medlicott* [1999] 1 WLR 727), unless there is reason to believe that such an application would be a waste of resources (see *Horsfall v Haywards* [1999] 1 FLR 1182) or ineffective to remedy the loss.

24.6 DATE FROM WHICH A WILL 'SPEAKS'

When interpreting any provision it is essential to ascertain the time at which a description is to be applied.

24.6.1 Subject matter

Generally, a will takes effect as if executed immediately before the death of the testator in relation to the subject matter of gifts (Wills Act 1837, section 24). Thus, a will 'speaks from death'. In the absence of a contrary intention, any description in the will of the subject matter of a gift is applied at the testator's death, whether the gift is specific or general.

Thus, a gift of 'all my shares in X Co Ltd', in the absence of contrary intention, is construed as a gift of such shares in X Co Ltd as the testator holds at the date of their death. This may include shares acquired after the date of the will and exclude shares disposed of after the date of the will.

A contrary intention is implied when the subject matter is described so particularly that it is plain an object in existence at the date of the will was intended. For example, a reference to 'my piano' in *Re Sikes* [1927] 1 Ch 364 was held to refer to the piano owned at the date the will was executed and not to the one that had replaced it by the date of death. The gift, therefore, failed by ademption.

Express words may also exclude section 24, by stating the date at which the subject matter is to be ascertained. However, words such as 'now' or 'at present' are inconclusive as to the testator's intention as, *prima facie*, the will speaks from death and the testator may have meant 'now' when the will was signed or 'now' when the will takes effect. In such a case the will must be considered as a whole to determine whether section 24 is to be excluded.

Where section 24 has been excluded by a contrary intention and a provision is to speak as from the date of the will, then, if the will is later republished by re-execution or a later codicil, the effect is that the will speaks from the date of the codicil or re-execution, unless a contrary intention is apparent.

24.6.2   Beneficiaries

When identifying beneficiaries, a will speaks from the date of its execution, unless a contrary intention is apparent. Thus, a gift to 'the eldest son of my sister' would be construed as a gift to the person who fulfilled that description at the date the will was executed and would lapse if that person predeceased the testator.

When the will is republished by a later codicil or re-execution then, in the absence of contrary intention, the gift speaks from the date of the republication.

24.7   THE FALSA DEMONSTRATIO DOCTRINE

The first limb of the doctrine of *falsa demonstratio* provides that where the description of a person or thing is partly true and partly false then, provided the part which is true describes the person or thing to a high degree of certainty, then the untrue part of the description is rejected and the gift is allowed to take effect.

The second limb provides that additional words are not rejected as false if they can be read as words of restriction. For example, in *Wrightson v Calvert* (1860) 1 John & H 250, a gift was made to the grandchildren of the testator living near another named person. Only two of the testator's grandchildren lived near the other person and the third grandchild was therefore not entitled to a share in the gift.

The doctrine also apparently covers descriptions which are wholly false if the context and surrounding circumstances show the testator's intention unambiguously. In such a case the whole erroneous description is rejected but the gift still takes effect. Thus in *Ellis v Bartrum* (1857) 25 Beav 107, the object of the gift was wrongly described as 'the resident apothecary' instead of 'the resident dispenser', but the gift was given effect, as the intention of the testator was apparent from the circumstances.

24.8 CONSTRUING THE SAME WORDS IN DIFFERENT PARTS OF THE SAME WILL

A word may not necessarily be used in the same sense throughout a will, but if it is used in one place with a clear and unambiguous meaning then it is presumed to have the same meaning if used ambiguously in another part of the same will, provided that meaning makes sense in the context (see *Re Birks* [1900] 1 Ch 417). Such a presumption arises only where there is ambiguity. In any event, words must be construed with reference to their subject matter and may therefore bear different meanings even within the same gift, for example when relating to realty and personalty.

24.9 MEANING OF PARTICULAR WORDS OF DESCRIPTION

24.9.1 Personal chattels and household effects

If used in its ordinary sense, the phrase 'personal chattels' has the meaning ascribed to it in Administration of Estates Act 1925, section 55(1)(x). It is common to incorporate the definition expressly into wills. However, the Inheritance and Trustees' Powers Act 2014 amended the section 55 definition. It is now as follows:

> tangible movable property, other than any such property which—
>
> > consists of money or securities for money, or
> > was used at the death of the intestate solely or mainly for business purposes, or
> > was held at the death of the intestate solely as an investment.

The first exception repeats the exclusion in the original section 55(1)(x).

The second slightly extends the original definition which excluded any item 'used for business purposes at the date of the intestate's death'. On a strict reading of the original wording, an item used even occasionally for business purposes would not be a personal chattel.

The third exception largely replicates existing case-law and is intended as a narrow exception for property held *solely* as an investment which had no personal use at the date of the deceased's death, and so would not include property which had some personal use but which the deceased also hoped might maintain or increase its value. Gold jewellery would normally be a personal chattel, even if bought with a view to its likely future increase in value. Gold bars would not.

Many wills refer to the section 55(1)(x) definition when making gifts of personal chattels. Inheritance and Trustees' Powers Act 2014, section 3(2) provides that, where a will or codicil, *executed* before 1 October 2014, contains a reference to personal chattels defined (in whatever form of words) by reference to Administration of Estates Act 1925, section 55(1)(x), subject to contrary intention, it will be read as referring to the old definition of personal chattels irrespective of the date of death. Wills executed on or after that date will be read as referring to the new definition, subject to contrary intention.

The word 'furniture' has been held to include ornaments, but not books. The phrase 'household effects' is wider in scope and may include books and sewing machines, for example, but has been held not to include pets or a collection of postage stamps. The word 'effects' has no fixed meaning and is construed in the light of the context of the will and the surrounding circumstances. The *ejusdem generis* rule applies, and thus if a number of personal chattels are listed, followed by words such as 'and all other effects', the word is restricted to such effects as are personal chattels.

A gift of 'the contents' of, for example, a desk includes the contents and any *choses in action* found in the desk, but not items in a separate box, the key of which is in the desk.

24.9.2   Money or cash

The word 'money' has many different meanings, depending on the context and circumstances in each case. It normally includes cash in hand (including notes) and cash at the bank, either on current account or on deposit where no notice of withdrawal is required.

The phrase 'moneys due' to the testator includes a balance at a bank (except deposits requiring notice of withdrawal), stock, money receivable under a life assurance policy on the testator's life, and money payable to the testator from the estate of another deceased person provided that estate has been 'got in' at the time of the testator's death. It does not include money due under a service contract which has not been completed at the time of the testator's death.

The phrase 'moneys owing' includes all items included in the phrase 'money due' and also money on deposit at a bank where notice of withdrawal is required.

'Moneys on deposit' include National Savings Accounts and Certificates. The phrase 'ready money' is the rough equivalent of 'moneys due', including cash. 'Cash' is normally taken to mean notes and other coins and does not include promissory notes, bonds or long annuities. It would not extend to cryptocurrencies (unless the context made it clear that it was intended to).

24.9.3   Land or house

Unless an intention to the contrary is apparent from the context or circumstances, the term 'land' generally includes any buildings on the land and any sale proceeds arising from the land if subject to a trust for re-investment in land. It also includes incorporeal hereditaments.

Without express provisions, a devise of land does not pass mortgage debts charged on land or other charges on land.

A devise of a 'house' passes with it everything belonging to the house for its enjoyment, such as a garden or orchard. The term 'messuage' includes any garden, orchard and curtilage.

Where a testator gives part of their land to A and the remainder, adjoining land, to B, leaving B's part land-locked, B is entitled to a necessary right of way over A's land.

24.9.4   Shares, investments and securities

The definition of 'stocks and shares' depends on the context and circumstances, but is generally taken to mean only stocks and shares in limited companies and not government securities, redeemable debentures or holdings in public limited companies. However, the phrase is given its widest possible construction where the testator demonstrates an intention to dispose of all their personal estate and the will contains no residuary gift.

Again, the scope of the term 'investments' depends on the circumstances and has been held to include money on deposit.

'Securities' may include such things as government stock, a lien for unpaid purchase money, money lent on a mortgage and a promissory note, but does not generally include money at a bank on current or deposit account, stocks and shares, life assurance policies and their proceeds or debts. If money has been lent on a mortgage where the legal estate is vested in trustees and the testator is entitled only to the residue of the repayments after the discharge of other payments, then the testator's interest does not pass as a 'security'.

24.9.5   Businesses and partnerships

Generally, a bequest of a business passes the whole of the business, both assets and liabilities. If the testator is not the sole proprietor of a business but is in partnership, then the disposal of their interest may be limited by the partnership deed and any bequest would be subject to those provisions. See also Chapter 13.

24.9.6   Other terms

'Probate valuation' means the valuation of items by valuers for the purpose of obtaining a grant of probate.

Unless a contrary intention is shown or the context requires otherwise, any reference to a 'month' is construed as a calendar month.

The word 'moiety', meaning half, may also be used to mean an equal share where there are two shares.

'Unmarried' may mean 'never having been married' or 'not now married', depending on the context.

24.9.7   Words of gift

The term 'devise' is generally limited to gifts of land. Although the terms 'legacy' and 'bequeathed' commonly refer to personalty, they may include gifts of land and interests in land in some circumstances.

Even words such as 'personal property' may not be limited to personalty if the context shows that the testator intended to pass some real property. Leaseholds are regarded as personalty but may pass under a gift of realty if the context shows that that was the testator's intention. The phrase 'worldly goods' may also include realty.

24.10   PER CAPITA AND PER STIRPES DISTRIBUTION

A gift intended to be distributed *per capita* among the beneficiaries results in each beneficiary taking an equal share of the whole.

A gift distributed *per stirpes* is divided according to family or stock. Each family (or branch of the family) takes an equal share and that share is then subdivided amongst the members of each family. Thus where one branch of a family has many members, all the members may receive a small share, whereas another branch may consist of a single beneficiary who may take a large share of the whole.

Unless the will demonstrates a contrary intention or gives rise to a contrary inference, then it is presumed that gifts to a number of donees are to be distributed *per capita* rather than *per stirpes*.

24.11   CHILDREN BORN AS A RESULT OF FERTILISATION TECHNIQUES

At common law a child's legal parentage is their genetic parents. Various statutes have amended the position.

Family Law Reform Act 1987, section 27 made the first change to this rule by providing that in the case of a child born to a married woman on or after 4 April 1988 as the result of her artificial insemination with donor sperm, the child was to be treated as the child of both parties to the marriage and of no one else unless the husband had not consented to the fertility treatment.

Unlike subsequent legislation the crucial date was the date of *birth* and not the date of the fertility treatment.

The Human Fertilisation and Embryology Act 1990 applies where:

(i)   a woman receives fertility treatment on or after 1 August 1991 and before 6 April 2009;
(ii)   embryos or sperm and eggs are placed inside her, or she receives artificial insemination; and
(iii)   the woman's partner is not the child's genetic father (and so would not be treated as the child's father at common law).

The woman who carries the child is always the mother (section 27) irrespective of whether or not there is any genetic connection between her and the child. Where her partner did not provide the sperm, the question is who is the child's father? A child may have only one father, so if someone else is treated as the father, the genetic father will not be the child's legal father (section 28(4)). A sperm donor is not a father in such cases, although his details will remain on the Human Fertilisation and Embryology Act Register of Information and the child may access these in adulthood.

Section 28(2) provides that if the woman was married at the time of her treatment, her husband is the father unless he did not consent to the treatment.

If the woman is unmarried at the time of her treatment (or married but her husband is not treated as the father, for example because he did not consent to the treatment), then if the treatment was provided to the woman and a man 'together', the man will be treated as the child's father (section 28(3)). The concept of treatment provided to the couple 'together' has caused problems where a couple started treatment together but separated later (see *Re D* [2005] UKHL 33).

Human Fertilisation and Embryology Act 2008 (HFEA 2008), Part 2 extends the meaning of 'parent' in the case of assisted reproduction taking place on or after 6 April 2009 to reflect the widening of the adoption law, the implications of the Civil Partnership Act 2004 and changes in social attitudes to same sex relationships. It allows a woman to be treated as the child's 'other parent'.

The HFEA 2008 applies where:

(i)   a woman receives fertility treatment on or after 6 April 2009;
(ii)   embryos or sperm and eggs are placed inside her, or she receives artificial insemination; and
(iii)   the woman's partner is not the child's genetic father.

As with the 1990 Act, the woman who carries the child is always the mother (HFEA 2008, section 33). There are no changes in relation to the rules for married couples. The woman's husband is the father unless he did not consent to treatment. What is new in HFEA 2008 is the introduction of provisions dealing with female civil partnerships. If the woman who carries the child is in a civil partnership at the time of her treatment, her civil partner is treated as the child's second parent unless the civil partner did not consent to the treatment (sections 42 and 48(6)).

In addition, the HFEA 2008 makes a change to the formalities required in the case of unmarried opposite sex couples and makes new provision for female unmarried couples.

Where the woman who carries the child is unmarried and not in a civil partnership (or is married/in a civil partnership, but her husband/civil partner is not treated as the other parent), the following will be treated as the child's other parent under the HFEA 2008:

•   a male partner who meets the agreed 'fatherhood' conditions (sections 36 and 37); or

- a female partner who meets the agreed 'female parenthood' conditions (sections 43 and 44).

The parenthood conditions are, broadly, that:

- the mother and her partner must both have consented in writing and not withdrawn the consent; and
- the parties must not be within the prohibited degrees of relationship (defined in section 58(2)).

The requirement for written consent is stricter than the rather loose concept of being treated 'together' which the 1990 Act had required for opposite sex unmarried couples.

The rules governing male civil partners and unmarried male couples remain unchanged under the HFEA 2008. The result is that a man who is not a child's genetic father will not be treated as the child's other parent unless he adopts the child (or if the couple can apply for a parental order following a surrogacy arrangement).

For married couples and civil partners, the rules apply wherever the treatment was given. For unmarried couples, the rules only apply if the treatment was given in the United Kingdom by a provider licensed under the Act. Hence, in cases where treatment is obtained outside the United Kingdom, the 'other partner' will not have automatic parental rights and will need to apply for an adoption order.

Unusually, both the Human Fertilisation and Embryology Acts have retrospective effect and apply to the construction of wills and trusts made before they came into force. The rules in both Acts apply to 'references to any relationship between two people in any enactment, deed or other instrument or document (whenever passed or made) (HFEA 2008, section 48(5), Human Fertilisation and Embryology Act 1990, section 29). HFEA 2008, section 53 makes express provision for references to a father in such documents to be construed as a reference to a female parent.

Although the Act does not expressly state that it can be excluded, it is always possible for an instrument to provide that terms are to be construed in a particular way or to state that a will is to be construed as though the Act had not been enacted. The latter course is not recommended as it would cause problems for trustees. Before distributing to a class, they would have to ask all parents of 'children' whether any assisted reproduction had taken place. Failure to do so would risk distributing to children who were, in fact, excluded. In most cases it is likely to be preferable to allow the provisions of the Act to apply but to give trustees power to add or exclude persons from the class of beneficiaries.

24.12   SURROGACY ARRANGEMENTS

Under Human Fertilisation and Embryology Act 1990, section 30, married couples were able to apply for a parental order where another woman carried a child produced from the eggs or sperm of at least one party to the marriage. The effect of such an order is broadly the same as an adoption (Parental Orders (Human Fertilisation and Embryology) Regulations 1994 (SI 1994/2767)).

To obtain an order, the conditions set out in section 30 must be satisfied. In particular the parties must apply within 6 months of the birth (section 30(2)); the child's home must be with the couple at the time of the application (section 30(3)); all parties involved must consent freely and with full understanding (section 30(5)) and no money or other benefit other than reasonable expenses must change hands without the court's authority (section 30(7)).

Section 30 was repealed as from 6 April 2010. Since HFEA 2008, section 54 came into force, parental orders are no longer limited to married couples. The section allows applications from civil partners and from two persons who are 'living as partners in an enduring family relationship and are not within prohibited degrees of relationship to each other'. In both cases, the child must have been produced from the eggs or sperm of at least one of the applicants.

24.13   CLASS GIFTS

Wills often contain gifts to a class of beneficiaries, for example, 'to the children of X' or to 'the children of X who reach twenty-one'.

When drafting such a gift, it is necessary to decide whether the class is to remain open until all possible members have been ascertained (in which case it will not be possible to distribute until all members have been ascertained), or whether the class should close early to allow distribution to take place. Convenience is in favour of early distribution. Fairness suggests keeping the class open as long as other members might be added.

The testator is free to make express provision for closing the class but, in the absence of such provision, certain rules of construction, known as the class-closing rules, apply. There are different rules for the different types of gift. The aim of all the rules is to close the class as soon as there is a beneficiary who is entitled to immediate distribution.

24.13.1 Individual gift to each member of a class

A gift such as '£1,000 to each of the children of X' is not, strictly speaking, a class gift as the size of each beneficiary's entitlement is fixed and does not vary according to the number of class members. However, such a gift shares many of the practical problems of true class gifts; the personal representatives are likely to have difficulty distributing the estate as they will not know how large a fund to retain.

In the absence of provision to the contrary, the class closes at the date of the testator's death and includes only children then living. If there are no children living the whole gift fails. The object of this drastic class-closing rule is to allow the personal representatives to distribute the estate. If the gift is preceded by a life interest, closure is postponed until the death of the life tenant. The class would then include all members alive at the date of death of the testator, together with those born before the death of the life tenant.

24.13.2 Immediate class gift

An example of an immediate class gift is 'to the children of X'. Here, the class closes at the testator's death if any class members are already in existence. If there are no members in existence, the class remains open indefinitely.

24.13.3 Postponed class gift

In a postponed class gift, such as 'to L for life and then to the children of X', the class closes at the life tenant's death if any class members are already in existence. It includes all members alive at the testator's death, together with those born before the death of the life tenant. If there are no class members by the time the life tenant dies, the class remains open indefinitely.

24.13.4 Contingent class gift

Under a contingent class gift, such as 'to the children of X who reach twenty-one', the class closes at the testator's death if any class members have already satisfied the contingency. If no class members have then satisfied the contingency, the class remains open until the first one does so and then closes immediately. Once the class closes any child within the class who subsequently fulfils the contingency can take.

24.13.5   Postponed contingent class gift

A postponed contingent class gift may take the form 'to L for life and then to the children of X who reach twenty-one'. Here the class closes at the life tenant's death if any class members have by then satisfied the contingency. If there are no class members by the time the life tenant dies, the class remains open until the first member satisfies the contingency and then closes immediately. It includes all members alive at the testator's death, together with those born before the class closes who subsequently satisfy the contingency.

24.13.6   Modifying the rules

The class closing rules are designed to facilitate the administration of the estate. But they can operate harshly in excluding members from benefit and can cause family disharmony. There may be cases where it is appropriate to provide that:

(i)   the class remains open after it would otherwise have closed;
(ii)   but that distributions can be made;
(iii) and that no beneficiary is to have their share reduced by later additions to the class.

Thus, later born beneficiaries would take less, but are more likely to take something. For example, a testator makes a gift to their grandchildren contingent on their reaching 18, with a direction in the form set out above. Three grandchildren, A, B and C are living at the date of death. A is 18:

- A takes one-third of the fund immediately;
- D and E are born;
- B, C, D and E take one-quarter of the remaining fund at age 18.

24A   CLASS GIFT FOR GRANDCHILDREN EQUALLY WITH PROVISION IN LIEU OF CLASS CLOSING

My Trustees shall hold the trust fund UPON TRUST absolutely for such of my grandchildren living at my death or born afterwards at any time during their parents' lifetime as reach the age of eighteen or marry under that age and if more than one in equal shares PROVIDED that the share in the trust fund of any grandchild who has attained a vested interest shall not be diminished by the birth or marriage of or the attainment of [eighteen] by any further grandchildren.

24.14   ABSOLUTE INTERESTS MADE SUBJECT TO RESTRICTIONS

Where an absolute gift is given and further words are added to describe the testator's intention when making the gift, then the subsequent words do not generally restrict the absolute interest. Where a particular interest is given to X with an additional power for X to dispose of the property, then the gift may take effect as an absolute gift, but normally only if the additional power is exercised.

The rule in *Lassence v Tierney* (1849) 1 Mac & G 551 provides that if there is an absolute gift to a legatee in the first instance, and trusts are engrafted or imposed on that absolute interest, and the trusts fail because of lapse or invalidity, or for any other reason, then the absolute gift takes effect so far as the trusts have failed, to the exclusion of the residuary legatee or next of kin as the case may be.

Similarly, if a life interest is settled upon trust for a wife for life with remainder to her children, and if there prove to be no children or no children eligible to take an interest, then the previous absolute interest remains and takes effect without qualification.

To determine that there has been an absolute gift which is capable of taking effect despite subsequent restrictions or powers, the court must be satisfied, first, that the subject matter of the gift has been segregated from the remainder of the testator's estate 'once and for all'; and, second, that behind any trusts or powers attached to the gift there remains an interest vested in the legatee which may take effect in so far as the engrafted trusts fail or do not exhaust the subject matter of the gift.

24.15   GIFTS TO LEGATEES AND THEIR CHILDREN

The effect of a gift 'to X and his children' depends on its construction. It may be a gift to X and his children concurrently; or to X and then to his children in succession; or the children may even be intended to take in substitution for X.

The court would first look to the intention of the testator as evidenced by the will as a whole. In general, such a gift takes effect in favour of both the parent and the children concurrently as joint tenants. However, the court leans towards the creation of successive interests.

24.16   GIFTS TO LEGATEES AND THEIR ISSUE

Before 1926, a gift of land to 'X and his issue' *prima facie* created an estate tail, as the word 'issue' was treated as a word of limitation. Where the context allowed, however, it was treated as a word of description only. Since 1926, such a gift passes the fee simple to the donee and, where the context admits, the issue take as joint tenants with the named legatees.

In respect of personalty, such a gift *prima facie* gives both the named donee and the issue concurrent interests as joint tenants. Such a gift may be construed as an absolute gift to the named donee, for example, where there is a gift over upon failure of issue.

Since 1925, the word 'issue' no longer creates an estate entail. This means that whenever such words are construed as words of limitation the donee takes an absolute interest.

24.17   GIFTS TO BENEFIT LEGATEES

Where the whole of the capital or income of a fund is given to a beneficiary or to trustees for the beneficiary, in the absence of a contrary intention, it is presumed that the testator intended to benefit that beneficiary to the full extent of the subject matter of the gift. In such circumstances the gift is held to be a valid gift of the whole fund, even where the testator expresses the gift to be for a particular purpose and where that purpose cannot be performed or does not exhaust the whole of the fund. The statement of the intended purpose is construed as a mere statement of motive (see *Re Osoba* [1979] 1 WLR 247).

Generally, there must be a clear indication in the will before a beneficiary becomes entitled to an interest, although some interests may arise by necessary implication. For example, if a gift is made to B after the death of A, then A takes a life interest by implication unless the will provides for the income of the property during A's life to form part of the residuary estate, or unless a contrary intention is otherwise demonstrated by the will. The implication arises because no other provision has been made regarding the income from the testator's death until A's death. For this life interest to arise by implication, B must be the sole person entitled on intestacy at the time the will was made and the intermediate income must not be caught by any residuary gift.

In any other case, undisposed of property passes under any residuary gift or, if there is no such gift, to the person entitled on intestacy.

Specific devises and bequests also carry the intermediate income to the devisees and legatees unless that income is expressly otherwise disposed of. A life estate by implication, therefore, never arises in the case of specific gifts.

24.18 GIFTS OVER

Where property is given to A absolutely with a gift over of that property in the event of A's death then, unless some other period is indicated by the context, the gift over takes effect if A dies before the distribution or vesting. Thus a gift over attached to an immediate gift takes effect only if A predeceases the testator, the gift over being in substitution for the gift to A.

If the gift to A is postponed to the life interests of B with a gift over to C, the gift over *prima facie* takes effect only if A dies during the life of the life tenant, B. The gift over to C takes effect on the death of B as an alternative to the gift to A.

If the gift is made to one person indefinitely, with a gift over to a second person on the death of the first then, *prima facie*, the first donee takes a life interest only and the gift over to the second donee takes effect on the death of the first by way of succession.

24.19 CONTINGENCIES RELATING TO GIFTS OVER ON DEATH

Generally, where a gift over is to take effect on the death of a prior donee and on the satisfaction of other contingencies, it is irrelevant whether the contingencies are satisfied or whether the prior donee dies before or after the testator's death. But this is not so if the will, on its true construction, refers to the occurrence of the events only after the testator's death or at some specified time. The gift would *prima facie* take effect once the prior donee has died and all the contingencies have been fulfilled. However, a gift over may be intended to be substitutional and the will may be construed to allow the gift over to take effect only if the prior donee dies within a specified period. There may be alternative gifts over.

24.20 DIVESTING

Wherever there is uncertainty, the court of construction construes divesting conditions strictly and restrictively, favouring the construction that leads to the vesting indefeasibly of the property as early as possible.

24.21   FAILURE OF ISSUE

Wills Act 1837, section 29 provides that where words in a gift import either the want or failure of issue of any person in their lifetime, or at the time of that person's death or indefinitely, then, unless a contrary intention is apparent in the will, such words are construed to mean a want or failure of issue during the lifetime or at the date of death of that person, as appropriate. Examples of such words are 'have no issue' or 'die without issue' or 'die without leaving issue'.

A contrary intention may be expressed within the will or may be evident from the context generally. Section 29 applies only where the words may bear the construction the section imposes. If the words written must import an indefinite failure of issue, then the section has no effect and the words must be construed accordingly.

Chapter 25

Failure of Gifts and Intestacy

A gift in a will may fail for a number of reasons:

(i)   the beneficiary is an attesting witness (see Chapter 4);
(ii) lapse (see Chapter 5);
(iii) the dissolution of the testator's marriage to or civil partnership with the beneficiary (see Chapter 7);
(iv) ademption (see Chapter 20);
(v) the beneficiary is guilty of the murder or manslaughter of the deceased (see Chapter 5).

Other reasons, not discussed elsewhere in this book, are examined in this chapter.

25.1 UNCERTAINTY

If, after considering any admissible evidence and applying the relevant rules of construction, it is impossible to identify the subject matter or the object of the gift, then the gift is void for uncertainty (see e.g. *Peck v Halsey* (1726) 2 PW 387 and *Re Stephenson* [1897] 1 Ch 75). But also see *Re Golay's Will Trusts* [1965] 1 WLR 969, where the court allowed a gift by a testator who directed his executors to let B enjoy one of his flats during her lifetime 'and to receive a reasonable income from my other property'. The words 'reasonable income' were held not to give rise to uncertainty since the court could, from the wording of the gift, make an objective assessment of reasonable income.

There are two principles that are sometimes used in cases of uncertainty.

The first is that unclear words which are added to a gift do not render the gift uncertain if it can be substantially ascertained from the nature of the case, for example, where the gift is stated to be for a particular purpose even though the amount of the gift is indefinite. The court can, by inquiry, ascertain what sum is sufficient or necessary to answer the purpose.

The second is that in cases where the words used are capable of two constructions, the construction to be adopted is that which tends to make the document effective, and a will should be construed to give effect, as far as possible, to every word.

Where there is a power in the nature of a trust, the intention to benefit the class is mandatory and the beneficiaries can compel the trustees to execute the trust if they are in default. It is essential that the beneficiaries should be known, in the sense that it must be possible to draw up a definitive and complete list of all the persons within the class of beneficiaries.

Where there is a fixed trust and it is not possible to ascertain the beneficiaries at the date of the document declaring the donor's intention, the trust fails for uncertainty. The position with regard to powers is different. Where there is doubt, the court may be required to assess the validity of any proposed appointment and be able to say with certainty whether a particular person is or is not within the permissible class of objects. This rule also applies to discretionary trusts.

25.2 DISCLAIMER

A beneficiary is free to disclaim any gift given to them in a will. They are likely to do this where the gift is subject to conditions or is of a burdensome character. A disclaimer affects only the interests given to the donee and does not affect any other right or interest given by the will, such as a charge on the property or a trust.

Where a beneficiary disclaims a gift, the property passes to the person next entitled under the terms of the will and the rules of inheritance.

The will may make express provision for the failure of the gift 'for any reason' or it may be limited to failure as a result of predeceasing. Well-drafted wills have for many years made gifts over contingent on the gift failing for any reason. This allows a substitutional gift to effect where, for example, a gift fails because the beneficiary witnesses the will.

The Estates of Deceased Persons (Forfeiture Rule and Law of Succession) Act 2011 amends the Wills Act 1837 for deaths on or after 1 February 2012 to provide that for the purposes of the Act a person who disclaims an entitlement under a will (or who is deprived of it by the operation of the forfeiture rule) is to be treated as having died immediately before the testator. The amendment appears to be limited to children and issue of the testator, so express provision will still be required to deal with forfeiture or disclaimer by any other person.

A beneficiary cannot disclaim part of a single gift unless the will provides otherwise. If a beneficiary is given two different properties, they are entitled to disclaim one and take the other even where the two are included in the same gift, but if, upon the true construction of the will, the two properties are intended to be taken together or not at all, they may not disclaim one and take the other. Where there is a single undivided gift, for example a gift of residue, the whole must be taken or none.

25A CLAUSE ALLOWING FOR A PARTIAL DISCLAIMER, THE PROPERTY DISCLAIMED DEVOLVING AS IF THE PERSON DISCLAIMING HAD PREDECEASED THE TESTATOR

> I DECLARE that any person may by notice in writing to my personal representatives disclaim in whole or in part any gift in [his] [her] favour contained in this my will or any codicil hereto and in the event of such disclaimer either in whole or part the gift or part thereof disclaimed shall devolve as if the person disclaiming had predeceased me.

The right to disclaim is lost once the beneficiary has accepted the benefit of the gift. Acceptance is generally inferred from the acts of the donee – acts amounting to ownership of the property given. On the other hand, the will may prescribe some specific act to be performed by the beneficiary to indicate acceptance.

Disclaimer must normally be in writing, but it is possible to disclaim by conduct. In any event, clear evidence of disclaimer is required (see *Cook v IRC* [2002] WTLR 1003, [2002] STC (SCD) 318).

A beneficiary who refuses to accept a gift is treated for inheritance tax purposes as making a transfer of value (see Chapter 27). The effect of this is that if the beneficiary were to die within 7 years of disclaiming, then, subject to inheritance tax exemptions and reliefs, they would be liable to pay inheritance tax on the disclaimed gift. However, Inheritance Tax Act 1984, section 142, provides that if a testamentary benefit is disclaimed by an instrument in writing within 2 years of death and the disclaimer is not made for consideration in money or money's worth, the disclaimer is not treated as a transfer of value. Likewise, for capital gains tax purposes, a disclaimer amounts to a disposal by the original beneficiary, but Capital Gains Tax Act 1979, section 49(6), provides that if the benefit is disclaimed by an instrument in writing within 2 years of death and the disclaimer is not made for consideration in money or money's worth, the disclaimer is not treated as a disposal. The property is treated as if left by the deceased to the person entitled once the disclaimer has taken effect.

25.3   FORFEITURE ON CONTESTING A WILL

It is possible to include a provision in a will that anyone who contests the will forfeits their entitlement. It was held in *Nathan v Leonard* [2003] EWHC 1701 (Ch), [2003] 1 WLR 827, [2002] WTLR 1061 that making an application under the Inheritance (Provision for Family and Dependants) Act 1975 (see Chapter 26) would amount to a challenge and so bring about forfeiture. Although the particular clause used in that case was held to be ineffective because its meaning was uncertain, the decision is significant. The court accepted that such a clause is not void as being contrary to public policy.

25B   PROVISION FOR FORFEITURE ON CONTESTING THE WILL OR ATTEMPTING TO INTERMEDDLE

PROVIDED THAT if any of [names or description of Beneficiaries] shall either (i) dispute the validity of this will or any of the dispositions of my estate effected by it or (ii) apply to court for a larger share of the estate under the Inheritance (Provision for Family and Dependants) Act 1975 or any Act that replaces it or (iii) at any time without reasonable cause interfere in or intermeddle with or attempt to interfere in or intermeddle with the administration or management of my estate then notwithstanding anything herein elsewhere provided that person shall forfeit their interest in [my residuary estate] and be deemed to have predeceased me for the purposes of the devolution of my estate.

25.4   THE EFFECT OF FAILURE

Where a legacy or specific devise fails, the subject matter of the gift passes under the residuary gift contained in the testator's will, provided such a clause is effectively drafted.

Where a residuary gift fails completely, the residuary estate devolves according to the rules of intestacy. If a gift of a *share* in the residuary estate fails, then *prima facie* that share goes on intestacy. This rule can be excluded if the will shows a contrary intention.

In the case of a class gift to persons who are to be ascertained at or after the testator's death, the gift does not necessarily fail if a presumptive member of the class dies in the testator's lifetime, or if such a member proves to be incapable of taking for any reason, provided in each case that at least one other member of the class can take. Similarly, where there is a gift to four beneficiaries as joint tenants and three die before the testator but one survives the testator, the gift does not fail and the survivor takes the whole gift.

25.5 ACCELERATION OF A SUBSEQUENT INTEREST

Acceleration of an interest occurs where a testator purports to give real or personal property to a tenant for life but the gift fails. If there is a vested gift in remainder after the tenant for life's interest, this remainder is accelerated and takes effect immediately in possession. This may be excluded by a contrary intention. The doctrine applies even where the vested gift in remainder is vested subject to being divested. In such a situation, under the doctrine of acceleration, the remainder interest takes effect immediately in possession, but the remainderman's interest remains liable to be divested in accordance with the terms of the will.

The remainder is not accelerated where, after the tenant for life's interest, there is only a contingent gift in remainder. If, however, the gift in remainder subsequently becomes vested, the remainder is accelerated and takes effect in possession.

25.6 INTESTACY

Total intestacy occurs where the testator fails to make an effective disposition of any of their property. A partial intestacy arises where the testator makes testamentary dispositions which fail to dispose of part or some interest in all or part of the property of which they are competent to dispose by will. It is beyond the scope of this book to discuss the rules on intestacy in detail and therefore only an outline is included.

Administration of Estates Act 1925, section 33(1) as amended provides that where a person dies with property undisposed of by will, such property is held in trust by their personal representatives with the power to sell it. The personal representatives must pay all funeral, testamentary and other administration expenses, the testator's debts and liabilities, and, in the case of a partial intestacy, any legacies given in the will. What is left after these payments is the testator's net estate to which the beneficiaries under the intestacy rules are entitled.

25.6.1 The rights of the surviving spouse or civil partner on intestacy

A 'spouse' for this purpose includes the surviving polygamous spouses of an intestate deceased provided the marriages were valid in the country in which they had been contracted. See *The Official Solicitor to the Senior Courts v Yemoh and Others* [2010] EWHC 3727 (Ch), [2011] 1 WLR 1450, where the surviving wives were together entitled to be recognised as the surviving spouse.

The entitlement of a surviving spouse or civil partner depends on what close relatives, if any, survive the intestate and on whether death occurred before or on or after 1 October 2014 when the Inheritance and Trustees' Powers Act 2014 came into force and amended some of the provisions relating to the entitlement of surviving spouses and civil partners.

This chapter deals with deaths on or after 1 October 2014 only.

Since the Family Law Reform Act 1987 came into effect on 4 April 1988, references to any relationship between two persons are construed without regard to whether the person was legitimate or illegitimate (section 18).

The remoter relatives, such as grandparents or uncles and aunts, have no rights to share in the estate.

Spouse or civil partner and issue

Where the intestate leaves a surviving spouse or civil partner and issue, the spouse or civil partner receives:

(i)   the deceased's personal chattels absolutely. The term 'personal chattels' is defined in Administration of Estates Act 1925, section 55(1)(x) as amended by the Inheritance and Trustees' Powers Act 2014;

(ii)   a statutory legacy of £270,000 tax-free absolutely;

(iii)   interest on the statutory legacy at the Bank of England rate applying at the end of the day of the deceased's death from the death of the deceased to the date of payment;

(iv)   half of the residue absolutely.

The issue take the rest of the estate on the statutory trusts.

The Inheritance and Trustees' Powers Act 2014 introduced new rules requiring the Lord Chancellor to review the level of the statutory legacy at least every 5 years. As a result, it was increased from £250,000 for deaths on or after 6 February 2020.

If the intestate and the surviving spouse or civil partner were joint tenants of the matrimonial home, it would automatically vest in the survivor by survivorship. If, however, the intestate were the sole owner of the home or if it were held under a tenancy in common, then the property would become part of the deceased's undisposed of estate. The surviving spouse or civil partner can, in such a case, acquire the matrimonial home under the provisions of Intestates' Estates Act 1952, Schedule II, and Administration of Estates Act 1925, section 41.

Spouse or civil partner and no issue

In this case the surviving spouse or civil partner receives all the undisposed of property.

25.6.2 The rights of the issue on intestacy

The issue take an appropriate share in the statutory trusts (Administration of Estates Act 1925, section 47). Under this section, the property is held equally for the children of the intestate who are either alive or *en ventre sa mère* at the date of the intestate's death. Children who satisfy this requirement have a contingent interest unless and until they attain 18 years of age or marry or form a civil partnership under that age. If a child dies under the age of 18, unmarried or without forming a civil partnership, the child is treated as if they had never existed.

Where a child predeceases the intestate and leaves issue alive at the date of the intestate's death, those grandchildren or their issue take *per stirpes* the share the parent would have taken, provided they attain the age of 18 or marry or form a civil partnership under that age.

For deaths on or after 1 February 2012, the Estates of Deceased Persons (Forfeiture Rule and Law of Succession) Act 2011 makes two changes to the intestacy rules.

First, where a person disclaims an entitlement under the intestacy rules or is precluded by the forfeiture rule from acquiring an interest, section 1 of the Act provides that the person is to be treated for the purposes of this Part as having died immediately before the intestate, thus allowing their issue to take the share they would have taken.

Second, where a child (or remoter issue) survives the intestate but dies without attaining 18 or marrying earlier but with an illegitimate child, section 3 of the Act allows the illegitimate child to take the share the deceased parent would have taken. Slightly oddly, this is only the case if the illegitimate child was itself alive at the date of death of the intestate.

25.6.3 The rights of others on intestacy

Other relatives who take on the statutory trusts must fulfil the same requirements as must the issue, that is, they must be living at the intestate's death and reach the age of 18 or marry or form a civil partnership earlier.

25.6.4   Effect of adoption

The general rule, set out in Adoption and Children Act 2002, section 67(3), is that after adoption a child is regarded for all purposes as the legal child of the adopter or adopters, and has no other legal parents. This can mean that an adopted child loses the right to property held contingently on the statutory trusts arising on intestacy or under a will.

Applications can be made for a variation of the terms of the trust before adoption (see *S v T* [2006] WTLR 1461 for a successful application to vary the statutory trusts), but obviously this is expensive and the need for the application may well be overlooked.

Adoption and Children Act 2002, section 69(4) contains provisions to preserve a child's rights to interests vested in possession or in remainder in an adopted person before an adoption. It provides that adoption shall not prejudice:

(a)   any qualifying interest, or

(b)   any interest expectant (whether immediately or not) upon a qualifying interest.

'Qualifying interest' means an interest vested in possession in the adopted person before the adoption.

The Inheritance and Trustees' Powers Act 2014 extended this protection to a contingent interest by adding to section 69(4):

or

(c)   any contingent interest (other than a contingent interest in remainder) which the adopted person has immediately before the adoption in the estate of a deceased parent, whether testate or intestate.

The effect is that where, before adoption, a child's legal parent has died and some or all of that parent's estate is held on contingent trusts – whether created by will or arising on intestacy – for the child, the interest of the child will not be affected by the adoption.

The effect of the amendment is limited. It applies only to an interest in '*the estate of a deceased parent*, whether testate or intestate'. A contingent interest in the estate of a deceased grandparent would, therefore, not be saved. Neither would a contingent interest following an interest in possession. Contingent interests in remainder no longer arise under the intestacy rules but may be created by will.

For example, a parent makes a will leaving their estate in trust so that X has a right to the income for life and subject to that the child will take the estate if they reach 25. The child's interest is contingent, but (if X is living at the date of the adoption) it is in remainder to X's interest and therefore not preserved by new paragraph (c).

25.6.5   Presumption of death

Family Law Reform Act 1987, section 18(2) operates where a person dies intestate and their parents were not married to each other at the time of their birth. It contains a presumption that the intestate is deemed to have been predeceased by an unmarried father or second female parent and by any other person to whom the intestate was related only through their father or second female parent. This assists personal representatives of an intestate child to distribute the estate where nothing is known of the father or second female parent.

The presumption is disapplied by Family Law Reform Act 1987, section 18(2ZA) where the father (or second female parent) is registered as the child's parent.

25.7   ACCRUER CLAUSES

Clauses in a will which divest and dispose of the share of a donee dying before a particular time or event, in the absence of evidence to the contrary, refer only to that donee's original share and do not extend to shares which have accrued under another such clause so as to pass them a second time. For example, the testator leaves a gift to A, B, C, D, E and F to be paid to them at the age of 21, with a direction that if any dies under the age of 21, the share is to devolve to the others. A and B die under the age of 21 and predecease the testator. A dies first, then B. B's original share goes to the survivors, but the share which has accrued to B on the death of A does not pass to the survivors (see *Rickett v Guillemard* (1841) 12 Sim 88).

In the absence of an express or inferred intention to the contrary, conditions which apply to the original share are not applicable to the accrued share under such a clause, although they may be held to be applicable to prevent the accruing shares from being void under the rule against perpetuities.

The original shares may not be equal but, in the absence of a contrary provision, an accruing share is divided and accrues to each survivor equally.

There are several situations, however, when the accrued share devolves with the original share:

(i)   where there is express direction to that effect;
(ii)   where there is a gift of residue, the presumption against an intestacy may allow the accrued share to devolve with the original share;
(iii)   where the testator, although they speak of individual shares, treat the fund as an aggregate (see *Re Lybbe* [1954] 1 WLR 573).

25C   ACCRUER OF SHARES

I DECLARE that if the foregoing trusts shall fail in relation to any share by reason of the failure of any person to attain a vested interest therein then the said shares and any shares which may accrue thereto either under the provisions of this my will or otherwise shall be held on trust by my Trustees subject to the trusts powers and provisions previously set out and such trusts powers and provisions as may be implied by statute as an accretion to the other share or shares ([equally] [proportionally] if more than one) the trusts whereof shall not at the date of such accruer have failed as aforesaid and upon the same terms as previously set out in so far as the same shall be capable of taking effect.

Chapter 26

Family Provision

26.1 INTRODUCTION

When drafting a will the provisions of the Inheritance (Provision for Family and Dependants) Act 1975 must be borne in mind, since the concept of complete testamentary freedom has been eroded, at least to some extent, by this Act. The Act gives the court limited powers to order financial provision from the net estate of a deceased for the benefit of certain categories of applicant.

Significant changes have been made to the Act by the Inheritance and Trustees' Powers Act 2014 for deaths occurring on or after 1 October 2014. This chapter deals only with the position for deaths on or after that date.

To bring a successful application four conditions must be met:

(i)   the deceased must have died domiciled in England and Wales after 31 March 1976;
(ii) the application must be made within a prescribed time limit;
(iii) the applicant must fall into one of the six possible categories of applicant;
(iv) the will (or intestacy) must not have made reasonable provision for the applicant.

If these conditions are met the court may make an order for financial provision for the applicant.

The right of action under the Inheritance (Provision for Family and Dependants) Act 1975 is personal to the applicant, so that if both parties to a marriage or civil partnership die, the right to claim against the estate of the deceased's spouse or civil partner no longer exists (see *Re Bramwell Deceased; Campbell v Tobin* [1988] 2 FLR 263 and *Roberts and Another v Fresco* [2017] EWHC 283 (Ch)).

26.2   TIME LIMIT FOR APPLICATIONS

Applications should usually be made within 6 months of the date of the general grant of representation (section 4). The court has a discretion to extend this time limit. The cases of *Re Salmon Deceased* [1981] Ch 167 and *Re Dennis deceased* [1981] 2 All ER 140 outlined the guidelines the court should take into account in the exercise of its discretion. In *Re Salmon* Megarry J listed the following:

(i)   the discretion is to be exercised judicially;
(ii)   the onus is on the applicant to make out a substantial case for the court to exercise its jurisdiction;
(iii)   the court should consider how promptly and in what circumstances the applicant applied for an extension and warned the defendant of the proposed application;
(iv)   the court should ascertain whether negotiations have started within the time limit;
(v)   the court is to look at whether the estate has been distributed before the claim has been notified;
(vi)   the court should consider whether a refusal to extend the time would leave the applicant without redress against anyone, including their own solicitors for negligence.

Re Dennis Deceased [1981] 2 All ER 140 added a further guideline. Applicants must show that they have an arguable case, a case fit to go to trial. In deciding this, the court's approach is similar to that when considering whether a defendant ought to have leave to defend in proceedings for summary judgment.

Personal representatives who distribute the estate of the deceased having waited 6 months from the date of the grant are not liable to subsequent applicants who are given leave to apply out of time. This does not, though, prejudice the applicant's power to recover any part of the estate so distributed (section 20).

26.3   THOSE WHO CAN APPLY

The following persons may apply to the court for an order under the Act.

26.3.1   The deceased's spouse or civil partner

The deceased's spouse or civil partner must show that the marriage or civil partnership subsisted at the time of the deceased's death.

A judicially separated spouse or civil partner, a party to a voidable marriage or civil partnership which was not annulled before death, and a wife in a polygamous marriage come within this category (see *Re Sehota* [1978] 1 WLR 1506). A person also comes within this category where the marriage or civil partnership was void but the applicant entered into it in good faith, unless, during the deceased's lifetime, the marriage or civil partnership was annulled or dissolved, or the applicant entered into a later marriage or civil partnership (section 25(4) and (4A)). The Act provides that a court may bar a claim under the Act when making a decree of judicial separation (section 15).

26.3.2 A former spouse or civil partner

A former spouse or civil partner is a person whose marriage or civil partnership with the deceased was dissolved or annulled during the deceased's lifetime by a decree of divorce, dissolution or nullity made in the courts of England and Wales, the British Islands, and this under section 25(1) (as amended) means the United Kingdom, Channel Islands and Isle of Man; or by a decree of divorce or nullity or an order which is entitled to be recognised as valid by the law of England and Wales. The court may impose a bar against applications for financial provision by a former spouse under section 15 or by a civil partner under section 15ZA with the agreement of both parties on the granting of a decree of divorce, dissolution or nullity. It also has power to impose such bars when making a property adjustment order following a decree made overseas under sections 15A and 15B.

The bar extends only to applications as a former spouse or civil partner. It does not prevent applications as a cohabitee, person maintained or, in the case of remarriage, as a surviving spouse or civil partner (see *Chekov v Fryer and Another* [2015] EWHC 1642 (Ch)).

Applications by former spouses and civil partners are rare. Even when there is no bar, they are unlikely to succeed. The Court of Appeal observed, in *Re Fullard (Deceased)* [1982] Fam 42, that in view of the wide powers of the court to make financial arrangements on divorce, the number of cases in which it would be appropriate for a former spouse to apply would be small. But such a claim might succeed, for example, where the deceased's estate receives the proceeds of a large insurance policy, or where the applicant was provided for in the divorce proceedings by means of periodical payments rather than a lump sum.

In *Barrass v Harding and Another* [2000] EWCA Civ 521, [2001] 1 FLR 138, the Court of Appeal refused to allow a modest order made in favour of a divorced woman. She was in dire financial straits and living with her son who was also badly off, but there was no indication of any continuing relationship between her and the deceased. The Court of Appeal said there was no reason for the approach adopted in *Re Fullard (Deceased)* [1982] Fam 42 not to apply. On the other hand, in *Parnall v Hurst and Others* [2003] WTLR 997, an application for interlocutory relief in a claim by a former wife against the executors of her former husband's estate was allowed. The points in her favour were:

(i)   she was being maintained by the deceased at the rate of £6,000 a year and that income had been abruptly terminated;
(ii)   she was in a parlous financial state as a result of the cessation of maintenance;
(iii) the relatively short duration of the deceased's marriage to his second wife and the fact that the second wife had the benefit of the deceased's occupational pension.

26.3.3   A person living as the spouse or civil partner of the deceased

A person living as the spouse or civil partner of the deceased was added as a category of claimant (under Inheritance (Provision for Family and Dependants) Act 1975, section 1(1)(ba)) by the Law Reform (Succession) Act 1995 and a person living as a civil partner was added by the Civil Partnership Act 2004. Claimants must fulfil the requirements of section 1A, which provides as follows:

> The deceased must have died on or after 1st January 1996 and, during the whole of the period of two years ending immediately before the date when the deceased died, the person was living—
>
> (a)   in the same household as the deceased, and
> (b)   as if that person and the deceased were a married couple or civil partners.

The parties must be living together *as spouses or as civil partners*. This requires a 'commitment to permanence' at some point in the relationship (see the House of Lords' decision in *Ghaidan v Godin-Mendoza* [2004] UKHL 30, [2004] AC 557). Moreover, marriage and civil partnerships are publicly acknowledged relationships which must be openly and unequivocally displayed to the outside world. It is not possible for two persons to live together as spouses or civil partners unless their relationship as a couple is an acknowledged one (see *Baynes v Hedger and Others* [2008] EWHC 1587 (Ch), [2008] 2 FLR 1805 and *Lindop v Agus and Others* [2009] EWHC 1795 (Ch), [2010] 1 FLR 631).

The 2-year period must be unbroken, and an application is bound to fail if the applicant ceased, but then resumed, living with the deceased but failed to 'clock up' a full 2-year period before the death. Separations brought about by external circumstances, such as illness necessitating a stay in hospital or hospice care are, however, irrelevant. A temporary separation which does not break the relationship will similarly be irrelevant even if it is existing at the date of death (see *Gully v Dix* [2004] EWCA Civ 139, [2004] 1 FLR 918) or lengthy (see *Kaur v Dhaliwal and Another* [2014] EWHC 1991 (Ch)).

26.3.4 A child of the deceased

A child of the deceased includes an illegitimate, legitimated or adopted child and a child *en ventre sa mère* at the deceased's death.

Some cases appeared to suggest that in claims by adult able-bodied children, there is an additional 'threshold' requirement of a special obligation owed by the deceased to the claimant. This was a misunderstanding of the decision in *Re Coventry* [1980] Ch 461 and was categorically rejected by the Court of Appeal in a number of later cases (see *Re Hancock Deceased* [1998] 2 FLR 346, *Re Pearce Deceased* [1998] 2 FLR 705, *Espinosa v Bourke* [1999] 1 FLR 747 and, most recently, *Ilott v Mitson and Others* [2015] EWCA Civ 797 and [2011] EWCA Civ 346).

The approach is that the court, in reaching its decision, considers the circumstances in their entirety, seeking to balance all the factors set out in section 3 of the Act. In *Gold v Curtis* [2005] WTLR 673 and *Re Myers, Myers v Myers and Others* [2004] EWHC 1944 (Fam), [2005] WTLR 851, the court accepted that parents owe continuing obligations and responsibilities to their children. Nevertheless, an adult able-bodied child who cannot produce any argument to buttress a claim beyond being badly off is unlikely to be successful if there are other deserving applicants (see *Re Coventry* [1980] Ch 461, and *Ilott v Mitson and Others* [2015] EWCA Civ 797 and [2011] EWCA Civ 346). *Ilott v Mitson and Others* proceeded to the Supreme Court under the name *Ilott v The Blue Cross and Others* [2017] UKSC 17. The Supreme Court confirmed that in the case of applications by adult children there is no requirement for a moral claim as a *sine qua non*. However, the presence or absence of a moral claim may be relevant to a decision in relation to any applicant.

26.3.5 A child treated as a child of the family

A person (not being a child of the deceased) treated by the deceased as a child of the family in relation to any marriage or civil partnership to which the deceased was at any time a party, or in relation to any family in which the deceased at any time stood in the role of a parent, may make a claim. Section 1(2A) provides that 'a family in which the deceased stood in the role of a parent includes a family of which the deceased was the only member (apart from the applicant)'. Hence, a child cared for by the deceased as a single parent comes within the category.

26.3.6   Persons maintained

Any person (other than one falling within the above paragraphs) who, immediately before the death of the deceased, was being maintained wholly or partly by the deceased, may claim. Section 1(3) provides that:

> a person shall be treated as being maintained by the deceased, either wholly or partly ... only if the deceased, was making a substantial contribution in money or money's worth towards the reasonable needs of that person, other than a contribution made for full valuable consideration pursuant to an arrangement of a commercial nature.

It is difficult to say with certainty what amounts to 'a substantial contribution', but in *Jelley v Iliffe* [1981] Fam 128, the court said that the provision of rent-free accommodation was sufficient. See also *King v Dubrey and Others* [2014] EWHC 2083 (Ch) (reversed in part, but not on this point).

The burden is on the applicant to show that the deceased was making a substantial contribution towards their reasonable needs.

The words 'pursuant to an arrangement of a commercial nature' were added by the Inheritance and Trustees' Powers Act 2014 for death on or after 1 October 2014 to prevent the court having to weigh up the respective contributions made by each party in cases of mutual dependency.

Section 1(1)(e) expressly provides that the applicant must have been maintained 'immediately before the death' of the deceased. This need not be literally interpreted where the deceased had been maintaining the applicant but had been unable to do so in the few weeks before their death when the applicant was taken into hospital. Megarry VC said in *Re Beaumont Deceased* [1980] Ch 444 that the court must look at 'the settled basis or ... arrangement between the parties'.

26.4   REASONABLE FINANCIAL PROVISION

The Inheritance (Provision for Family and Dependants) Act 1975 sets out two standards of provision, the first applicable to a surviving spouse or civil partner, and the second applicable in all other cases.

26.4.1   The surviving spouse standard

Reasonable financial provision in this case is (section 1(2)(a)):

> such financial provision as it would be reasonable in all the circumstances ... for a husband or wife or civil partner to receive, whether or not that provision is required for his or her maintenance.

Under section 14, the court has a discretion to apply the surviving spouse standard to a former spouse or civil partner where a decree of judicial separation, nullity, divorce or dissolution was made within 12 months of the death of the deceased and no order for financial provision was made (or refused) in the matrimonial or dissolution proceedings. In *Re Farrow Deceased* [1988] 1 FLR 205, a former spouse was awarded a lump sum payment to take account of the fact that for some 7 years she was without periodical payments, as financial provision was not finalised for such a time.

26.4.2 The ordinary standard

In all cases where the 'surviving spouse' standard is not applied, 'reasonable provision' means (section 1(2)(b)):

> such financial provision as it would be reasonable in all the circumstances of the case for the applicant to receive for his maintenance.

Buckley LJ, in *Re Coventry* [1980] Ch 461, said that it could be regarded as:

> such financial provision as would be reasonable in all the circumstances of the case to enable the applicant to maintain himself in a manner suitable to those circumstances.

In the case of cohabitees, 'reasonable financial provision for maintenance' will be assessed in the light of the applicant's lifestyle during the cohabitation and not their previous lifestyle (see *Negus v Bahouse* [2007] EWHC 2628 (Ch)).

The limitation to maintenance is significant. The court is not free to vary the disposition of the estate if the applicant is able to maintain themselves appropriately. In *Ilott v The Blue Cross and Others* [2017] UKSC 17, Lord Hughes emphasised this point at [13], saying that 'This limitation to maintenance provision represents a deliberate legislative choice and is important'. At [14] he said:

> The concept of maintenance is no doubt broad, but the distinction made by the differing paragraphs of s 1(2) shows that it cannot extend to any or every thing which it would be desirable for the claimant to have. It must import provision to meet the everyday expenses of living.

At [15], Lord Hughes said that the level at which maintenance may be provided for is clearly flexible and falls to be assessed on the facts of each case. It is not limited to subsistence level. Nor, although maintenance is by definition the provision of income rather than capital, need it necessarily be provided for by way of periodical payments, for example under a trust. It will very often be more appropriate, as well as cheaper and more convenient for other beneficiaries and for executors, if income is provided by way of a lump sum from which both income and capital can be drawn over the years.

There will often be cases where the applicant has a need for housing. Lord Hughes made the important point that in the case of an applicant entitled only to provision for maintenance, it will normally be appropriate to make provision for housing by way of a life interest rather than by a capital sum.

In *Thompson v Ragget and Others* [2018] EWHC 688 (Ch), the first case reported on a housing need after the Supreme Court's decision in *Ilott*, the judge made an outright award of the deceased's house to his cohabitee, but there were unusual circumstances. The decision in *Banfield v Campbell* [2018] EWHC 1943 (Ch) is probably more typical. Master Teverson refused to make a capital award for housing to the disabled cohabitee, aged 66 at the time of the application. The estate was about £725,000, the major portion being the house which had been inherited from the deceased's husband. It was accepted that provision for housing was appropriate, but Master Teverson ordered that the property should be sold and the applicant to be granted a life interest in one half of the net proceeds of sale, which were to be used in or towards providing alternative accommodation for him.

26.5   THE GUIDELINES

If the court decides that reasonable provision has not been made for the applicant in the will, it must then consider whether or not to exercise its discretion to make an order and, if so, decide what order to make. The court is helped by two sets of guidelines, general and particular.

26.5.1   The general guidelines

By section 3(1) the court must have regard to:

(a)   the financial resources and the needs of the applicant;
(b)   the financial resources and the needs of any other applicant;
(c)   the financial resources and the needs of the beneficiaries of the estate;
(d)   any obligations and responsibilities of the deceased towards the applicant or towards any beneficiary;
(e)   the size and nature of the estate;
(f)   any physical or mental disability of any applicant or beneficiary;
(g)   any other matter, including the conduct of the applicant or any other person which the court may consider relevant.

The court will consider each relevant guideline and assess its significance. A guideline of little significance in one case may be of overwhelming importance in another. See, for example, *Wright v Waters and Another* [2014] EWHC 3614 (Ch), where the applicant's dreadful conduct towards her mother completely outweighed other factors which were in her favour.

The first three guidelines are balancing guidelines, so the absence of a beneficiary or other applicant with a strong claim will assist the applicant. In *Ilott v Mitson and Others* [2015] EWCA Civ 797, the applicant adult daughter's financial position was poor and the only beneficiaries were charities. The Court of Appeal considered that the charities had no resources and needs to be taken into account. Arden LJ said at [47] 'For the Charities, any money from this estate is a windfall'. In *Ilott v The Blue Cross and Others* [2017] UKSC 17, the Supreme Court strongly disagreed. Lord Hughes said at [46] that while the charities had no personal need:

> charities depend heavily on testamentary bequests for their work, which is by definition of public benefit and in many cases will be for demonstrably humanitarian purposes. More fundamentally, these charities were the chosen beneficiaries of the deceased. They did not have to justify a claim on the basis of need under the 1975 Act, as Mrs Ilott necessarily had to do. The observation, at para 61 of the Court of Appeal judgment, cited above, that, because the charities had no needs to plead, they were not prejudiced by an increased award to Mrs Ilott is, with great respect, also erroneous; their benefit was reduced by any such award. That may be the right outcome in a particular case, but it cannot be ignored that an award under the Act is at the expense of those whom the testator intended to benefit.

26.5.2 The particular guidelines

Section 3(2) sets out additional guidelines which are appropriate to particular categories of applicant; these guidelines are to be used in conjunction with, but without prejudice to, the general guidelines.

The surviving spouse or civil partner

The court must consider the following guidelines:

(i) the age of the applicant and the duration of the marriage or civil partnership;
(ii) the contributions made by the applicant to the welfare of the family of the deceased, including any contributions made by looking after the home or caring for the family; and

(iii) the provision the applicant might reasonably have expected to receive if, on the day on which the deceased died, the marriage or civil partnership, instead of ending in death, had ended by a decree of divorce or dissolution.

The guideline in point (iii) does not mean that the court is to make the same provision as if there had been a divorce on the day of the death. A number of cases made this point (see *Re Besterman; Besterman v Grusin* [1984] Ch 458, *Re Krubert (Deceased)* [1997] Ch 97 (CA), *Fielden v Cunliffe* [2005] EWCA Civ 1508, *sub nom Cunliffe v Fielden and Others* [2006] 2 WLR 481, and *P v G (Family Provision: Relevance of Divorce Provision)* [2004] EWHC 2944 (Fam), [2006] 1 FLR 431). The likely provision on divorce is merely one of the factors to which the court is to have regard. This had been thought to be the case, but the Inheritance and Trustees' Powers Act 2014 amended the sub-section to provide expressly that the court is not required to treat the provision that would be made on divorce 'as setting an upper or lower limit on the provision which may be made'. The overriding consideration is what is 'reasonable' in all the circumstances.

Inevitably, the increased amounts paid to non-working spouses as a result of the House of Lords' decision in *White v White* [2000] UKHL 54, [2001] 1 AC 596 affects the approach taken in Inheritance Act claims (see *Adams v Lewis* [2001] WTLR 493, [2001] All ER (D) 274 (Jan), *McNulty v McNulty* [2002] EWHC 123 (Ch), [2002] WTLR 737 and *Fielden v Cunliffe* [2005] EWCA Civ 1508, *sub nom Cunliffe v Fielden and Others* [2006] 2 WLR 481). It seems from *Cunliffe* that the short duration of a marriage is likely to be less important in family provision cases than it would be in the case of a divorce. A divorce involves a conscious decision by one or both of the spouses to bring the marriage to an end. That process leaves two living former spouses, each of whom has resources, needs and responsibilities. In such a case the length of the marriage and the parties' respective contributions to it assume a particular importance. Where a marriage ends with death, the surviving spouse can legitimately claim that it would have continued indefinitely.

Since, on divorce, there will normally be capital provision, a surviving spouse who is left only an income entitlement is likely to be successful in a claim that they have not received reasonable provision. In *Cowan v Foreman and Others* [2019] EWCA Civ 1336, [2020] Fam 129, the deceased's widow was left a life interest in part of the estate and was a beneficiary of the discretionary trust over the rest of the estate. The Court of Appeal gave her leave to apply outside the normal 6-month period, partly on the basis that she had a real prospect of success. She had no autonomy and no security and had no direct interest, even in the property which had been her home for more than 20 years.

Where a marriage was effectively over before death although the parties have not yet obtained a divorce or dissolution, the amount the survivor would have received on divorce or dissolution will be particularly significant. The court is unlikely to order more than they would have received on divorce or dissolution (see *Aston v Aston* [2007] WTLR 1349 and *Goenka v Goenka and Others* [2014] EWHC 2966 (Ch)).

If the parties have, with proper advice, entered into a pre-nuptial agreement limiting the amount to be obtained in the event of divorce, the courts will take this into account (see *Hendry v Hendry and Others* [2019] EWHC 1976 (Ch)).

The former spouse

Guidelines (i) and (ii) above apply to an application by a former spouse, but (iii) above is not relevant unless the court has exercised its discretion to apply the surviving spouse standard.

Person living as spouse or civil partner

The following are to be taken into account:

(i) the age of the applicant and the length of time the applicant lived as the spouse or civil partner of the deceased and in the same household as the deceased;

(ii) the contribution made by the applicant to the welfare of the family of the deceased, including any contribution made by looking after the home or caring for the family.

As in the case of a spouse or civil partner, a cohabitee is entitled to have the standard of living enjoyed with the deceased taken into account. In *Negus v Bahouse*, the Court of Appeal refused an appeal from the first instance decision at [2007] EWHC 2628 (Ch) made on the basis that the award was excessive reflecting the extravagant lifestyle enjoyed by the couple. The court held that it was necessary to be flexible to suit the circumstances of the case and that meant looking at the lifestyle the cohabitee had been accustomed to during the deceased's lifetime.

A child of the deceased

Where the applicant is a child of the deceased the court must consider the manner in which the applicant was being, or might have expected to be, educated or trained.

A person treated by the deceased as a child of the family

If the applicant is a child the court must consider their education and training, as for a child of the deceased, and:

(i)   whether and, if so, to what extent the deceased assumed responsibility for the maintenance of the applicant; and

(ii)   whether in maintaining or assuming responsibility for maintaining the applicant the deceased did so knowing that the applicant was not the deceased's own child; and

(iii) the liability of any other person to maintain the applicant.

A person maintained by the deceased

Where an applicant was being maintained by the deceased immediately before the deceased's death, the court must consider:

(i)   the length of time for which, and basis on which, the deceased maintained the applicant, and the extent of the contribution made by way of maintenance;

(ii)   whether and, if so, to what extent the deceased assumed responsibility for the maintenance of the applicant.

26.6   PROPERTY AVAILABLE FOR FINANCIAL PROVISION

All the orders that the court can make are against the net estate. This is after payment of debts (including tax), but potentially including the deceased's share of property nominated, subject to a *donatio mortis causa* or passing by survivorship (sections 8 and 9) and property covered by the anti-avoidance provisions set out in sections 10 and 11. An estate which appears large may be reduced to virtually nothing if the deceased owed an accumulation of income tax, together with interest and penalties. Conversely, an estate may appear to be very small but there may be assets which can be added to it under sections 8 to 11 (see **26.6.1** to **26.6.3**).

26.6.1   The net estate

Section 25 defines the 'net estate' as comprising:

(i)   all property of which the deceased had power to dispose by their will (otherwise than by virtue of a special power of appointment), less the amount of the funeral, testamentary and administration expenses, debts and liabilities including any inheritance tax payable out of their estate on death;

(ii)   any property in respect of which the deceased held a general power of appointment (not being a power exercisable by will) which has not been exercised;

(iii) any property nominated by the deceased to any person under a statutory nomination or received by a person as a result of a *donatio mortis causa*, less any inheritance tax payable in respect thereof and borne by the nominee or donee (section 8);

(iv) the deceased's severable share of a joint tenancy, in so far as the court deems fit (section 9);

(v)   any property in respect of which the court exercises its anti-avoidance powers and orders to be available (sections 10 and 11).

26.6.2   Joint property

Section 9 provides that the court may, for the purpose of facilitating the making of financial provision, order that the deceased's severable share in any property held by them under a joint tenancy immediately before their death (or the value thereof immediately before their death) is to be treated as part of the deceased's net estate to such extent as appears just in all the circumstances (and after deducting any inheritance tax payable).

In the case of deaths on or after 1 October 2014, it is no longer necessary for an application under section 9 to be made within 6 months of the date of the grant. The court can exercise its discretion to allow an application out of time in relation to an interest passing by survivorship.

However, where an application is made significantly after the date of death, there may be issues as to how to value the interest.

In the case of deaths on or after 1 October 2014, the matter is dealt with as follows in section 9:

> the value of the deceased's severable share of the property concerned is taken for the purposes of this Act to be the value that the share would have had at the date of the hearing of the application for an order under section 2 had the share been severed immediately before the deceased's death, unless the court orders that the share is to be valued at a different date

It can be difficult to ascertain whether or not particular assets are held jointly. In relation to life policies, compare *Powell v Osbourne* [1993] 1 FLR 1001 (CA), *Murphy v Holland; Holland v Murphy and Others* [2003] EWCA Civ 1862, [2004] 1 FCR 1 and *Lim v Walia* [2014] EWCA Civ 1076).

Section 9(4) expressly provides that for the purposes of that section there may be a joint tenancy of a *chose in action*.

26.6.3   Nominated property

Nominated property is part of the net estate if it is nominated 'in accordance with the provisions of any enactment'.

Clearly, a nomination under primary legislation is included, but is any other sort of nomination?

Howard v Cairnes (1983) 4 FLR 225 held that a nomination made in relation to a private employment scheme was not within the section: the term 'enactment' is inapt to describe a mere trust deed which is the creature of a contract between employer and employee.

In *Goenka v Goenka and Others* [2014] EWHC 2966 (Ch), HHJ Hodge QC (sitting as a Judge of the High Court) had to consider whether a nomination under the National Health Service Pension Scheme Regulations 1995 (SI 1995/300) (which were made under powers conferred by the Superannuation Act 1972) was made under an 'enactment'. The Court of Appeal had held in *Rathbone v Bundock* [1962] QB 260 that whether the term 'enactment' extended to secondary legislation depended on context.

HHJ Hodge QC said he could see no reason why Parliament should have wished to discriminate between a nomination made under primary legislation and one made under secondary legislation. There was no immediate statutory context within the 1975 Act, to lead the court to view the reference to any 'enactment' as not extending to secondary legislation by way of statutory instrument. He, therefore, concluded that, since the nomination was made pursuant to rules made under a power conferred by a statute, the nomination should be regarded as made 'in accordance with the provisions of any enactment' and within section 8.

26.7   ORDERS WHICH THE COURT MAY MAKE

The types of order available to the court are set out in section 2(1) as follows.

26.7.1   Periodical payments

An order for periodical payments may direct a specified part of the net estate to be set aside or appropriated for making periodical payments for the term specified from the income (section 2(3)). Only that needed to produce the income at the date of the order can be set aside. In the case of a former spouse, an order ceases to have effect on that person's remarriage (section 19(2)). In any other case, the court must decide the date of termination when it makes the order.

The amount of the payments may be expressed as a specified sum to be paid at regular intervals; or may be the income of the whole or a proportion of the net estate; or may be the whole of the income from a specific part of the net estate; or may be determined in any other way the court thinks fit.

During the term of the order an application for its variation may be made by the original recipient, a former applicant, a beneficiary of the estate or the personal representatives of the estate.

On an application for variation the court considers all the circumstances of the case and any change in the circumstances that existed at the time of the original order (section 6(7)). Only property already set aside for the purposes of paying periodical payments ('relevant property') can be the subject of the variation. The court cannot increase the amount of relevant property set aside.

Periodical payments are unpopular with courts because they are expensive to provide (requiring trust machinery to operate them) and lack finality. Lump sums are more commonly ordered.

26.7.2   Lump sum payment

A lump sum order cannot generally be varied but, where it is made payable by instalments, the number, amount and dates for payments of those instalments may be the subject of an application for variation (section 7).

26.7.3   Transfer of property

The court may order the transfer of a particular asset to an applicant, which may be preferable to a sale. Once made, the order cannot be varied.

26.7.4   Settlement of property

A settlement of property order is useful in respect of minors or persons under a disability. Such an order cannot subsequently be varied.

26.7.5   Acquisition of property for transfer or settlement

The court has power to order the acquisition of a specified property using the assets of the net estate. That property may be either transferred to or settled on an applicant. Again, the order cannot be varied. This can be a useful power, particularly where minors are concerned, as it allows the court to direct the purchase of a dwelling house.

26.7.6   Variation of marriage settlements

The court may vary any ante-nuptial or post-nuptial settlement so as to benefit the surviving spouse of the marriage or any person who was treated by the deceased as a child of that marriage. Once the order varying the settlement has been made, that order cannot itself be varied.

A provision in a pension scheme allowing an employee to direct benefits to a spouse may mean that the scheme can be regarded as a nuptial settlement for this purpose (see *Brooks v Brooks* [1996] AC 375). Given that, for many people, pension rights are one of their most valuable assets, this is clearly an important provision.

Similarly, the court can, for the benefit of the surviving civil partner, or any child of both the civil partners, or any person who was treated by the deceased as a child of the family in relation to that civil partnership, vary a settlement made:

(i)   during the subsistence of a civil partnership formed by the deceased, or
(ii)   in anticipation of the formation of a civil partnership by the deceased,

on the civil partners.

26.7.7   Variation of trust of property

The court can make an order varying for the applicant's benefit the trusts on which the deceased's estate is held (whether arising under the will, or the law relating to intestacy, or both). This is a new provision introduced by the Inheritance and Trustees' Powers Act 2014.

26.8   INTERIM PAYMENTS

An interim order in favour of an applicant may be made under section 5 if it appears to the court that:

(i) the applicant is in immediate need of financial assistance but it is not yet possible to determine what order (if any) should be made; and

(ii) the property forming part of the deceased's net estate is or can be made available to meet the needs of the applicant.

Inevitably, the court is cautious about making such an order as the funds will be lost to the estate and the applicant may not be successful. See *T v V* [2019] EWHC 214 (Fam), which made this point. However, in *Weisz v Weisz and Others* [2019] EWHC 3101 (Fam), Francis J said that the position was different where it was clear that the applicant was going to achieve something from the litigation.

26.9 ANTI-AVOIDANCE

Sections 10 and 11 of the Act enable the court to prevent lifetime dispositions reducing the deceased's net estate for the purpose of evading the Act. Section 10 covers dispositions made:

(i) after 31 March 1976 and less than 6 years before the date of the death of the deceased; and

(ii) with the intention of defeating an application under the Act; and

(iii) for less than full valuable consideration.

A 'disposition' for this purpose includes any conveyance of property or payment of money (including insurance premiums), but not a statutory nomination, *donatio mortis causa* or appointment.

Section 11 of the Act covers a contract:

(i) entered into after 31 March 1976; and

(ii) under which the deceased agreed to leave money or other property by will or agreed that money or other property would be paid or transferred to any person from their estate; and

(iii) the deceased made the contract with the intention of defeating an application under the Act; and

(iv) full valuable consideration was not given or promised.

There is no time limit to the operation of section 11.

The court may order the donee of a disposition under section 10 to provide such sum of money or other property as it may specify, subject to the following limitations:

(i) if the donee was given money, they cannot be ordered to provide more than was paid to them by the deceased less any inheritance tax borne by them;

(ii)   if the donee was given property, they cannot be ordered to provide more than the value of the property at the date of death of the deceased (or the date of the disposal of the property if disposed of before the deceased's death) less any inheritance tax borne by them in respect of the property.

Where the testator has entered into a contract caught under section 11 and, before the date of the application, the personal representatives have not transferred money or property to the donee in accordance with the provisions of the contract, the court may order them to make no payment, or no further payment, or a reduced payment (section 11(2)(ii)).

If, before the date of the application, the personal representatives of the deceased have already transferred money or property to the donee in accordance with the provisions of the contract, the court may order the donee to provide such sum of money or other property as it thinks fit (section 11(2)(i)).

The court can make orders only to the extent that the property transferred under the contract exceeds the value of any consideration given. The valuation is to be made at the date of the hearing (section 11(3)).

Where a donee has died, the court has the same powers against the donee's personal representatives until the property has been distributed by those personal representatives. At that time the court's power ceases (section 12(4)). Orders to provide property may also be made (subject to some limitations) against trustees to whom property has been transferred by the deceased with the intention of defeating an application (section 13(1) and (3)).

In *Hanbury v Hanbury* [1999] 2 FLR 255, the court used sections 9 and 10 to recover more than £50,000 of assets from the deceased's second wife to make provision for his mentally and physically disabled daughter for whom he had made virtually no provision.

26.10   TAX IMPLICATIONS

Where the court makes an order for provision from the estate, the property shall for the purposes of inheritance tax be treated as if it had on the deceased's death devolved subject to the provisions of the order (see Inheritance Tax Act 1984, section 146).

It is desirable that any provision made by the court should be efficient from an inheritance tax point of view. Section 2(4) gives the court power to order such consequential and supplemental provisions as it thinks necessary or expedient, to give effect to an order, or to secure that the order operates fairly as between one beneficiary and another. It can, in particular, but without prejudice to the generality of the subsection:

(i)   order a transfer of property from the deceased's net estate;
(ii)   vary the disposition of the deceased's estate; or
(iii) confer on the trustees of any property which is the subject of an order under section 2 such powers as appear to the court to be necessary or expedient.

The comments made by the Court of Appeal in *Re Goodchild; Goodchild v Goodchild* [1997] 1 WLR 1216, however, suggest that the courts are not always prepared to exercise their powers under section 2(4). At first instance the court made an order, on 20 February 1996, directing that the testator's will was to be treated as if it had always left £185,000 to trustees to pay the income to the deceased's second wife until her death or until 1 March 1996, whichever was the earlier, and, subject thereto, for the applicant absolutely. The purpose of the order was to have the benefit of the spouse exemption and avoid the inheritance tax which would have been payable had the property been left directly to the applicant. The applicant took the risk of an inheritance tax liability arising on the death of the second wife if she died within 7 years of the termination of the interest in possession. The Court of Appeal expressed some reservations about the use of variation orders under section 2(4) to obtain a tax benefit, and suggested that if such orders were made, 'the grounds on which it is thought to be authorised by section 2(4) should be clearly demonstrated for the consents and wishes of the parties are not enough'.

There is no corresponding provision in the Taxation of Chargeable Gains Act 1992. However, Inheritance (Provision for Family and Dependants) Act 1975, section 19 provides that orders of the court made under section 2 of the Act are deemed to have applied from the date of death for all purposes. There is therefore no capital gains tax disposal as a result of the making of the order and assets will vest in the persons named in the order at market value at the date of death. However, this is not the case where a compromise settlement is agreed by the parties. The court will normally stay or dismiss the proceedings on terms scheduled to the order (a 'Tomlin order').

If the order includes a positive requirement to carry out the terms of the compromise, HM Revenue & Customs accepts that this is an order within section 2 of the 1975 Act (see HM Revenue & Customs, *Capital Gains Tax Manual* at CG31810, available at www.gov.uk/hmrc-internal-manuals/capital-gains-manual). However, this is normally only done in cases where the interests of minors are involved. If the order merely permits the parties to carry out the terms of the agreement, it has no retrospective effect. If the agreement is reached within 2 years of death it may be possible to treat it as a variation of the disposition of the estate having retrospective effect under Taxation of Chargeable Gains Act 1992, section 62(6). Where this is not possible, there is a disposal and acquisition by the parties (see the *Capital Gains Tax Manual* at CG31900 *et seq*).

26.11 MINIMISING THE CHANCES OF A SUCCESSFUL CLAIM

A testator who wants to leave nothing to a person who is within a category of potential claimants should always leave a statement of reasons. It is preferable to do this as a separate document rather than to include it in the will itself which is a public document.

26A DECLARATIONS UNDER THE INHERITANCE (PROVISION FOR FAMILY AND DEPENDANTS) ACT 1975 OF REASONS FOR MAKING NO PROVISION

I DECLARE that the reason[s] I am making no [further] provision for:

(a) my [spouse] [civil partner] [name] is that by a deed of separation dated ... and made between [parties] I covenanted to pay [him] [her] a clear annuity of £ ... during [his] [her] life and such annuity will after my death be a charge upon my estate.

(b) my life partner [name] with whom I am living are set out in a statement signed by me and deposited with ....

(c) my present [spouse] [civil partner] [name] or the minor children of my present marriage/civil partnership is that the whole of my real and personal estate consists of property inherited from my first [spouse] [civil partner] [name] and I consider that the whole of the beneficial interest therein should go to the children of my first marriage/civil partnership [more especially as my present [spouse] [civil partner] has adequate means].

(d) my [son] [daughter] [name] is that [he] [she] left home many years ago and I consider that my [son] [daughter] [name] with whom I have made my home for many years has a much greater claim on me.

(e) my minor [son] [daughter] [name] is that [he] [she] is already well provided for under the will of [his] [her] godfather the late [name] while my other children have no means of their own.

26B DECLARATION UNDER THE INHERITANCE (PROVISION FOR FAMILY AND DEPENDANTS) ACT 1975 OF REASON FOR MAKING NO FURTHER PROVISION

I DECLARE that my reason for making no greater provision in this my will for [name] with whom I have lived for many years is that [he] [she] has [his] [her] own financial resources and has never been maintained by me during my lifetime.

Testators may reduce the chance of an application being successful if they leave the estate to a beneficiary with competing needs rather than to charity.

If testators are willing to leave the potential claimant something, they may consider a forfeiture clause. There had been fears that such clauses were void for public policy reasons as seeking to oust the jurisdiction of the court, but in *Nathan v Leonard* [2002] EWHC 1701 (Ch), [2003] 1 WLR 827, [2002] WTLR 1061, the court said that, in principle, such a condition is valid and is not contrary to public policy. The condition does not *prevent* a claim being made. The claimant is free to bring the claim if he is prepared to take the risk of receiving nothing from the court and losing the entitlement under the will.

26C FORFEITURE CLAUSE

> I DECLARE that any person who would otherwise benefit under my Will but who:
> (a) institutes any proceedings to set aside or contest the validity of my Will or any of its provisions, or
> (b) lodges any formal objections to the issuing of a grant of a representation, or
> (c) brings any proprietary estoppel claim, or
> (d) claims under the Inheritance (Provision for Family and Dependants) Act 1975 in relation to my Estate
> shall immediately be excluded from receiving any benefit under my Will and my Will shall take effect as if no provision had been made for the benefit of that person.

For an alternative version of a similar clause, see Precedent 25B.

In cases where the client is not willing to give anything to the family member directly, perhaps because of problems with alcohol or drug abuse, a discretionary trust with a clear letter of wishes is probably the best course.

Chapter 27

Inheritance Tax

This chapter can, of necessity, only provide a summary of the principles of inheritance tax. Readers requiring more detail should consult one of the specialist tax textbooks.

27.1 THE CHARGE TO TAX

Inheritance tax is charged not only on the assets in an estate at the time of a person's death, but also upon some lifetime transfers.

The rate of tax charged depends on the 'cumulative total' of the assets of the transferor at the time of the transfer. There is a nil rate band, and transfers which fall within that band are taxed at 0%.

The Finance Act 2010 'froze' the nil rate band at £325,000 until 2014–15; it was frozen again until 2020–21 to help fund the new RNRB and frozen again until 2026–27 as a result of the cost of the COVID-19 pandemic.

Some lifetime transfers (known as 'chargeable' transfers) are chargeable to tax at the time of the transfer; others (known as 'potentially exempt' transfers) are chargeable only if the transferor dies within 7 years of making the transfer.

27.2 TRANSFERS OF VALUE

Inheritance Tax Act 1984, section 3(1) states:

> A transfer of value is a disposition made by a person (the transferor) as a result of which the value of the estate immediately after the disposition is less than it would be but for the disposition.

'Disposition' is not defined. The term includes an omission to exercise a right (section 3(3)) and a disposition effected by 'associated operations' (section 272).

Note that the transfer of value is measured by the loss to the estate. This is sometimes overlooked.

Examples

(1) Fred has 52 of the 100 shares in a company and, therefore, has control. If he gives away two shares, he loses control. The value transferred is not the value of two shares, it is the reduction in value of Fred's estate caused by the loss of the two shares and the loss of control.

(2) Freda has a house worth £400,000. She gives her daughter a 50% interest in the house. The value transferred is not £200,000. It is the difference in market value between a whole house and a 50% share of a house.

Certain events, for example, death and the termination of an interest in possession, are 'deemed' to be transfers of value (see section 3(4)). On death, a person is deemed to make a transfer of value of the value of their estate immediately before death (see section 4(1)). In the case of settled property, a beneficiary entitled to certain types of interest in possession in settled property is treated for inheritance tax purposes as if beneficially entitled to the property in which he has the interest. See Chapter 29.

Section 5(1) of the 1984 Act provides that, when determining the value transferred by a transfer of value, 'a person's estate is the aggregate of all the property to which he is beneficially entitled'.

Under section 5(2), property over which the transferor has a power of appointment or disposition by will is also included in the term 'estate'. 'Property' includes all rights and interests of any description (section 272).

27.3 VALUE TRANSFERRED

We saw at **27.2** that the deceased is deemed to have made a transfer of value equal to the value of their estate immediately before their death (Inheritance Tax Act 1984, section 4(1). The value of property comprised in the estate is the price which the property might reasonably be expected to fetch if sold on the open market at that time, provided that such price is not assumed to be reduced on the ground that the whole property is to be placed on the market at the same time (section 160). In other words, the value will be the open market value of the property immediately before the death.

There are special rules for taking into account changes in value which occur by reason of the death, for example to life policies (Inheritance Tax Act 1984, section 171), for valuing related property (see section 161) and for sale of land and qualifying investments for less than probate value (sections 178 to 198).

It is important that assets are valued correctly as HM Revenue & Customs has power to impose penalties where there are careless or deliberate errors in accounts. Valuers should be instructed to value at open market value and, in the case of land, to include a value for any hope or development value that may exist. Where a value has to be estimated because there is a need to obtain a grant before the value can be finalised, it is important to identify the value clearly as an estimate and to inform HM Revenue & Customs of the reason for the use of an estimate (see *Robertson v IRC* 2002 STC (SCD) 182 and *Cairns v RCC* [2009] UKFTT 67 (TC), [2009] STC (SCD) 479). See also the guidance in HM Revenue & Customs, *Inheritance Tax Toolkit: IHT400 (2022 to 2023)* at page 16 (available at www.gov.uk/government/publications/hmrc-inheritance-tax-toolkit).

27.4 TRANSFERS WHICH ARE NOT TRANSFERS OF VALUE

Not all dispositions are transfers of value, and some dispositions are deemed not to be transfers of value even though the transferor's estate is reduced. Inheritance tax is chargeable on transfers of value only.

27.4.1 Transfers without gratuitous intent

Inheritance Tax Act 1984, section 10(1) states that:

> A disposition is not a transfer of value if it is shown that it was not intended, and was not made in a transaction intended, to confer any gratuitous benefit on any person and either—
>
> (a) that it was made in a transaction at arm's length between persons not connected with each other, or
> (b) that it was such as might be expected to be made in a transaction at arm's length between persons not connected with each other.

If a transferee provides full value to the transferor then there can be no transfer of value as there has been no net reduction in the transferor's estate. But section 10(1) applies to sales of unquoted shares or debentures only if it can be shown that the sale price was freely negotiated or was equivalent to a price that could have been expected to be freely negotiated at the time of sale.

The section was considered by the Supreme Court in *RCC v Parry and Others* [2020] UKSC 35, [2021] 1 All ER 365. The Supreme Court rejected HM Revenue & Customs' argument that all that was necessary was a transaction which objectively transferred a benefit. The question is not simply, 'Was a gratuitous benefit conferred on any person?' The search is for what the disponor *intended*, and, in particular, for whether the disponor intended to confer any gratuitous benefit on any person.

27.4.2 Gifts for family maintenance

Inheritance Tax Act 1984, section 11 sets out various situations in which a lifetime disposition made for the maintenance of another person will not be treated as a transfer of value if:

(1) … it is made by one party to a marriage or civil partnership in favour of the other party or of a child of either party and is—

  (a) for the maintenance of the other party, or
  (b) for the maintenance, education or training of the child for a period ending not later than the year in which he attains the age of eighteen or, after attaining that age, ceases to undergo full-time education or training.

(2) … it is made in favour of a child who is not in the care of a parent of his and is for his maintenance, education or training for a period ending not later than the year in which—

  (a) he attains the age of eighteen, or
  (b) after attaining that age he ceases to undergo full-time education or training;

  but paragraph (b) above applies only if before attaining that age the child has for substantial periods been in the care of the person making the disposition.

(3) … it is made in favour of a dependent relative of the person making the disposition and is a reasonable provision for his care or maintenance.
(4) … it is made in favour of an illegitimate child of the person making the disposition and is for the maintenance, education or training of the child for a period ending not later than the year in which he attains the age of eighteen or, after attaining that age, ceases to undergo full-time education or training.

'Child' includes a step-child and an adopted child.

The main application of section 11 is to dispositions made on divorce or dissolution of a civil partnership, although such transfers may also fall within section 10. The section will also cover a disposition in favour of a child of a former marriage or civil partnership if the disposition is made on the occasion of the dissolution or annulment of the marriage or civil partnership, or if it varies a disposition so made.

The test of 'reasonable' in (3) above is not all or nothing. Where a disposition exceeds what is required for 'maintenance', the disposition can be apportioned so that only the excess will be a transfer of value. In *McKelvey v RCC* [2008] STC (SCD) 944, an adult daughter transferred assets to her elderly mother to provide for her care and died within 7 years. The amount given was clearly for the purposes of maintenance and the only issue was whether it was excessive. The test is objective and, as the amount given was more than was reasonably necessary, it was apportioned. The portion that fell within the section was not a transfer of value.

Where a person is terminally ill and wants to make tax effective provision for minor children falling within the terms of the section, it is preferable to make use of section 11 to make some lifetime provision rather than leaving everything by will. A transfer can be made to a lifetime settlement expressed to be for the maintenance, education and training of the child. The trustees must have power to use capital as well as income and the trust must be drafted to terminate when the child attains 18 or completes full-time education or training, whichever is the later.

27.4.3   Retirement benefit schemes

Section 12 provides that a disposition is not a transfer of value if it is a contribution under a registered pension scheme, a qualifying non-UK pension scheme or a section 615(3) scheme in respect of an employee of the person making the disposition. Failing to exercise rights in connection with a registered pension scheme when under age 75 will not be a transfer of value (see **27.5**).

27.4.4   Agricultural tenancies

Section 16 provides that a grant of an agricultural tenancy for agricultural purposes in the United Kingdom, the Channel Islands or the Isle of Man is not treated as a transfer of value provided it is made for full consideration in money or money's worth.

27.5 CHARGEABLE TRANSFERS

Lifetime transfers, unless exempt, become chargeable to tax if the transferor dies within 7 years of the transfer. Lifetime transfers to relevant property settlements are immediately chargeable to inheritance tax at half the death rates. Credit is given for tax already paid in the event of death within 7 years. Inheritance tax is also charged on the estate at death.

Thus, on a transferor's death, the starting point for tax assessment is the transferor's cumulative total of chargeable transfers during the preceding 7 years, together with the value of their estate immediately before death. Generally, the value of the estate is reduced by taking into account any liabilities outstanding at the transferor's death (section 5(3)).

By Inheritance Tax Act 1984, section 160:

> the value at any time of any property shall for the purposes of this Act be the price which the property might reasonably be expected to fetch if sold in the open market at that time; but that price shall not be assumed to be reduced on the ground that the whole property is to be placed on the market at one and the same time.

The value of property can be substantially reduced by imposing conditions as to its disposal and thereby avoiding tax by artificial restrictions. Section 163 provides that where, by a contract made at any time, the right to dispose of any property has been excluded or restricted, then for the purposes of determining the value of the property for the first chargeable transfer after that time, the exclusion or restriction will reduce the value of the property only to the extent that consideration in money or money's worth was given for it. In determining the value transferred, expenses incurred by the transferor in making the transfer are to be left out of account (section 163).

Inheritance Tax Act 1984, section 3(3) provides that where the value of a person's (A's) estate is diminished and another person's (B's) is increased by A's omission to exercise a right, A is treated as having made a disposition at the latest time when they could have exercised that right, unless it can be shown that the omission was not deliberate. In *RCC v Parry and Others* [2020] UKSC 35, [2021] 1 All ER 365, the Supreme Court considered how section 3(3) should be interpreted. Lady Black said at [94] that it was not appropriate to adopt a narrow and legalistic approach to the section. The question should be, 'Was the omission the operative cause of the increase in the other person's estate?'

Section 3(3) could be significant in relation to pension lump sums. Members of registered pension schemes who choose not to take their pensions, thereby causing enhanced death benefit to be paid to their beneficiaries, are omitting to exercise a right. This was one of the points in issue in *RCC v Parry and Others* [2020] UKSC 35, [2021] 1 All ER 365. The deceased had omitted to draw benefits from her pension scheme and in a letter of wishes had nominated her sons to take the death benefit. Her personal representatives argued unsuccessfully that there was a material break in the chain of causation between the deceased's omission and the increase in value in her sons' estates, by virtue of the fact that the payment to the sons resulted from the exercise of a discretion by the pension scheme administrator. Lady Black said at [94] that she did not see the limited discretion of the scheme administrator as breaking the chain connecting the two events. The increase in the sons' estates could also be said to be brought about 'by' the exercise of the administrator's discretion, but that did not preclude a finding that they were increased 'by' the omission.

However, section 12(2ZA) has changed the position in relation to omissions to take pension benefits. It provides that where a member of a registered pension scheme, a qualifying non-UK pension scheme or a section 615(3) scheme omits to exercise pension rights under the pension scheme, section 3(3) above does not apply in relation to the omission. Section 12(2ZA) applies to dispositions made (or treated as made) on or after 6 April 2011.

27.5.1 Potentially exempt transfers

The provisions relating to potentially exempt transfers are contained in Inheritance Tax Act 1984, section 3A (as amended by Finance Act 1986, Schedule 19, paragraph 1).

If certain conditions are satisfied, transfers of value may be potentially exempt from inheritance tax. If the transferor survives for 7 years following the date of the gift, it becomes completely exempt. If the transferor does not survive for the requisite 7 years then the gift is charged to tax on their death, although the amount is reduced if the transferor survives for between for 3 and 7 years. To be a potentially exempt transfer, the conditions to be met are that the gift must be made on or after 18 March 1986, by an individual, to another individual or into a disabled person's trust (see below and **27.5.2**).

Once a potentially exempt transfer has been made for 7 years it becomes fully exempt and is no longer included in the individual's cumulative total of lifetime gifts (Inheritance Tax Act 1984, section 7(4), as amended by Finance Act 1986, Schedule 19, paragraph 2(4)).

If the transferor dies within 7 years of making a potentially exempt transfer, the transfer is liable to tax at the death rate. If, however, the transferor survives more than 3 years after the transfer, only the following percentage of the tax is payable:

(i)   transfer 3 to 4 years before death: 80% of tax is payable;
(ii)   transfer 4 to 5 years before death: 60% of tax is payable;
(iii) transfer 5 to 6 years before death: 40% of tax is payable;
(iv)   transfer 6 to 7 years before death: 20% of tax is payable.

The gift is cumulated with other transfers made in the 7 years preceding the potentially exempt transfer. As the potentially exempt transfer is no longer exempt it affects any other chargeable gifts made after the potentially exempt transfer by increasing the cumulative total on which the charge to tax is based, therefore increasing the inheritance tax payable in respect of subsequent gifts. Similarly, the cumulative total applicable when calculating inheritance tax on the death estate is also increased by the potentially exempt transfer which was made within 7 years of death.

27.5.2   Lifetime chargeable transfers

Since 22 March 2006, all transfers to trusts are lifetime chargeable transfers, unless they are for the benefit of a person who is disabled within the meaning of Inheritance Tax Act 1984, section 89, or created for the settlor's own benefit at a time when the settlor is suffering from a condition that it is reasonable to expect will lead to their becoming disabled within the meaning of section 89.

As mentioned at **27.2**, the value of lifetime gifts is determined by the amount of the reduction of the value of the donor's estate, not the gain to the donee's estate. The gift element of a sale at an undervalue is therefore taxable. Where sales are made to connected persons, the onus is on the taxpayer to show that there is no gratuitous element. Because the tax is primarily payable by the donor of a gift, the tax itself also reduces the value of the estate. Thus, unless the donee agrees with the donor that the former will pay any tax chargeable, the amount of any gift is 'grossed up' to represent the reduction in value, inclusive of the tax. Tax is charged on the grossed up amount, resulting in more tax being payable than would have been on the gift itself.

27.5.3 Transfers made on death

The estate on death

On the death of any person, tax shall be charged as if, immediately before their death, they had made a transfer of value and the value transferred by it had been equal to the value of their estate immediately before their death (Inheritance Tax Act 1984, section 4).

As explained at **27.2**, Inheritance Tax Act 1984, section 5(1) defines a person's estate as 'the aggregate of all the property to which he is beneficially entitled' other than excluded property (excluded property is defined in Inheritance Tax Act 1984, sections 6 and 48 and includes reversionary interests). Section 5(3) states that 'in determining the value of a person's estate at any time his liabilities at that time shall be taken into account except as otherwise provided by this Act'. An increasing number of liabilities have been made non-deductible (see 'Non-deductible debts' below). Although the general rule is that the estate must be valued immediately before death, funeral expenses can be deducted (including a reasonable sum for a 'wake' and the cost of a gravestone).

The following points should be noted:

(i)   property over which the transferor has a general power of appointment is included in their 'estate' unless it is held in a settlement (Inheritance Tax Act 1984, section 5(2));

(ii) the estate includes property in which the deceased had reserved a benefit at the time of their death (see **27.10**);

(iii) the estate includes property which the deceased is deemed to own by virtue of enjoying a qualifying interest in possession (Inheritance Tax Act 1984, section 49(1));

(iv) as the transfer is deemed to occur immediately before the death, the estate includes a share of the deceased in jointly owned property that passes by survivorship to the surviving joint tenants;

(v)   the estate also includes a gift made before death in anticipation of death and conditional upon it occurring (a '*donatio mortis causa*').

Transfers made on death are charged at the death rate. Transfers made within 7 years of death become chargeable at the full death rate, although tapering relief will reduce the tax payable on gifts made more than 3 years before death. In each case, the cumulative total for the 7 years preceding the date of the gift is applied to determine the starting point.

Take, for example, a series of gifts by T who dies on 2 January 2022, assuming that the current tax rates apply throughout the period. No exemptions are available to cover any part of the gifts:

Date of gift	Amount (gross)	Tax at time of gift	Tax on death
1 July 2013	100,000 to A, an individual	PET; no IHT	No IHT; T survived more than 7 years after the gift
2 August 2016	£100,000 to a discretionary settlement	Lifetime chargeable transfer because the donee is not an individual nor a privileged trust. There is no tax to pay because the transfer is within the nil rate band	Recalculate on death. There is nothing to cumulate as the 2013 PET has become fully exempt. There is no tax to pay because the transfer is within the nil rate band. Only £225,000 of the nil rate band is available for later transfers
1 January 2018	£300,000 to B, an individual	PET; no IHT	Recalculate on death. The first £225,000 is within the nil rate band. The remaining £75,000 is taxed at 40%. Taper relief is available as death is more than 4 but less than 5 years after the transfer, so only 60% of the full tax bill is payable
1 January 2019	£250,000 to a discretionary settlement	This is a lifetime chargeable transfer because the donee is not an individual nor a privileged trust. The 2018 PET is initially treated as exempt, so only the 2016 chargeable transfer has to be cumulated. The first £225,000 of the current transfer is within the nil rate band. The remaining £25,000 is taxed at the lifetime rate of 20%	Recalculate on death. Because the 2018 PET has become chargeable, there is no nil rate band available for the current transfer. The whole £250,000 is now chargeable at 40%. Taper relief is available at death more than 3 years but less than 4 years after transfer, so only 80% of the full tax bill is payable. Credit is given for the tax paid at the time of the transfer

Notes: PET = potentially exempt transfer; IHT = inheritance tax.

If, when T dies on 2 January 2022, T's death estate is £100,000, inheritance tax is charged at 40% on the whole of the death estate, as the transfers made within 7 years of death have exhausted the nil rate band at death.

Assets outside the estate

It is good tax planning to try to get assets outside the death estate. The taxpayer may not be sufficiently wealthy to be able to make significant lifetime gifts. However, it may be possible to afford life assurance premiums on a life policy to pay out on the taxpayer's death. The premiums will normally be exempt under the normal expenditure out of income exemption (see **27.7.1**) and if the policy is assigned when first taken out, the value transferred will be nil.

Note that the assignment must be irrevocable if it is to remove the property from the estate. In *Kempe v IRC* [2004] STC (SCD) 467, the deceased had worked in the USA and had taken out a life policy there, the terms of which allowed him to designate beneficiaries, alter a designation, and ensure, if he wished, that the sum assured was paid to his estate by failing to leave a valid designation. It was held that, although he had in his lifetime designated family members to receive the proceeds of the policy, he had a general power of appointment over the policy which, therefore, remained part of his estate under Inheritance Tax Act 1984, section 5(2).

Planning with pension benefits

Death benefits payable under a discretionary pension scheme will normally be outside the estate for inheritance tax purposes as, although the scheme member can nominate a person to receive the death benefit, that nomination is not binding on the scheme trustees or provider; the lump sum is not treated as part of the member's estate so no inheritance tax charge arises.

Although no inheritance tax is payable, in some cases a charge to tax, occasionally referred to as a death tax, arises when benefits are taken.

The changes to the legislation relating to pensions (which take effect for pension fund death benefits payable on or after 6 April 2015) contained in the Taxation of Pensions Act 2014 are important for estate planning purposes. Not only do they allow much more flexibility in the way taxpayers can access their pension funds during their lifetime but, crucially, they allow undrawn pension funds:

- to be passed on;
- more than once; and
- sometimes, completely tax free.

Scheme members can nominate a person to take benefits under a pension scheme. Benefits can be taken either as a lump sum or if the pension scheme permits, the fund can remain within the pension scheme allowing the nominated beneficiary to draw funds from the pension as desired. The tax consequences are different and depend on the age of the pension scheme member at death:

(i) *Death below 75* – there will be no charge to tax on the member's death whether the nominated beneficiary takes a lump sum or the funds remain invested. In the latter case, there will be no charge to tax of any kind as and when the nominated beneficiary draws on the fund.

(ii) *Death at 75 or above* – if a nominated beneficiary takes a lump sum, it will be taxed at their marginal income tax rate. Note that if the lump sum is substantial, this will probably take the nominated beneficiary into the additional rate of tax which is 45%.

If the nominated beneficiary leaves the funds within the pension wrapper and draws an income from the invested funds, they will pay income tax at their marginal rate.

In the case of deaths at 75 or above, unless the nominated beneficiary needs a lump sum for a specific purpose, the income drawdown option is likely to be more attractive. Income can be manipulated to allow the nominated beneficiary to remain in the lower tax bands.

Where funds remain invested on the death of the first nominated beneficiary, that beneficiary can nominate a further beneficiary and so on until the funds are fully withdrawn. On each transfer, the tax position will depend on the age of the person nominating the next beneficiary. In the unlikely event of a series of deaths below 75, the funds could be passed on every time without any tax being payable.
Note that once a lump sum is taken, the link with the pension is broken and the lump sum will simply be a normal part of the beneficiary's estate.

Before the changes to the pension rules, the standard estate planning advice was to set up a lifetime discretionary trust in pilot form and to ask the pension trustees to pay the death benefit to the trust. The sum would then be available to family members but would not be part of their estate for inheritance tax purposes.

This advice is not necessarily correct in the light of the new rules. Payments can only be made to a trust in the form of a lump sum so if the member dies at 75 or over, there will be a charge to tax at 45%.

Within the trust the funds will be subject to the higher rates of income tax and capital gains tax payable by trusts.

Lastly, the funds will be subject to inheritance tax anniversary and exit charges. Because the lump sum is paid from one trust (the original pension trust) to another trust, the funds are treated as remaining in the original trust for inheritance tax purposes (Inheritance Tax Act 1984, section 81). According to the Privy Council in *Air Jamaica Ltd v Charlton* [1999] 1 WLR 1399, as each member joins a pension scheme, a new settlement is created for that member irrespective of when the scheme itself began. In a worst-case scenario, therefore, a 10-year anniversary could fall weeks or days after the death of the member.

In view of all these disadvantages, is there any reason for using a trust? The answer is 'yes'. A trust gives the original member control over what happens to the pension funds.

Example

Janet has the benefit of a substantial pension and dies aged 70. She nominates it to her husband, Ralph, in the expectation that he will leave the funds invested and draw what he needs, leaving any undrawn surplus to their daughter, Naomi.

There is no certainty that Ralph will do this. He might withdraw the whole lot and blow it on a fast car.

He might marry again and nominate the undrawn funds to his new wife who in turn nominates them to her own children and not to Naomi.

Had Janet nominated the lump sum to be paid to a discretionary trust for the benefit of Ralph and Naomi, this could not have happened.

It is possible to avoid the high rates of income tax and capital gains tax payable by trusts by either giving a beneficiary a right to income or lending the trust assets to a beneficiary so that tax is payable at the beneficiary's rates.

It is not possible to avoid the 10-year anniversary charges but, given that the maximum rate of inheritance tax payable on anniversaries is 6%, many people would regard this as a price worth paying to retain some control.

Liabilities

Liabilities are only deductible if incurred for consideration in money or money's worth (Inheritance Tax Act 1984, section 5(5)).

Personal debts of the deceased can only be deducted from their personal estate, and so surplus liabilities cannot be set against property which is deemed to be part of the estate such as property subject to a reservation or property in which the deceased had a qualifying interest in possession (see *St Barbe Green and Another v IRC* [2005] EWHC 14 (Ch)). Once the personal estate is reduced to zero, there can be no further deductions.

Non-deductible debts

(i) *Finance Act 1986, section 103* – so-called 'artificial' debts are non-deductible. The section provides that, when determining the value of a deceased person's estate, a debt incurred by them or incumbrance created by them is not deductible for inheritance tax purposes to the extent that the consideration given for the debt or incumbrance consisted of property derived from the deceased.

Property 'derived from the deceased' means any property which was the subject matter of a disposition by the deceased other than a disposition which does not amount to a transfer of value (such as transfers without gratuitous intent and dispositions for family maintenance).

Example

Dad gives £100,000 to son and subsequently borrows the money back. The £100,000 debt is not deductible when Dad dies.

(ii) *Inheritance Tax Act 1984, section 162A* – liabilities attributable to financing excluded property are non-deductible. Excluded property includes overseas property owned by a person not domiciled in the United Kingdom (see **27.6**).

Example

Alfredo, a non-UK domiciliary, raised a loan on his London home to acquire non-UK-situated property which will be excluded property and so outside the UK tax net. The liability charged against the UK property will be ignored in calculating the inheritance tax liability of Alfredo's estate

---

The date the liability was incurred is irrelevant. The non-deductibility rule applies where death (or other chargeable event) occurs on or after 17 July 2013.

(iii) *Inheritance Tax Act 1984, section 162AA* – liabilities attributable to financing non-residents' foreign currency accounts are non-deductible. This amendment has effect in relation to transfers of value made, or treated as made, on or after 17 July 2014.

(iv) *Inheritance Tax Act 1984, section 162B* – liabilities attributable to financing property eligible for business or agricultural property relief or woodlands relief. This amendment was introduced to prevent a common tax-saving arrangement by which an elderly taxpayer would raise a mortgage on (say) their main residence using the proceeds to purchase an AIM portfolio which will, after 2 years, qualify for 100% business property relief.

In the case of liabilities incurred on or after 6 April 2013, the liability is treated as reducing the value of the relievable property (in effect it becomes a charge on that property) so that it is only the excess value (if any) which is deducted against other assets. These rules apply to liabilities incurred on and after 6 April 2013, although to stop a tax-saving manoeuvre if an existing loan agreement is varied on or after that date to make additional funds available, the additional liability is treated as having been incurred on the date the agreement was varied.

(v) *Inheritance Tax Act 1984, section 175A* – in valuing the estate on death, a liability is only deductible if 'it is discharged on or after death, out of the estate, in money or money's worth'. In other cases when the liability is not discharged, a liability is only deductible where 'there is a real commercial reason for the liability or the part not being discharged' and it must not be left outstanding as part of arrangements for 'the main purpose, or one of the main purposes' of which is to secure a 'tax advantage'. 'Tax' includes income tax and capital gains tax.

Discharging 'out of the estate' includes the situation where the personal representatives borrow money to discharge the liability. The date the liability was incurred is irrelevant. The restriction applies where death (or other chargeable event) occurs on or after 17 July 2013.

There was concern as to how the section 175A restriction would operate in practice: in completing Form IHT400, would a deduction only be allowed for a liability which has then been discharged? But until a grant has been obtained it is usually not possible to pay off the deceased's debts. Did that mean that it would be impossible to deduct utility bills and similar mundane liabilities until after payment?

HM Revenue & Customs guidance (see *Inheritance Tax Manual* at IHTM28027, available at www.hmrc.gov.uk/manuals/ihtmanual) says that the starting assumption is that all commercial liabilities (such as utility bills, credit card bills, council tax, payments due to HM Revenue & Customs, outstanding care fees, professional fees to the date of death, overpaid pension, payments for goods and services) will be repaid and will make no enquiries as to their payment. So, unless the personal representatives are aware that a liability is not going to be repaid, the Form IHT400 Notes allow the personal representatives to include all the deceased's liabilities when completing the form.

Where non-arm's-length liabilities are deducted (e.g. a loan from a nil rate band discretionary trust to a surviving spouse), HM Revenue & Customs will ask for evidence that the money has been repaid out of the estate.

27.6 EXCLUDED PROPERTY

Where property is 'excluded' property it does not form part of an individual's estate on death for inheritance tax purposes, neither is a lifetime transfer of excluded property either a chargeable or a potentially exempt transfer. But where a lifetime transfer of *excluded* property gives rise to a reduction in the value of the donor's non-excluded property, then that reduction is treated as a potentially exempt transfer or a chargeable transfer, as appropriate (Inheritance Tax Act 1984, section 3(2)).

The most common examples of excluded property are (Inheritance Tax Act 1984, section 48(1)):

(i)   most property situated outside the United Kingdom and owned by a person whose domicile is outside the United Kingdom (Inheritance Tax Act 1984, section 6(1));

(ii)   settled property situated outside the United Kingdom where the settlor was domiciled outside the United Kingdom at the date they created the settlement unless one of two anti-avoidance provisions applies:

–   a person domiciled in the United Kingdom has, at any time, had an interest in possession in it, and that interest arose from a disposition in money or money's worth made on or after 5 December 2005 (Inheritance Tax Act 1984, section 48(3), (3B), (3C)); or

–   a person formerly domiciled in the United Kingdom but who has obtained a domicile of choice elsewhere and who has created a settlement non-UK domiciled, returns to the United Kingdom and becomes an FDR: see below – the trust ceases to be excluded property while the settlor is an FDR (Inheritance Tax Act 1984, section 267).

(iii) reversionary interests on settled property provided that:

–   the interest is vested in neither the settlor nor their spouse or civil partner; and

–   the interest has not been acquired for money or money's worth; and

–   the interest is not expectant on a lease for life at a nominal rent.

Note that a person can be deemed domiciled for inheritance tax purposes in certain circumstances when they would not be domiciled in the United Kingdom under the general law. These include being 'long term' resident in the United Kingdom. The period is 17 out of the previous 20 years until 5 April 2017 and, as from 6 April 2017, 15 of the previous 20 years (see Inheritance Tax Act 1984, section 267). A person will also be deemed domiciled in the United Kingdom if they are an FDR. A person is an FDR if they were born in the United Kingdom, had a domicile of origin in the United Kingdom, acquired a domicile of choice elsewhere and then became resident in the United Kingdom. The deemed domicile takes effect for inheritance tax purposes in the tax year following the year in which they became resident. Residence is determined as for the purposes of income tax (section 267(4)).

27.7 EXEMPTIONS AND RELIEFS

Where a transfer, whether lifetime or on death, is exempt from inheritance tax, it is not included in the individual's cumulative total assets. Where potentially exempt transfers become chargeable on the death of the donor within 7 years, the appropriate lifetime exemption may be applied to the transfer.

27.7.1 Exemptions and reliefs: lifetime transfers only

Annual exemption

Under Inheritance Tax Act 1984, section 19 an individual may make lifetime transfers of up to £3,000 in any tax year without liability to tax. The value of the transfer is not grossed up (see **27.5.2**). The exemption may be carried forward for 1 year only in so far as it is not used. Potentially exempt transfers are ignored for the purposes of the exemption but, if the potentially exempt transfers become chargeable, the annual exemptions are taken into account when re-assessing the inheritance tax payable on those transfers at the donor's death. The exemption is applied to non-potentially-exempt transfers in priority to potentially exempt transfers that become chargeable subsequently, regardless of the date order of the transfers. Both parties to a marriage have full individual exemptions.

Small gifts

Under section 20, outright gifts of up to £250 to any one person are exempt from tax.

Normal expenditure out of income

Under section 21, lifetime gifts paid by a donor out of income which form part of the donor's usual expenditure are exempt provided the donor is left with sufficient income to maintain their usual standard of living.

The most common application of this exemption is the payment by the donor of premiums for a life policy taken out on their own life for the benefit of another, or others, such as their children. The premium payments, although gifts to the donee, are exempt and the policy proceeds pass directly to the children without forming part of the donor's estate and without being liable to inheritance tax. The exemption may also cover regular allowances made to the donor's children during the donor's lifetime.

To be part of normal expenditure, it must be shown either that there was a settled pattern of gifts (such as a £1,000 Christmas present each year) or that the transfer was made under a legal obligation to make regular payments, such as a deed of covenant or the regular payment of life assurance premiums or that the giver intended to make a series of gifts from income. In *Bennett v IRC* [1995] STC 54, shares which produced a small income were held on trust for the deceased's widow for life. In 1987, the trustees sold the shares and this resulted in a great increase in the income of the trust. In 1989, the life tenant instructed the trustees to give her sons all the income of the trust which was surplus to her requirements. On 14 February 1989, the trustees gave £9,300 to each son. On 5 February 1990, the trustees gave £60,000 to each son. On 20 February 1990, the life tenant died. It was held that the gifts were exempt under the normal expenditure out of income exemption. There was a settled pattern of expenditure. Such a pattern may be established by a sequence of payments or by proof of prior commitment.

The decision in *Bennett v IRC* is to be contrasted with that in *Nadin v IRC* [1997] STC (SCD) 107, where the deceased made various gifts to the family between 1988 and 1993. It was held that the exemption did not apply because there was no evidence of prior commitment and no settled pattern of expenditure.

In *McDowall's Executors v IRC* [2004] STC (SCD) 22, a commitment to distribute future surplus income was held to be sufficient. An attorney made gifts on behalf of his mentally incapacitated father-in-law, Mr McDowall. The gifts were, in fact, held to be void as outside his powers, but the special commissioner considered the question whether, had they been valid, the normal expenditure exemption would have applied. The attorney declared that he was going to use surplus income to make gifts to Mr McDowall's children. He had the chance to make only one set of payments of £12,000 to each of the children before Mr McDowall died. The Commissioner held that the attorney had made a commitment to make payments; the first payments demonstrated that the commitment was being implemented; and, but for Mr McDowall's death, the attorney would have continued to make similar, even if much smaller, payments. The payments in issue were particularly substantial because of the build-up of excess income in previous years.

Gifts made in consideration of marriage or formation of a civil partnership

Section 22 provides family members with an opportunity to make tax-free gifts to a couple who are marrying or forming a civil partnership. The following one-off gifts are exempt:

(i)   gifts of up to £5,000 by a parent of the prospective bride or groom or civil partner (section 22(1)(a));
(ii) gifts of up to £2,500 by a grandparent of the prospective bride or groom or civil partner or by a remoter lineal ancestor (section 22(1)(b) and (2)(b));
(iii) gifts of £2,500 between the prospective bride and groom or civil partners and *vice versa* (section 22(1)(b) and (2)(c)); and
(iv) any other gift to the prospective bride or groom up to the value of £1,000 (section 22(1)(c)).

27.7.2   Exemptions and reliefs: both lifetime transfers and death transfers

Transfers between spouses or between civil partners

Transfers between spouses and between civil partners are exempt from inheritance tax provided the gift has immediate effect (section 18). Such gifts include gifts settled on a spouse or civil partner for life.

The only limit arises where the donor spouse or civil partner is domiciled in the United Kingdom and the recipient is not. In such a case, section 18(2) as originally written limited the amount of the exemption to £55,000 in total. In October 2012, the European Commission formally requested the United Kingdom to review the exemption on the grounds that the £55,000 limit was discriminatory. This was followed by amending legislation in the Finance Act 2013. The amendments were not limited to EU spouses.

There are two changes:

(i) Section 18(2) is amended to link the exemption to the level of the nil rate band applying at the date of death of the recipient spouse or civil partner.
(ii) A non-domiciled spouse or civil partner can elect to be treated as UK domiciled in order to benefit from an unrestricted spouse exemption on gifts from the domiciled spouse or civil partner (inserted as Inheritance Tax Act 1984, sections 267ZA and 267ZB).

HM Revenue & Customs has produced guidance which is found in the *Inheritance Tax Manual* at IHTM13040–13049, available at www.hmrc.gov.uk/manuals/ihtmanual.

There is a downside to making an election as the worldwide estate of the previously non-domiciled spouse is brought into the inheritance tax net. Not only does this mean that inheritance tax will be payable if they die while the election remains in force, but also gifts made after the date the election comes into effect are potentially brought within the inheritance tax charge. As a result, the election should not be exercised without careful thought as to whether it will be advantageous.

There are two types of election (Inheritance Tax Act 1984, section 267ZA):

- *A lifetime election* – made by the non-domiciled spouse or civil partner during the lifetime of the other partner.
- *A death election* – made either by a surviving non-domiciled spouse or civil partner following the death of the UK domiciled partner, or by the personal representatives of the non-UK domiciled partner.

The death election must be made within 2 years of the death of the spouse or such longer period as an officer of HM Revenue & Customs may in the particular case allow.

Gifts to political parties

Inheritance Tax Act 1984, section 24, as amended by the Finance Act 1988, makes all gifts to political parties wholly exempt from inheritance tax (see Chapter 5).

Gifts to charities and national institutions

Gifts to charities are totally exempt from inheritance tax whenever made and regardless of amount (section 23). Similarly, gifts to certain named institutions, including certain museums, the National Trust, government departments, local authorities and universities in the United Kingdom, are also exempt under section 25.

Heritage property

Inheritance Tax Act 1984, sections 30 to 35, as amended, make provision for inheritance tax on 'heritage property' to be postponed provided undertakings are given to take reasonable steps for its preservation, to secure reasonable access by the public and, in the case of category 1 items, to keep the property in the United Kingdom. Property must be designated by the Treasury as falling into one of the categories set out in section 31(1):

(i)   items of pre-eminent national, scientific, historic or artistic interest; or
(ii) land of outstanding scenic, historic or scientific interest; or
(iii) buildings of outstanding historic or architectural interest and their amenity land and chattels historically associated with such buildings.

The Finance Act 1998 inserted a new section 31(FA) and (FB) into the Inheritance Tax Act 1984 to ensure extended access for the public and for greater disclosure of information.

Undertakings must be given by such person as the Treasury thinks appropriate. In practice this will be the lifetime donee or person inheriting on death. Where relief is given the item is conditionally exempt. So long as the undertakings are observed and the property is not further transferred, inheritance tax liability will be postponed. During the COVID-19 pandemic, HM Revenue & Customs recognised that pre-eminent land and buildings which would otherwise be open to the public were forced to close to the public. A temporary relaxation of the rules was allowed.

The deferral can be renewed on transfer if further undertakings are given. The deferred tax will become payable on sale, breach of an undertaking or failure to give undertakings on a subsequent transfer. Where inheritance tax is deferred there is also a deferral of capital gains tax (see Taxation of Chargeable Gains Act 1992 (TCGA 1992), section 258, and Chapter 28).

Heritage property can be given for national purposes or for the public benefit without any inheritance tax charge (section 23). Alternatively, the property can be sold by private treaty to heritage bodies listed in Inheritance Tax Act 1984, section 25(1) and Schedule 3. Such a sale does not lead to an inheritance tax charge nor is there any liability to capital gains tax (see TCGA 1992, section 258, and Chapter 28).

Reliefs for businesses

Where 'relevant business property' is transferred, whether by way of lifetime transfer or on death, business property relief may be applicable in accordance with Inheritance Tax Act 1984, sections 104 to 106. The relief operates by reducing the market value of the property transferred by a given percentage when assessing the tax chargeable. In general property must have been owned by the transferor for at least 2 years before the transfer. If a transfer of a business has been made from one spouse to another on death, the ownership period of the deceased spouse is treated as that of the recipient spouse, but this is not the case for lifetime transfers (section 108).

Section 105(3) provides that relief is not available if the business consists wholly or mainly of one or more of the following:

(i)   dealing in securities, shares, land or buildings; or
(ii)   making or holding investments.

Taking an income from land is regarded as an investment activity (see *McCall and Another v RCC* [2009] NICA 12, [2009] STC 990 and *George and Another v IRC* [2003] EWCA Civ 1763). So the following businesses are unlikely to qualify for the relief:

- residential and commercial lettings;
- holiday lettings;
- grazing licences;
- caravan sites;
- marinas;
- car parks;
- markets;
- do-it-yourself livery stables.

The relief is available or unavailable on the whole of the business, so, for example, a business may have a mixture of activities but the question is whether the business does or does not consist 'mainly' of one of the ineligible activities. If it does, no relief at all is available. If it does not, property relating to all the activities is eligible for relief. See, for example, *RCC v Brander* [2010] UKUT 300 (TCC), [2010] STC 2666, where relief was held to be available on a landed estate carrying out a mixture of activities. A substantial part of the turnover and profit was from let properties, but the Upper Tribunal concluded that the First-tier Tribunal had been entitled to conclude that the activities carried out did not consist mainly of holding investments.

Finding and dealing with tenants, and keeping the property in repair is part and parcel of taking an income from land and does not constitute an 'additional' service. Where services are genuinely additional to the core rental element, Carnwath LJ made it clear in *George and Another v IRC* [2003] EWCA Civ 1763, [27] that they are 'unlikely to be material' because they will not be enough to prevent the business remaining mainly one of property investment. Nonetheless, in that case, the Court of Appeal allowed relief on a caravan business which consisted of a range of different activities, and in *Executors of Piercy (Deceased) v RCC* [2008] UKSPC SPC00687, [2008] STC (SCD) 858, relief was available for a property development company despite the fact that the bulk of its income had come from rentals because this was a temporary deviation from the norm caused by planning difficulties.

There are an enormous number of cases dealing with the point at which a business tips into 'mainly' ineligible activities. See, for example, *McCall and Another v RCC* [2009] NICA 12, [2009] STC 990, where farmland was let out for grazing. The owner was responsible for maintaining fences and water troughs. Agricultural property relief was available on the land's agricultural value but it had a substantial development value in excess of that so on the death of the owner an application was made for business property relief. The Court of Appeal accepted that the activities of tending the land were sufficient to constitute a business. However, it was one which consisted wholly or mainly of the making of investments and hence relief was not available.

Building and property developing are trading businesses. However, buying and selling property without developing it in any way is an investment business, as is renting out property. Hotels and bed and breakfast establishments are usually regarded as mainly non-investment businesses (as are care homes for the elderly) because the bulk of the income is attributable to the services provided rather than to the room rental. However, HM Revenue & Customs has said that it will look critically at the nature of the business and not just at the label attached. 'Budget' hotels and hotels offering accommodation for local authorities housing vulnerable adults offer very little in the way of additional services and may be regarded as investment businesses.

Holiday letting businesses will normally be regarded as mainly investment businesses not qualifying for relief (see *RCC v Lockyer and Another* [2013] UKUT 50 (TCC), *Green v RCC* [2015] UKFTT 0236 (TC) and *Executors of the Late Sheriff Graham Loudon Cox v RCC* [2020] UKFTT 442 (TC)) unless they are providing exceptional levels of services making them more akin to a hotel (see *The Personal Representatives of Graham (Deceased) v RCC* [2018] UKFTT 306 (TC)).

Businesses are often a mixture of these activities, and the proportions may vary over time, so a business which used to be 'mainly' a trading business may become an investment one.

Section 112 provides that only the value of assets used in the business is eligible for relief. It is not, therefore, possible to shelter large amounts of cash within a business unless the taxpayer can demonstrate that the cash was being accumulated for a legitimate business purpose such as the acquisition of assets for business purposes.

It is tax-efficient to leave property eligible for relief to non-exempt beneficiaries and other assets to spouses or civil partners. However, testators are frequently uncertain whether or not business assets qualify for relief. It is not advisable to leave such assets 'to my children if they qualify for relief and, if not, to my spouse', as HM Revenue & Customs normally refuses to determine whether or not relief is available since no tax turns on the issue. The best solution is to leave the assets to a discretionary trust. The trustees can then appoint appropriately once HM Revenue & Customs has determined the issue of relief. Provided the appointment is made within 2 years of death, the appointment will be read back into the will (section 144).

The Act sets out what constitutes 'relevant' business property:

(i)   a business or an interest in a business;
(ii)   quoted shares which give the transferor control;
(iii)   unquoted shares in a company;
(iv)   land, buildings, plant and machinery, owned by the transferor but used by a partnership in which the transferor was a partner or a company of which the transferor had control.

Relief is at the rate of 100% on property in categories (i) and (iii) and at 50% on property in categories (ii) and (iv).

Agricultural property relief

Relief is given on transfers of value of agricultural property as defined in Inheritance Tax Act 1984, section 115(2). There are three parts to the definition:

(i)   agricultural land or pasture;
(ii)   woodland and any building used in connection with the intensive rearing of livestock or fish if the woodland or building is occupied with agricultural land or pasture and the occupation is ancillary to that of the agricultural land or pasture;
(iii)   such cottages, farm buildings and farmhouses, together with the land occupied with them, as are of a character appropriate to the property.

To qualify as agricultural land, the land must be reasonably substantial and used for agricultural purposes; an extended garden does not qualify. Problems arise where a working farmer disposes of the bulk of his farm, keeping only a small portion (see *Starke v IRC* [1994] 1 WLR 888 and *Rosser v IRC* [2003] STC (SCD) 311). *Williams v RCC* [2005] SpC 500 makes clear that, in the case of buildings used for intensive rearing of livestock, agricultural property relief is available only where the use of the buildings is the 'junior partner' in a farming enterprise. Where this is not the case, business property relief may be available.

There are many cases on the questions 'What is a "farmhouse"?' and 'What is "a character appropriate"?'. The decision in *Lloyds TSB as Personal Representative of Antrobus (Deceased) v IRC* [2002] UKSC SPC00336, [2002] STC (SCD) 468 (*Antrobus*) is the most important in laying down general principles. In that decision, the special commissioner set out the guidelines as follows:

(i)   the house should be appropriate by reference to its size, content and layout with the farm buildings and the particular area of farmland being farmed;
(ii)   the house should be proportionate in size and nature to the requirements of the farming activities conducted on the agricultural land or pasture in question;
(iii) although impossible to define, one knows a 'character appropriate' farmhouse when one sees it (the 'elephant test');
(iv)   would the educated rural layman regard the property as a house with land or a farm?;
(v)   how long has the house been associated with the agricultural property and was there a history of agricultural production?

In addition, when *Antrobus* went to the Lands Tribunal for valuation purposes, the Tribunal said that a farmhouse was a property occupied by someone who earned his living in agriculture, suggesting that a property owned by a 'lifestyle' farmer who earned his living elsewhere, employing a manager to run the farm, would not qualify as a farmhouse.

In *Arnander v RCC* [2006] STC (SCD) 800, the special commissioner added a further factor: the relationship between the price of the house and the profitability of the land. She concluded that the return from agriculture would not provide a living income for a person who paid the asking price for the whole estate and so would not attract demand from a commercial farmer. The house was too expensive. This new factor was a great concern since many elderly farmers have to scale down their farming activities towards the end of their lives, making relatively small profits. However, in *Golding and Another v RCC* [2011] UKFTT 351 (TC), the Tribunal said at [28] that profitability is only one factor and no one factor is determinative. 'It seems to us that the question to be asked is "was the deceased farming"? ... We suspect that as farming is very much a vocational activity, farmers are prepared to forego luxuries'.

In *Arnander v RCC*, the special commissioner found that a house was not a farmhouse because it was not the main dwelling from which agricultural operations were conducted. The day-to-day farming activities were carried on by contractors who were managed by an employee. Even if the house were a farmhouse, it was not 'of a character appropriate to the property', within the meaning of section 115(2), in that its value was disproportionate to the profitability of the farm. In any event the house was not occupied by the taxpayers for agricultural purposes throughout the 2 years ending with their dates of death. They were elderly and frail and had been unable engage in farming throughout those 2 years. Note the more generous approach to 'occupation' taken in *Atkinson and Another v RCC* [2010] UKFTT 108 (TC) in relation to a farm cottage.

It is the agricultural value of the property which is subject to relief. This is defined as the value which the property would have if subject to a perpetual covenant prohibiting its use otherwise than as agricultural property (section 115(3)). In *Antrobus*, the Lands Tribunal considered the terms of such a covenant and concluded that the property had to be regarded as subject to a covenant that it could be occupied only by someone who earned their living in agriculture. It also concluded that such a person would not be willing to pay as much for the property as would a 'lifestyle farmer'. Therefore, the agricultural value of the property is less than the full market value.

Where agricultural land has a development value, agricultural property relief will not be available on the development value. Business property relief will be available provided the business is not mainly an investment business. As seen earlier, this was the problem in *McCall and Another v RCC* [2009] NICA 12, [2009] STC 990, where farmland was let out for grazing. A further problem is that if the deceased was not a hands-on farmer at the date of death but was merely taking an income from land, the house in which the deceased lived will not qualify as a 'farmhouse'.

However, the facts are always important. In *Charnley and Another v RCC* [2019] UKFTT 650 (TC), an elderly farmer did not want to deal with the paperwork attached to livestock and let his land on grazing licences. HM Revenue & Customs had allowed agricultural property relief on the land but refused it on the house and buildings occupied with the land, on the basis that the house was not a farmhouse and neither the house nor the other buildings were occupied by the deceased 'for the purposes of agriculture'. Business property relief was refused on the basis that the business was mainly an investment business. However, the evidence showed that it was the deceased who had carried out the work of caring for the livestock and making the decisions about their welfare. He was described as 'the boots on the ground' by the owner of the livestock. Hence, he was carrying out a farming business and the reliefs were available.

The level of relief is 100% of the agricultural value where the interest of the transferor in the property immediately before the transfer carries the right to vacant possession, or the right to obtain vacant possession within 12 months. Extra-statutory concession F17 extends 100% relief to cases where there is a right to vacant possession within 24 months of the relevant transfer or where, despite the existence of a tenancy, the property is broadly valued at vacant possession value. In other cases relief is 50% of the agricultural value.

No relief is available, however, unless the further requirements of section 117 are satisfied. These are that the property was:

(i)   occupied by the transferor for the purposes of agriculture throughout the period of 2 years ending with the date of the transfer; or

(ii)   owned by the transferor throughout the period of 7 years ending with that date and occupied by the transferor or another for the purposes of agriculture.

27.7.3   Exemptions and reliefs applicable only on death

Death on active service

Under Inheritance Tax Act 1984, section 154 as originally drafted, there was an exemption from the inheritance tax payable on the death estates of members of the armed forces who die as a result of (or whose death is hastened by) a wound inflicted, injury sustained or disease contracted while:

(i)   on active service against the enemy; or

(ii)   on other service of a warlike nature.

Death may occur many years after the injury. The test is whether or not the wound or disease was 'a' cause. It does not have to be 'the' cause (see *Barty-King v Ministry of Defence* [1979] 2 All ER 80 (QBD)).

For deaths on or after 19 March 2014, section 154 is amended to apply not just to the transfer on death, but also to tax payable as a result of death on potentially exempt transfers and lifetime chargeable transfers.

In addition, the inheritance tax exemption is extended by a new section 153A for deaths on or after 19 March 2014 to persons 'responding to emergency circumstances in that person's capacity as an emergency responder'.

'Emergency circumstances' are defined widely and include circumstances which are present or imminent and are causing or likely to cause death, serious injury or illness of a person or animal or serious harm to the environment, buildings or other property, or a worsening of any such injury, illness or harm.

A person is 'responding to emergency circumstances' if dealing with emergency circumstances, preparing to do so imminently, dealing with the immediate aftermath or going anywhere for the purpose of dealing with emergency circumstances occurring there.

'Emergency responder' includes persons employed as firefighters, providers of search and rescue services, medical, ambulance or paramedic services, services for the transportation of organs, blood, medical equipment or medical personnel, or humanitarian assistance. It is immaterial whether the employment or engagement is paid or unpaid.

A new section 155A extends the section 154 relief for deaths on or after 19 March 2014 to a constable or service person deliberately targeted by reason of their status as a constable or service person. It is immaterial whether the deceased was acting in the course of their duties as a constable or service person when the injury was sustained or the disease was contracted.

Quick succession relief (section 141)

This relief is designed to mitigate the effect of a double charge to inheritance tax where property passes through two estates due to the death of a donee within 5 years after the death of the original donor. The relief is based on a sliding scale depending on the time between the two deaths. A percentage of the tax charged on the property on the first occasion is deducted from the amount payable on the same property on the subsequent death. The percentage deductions are as follows (Inheritance Tax Act 1984, section 141(3)(a) to (e)):

- 100% if the donee dies within 1 year of the previous transfer;
- 80% if the death of the donee is between 1 and 2 years of the transfer;
- 60% if the death of the donee is between 2 and 3 years of the transfer;
- 40% if the death of the donee is between 3 and 4 years of the transfer;
- 20% if the death of the donee occurs between 4 and 5 years of the transfer.

27.8 THE TRANSFERABLE NIL RATE BAND

Most inheritance tax planning for the moderately wealthy is for married couples with children who want to provide efficiently for the survivor and the children (and perhaps grandchildren).

The main concern used to be allowing the survivor to have access to the couple's joint wealth while making use of the nil rate band of the first to die. Because the survivor needed access to all the assets, it was usual to include a nil rate band discretionary trust in the will of the first to die for the benefit of the surviving spouse and issue. The terms of the trust would often allow the executors to transfer all the assets of the estate to the surviving spouse charged with a debt for the nil rate sum. The trustees of the discretionary trust would be required to accept the charge instead of assets. On the death of the survivor, their estate would be reduced for inheritance tax purposes by the value of the debt owed to the discretionary trust.

Such arrangements worked moderately well but were complicated to administer and ran into problems if the debt was non-deductible because of Finance Act 1986, section 103. This provides that a debt incurred by the deceased or a charge created by them is non-deductible for inheritance tax purposes where the consideration for it consisted of property derived from the deceased (see Chapter 30 for a discussion, and Appendix 2).

The need for such complex arrangements has largely disappeared as a result of the introduction of the transferable nil rate band.

Where a surviving spouse or civil partner dies on or after 9 October 2007, their personal representatives can claim an increase in their nil rate band if the first spouse to die had any nil rate band unused. The survivor's nil rate band is increased by the proportion that was unused on the first death.

Example

Assume Bill died in 2002–03 when the nil rate band was £250,000, leaving everything to his wife, Jane.

He had made lifetime chargeable transfers of £100,000, which means that 40% of his nil rate band was used and 60% was unused.

Jane dies in a tax year when the nil rate band has increased to £400,000. Her personal representatives will be able to claim an additional nil rate band of 60% of £400,000 which amounts to £240,000.

The introduction of the nil rate band led many spouses and civil partners to make simpler wills leaving everything to the other absolutely or, if they want to achieve some capital protection, to leave the survivor a terminable life interest in some or all of their estate. However, there is still merit in using a nil rate band discretionary trust. Assets sit outside the estate of the beneficiaries. This reduces the tax payable on death and may mean that the estate is able to benefit from the RNRB which starts to be withdrawn once the estate exceeds the taper threshold of £2 million. See **27.9**.

Unused nil rate band can be claimed whenever the first spouse died and it is irrelevant that the first death was in the days of capital transfer tax or estate duty. However, for estate duty there was no spouse exemption before 21 March 1972 so if a spouse died in 1970 leaving everything to the spouse but with an estate in excess of the nil rate band, there will be no unused nil rate band available for transfer to the surviving spouse. On 21 March 1972, a £15,000 spouse exemption was introduced. This limit was removed for deaths on or after 13 November 1974, giving a full spouse exemption for estate duty which continued until estate duty was replaced by capital transfer tax on 13 March 1975. Capital transfer tax had a full spouse exemption in the same way that inheritance tax does.

A list of historic nil rate bands is available at www.gov.uk/government/publications/rates-and-allowances-inheritance-tax-thresholds-and-interest-rates/inheritance-tax-thresholds-and-interest-rates#estate-duty-inheritance-tax-thresholds. It is titled 'Inheritance Tax thresholds and interest rates', but includes capital transfer tax and estate duty thresholds.

27.9 THE RESIDENCE NIL RATE BAND

The RNRB has its roots back in 2007 when the Conservative Party said at its Party Conference that it was in favour of increasing the nil rate band to £1 million.

Although newspaper headlines suggested that the RNRB has that effect, this is very far from correct. A few people have a combination of nil rate bands that add up to £1 million, but they are in the minority.

Because the RNRB is very closely targeted, being tied to homes and lineal descendants, it can work in an illogical and, some would say, unfair fashion.

27.9.1 The effect of the legislation

The Finance (No 2) Act 2015 inserts new sections 8D to 8M into the Inheritance Tax Act 1984. There are also downsizing provisions which were added by the Finance Act 2016 (see **27.9.2**). Sections 8D to 8M have the effect set out below (references are to the Inheritance Act 1984):

(i)   Extra nil rate band equal to the residence nil rate amount is available for deaths on or after 6 April 2017 when a residence or interest in a residence is 'closely inherited'. The additional amount (the RNRB) has to be claimed by the personal representatives of the deceased.

(ii)   'Closely' means that the residence or interest in a residence must pass to a lineal descendant or, following an amendment at Committee stage, to a spouse or civil partner of a lineal descendant. Where the gift is to the spouse or civil partner of a lineal descendant who predeceased the deceased, the RNRB is available provided the surviving spouse or civil partner has not married or entered into a civil partnership following the death of the predeceased lineal descendant (section 8K).

(iii) The definition of a child in section 8K is very wide and includes step-children, foster children and natural children who have been adopted by a third party.

(iv)   'Inherited' is defined in section 8J as a disposition effected by will, the intestacy rules or otherwise (presumably by survivorship). Post-death variations passing a residential interest to lineal descendants will attract the RNRB (other requirements being satisfied) because there is reading back under section 142 for all inheritance tax purposes (see **27.13**). Events occurring after inheritance such as a sale of the property are irrelevant.

(v)   Property left to certain sorts of settlement will be treated as 'inherited' under section 8J(4). The settled property must be held for the lineal descendant ('B') on trusts which create one of the following:

       – an immediate post-death interest, under section 49A, or
       – a disabled person's trust under section 89, or
       – a bereaved minor or bereaved young person trust under section 71A or section 71D.

       Note how few settlements qualify. A discretionary settlement is not included even if all the beneficiaries are lineal descendants. A typical grandparental settlement, 'to such of my grandchildren as reach 21' will not qualify because it is a relevant property trust. However, an appointment made within 2 years of death to the lineal descendants would be read back into the will under section 144 and so trustees could retrospectively secure the RNRB for the estate.

(vi)   The value of the RNRB was £100,000 in 2017–18, rising by £25,000 each tax year until it reached £175,000 in 2020–21. It was then to increase in line with the Consumer Price Index, but is frozen until the end of 2025–26.

(vii) The values set out above are *maxima*. The RNRB is capped at the value of the deceased's residential interest. Debts charged on a property are deducted, so only the net value is relevant.

(viii)   Note that there is no requirement that it be the deceased's *main* residence or a UK property. A second home will qualify. Non-UK residences can qualify provided the deceased was domiciled in the United Kingdom and so is paying tax on their worldwide assets.

(ix)   The RNRB is limited to one residential property. Where an estate includes more than one, the personal representatives must nominate which residential property should qualify. If the deceased had two residential properties, one worth more and one worth less, then the personal representatives are likely to choose the more valuable. If both properties are worth less than the RNRB, the claim is limited to one, so some of the RNRB will be wasted.

(x)   A property which was never a residence of the deceased, such as a buy-to-let property, will not qualify. However, the property does not have to have been a residence throughout the period of ownership. It is sufficient that it was a residence at some point.

> **Example**
>
> The RNRB will be available if, shortly before death, the deceased moves into a property originally bought as a buy-to-let investment or if they move into care and the family rent out the former residence to provide funds to pay the care fees.

(xi)   When the net value of an estate is more than the taper threshold, the RNRB (made up of the deceased's own allowance plus anything transferred from a predeceased spouse or civil partner – see (xiii) below) is withdrawn by £1 for every £2 that the value of the estate exceeds the taper threshold. The adjusted amount (which may be nothing) is called the 'adjusted allowance'. The taper threshold is currently £2 million. It is frozen until the end of 2025–26.

(xii)   Note that the threshold looks only at the value of the 'estate' which is defined as assets less liabilities. Exemptions and reliefs are ignored but so are lifetime gifts.

> **Example**
>
> A wealthy individual leaves his entire estate worth £5 million to his children. £4 million attracts business property relief, but the relief is ignored so his estate remains at £5 million and exceeds the taper threshold to such an extent that no RNRB would be available.
>
> However, if on his deathbed he gives away £4 million, his death estate is reduced to £1 million and a full RNRB would be available.

(xiii)   Any unused RNRB can be transferred to a surviving spouse or civil partner (section 8F). If a person dies without a residential interest or without one which is closely inherited, the whole RNRB (adjusted by taper if necessary) can be transferred to a surviving spouse or civil partner.

Inevitably, anyone who died before 6 April 2017 cannot have used their RNRB and so it will be available for transfer. The carry forward is irrespective of how long ago the death was, what they owned and who they left their estate to. The only issue is whether the estate of the predeceased spouse or civil partner exceeded £2 million, in which case their carried forward allowance is tapered. Where the predeceased spouse or civil partner died before 6 April 2017, the carried forward allowance is deemed for the purposes of taper to be £100,000.

Examples

Fred dies in 2006 with an estate of £2.1 million, all of which he leaves to his wife, Selina.

She dies in March 2020 when the RNRB is £150,000. The size of Fred's estate means that he is treated as losing half of his deemed RNRB of £100,000.

Selina's RNRB will be enhanced by 50% of £150,000 available for transfer from Fred (though if her estate exceeds £2 million she will start to lose her enhanced RNRB).

(xiv)   Spouses and civil partners who want their estates to benefit from the RNRB may want to consider leaving assets away from the survivor to ensure that the survivor's estate does not exceed the taper threshold. Alternatively, the survivor can consider varying the disposition of the estate of the predeceased spouse to create a nil rate band discretionary trust or making lifetime gifts to reduce their death estate.

(xv)   As with the existing transferred nil rate band, the brought forward RNRB has to be claimed. See section 8L.

(xvi)   A residence that was held in trust for the deceased can qualify for RNRB if the deceased is treated as owning the property for inheritance tax purposes (i.e. the trust must be either an immediate post-death interest or a trust for the disabled). On the death of the beneficiary, a lineal descendant must 'inherit' it under the terms of the trust. Section 8J(5) states that a person inherits for this purpose if they become beneficially entitled 'to it'. This is not entirely clear but suggests that the new beneficiary must take absolutely as opposed to taking an interest under a trust in the property.

> **Example**
>
> W leaves her estate, which includes a residence, on immediate post-death interest trusts for H and following his death to their daughter absolutely. H's estate will benefit from the RNRB.
>
> But if, on H's death, trusts then arise, whether discretionary or giving a flexible life interest to the daughter, no RNRB will be available to H's estate because the daughter is not 'inheriting' within the meaning of section 8J. In such a case, the trustees should use any powers of appointment they have available under the terms of the trust to modify the gift over during H's life to create an absolute entitlement for the daughter.

Section 8H(3) provides that where a person has more than one interest in a dwelling, the interests are added together. For example, a surviving spouse who dies with an immediate post-death interest in half a residence and an absolute interest in the other half is treated as owning the whole residence.

(xvii) The RNRB is only available on the death estate, not on lifetime transfers, so, for example, if a father gives his son a house in 2018 and dies in 2021, the transfer is chargeable but no RNRB is available to the father's estate. There are two cases where an estate may benefit from the RNRB even though a residence has been given away:

- where the gift is made on or after 8 June 2015, and the downsizing provisions apply (see below);
- where because of a reservation of benefit, a residence is taxed as part of the death estate *but only if* the lineal descendant is 'the person to whom the disposal was made' (section 8J). This produces some inconsistent results.

> **Example**
>
> If a father gives his house to his son in 2014, moves in with his son in 2016 and dies in May 2022, the RNRB is available because the disposal was made to the son.
>
> However, if in 2014 the father settles property on himself for life, remainder to his son absolutely, even though there is a reservation of benefit, the RNRB is not available because the disposal was not to the son.

27.9.2   The downsizing legislation

The government recognised at an early stage that if taxpayers had to own a residence at the date of death in order to benefit from the RNRB, this would result in elderly people clinging onto properties when they ought to be selling them and moving into smaller accommodation or into care. It undertook to introduce a mechanism to allow taxpayers to benefit from the RNRB despite having disposed of a residence completely or moving to cheaper accommodation. This was done in the Finance Act 2016, which inserted new sections 8FA to 8FE and 8HA into the Inheritance Tax Act 1984. The new provisions apply where a person disposes of a residential property on or after 8 July 2015 either completely or by moving to a less valuable property.

The chargeable transfer on death must exceed the value of any residence owned at the date of death and there must be assets which are closely inherited. The downsizing addition is capped at the value of the assets which are closely inherited.

The legislation is impenetrable in detail, but reasonably straightforward in outline.

It is necessary to calculate the 'lost relievable amount' by expressing the value of the 'former residential interest' as a percentage of the 'former allowance'. The maximum percentage allowed is 100%.

There are five steps to work out the amount of additional threshold that has been lost:

- *Step 1* – Work out the additional threshold that would have been available when the disposal of the former home took place. This figure is made up of the maximum additional threshold due at the date of disposal (or £100,000 if the disposal occurred before 6 April 2017) plus any transferred additional threshold which is available at the date of death.

- *Step 2* – Divide the value of the former home at the date of disposal by the figure in step 1 and multiply the result by 100 to get a percentage. If the value of the former home is greater than the figure in step 1, the percentage will be limited to 100%. If the value of the home disposed of is less than the figure in step 1, the percentage will be between 0% and 100%.

- *Step 3* – If there is a home in the estate on death, divide the value of the home on death by the additional threshold that would be available at the date of death (including any transferred additional threshold). Multiply the result by 100 to get a percentage (again this percentage is limited to 100%). If there is no home in the estate at death this percentage will be 0%.

- *Step 4* – Deduct the percentage in step 3 from the percentage in step 2.

- *Step 5* – Multiply the additional threshold that would be available at the date of death by the figure from step 4. This gives the amount of the lost additional threshold.

Example

Darius, who is divorced, sells a property for £250,000 in 2022 and moves into residential accommodation. The downsizing addition is calculated as follows:

- The value of the former residence exceeded the RNRB available at the date of sale (£175,000). It is 142.85% of the RNRB. Darius is therefore treated as having a downsizing addition of 100% of the available RNRB on death.
- If Darius dies in 2023–24 the downsizing allowance available to his estate will be £175,000, but it will be limited to the value of assets which are closely inherited.

The calculation is more complicated when there is transferred RNRB available. HM Revenue and Customs, *Inheritance Tax Manual* has useful examples at IHTM6066 (available at www.hmrc.gov.uk/manuals/ihtmanual).

There was a problem where a married couple (or civil partners) jointly disposed of a residence. If the first to die did not make use of the downsizing allowance (because, for example, they left everything to the survivor), the survivor got little benefit from the transferred downsizing allowance. Due to a quirk in the drafting, the problem did not arise if the couple have moved to a cheaper property.

However, the Finance Act 2019 removed this problem for deaths on or after 29 October 2018 by amending section 8FA.

When the original draft downsizing provisions were published in December 2015, there were oddities in the way they worked in relation to the disposal of a property held in a trust in which the deceased had a qualifying interest in possession such as an immediate post-death interest.

Significant amendments were made to the downsizing provisions (see section 8H(4A) to (4F) and section 8HA) in relation to settlements which include a residence or interest in a residence in which a beneficiary has a qualifying interest in possession. As a result:

(i)   Where trustees dispose of the residence or interest in a residence and the beneficiary continues to have a qualifying interest in the settlement, the beneficiary will be treated as having disposed of the residence.
(ii) Where trustees terminate the beneficiary's interest or the beneficiary disposes of their interest during their lifetime, the beneficiary will be treated as having disposed of the residence.
(iii) Where a person has two or more interests in a residence (such as a half share owned outright and an interest in possession in half) and disposes of them

on the same day, they will be added together for the purposes of the downsizing allowance. This will not be the case if they are disposed of on different days.

A further amendment provides that a gift of a residence which creates a reservation of benefit is not a disposal for the purposes of the downsizing allowance. However, if the reservation ceases (e.g. because the donor moves out of the property), there is a disposal for downsizing purposes at that point.

27.10   RESERVATION OF BENEFIT

27.10.1   The principles

The Finance Act 1986 introduced the concept of the potentially exempt transfer and, to accompany it, the concept of reservation of benefit. This was required to prevent a person from making a potentially exempt transfer to take property out of their estate for inheritance tax purposes, and then continuing to benefit from the property until death.

Finance Act 1986, section 102 provides that where a donor disposes of property by way of gift on or after 18 March 1986 and either:

(a)   possession and enjoyment of the property is not *bona fide* assumed by the donee at or before the beginning of the relevant period; or

(b)   at any time in the relevant period the property is not enjoyed to the entire exclusion, or virtually to the entire exclusion, of the donor and of any benefit to him by contract or otherwise;

the property is property subject to a reservation.

The 'relevant period' means a period ending on the date of the donor's death and beginning 7 years before that date or, if it is later, on the date of the gift.

Property which is subject to a reservation is treated as part of the donor's estate on death for inheritance tax purposes. If the benefit is released before the donor's death, the gift is treated as a transfer of the whole as from the time of the release.

Under the reservation of benefit rules, the donor is not treated as the actual owner for all tax purposes. The property is treated as the donor's for inheritance tax purposes, but for capital gains tax purposes, it remains the property of the donee. In the case of a house in which the donor continues to reside, the principal private dwelling house exemption is not available if the house is sold during the donor's lifetime, nor would there be any uplift in value on the donor's death.

Thus it is important that the donee of any gift takes full possession of the property and enjoys it so that the donor is excluded or virtually excluded from the benefit and enjoyment of the property. The term 'virtually excluded' is statutory but open to judicial interpretation. See *Buzzoni and Others v RCC* [2013] EWCA Civ 1684, where the Court of Appeal held that the donee's enjoyment is to the entire exclusion of benefit to the donor within the meaning of section 102 even though the donor retains a benefit, provided that benefit is not obtained at the expense of the donee. However, small differences are important here. In *Hood v RCC* [2018] EWCA Civ 2405, [2018] STC 2355, on similar facts there was held to be a reservation of benefit because, unlike *Buzzoni*, there was held to be an expense to the donee.

27.10.2 Cases where reservation of benefit rules do not apply

It is important to remember that if a taxpayer gives away 'X' and retains 'Y' the reservation of benefit rules do not apply to any benefit enjoyed in 'Y'. As Lord Simonds said in *Attorney General v St Aubyn* [1952] AC 15:

> … if A gives to B all his estates in Wiltshire except Blackacre, he does not except Blackacre out of what he has given; he just does not give Blackacre.

So called 'shearing' arrangements can sometimes be used to achieve a tax saving but the government has introduced a series of anti-avoidance provisions to try to prevent fragmenting arrangements which have allowed taxpayers to divide property into different interests, giving away some and retaining others. It also introduced the charge on pre-owned assets which has made lifetime tax planning more difficult.

Where there is a gift of land or a chattel, occupation of the land or possession of the chattel by the donor is disregarded if it is for full consideration in money or money's worth (Finance Act 1986, Schedule 20, paragraph 6(1)(a)). Thus if the donor gives their house away, but continues to occupy it for the payment of a full rent to the donee, the gift of the house is not property with a reservation. Care must be taken to ensure that the rent is a full rent, and there should be appropriate rent review clauses.

There is also relief where a gift of land is made and the donor subsequently occupies the land as a result of becoming unable to maintain themselves (Finance Act 1986, Schedule 20, paragraph 6(1)(b)). Thus if a father gives away his house to his son, and later becomes infirm so that he returns to the house to be looked after by his son, the gift with reservation rules would not apply. It must be shown that the change in circumstances was unforeseen at the time of the gift; that the return of the donor to the house represents reasonable provision by the donee for the donor's maintenance; and that the donor and donee are related.

Although it is safest if the donor is entirely excluded from the property they give away, the gift with a reservation rules do not apply if the donor is 'virtually' entirely excluded from the property. The *Inheritance Tax Manual* at IHTM 14333 (available at www.hmrc.gov.uk/manuals/ihtmanual) gives interesting insight into HM Revenue & Customs' view of the meaning of 'virtually'. It suggests that a gift is not a gift with a reservation solely because the donor subsequently stays, in the absence of the donee, for not more than 2 weeks each year, or stays with the donee for less than one month each year, or stays for the purpose of convalescence from medical treatment or to look after the donee who is convalescing, or while the donor's house is being redecorated. Visits to the house for the purpose of baby-sitting, or visits to the library in the house fewer than five times a year, are also ignored. A gift of a car is not considered a gift with a reservation if the donee gives the donor lifts no more than three times a month, and a gift of land is not taxed as property with a reservation solely because the donor continues to walk their dogs or ride their horses over the land.

27.10.3   Sharing arrangements

Finance Act 1986, section 102B provides that there is no reservation of benefit where a donor gives away an undivided share of an interest in land in two cases:

(i)   The donor does not occupy the land (section 102B(3)(a)). This would allow a donor to give away an interest in land but retain the income it produces without being caught by the reservation of benefit rules.

(ii)   The donor and the donee occupy the land and the donor does not receive any benefit, other than a negligible one, provided by or at the expense of the donee for some reason connected with the gift (section 102B(4). This allows, for example, a parent to give an interest in the family home to a child and continue to occupy the property. It is important that both parties 'occupy' the property.

If the donee moves out, the reservation of benefit rules will apply unless the donor can afford to pay full consideration in money or money's worth (section 102B(3)(b)).

It is also important that the donor receives no benefit so the donee must not pay more than their share of the expenses.

27.10.4   Exclusion of the rule: IRC v Eversden and Another

Property is not subject to a reservation if any of the exemptions set out in Finance Act 1986, section 102(5) apply. These exemptions include the spouse exemption, the small gift exemption, the exemption for wedding gifts and the exemptions for gifts to charity and similar bodies (see **27.7.1**), but the annual £3,000 exemption and the exemption for normal gifts out of income do not prevent the reservation rules applying.

In *IRC v Eversden and Another* [2003] EWCA Civ 668, [2003] STC 822, the Court of Appeal held that the reservation of benefit rules did not apply where a taxpayer had settled property on her husband for life, with remainder to discretionary trusts for beneficiaries including herself. HM Revenue & Customs argued unsuccessfully that when the husband's life interest came to an end on his death, there was another gift to the discretionary trusts to which the gift with reservation rules applied. The case opened the way to avoid the reservation of benefit rules by one spouse settling a house on the other spouse with remainders over to children or to a discretionary trust. The donee spouse's life interest could be determined early in favour of other beneficiaries, but the settlor spouse could continue to occupy the house without it becoming property with a reservation of benefit.

The Finance Act 2003, however, made provision to counter the *Eversden* decision in the case of gifts made on or after 20 June 2003. For the purposes of the gift with reservation rules, the gift is taken to be made when the donee spouse's life interest comes to an end. If the settlor continues to benefit after this time, the gift with reservation rules may be brought into play.

27.11   THE REDUCED RATE FOR CHARITABLE GIVING

Where a testator wishes to make gifts to charity, it is possible in certain cases to obtain a reduced rate of inheritance tax on the rest of the estate.

27.11.1   The legislation in outline

The Finance Act 2012 inserted into the Inheritance Tax Act 1984 a new Schedule 1A to reduce the inheritance tax rate from 40% to 36% for taxpayers leaving 10% or more of their net estate to charity.

The reduced rate applies where death occurs on or after 6 April 2012. HM Revenue & Customs, *Inheritance Tax Manual* has a helpful section on the reduced rate at IHTM4500 onwards (available at www.hmrc.gov.uk/manuals/ ihtmanual). The 10% is not necessarily 10% of the whole estate. The legislation reflects the fact that a person's estate is made up of different types of property, some of which can be left by will and some of which cannot.

Schedule 1A, paragraph 3 divides the taxpayer's estate into three 'components' as follows:

(i)   *The survivorship component* – 'all the property comprised in the estate that, immediately before D's death, was joint (or common) property liable to pass on D's death ... by survivorship ...'.
It is unlikely that property in this component will pass to charity on the taxpayer's death; this will only happen if:

  –   the charity was a joint tenant with the deceased; or
  –   the joint tenancy is 'severed' by a post-death deed of variation and the share of the deceased redirected to charity.

This component applies to all joint property owned by the deceased. For instance, the deceased may jointly own a seaside cottage with their brother and an investment property in Spain with their son. The value of the deceased's interest in these two properties is comprised in the survivorship component.

(ii) *The settled property component* – this is made up of the value of all the settled property in which the deceased was entitled to an interest in possession. Since the 2006 changes in the inheritance tax treatment of settlements, it is only 'qualifying' interests in possession which result in the beneficiary being deemed to own the settled property under Inheritance Tax Act 1984, section 49(1).
A deceased may, of course, have been entitled to an interest in more than one settlement. If so, the values will be aggregated to form the settled property component.

(iii) *The general component* – this is made up of all the property comprised in the estate other than property in the other two components (joint and settled property) and reservation of benefit property.

Reservation of benefit property forms part of none of the components although, as discussed below, it may (if a merger election is made) benefit from the reduced inheritance tax rate. The general component is therefore made up of what is often called the 'free estate', i.e. property capable of passing under the deceased's will.

If the 10% test is met for any one of the three statutory components of the estate, that component is taxed at the reduced rate. The test is 'all or nothing' so that a gift of 9% of the component to charity will not give rise to any relief. It is most likely that the test will be met in respect of the free estate.

The division of the estate into the three components makes it easier for the relief to be obtained since:

(i)   if all the components were to be treated as one, the 10% test would have to be met in respect of the total value;

(ii)   it is unlikely that any charitable giving will occur in the survivorship and settled property components;

(iii) reservation of benefit property does not belong to the deceased (albeit that it is deemed to form part of their estate) so there is no question of it meeting the charitable giving condition.

When calculating whether the 10% test is met for any component, it is necessary to compare the amount given to charity with 'the baseline amount' for each component. The 'baseline amount' is the net value (i.e. after debts) of the assets included in the component after deducting:

- any available nil rate band (or transferred nil rate band);
- any exemptions (other than the charity exemption); and
- any reliefs.

The nil rate band is allocated proportionally amongst the components of the estate. Any additional RNRB available to the estate is ignored when calculating the baseline amount.

Example

Fahim dies with a chargeable estate of £800,000 plus property eligible for business property relief of £1 million. He has unused nil rate band of £300,000. He leaves a legacy to charity, his house worth £400,000 to his wife and the residue to his son.

If his estate is to benefit from the reduced rate, how large must the charitable legacy be?

The spouse exemption and property eligible for business property relief are deducted leaving £400,000 (the gift to charity is included when calculating the baseline amount). After deducting the available nil rate band of £300,000 the baseline amount of the general component is £100,000 so the charitable legacy must be at least £10,000.

Without the legacy, Fahim's son would take £400,000 less inheritance tax at 40% on £100,000 (£40,000) so £360,000.

With the legacy and the benefit of the reduced rate Fahim's son will take £390,000 less inheritance tax at 36% on £90,000 (£32,400) so £357,600.

Notice that in the above example, Fahim's son takes less than he would have taken had no legacy at all been given. However, where a will contains a charitable legacy of less than 10% but more than 4%, increasing it to reach the magic 10% can actually increase the amount taken by the non-exempt beneficiaries.

Example

If Fahim had given a legacy of say 9% to charity, it would benefit Fahim's son to increase the legacy to 10% by means of a post-death variation.

For post-death variations, see **27.13**.

HM Revenue & Customs has a helpful calculator available, which can calculate the size of legacy required to obtain the rate reduction (see www.gov.uk/inheritance-tax-reduced-rate-calculator).

27.11.2 Merger and opt-out elections

Schedule 1A, paragraph 7 allows components to be merged. Merger is useful if, for example, a substantial charitable gift is made by the deceased's will which exceeds 10% of the baseline amount for the general component and the deceased had also either enjoyed a qualifying life interest in settled property (the settled property component) or had owned joint property (the survivorship component). The effect of the election is to treat the merged components as one so that the 10% test is then applied to the merged components. This election can also be made in respect of reservation of benefit property which forms part of the deceased's estate but does not come within any of the three components.

The election must be made by the 'appropriate persons', who are the personal representatives (for the free estate), the surviving joint owners (for the joint property component), the trustees (for the settled property component) and the donee (owner) of the reservation of benefit property. The election must be made by notice in writing to HM Revenue & Customs within 2 years after the death of the deceased. It can be withdrawn by the same parties within the period of 2 years and one month of the deceased's death. (HM Revenue & Customs has a discretion to extend these time limits if, for example, asset values cannot be agreed.)

An opt-out election (contained in Inheritance Tax Act 1984, Schedule 1A, paragraph 8) is available because there may be cases where the cost of claiming the reduction (e.g. additional valuations) may exceed the benefit obtained from the rate reduction. The opt-out election is made by the same 'appropriate persons' who would make a merger election and the time limits are the same. It is questionable how often an opt-out election will be appropriate. It is probably most likely when private company shares not attracting business property relief are left to charity, but this rarely happens.

27.11.3   Practical implications

The legislation is complex and imposes burdens on personal representatives and will drafters. Whether the 10% test is met normally depends on factors at the time of the deceased's death. However, asset values may change during the administration, for example if land is sold for less than its value at the time of death, so that although the reduced rate had not originally applied it may, as a result of the reduced value, come to apply. The will drafter may therefore use a discretionary trust so that account can be taken of the position at the time of death, with the trustees making an appointment of the requisite size in favour of charity to obtain reading back under Inheritance Tax Act 1984, section 144. It is more likely, however, that a formula will be used to ensure that the conditions for the relief are met. See Precedent 27A.

After a death, beneficiaries may be able to achieve a tax saving by varying the dispositions of the estate to give more to charity thereby obtaining the benefit of the reduced rate.

To avoid the need to continually revise charitable legacies in wills, a clause may be worded so that a specific legacy to charity will always meet the 10% test. HM Revenue & Customs includes the following approved wording in the *Inheritance Tax Manual* at IHTM45008 (available at www.hmrc.gov.uk/manuals/ihtmanual).

27A   LEGACY TO CHARITY USING FORMULA TO SECURE REDUCED RATE OF INHERITANCE TAX

I GIVE to [name of charity] such a sum as shall constitute a donated amount equal to 10 [or larger figure] % of the baseline amount in relation to the [general component] [aggregate of the general, [survivorship], [settled property] components and [reservation of benefit property]] of my estate.

The legacy given by this clause shall in no event:

(i)   be less than £ ... whether or not the lower rate of tax shall be applicable; and

(ii)   exceed £ ... (the upper limit) even if in consequence of this restriction in the value of the legacy the lower rate shall not apply.

[If this proviso shall apply and in consequence the lower rate of tax shall not be payable, the amount of this legacy shall [be equal to the amount of the upper limit] [be reduced to £ ...] [lapse]].

Notes:

The clause may include other administrative provisions, but the essential wording to qualify for the reduced rate is that shown above. It follows from the wording of this clause that the amount of the legacy may not be known until the value of the estate is settled and the amount of charity exemption will change as the value of the estate changes.

The first paragraph of the clause ensures that the charitable legacy will meet the requirements for the reduced rate. The legacy is set by the reference to the components of the estate listed; but this only fixes the size of the legacy to be paid under the will – it does not override the requirement for those liable for the tax at the different components to elect for the components to be merged before other components can benefit from the reduced rate.

Proviso (i) ensures that even if the estate is not liable to inheritance tax, the legacy is still payable to the charity.

Proviso (ii) ensures that charitable legacy does not exceed a fixed amount, even though that may mean the estate does not qualify for the reduced rate.

The Society of Trust and Estate Practitioners has developed a model clause for wills. The clause can be accessed from HM Revenue & Customs, *Inheritance Tax Manual* at IHTM45008 (available at www.gov.uk/hmrc.gov.uk/manuals/ihtmanual).

27.12   GENERAL TAX PLANNING

The structure of inheritance tax and its interaction with capital gains tax can lead to dilemmas in tax planning. Lifetime gifts may often be potentially exempt transfers and, if the donor survives for 7 years after the transfer, all inheritance tax can be saved, but the gift is likely to be subject to capital gains tax. On the other hand, if an individual retains their wealth until death, inheritance tax is payable at the death rate on their estate.

As a general rule, more wealthy individuals should seek to take advantage of potentially exempt transfers as early as possible. Even if the transferor fails to survive the full 7-year period, some tax is saved if the gift exceeds the nil rate band and the transferor survives for 3 years or more, and lifetime exemptions and reliefs may help to reduce the liability further. However, if the gift is less than the nil rate band, no benefit is obtained from taper relief because the relief reduces the tax payable.

Example

Madhur gives her daughter £225,000, having used her annual exemptions for the current and previous tax years. She dies with an estate of £1 million:

- 2 years later;
- 6 years later.

In neither case is any tax payable on the gift. However, Madhur's nil rate band is eroded in both cases. Only £100,000 of nil rate band is left for her death estate.

However, if the gift is £825,000, the position is different.

If Madhur dies after 2 years, tax on the lifetime gift is 40% of £500,000 = £200,000. There is no nil rate band left for the death estate.

If Madhur dies after 6 years, the tax on the lifetime gift is tapered so only 20% is payable (£40,000). There is no nil rate band left for the death estate.

There is also the important consideration that the RNRB starts to be withdrawn once the death estate exceeds £2 million (see **27.9**). This can be a reason for making lifetime gifts. However, capital gains tax is a concern and, if possible, gifts of assets which have not increased significantly in value since acquisition or which are exempt from capital gains tax should be made (see below).

See Chapter 30 for a discussion of tax and planning issues affecting will drafting.

27.13   POST-DEATH VARIATIONS

Beneficiaries are always free to refuse to accept or to give away property they are entitled to as a result of someone's death. In the normal course of events this would not alter the inheritance tax position of the deceased but would give rise to a transfer of value from the original to the new beneficiary. (There would also be a disposal for capital gains tax purposes and a charge to capital gains tax on any increase in value from the date of death to the date of disposal.)

These consequences are avoided by Inheritance Tax Act 1984, section 142, and TCGA 1992, section 62(6), which provide that any variations made within 2 years of the date of death of the deceased are treated for the purposes of inheritance tax and capital gains tax on death as if the variations had been made by the deceased themselves. The provisions extend to property passing by survivorship as well as to property passing by will or on intestacy. The variation should state that the property is to pass as if the deceased had severed the joint tenancy before death and left the property to the 'new' beneficiary.

Variations which comply with the requirements of section 142 are effective for all inheritance tax purposes. As can be seen in Chapter 28, they have a more limited effect for capital gains tax purposes.

The requirements are as follows:

(i)   any variation must be made in writing and within 2 years of the deceased's death;
(ii)   the variation must state that section 142 and/or section 62 is to apply so that it is effective for inheritance tax and/or capital gains tax purposes;
(iii) any person giving up a benefit must consent to the variation. If the beneficiary is a minor or under a disability making them unable to consent, then the court must consent to the variation on the beneficiary's behalf.

In relation to the requirement for consent, a common query is whether the beneficiaries of a discretionary trust can, between them, vary the destination of the property left to the trust. In principle, the answer is 'yes', *provided* all the beneficiaries are of full age and capacity and are between them entitled to the whole beneficial interest. In practice, there will often be minor, unborn or unascertained beneficiaries so that a variation will not be possible. However, in such a case it will usually be possible for the trustees to make an appointment from the trust which will be read back into the will under Inheritance Tax Act 1984, section 144 (see **29.3**).

Where property has already been redirected by variation, its destination cannot be varied a second time, so it is important to get the variation right first time. Mistakes cannot be put right unless the court will agree to rectify the document on the basis that it does not carry out the true agreement of the parties. The evidence in support of a claim in rectification must be 'strong irrefragable evidence' (see *Lake v Lake* [1989] STC 865). However, there have been a number of cases where rectification has been obtained (e.g. *Giles v The Royal National Institute for the Blind and Others* [2014] EWHC 1373 (Ch), *Wills v Gibbs* [2007] EWHC 3361 (Ch) and *Vaughan-Jones and Another v Vaughan-Jones and Others* [2015] EWHC 1086 (Ch)).

A variation is effective for all inheritance tax purposes. Thus, if it creates a settlement, the deceased – not the person making the variation – is regarded as the settlor for inheritance tax purposes. The reservation of benefit rules do not affect the person making the variation as the transfer is treated as made by the deceased for all inheritance tax purposes.

Beneficiaries are permitted to 'exchange' their respective interests under the will or the intestacy rules, but if there is any other form of consideration in money in respect of such a variation or disclaimer then the statutory provisions do not apply and the transfer or disposition is liable to tax in the usual way (see *Lau v RCC* [2009] UKVAT SPC00740, [2009] STC (SCD) 352 and *Vaughan-Jones and Another v Vaughan-Jones and Others* [2015] EWHC 1086 (Ch)).

It is possible for the personal representatives of a deceased beneficiary to vary on behalf of the deceased. This can often be extremely useful.

Example

Ben dies in May 2021 when the nil rate band is £325,000. He leaves his estate (value £325,000) to his divorced sister, Sally.

Sally dies in March 2022 with £325,000 of her own assets. She leaves her estate to her daughter, Dee.

Neither Ben nor Sally made any lifetime gifts.

If nothing is done, substantial inheritance tax will be payable on Sally's death. If Ben's will is varied on behalf of Sally to leave Ben's estate to Dee, no inheritance tax will be paid on either estate.

In the above example, who should vary on behalf of Sally? HM Revenue & Customs, *Inheritance Tax Manual* at IHTM35042 (available at www.hmrc.gov.uk/manuals/ihtmanual) says that the personal representatives of a person who has died may make a variation redirecting that person's entitlement on an earlier death. Where the variation reduces the entitlement of the beneficiaries of the second deceased then the beneficiaries should also agree to the variation. If the beneficiaries are not a party to the deed of variation then HM Revenue & Customs will request other written evidence of their consent. In the above example, therefore, Sally's personal representatives can vary the disposition of Ben's estate, but Dee must either be a party or provide written agreement.

HM Revenue & Customs considers that it is not possible to vary a will creating a life interest if the life tenant has died (see HM Revenue & Customs, *Inheritance Tax Manual* at IHTM35042, available at www.hmrc.gov.uk/manuals/ihtmanual). This is supposedly because, after the life tenant's death, the life interest ends and there is no property that can form the basis of such a variation. The argument seems misconceived since there will often be income produced by the settlement which can be redirected in the variation. The Scottish case of *Soutter's Executry v IRC* [2002] STC (SCD) 385 supported HM Revenue & Customs' argument, although, as the interest was a right to occupy property, the argument as to income was not aired. HM Revenue & Customs does accept that the life tenant's personal representatives can *disclaim* the life interest on behalf of the life tenant under Inheritance Tax Act 1984, section 93 (but only if the life tenant accepted no benefit from the interest) (see HM Revenue & Customs, *Inheritance Tax Manual* at IHTM35165, available at www.hmrc.gov.uk/manuals/ihtmanual). Where possible, therefore, disclaimer will clearly be the better course to take.

Chapter 28

Capital Gains Tax

As is the case with inheritance tax, this chapter provides only a summary of the principles of capital gains tax. Readers requiring more detail should consult a specialist textbook.

28.1 INTRODUCTION

Capital gains tax is charged on individuals resident in the United Kingdom, personal representatives and trustees (TCGA 1992, section 1A).

New provisions were introduced to the Act (sections 1A to 1D and Schedule 1A) under which non-UK residents are chargeable to capital gains tax in limited cases. Non-UK residents are chargeable on gains made on the disposal of:

(i) assets situated in the United Kingdom that are connected to the person's UK branch or agency and are disposed of at a time when the person has that branch or agency;
(ii) interests in UK land; and
(iii) assets (wherever situated) that derive at least 75% of their value from UK land where the person has a substantial indirect interest in that land.

The charge is on the amount by which an asset increases in value while owned by the taxpayer. Thus, if an individual purchases an asset for £20,000 and sells it (or gives it away) when its value has reached £50,000, there is a gain of £30,000 which may be chargeable to capital gains tax. The tax is triggered by a 'disposal' of the asset (TCGA 1992, section 1). The disposal usually consists of the sale of the asset, but the term has a wide meaning and includes gifts and transfers into settlements (TCGA 1992, section 70) as well as part disposals. The Act extends the term to include situations where a capital sum is derived from assets (TCGA 1992, section 22), the total loss or destruction of an asset (TCGA 1992, section 24(1)) as well as certain deemed disposals under settlements (TCGA

1992, sections 71 and 72). If the profit on the transaction is charged to income tax it is not chargeable to capital gains tax (TCGA 1992, section 37).

No allowance has been made for the effects of inflation since 6 April 2008 although the rate of tax was reduced in the Finance Act 2008.

Incidental expenses incurred on acquisition and disposal are deductible when calculating the gain, as is any expenditure wholly and exclusively incurred for the purpose of enhancing the value of the asset (being reflected in the state or nature of the asset at the time of the disposal), and any expenditure wholly and exclusively incurred in establishing, preserving or defending title to, or to a right over, the asset (TCGA 1992, section 38).

Business assets disposal relief and investors' relief, when available, reduce the rate of tax charged. See **28.2.2**.

Each tax year gains made by an individual up to a specified figure are exempt from tax. For tax year 2022–23, the annual exemption is £12,300 and is frozen until the end of 2025–26 (TCGA 1992, section 1K).

Since capital gains tax is normally charged only on individuals who are resident in the United Kingdom (TCGA 1992, section 1A), it is possible to avoid the tax by moving abroad before making a disposal. Provided the individual making the disposal is not resident in the United Kingdom in the tax year of the disposal, the disposal is not charged to capital gains tax (unless the disposal is of UK residential land). However, unsurprisingly anti-avoidance provisions exist. TCGA 1992, section 1M provides that an individual who leaves the United Kingdom is liable to capital gains tax on realising assets owned before departure if the individual is a 'temporarily non-resident'. This is defined in Finance Act 2013, Schedule 45, paragraph 110:

(i)   had sole residence in the United Kingdom for any part of at least 4 out of the 7 years before departure; and
(ii) the temporary period of non-residence is less than 5 years.

An individual who has been resident in the United Kingdom for 4 of the previous 7 years would therefore have to be prepared to become non-resident for at least 5 years to take advantage of the exemption. If the individual does move abroad, they should delay the disposal until the tax year following their departure. Although concession D2 provides that the individual will not be charged to capital gains tax on disposals after the day of departure, the concession cannot be relied on for the purposes of tax avoidance.

Current HM Revenue & Customs guidance on residence and domicile is contained in its booklets, *Guidance Note: Residence, Domicile and the Remittance Basis*, RDR1 (July 2018) (see www.gov.uk/government/publications/residence-domicile-and-remittance-basis-rules-uk-tax-liability), and *Guidance Note: Statutory Residence Test (SRT)*, RDR3 (January 2020) (see www.gov.uk/government/publications/rdr3-statutory-residence-test-srt).

Legislation was introduced in the Finance Act 2016 to deem persons to be domiciled in the United Kingdom for all tax purposes once they have been resident for at least 15 of the previous 20 years. The provisions took effect from 6 April 2017. The legislation also introduces the concept of the formerly domiciled resident (FDR). For income tax and capital gains tax purposes, these are individuals who were born in the United Kingdom with a UK domicile of origin, but who subsequently left the United Kingdom and acquired a domicile of choice outside the United Kingdom. Such FDRs are deemed domiciled in the United Kingdom during any period when they are subsequently UK tax resident (Income Tax Act 2007, section 835BA(3)).

28.2 RATES OF TAX

28.2.1 The general rules

For gains arising on or after 23 June 2010, gains made by individuals are added to taxable income.

For gains made by individuals on or after 23 June 2010 and before 6 April 2016, the rate charged is 28% to the extent that gains exceed the upper limit of the basic rate tax band. Gains below that level are taxed at 18%.

Gains made by trustees and personal representatives between those dates are charged at a flat rate of 28%.

For later tax years, the rates are reduced and there are differential rates for certain types of property. The rates are generally:

(i)   10% and 20% tax rates for individuals on assets other than residential property and carried interest;
(ii) 18% and 28% tax rates for individuals for residential property and carried interest;
(iii) 20% for trustees and for personal representatives on assets other than residential property;
(iv) 28% for trustees or for personal representatives for disposals of residential property.

28.2.2   Business assets disposal relief and investors' relief

Business assets disposal relief replaces entrepreneurs' relief for disposals on or after 11 March 2020.

Entrepreneurs' relief was introduced by Finance Act 2008, section 9 and is contained in TCGA 1992, sections 169H to 169V. Initially, the first £1 million of gains made by individuals on the disposal of certain business assets was charged at 10%. The limit was increased on a number of occasions and was £10 million for disposals occurring on or after 6 April 2011 and before 11 March 2020.

As the name suggests, the relief was intended to stimulate entrepreneurial activity, but it became apparent that it was not working as intended and as a result significant changes have been made. The Finance Act 2020 changed the name to 'business assets disposal relief' and reduced the limit to £1 million for disposals on or after 11 March 2020.

To encourage an investment culture and help companies access the capital they need to expand and create jobs, the Finance Act 2016 amended TCGA 1992, Part V to extend entrepreneurs' relief to gains accruing on the disposal of ordinary shares in an unlisted trading company held by individuals. It is referred to as 'investors' relief '.

28.2.3   Annual tax on enveloped assets

Where the Annual Tax on Enveloped Dwellings is payable (dwellings owned by offshore entities), gains on sales are now subject to the normal capital gains tax rules for UK or non-UK residents.

28.3   DISPOSAL OF ASSETS

Capital gains tax is charged on the disposal of an asset; 'disposal' includes any transfer of the beneficial title by one party to another, whether gratuitous or for value. 'Assets' are defined by TCGA 1992, section 21:

> All forms of property shall be assets for the purposes of this Act, whether situated in the United Kingdom or not, including—
>
> (a)   options, debts and incorporeal property generally, and
> (b)   any currency other than sterling, and
> (c)   any form of property created by the person disposing of it, or otherwise coming to be owned without being acquired.

The chargeable gain is generally calculated as the difference between the sale price and the acquisition cost, as adjusted by the indexation allowance, if appropriate. Also deducted is expenditure on improvements and other allowance costs.

Where, however, the sale is not for full market value or the transfer is by way of a gift or settlement, the chargeable gain is calculated with reference to the market value of the asset at the time of the gift and there is deemed to be a disposal at the price on that date. Conversely, the deemed disposal price is used as the acquisition cost when calculating the gains on the asset in the hands of the donee.

Sales made at an undervalue are treated as gifts of the difference between the sale price and the market value, in which case the market value is deemed to be the consideration on disposal. This is especially relevant in the case of disposals between 'connected persons'. Disposals between connected persons are presumed not to be at arm's length and the onus is on the taxpayer to prove that a transaction was based on the full market value. 'Connected persons' include spouses, civil partners, relatives and partners, settlors and trustees.

28.4   EFFECT OF DEATH

Death is not a disposal by the deceased to their personal representatives and there is therefore no charge to capital gains tax by reason of a person's death. The personal representatives are deemed to have acquired the deceased's assets at the date of their death at full market value (TCGA 1992, section 62(1)). This gives rise to an 'uplift' which may save a considerable amount of tax if assets are retained until death. If the personal representatives transfer assets to the beneficiaries, there is no disposal on the transfer for capital gains tax purposes and the beneficiaries are deemed to acquire the assets at the market value at the date of the deceased's death (TCGA 1992, section 62(4)).

Similarly, property passing under a *donatio mortis causa*, a nomination or the right of survivorship in the case of joint property is not subject to capital gains tax as there is no deemed disposal, but the recipient is deemed to have acquired the property at the market value at the time of the deceased's death.

If the personal representatives appropriate assets to a beneficiary, the beneficiary acquires them at probate value.

Where personal representatives sell estate property, the chargeable gain is calculated by deducting from the sale price the deemed acquisition cost and any allowable subsequent expenditure and disposal costs. Personal representatives are liable to capital gains tax even if the beneficiaries of the estate would not be, for example where they are UK charities. It is, therefore, important that they consider the capital gains tax position of beneficiaries and, where appropriate, transfer assets to the beneficiaries so that they can make the disposal. Alternatively, it is possible to appropriate assets to beneficiaries and make the sale as a bare trustee on their behalf. HM Revenue & Customs requires evidence of the appropriation and of the approval of the beneficiary for the sale.

Losses in the same year of assessment can be set off against the gains, and any excess losses may be carried forward to the following year. They cannot be transferred to beneficiaries, so there may be cases where it is preferable to vest the asset in the beneficiary and let the beneficiary make the disposal.

Personal representatives have an annual exemption equal to that of an individual in the tax year of death and the following 2 tax years. After that period, no further exemption is available and gains are charged at the full rate(s).

Personal representatives pay capital gains tax at the higher rates (20% and 28% on residential land) irrespective of the level of income and gains.

28.5 EXEMPTIONS AND RELIEFS

28.5.1 Annual exemption

It has already been seen that individuals have an annual exemption (£12,300 in tax year 2022–23 and frozen until the end of tax year 2025–26) to set off against total net gains, and that personal representatives have the same exemption for the year of assessment which includes the date of death, and for the following 2 years. Thereafter personal representatives have no annual exemption. They should, therefore, try to time disposals so as to take advantage of the annual exemptions available in the first 3 tax years of the administration.

Trustees have an annual exemption which is half that of an individual (unless the settlor created more than one settlement, in which case the annual exemption is divided among the trusts with a minimum of one tenth of the full annual exemption per trust).

28.5.2 Money

Money held in sterling is not an asset for capital gains tax purposes and is not therefore subject to capital gains tax.

28.5.3   Chattels disposed of for £6,000 or less

If the amount or value of the consideration for an article or a set of articles is equal to or less than £6,000 at the time of disposal then, provided the asset being disposed of is tangible, movable property, no capital gains tax is payable on any gain accruing on the disposal.

28.5.4   Private dwelling houses

The exemption in respect of a private dwelling house is one of the most important exemptions in practice, and is contained in TCGA 1992, section 222. A person's only or main residence may be disposed of, and the whole of any gain arising is exempt from capital gains tax. The exemption includes the garden and grounds of up to 0.5 hectare or such larger area as is required for the reasonable enjoyment of the dwelling house. Provided the dwelling house is covered by the exemption, a gain made on the disposal of part of the grounds or garden is also exempt from capital gains tax where the house itself is retained. If a dwelling house is to be sold separately from part of its grounds, the grounds should always be sold first to take advantage of the exemption in respect of both disposals (see *Varty (Inspector of Taxes) v Lynes* [1976] 3 All ER 447).

Qualifying residence

For relief to be available, the dwelling house in question must have been the individual's only or main residence throughout the period of ownership, except that for disposals on or after 6 April 2020, the last 9 months of ownership, for example where the owner moves into new property and experiences delay in selling the former.

(For disposals before 6 April 2020 and on or after 6 April 2014, the period was 18 months. For disposals before 6 April 2014, the last 3 years of ownership were ignored. This period will continue to apply after 6 April 2014 in some situations where the person disposing of the property is a disabled person or has gone into care.)

While it is usually apparent whether particular property has been used as the main dwelling house of the individual, or forms part of it, this is not always the case.

Where a dwelling house has been occupied as a main residence for part only of the individual's ownership (after March 1982) then only a corresponding proportion of any gain is exempt. The taxpayer is entitled to have a total of 3 years disregarded in respect of periods of absence – and longer periods if the absence was necessitated by employment – provided the house was the main residence of the taxpayer both before and after each such period of absence.

Where the whole or part of the property has been let as residential accommodation, this may result in a partial loss of the exemption. However, the gain attributable to the letting (calculated according to how much was let and for how long) is exempt up to the lesser of £40,000 and the exemption attributable to the owner's occupation. This relief does not apply if the let portion forms a separate dwelling (TCGA 1992, section 223(4)). HM Revenue & Customs has stated that taking in a lodger does not result in loss of the exemption provided the lodger lives as part of the family and shares living accommodation (SP14/80) (see also HM Revenue & Customs, *Capital Gains Manual* at CG64702, available at www.gov.uk/hmrc-internal-manuals/capital-gains-manual).

The exemption is available to non-resident individuals disposing of a UK residential property that has been their main or only residence, but only in respect of gains attributed to tax years during which they have stayed (or they and their spouse or civil partner have between them stayed) overnight on least 90 occasions in their UK property or UK properties (TCGA 1992, section 222C). The exemption is also available to non-resident trustees disposing of a UK residential property that has been the main or only residence of a trust beneficiary, but where that beneficiary is a non-resident they must satisfy the 90-day test.

Nomination of main residence

Where a taxpayer has more than one residence, they may nominate which is to be the main residence for capital gains tax purposes. Spouses and civil partners who live together may nominate only one residence between them (TCGA 1992, section 222(6)).

For periods of occupation up to and including 6 April 1988 a further exemption may be claimed in respect of property owned by the taxpayer and occupied rent-free by a dependent relative of theirs. This exemption, contained in Capital Gains Tax Act 1979, section 105, was abolished by the Finance Act 1988 for all periods after 6 April 1988.

Personal representatives

Section 225A extends the main residence to disposals by personal representatives in limited circumstances. The dwelling-house must have been the only or main residence of one or more individuals who are entitled as to at least 75% of the net proceeds of disposal of the property.

Trustees

TCGA 1992, section 225 extends the private residence exemption to trustees disposing of a dwelling house which has been the only or main residence of a person entitled to occupy it under the terms of the settlement during the trustee's period of ownership.

The exemption clearly applies to life tenants. In *Sansom v Peay* [1976] 1 WLR 1073, the court held that the exemption was available where a beneficiary occupied a property held on discretionary trusts even though occupation was a matter for the trustees' discretion.

28.5.5 Other exempt property

Statutory provisions exempt from capital gains tax on a disposal certain other property, for example private motor cars; decorations awarded for valour unless acquired for money or money's worth; National Savings certificates and government stocks; shares in personal equity plans and individual savings accounts. Where heritage property is given or sold by private treaty to a charity or other national institution, any gain will be exempt from capital gains tax provided the Treasury so directs (TCGA 1992, section 258(2)). As in the case of inheritance tax, gains on gifts of heritage property will be conditionally exempt provided the requisite undertakings are given as to maintenance, preservation and access (TCGA 1992, section 258(3)(4)). Gains on any property accepted by the Treasury in satisfaction of inheritance tax is exempt from capital gains tax (TCGA 1992, section 258(2)(b)). See Chapter 27 for details of the equivalent inheritance tax exemption.

28.5.6 Charities

Disposals to charities and by charities and certain national institutions are exempt from capital gains tax (TCGA 1992, section 257).

28.5.7 Spouses and civil partners

Spouses and civil partners are each entitled to a full annual exemption, and are each taxed separately on their own gains. Where assets are transferred from one party to a marriage or civil partnership to the other, they are treated as disposed of for a consideration which produces neither a gain nor a loss (TCGA 1992, section 58). Thus the exemption cannot be used to 'uplift' the acquisition cost, but if the 'donee' spouse receives the property by reason of the death of the other, there is the usual 'uplift' on death.

Assets can therefore be freely transferred between spouses and civil partners without any charge to capital gains tax (except in the case of trading stock or where the transfer is by way of *donatio mortis causa*). When the donee spouse or civil partner disposes of the asset to someone other than the donor spouse or civil partner, the entire gain since the asset was acquired by the donor spouse or civil partner becomes chargeable.

The special treatment of disposals between spouses and civil partners applies only where the parties were living together in the year of assessment in which the disposal was made. If the parties have separated and the disposal is made in the following tax year, the no gain/no loss rule does not apply. Transfers between cohabitees cannot benefit from the no gain/no loss provision.

28.5.8 Life policies

Gains from the disposal of life insurance policies are exempt if the disposal is made by the original beneficial owner (TCGA 1992, section 210). But if the person making the disposal is not the original beneficial owner and acquired the policy for value, the gain is chargeable.

28.5.9 Holdover relief

Holdover relief operates by allowing a transferee to elect not to pay capital gains tax at the time of receiving a gift but instead to 'hold over' or defer payment of the tax. The effect is that the transferee is deemed to acquire the property at the acquisition cost of the transferor, and is therefore liable for tax on the whole gain from the date the transferor acquired the property to the time of disposal by the transferee. If the transferee makes a disposal by way of a gift, the subsequent transferee may also elect to hold over the gain. If this continues until a transferee dies, the uplift on death would mean that the tax never becomes payable.

The charge to capital gains tax can normally be held over under TCGA 1992, section 260, where the charge is on a transfer which is a chargeable transfer for inheritance tax purposes. Thus, after 22 March 2006, lifetime transfers to settlements other than those for the disabled can qualify for holdover relief, as they do not qualify as potentially exempt transfers. So too can appointments on the determination of a relevant property trust. Disposals from accumulation and maintenance trusts, bereaved minor trusts and bereaved young person trusts also attract holdover relief under TCGA 1992, section 260.

The charge may also be held over under TCGA 1992, section 165, as amended by Finance Act 2000, section 90, on a gift or transfer of business assets to an individual or a trust, but not a transfer of shares or securities to a company.

Changes introduced by the Finance Act 2006 substantially limited the availability of holdover relief. The relief is not available if the settlement is 'settlor interested'. From 6 April 2006 a settlement is settlor interested if any property 'is or will or may become payable to or applicable for the benefit of a child of the [settlor] at a time when the child is a dependant of his'. For this purpose, a dependent child is a child of the settlor (including a step-child) who is under the age of 18 and unmarried and does not have a civil partner (TCGA 1992, section 169F(3A), (4A) and (4B), inserted by Finance Act 2006, Schedule 12, paragraph 4).

If having claimed holdover relief, the settlement becomes settlor interested within 6 years of the end of the tax year in which the disposal was made (e.g. where the class of beneficiaries includes the settlor's children, all of whom are adult at the date of creation, but an additional child is born after creation or the settlor remarries and acquires a minor step-child), the relief is clawed back (TCGA 1992, section 169C).

It is common to include a clause excluding the settlor, the settlor's spouse or civil partner by providing that the following are not to benefit:

> during the Settlor's life, the Settlor's children and step-children who:
> (i)   are under eighteen; and
> (ii) are not married or in a civil partnership.

28.6   ACCELERATED PAYMENT OF TAX

Finance Act 2019, section 14 and Schedule 2 introduced accelerated reporting and payment dates for capital gains tax on UK land disposed of by *non-residents* starting in tax year 2019–20.

The change has been extended and now applies to all disposals of UK residential land on or after 6 April 2020 *where tax is due*. It applies to disposals made by personal representative and trustees as well as to disposals by individuals.

The date of disposal is fixed by reference to the date of unconditional exchange of contracts. The return and payment must be submitted within 60 days of completion of the disposal (30 days where completion was before 27 October 2021).

No returns are required for disposals where no tax is due, for example because the gain:

- is within the annual exemption;
- is covered by existing losses;

- attracts main residence relief; or
- is to a spouse or civil partner (no gain/no loss disposal).

The calculation of tax is made on the basis of events so far in the tax year with an approximation of the level of income expected during the year. The payment made is on account of the tax due at the end of the year. However, it is not necessary to submit a self-assessment tax return if the tax paid was correct and there is no further need for a return.

The payment may turn out to be too little (e.g. where the taxpayer's combined income and gains unexpectedly exceeds the higher rate limit) or too much (e.g. where income is less than expected or losses are made later in the tax year). Where too little has been paid, the additional amount is simply paid with the rest of the tax.

HM Revenue & Customs has confirmed that, provided reasonable estimates were used at the time of the report, interest will not be charged if the payment on account is subsequently found to be insufficient – as long as the box highlighting that the tax return contained an estimate was ticked. HM Revenue & Customs has said it will charge interest if an estimate was used, but not indicated on the tax return.

In practice, since it will be necessary to estimate the income figure at the time of the tax return in almost all cases as the tax return is being made before the end of the tax year, most tax returns will need to indicate that an estimate has been used. The accelerated payment rules apply to personal representatives and trustees as well as to personal representatives.

28.7   REARRANGING SUCCESSION PROVISIONS AFTER DEATH

Post-death variations, which are effective for capital gains tax purposes, can be entered into. TCGA 1992, section 62(6) is, however, more limited than the corresponding inheritance tax provision. The disposition is treated as the deceased's for the purposes of section 62 as a whole, but for other capital gains tax purposes, the person making the variation is treated as the person making the disposition. For example, if the variation creates a settlement, the person making the variation is regarded as the settlor. This was known to be the position as the result of the decision in *Marshall v Kerr* [1995] 1 AC 148, but Finance Act 2006, Schedule 12 inserted a new section 68C into the TCGA 1992 which sets this out expressly.

The requirements for a variation to be effective for capital gains tax are the same as those for an effective inheritance tax variation (see **27.13**). The instrument must state that TCGA 1992, section 62(6) is to apply. The person making the variation is free to choose that the disposition be treated as the deceased's for one tax, but not the other.

It is usually desirable to choose that the disposition be the deceased's for capital gains tax purposes. There are, however, occasions when it may be beneficial for the property to be treated as passing first to the original beneficiary and then to the new beneficiary. For example:

(i) Where the asset has increased by less than the level of the annual exemption and the person making the variation has made no other disposals that tax year. The person making the variation will acquire the asset at probate value, and will then be treated as making a disposal to the new beneficiary at current market value. The gain will be covered by the annual exemption of the person making the variation so no tax will be payable. The new beneficiary will have the benefit of an increased acquisition value.
(ii) Where the person making the variation has unused losses which can be offset against the increase in value since the death.

To be effective:

(i) any variation must be made in writing and within 2 years of the deceased's death;
(ii) the variation must state that it is to be effective for capital gains tax purposes;
(iii) there must be no consideration other than the making of another variation;
(iv) any person giving up a benefit must consent to the variation. If the beneficiary is a minor or under a disability making them unable to consent, then the court must consent to the variation on the beneficiary's behalf.

If the variation creates a settlement, the person making the variation is regarded as the settlor for capital gains tax purposes (Finance Act 2006), but not for inheritance tax purposes.

28.8 BASIC TAX PLANNING

The tax implications of the retention or disposal of assets must be looked at as a whole, taking both inheritance tax and capital gains tax into consideration. It is often a balancing exercise. One advantage of retaining assets which have substantially increased in value since acquisition is the 'uplift' on death which exempts such property from capital gains tax on gains during the deceased's lifetime. Assets can then be passed to beneficiaries by will or on intestacy.

If lifetime gifts are to be made, then gifts of money may be made free of capital gains tax. Where cash is not available, it is advisable to make gifts of items exempt from capital gains tax or subject to reliefs and, if possible, to give assets which are likely to appreciate in value, but which have yet to do so.

Chapter 29

Settlements

Settlements are widely used as part of standard will drafting and estate planning. Often the motive is asset protection rather than tax saving. However, it is important to understand the tax consequences of creating and running settlements so that settlements are used only in appropriate circumstances.

29.1 LIABILITY TO INHERITANCE TAX

29.1.1 Introduction

A settlement is defined for inheritance tax purposes by Inheritance Tax Act 1984, section 43 as any disposition whereby property is:

(i) held in trust for persons in succession or subject to a contingency; or
(ii) held by trustees on trust to accumulate the whole or part of any income or with power to make discretionary payments; or
(iii) charged (otherwise than for full consideration in money or money's worth) with the payment of an annuity or other periodical payment payable for a life or any other limited or terminable period.

Thus, it does not include property held on a bare trust or as a nominee, or property held by persons as co-owners.

Substantial changes to the taxation of settlements were made by the Finance Act 2006.

29.1.2 Settlements created before 22 March 2006

Until the Finance Act 2006, there were two groups of settlements – those with an interest in possession and those without.

Lifetime transfers to settlements with an interest in possession were treated as potentially exempt transfers (Inheritance Tax Act 1984, section 3). Whether the settlement was created by lifetime transfer or on death, the beneficiary with the interest in possession was treated under section 49 of the 1984 Act as beneficially entitled to the underlying capital. Any termination of the interest in possession was a transfer of value by that beneficiary.

Settlements without an interest in possession were sub-divided into those which qualified for privileged inheritance tax treatment and those which did not. Those qualifying for privileged treatment were accumulation and maintenance trusts and trusts for a disabled beneficiary. Settlements not qualifying for privileged treatment (broadly, discretionary trusts and contingent trusts not qualifying as accumulation and maintenance trusts) were subject to three possible charges to inheritance tax:

(i)   an entry charge when property was transferred to the settlement;
(ii) a 10-year anniversary charge at 10-yearly intervals from the creation of the settlement;
(iii) an exit charge when property ceased to be held on relevant property trusts.

This regime, often called the 'relevant property' regime, continues after the Finance Act 2006 for settlements created before the Act came into force and, as set out below, has been extended to other types of lifetime settlement created afterwards. The method of calculation of tax is described at **29.1.3**.

Accumulation and maintenance trusts had to satisfy the three requirements of Inheritance Tax Act 1984, section 71 that:

(i)   beneficiaries would become entitled to income or capital at or before the age of 25;
(ii) no interest in possession existed;
(iii) either the beneficiaries were children of a common grandparent, or the settlement had not lasted for more than 25 years.

If the settlement qualified as an accumulation and maintenance trust, it benefited from the following privileges:

(i)   the lifetime creation would be a potentially exempt transfer rather than a lifetime chargeable transfer;
(ii) there would be no periodic charge on each 10-year anniversary of the settlement's creation;
(iii) there would be no exit charge when beneficiaries became entitled to income or capital.

Accumulation and maintenance trusts in existence on 15 March 2006 were able to retain their privileged status but had to fulfil more stringent requirements (see **29.1.4**). A number of such trusts still continue.

Trusts for a disabled beneficiary had to fulfil the then requirements of Inheritance Tax Act 1984, section 89. The beneficiary had to be incapable by reason of mental disorder within the meaning of the Mental Health Act 1983 of administering their property or managing their affairs, or in receipt of attendance allowance or disability living allowance. There were no restrictions on the application of income, but at least half the capital had to be paid to the disabled beneficiary. Assuming all the requirements were satisfied, the trust would be treated as a trust with an interest in possession. The requirements were significantly amended by the Finance Act 2013.

29.1.3   Settlements created after 22 March 2006

The rules have changed substantially since the Finance Act 2006. Transitional provisions apply to existing accumulation and maintenance trusts and interest in possession trusts. These are dealt with **29.1.4**.

In relation to transfers made after 22 March 2006, liability to inheritance tax depends largely on whether the settlement was created by lifetime settlement or on death. Many more settlements are subject to the relevant property regime.

All settlements created by lifetime transfer are subject to the relevant property regime unless they qualify as a trust for a disabled beneficiary. Trusts created on death are subject to the relevant property regime unless they qualify as a trust for a disabled beneficiary, a trust with an immediate post-death interest or a trust for a bereaved minor or bereaved young person (see below).

The method for calculating the rate of tax has changed for charges on relevant property settlements arising on or after 18 November 2015, as to which see Chapter 16. In this chapter, we consider only the new rules.

The relevant property regime

As explained at **29.1.2**, there are three points at which inheritance tax is chargeable:

(i)   when property is transferred to the settlement (lifetime transfers are charged at half the death rates);

(ii)   on each 10-year anniversary of the creation of the settlement;

(iii) an exit charge when property ceases to be held on relevant property trusts (calculated on the number of completed quarter years since the last anniversary, using the rate of tax calculated on the last anniversary).

The anniversary charge is calculated on the value of the property in the settlement at the date of the anniversary.

The rate to be charged is calculated by working out the tax that would be charged at lifetime rates on a 'hypothetical chargeable transfer', turning it into an average rate and then applying 30% of the average rate to the value of the relevant property in the settlement.

The hypothetical chargeable transfer is found by adding together:

- the value of the relevant property in the settlement;
- the value immediately after the settlement of any relevant property in a related settlement (one created on the same day, usually nil);
- the value of any 'same day addition' as defined in Inheritance Tax Act 1984, section 62A (as to which, see **16.3**).

The table of rates is joined at the point reached by the settlor's chargeable transfers in the 7 years before creating, or adding to, the settlement plus any chargeable transfers from the settlement in the last 10 years.

Hence, where the settlor's nil rate band is unused at creation, the settlement inherits that full nil rate band. (Note that if the settlor adds funds later at a time when they have used some or all of their nil rate band, the settlement's nil rate band is similarly reduced.)

The rate of tax applied to the hypothetical chargeable transfer is always the lifetime rate, even where the settlement was created on death.

The tax calculated is converted into an average or estate rate and the tax actually charged is at 30% of that average rate. The maximum rate charged is, thus, 30% of 20% = 6%. The maximum rate is only chargeable when the settlor had no nil rate band available at creation for the settlement to inherit.

The exit charge is calculated at the previous anniversary rate. It is charged on the value of the property leaving the settlement. The number of complete quarters (3-month periods) since the last anniversary is used to ascertain the appropriate proportion of the periodic charge.

> **Example**
>
> Trustees appoint £20,000 from a discretionary trust exactly 2 years after the last anniversary.
>
> Assume the average rate charged on the last anniversary was 4.5%.
>
> There are eight complete quarters since the last anniversary, so the rate of tax for the exit charge is calculated as:
>
> 8/40 x 4.5% = 0.9%
>
> This rate is applied to the £20,000, leaving the settlement:
>
> 0.9% x £20,000 = £180

If a transfer is made within the first 3 months after an anniversary, there is no charge to tax as there are no completed quarters.

During the first 10 years, the rate for the exit charge has to be calculated in a special way as there is no previous anniversary charge on which to base it. The rate is calculated by reference to the settlor's cumulative total immediately before the creation of the settlement. No account is taken of any earlier transfers made from the settlement. The value is the value of the property in the settlement at the date of creation. The result is that if the property settled was within the settlor's nil rate band, all transfers from the settlement are at 0% during the first 10 years.

> **Example**
>
> A settlor creates a settlement in May 2020 of £325,000 at a time when their cumulative total is nil.
>
> The trustees appoint £50,000 to a beneficiary in May 2025. The exit charge will be at 0%.
>
> In April 2030, just before the 10th anniversary of the settlement, the trustees decide to appoint the rest of the trust property, now worth £700,000 (significantly more than the nil rate band applying at that point), to a beneficiary. The exit charge will be at 0%.
>
> However, if the trustees wait until 6 months after the first 10-year anniversary to make the appointment of the £700,000 of trust property, there would be an anniversary charge and a small exit charge.

As seen in the above example, it is, therefore, important for trustees to review trusts shortly before each 10-year anniversary.

Lifetime settlements created on or after 22 March 2006

All lifetime settlements created on or after 22 March 2006 are subject to the relevant property regime previously applicable to discretionary trusts, unless created for a disabled beneficiary (Inheritance Tax Act 1984, section 89), or a 'self-settlement' created by a settlor suffering from a condition reasonably expected to lead to such disability (Inheritance Tax Act 1984, section 89A), in which case they are treated as settlements with an interest in possession under Inheritance Tax Act 1984, section 49.

Thus, property settled on a spouse for life on or after 22 March 2006 is subject to the relevant property regime, as is property settled on children contingent on reaching a specified age. The surviving spouse exemption is not available. Transfers to such settlements attract an immediate charge to inheritance tax at half the death rates. There are anniversary and exit charges.

The only potentially exempt transfers that remain are transfers from one individual to another individual absolutely or to a settlement qualifying as a trust for a disabled beneficiary under Inheritance Tax Act 1984, section 89 or section 89A.

For a discussion of trusts for a disabled beneficiary, see **18.10**.

Settlements created on death on or after 22 March 2006

Certain trusts created on death qualify for privileged inheritance tax treatment. These exceptional cases are:

- bereaved minor trusts (satisfying the requirements of Inheritance Tax Act 1984, section 71A trusts);
- bereaved young person trusts (satisfying the requirements of Inheritance Tax Act 1984, section 71D trusts);
- trusts for the disabled (satisfying the requirements of Inheritance Tax Act 1984, section 89);
- immediate post-death interests (satisfying the requirements of Inheritance Tax Act 1984, section 49A).

All other trusts are subject to the relevant property regime outlined above.

Settlements for bereaved minors (Inheritance Tax Act 1984, section 71A)

Settlements for bereaved minors are settlements established on intestacy for the deceased's issue or under the will of a deceased parent for their own minor child, or established under the criminal injuries compensation scheme, which comply with the following conditions:

(i) that the bereaved minor will become entitled to the capital, together with any income arising from it or already accumulated, at latest at age 18; and

(ii) that all income applied while the bereaved minor is living and under 18 is applied for the benefit of the bereaved minor; and

(iii) that, while the bereaved minor is living and under 18, either the minor is entitled to all the income arising, or no such income may be applied for any other person.

Provided the conditions are complied with, there is no charge to tax when:

(i) the bereaved minor becomes absolutely entitled to capital at or below age 18; or

(ii) the bereaved minor dies under that age; or

(iii) capital is paid or applied for the advancement or benefit of the bereaved minor.

Capital gains tax holdover relief is available under TCGA 1992, section 260, when the beneficiary becomes absolutely entitled as against the trustees.

Inheritance Tax Act 1984, section 71A(4)(c) provides that the existence of a power of advancement under Trustee Act 1925, section 32, or an express power to like effect, does not prevent the trust from fulfilling the capital condition.

It is possible, in appropriate cases, for the trustees to advance capital for the benefit of the beneficiary on new trusts. The existence of that power does not prejudice the status of the trust, but once exercised, the new settlement created would not be a bereaved minor settlement and would be subject to anniversary and exit charges.

Settlements for bereaved minors are relatively inflexible. There are the following limitations:

(i) to qualify as a bereaved minor's settlement, a settlement created by will must be for the parent's *own* child. Although it is possible to include a substitutional gift to children of a deceased child without prejudicing the status of the rest of the settlement, if a grandchild takes in substitution for a deceased child, that part of the settlement is held on relevant property trusts;

(ii) the beneficiaries must become entitled to *capital* at 18. It is not enough to become entitled to income.

Inheritance Tax Act 1984, section 71A and section 71D are drafted by reference to a single beneficiary (in section 71A called the 'bereaved minor' and in section 71D called 'B'). This suggests that each beneficiary must be entitled to a fixed share and that there can be no 'switching' of funds between beneficiaries. However, on 20 June 2007, HM Revenue & Customs agreed guidance on sections 71A and 71D and accumulation and maintenance trusts with Emma Chamberlain and Chris Whitehouse, both then of 5 Stone Buildings, Lincoln's Inn. In this guidance, HM Revenue & Customs said that it is possible to pluralise the 'bereaved minor' or 'B' to include all beneficiaries within the relevant class provided they are *alive* at the date the section 71A or section 71D trusts take effect and are under the specified age. That guidance is now contained in HM Revenue & Customs, *Inheritance Tax Manual* at IHTM 42816 (available at www.hmrc.gov.uk/manuals/ihtmanual) (though, oddly, only in relation to bereaved young persons).

The guidance said a will trust in the following terms can qualify as an Inheritance Tax Act 1984, section 71A trust:

> to such of my children alive at my death as attain the age of 18 years and if more than one in such shares as the trustees shall from time to time by deed or deeds revocable or irrevocable appoint and in default of such appointment in equal shares absolutely at 18 provided that no such appointment shall be made and no such appointment shall be revoked so as to either diminish or to increase the share (or the accumulations of income forming part of the share) of or give a new share (or new accumulations of income) to a child who at the date of such appointment or revocation has reached the age of 18 nor to benefit a child who has been excluded from benefit as a result of the exercise of the power.

The following should be noted:

- It is not necessary to fix the shares in which each child takes income and capital while they are all under 18. Hence it is possible to pay out income and capital to the minor children in unequal shares.
- The power of selection must not be capable of being exercised so as to vary the share of a child who has *already* reached 18. Assume three beneficiaries B1, B2 and B3. It is possible to specify at any time before the eldest (B1) reaches 18 the share B1 is to take but once B1 reaches 18 any further power of selection can only be exercised between B2 and B3. B1 ceases to be within the definition of 'B' in these circumstances.
- If the power of selection is exercised revocably then it is not possible by revoking that exercise to benefit someone who has been wholly excluded from benefit albeit revocably. If, for example, the whole relevant share is appointed revocably to B3 (but on terms that the appointment could be revoked to confer benefits on B1 or B2) then even though B1 and B2 are under 18 the trust ceases to qualify for section 71A status. HM Revenue &

Customs considers that it is not possible under the section 71A regime for someone who is not currently benefiting to become entitled in the future. Practitioners will therefore need to be careful before exercising any power of appointment revocably.

- HM Revenue & Customs does not consider that section 71A is breached merely because a power of appointment might be exercised in this way. Nor is it a problem if, in the above example, the power of appointment is exercised revocably so as to give B1 5%, B2 5% and B3 90%. Since B1 and B2 are not wholly excluded, HM Revenue & Customs takes the view that they can still benefit under a future exercise of the power since they remain within 'B'.

- Nor is there a problem if a beneficiary dies under 18 leaving children in whose favour there will be incorporated substitutionary provisions. Hence if B1 dies before 18 leaving children and B1's presumptive or fixed share passes to those children under the terms of the will, it is only *from that point* that the presumptive share of B1 will cease to qualify under section 71A and fall within the relevant property regime. The mere possibility that B1 could die before 18 with children taking B1's share does not breach the section 71A conditions. Any power of selection, though, must not be capable of varying the presumptive share of the deceased B1 once he has died – because B1's children are not within the definition of B and their share must not be increased or decreased after B1 has died.

- No overriding powers of appointment can be included which might allow 'B's' absolute entitlement to be defeated at 18 although the legislation provides that the existence of an extended power of advancement (i.e. an express or statutory power of advancement that could be used to defer the beneficiary's capital entitlement by, for instance, providing that B's share was to be held on life interest trusts beyond the age of 18) will not in itself cause the trust to fail to satisfy the section 71A conditions from the outset. However, if the settled power of advancement is exercised so as to defer vesting of capital at 18 (e.g. by the making of a settled advance) then although there is no charge under section 71A on the ending of the bereaved minor trust, the relevant share from that point falls within the relevant property regime.

All the points above apply to Inheritance Tax Act 1984, section 71D trusts set up by will and to accumulation and maintenance trusts which are converted to fall within section 71D before 6 April 2008 (or before a beneficiary has attained an interest in possession if earlier). Hence it will be necessary to ensure that any powers of appointment that are retained do not permit a beneficiary's absolute share to be altered after they have reached 25 or defeated on reaching that age and if a power of appointment is exercised revocably it must not be capable of benefiting anyone who has been wholly excluded (even if under 25 and even if the exclusion was revocable).

A very simple clause suffices to comply with the requirements of Inheritance Tax Act 1984, section 71A. Precedent 17N does so, provided the age contingency for the children is fixed at 18. If any issue are substituted for a deceased child, the portion of the trust fund in which the issue take an interest would not qualify as a bereaved minor trust.

Settlements for bereaved young people – 'age 18-to-25 trusts' (Inheritance Tax Act 1984, section 71D)

These settlements were introduced to counter criticisms that 18 was too early an age to allow children access to capital. The requirements are the same as for Inheritance Tax Act 1984, section 71A trusts, so these settlements can be created by will only for the deceased's own children, but instead of the children having to become entitled to capital at 18, the children can become entitled to capital at any age before 25. Pending entitlement to capital, either the beneficiary must be entitled to the income, or the income must be accumulated for their benefit, and there must be no power to apply income for the benefit of any other person.

As with Inheritance Tax Act 1984, section 71A settlements, the existence of the section 32 power to advance capital to the beneficiary (or an express power in similar terms) does not prejudice the status of the trust.

As with Inheritance Tax Act 1984, section 71A settlements, the power of advancement can be used to make a settled advance deferring entitlement beyond 25. At that point the settlement will cease to qualify as a section 71D settlement and will enter the relevant property regime.

While the beneficiary is under 18 there are no periodic or exit charges. Once the beneficiary reaches 18 a special charging regime set out in Inheritance Tax Act 1984, section 71F applies. Tax is calculated in broadly the same way as the exit charge applying to other trusts. The value of the property to which the beneficiary becomes entitled is charged at 30% of lifetime rates multiplied by the number of complete quarters which have elapsed since the beneficiary's 18th birthday.

Most clients who are making provision for their children will prefer to leave their property on Inheritance Tax Act 1984, section 71D trusts rather than on section 71A trusts. With section 71D trusts, the trustees are free to advance the trust property to the beneficiaries at 18 if that seems appropriate, in which case no inheritance tax is payable. If, however, it seems appropriate to defer entitlement to 25 or beyond, they can do so at the cost of a charge to tax for the period following the beneficiary's 18th birthday.

Precedent 17N creates an Inheritance Tax Act 1984, section 71D settlement if the age contingency for the children is fixed at 25. If any issue are substituted for a deceased child, the portion of the trust fund in which the issue take an interest would not qualify as a section 71D settlement.

Immediate post-death interests (Inheritance Tax Act 1984, section 49A)

A beneficiary qualifies under section 49 as beneficially entitled to the trust capital of the trust only if their interest qualifies as an immediate post-death interest under section 49A.

To qualify as an immediate post-death interest the following conditions must be fulfilled:

(i)   the settlement must be created by will or on intestacy;
(ii)   the beneficiary must have become beneficially entitled to the interest in possession on the death and have continued to be so entitled without interruption;
(iii) the settlement must not be a bereaved minors' trust or a trust for the disabled.

The existence of overriding powers which allow the trustees to terminate the interest in possession does not prejudice the status of the trust. If the trustees exercise those powers to transfer property to another beneficiary outright, the beneficiary with the interest in possession is treated as making a potentially exempt transfer. If the trustees appoint some or all of the trust property on continuing trusts, the beneficiary is treated as making a chargeable transfer of value (unless the trusts are for a disabled beneficiary, in which case the transfer would be potentially exempt). If the original beneficiary is included as a beneficiary of the new trusts, the original beneficiary is treated as making a gift for the purposes of the reservation of benefit rules (Finance Act 1986, section 103ZA).

The ability to create an immediate post-death interest for a surviving spouse (or civil partner) with a power to terminate it at a later stage is a useful tax planning tool offering a variety of advantages which are not all tax related:

(i)   the spouse exemption will be available to the property subject to the interest when the first spouse dies;
(ii)   if the trust continues until the death of the survivor, the transferable nil rate band will be available on the survivor's death;
(iii) the fact that the property is settled gives the first spouse to die control over the ultimate destination of the capital (particularly helpful in the case of second marriages) and protection against nursing home fees;

(iv)   the power to terminate the interest gives flexibility and allows the trustees to make capital available to the survivor or to issue depending on circumstances and needs.

Interests in possession created by appointment from a relevant property trust within 2 years of death are read back to the date of death under Inheritance Tax Act 1984, section 144 (see Schedule 20, paragraph 27) and will retrospectively create an immediate post-death interest.

Immediate post-death interests are likely to be created most often for surviving spouses, but they are not limited to surviving spouses and can be created for anyone. Some clients may wish to create immediate post-death interests for their children as a way of deferring their capital entitlement without incurring anniversary and exit charges.

The introduction of the new RNRB which is only available where property is inherited by children or issue of the deceased absolutely or left to a trust for a disabled beneficiary, an Inheritance Tax Act 1984, section 71A or section 71D trust or on trusts creating immediate post-death interests means that there may be more interest in using immediate post-death interests for young people. Grandparents cannot create section 71A or section 71D trusts so, if they want the residence to be held on trust, an immediate post-death interest will be their only option.

The RNRB is available on the death of a beneficiary with an immediate post-death interest in a trust containing a residence or interest in a residence, provided that a lineal descendant of the beneficiary is beneficially entitled to the residence on the death of the beneficiary (Inheritance Tax Act 1984, section 8J(5)). It should be remembered that a lineal descendant includes a step-child.

The unwanted immediate post-death interest

A will creating a settlement for the deceased's own children contingent on reaching an age between 18 and 25 which also gives the children an interim right to income would qualify both as an immediate post-death interest as defined in Inheritance Tax Act 1984, section 49A and as a section 71A or section 71D settlement in the absence of statutory provision providing certainty. The legislation, therefore, introduces a 'pecking order' to decide the nature of the settlement. The rule is that if the conditions for more than one sort of settlement are satisfied, they will take effect in this order:

- section 71A (bereaved minor);
- section 49A (immediate post-death interest);
- section 71D (bereaved young person).

If a beneficiary of a section 71D trust obtains a right to income within 2 years of death (whether as a result of an appointment by trustees or the right to income at 18 created by Trustee Act 1925, section 31), the writing back effect of Inheritance Tax Act 1984, section 144 means that an immediate post-death interest is created.

The tax effects of having an immediate post-death interest rather than an interest in an Inheritance Tax Act 1984, section 71D trust are significant:

- the value of property in which a beneficiary has an immediate post-death interest is part of their estate for inheritance tax (Inheritance Tax Act 1984, section 49);
- for capital gains tax purposes when the beneficiary becomes entitled to capital (e.g. at the age of 25), there is a deemed disposal. In the case of a section 71D settlement, holdover relief is available (TCGA 1992, section 260) but in the case of a settlement with an immediate post-death interest no holdover relief is available under section 260.

Example

T's will leaves property to be held for her sons contingent on reaching 21. Trustee Act 1925, section 31 applies to the settlement.

When she dies there are three children:

- A aged 19;
- B aged 17; and
- C aged 14.

A has an immediate post-death interest from the date of death because he is entitled to income.

B will become entitled to income at 18 under Trustee Act 1925, section 31 but because this event is within 2 years of death, there will be automatic reading back into the will under Inheritance Tax Act 1984, section 144(3) as a result of which B will be treated as acquiring an immediate post-death interest.

C will become entitled to income at 18 four years after the death so there will be no reading back under section 144(3) and he will be a beneficiary of a section 71D settlement.

The solution to this problem lies in the drafting. The will should exclude the right to income under Trustee Act 1925, section 31(1)(ii) and allow the trustees' discretion to continue until the children become entitled to capital. The trustees must not use any express powers to appoint interests in income until 2 years after the death.

A similar problem arises if a beneficiary of a relevant property settlement created on death is given a right to income by the trustees within 2 years of death. The appointment is read back to the date of death under Inheritance Tax Act 1984, section 144 and will create a retrospective immediate post-death interest. See *Payne and Another v Tyler and Another* [2019] EWHC 2347 (Ch) for an example of the accidental creation of an immediate post-death interest in this way.

29.1.4 Transitional provisions

Accumulation and maintenance trusts already in existence at 22 March 2006 continued to enjoy privileged tax treatment until 6 April 2008. After that, their privileged tax treatment ceased, unless the trusts in place at that time provided for beneficiaries to become absolutely entitled to the trust property either:

(i)   at 18, in which case they remained as accumulation and maintenance trusts; or
(ii) at 25, in which case they became section 71D trusts.

(This is so even though the settlement in either case may have been a lifetime settlement and/or may have been created by a non-parent.)

Where the trusts did not satisfy either of those requirements, the settlements entered the relevant property regime. Periodic charges for such settlements are assessed on the 10th and subsequent anniversaries of the creation of the settlement, although the first charge is calculated in relation only to the period commencing on 6 April 2008. Thus, an accumulation and maintenance trust created in May 2002 for children, contingent on reaching age 25, which continued after 6 April 2008 became liable for its first periodic charge on 1 May 2012. The charge was two-tenths of the normal charge.

The pre-2006 rules for interest in possession trusts continue until the interest in existence at 22 March 2006 comes to an end. If the property passes to someone absolutely at that point, there is a transfer by the person whose interest in possession comes to an end. It will be either a transfer on death, or a potentially exempt transfer if made during the lifetime of the person whose interest is ending.

If the property remains in trust, this is treated as the creation of a new settlement and subject to the new rules.

The Finance Act 2006 contained provisions which allowed 'transitional serial interests' to be treated as qualifying interests in possession for the purposes of Inheritance Tax Act 1984, section 49.

A transitional serial interest arises in the following circumstances:

(i)   under Inheritance Tax Act 1984, section 49C, where an interest in possession existed before 22 March 2006 and came to an end after that date but before 6 April 2008 and someone obtained an interest in possession at that time; or

(ii) under Inheritance Tax Act 1984, section 49D, where an interest in possession existed before 22 March 2006 and came to an end on or after 6 April 2008 with the death of the beneficiary and the spouse of the original beneficiary obtaining an interest in possession; or

(iii) under Inheritance Tax Act 1984, section 49E, where there are successive interests in life assurance and the settlement existed before 22 March 2006.

29.1.5   Implications for will drafting

Clients who wish to benefit their children or grandchildren and avoid unnecessary charges to inheritance tax should consider how they want to leave their property. If there is a surviving spouse or civil partner, the simplest solution is to leave everything to the survivor in order to benefit from the spouse exemption on the first death and the transferable nil rate band on the second. The gift of residue can be absolute or, if the testator wants more control, can be a flexible life interest followed by a gift to the children contingent on reaching an age no greater than 25. The initial life interest to the spouse attracts the spouse exemption. The settlement can contain power for the trustees to apply capital for the benefit of the spouse or children. If the trustees appoint to the spouse, there is no inheritance tax effect. If they appoint to the children absolutely, the spouse is treated as making a potentially exempt transfer. If they appoint on continuing trusts for the children, the spouse is treated as making a lifetime chargeable transfer.

Leaving everything to the spouse whether absolutely or as an immediate post-death interest means that the first to die does not use their RNRB. It can be claimed by the personal representatives of the survivor. However, if the aggregated estates exceed the taper threshold (£2 million until 2025–26), the RNRB will be withdrawn by £1 for every £2 of excess.

If this is a concern, the first to die can consider:

(i)   creating a nil rate band discretionary trust to reduce the value in the aggregated estate; or

(ii) leaving assets to the survivor on flexible life interest trusts with a letter of wishes asking the trustees to terminate part of the interest by advancing capital to the issue if the estate approaches the taper threshold (this is preferable to relying on the spouse to make gifts from an absolute entitlement as the spouse may lose capacity);

(iii) leaving a residential property interest to the issue, but if the only residential property is the matrimonial home this will create problems if the children have divorce or debt problems (an immediate post-death interest for the issue with power for the trustees to advance capital may also be useful here).

Where testators want to leave substantial amounts to issue who are young at the time the will is executed, they rarely wish to make the gifts absolute, but will prefer to leave the assets on trust. Traditionally, such a trust would be made contingent on the beneficiaries reaching a stated age. However, unless the gifts are to the testator's own children and are contingent on them reaching an age no greater than 25, periodic and exit charges will be charged. Many testators may decide that they are willing to accept those charges in exchange for the benefit of deferring the beneficiary's entitlement to capital. Factors to consider are:

(i) the maturity of the beneficiary;
(ii) the extent to which the settled sum exceeds the nil rate band;
(iii) the length of time the property is likely to remain settled;
(iv) whether the rate of tax levied on periodic and exit charges remains relatively benign (at the time of writing the maximum is 30% of $20\% = 6\%$), or whether it is increased.

Alternatives are to leave the children or issue immediate post-death interests or to leave property on a bare trust. Such gifts will also allow the estate to benefit from the RNRB where the property settled includes a residence or interest in a residence. In the case of an immediate post-death interest, the trustees can be given power to advance capital to the beneficiaries. This has the advantage of giving control of the capital to the trustees, but it has the disadvantage that the property in which the child has an interest would be aggregated with their own estate in the event of death. The settlor can, though, control the ultimate destination of the trust funds.

A bare trust does not fall within the definition of a settlement for inheritance tax purposes, so there would be no continuing inheritance tax charges. The beneficiary is able to claim the property at 18 without a charge to inheritance tax. The property is treated as the child's for income and capital gains tax purposes, which is beneficial. But if the child dies before claiming the property at 18, the property is included in their estate for inheritance tax purposes. A further disadvantage is that the testator cannot control the destination of the property if the child dies before 18. It would pass with the rest of the child's assets – normally to the child's next of kin.

29.2 LIABILITY TO CAPITAL GAINS TAX

29.2.1 Definition of settled property

'Settlement' is not defined in the legislation on capital gains tax, but TCGA 1992, section 68, as amended by the Finance Act 2006, provides a definition of settled property:

> any property held in trust other than property to which section 60 applies and references, however expressed, to property comprised in a settlement, are references to settled property

Thus, references to property comprised in a settlement are always to be construed as references to settled property.

Section 60 applies to assets held by a person or persons as nominee for another, or as bare trustee for another or others, or as trustee for someone who would be absolutely entitled as against the trustee but for infancy or other disability. Where section 60 applies, the property is not settled property and is treated as if belonging to the beneficiary.

29.2.2 Creation of the settlement

While a settlement is created by a lifetime transfer, there is a deemed disposal by the settlor/donor to the trustee which gives rise to a charge to capital gains tax in the usual way. If the settlement is created on death, by will or intestacy, there is no capital gains tax and the acquisition values are uplifted so that the trustees are deemed to acquire the settled assets at their market value as at the settlor's death.

29.2.3 Actual disposals by trustees

A sale of settled assets by trustees gives rise to a charge to capital gains tax on the gain, taken to be the difference between the consideration on sale and the acquisition cost (or deemed acquisition cost), taking into account any allowable costs. Trustees have an annual exemption which is half that of an individual (if the settlor created more than one settlement, the exemption is divided among the group of settlements, with a minimum of one tenth of the full annual exemption).

The rate of capital gains tax paid by trustees is 18% on assets other than residential land which is charged at 28%.

29.2.4   Deemed disposal when beneficiary becomes absolutely entitled

When a beneficiary becomes absolutely entitled as against the trustees, there is a deemed disposal of that part of the property from the trustees to the beneficiary. Capital gains tax is chargeable on any gain in value between the acquisition by the trustees and the deemed disposal (TCGA 1992, section 71).

When a beneficiary becomes absolutely entitled on the death of a person with an interest in possession, there is a death uplift and no charge to capital gains tax. The beneficiary is deemed to acquire the property at its market value at the date of becoming absolutely entitled (TCGA 1992, section 72(1)).

Where the interest in possession is created on or after 22 March 2006, the death uplift and no-charge provisions apply only if the interest terminating is:

- an immediate post-death interest; or
- a transitional serial interest; or
- a trust for a bereaved minor.

In other cases, there is a deemed disposal if a beneficiary becomes absolutely entitled, with a consequent charge on any increase in the value of the trust property. If no beneficiary becomes absolutely entitled, there is no disposal and no charge.

29.2.5   Holdover relief

Holdover relief is available under TCGA 1992, section 260 on disposals which are immediately chargeable to inheritance tax. The changes to the taxation of trusts introduced by the Finance Act 2006 mean that most lifetime transfers to trusts made after 22 March 2006 are immediately chargeable, and holdover relief under TCGA 1992, section 260 is therefore available (unless the trust is settlor interested; see below).

Holdover relief under TCGA 1992, section 165 is available on all transfers of assets attracting business or agricultural property relief (again unless the trust is settlor interested; see below). It is also available on transfers from accumulation and maintenance trusts under TCGA 1992, section 260(2). This continues to be available to trusts which fulfil the requirements for accumulation and maintenance status. Holdover relief is also available under TCGA 1992, section 260 on disposals from trusts for bereaved minors and young persons.

Changes introduced by the Finance Act 2006 have substantially limited the availability of holdover relief. The relief is not available if the settlement is 'settlor interested'. From 6 April 2006, a settlement is 'settlor interested' if any property 'is or will or may become payable to or applicable for the benefit of a child of the [settlor] at a time when the child is a dependant of his'. For this purpose, a dependent child is a child of the settlor (including a step-child) who is under the age of 18 and unmarried and does not have a civil partner (TCGA 1992, section 169F(3A), (4A) and (4B), inserted by Finance Act 2006, Schedule 12, paragraph 4).

29.3   INHERITANCE TAX ACT 1984, SECTION 144: APPOINTMENTS FROM TRUSTS WITHIN 2 YEARS OF DEATH

The introduction of the transferable nil rate band in 2007 meant that Inheritance Tax Act 1984, section 144 was much more widely used, as many trustees decided that rather than having the bother of an ongoing trust when the first spouse or civil partner died, they would get rid of the trust by appointing the settled assets to the survivor. The section has been used even more frequently as a result of the introduction of the RNRB. It allows trustees to redistribute assets in a more tax-efficient way.

Inheritance Tax Act 1984, section 144(1) provides that where property comprised in a person's estate immediately before death is settled by will and within 2 years of their death, and before any interest in possession has subsisted in the property, an event occurs on which tax would otherwise be chargeable, no tax shall be charged and the Act shall apply as if the will had provided that on the testator's death the property should be held as it is after the event.

Examples

(1) T, who has made no chargeable lifetime transfers, leaves his substantial estate on discretionary trusts for the benefit of his wife and family.

Eight months after his death the trustees appoint everything to his wife. The whole estate will be treated as left to his wife and so will attract the spouse exemption. T's unused nil rate band will be transferred to his wife.

(2) A grandmother leaves her estate which includes a residence to her grandchildren contingent on reaching the age of 21.

When she dies, her grandchildren are aged 10 and 8. The trust is a relevant property settlement and so her estate will not benefit from the RNRB.

Within 2 years of death if the trustees appoint the residence to the grandchildren either on bare trusts or on immediate post-death interests in the residence, the estate will get the benefit of the RNRB.

Where the testator dies on or after 22 March 2006, 'interest in possession' is to be construed as an immediate post-death interest or a disabled person's interest (Inheritance Tax Act 1984, section 144(1A)).

It used to be crucial to make no appointments within the first 3 months of death. This was because the reading back provisions of Inheritance Tax Act 1984, section 144 apply only where there would otherwise be a charge to inheritance tax. There is no exit charge when property leaves a discretionary trust made within the first 3 months of creation of the settlement so there would be no reading back. This could be disastrous. See *Frankland v IRC* [1997] STC 1450, where trustees were unable to claim the spouse exemption on a very large appointment to a spouse made within the first 3 months of death.

Fortunately, the Finance (No 2) Act 2015 amended Inheritance Tax Act 1984, section 144 so that reading back does now take place if an appointment is made within 3 months of death.

Finance Act 2006, Schedule 20, paragraph 27 amended Inheritance Tax Act 1984, section 144 to make clear that appointments creating an immediate post-death interest and section 71A and section 71D trusts would be read back into the will.

Where trustees wish to appoint capital from the will trust, they can do so before the executors have vested assets in them. The trustees have a *chose in action* from the date of death – the right to the assets if not required by the executors for the payment of debts or expenses – and the trustees can appoint their rights under the will to the appointee. An early appointment can be advantageous for capital gains tax (see **29.3.1**).

Inheritance Tax Act 1984, section 144 does not impose any requirements as to form or wording and indeed talks in terms of 'events' so an informal advancement of capital is sufficient to engage section 144. However, the terms of a will trust often require the use of a deed to exercise a power of appointment; where this is the case the trustees must comply with the requirements if the appointment is to take effect.

It is important that the deed (or trustees' minute confirming an informal advancement of assets) is kept safe as this is proof that the terms of the will have been varied. Often the motive for the appointment is to get the spouse exemption with a view to claiming an additional nil rate band on the death of the surviving spouse. When making the claim on the death of the survivor, it will be necessary to demonstrate to HM Revenue & Customs that the will of the first to die was altered by Inheritance Tax Act 1984, section 144.

29.3.1 Capital gains tax and Inheritance Tax Act 1984, section 144

Section 144 applies only for inheritance tax purposes and there is no corresponding capital gains tax provision. General principles therefore apply.

An appointment from a settlement is a disposal and if assets have increased in value by more than the trustees' annual exemption since the trustees acquired them, there will be a charge to capital gains tax. Because section 144 appointments are read back into the will for inheritance tax purposes and are not chargeable to inheritance tax, holdover relief under TCGA 1992, section 260 is not available.

However, in a case where capital gains tax may be an issue, early planning can prevent an unnecessary charge. See HM Revenue & Customs, *Capital Gains Tax Manual* at CG31430 (available at www.gov.uk/hmrc-internal-manuals/capital-gains-manual). The paragraph states that if the trustees exercise their powers of appointment while the assets are still in the hands of the personal representative, the asset(s) should be treated as passing direct to the appointee from the estate. The trust disappears. The appointee is treated in the same way as any legatee of an estate and will take the assets at their death value.

29.3.2 Combining a post-death variation and an Inheritance Tax Act 1984, section 144 appointment

HM Revenue & Customs accepts that it is possible for both section 144 and section 142 of the Inheritance Tax Act 1984 to apply to the same assets to achieve 'double reading back' (see HM Revenue & Customs, *Inheritance Tax Manual* at IHTM35085, available at www.hmrc.gov.uk/manuals/ihtmanual). This is extremely useful.

For example, an adult beneficiary could use Inheritance Tax Act 1984, section 142 to vary their entitlement and create a discretionary trust. If the trustees exercise their power of appointment within 2 years of death in favour of a beneficiary of the trust, their appointment will be read back into the will.

Alternatively, if the terms of the will trust created on death are unsatisfactory, the trustees can appoint assets to an adult beneficiary absolutely. The appointee then uses Inheritance Tax Act 1984, section 142 to vary the terms of their entitlement to create a new discretionary trust with different terms. The new trust will be treated as created in the will.

29A   CLAUSE FOR INCLUSION IN A DISCRETIONARY WILL TRUST TO ENCOURAGE TRUSTEES TO TAKE ADVANTAGE OF INHERITANCE TAX ACT 1984, SECTION 144 OR OTHERWISE APPOINT BEFORE THE FIRST 10-YEAR ANNIVERSARY

[x]   Without imposing any binding trust or legal obligation on my Trustees I REQUEST them in exercising any powers afforded to them by this clause to consider the advisability or otherwise of exercising such powers prior to the second anniversary of my death and failing their so doing then prior to the tenth anniversary of my death.

Note: This provision may be included in any precedent where the will creates a relevant property trust (see e.g. Precedent 18F or Precedent 18H) purely by way of reminding the trustees to consider the merits of ending the trust within 2 years of death (to take advantage of Inheritance Tax Act 1984, section 144) or, alternatively, before the first 10-year anniversary charge falls due. The latter reminds the trustees of the advantage of a 9-year discretionary trust where the tax rate for any exit charge will be based on values at the date of death, i.e. historic values, rather than on the then current values.

29B   DEED OF APPOINTMENT BY TRUSTEES OF DISCRETIONARY WILL TRUST TO SPOUSE OR CIVIL PARTNER WITHIN 2 YEARS OF DEATH COMPLYING WITH INHERITANCE TAX ACT 1984, SECTION 144

THIS DEED OF APPOINTMENT made the [date]* by [name of first Trustee] of [address] and [name of second Trustee] of (address) (together 'the Appointors')
IS SUPPLEMENTAL to the will dated [date] ('the Will') of [name]) ('the Testator') who died on [date] which was proved on [date] by the Appointors [or as the case may be] at [name of probate registry]
WHEREAS
(i)   By clause [number] the Will established a discretionary trust [of the residue] of the Testator's estate ('the Will Trust').
(ii)   [name of Testator's surviving spouse or civil partner] ('the Beneficiary') is a member of the class of Beneficiaries as defined in clause [number] of the Will.
(ii)   The Appointors are the present Trustees of the Will Trust and are desirous of appointing [all] [such of] the assets comprised in the Will Trust as listed in the Schedule to this deed to the Beneficiary absolutely* within two years of the Testator's death so that such appointment will comply with the provisions of Inheritance Tax Act 1984, section 144.
NOW THIS DEED WITNESSES AS FOLLOWS
1   In exercise of their power under clause [number] and all other relevant powers, the Appointors hereby irrevocably appoint the property set out in the Schedule to the Beneficiary so that as from

the date of this deed such property is held on trust as to both capital and income for the Beneficiary absolutely.*

2   All income received by or on behalf of the Appointors or such of the Trustee or Trustees for the time being of the Will Trust from and after the date of this deed shall be treated as if it had arisen wholly after such date and the Apportionment Act 1870 shall not be applicable to it.**

SIGNED and DELIVERED as a deed, etc

(Signatures of the Appointors)

(Signatures of witnesses)

SCHEDULE

[Identify property to be appointed from the Will Trust]

* An appointment does not have to be an absolute one. The trustees of a discretionary trust can appoint the capital to trustees to hold for the spouse or civil partner on terminable interest in possession trusts (as in Precedent 18G). If the appointment is within 2 years of death, the reading back effect of section 144 will create an immediate post-death interest.

** An express reference to the disapplication of the Apportionment Act 1870 is included for clarity but is no longer required in relation to trusts created or arising on or after 1 October 2013 because Trusts (Capital and Income) Act 2013, section 1 provides that any entitlement to income is to income as it arises (and accordingly Apportionment Act 1870, section 2, which provides for income to accrue from day to day, does not apply).

29.4   THE NEED TO REGISTER SETTLEMENTS

29.4.1   The Fourth Money Laundering Directive

The Money Laundering, Terrorist Financing and Transfer of Funds (Information on the Payer) Regulations 2017 ('the 2017 Regulations') (SI 2017/692) came into force on 26 June 2017 and implemented in the United Kingdom the Fourth Money Laundering Directive ('4MLD' – Directive 2015/849/EU of the European Parliament and of the Council of 20 May 2015 on the prevention of the use of the financial system for the purposes of money laundering or terrorist financing, as amended by Directive 2018/843 of the European Parliament and of the Council of 30 May 2018).

The principle behind 4MLD is that anonymous structures (companies and trusts) should be prevented from financing terrorism and laundering money. 4MLD imposed the following obligations:

• Trustees of 'relevant trusts' must keep and provide information about the beneficial owners of trusts.

- HM Revenue & Customs must maintain a Register of 'taxable relevant trusts'.
- Trustees of 'taxable relevant trusts' had to register information about beneficial owners.

There was therefore a crucial distinction between trusts which were merely relevant trusts and those which were *taxable* relevant trusts. All relevant trusts were required to gather and store identity information and make it available to the appropriate authorities but, in addition, *taxable* relevant trusts had to register the information gathered.

All UK express trusts were 'relevant trusts'. Non-express trusts, such as the statutory trust created on intestacy or a trust imposed by a court order, were not within 4MLD.

A trust is a taxable relevant trust in any tax year in which it has a liability to pay one or more of the specified taxes: income tax, capital gains tax, inheritance tax, stamp duty land tax, land and buildings transaction tax (Scotland only), land transaction tax (Wales only), stamp duty reserve tax.

A non-UK express trust was a 'relevant trust' if it: (i) received income from a source in the United Kingdom; or (ii) was liable to pay one or more of the specified taxes.

Although non-express trusts are not within 4MLD, HM Revenue & Customs decided to use the Register in place of the paper Form 41G as the means of obtaining self-assessment tax returns. As a result, non-express trusts and estates requiring a return (referred to by HM Revenue & Customs as 'complex' estates) had to register under 4MLD.

Statutory trusts and complex estates that are required to register simply to obtain a tax return are not required to keep the information on the Register up to date and are not subject to the third-party access provisions (see HM Revenue & Customs, *Trust Registration Service Manual* at TRSM26040, available at www.gov.uk/hmrc-internal-manuals/trust-registration-service-manual).

29.4.2   The Fifth Anti-Money Laundering Directive

The Money Laundering and Terrorist Financing (Amendment) (EU Exit) Regulations 2020 (SI 2020/991) (the '2020 Regulations') amend the 2017 Regulations to implement the changes to the Register required by the Fifth Anti-Money Laundering Directive ('5MLD' – Directive (EU) 2018/843 of the European Parliament and of the Council of 30 May 2018 amending Directive

(EU) 2015/849 on the prevention of the use of the financial system for the purposes of money laundering or terrorist financing, and amending Directives 2009/138/EC and 2013/36/EU). They came into force on 6 October 2020. The Register became open for registration and updates of information from September 2021. 5MLD expands the scope of this Register in two ways:

(i)   The Register must be available to anyone with a 'legitimate interest'. Under 4MLD the Register was only open to government agencies. This raised the spectre of open public access to the Register, causing a great deal of concern to private client practitioners. However, the United Kingdom is taking a narrow view on this requirement and restricts access to those involved in fighting money laundering and terrorist financing.

(ii) Trustees of all non-excluded UK express trusts must register details of the trust and its beneficial owners on the Trusts Register, *whether or not the trust has incurred a UK tax liability*.

The extension of the registration requirement is a huge change and, although some trusts are excluded, an enormous number of small family trusts will have to enter details on the Register.

The 2020 Regulations insert a new Schedule 3A into the 2017 Regulations setting out the UK non-taxable trusts which are excluded from the registration requirement.

Particularly important exclusions for private client practitioners are:

- *Paragraph 5 – charitable trusts*:

    A trust for charitable purposes which—

    (a)   in Scotland or Northern Ireland, is registered as a charity; or
    (b)   in England and Wales, is registered as a charity or not required to register by virtue of section 30(2)(a) to (d) of the Charities Act 2011.

- *Paragraph 6 – pilot trusts*: a trust which holds property with a value not exceeding £100, and created before the Regulations comes into force (6 October 2020). Note that pilot trusts created on or after that date are not excluded.

- *Paragraph 6A – bank accounts for minors and those lacking capacity*: a trust which is created as a requirement of opening a relevant account for the sole benefit of a minor or a person who lacks capacity within the meaning of section 2 of the Mental Capacity Act 2005 (or the equivalent legislation in Scotland or Northern Ireland).

- *Paragraph 7 – trusts having effect on death*:

    A trust effected by will where—

    (a)   the trust is holding only the property comprised in a person's estate on death, and

    (b)   less than two years has passed since that person's death.

    The exclusion for will trusts is very welcome but note that it is limited to a maximum of 2 years so, unless the trust is wound up within 2 years of death, it will have to be registered at the end of that period – or earlier, if at any date beforehand the trust accepts an addition of property from outside the estate, in which case it will need to register from that date.

    The exclusion is limited to trusts created by will. If a testator leaves property by will to a trust created in their lifetime (e.g. a pilot trust), the exclusion from registration does not apply. The pilot trust will be already registered unless it was created before 6 October 2020.

    Similarly, a trust created by post-death variation is not within this exclusion. The trust is created by the person varying and they are the settlor for the purposes of registration (see HM Revenue & Customs, *Trust Registration Service Manual* at TRSM23020, available at www.gov.uk/hmrc-internal-manuals/trust-registration-service-manual).

    HM Revenue & Customs deals with the question of when a will trust comes into effect at TRSM23020. The paragraph says: 'A careful examination of the wording of the will is needed to understand what type of trust it creates and when it arises'. It gives the following examples:

    (1)   A trust of a specific asset or sum of money commences at death so if the personal representatives are still holding the assets on the 2-year anniversary, details must be registered.

    (2)   The whole estate may be left to the executors on trust:

    > I give my estate to my executors on trust with power at their discretion to sell all or any part of parts of such property when they think fit. My executors shall pay my funeral and testamentary expenses my debts and any legacies given by this will out of such property or its proceeds of sale and hold the balance upon trust for such of Donald, Harold and Michaela as are living at my death and if more than one in equal shares.

    This is an express trust which covers the administration period and therefore starts from the date of death. So, if the administration of the estate continues after 2 years from date of death it must be registered. This trust would continue until all of the assets are paid outright to the residuary beneficiaries.

(3)   The executors may be directed to pay debts, etc and hold the residue on trust.

In such cases the trust is not required to register until assets have been transferred from the estate to the trust, and only from 2 years following the date of death. For example:

> I appoint Sophie as my executor to pay my debts, funeral expenses and to hold the balance upon trust for Gisele absolutely.

Here, the trust technically comes into existence when the administration period has ended and Sophie switches role from executor to trustee. It may be difficult to ascertain when this occurs. If the assets have not been transferred to Gisele within 2 years of death than the trust needs to be registered at that point if the administration period has ended or at the date when the administration period ends if later.

Paragraph 9 – co-owned property: a trust of jointly held property where the trustees and the beneficiaries are the same persons. HM Revenue & Customs states in the *Trust Registration Service Manual* at TRSM23050 (available at www.gov.uk/hmrc-internal-manuals/trust-registration-service-manual) that the proportions in which co-owned property is held are not relevant for registration purposes nor are changes from joint tenancy to tenancy in common. Note that HM Revenue & Customs states at TRSM23020 that if the new beneficiary is appointed as a co-trustee, the trust would again be an excluded co-ownership trust.

In addition, if a tenant in common makes a gift of their share to someone else or dies and leaves their share away from the co-owner, the co-ownership exclusion will no longer apply so details of the co-ownership trust will have to be registered by the owner of the legal title.

If the co-ownership interest is left by will on trust, the will trust has to be registered if it lasts for more than 2 years. There are useful examples in HM Revenue & Customs' *Trust Registration Manual* at TRSM23020 (available at www.gov.uk/hmrc-internal-manuals/trust-registration-service-manual).

- *Paragraph 16 – trusts meeting legislative requirements*: trusts for bereaved minors or bereaved young persons (Inheritance Tax Act 1984, section 71A or section 71D).

- *Paragraph 17 – heritage funds.*

- *Paragraph 18 – personal injury trusts.*

- *Paragraph 19 – trusts for tenants' service charges.*

- *Paragraph 22 – trusts for a disabled beneficiary*: a trust holding property for a beneficiary who is a disabled person within the meaning given by Finance Act 2005, Schedule 1A.

Bare trusts are not taxable trusts as income and gains are treated as belonging to the beneficiary. There is no general exclusion from the need to register. HM Revenue & Customs, *Trust Registration Service Manual* at TRSM10030 (available at www.gov.uk/hmrc-internal-manuals/trust-registration-service-manual) says:

> There is no specific exclusion from registration for bare trusts. In general, if a bare trust is an express trust it should register on TRS.

What about transfers of land to minors?

Originally, there was no guidance on this point. However, HM Revenue & Customs, *Trust Registration Service Manual* at TRSM 23050 (available at www.gov.uk/hmrc-internal-manuals/trust-registration-service-manual) now says that registration is not required where one of a number of co-owners is a minor:

Property held on behalf of minor children

Where property is owned by two or more persons and one of those persons is under the age of 18, Schedule 1(2) of the Trusts of Land and Appointment of Trustees Act 1996 provides that the land is held in trust by the persons over the age of 18 for the benefit of themselves and the person or persons under the age of 18. Trusts created in this way are excluded from registration as trusts imposed by legislation (see TRSM23140).

Example

Francisco transfers the legal and beneficial interest in a property to his three children Antonia, Sofia and Dolores to hold equally as joint tenants. Dolores is under the age of 18 and is unable to hold the legal title to the land. Antonia and Sofia therefore are treated by the Trusts of Land and Appointment of Trustees Act 1996 as holding the property on bare trust for the benefit of themselves and Dolores, until such time as Dolores reaches the age of 18. As a trust imposed by legislation, this trust is not required to register on TRS.

What about a bare trust where land is conveyed to a minor or minors without adults?

There is no specific guidance in the Manual at the time of writing. It is not entirely clear, but it is probably the case that it has to be registered. The legislation deals rather differently with conveyances to a minor. Schedule 1, paragraph 2 provides that a purported conveyance of a legal estate in land to a minor 'operates as a declaration that the land is held in trust for the minor'. So this would appear to be a sort of deemed express trust.

29.4.3   The details required for the Register

This is really beyond the scope of this book. HM Revenue & Customs, *Trust Registration Service Manual* (available at www.gov.uk/hmrc-internal-manuals/trust-registration-service-manual) sets out the information required on beneficial owners and on the trust itself at TRSM30000 onwards.

The 'beneficial owners' are listed by regulation 6 of the 2017 Regulations as:

- the settlor;
- the trustees;
- the beneficiaries;
- where some or all of the individuals benefiting from the trust have not been determined, the class of persons in whose main interest the trust is set up, or operates;
- any individual who has control over the trust.

More detailed information is required in the case of taxable trusts (see HM Revenue & Customs, *Trust Registration Service Manual* at TRSM32080 and 32090).

Trusts with a tax liability in a tax year are required to update the information on the Register within 90 days of changes to the trust details or beneficial ownership.

Trustees are required to confirm that the information held on the Register is up to date by 31 January after the end of the tax year in which the trustees are liable to pay tax. This is also confirmed by the trustees on the SA900 return form.

If the trustees are not liable (in respect of any given tax year) to pay any of the relevant UK taxes, then there is no requirement to confirm the Register is up to date for that tax year. Trustees will be required to provide an update by 31 January after the end of the tax year in which the trustees become liable to pay any of the relevant UK taxes.

29.4.4   Deadlines

Registrable taxable trusts

Registrable taxable trusts are required to register by 31 January (or 5 October if they need a self-assessment tax return for the first time) following the end of the tax year in which the trust had a liability to UK taxation.

An express trust which is excluded from the registration requirement will have to register if it incurs a tax liability.

Deadlines for registrable express trusts

- Registrable non-taxable express trusts in existence on or after 6 October 2020 must register by 1 September 2022.
- Where the trust is set up or otherwise becomes registrable in the 90 days immediately prior to 1 September 2022 they must instead register within 90 days of the date of creation.
- Registrable non-taxable trusts created after 1 September 2022 must register within 90 days of creation.

Where an excluded trust becomes taxable, it must register by 31 January (or 5 October if they need a self-assessment tax return for the first time) following the end of the tax year in which the trust had a liability to UK taxation.

29.4.5   Conclusions for will drafters

The requirement to register is likely to be a disincentive to the creation of trusts as it introduces complexity and cost. There are penalties for non-registration.

In the consultations on the extension of the registration requirement to non-taxable trusts, HM Revenue & Customs accepted that an enormous number of trusts would be affected and indicated that it will take a 'light touch' approach. It will take a pragmatic and risk-based approach to charging penalties. At the time of writing, the level of penalties has not been fixed at the time of writing.

Chapter 30

Tax-efficient Will Planning

30.1   INTRODUCTION

The Finance Act 2006 substantially restricted the lifetime possibilities for saving inheritance tax through the use of lifetime settlements. By contrast, the will drafter still has many of the old tax saving options available, most of which continue to feature settlements. A will drafter can make use of settlements to minimise a family's tax liability in a number of ways. Saving tax is normally a concern for families with children, the parents wishing to pass assets on to children or grandchildren as efficiently as possible.

The introduction of the new RNRB presents fresh problems as the use of many popular forms of settlement may mean the loss of the new nil rate band.

The suggestions made in the text below are based on the assumptions that:

(i)   the clients are married (or in a civil partnership);
(ii)   one or both has children;
(iii) both clients have assets in excess of the nil rate band but are not overburdened with wealth, and have the bulk of their joint assets tied up in the family home;
(iv)   both clients are concerned that the surviving spouse or civil partner should have enough to live on, but are anxious to pass on as much as possible to the children.

There are several possibilities, but most clients prefer to avoid substantial costs. The use of a settlement introduces additional cost elements, such as the need to register with HM Revenue & Customs (see **29.4**).

Advisers should be cautious, particularly when dealing with the family home. It is important to warn clients that the tax rules may change and that very few tax saving schemes can be guaranteed.

Insurance policies can be used to make funds available to children for paying inheritance tax or to give them a lump sum not liable to inheritance tax. This can be achieved by means of a joint lives policy. Premiums will be exempt if the payments fall within the normal expenditure from income exemption (Inheritance Tax Act 1984, section 21). The policy will mature on the death of the last surviving spouse and, provided the benefit of the policy has been assigned to the children, the proceeds will pass directly to them.

When dealing with elderly clients who are accompanied by adult children, it is important to establish what the clients (as opposed to their children) want, and it is desirable, if possible, to see the clients in the absence of those who may benefit from the transaction. Allegations of undue influence in relation to lifetime gifts are increasing, and solicitors have been criticised in court for failing to give independent legal advice to clients in relation to proposed gifts.

The simplest option is for the first spouse to die to leave everything to the survivor, relying on the survivor to leave the combined assets to the children. The whole of the first estate will be spouse exempt and the survivor's estate will benefit from the transferable nil rate band.

The disadvantages of such an arrangement are that the survivor may remarry, spend or lose the combined assets or go into a care home leading to the loss of the estate in fees. Many people, therefore, choose to make use of trusts for asset protection purposes. The use of a flexible life interest trust for some or all of the assets (Option 4 below, see **30.2.4**) can be particularly useful.

Although the use of nil rate band discretionary trusts became less popular with the introduction of the transferrable nil rate band, there is still much to be said for creating a nil rate band discretionary trust with spouse and issue as beneficiaries, and leaving the residue on trust for the surviving spouse for life, giving the trustees wide powers to appoint capital to the life tenant or to the issue. Such an arrangement has the following advantages:

(i)   the first spouse to die makes use of their nil rate band (this is useful both where future growth in the value of assets may outstrip the value of the nil rate band transferred to the survivor and where the survivor's estate may exceed the taper threshold leading to loss of the RNRB);

(ii)   the trustees can give the surviving spouse all the income of the estate if that is appropriate;

(iii) the trustees can appoint all the capital of the estate to the surviving spouse, if appropriate;

(iv)   the trustees have the flexibility to appoint income and capital to other beneficiaries, if appropriate;

(v)   the trust capital can be preserved for the issue.

30.2   ESTATE PLANNING OPTIONS

30.2.1   Option 1 – Maximising the benefits of 100% business or agricultural relief

There are specific tax rules on how to apply the business and agricultural reliefs. If property eligible for relief is specifically bequeathed, the legatee alone benefits from the relief. From a tax planning point of view, it is preferable, therefore, to pass property eligible for relief to non-exempt beneficiaries, and assets not attracting relief to the exempt beneficiaries. An appropriation is not a specific gift for this purpose.

It may be beneficial to give a surviving spouse an option to purchase the property attracting relief from the children at market value. This will allow cash to be made available to the children effectively tax free. Provided the surviving spouse survives for 2 years, the assets will attract relief in the spouse's estate and can be left or transferred to the children without a charge to inheritance tax. It may be worth insuring against the spouse's death to cover the possibility of death within 2 years.

Where the property eligible for relief is not specifically given, Inheritance Tax Act 1984, section 39A provides that the benefit of the relief is apportioned through the estate using the formula:

$$\frac{\text{Reduced value of estate (after deducting any specific gifts qualifying for relief)}}{\text{Unreduced value of the estate (after deducting any specific gifts qualifying for relief)}}$$

This means that all property in the estate benefits from a proportion of the relief. The inheritance tax value of all gifts is reduced by a share of the relief. The result can be surprising.

Example

Dougal who had exhausted his nil rate band, left a pecuniary legacy of £600,000 to his daughter and the residue of his estate to his wife. His estate consisted of shares eligible for 100% relief worth £500,000 and other assets worth £1 million. His personal representatives must apportion the relief through the estate under Inheritance Tax Act 1984, section 39A. The effect of apportioning the relief is that the inheritance tax value of the daughter's legacy and of the residue is reduced. It is necessary to multiply the legacy by the R/U (reduced value over the unreduced value), as follows:

$$£600,000 \times \frac{£1\text{ million}}{£1.5\text{ million}} = £400,000$$

There is an inheritance tax saving even though the daughter does not take the property eligible for relief. However, as some of the relief is allocated to the residue (using the same formula), the result is not as beneficial in tax terms as a specific gift to the daughter of the property eligible for relief.

The section can work against the interests of the estate where, for example, assets attracting relief are part of the residue and there are specific or pecuniary legacies passing to exempt beneficiaries. The benefit of some of the relief will be wasted as it will have to be allocated to the exempt legacies.

Inheritance Tax Act 1984, section 39A can also affect the taxable value of nil rate band legacies where assets attracting relief are passing as part of the residue of the estate (see the Example on the following page).

As an alternative, and probably a preferable one, the will can be drafted to leave the property eligible for relief specifically to a discretionary trust. This is particularly useful in cases where it is uncertain whether or not property will be eligible for relief at the date of death. Businesses frequently change the focus of their activities over time, and a business which is clearly wholly or mainly a trading business at the date the will is made may have become a business which is wholly or mainly the holding of investments by the date of death. It is not advisable to direct that the property is to pass to the children if it attracts relief, and to the spouse if it does not. HM Revenue & Customs will refuse to decide whether or not the property is eligible for relief as it will get no tax either way. In such a case, the best solution is to leave the assets on discretionary trusts. Inheritance Tax Act 1984, section 144 allows an appointment made within 2 years of death to be read back into the will so the trustees can appoint the property appropriately once HM Revenue & Customs has determined whether or not relief is available.

Example

Toyah dies with an estate of £1 million which includes property eligible for relief worth £500,000. She leaves a nil rate band legacy in the form set out below to her daughter, residue to her husband:

> I give to my daughter such sum as at my death equals the maximum amount which could be given by this will without inheritance tax becoming payable on my estate.

At the date of death Toyah has a full nil rate band of £325,000 available.

At first sight, it may appear that Toyah's daughter will take £325,000, but she will actually take more than that. The inheritance tax value of the legacy is reduced by multiplying by R/U. On these figures, the daughter would receive twice the nil rate band, i.e. £650,000:

$$£650,000 \times \frac{£500,000}{£1 \text{ million}} = £325,000$$

This may be highly desirable, as more assets are passed to the daughter tax-free. But if Toyah is concerned that her husband may be left with too little, it is possible to include a cap on the amount to pass under the legacy by adding the words 'such sum not to exceed the upper limit in the Table of Rates of Tax contained in Schedule 1 to the Inheritance Tax Act 1984'.

30.2.2 Option 2 – A nil rate band discretionary trust for the benefit of surviving spouse or civil partner, children, grandchildren and their spouses and civil partners

The introduction of the transferable nil rate band has made the nil rate band discretionary trust much less popular.

However, many practitioners still like to include one because it gives flexibility and, if unwanted on the death of the first spouse or civil partner, can be removed by the use of an appointment of capital which will be read back to the date of death under Inheritance Tax Act 1984, section 144.

A nil rate band discretionary trust should always be used where a spouse or civil partner has the benefit of an additional nil rate band transferred from a previous deceased spouse or civil partner as it is not possible for the survivor to 'inherit' more than one nil rate band (Inheritance Tax Act 1984, section 8A(7)).

> **Example**
>
> Henry has a nil rate band inherited from Felicity and marries
> Susan. From an inheritance tax planning point of view, Henry
> should leave assets equal to one nil rate band to a discretionary
> trust and the residue to Susan.
>
> On Henry's death, the assets left to the trust will be outside
> Susan's estate. She will benefit from one additional nil rate
> band transferred from Henry.
>
> On Susan's death, her personal representatives can claim one
> additional nil rate band transferred from Henry.

If assets other than the matrimonial home (or a share in it) are available, it is simpler to use them to fund a discretionary trust. The surviving spouse or civil partner will be a beneficiary and hence can benefit from both income and capital. Accordingly, putting the assets into the discretionary trust need not present any financial problems for the survivor. If the survivor is to be a trustee, a clause providing that trustees can exercise their fiduciary powers so as to benefit themselves should be included.

Because the trust is within the settlor's nil rate band, there are no exit charges during the first 10 years. The first possible charge to tax is on the 10th anniversary, and only then to the extent that the assets exceed the nil rate band current at that date.

It used to be important that trustees of a nil rate band discretionary trust did nothing to confer an interest in possession on the surviving spouse or civil partner, as this would mean that the survivor would be treated as beneficially entitled to the trust property. Since the changes to the taxation of trusts introduced by the Finance Act 2006, this is not the case unless the interest in possession is an immediate post-death interest as defined in section 49A. Trustees cannot normally create such an interest as the interest has to be 'immediate' to qualify. The only exception is if the trustees make an appointment of an interest in possession within 2 years of death which is read back into the will under Inheritance Tax Act 1984, section 144. Trustees do, therefore, need to be cautious in the first 2 years after death that they do nothing that can be construed as an appointment but, thereafter, they can give a surviving spouse or civil partner a right to receive trust income or occupy the former matrimonial home secure in the knowledge that the property will not be aggregated with the spouse's estate.

From an income tax point of view, it is beneficial for trustees of any discretionary trust to give one or more beneficiaries rights to income rather than making discretionary appointments. For the tax year 2016–17 onwards, trusts where beneficiaries are not entitled to income as it arises are subject to the trust rate of income tax on all income in excess of £1,000. For 2022–23 this is 39.35% on dividends and 45% on other income. Beneficiaries receive a tax credit of 45% on the trust income received, but because the income is classified as trust income, they cannot benefit from the tax-free dividend allowance. The trustees have to meet the difference between the tax actually paid and the 45% tax credit claimed by the beneficiaries. The result is that trusts which receive dividend income lose the benefit of the lower dividend rate of income tax. Granting beneficiaries a right to income is beneficial as:

(i)   there is a cash flow advantage as the trustees are only liable at basic rate;
(ii)   because the income is received in its original form rather than as trust income, the beneficiaries have the possibility of using their tax-free dividend (and other) allowances; and
(iii)   the disproportionate rate of income tax on dividends is avoided.

In cases where the intention of the couple is that the RNRB of the first to die will be claimed by the survivor's personal representatives, a nil rate band discretionary trust will be useful to keep assets out of the estate of the survivor in cases where the aggregated estates may exceed the taper threshold.

30.2.3   Option 3 – Nil rate band discretionary trust with debt provisions

Before the introduction of the transferable nil rate band, the debt or charge scheme became very popular as a way of allowing surviving spouses or civil partners to enjoy the combined assets of the couple while making use of the nil rate band of the first to die. The scheme worked as follows:

(i)   The first spouse or civil partner to die created a nil rate band discretionary trust and left the residue to the survivor.
(ii)   Instead of transferring assets to the trust, the executors transferred all assets to the survivor; the trustees received either an IOU from the survivor or, more commonly (because of stamp duty land tax problems), the benefit of a charge placed on the assets by the executors.
(iii)   The debt reduced the estate of the survivor.

There is normally no compelling reason for the creation of such arrangements after the introduction of the transferable nil rate band, but practitioners will continue to encounter estates where the survivor's estate is charged with such a debt and will do so for many years. Also, in a case where the first spouse to die has an additional nil rate band transferred from a deceased spouse, creating a discretionary trust equal to one nil rate band is the only way to make use of the additional nil rate band and allow the new surviving spouse to benefit from the couple's combined assets (see Option 2, **30.2.2**). In a case where much of the couple's wealth is tied up in the matrimonial home, debt/charge arrangements will be helpful.

As explained at Option 2 (**30.2.2**), the use of a nil rate band discretionary trust will be useful in cases where the survivor's estate might otherwise exceed the taper threshold leading to loss of the RNRB. In such cases debt/charge provisions will be useful in reducing the burden of administering a trust containing 'live' assets requiring management.

See Appendix A2A for a summary of points relevant to such arrangements.

30.2.4 Option 4 – Leaving some or all of the estate to surviving spouse or civil partner on flexible life interest trusts

Instead of leaving property to a spouse or civil partner absolutely, it can be left to the spouse or civil partner on flexible life interest trusts. The will should give the trustees power to terminate all or part of the life interest.

The advantages of flexible life interest trusts are that:

(i)   the residue passes to a spouse or civil partner initially and, therefore, is exempt from inheritance tax;
(ii) the nil rate band of the first to die will be transferred to the survivor;
(iii) the surviving spouse has the benefit of all the income but the capital is protected for the issue;
(iv) the trustees have power to appoint capital to the spouse or issue, depending on the circumstances.

If the trustees use their powers to terminate all or part of the spouse's interest in possession to create a discretionary trust, the spouse is treated as making a gift for the purposes of the reservation of benefit rules (Inheritance Tax Act 1984, section 102ZA). The spouse should not, therefore, be included in the class of beneficiaries.

30.3 PROBLEMS WITH USING THE RESIDENCE NIL RATE BAND

It is not necessary to make a specific gift of a residence to lineal descendants to obtain the RNRB. It can be left as part of the residue of the estate. If residue is divided between lineal descendants and others, each is treated as inheriting a proportional share of the residence.

Example

Ted leaves his entire estate (which includes a residence) equally to his two children and one nephew. He is entitled to a single RNRB of £175,000.

His children are inheriting two-thirds of the value of the residence. If it is worth £300,000, the children inherit £200,000 and a full RNRB will be available to the estate. If the residence is worth £180,000, the children inherit £120,000 and the RNRB is capped at £120,000.

In cases where it will achieve a tax saving, the children and nephew should vary so that the children take more of the residence and the nephew takes more of the other assets.

However, even the simplest gifts can cause problems. A straightforward substitutional gift to children of a predeceased child may lead to loss of the RNRB if the substitutional gift is contained in a trust contingent on reaching a stated age.

Example

Tracey leaves the residue of her estate (which includes a house) to trustees to hold for:

> such of my three children as survive me, equally if more than one, but if any child predeceases me the share which he would have taken had he survived me shall pass to such of his children that reach 21 and if more than one equally

Tracey had three children, one of whom predeceased her leaving two minor children of his own. The substitutional trust for the grandchildren does not attract the RNRB because it is not one of the permitted trusts.

If the house is worth £300,000, £200,000 of the house is inherited by the children and £100,000 goes to the trust for the grandchildren. Obviously, if all the children predeceased and were replaced by minor grandchildren, the RNRB would be wasted. This is unfortunate considering what a standard gift this is.

The drafting solution is either to remove the age restriction to create a bare trust for the grandchildren or to leave the grandchildren's share on flexible life interest trusts. If the latter approach is taken, the trustees can use their powers to appoint capital to the grandchildren at an appropriate age.

To ensure that the trust creates immediate post-death interests for the substituted grandchildren, vary Trustee Act 1925, section 31 to remove the possibility that if a minor dies before 18, any accumulated income passes with the capital. That possibility would prevent the minor having a right to income.

30A   VARIATION OF THE TRUSTEE ACT 1925 TO ENSURE IMMEDIATE POST-DEATH INTEREST

During the minority of a Beneficiary, Trustee Act 1925, section 31 shall not apply and my Trustees may apply income for the Beneficiary's maintenance, education and benefit at their discretion *and to the extent that they do not shall retain the balance for the Beneficiary absolutely*.

Appendix 1

Complete Wills and Miscellaneous Precedents

A1A   STANDARD WILL: FULL FORM (LONG)

THIS IS THE LAST WILL of me [AB of ...].

1.   I HEREBY REVOKE all former testamentary dispositions made by me.

2.

    (1)   I APPOINT [CD of ...] and [EF of ...] (hereinafter referred to as 'my Trustees' which expression shall include the Trustees for the time being hereof) to be the executors and trustees of this my will.

    (2)   If the said [CD] and [EF] shall both fail to survive me or if the survivor or survivors of them shall decline to act as my trustee or if the appointment shall fail for any other reason then I APPOINT [the equity partners directors or members as appropriate at the date of my death in the firm of [YZ and Co] solicitors of ... or the firm which at that date has succeeded to and carries on its practice to be the executors and trustees hereof and I DIRECT that no more than two of the said partners directors or members shall prove my will and act initially in its trusts] *or* ...

    (3)   [Professional charging clause, see for example Precedent 22R.]

3.   [Gift of personal chattels to spouse or civil partner and two children, see Precedent 12D.]

4.   I GIVE the following specific legacies:

    (1)   [Gift of stamp collection, see Precedent 12R.]

    (2)   [Gift of stock, see Precedent 12J.]

5.   I GIVE the following pecuniary legacies payable on my death:

    (1)   [Immediate legacy to individual, see Precedent 12V.]

    (2)   [Simple legacy to individual, see Precedent 12W.]

    (3)   To each of my Trustees [not being a professional trustee] who shall prove this my will and act in the trusts hereof I give the sum of [£1,000].

6.   [Specific gift of freehold property, see for example Precedent 14B.]

7.   [Residuary gift to Trustees upon trust, see Precedent 17E.]

8.   [Residuary gift to spouse with substitutional gift to children, see Precedent 17I.]

9.   [Power of appropriation, see Precedent 22A.]

10.   [Power to insure, see Precedent 22EE.]

11.   [Power to defer payment of debts, see Precedent 22FF.]

12.   [Power to carry on business, see Precedent 22GG.]

13.   [Power to borrow, see Precedent 22HH.]

14.   [Power to make loans, see Precedent 22NN.]

15.   [Direction to act by majority, see Precedent 22H.]

16.   [Power to act on counsel's opinion, see Precedent 22L.]

17.   [General indemnity to trustees, see Precedent 22M.]

18.   [Provision for receipts of minors, see Precedent 22II.]

19.   [Power of investment, including power to buy land, see Precedent 22W.]

20.   [Clause for maintenance of child, see Precedent 22JJ.]

21.   [Power of advancement, see Precedent 22LL.]

22.   [General survivorship condition, see Precedent 17M.]

23.   I DECLARE that any powers conferred on my Trustees by the provisions of this my will and any codicil hereto shall be construed as being in addition to and not in substitution for any power discretion or trust which in the absence of the powers herein contained or any of them would be vested in my Trustees by any law or statute.

[Attestation clause, see Precedent 4A.]

A1B   MUTUAL WILLS

THIS IS THE LAST WILL AND TESTAMENT of me [name] of [address].

1.   I HEREBY REVOKE all former testamentary dispositions made by me.

2.   I APPOINT my [spouse] [civil partner] [partner] [name] and [X of …] to be the executors and trustees hereof (hereinafter referred to as 'my Trustees' which where the context admits shall include the trustees for the time being hereof).

3.   WHEREAS my [spouse] [civil partner] [partner] and I have agreed with one accord to execute like wills in similar terms and whereas we have further agreed that each such respective will shall not be altered or revoked either during our joint lives or by the survivor of us so in reliance upon the said agreement I HEREBY GIVE all my property whatsoever and wheresoever situate [including any property over which I may have a general power of appointment or disposition by will] to my Trustees UPON TRUST to sell call in and convert the same into money with power to postpone the said sale calling in and conversion thereof for so long as they shall in their absolute discretion think fit without being liable for loss and to hold the proceeds of such sale calling in and conversion and my ready money upon the following trusts:

(1) UPON TRUST to pay thereout my debts and funeral and testamentary expenses and subject thereto UPON TRUST for my [spouse] [civil partner] [partner] during [his] [her] lifetime;

(2) upon the death of my [spouse] [civil partner] [partner] or if [he] [she] shall die before me or if the foregoing trust fails for any reason IN TRUST … [continue as in Precedent 6C].

4.   [Charging clause, see Precedent 22T.]

5.   [Power of investment, including power to buy land, see Precedent 22W.]

6.   [General indemnity, see Precedent 22M.]

[Attestation clause, see Precedent 4A.]

Note

It is only in rare circumstances that mutual wills are the best testamentary solution. If the agreement relates to land, it is necessary to comply with the requirements of Law of Property (Miscellaneous Provisions) Act 1989. This means having a side document setting out the terms of the agreement in relation to the land and signed by both parties. If wills are *not* intended to be mutual, it may be helpful to include a declaration that they are not intended to be mutual and that each party is free to revoke their own will (see Precedent 2D).

A1C   WILL DISPOSING OF A BUSINESS

This form is appropriate if the deceased's estate includes a business run as a sole trader. The business is to be carried on after death with a view to sale at an appropriate opportunity, perhaps because no one in the family is interested in taking it over. The business would normally attract business property relief at 100% so long as the deceased had owned it for at least 2 years before death and the business does not consist wholly or mainly of the making or holding of investments.

THIS IS THE LAST WILL AND TESTAMENT of me [AB of …]

1.   I HEREBY REVOKE all former testamentary dispositions made by me.

2.   [Appointment of executors and trustees, see Precedent 9C.]

3.   [Gift of business to trustees, see Precedent 13B (or Precedent 13A if a specific beneficiary is contemplated).]

4.   [Power to carry on business without interference, see Precedent 13E.]

5.   [Provision of salary for trustees managing business, see Precedent 13G.]

6.   [Provision allowing trustees to exercise powers whether or not they have an interest in the business, see Precedent 13H.]

7.   [Indemnity for trustees running business, see Precedent 13I.]

8.   (i)   Subject as aforesaid … [continue as in Precedent 17D giving residuary estate to trustees UPON TRUST].

          (ii)   Trust for testator's children [see Precedent 17N.]

[Attestation clause, see Precedent 4A.]

A1D   WILL OF WIDOW(ER) EXERCISING POWER OF APPOINTMENT GIVEN BY WILL OF PRE-DECEASED SPOUSE OR CIVIL PARTNER

THIS IS THE LAST WILL AND TESTAMENT of me [name] of …

1.   I HEREBY REVOKE all former testamentary dispositions made by me.

2.   I APPOINT [name] of … and [name] of … to be the Executors and Trustees hereof (those being the Trustees of my late [spouse's] [civil partner's] will).

3.   [Specific gifts and pecuniary legacies, see for example Precedents 12A to 12GG.]

4.   In exercise of a power of appointment vested in me by the will of my late [spouse] [civil partner] dated the [date] over and in respect of the proceeds of sale and conversion of their residuary estate both real and personal and the investments for the time being representing the same in favour of the children and issue of our [marriage] [civil partnership] I HEREBY DIRECT AND APPOINT that the Trustees of the will of my said [spouse] [civil partner] shall stand possessed of my [spouse's] [civil partner's] residuary estate as from the date of my death upon the following trusts:

        (1)   as to one half thereof UPON TRUST for my [son] [name] absolutely;

        (2)   as to one half UPON TRUST to pay the income thereof to my [daughter] [name] during her life and after her death to hold the capital and income for all or any children or child of my said daughter who attain or attains the age of eighteen years and if more than one in equal shares.

5.   I GIVE to my Trustees as aforesaid all my real and personal property not otherwise disposed of hereunder UPON TRUST to sell call in and convert the same with full power to postpone the said sale calling in and conversion for so long as they shall in their absolute discretion think fit without being liable for any loss occasioned thereby and I DIRECT that my Trustees shall pay out of the net proceeds of sale and conversion all my debts funeral and testamentary expenses and all taxes payable upon my estate and shall thereafter hold the balance of my estate upon the trusts of my late [spouse's] [civil partner's] residuary estate as if an accretion to that estate.

[Attestation clause, see Precedent 4A.]

A1E   WILL GIVING NIL RATE BAND LEGACY TO DISCRETIONARY TRUST

THIS IS THE LAST WILL AND TESTAMENT of me [name] of …

1.   I HEREBY REVOKE all former testamentary dispositions made by me.

2.

    (1)   [Appointment of professional executors and trustees, see Precedent 9F.]

    (2)   [Professional charging clause, see Precedent 22S.]

3.   [Specific gifts, see for example Precedents 12A to 12U.]

4.   [Pecuniary legacy, see for example Precedents 12V to 12GG.]

5.   [Gift of nil rate sum to discretionary trust, see Precedent 18H.]

6.   [Gift to trustees upon trust, see Precedent 17E.]

7.   [Gift of residue to spouse or civil partner absolutely and substitutional gift to issue, see Precedent 17I]

8.   [Power of appropriation, see Precedent 22A.]

9.   [Power to insure, see Precedent 22EE.]

10.   [Power to defer payment of debts, see Precedent 22FF.]

11.   [Power to borrow, see Precedent 22HH.]

12.   [Direction to act by majority, see Precedent 22H.]

13.   [Power to act on counsel's opinion, see Precedent 22L.]

14.   [General indemnity to trustees, see Precedent 22M.]

15.   [Provision for receipts of minors, see Precedent 22II.]

16.   [Power of investment, including power to buy land, see Precedent 22W.]

17.   [Clause for maintenance of child, see Precedent 22JJ.]

18.   [Power of advancement, see Precedent 22LL.]

19.   [Power to make loan, see Precedent 22NN.]

20.   [General survivorship condition, see Precedent 17M.]

21.   I DECLARE that any powers conferred on my Trustees by the provisions of this my will and any codicil hereto shall be construed as being in addition to and not in substitution for any power discretion or trust which in the absence of the powers herein contained or any of them would be vested in my Trustees by any law or statute.

[Attestation clause, see Precedent 4A.]

Note
If wanting to include debt/charge provisions, include additional clauses in clause 5 (see Appendix 2).

A1F SIMPLE WILL GIVING ALL PROPERTY TO ANOTHER OF FULL AGE ABSOLUTELY

THIS IS THE LAST WILL AND TESTAMENT of me [name] of …

1.   I HEREBY REVOKE all former testamentary dispositions made by me.

2.   I GIVE all my real and personal property whatsoever and wheresover situate (including any property over which I may have a power of appointment or disposition by will) to [name] absolutely and I appoint [him] [her] to be the sole Executor of this my will.

[Attestation clause, see Precedent 4A.]

A1G CODICIL MADE ON SEPARATION FROM SPOUSE OR CIVIL PARTNER PRIOR TO DIVORCE OR ANNULMENT

I [name] of … DECLARE this to be the [first] codicil to my will made on the [date].

WHEREAS:

1.   By my said will dated [date] I have made various bequests and provisions in favour of my [spouse or civil partner] [name].

2.   My [spouse or civil partner] and I have separated [with a view to commencing [divorce] [annulment] proceedings] and I HEREBY REVOKE all bequests made to my [spouse or civil partner] in my will and declare that for all purposes in connection with my will and its provisions my will shall take effect as if my [spouse or civil partner] had died immediately prior to my death. I hereby confirm my will as modified by this codicil.

[Attestation clause, see Precedent 4A.]

Note

When spouses or civil partners separate, it is good practice to consider whether their respective wills should be altered immediately. Wills Act 1837, section 18A (inserted by the Administration of Justice Act 1982) provides that on dissolution of a marriage or civil partnership, any gift to the spouse or civil partner in a pre-existing will lapses. However, this does not happen until the decree absolute, so it is normally preferable to make express provision at an earlier stage. It is generally preferable to make a complete new will rather than a codicil to an existing one.

A1H   WILL PROVIDING FOR DISCRETIONARY TRUST OF INCOME DURING PERPETUITY PERIOD WITH DIVISION OF CAPITAL AT THE END OF PERIOD BETWEEN SURVIVING BENEFICIARIES

THIS IS THE LAST WILL AND TESTAMENT of me [name] of ...

1.   I HEREBY REVOKE all former testamentary dispositions made by me.

2.

  (1)   [Appointment of professional executors and trustees, see Precedent 9F.]

  (2)   [Professional charging clause, see Precedent 22S.]

3.   [Specific gifts, see for example Precedents 12A to 12U.]

4.   [Pecuniary legacy, see for example Precedents 12V to 12GG.]

5.   [Gift to trustees upon trust, see Precedent 17E.]

6.   [Discretionary trust for testator's family, see Precedent 18F.]

7.   [Power of appropriation, see Precedent 22A.]

8.   [Power to insure, see Precedent 22EE.]

9.   [Power to defer payment of debts, see Precedent 22FF.]

10.   [Power to borrow, see Precedent 22HH.]

11.   [Power to loan money, see Precedent 22NN.]

12.   [Direction to act by majority, see Precedent 22H.]

13.   [Power to act on counsel's opinion, see Precedent 22L.]

14.   [General indemnity to trustees, see Precedent 22M.]

15.   [Power of investment, including power to buy land, see Precedent 22W.]

16.   [Clause for maintenance of child, see Precedent 22JJ.]

17.   [Power of advancement, see Precedent 22LL.]

18.   [General survivorship condition, see Precedent 17M.]

19.   I DECLARE that any powers conferred on my Trustees by the provisions of this my will and any codicil hereto shall be construed as being in addition to and not in substitution for any power discretion or trust which in the absence of the powers herein contained or any of them would be vested in my Trustees by any law or statute.

[Attestation clause, see Precedent 4A.]

A1I   LETTER OF WISHES TO TRUSTEES

Note

A letter such as this may be made available to assist the trustees in any situation if they will be required to exercise discretions given to them by the will. Whilst it is not binding on the trustees, it can be particularly helpful if guidance is required as to the future welfare and support of a beneficiary with special needs or requirements, or in a general case if there is a wide range of beneficiaries but the testator regards one of them as the main object.

Of course, in all cases the wording must be adapted to reflect the circumstances and the testator's current wishes. If circumstances should change, there is no reason why an initial letter of wishes should not be replaced, or supplemented, with a further letter prior to the testator's death.

To the Trustees of my will

In clause [...] of my will dated [...], I have left the residue of my estate to my children. I have left both [...] and [...] a one third absolute share and the other one third share which I might otherwise have left absolutely to my daughter [...], I have instead left to you in paragraph [...] of clause [...] on a special discretionary trust. The objects of this trust are my daughter [...], my other two children [...] and [...] and also their respective families.

I have decided to create this special trust because [...] is, and will always be, unable to deal with her own financial affairs and I want to ensure that I make the best possible provision for her for the rest of her life. However, I do not have the resources to ensure that she can be financially independent for the rest of her life. Due to her present condition, which will not improve, she is ever reliant on financial entitlements which are dependent on means-tested state benefits and other provision that is, or might in future be, available to her. Her condition also requires support to look after her health and welfare which is provided by individuals and specialist bodies.

In giving effect to this special trust, it is my wish that you use your wide powers to promote the welfare and independence of [...] by giving her the financial support that she needs. You should supplement any provision that is otherwise available to her by using your discretion to pay her income for her maintenance and, if necessary, please use the capital as well to improve her environment and the standards of amenity that she enjoys or would like. For those who provide her with personal care, I would like you to see that they receive whatever practical and financial support they may need so far as your powers allow and I hope that you will provide similar assistance to any organisation or body that can achieve the same outcome.

I have made the trust provisions as flexible as I can so that you can fulfil my wishes by using your powers to the widest extent permissible. The most important thing I want you to keep in mind is that whilst she is alive, you are to regard and treat my daughter as the principal beneficiary of the trust and so consider her as the main object of your discretion. Subject thereto, you may also benefit [my other children and their respective families] who are also potential objects of the trust.

Signed [testator]

Dated [...]

A1J   DEED OF VARIATION TO SEVER BENEFICIAL JOINT TENANCY AND CREATE NIL RATE BAND LEGACY

THIS DEED OF VARIATION is made the ... day of ... by [...] of [...] ('the [widow] [widower] [surviving civil partner]') of the one part and [....] of [....] ('the executor') of the other part and is SUPPLEMENTAL TO the will of [...] ('the deceased') dated [...] ('the will').

WHEREAS:

1.   The deceased died on [...] and probate of the will was granted to the executor out of the District Registry at [...] on [...];

2.   At the date of his/her death the deceased and the [widow] [widower] [surviving civil partner] owned as beneficial joint tenants (1) two accounts with the [...] Bank numbers [...] ('the accounts') and (2) [...] ('the property') all of which assets passed to the [widow] [widower] [civil partner] by survivorship.

3.   In the events which have happened the [widow] [widower] [civil partner] is the sole residuary beneficiary of the deceased's estate and is now desirous of varying the dispositions of assets comprised in the deceased's estate in accordance with the provisions set out in this deed.

NOW THIS DEED WITNESSES:

1.   That it shall be deemed that the [widow] [widower] [civil partner] had immediately prior to the death of the deceased severed their beneficial joint tenancy in the accounts and in the property so that at the date of the deceased's death his/her beneficial half share in the said accounts and property formed part of his/her free estate.

2.   That the will shall be varied as if there were inserted immediately before clause [...] the following pecuniary legacy.

[Continue with gift of nil rate band legacy, see Precedent 12HH.]

3.   In accordance with Inheritance Tax Act 1984, section 142(2) and Taxation of Chargeable Gains Act 1992, section 62(7), the parties hereto state that they intend that the provisions of Inheritance Tax Act 1984, section 142(2) and Taxation of Chargeable Gains Act 1992, section 62(7) shall apply in relation to the variation effected by this deed to the intent that such variation shall be treated as if it were made by the deceased for the purposes of inheritance tax and capital gains tax.

IN WITNESS whereof the parties hereto have executed this deed the day and year first before written

SIGNED and DELIVERED as a deed by the said

[widow] [widower] [surviving civil partner] in the presence of

SIGNED and DELIVERED as a deed by the said
executor in the presence of

Notes:

(i) There is strictly no need for the personal representative to be a party to an instrument of variation because the variation is made by the beneficiary. However, it is good practice to include the personal representative as an additional party if, as here, the variation affects the terms of the will (or an intestacy). Doing so ensures the personal representative is made aware of the change to beneficial entitlement and acts accordingly.

(ii) If the intended 'reading back' is to be achieved, it is crucial that the deed contains a certificate in the form of clause 3, failing which the transfer would be treated as a transfer of value by the original beneficiary for inheritance tax purposes. Similarly, it would be treated as a disposal by the original beneficiary for capital gains tax. The certificates are mutually exclusive and it may be that the consequences of one is not such as to make it beneficial to include it. It is possible to include a certificate for one tax and not the other which produces a better tax result. Typically, there may be cases where the value of the property has risen since the date of death but not by an amount which would trigger a charge to capital gains tax if the disposal was attributed to the person making the variation (e.g. within annual exemption, gain extinguished by availability of loss relief, etc). In such a case, the section 62(7) certificate should be omitted, so there will be no reading back for capital gains tax purposes and the donee will acquire at the higher value. Provided the inheritance tax certificate is included, there will be a reading back for inheritance tax purposes, so that the transfer will be treated as the deceased's.

A1K   DEED OF VARIATION OF A WILL

This DEED OF VARIATION is made [date] between:

[name of original beneficiary] of [...] (hereinafter called [X]) of the first part;

[name of first donee] of [...] (hereinafter called [Y]) of the second part;

[name of second donee] of [...] (hereinafter called [Z]) of the third part; and

[name of first Executor] of [...] and [Y] [*or* name of second Executor, etc as the case may be] (hereinafter called 'the Personal Representatives') of the fourth part

And IS SUPPLEMENTAL to the Will (hereinafter called 'the Will') dated [date] of [name of Testator] late of [address] (hereinafter called 'the Testator').

WHEREAS

1.   The Testator died on [date] and the Will was proved on [date] at [insert details of probate registry] by the Personal Representatives.

2.   By the Will the Testator gave all the residue of their real and personal property whatsoever and wheresoever to their daughter X absolutely.

3.   X is desirous of disposing of part of his/her entitlement under the Will in favour of his/her sons Y and Z and to effect such disposal, X, Y and Z have agreed to vary the terms of the Will in so far as they relate to the entitlement of X as follows.

NOW THIS DEED WITNESSETH as follows:

1.   It is agreed and declared by the parties hereto and X directs that the Personal Representatives shall henceforth administer the estate of the Testator as if the Will was varied in the following manner:

   1.1   As if the Will contained pecuniary legacies of two hundred thousand pounds (£200,000) in favour of each of them the Testator's two grandsons Y and Z absolutely, and

   1.2   Contained a declaration that such pecuniary legacies were free of all inheritance tax payable by reason of the Testator's death and that such tax attributable to the value thereof should be paid out of the residue of the Testator's estate.

2.   Nothing herein contained shall affect entitlement to income of the Testator's estate and no interest shall be payable on or in respect of the pecuniary legacies mentioned in sub-clause 1.1 hereof whether or not such pecuniary legacies shall be paid more than one year after the date of the Testator's death.

3.   Save in so far as expressly varied by clause 1 hereof the provisions of the Will shall continue to have full force and effect.

4.   In accordance with Inheritance Tax Act 1984, section 142(2) and Taxation of Chargeable Gains Act 1992, section 62(7) the parties hereto state that they intend that the provisions of Inheritance Tax Act 1984, section 142(2) and Taxation of Chargeable Gains Act 1992, section 62(7) shall apply in relation to the variation effected by this deed to the intent that such variation shall be treated as if it were made by the deceased for the purposes of inheritance tax and capital gains tax.

IN WITNESS whereof the parties hereto have executed this deed the day and year first before written

SIGNED and DELIVERED as a deed, etc

[execution by all parties]

Note

A deed of variation must be drafted so as to reflect the circumstances and desired outcome. This is simply an example based on a principal beneficiary wanting to give away part of their inheritance to their two children – a case of 'generation skipping'. If the intended 'reading back' is to be achieved, it is crucial that the deed contains a certificate in the form of clause 4, failing which the transfer would be treated as a transfer of value by the original beneficiary for inheritance tax purposes. Similarly, it would be treated as a disposal by the original beneficiary for capital gains tax purposes, although since the subject matter of the disposal in this case is cash, that would not cause any problems. (See also the notes to Precedent A1J.) It is important, but often overlooked, that miscellaneous matters are clarified; in this case it is made clear that the new legacies are to be free of tax (sub-clause 1.2) and that no interest can be claimed on those legacies (clause 2).

Appendix 2

Nil Rate Band Discretionary Trusts with Debt/Charge Provisions

A2A EXPLANATORY NOTE

As explained in Chapter 30, before the introduction of the transferable nil rate band, the debt or charge scheme was a popular way of allowing surviving spouses or civil partners to enjoy the combined assets of the couple while making use of the nil rate band of the first to die. Such arrangements may become popular again as a means of keeping the estate of the survivor below the level of the taper threshold for the purposes of the RNRB:

(i)   The first spouse or civil partner to die creates a nil rate band discretionary trust and leaves the residue to the survivor.
(ii) Instead of transferring assets to the trust, the executors transfer all assets to the survivor; the trustees receive either an IOU from the survivor or, more commonly (because of stamp duty land tax problems) the benefit of a charge placed on the assets by the executors for the debt.
(iii) The debt reduces the estate of the survivor.

In the simplest arrangements, the surviving spouse or civil partner gives the trustees of the discretionary trust an IOU. This is satisfactory from an inheritance tax point of view (with one exception, see Finance Act 1986, section 103 below), but, if land is transferred, this will result in a charge to stamp duty land tax because an interest in land is being obtained for consideration. To prevent such a liability, the executors should transfer the assets to the survivor charged with the debt owing to the nil rate band discretionary trustees. The charge must be a non-recourse charge, meaning that the trustees have no rights to recover the debt from the survivor, only from the proceeds of sale. HM Revenue & Customs accepts that this avoids stamp duty land tax issues. See HM Revenue & Customs, *Stamp Duty Land Tax Manual* at SDLTM04045 (available at www.gov.uk/hmrc-internal-manuals/stamp-duty-land-tax-manual). The non-recourse charge also avoids any danger of falling foul of the artificial debt provisions contained in Finance Act 1986, section 103 although these are rarely a problem.

A debt charged on an asset reduces its value for inheritance tax purposes (see Inheritance Tax Act 1984, section 162). Hence on the survivor's death the value of the residence will be reduced by any debt charged on it. The residence nil rate allowance is capped at the value of any residence left to lineal descendants (see Chapter 27), with the result that a full RNRB may not be available to the survivor's estate.

There is a particular problem in relation to the simple IOU arrangement where the first spouse or civil partner to die received substantial transfers from the survivor. Finance Act 1986, section 103 provides that a debt incurred by the deceased or a charge created by them is non-deductible for inheritance tax purposes where the consideration for it consisted of property derived from the deceased, the artificial debt problem. In *Phizackerley v RCC* [2007] UKSPC SPC00591, [2007] STC (SCD) 328, HM Revenue & Customs argued successfully that a debt created by IOU was non-deductible under section 103. However, the facts were unusual.

Mr Phizackerley had been the sole breadwinner as his wife had never worked. The couple had lived in university accommodation for most of their married life. Mr Phizackerley bought the couple's first home in joint names with funds provided by him alone. Mrs Phizackerley died first and left her half interest in the house to a nil rate band discretionary trust and the rest of the estate to her husband. Her half interest in the house was transferred to Mr Phizackerley in consideration for an IOU. The special commissioner agreed with HM Revenue & Customs that Mrs Phizackerley's half interest in the house was property derived from her husband and, therefore, the debt was non-deductible under section 103.

Despite the *Phizackerley* decision, section 103 is only rarely a problem for the following reasons:

(i) It probably applies only where one spouse or civil partner has transferred particular property to the other (as Mr Phizackerley had done with the half interest in the house) and the donee then leaves that property to the survivor.
(ii) The donee must die first.
(iii) It applies only where the survivor incurs the debt or creates the incumbrance. If assets are transferred to the survivor by the executors subject to a charge or if residue is left to trustees to hold for the surviving spouse for life, the survivor has neither incurred a debt nor created the incumbrance.

The mere fact that the survivor was one of the executors who created the charge over the assets transferred should not give rise to a section 103 problem despite the apparent creation of an incumbrance. The charge is created in a representative capacity whereas section 103 clearly contemplates personal debts and incumbrances.

A section 103 problem can arise after assets have been transferred to the survivor charged with a debt, if the spouse wants to sell the property subject to the charge. At that point the survivor will have to pay off the charge. The trustees of the nil rate band discretionary trust cannot simply lend the property back to the survivor in return for an IOU as this will create a section 103 problem. However, the trustees can buy an interest in the replacement property together with the surviving spouse (provided they have powers in the trust instrument) and prepare a trust deed permitting the spouse to go into occupation.

Another problem that can arise in connection with old debt/charge arrangements is the discovery when the survivor dies that there is no supporting documentation. One would normally hope to see some or all of the following by way of documentation:

(i)   A properly drafted will.

  –   The executors should be given power to transfer all of the assets to the survivor subject to a charge or in return for an IOU plus a requirement that the trustees must accept a debt or charge. They should be given an express power to assent assets to beneficiaries subject to a charge, as Administration of Estates Act 1925, section 36 may not be sufficient for this purpose. The executors must be relieved from liability for recovering the debt. They should be allowed to let it remain outstanding for as long as they wish and relieved from liability if the security becomes inadequate or if the surviving spouse is unable to repay. For stamp duty land tax reasons, the charge must not make the spouse personally liable for the debt. It should state that the nil rate band trustees have recourse only to the asset charged, otherwise there will be a charge to stamp duty land tax (unless the charge is created by variation).
  –   The trustees should be required to accept a debt or charge and the will should authorise the trustees to impose such terms as to interest or index-linking as they wish.

(ii) A letter from the executors to the trustees explaining what steps they are taking in relation to the nil rate sum.

  –   If the executors are proceeding by way of charge, there should be a charge. This will be a legal charge if over assets in the sole name of the deceased. If over the deceased's equitable interest in the matrimonial home, it will have to be an equitable charge.
  –   If the executors are proceeding by way of debt, there should be an IOU from the survivor.

(iii) A trustees' minute noting that they are accepting an IOU or charge instead of assets and setting out whether they are requiring interest or index-linking.

It is unusual to find perfect documentation. Even in the absence of any supporting documentation at all, if all the assets have been transferred to a surviving spouse when the will clearly states that there is a nil rate band discretionary trust, consider two possible lines of argument to convince HM Revenue & Customs that the value of the survivor's estate should be reduced:

(i)   The trustees allowed the survivor to take assets which were due to the trust. This was in breach of trust and there is, therefore, a right of recovery for the trust beneficiaries.

(ii)   The trustees of the nil rate band discretionary trust may have had power to advance assets informally to beneficiaries, as opposed to a requirement to appoint assets out of the trust by deed. If so, HM Revenue & Customs may accept that the trustees advanced the trust assets to the survivor. This is a good result if the survivor died on or after 9 October 2007 as the nil rate band of the first to die will be transferred to the survivor.

Treatment of interest/index-linking

The trustees may have required interest to be paid on the debt. This will normally be rolled up and paid when the survivor dies. The interest will be income of the trust and, if in excess of £1,000, will be taxed at the trust rate of tax, which for 2022–23 is 45%. The trustees may be able to pay the trust income to beneficiaries who are not taxpayers or who are liable to lower rates of tax, in which case the beneficiaries can recover tax from HM Revenue & Customs. If there are no such beneficiaries, the trustees should disclaim the interest. If interest is neither claimed nor paid, there is no income to be assessed (see *Dewar v IRC* [1935] 2 KB 351).

The position in relation to indexation is much less clear.

A payment resulting from the indexation of the sum owed is, in the view of HM Revenue & Customs, also liable to income tax. It argues that the index-linked uplift constitutes interest on which income tax is payable as a result of Income Tax (Trading and Other Income) Act 2005, sections 369(1) and 381. These sections extend the meaning of interest to include the payment of discounts and premiums.

HM Revenue & Customs, *Savings and Investments Manual* at SAIM2240 (available at www.gov.uk/hmrc-internal-manuals/savings-and-investment-manual) says:

> Where the lending carries a reasonable commercial rate of interest and is either issued at a discount or repayable at a premium, it may normally be assumed that the discount or premium is not in the nature of income. The discount or premium may reflect factors other than the time value of money, such as market risk.
> However, where there is no interest, or the rate of interest is below a commercial rate,
>
> •   a discount should be treated as falling within ITTOIA05/S381,
> •   a premium should be treated as being interest, chargeable under ITTOIA05/S369 (1).

In the April 2017 *Trusts and Estates Newsletter*, HM Revenue & Customs announced that it had issued closure notices on a number of cases, but none have been appealed. It then said:

> Going forward we will be writing to all taxpayers who we know have entered into these arrangements, inviting them to consider their position and settle the income tax payable with HMRC. In cases where the trustees elect not to settle, we will be issuing closure notices, against which there is the right of appeal. On receipt of an appeal, we will consider any additional information provided. In the absence of agreement, we intend to defend any resulting appeals before the tribunal.

HM Revenue & Customs is not necessarily right.

In *Westminster Bank Ltd v Riches* (1945) 28 TC 159, 189, Lord Wright said:

> the essence of interest is that it is a payment which becomes due because the creditor has not had his money at the due date. It may be regarded either as representing the profit he might have made if he had had the use of the money, or conversely the loss he suffered because he had not that use. The general idea is that he is entitled to compensation for the deprivation.

Indexation is simply aimed at preserving the value of the money outstanding.

In *Lomax v Peter Dixon & Son* [1943] KB 671, although Lord Greene MR said at 682 that where no interest is payable a 'discount' will normally, if not always, be chargeable to income tax, he also said:

> there can be no general rule that any sum which a lender receives over and above the amount which he lends ought to be treated as income.

He gave an example of loans where the amount to be repaid was fixed by reference to the price of gold at the repayment date, and if the currency depreciated in terms of gold there was to be a corresponding increase in the amount of sterling to be repaid at the maturity of the loan saying:

> it could scarcely be suggested that this excess ought to be treated as income when the whole object of the contract was to ensure that the lender should not suffer a capital loss due to the depreciation of the currency.

Unfortunately, few are prepared to challenge HM Revenue & Customs over what is often a relatively small amount of tax, so unless a test case is taken (which had not happened at the time of writing), the choice for trustees seems to be to:

- pay the tax, or
- disclaim the indexation, or
- distribute to beneficiaries who are subject to income tax at a rate less than the 45% trust rate and who are therefore able to obtain a tax refund.

A2B ADDITIONAL CLAUSES FOR A WILL CONTAINING A NIL RATE BAND DISCRETIONARY TRUST WHICH IS TO INCLUDE DEBT/CHARGE PROVISIONS

Note

These clauses should be added to that part of the will containing a conventional nil rate band discretionary trust (see Precedent 18H and Appendix A1E).

A. Instead of satisfying the Nil Rate Sum wholly by the payment of cash (or by the appropriation of property) to the Legacy Fund Trustees my Trustees may:

(1)   require the Legacy Fund Trustees to accept in place of all or any part of the Nil Rate Sum a binding promise of payment made by my Trustees as Trustees of any residuary property given by this will or any codicil hereto on trusts under which my [spouse] [civil partner] has an interest in possession for the purposes of inheritance tax which debt shall be repayable on demand;

(2)   charge all or any part of the Nil Rate Sum on any property which is (or but for this clause would be) given by this will or any codicil to it on trusts under which my [spouse] [civil partner] has an interest in possession for the purposes of inheritance tax.

B. In amplification of the foregoing provisions:

(1)   if my Trustees exercise their powers under A(1) above they shall be under no further liability to see that the Legacy Fund Trustees receive the sum promised and if they exercise their powers under A(2) they shall (to the extent of the value at my death of the property charged) be under no further liability to see that the Legacy Fund Trustees receive the sum secured;

(2)   if my Trustees exercise their powers under A(2) above they may give an assent of the property subject to the charge and no one in whose favour the assent is made shall become personally liable for the sum secured;

(3)   the Legacy Fund Trustees may require security to be given for any debt to be created by a promise within A(1) above or by a loan within [identify clause such as Precedent 18H, clause 10] and in relation both to such debts (whether or not secured) and to any debt to be secured by a charge within A(2) (all of which shall be debts payable on demand) they:

(a)   may (subject to the foregoing provisions) impose such terms (if any) as they think fit including terms as to interest and the personal liability of the borrower and terms linking the debt to the Index of Retail Prices or Consumer Price Index otherwise providing for its amount to vary with the passage of time according to a formula; and

(b)   may subsequently leave the debt outstanding for as long as they think fit and refrain from exercising their rights in relation to it and waive the payment of all or any part of it or of any interest or index-linked increment due in respect of it;

and they shall not be liable if my Trustees are or become unable to pay the debt or a security is or becomes inadequate or for any other loss which may occur through their exercising or choosing not to exercise any power given by this sub-clause;

(4)   the powers given by this clause are without prejudice to any other powers given by this will or any codicil to it or by the general law and are exercisable even though my Trustees and the Legacy Fund Trustees may be the same persons and my [spouse] [civil partner] may be among them (but they are not exercisable while my [spouse] [civil partner] is the sole Legacy Fund Trustee) and any of the Legacy Fund Trustees may exercise or concur in exercising all powers and discretions given to him or her by this clause or by law notwithstanding that he or she has a direct or other personal interest in the mode or result of any such exercise.

A2C   DEBT SCHEME: DRAFT LETTER FROM THE EXECUTORS TO THE TRUSTEES OF THE LEGACY FUND (WHEN A CHARGE IS BEING IMPOSED BY THE EXECUTORS)

This letter records the agreement that has been reached between us as to the way in which the Legacy Fund is to be constituted.

Under the will of [...] deceased they provided that the Legacy Fund should have a value equal to the unused portion of their nil rate band and gave the Executors power to require the Legacy Fund Trustees of that fund to accept in place of either cash or other property either a binding promise of payment by the surviving [spouse] [civil partner] or a charge over any property passing to that surviving spouse or civil partner. At the same time those Trustees may, *inter alia*, impose terms as to the payment of interest or linking the sum outstanding to an appropriate index.

It has now been agreed that you as Legacy Fund Trustees will be entitled to the Nil Rate Sum (£ ...) which will be charged over property which will pass to the deceased's surviving [spouse] [civil partner]. In line with the provisions in the will we as Executors will have no further liability to ensure that you receive this amount and when the assets comprised in the residue are transferred to the surviving [spouse] [civil partner] [he] [she] will likewise have no personal responsibility to ensure that you receive the relevant property. Your only recourse therefore is against the charged property.

It is also confirmed that the sum outstanding is repayable on a written demand being made by yourselves either to the Executors or, once the assets have been transferred to the surviving [spouse] [civil partner] to that [spouse] [civil partner]. [You have further agreed that the debt shall not carry interest nor be linked to an index.]

A2D   DEBT SCHEME: SECURING THE DEBT

Note

The trustees of a nil rate band discretionary trust normally wish to charge the assets of the deceased which are passing to the surviving spouse or civil partner to protect the beneficiaries. Frequently, the deceased owned the matrimonial home as beneficial tenant in common with the surviving spouse or civil partner. It is not possible to impose a legal charge on an equitable interest, but it is possible to impose an equitable charge and this should normally be done. For further guidance on the conveyancing aspects and Land Registry requirements, see Land Registry, *Practice guide 70: nil-rate band discretionary trusts* (June 2015) (available at www.gov.uk/government/publications/nil-rate-band-discretionary-trusts/practice-guide-70-nil-rate-band-discretionary-trusts).

Where the deceased had been sole legal and equitable owner of the house a standard legal charge may be employed.

EQUITABLE CHARGE

THIS CHARGE is made the ... day of ... between [...] ('the Executors') of the one part and [...] and [...] ('the Trustees') of the other part SUPPLEMENTAL to the will ('the Will') of [...] deceased ('the Testator').

WHEREAS:

(1)   The Testator died on [...] and the Will was proved by the Executors in the [...].

(2)   The 'Legacy Fund' and the 'Nil Rate Sum' have the same meanings as in the Will and the Nil Rate Sum amounts to [£ ...].

(3)   The Trustees were appointed Trustees of the Legacy Fund by clause [...] of the Will.

(4)   The Executors hold the property described in the schedule ('the Property').

(5)   In exercise of the powers given to them by clause [...] of the Will the Executors have required the Trustees to accept in place of the Nil Rate Sum a debt to be secured by a charge over the Property [and the Trustees have required this sum to be index-linked by reference to the [Retail Prices] [Consumer Price] Index at the date of the Testator's death].

NOW THIS DEED WITNESSES as follows:

In this deed 'the sum owing' shall mean the Nil Rate Sum multiplied by the index figure in the [Retail Prices] [Consumer Price] Index for the month in which the sum owing is being calculated and divided by the index figure in the Retail Prices Index for the month in which this deed is executed.

The Executors hereby charge the Property with the payment to the Trustees of the sum owing and the Executors are under no further liability to ensure that the same is paid to the Trustees who accept that their only recourse in respect of the sum owing is against the charged Property.

It is confirmed that in the event that the Executors vest the Property in the residuary beneficiary ('the Beneficiary') of the Testator's estate:

(a)   they will serve notice in writing on the Trustees; and

(b)   the Beneficiary shall not be under any personal liability to ensure that the sum owing is paid to the Trustees.

If the [Retail Prices] [Consumer Price] Index shall have been replaced by another official index and/or if there shall be any change in the manner in which the [Retail Prices] [Consumer Price] Index operates the Trustees shall have power in their absolute discretion to determine the amount of the sum owing in accordance with such formula as seems to them to be just and reasonable in the circumstances.

IN WITNESS whereof the parties have executed these presents as a deed the date and year first before written

SCHEDULE

(the Property)

Signed, etc

Appendix 3

Temporary changes to Wills Act 1837, section 9 to allow remote witnessing

This Appendix sets out temporary changes introduced during the 2020–22 COVID-19 pandemic allowing the remote witnessing of wills. While it is hoped there will be no repeat of the lockdown and social distancing rules that gave rise to these temporary changes, they are included here so practitioners may be aware of the amending legislation. It may, in due course, become the blueprint for permanent changes to the way in which wills can be executed.

In July 2017, the Law Commission issued a consultation paper on modernising the way wills are made and interpreted. One of its specific aims was to 'pave the way for the introduction of electronic wills, to better reflect the modern world, once the technology is in place which would enable fraud to be prevented'. According to the Law Commission's Annual Report 2020–21, work on that consultation was suspended in light of the COVID-19 pandemic, so any permanent change in the law is probably some way off. However, in developing its response to the execution issue raised by COVID-19 as described below, the Government consulted with the Law Commission on its findings to date. Consequently, when the Law Commission does report (the timetable for publication is 'under review'), it is likely to reflect aspects of these temporary changes permitted by the amending legislation.

A3.1 THE POSITION IN MARCH 2020 AT THE BEGINNING OF THE COVID-19 LOCKDOWN

At the beginning of the COVID-19 lockdown, there was concern as to how wills were to be witnessed during a period of social isolation and differing views were expressed as to whether 'presence' in Wills Act 1837, section 9 could be construed as extending to virtual presence.

Section 9 provides as follows:

> No will shall be valid unless—
>
> (a)   it is in writing and signed by the testator or by some other person in his presence and by his direction; and
> (b)   it appears that the testator intended by his signature to give effect to the will; and
> (c)   the signature is made or acknowledged by the testator in the presence of two or more witnesses present at the same time; and
> (d)   each witness either attests and signs the will or acknowledges his signature in the presence of the testator (but not necessarily in the presence of any other witness),
>
> but no form of attestation shall be necessary.

Although the word 'presence' is used in (a), (b) and (c), there is no statutory definition of what it means.

In the well-known case of *Casson v Dade* (1781) 1 Bro C C 99, the short note says:

> Being asthmatical, and the office very hot, she retired to her carriage to execute the will, the witnesses attending her: after having seen the execution, they returned into the office to attest it, and the carriage was accidentally put back to the window of the office, through which, it was sworn by a person in the carriage, the testatrix might see what passed.

The witnesses then brought out the will, handed it to the testatrix, telling her that they had attested it. The Lord Chancellor accepted that it was properly attested.

The case is generally accepted as authority that what is required for 'presence' is a line of sight.

However, a line of sight is not sufficient. It is also necessary that there is consciousness of what is going on. Gorell Barnes J said in *Brown v Skirrow* [1903] P 3, 5:

> You cannot be a witness to an act that you are unconscious of; otherwise the thing might be done in a ball-room 100 feet long and with a number of people in the intervening space. In my view, at the end of the transaction, the witness should be able to say with truth, 'I know that this testator or testatrix has signed this document'.

It is clearly possible to argue that remote witnessing amounts to presence. In its report *Electronic Execution of Documents* (Law Com No 386), the Law Commission's view was that the law in this area is uncertain.

In the unreported First-tier Tribunal decision, *Yuen v Wong First-tier Tribunal* 2016/1089, 8 January 2020, Daniel Gatty J considered the meaning of 'presence' in relation to Law of Property (Miscellaneous Provisions) Act 1989, section 1. The Act requires a deed to be signed in the presence of a witness. He acknowledged that the current state of the law was uncertain and said at [63]:

> The question whether attestation of a deed via video-link should be allowed is one of policy – a balancing of risk and convenience. The question whether it is permissible under the present law permits of more than one conceivable answer as the Law Commission acknowledged.

Most professional bodies (e.g. the Law Society of England and Wales) advised that remote witnessing was not acceptable in the context of wills.

During the course of the first COVID-19 lockdown, most practitioners became adept at ways of procuring 'safe' execution. For example, witnesses can stand outside a window or on the outside of an open door. Some testators have executed wills in parks sitting on adjacent benches or inside a car with the witnesses signing on the bonnet.

However, there continued to be pressure for a change in the law. On 25 July 2020, the Ministry of Justice announced that there would be legislation to allow remote witnessing for a limited period.

A3.2   THE AMENDING LEGISLATION

The Wills Act 1837 (Electronic Communications) (Amendment) (Coronavirus) Order 2020 (SI 2020/952) ('the 2020 Order') was laid before Parliament on 7 September 2020 and came into force on 28 September 2020. It amends the Wills Act 1837 as follows.

The existing section 9 becomes section 9(1) and a new section 9(2) provides as follows:

> For the purposes of paragraphs (c) and (d) of subsection (1), in relation to wills made on or after 31 January 2020 and on or before 31 January 2022, 'presence' includes presence by means of videoconference or other visual transmission.

The date of the 31 January 2022 was extended to 31 January 2024 by the Wills Act 1837 (Electronic Communications) (Amendment) Order 2022 (SI 2022/18).

The only other provision in the 2020 Order is an exclusion (article 3) providing that the 2020 Order does not affect any grant of *probate* or anything done pursuant to a grant of probate prior to the 2020 Order coming into force on 28 September 2020.

Example

Tom makes a conventionally witnessed will in 2015.

On 1 February 2020 he makes a will which is witnessed remotely and complies with the requirements of the amending Order.

Tom dies on 1 April 2020. Everyone believes that the remotely witnessed will is invalid so the executor of the 2015 will obtains a grant of probate on 30 June 2020.

In July, the government announces that wills witnessed remotely are valid.

The 2020 Order does not allow the remotely witnessed will to be proved because a grant of probate was obtained before 28 September 2020.

The reference to a grant of 'probate' is a little odd. The policy decision was apparently that a grant of administration on intestacy is to be overturned by a valid video witnessed will. But what about a grant of administration with will annexed?

Taken literally, only grants of *probate* are unaffected by a later remotely witnessed will. So, in the example above, if there was no executor appointed (or no executor able and willing to take the grant), a grant of letters of administration with will annexed would have been obtained and apparently that grant would be overturned by the remotely witnessed will.

This seems illogical and the reference to grants of 'probate' may be an error.

In any event, note that article 3 merely says that *nothing in the 2020 Order* affects an earlier grant of probate leaving it open, presumably, for a beneficiary of a remotely witnessed will to argue that a grant of probate issued before 28 September 2020 should be overturned under the terms of the unamended section 9.

The chances of encountering an earlier will which has been proved, despite there being a valid remotely witnessed subsequent will, are not high so practitioners probably do not need to dwell further on this issue. The best of luck should you encounter the problem!

A3.3   THE PROCEDURE FOR REMOTE WITNESSING

Anyone thinking of taking advantage of virtual witnessing should look at the Law Society Practice Note 'Video-witnessing wills' in the Topics and Resources/Private Client section of the Law Society website (available at www.lawsociety.org.uk/Topics/Private-client/Guides/Video-witnessing-wills).

This provides guidance on the witnessing of wills using real time video and incorporates advice issued by the Ministry of Justice published on 25 July 2020 when the change to the legislation was announced. It also includes suggested precedents for attestation clauses and additional practical steps that are advisable to support the validity of a will made under this provision, as well as guidance on issues affecting subsequent applications for a grant of representation.

A3.3.1   Set-up

- The type of video-conferencing or device used is not important.
- Witnessing pre-recorded videos is not permitted – the witnesses must see the will being signed in real-time.
- The witnesses and testator can all be at different locations, on a three-way link, or two can be physically together with one at a remote location.
- If possible, the procedure should be recorded.
- The attestation clause should be amended to state that one or both witnesses are witnessing remotely.

A3.3.2 The testator signs

- Before the testator signs, the will drafter should ensure that the witnesses are able to see the testator actually signing the will, not just the testator's head and shoulders.
- The witnesses should confirm that they can see, hear (unless they have a hearing impairment) and acknowledge they understand their role in witnessing the signing of a legal document.
- The testator should hold the front page of the will document up to the camera to show the witnesses, and then turn to the page they will be signing and hold this up as well.
- The testator must physically sign the will (or acknowledge an earlier physical signature). Electronic signatures are not permitted. The testator will date the will with the date of signature.
- If the witnesses do not already know the testator, the testator should hold up photographic identification such as a passport or driving licence.

A3.3.3 Witnessing the will

- The will must then be taken or posted to the witnesses.
- The witnesses must physically sign the will in the virtual presence of the testator, and, if possible, in the virtual or physical presence of each other.
- As with the testator, they should hold up the will to the testator and sign (or acknowledge an earlier signature) (again, the testator should see them writing their names, not just see their heads and shoulders).
- The witnesses will sign with the date on which they are signing, which may be different from the date on which the testator signed and the date on which the other witness signs. *The execution process is not complete until everyone has signed.*

When the change to the Wills Act 1837 was announced, the guidance said:

> The advice remains that where people can make wills in the conventional way they should continue to do so.

The accompanying press release said:

> The use of video technology should remain a last resort, and people must continue to arrange physical witnessing of wills where it is safe to do so.

However, there is no means of enforcing this, so people are free to choose this method if they wish to.

The procedure is cumbersome. Execution is not complete until both witnesses have signed. If the will has to be posted to the witnesses, there is the risk that the testator will die before the witnesses sign. If this happens, the will is invalid. Anyone who can arrange physical witnessing would be better off doing so.

Having said that, there will be occasions when the procedure will be useful. For example, where someone has tested positive for COVID-19 and wants to proceed with execution.

Life will be much easier if the two witnesses can be physically together as that will reduce the occasions when the parties have to be in communication with each other and speed up the process.

A3.4 POSSIBLE ATTESTATION CLAUSE WHERE BOTH WITNESSES ARE WITNESSING REMOTELY

While not essential for validity, it is desirable that the attestation clause should be amended to recite that remote witnessing took place and that the necessary formalities were complied with. If it is not, the witnesses are likely to have to provide statements as to what occurred. The following is probably the minimum necessary.

Testator
Signed by me in the joint virtual presence of these two witnesses, who are witnessing me doing this remotely via a video conferencing link
[signature of testator or testatrix]
[Date]

Witnesses
Signed by me in the virtual presence of [testator/testatrix] and the [actual] [virtual] presence of [other witness] having watched [testator/testatrix] sign remotely via a video conferencing link on [date]
[signature of witness]
[Date]

The Ministry of Justice in its guidance included a declaration to be made by the testator and witnesses which could be included in the will or attached to it. The declaration is set out below.

Witnesses may not feel comfortable making the statements at paragraphs (3) and (4) of the declaration.

However, it is sensible to prepare a supporting document setting out:

- The reason the will was executed remotely.
- Evidence suggesting that:

  - the testator appeared to have testamentary capacity when giving instructions and when executing;
  - the testator knew and approved the contents of the will;
  - the testator was not subject to undue influence.

Ministry of Justice Declaration
We, the undersigned testator and the undersigned witnesses, respectively, whose names are signed to the attached or foregoing instrument declare:

(1)   that the testator executed the instrument as the testator's will;
(2)   that, [on x date], in the presence [by video conference] of both witnesses, the testator [signed the instrument]/[acknowledged the signature already made on the instrument]/[the instrument was signed by [X/another] in the physical presence of the testator as directed by the testator];
(3)   that, to the best of our knowledge and belief, the testator executed the will as a free and voluntary act for the purposes expressed in it;
(4)   that, to the best of the witnesses' knowledge and belief, the testator was of sound mind when the will was executed.

A3.5   PROBLEMS

(i)   If the will is executed remotely, instructions were probably given remotely. It is more difficult to assess capacity and to spot undue influence remotely. Full attendance notes of both stages are essential. It is also advisable to ask the will drafter to try to rotate the screen to show whether anyone else is in the room. If a third party is with the will drafter, for example a younger family member who is there to assist the will drafter in setting up the video facility and is on standby to deal with any glitches, they should be asked to leave the room.

(ii)   General misunderstandings are more likely when instructions are taken remotely.

(iii)   Firms should have a policy as to the circumstances in which they will make remotely witnessed wills and the level of fee earners allowed to oversee virtual execution. The Law Society Practice Note 'Video-witnessing wills' suggests consulting the practice's insurer to ensure adequate indemnity insurance and processes and procedures to protect from the risk due to the novel measures the 2020 Order permits.

(iv)   Firms should also consider who is to be responsible for recording the execution process and who is to be responsible for storing it. It is likely to be necessary to amend the retainer to spell this out and perhaps to exclude liability for any damage to the recording.

(v) Before the firm agrees to be responsible for recording and storage, it should make sure the firm's IT team is happy.

(vi) Lastly, the firm should consider a re-execution of the will in conventional manner as soon as circumstances permit. This is particularly important if it is thought there might be contention over the validity of the will that has been witnessed remotely.

Index

marriage, gifts made in consideration
of   411
normal expenditure out of income
409–10
small gifts   409
see also lifetime transfer and death
transfer, exemption for *below*
lifetime transfer and death transfer,
exemption for
agricultural property, relief for *see*
agricultural property relief *above*
business, relief for *see* business
property relief *above*
charities and national institutions, to
412
civil partners, transfers between
411–12
heritage property   412–13
political parties, gifts to   412
spouses, transfers between   411–12
loss to estate, determining   394
post-death variations
deceased, on behalf of   440
discretionary trust   439
effectiveness   439
exchange of interests   440
generally   438–41
Inland Revenue guidance   440
life tenant's death, no variation on
life interest   440–1
mistake, court's power to rectify
439
personal representatives, by   440
requirements   439
reservation of benefit rules   439
right to make   438
second variation, prohibition on
439
statutory provisions   438–9
potentially exempt transfer   393, 399–
400, 437
property: meaning   394
rate   393
reservation of benefit
donor
need to exclude from benefit, etc
of property   430

tax treatment   429
inapplicable, where
Finance Act 1986 exemptions
431–2
generally   430–1
sharing arrangements   431
potentially exempt transfer, and
429
principles   429–30
release of benefit before donor's
death   429
relevant period: meaning   429
sharing arrangements   431
statutory provisions   429
residence nil rate band
downsizing legislation   426–9
effect of legislation   422–6
generally   422
withdrawal   438
residuary gift *see under* Residuary gift
settlement, on *see under* Settlement
transfer made on death
assets outside estate, moving   402–
3
death rate, chargeable at   401
estate on death, determining   401
example   401–2
liabilities   405
non-deductible debts   405–7
planning with pension benefits
anniversary and exit charges   404
death at 75 or above   404
death below 75   403
funds remaining invested   404
generally   403–5
trust, benefits of using   405
rate   402
tapering relief   401
transfer of value
deemed   394
exclusions *see* excluded transfer
above
generally   393–4
meaning   393
measurement   394
transferable nil rate band   420–2
value transferred   394–5